TANS:

...OSE DIVINES WHO
...N THE CAUSE

...ry,

...QUEEN ELIZABETH,
...EMITY,

...ROOK.

THE

LIVES

OF

THE PURITANS:

CONTAINING

A BIOGRAPHICAL ACCOUNT OF THOSE DIVINES WHO DISTINGUISHED THEMSELVES IN THE CAUSE

OF

Religious Liberty,

FROM THE REFORMATION UNDER QUEEN ELIZABETH, TO THE ACT OF UNIFORMITY, IN 1662.

BY BENJAMIN BROOK.

IN THREE VOLUMES.

VOL. I.

The memory of the just is blessed.—SOLOMON.

The precious spark of liberty had been kindled, and was preserved, by the PURITANS ALONE; and it was to this *Sect* that the English owe the whole freedom of their constitution.—HUME.

London:

PRINTED FOR JAMES BLACK,

YORK-STREET, COVENT-GARDEN.

1813.

DEDICATION.

TO THE

RISING GENERATION

AMONG THE VARIOUS DENOMINATIONS OF

PROTESTANTS.

MY YOUNG FRIENDS,

THE formation of your principles, the instruction of your minds, and the salvation of your souls, are, unquestionably, objects of high importance to yourselves, to your connexions, and to the protestant interest at large. When your fathers are translated from the church militant to the church triumphant, you will inherit their property, and will occupy their stations. On you it will devolve to manage the affairs of religion, to be zealous for its interests, and active for its prosperity.

But, if you be ignorant of its principles and destitute of its blessings, this zeal and activity cannot be expected. By enlightening your understandings with truth, and by impressing your hearts with the power of religion, we hope to secure your attachment to the cause of God, and to engage your talents and your future influence in its service.

Of all books which can be put into your hands, those which relate the labours and sufferings of good men are the most interesting and instructive. In them you see orthodox principles, christian tempers, and holy duties, in lovely union and in vigorous operation. In them you see religion shining forth in real life, subduing the corruptions of human nature, and inspiring a zeal for every good work. In them you see the reproaches and persecutions which the servants of God have endured; those gracious principles which have supported their minds; and the course they have pursued in their progress to the kingdom of heaven. Such books are well calculated to engage your attention, to affect your feelings, to deepen your best impressions, and to invigorate your noblest resolutions. They are well calculated to fortify you against the allurements of a vain world; to assimilate your characters to those of the excellent of the earth; to conform your lives to the standard of holiness; and to educate your souls for the mansions of glory.

The Puritans were a race of men of whom the world was not worthy. They devoted their days and nights to hard study; they cherished devotional feelings; and they enjoyed intimate communion with God. The stores of their minds were expended, and the energy of their souls was exerted, to separate the truths of the gospel from the heresies of the times in which they lived; to resist the encroachments of arbitrary power; to purify the church from secularity and corruption; and to promote the power of religion among the people. They persevered in this course amidst a host of difficulties, and in defiance of the most powerful opposition. The rulers of those times persecuted them with wanton cruelty, in total contempt of every sacred law, of every just principle, and of every humane feeling.

From these volumes you will learn, that the glorious cause of Nonconformity has been adorned by the holy lives of a multitude of good men; has been consecrated by the blood of martyrs; and has been sanctioned by the approbation and protection of heaven.

For their exalted attainments in piety, their assiduous researches in literature and divinity, and their unwearied exertions in the cause of God and their country, the Puritan divines are entitled to the admiration and reverence of every succeeding age. Our political freedom, our religious liberty, and our christian privileges, are to be ascribed to them more than to any other body of men that England ever produced. When you learn by what struggles these blessings have been acquired, and at what price they have been obtained, you will know how to estimate their value; and you will regard the men to whom we are indebted for them as distinguished benefactors to the English nation and the church of God.

For the sacred cause of religion, the Puritan divines laboured and prayed, wrote and preached, suffered and died; and they have transmitted it to us to support it, or to let it sink. With what feelings will you receive this precious inheritance? Will you lightly esteem what they so highly valued? Will you stand aloof from the cause which they watched with jealous vigilance, and defended with invincible courage? If the blood of these men run in your veins, if the principles of these men exist in your souls, most assuredly you will not.

That you may learn the wisdom, and imbibe the spirit of the Puritans;—that you may take them as patterns, imitate them as examples, and follow them as guides, so far as they followed Christ;—that you may adhere to the cause of religion with the same firmness, adorn it with the same holiness, and propagate it with the same zeal, is the fervent prayer of

Yours respectfully

and affectionately,

BENJAMIN BROOK.

TUTBURY,
October 6, 1813.

PREFACE.

At no period has biographical history been so much esteemed and promoted as in these days of christian freedom. The memoirs of wise and good men, especially such as have suffered for the testimony of a good conscience, afford interesting entertainment and valuable instruction. To rescue from oblivion impartial accounts of their holy actions, their painful sufferings, and their triumphant deaths, will confer a deserved honour upon their memory: and there is, perhaps, no class of men whose history better deserves to be transmitted to posterity than that of the persons stigmatized by the name of Puritans.

The cruelties exercised upon them were indeed very great. **They suffered for the testimony of a good conscience**, and an **avowed attachment to the cause of Christ**. The proofs which they gave of their zeal, their fortitude, and their integrity, were certainly as great as could be given. They denied themselves those honours, preferments, and worldly advantages by which they were allured to conformity. They suffered reproach, deprivation, and imprisonment; yea, the loss of all things, rather than comply with those inventions and impositions of men, which to them appeared extremely derogatory to the gospel, which would have robbed them of liberty of conscience, and which tended to lead back to the darkness and superstitions of popery. Many of them, being persons of great ability, loyalty, and interest, had the fairest prospect of high promotion; yet they sacrificed all for their nonconformity. Some modestly refused preferment when offered them: while others, already preferred, were prevented from obtaining higher promotion, because they could not, with a good conscience, comply with the ecclesiastical impositions. Nor was it the least afflictive circumstance to the Puritan divines, that they were driven from their flocks, whom they loved as their own souls; and, instead of being allowed to labour for their spiritual and eternal advantage, were obliged to spend the best of their days in silence, imprisonment, or a state of exile in a foreign land.

The contents of these volumes tend to expose the evil of bigotry and persecution. When professed Protestants oppress and persecute their brethren of the same faith, and of the same communion, it is indeed marvellous. The faithful page of history details the fact with the most glaring evidence, or we could scarcely have believed it. A spirit of intolerance and oppression ever deserves to be held up to universal abhorrence. In allusion to this tragic scene, Sir William Blackstone very justly observes, "That our an-" cestors were mistaken in their plans of compul-" sion and intolerance. The sin of schism, as such, " is by no means the object of coercion and " punishment. All persecution for diversity of " opinions, however ridiculous or absurd they " may be, is contrary to every principle of sound " policy and civil freedom. The names and sub-" ordination of the clergy, the posture of devo-" tion, the materials and colour of the minister's " garment, the joining in a known or unknown " form of prayer, and other matters of the same " kind, must be left to the opinion of every man's " private judgment. For, undoubtedly, all per-" secution and oppression of weak consciences, " on the score of religious persuasions, are highly " unjustifiable upon every principle of natural " reason, civil liberty, or sound religion."*

Perhaps no class of men ever suffered more reproach than the Puritans. Archbishop Parker stigmatizes them as "schismatics, belly-gods, deceivers, flatterers, fools, having been unlearnedly brought up in profane occupations, being puffed up with arrogancy."† His successor Whitgift says, "that when they walked in the streets, they hung down their heads, and looked austerely; and in com-

* Blackstone's Comment. vol. iv. p. 51—53. Edit. 1771.

† Strype's Annals, vol. i. p. 481.—Peirce's Vindication, part i. p. 61.

pany they sighed much, and seldom or never laughed. They sought the commendation of the people; and thought it an heinous offence to wear a cap and surplice, slandering and backbiting their brethren. As for their religion, they separated themselves from the congregation, and would not communicate with those who went to church, either in prayer, hearing the word, or sacraments; despising all, who were not of their sect, as polluted and unworthy of their company."* Dugdale denominates them "a viperous brood, miserably infesting these kingdoms. They pretended," says he, "to promote religion and a purer reformation; but rapine, spoil, and the destruction of civil government, were the woeful effects of those pretences. *They were of their father the devil, and his works they would do.*"† A modern slanderer affirms, "that they maintained the horrid principle, that the end sanctifies the means; and that it was lawful to kill those who opposed their endeavours to introduce their model and discipline."‡ Surely so much calumny and falsehood are seldom found in so small a compass.

Bishop Burnet, a man less influenced by a spirit of bigotry and intolerance, gives a very different account of them. "The Puritans," says he, "gained credit as the bishops lost it. They put on the appearance of great sanctity and

* Strype's Annals, vol. ii. p. 5.

† Dugdale's Troubles of Eng. Pref.

‡ Churton's Life of Nowell, p. 215.

gravity, and took more pains in their parishes than those who adhered to the bishops, often preaching against the vices of the court. Their labours and their sufferings raised their reputation and rendered them very popular."* Hume, who treats their principles with ridicule and contempt, has bestowed upon them the highest eulogium. "So absolute," says he, "was the "authority of the crown, that the precious spark "of liberty had been kindled, and was preserved, "by the *Puritans alone;* and it was to this sect "that the English owe the whole freedom of their "constitution."†

It is granted that they had not all equally clear views of our civil and religious rights. Many of their opinions were confused and erroneous; yet their leading principles were the same. Though they had, in general, no objection to a national establishment, many of them maintained, "That all true church power must be founded in a divine commission: that where a right to command is not clear, evidence that obedience is a duty is wanting: that men ought not to make more necessary to an admittance into the *church* than God has made necessary to an admittance into *heaven:* that so long as unscriptural impositions are continued, a further reformation of the church will be necessary: and that every one who must answer for himself *hereafter,* must

* Burnet's Hist. of his Time, vol. i. p. 17, 18.

† Hume's Hist. of Eng. vol. v. p. 134.

judge for himself *now*."* These were the grand principles of their nonconformity.

The author of these volumes has spared no labour nor expense in the collection of materials, and has used the utmost care to retain whatever appeared interesting, curious, and useful. Not writing to please any particular sect or party, he has endeavoured to observe the strictest impartiality. In the lives of these worthies, he has not suppressed their imperfections, nor even the accusations of their adversaries; but has constantly stated their faults, as well as their excellencies, without reserve. Neither has he at any time connived at bigotry and persecution, whether found among prelates, presbyterians, or any others. Whoever were the persecutors or aggressors, their case is represented, as near as possible, as it is found in the faithful pages of history. His sole object has been to give a lucid and impartial statement of *facts*. Indeed, the documents are frequently transcribed in the very words of the authors; and, wishing to retain the genuine sense and originality of the whole as entire as possible, he has constantly avoided dressing them in any garb of his own.

Through the whole, he has invariably given his authorities. These might easily have been multiplied; but, when two or more authors have given accounts of the same facts, he has invariably chosen that which appeared the most authentic:

* Calamy's Contin. vol. i. Pref.

or, when they have at any time contradicted each other, he has always given both, or followed that which appeared most worthy of credit. In the Appendix, a correct list is given of the principal books consulted; and, for the satisfaction of the more critical reader, the particular edition of each is specified. In numerous instances, reference will be found to single lives, funeral sermons, and many other interesting articles, of which the particular edition is mostly given. In addition to the numerous *printed* works, he has also been favoured with the use of many large *manuscript collections*, a list of which will be found at the close of the Appendix. From these rare documents he has been enabled to present to the public a great variety of most interesting and curious information never before printed.

After all, many lives will be found very defective, and will leave the inquisitive reader uninformed in numerous important particulars. Such defect was unavoidable at this distance of time; when, after the utmost research, no further information could possibly be procured. The author has spent considerable labour to obtain a correct list of the works of those whose lives he has given, and to ascertain the true orthography of the names of persons and places. Though, in each of these particulars, he has succeeded far beyond his expectations, yet, in some instances, he is aware of the deficiency of his information. He can only say, that he has availed himself of every advantage within his reach, to render the whole as complete and interesting as possible.

The lives of these worthies are arranged in a chronological order, according to the time of their deaths.* By such arrangement, the work contains a regular series of the History of Nonconformists during a period of more than a hundred years. It does not in the least interfere with any other publication; and forms a comprehensive appendage to Neal's "History of the Puritans," and a series of biographical history closely connected with Palmer's "Nonconformist's Memorial," containing a complete memorial of those nonconformist divines who died *previous* to the passing of the Act of Uniformity. To this, however, there are some exceptions. There were certain persons of great eminence, who lived *after* the year 1662; yet, because they were not *in the church* at that period, they come not within the list of *ejected* ministers, but are justly denominated Puritans. Memoirs of these divines will therefore be found in their proper places.

It was requisite, in a work of this nature, to give some account of the origin and progress of Nonconformity, together with a sketch of the numerous barbarities exercised upon the Puritans. This will be found in the Introduction, which may not prove unacceptable to the inquisitive and

* It should here be remembered, that, in all cases, when the particular period of their deaths could not be ascertained, the *last* circumstance noticed in their lives is taken for that period.

and freedom they sought, though in the most peaceable manner, to have the church of England purged of all human invention and error, they were stigmatized with the odious name of [illegible], and many of them, on account of their nonconformity, were suspended, [illegible], and [illegible] unto death. These volumes, therefore, present to the reader a particular account of the origin and gradual struggle for religious freedom, during the successive reigns of Queen Elizabeth, King James, [illegible] Charles I., to the [illegible] of King Charles II.

The reader will here find a circumstantial account of the proceedings of the High Commission and the Star Chamber, the [illegible] engines of [illegible]. The members of these tribunals assumed the power of administering an oath ex officio, by which persons were constrained to answer all questions proposed to them, though ever so prejudicial to themselves or others; if they refused the oath, they were cast into prison for contempt; or if they took it, they were convicted upon their own confession. The [illegible] and [illegible] of [illegible] of these courts [illegible] without [illegible] to the [illegible] [illegible] [illegible] [illegible] [illegible]

And because they sought, though in the most peaceable manner, to have the church of England purged of all its antichristian impurities, they were stigmatized with the odious name of *Puritans*, and many of them, on account of their nonconformity, were suspended, imprisoned, and persecuted even unto death. These volumes, therefore, present to the reader a particular detail of the arduous and painful struggle for religious freedom, during the arbitrary reigns of Queen Elizabeth, King James, and King Charles I., to the restoration of King Charles II.

The reader will here find a circumstantial account of the proceedings of the *High Commission* and the *Star Chamber*, the two terrible engines of cruelty and persecution. The former of these tribunals assumed the power of administering an oath *ex officio*, by which persons were constrained to answer all questions proposed to them, though ever so prejudicial to themselves or others: if they refused the unnatural oath, they were cast into prison for contempt; and if they took it, they were convicted upon their own confession. The tyrannical oppressions and shocking barbarities of these courts are without a parallel in any Protestant country, and nearly equal to the Romish inquisition. The severe examinations, the numerous suspensions, the long and miserable imprisonments, with other brutal usage, of pious and faithful ministers, for not wearing a *white surplice*, not baptizing with a *cross*, not *kneeling* at the sacrament, not [illegible] without foundation in [illegible] circumstances [illegible] quitous proceedings [illegible]

These [illegible] of reconciling the [illegible] them farther from [illegible] too weak to [illegible] consciences, [illegible] admire and esteem [illegible] weapons. [illegible] the nation a [illegible] continues in [illegible] ing prelates [illegible] the number [illegible] increased [illegible] into their own [illegible] yoke.

That the [illegible] learning, [illegible] to the [illegible] no one will [illegible] true character [illegible] which they [illegible] ledged, [illegible] but little [illegible] ence; and [illegible] superiors [illegible] the deprivation [illegible] of them to death [illegible] attempted to be [illegible]

The author is aware, however, of the delicacy of many things here presented to the public, and of the difficulty of writing freely without giving offence. But, as honest truth needs no apology, so the pernicious influence of bigotry, superstition, and persecution, he thinks, can never be too fairly and openly exposed. He also believes that all professing Christians, except those who are blind devotees to superstition, or persecutors of the church of God, will rejoice to unite with him in holding up these evils as a warning to posterity.

The work is not to be considered as a medium, or a test of religious controversy, but an historical narrative of facts. It is not designed to fan the flame of contention among brethren, but to promote, upon genuine protestant principles, that christian moderation, that mutual forbearance, and that generous affection, among all denominations, which is the great ornament and excellency of all who call themselves Protestants. A correct view of the failings and the excellencies of others, should prompt us to avoid that which is evil, and to imitate that which is good.

When we behold the great piety and constancy with which our forefathers endured the most barbarous persecution, will not the sight produce in our minds the most desirable christian feelings? Though we shall feel the spirit of indignity against the inhumanity and cruelty of their persecutors, will not the sight of their sufferings, their holiness, and their magnanimity, awaken in our breasts the

denominations, to a zealous imitation of the excellent qualities of their worthy ancestors, he will in no wise lose his reward.

The author wishes here to present a tribute of gratitude to his numerous friends, who have favoured him with the use of books and other materials for the work; and, under a deep sense of his multiplied obligations, he now requests them to accept his most grateful acknowledgments.* He desires particularly to express his special obligations to the Trustees of Dr. Williams's Library, Red-Cross-Street, London, for the use of several volumes of most curious and valuable manuscripts.

* Valuable communications of books or manuscripts have been received from the following ministers:—The late Dr. Edward Williams, Rotherham—Dr. Joshua Toulmin, Birmingham—Dr. Abraham Rees, London—Dr. John Pye Smith, Homerton—Mr. Timothy Thomas, Islington—Mr. Joseph Ivimey, London—Mr. John Sutcliff, Olney—Mr. William Harris, Cambridge—Mr. James Gawthorn, Derby—Mr. Joshua Shaw, Ilkeston—Mr. Thomas Roome, Sutton in Ashfield—Mr. William Salt, Lichfield—Mr. John Hammond, Handsworth—Mr. Samuel Bradley, Manchester—Mr. John Cockin, Holmfirth—Mr. John Tallis, Cheadle. Also from the following gentlemen:—Francis Fox, M. D. Derby—John Audley, Esq. Cambridge—Mr. Walter Wilson, London—Mr. J. Simco, ditto—Mr. Joseph Meen, Biggleswade—Mr. T. M. Dash, Kettering—Mr. James Ashton, Leek—Mr. Isaac James, Bristol—Mr. William Daniel, Lichfield.

CONTENTS OF VOL. I.

INTRODUCTION, containing a Sketch of the History of Nonconformity, from the Reformation to the passing of the Act of Uniformity, in 1662.

SECTION		PAGE
I.	From the Commencement of the Reformation, to the Death of Queen Mary,	1
II.	From the Death of Queen Mary, to the Death of Queen Elizabeth,	17
III.	From the Death of Queen Elizabeth, to the Death of King James I.,	60
IV.	From the Death of King James I., to the Death of King Charles I.,	70
V.	From the Death of King Charles I., to the passing of the Act of Uniformity,	94

John Bale	101
John Pullain	114
John Hardyman	116
Miles Coverdale	117
William Turner	128
Robert Hawkins	133
Andrew Kingsmill	149
Christopher Colman	150
William Axton	151
Thomas Becon	166
Gilbert Alcock	170
David Whitehead	172
Mr. Millain	174
William Bonham	ib.
Robert Johnson	176
Richard Taverner	189
R. Harvey	191
Edward Deering	193
Thomas Aldrich	211
Thomas Lever	213
Francis Merbury	223
William Whittingham	229
Mr. Lawrance	237
John Handson	238
Robert Wright	239
Bernard Gilpin	248
John Copping	262
Thomas Underdown	264
Mr. Sanderson	273
John Hilt	274
Nicholas Brown	275
Richard Crick	278
Anthony Gilby	ib.
John Edwin	285
Edward Brayne	289
Barnaby Benison	292
William Negus	296
John Stroud	ib.
John Browning	302
Stephen Turner	305

	PAGE
John Ward	305
Edmund Rockrey	306
H. Gray	308
Robert Moore	309
Edward Gellibrand	311
Edward Glover	313
John Walward	314
John Gardiner	316
Nicholas Standen	317
John Field	318
John Huckle	324
John Fox	326
John Wilson	339
John Elliston	355
Robert Crowley	357
Nicholas Crane	362
Lawrence Humphrey	363
Thomas Sampson	375
William Fulke	385
John Garbrand	392
Dudley Fenner	ib.
Cuthbert Bainbrigg	396
Edmund Littleton	405
Edward Lord	407
Andrew King	ib.
Malancthon Jewell	408
Edward Snape	409
John Holmes	414
Richard Greenham	415
Giles Wigginton	418
Thomas Barber	429
Robert Cawdrey	430
Lever Wood	444
Humphrey Fenn	ib.
Daniel Wright	447
William Proudlove	448
John More	449

CONTENTS OF THE NOTES.

Anecdote of Henry VIII. and his jester	2
John Hooper nominated Bishop of Gloucester	7
Joan Bocher's distribution of the New Testament	10
The number of sufferers in the days of Queen Mary	12
Cranmer and Ridley wished the habits to be abolished	ib.
Ridley a famous disputant	13
The deliverance of the protestant congregation	14
John Rough a celebrated preacher	ib.
———'s remarkable dream	15
A curious petition to Queen Elizabeth	18
The Act of Uniformity in the reign of Queen Elizabeth	ib.
Robert Cole preferred for his conformity	24
Whitgift at first a friend to the nonconformists	26
Title of a letter from Scotland	27
Bishop Maddox's false insinuation	33
The character of Archbishop Parker	37
——— Archbishop Grindal	45
The ministers suspended in Suffolk	46
——— in Essex	49

	PAGE
Lord Gray wished to have the bishops expelled	54
Anecdote of Martin Mar-Prelate	55
Bancroft's famous sermon at Paul's-cross	ib.
Sir Walter Raleigh's estimate of the Brownists	58
The nobility patrons of the puritans	ib.
The number of ministers suspended or deprived	60
Bancroft's flattery of King James	61
Whitgift's magnificent train	62
The number of ministers suspended	64
The cruel oppressions of the puritans	65
The character of Archbishop Bancroft	ib.
King James kicked Legatt with his royal foot	ib.
Thomas Legatt died in Newgate	ib.
John Selden's great learning	66
Archbishop Abbot opposed the Book of Sports	69
The character of King James	70
The censure and preferment of Dr. Manwaring	72
Curious pictures in St. Edmund's church	76
The character of Archbishops Abbot and Laud	ib.
A minister's son excommunicated	80
The number of ministers driven to New England	81
Great sums paid for the release of nonconformists	82
Archbishop Laud called a little urchin	83
The oppressions of the convocation in 1640	85
The sub-committee to assist the committee	86
The character of the high commission	87
Debates about the remonstrance	88
The Book of Sports abolished	89
List of the assembly of divines	90
List of lords and commons to assist the assembly	91
Welwood's account of Archbishop Laud	92
A curious anecdote of Laud	93
London ministers declared against the king's death	94
Venner's insurrection and execution	99
Kennet's opinion of the Act of Uniformity	100
The character of Dr. Richard Cox	108
The death of the famous William Tindal	120
The fall of Lord Cromwell	121
The funeral of Queen Katharine Parr	122
The barbarities of Queen Mary's reign	125
Bishop Ridley in prison	129
The separatists released from prison	145

PAGE
The examination of William White 145
Sir Robert Corbet a friend to the puritans 151
A curious anecdote of the surplice 153
———— of kneeling at the sacrament 159
Account of Bishop Bentham 165
Becon's book against popery suppressed by Laud 170
Bishop Maddox's account of severe proceedings 171
The indictment of Mr. Johnson 181
Account of Cardinal Wolsey 189
Curious anecdotes of Queen Elizabeth 207
The character of Roger Ascham 217
Bishop Aylmer's foul language 228
Bishop Pilkington's excellent letter 233
The psalms turned into metre 236
Account of Bishop Aylmer 242
———— Peter Martyr 243
The character of Bishop Tonstal 254
A form of warrant to convene ministers 264
Christmas not conformably observed 273
Sir Edmund Anderson a furious persecutor 274
Lord Burleigh a friend to the puritans 292
Earl of Bedford a friend to do. 304
Fox's Book of Martyrs expelled from the churches 323
Eating flesh forbidden in lent 324
Dutch anabaptists burnt 325
Account of Mrs. Heniwood 327
An order from the high commission 340
Curious inscription on a coffin 362
Account of Sir Thomas Bodley 364
———— Bishop Jewel 369
Astrology greatly admired 375
Anecdote of Queen Elizabeth 377
Bishop Parkhurst a friend to the puritans .... ib.
Dr. Heylin's curious tale of Mr. Snape 411
Sir Walter Mildmay a friend to the puritans 416
Hume's character of Archbishop Whitgift 421
A warrant to the keeper of the Gatehouse 426
Attorney Morrice a zealous advocate for liberty 440
The imprisonment of Mary Queen of Scots 442
Account of Sir Francis Walsingham 444

LIVES OF THE PURITANS.

INTRODUCTION:

CONTAINING A SKETCH OF THE HISTORY OF NONCONFORMITY FROM THE REFORMATION, TO THE PASSING OF THE ACT OF UNIFORMITY, IN 1662.

SECT. I.

From the Commencement of the Reformation, to the Death of Queen Mary.

PREVIOUS to the accession of King HENRY VIII. popish darkness overspread the whole island of Britain. This was followed by a train of most unhappy consequences. Ignorance, superstition, immorality and persecution were predominant in every part of the kingdom. Those who presumed to think for themselves on religious subjects, and to dissent from the national church, underwent all the oppressions and severities of persecution. From the days of Wickliffe to this time, great numbers of excellent christians and worthy subjects, fell sacrifices to popish cruelty. This proud monarch being at first a most obedient son of the pope, treated the bold confessors of truth as obstinate rebels; and because their piety and integrity condemned his licentiousness, he put multitudes to cruel tortures and to death.

Soon after Luther arose in Saxony, England became affected by his bold and vigorous opposition to the errors of the church of Rome. The young king, vain of his scholastic learning, was unwise enough to meet the bold reformer on the field of controversy, and published a book against him.* Luther treated his royal antagonist with sarcastic contempt, contending that truth and science knew no difference between the prince and the plebeian. The pope, however, craftily flattered the vanity of the royal author, by conferring upon him the title of *Defender of the Faith*,† which Henry was weak enough to value as the brightest jewel in his crown. This pompous reward from his holiness was conferred upon him in the year 1521.‡

The haughty king soon discovered his ingratitude. He quarrelled with the pope, renounced his authority, and became his avowed enemy. Being weary of Queen Katharine his wife, with whom he had lived almost twenty years; and having long sought, but in vain, to be divorced by the pope, he was so much offended, that he utterly rejected the papal power, authority and tyranny in England. This was a dreadful blow against the Romish supremacy. But the king soon after procured the dignified and flattering title of *Supreme Head of the Church of England.* This additional jewel to his crown was conferred upon him, first by the clergy in convocation, then by act of parliament.§ Thus, in the year 1534, Henry VIII. having renounced the supremacy of the pope, and having placed himself in the chair of his holiness, at least as far as concerned the English church, did not fail to manifest his usurped power and authority. He did not intend to ease the people of their oppressions, but only change their foreign yoke for domestic fetters, dividing the pope's spoils betwixt himself and his bishops, who cared not for their father at Rome, so long as they enjoyed honours and their patrimony under another head.‖

* Mr. Fox observes, that though "this book carried the king's name in the title, it was another who ministred the motion, and framed the style. But whosoever had the labour of the book, the king had the thanks and the reward."—*Acts and Monuments of Martyrs*, vol. ii. p. 57.

† It has been said, that the jester whom Henry, according to the custom of the times, retained at court, seeing the king overjoyed, asked the reason; and when told, that it was because his holiness had conferred upon him this new title, he replied, "my good Harry, let thee and me defend each other, and let the faith alone to defend itself." If this was spoken as a serious joke, the fool was undoubtedly the wisest man of the two.

‡ Burnet's Hist. of Refor. vol. i. p. 19.—King Henry afterwards got this sacred title united to the crown, by act of parliament; and, curious and inconsistent as it may appear, it is retained to this day.—*Heylin's Hist. of Pres.* p. 235.

§ Burnet's Hist. of Refor. vol. i. p. 112. 136. 157.

‖ Memoirs of Col. Hutchinson, vol. i. p. 105. Edit. 1810.

On June 9, 1536, assembled the first reformed convocation in England; in which Lord Cromwell, prime secretary, sat in state above the bishops, as the king's vicegerent in all spiritual matters.* On this occasion, Cromwell, by order of the king, declared, "That it was his majesty's pleasure, that the rites and ceremonies of the church should be reformed by the RULES OF SCRIPTURE, and that nothing should be maintained which did not rest on that authority; for it was absurd, since the scriptures were acknowledged to contain the laws of religion, that recourse should be had to glosses or the decrees of popes, rather than to them."† Happy had it been, if the reformers of the church of England had invariably adhered to this sacred principle. Much, however, was done even at this early period. The pious reformers rejoiced to see the holy scriptures professedly made the only standard of faith and worship, to the exclusion of all human traditions. The immediate worship of images and saints was now renounced, and purgatory declared uncertain. But the corporeal presence in the sacrament, the preservation and reverence of images, with the necessity of auricular confession, were still retained.‡ The publication of Tindal and Coverdale's Translations of the Bible, greatly promoted the work of reformation; though it soon received a powerful check by the passing of the terrible and bloody act of the Six Articles. By this act, all who spoke against transubstantiation were to be burnt as heretics, and suffer the loss of all their lands and goods; and to defend the communion in both kinds, or the marriage of priests; or, to speak against the necessity of private mass, and auricular confession, was made felony, with the forfeiture of lands and goods.§ Towards the close of this king's reign, the popish party obtained the ascendancy; the severity of persecution was revived; and the Romish superstitions greatly prevailed. Till now, these superstitions had never been denominated *laudable ceremonies*, *necessary rites*, and *godly constitutions*. All who refused to observe them, were condemned as traitors against the king. To make the standing of the persecuting prelates more secure, and their severities the more effectual, this was ratified by act of parliament.‖ Many excellent persons were, therefore, condemned to the flames: among whom were the famous Mr. Thomas Bilney,

* Fuller's Church Hist. b. v. p. 207.
† Burnet's Hist. of Refor. vol. i. p. 214.
‡ Ibid. p. 218.
§ Strype's Cranmer, p. 72.
‖ Ibid. p. 130.

Mr. Richard Byfield, Mr. John Frith, and Dr. Robert Barnes, all highly celebrated for piety and zeal in the cause of the reformation.*

King Henry was succeeded by his son, EDWARD VI., a prince of most pious memory. Being only nine years and four months old when he came to the crown, he was free from bigotry and superstition, and ready to observe the instructions of Archbishop Cranmer and the Duke of Somerset, by whose aid and influence, he set himself to promote sound religion. Upon his accession, the penal laws against protestants were abolished, the chains of many worthy persons confined in prison were struck off, the prison-doors were set open, and the sufferers released. Others who had fled from the storm, and remained in a state of exile, now with joy returned home. Among the former were old Bishop Latimer and John Rogers;† and among the latter, were Hooper, afterwards the famous martyr, and Miles Coverdale, afterwards a celebrated puritan.‡ Men of real worth were esteemed and preferred. Hooper became Bishop of Gloucester, and Coverdale was made Bishop of Exeter. The monuments of idolatry, with the superstitious rites and ceremonies, were commanded to be abolished, and a purer form of worship introduced. Though, during this reign, the reformation made considerable progress, the greatest part of the parochial clergy were in a state of most deplorable ignorance: but to remedy, as far as possible, this evil, the pious reformers composed and published the book of Homilies for their use.§ The order of public worship was a Liturgy or Book of Common Prayer, established by act of parliament. Though this act did not pass without much opposition, especially from the bishops, some were so enamoured with the book, that they scrupled not to say, "it was compiled *by the aid of the Holy Ghost*."‖

In the year 1550, the altars in most churches were taken away, and convenient tables set up in their places.¶ "And as the form of a table," says Burnet, "was more likely to turn the people from the superstition of the popish mass, and bring them to the right use of the Lord's supper, Bishop Ridley, in his primary visitation, exhorted the

* Fox's Martyrs, vol. ii. p. 227, 241, 256, 445.
† Burnet's Hist. of Refor. vol. ii. p. 25.
‡ Fuller's Church Hist. b. vii. p. 371.
§ Burnet's Hist. of Refor. vol. ii. p. 25, 27. ‖ Ibid. p. 94.
¶ MS. Remarks, p. 51.

curates and churchwardens in his diocese, to have it in the fashion of a table, decently covered."* This was very congenial to the wishes of many of the pious reformers, who, at this early period, publicly avowed their nonconformity to the ecclesiastical establishment. Among the articles of the above visitation, the bishop inquired, "Whether any of the anabaptists' sect, or others, use any unlawful or private conventicles, wherein they use doctrine, or administration of sacraments, separating themselves from the rest of the church? And whether any minister doth refuse to use the common prayers, or minister the sacraments, in that order and form, as set forth in the Book of Common Prayer?"† The disputes about conformity were carried into the pulpits; and whilst some warmly preached against all innovations, others as warmly preached against all the superstitions and corruptions of the old Romish church; so that the court prohibited all preaching, except by persons licensed by the King or the Archbishop of Canterbury.‡

In the convocation of 1552, forty-two Articles of Religion were agreed upon by the bishops and clergy, to which subscription was required of all ecclesiastical persons, who should officiate or enjoy any benefice in the church. And all who should refuse, were to be excluded from all ecclesiastical preferment. This appears to be the first time that subscription to the articles was enjoined.§ Here the reformation under King Edward made a stand.

During this king's reign, there were numerous debates about the habits, rites and ceremonies; and many divines of great learning and piety, became zealous advocates for nonconformity. They excepted against the clerical vestments, kneeling at the communion, godfathers and their promises and vows in baptism, the superstitious observance of Lent, the oath of canonical obedience, pluralities and nonresidence, with many other things of a similar description.‖ At this early period, there was a powerful and very considerable party disaffected to the established liturgy.¶ Though the reformation had already made considerable progress, its chief promoters were concerned for its further advancement. They aimed at a more perfect work; and

* Burnet's Hist. of Refor. vol. ii. p. 158.
† Sparrow's Collection, p. 36.
‡ Burnet's Hist. of Refor. vol. iii. p. 195.
§ Sparrow's Collection, p. 39.—Strype's Eccl. Mem. vol. ii. p. 420.
‖ MS. Remarks, p. 51. ¶ Fuller's Church Hist. b. vii. p. 426.

manifested their disapprobation of the numerous popish ceremonies and superstitions still retained in the church. King Edward desired that the rites and ceremonies used under popery, should be purged out of the church, and that the English churches might be brought to the APOSTOLIC PURITY. Archbishop Cranmer was also very desirous to promote the same;* and he is said to have drawn up a book of prayers incomparably more perfect than that which was then in use; but he was connected with so wicked a clergy and convocation, it could not take place.† And the king in his diary laments, that he could not restore the primitive discipline according to his heart's desire, because several of the bishops, some through age, some through ignorance, some on account of their ill name, and some out of love to popery, were opposed to the design.‡ Bishop Latimer complained of the stop put to the reformation, and urged the necessity of reviving the primitive discipline.§ The professors of our two universities, Peter Martyr and Martin Bucer, both opposed the use of the clerical vestments. To Martyr the vestments were offensive, and he would not wear them. "When I was at Oxford," says he, "I would never use those white garments in the choir; and I was satisfied in what I did." He styled them *mere relics of popery*. Bucer giving his advice, said, "That as those garments had been abused to superstition, and were likely to become the subject of contention, they ought to be taken away by law; and ecclesiastical discipline, and a more thorough reformation, set up. He disapproved of godfathers answering in the child's name. He recommended that pluralities and nonresidences might be abolished; and that bishops might not be concerned in secular affairs, but take care of their dioceses, and govern them by the advice of their presbyters." The pious king was so much pleased with this advice, that "he set himself to write upon a further reformation, and the necessity of church discipline."‖ Bucer was displeased with various corruptions in the liturgy. "It cannot be expressed, how bitterly he bewailed, that, when the gospel began to spread in England, a greater regard was not had to discipline and purity of rites, in constituting the

* Neal's Puritans, vol. i. p. 73.—Strype's Cranmer, p. 299.
† Troubles at Frankeford, p. 43.
‡ King Edward's Remains, numb. 2. in Burnet, vol. ii.
§ Burnet's Hist. of Refor. vol. ii. p. 152.
‖ Ibid. vol. ii. p. 155—157.

churches."* He could never be prevailed upon to wear the surplice. And when he was asked why he did not wear the *square cap?* he replied, "Because my head is not square."† The famous Dr. Thomas Sampson, afterwards one of the heads of the puritans, excepted against the habits at his ordination, who, nevertheless, was admitted by Cranmer and Ridley.‡ But the celebrated John Rogers and Bishop Hooper, according to Fuller, were "the very ringleaders of the nonconformists. They renounced all ceremonies practised by the papists, conceiving (as he has expressed it) that such ought not only to be clipt with shears, but shaven with a razor; yea, all the stumps thereof pluckt out."§

The sad effects of retaining the popish habits in the church, began to appear at a very early period. In the year 1550, a debate arose, which to some may appear of small consequence; but, at this time, was considered of great importance to the reformation. The debate was occasioned by Dr. Hooper's nomination to the bishopric of Gloucester. Burnet denominates him a pious, zealous, and learned man. Fuller says, he was well skilled in Latin, Greek, and Hebrew.‖ He was some time chaplain to the Duke of Somerset, and a famous preacher in the city of London;¶ but declined the offered preferment for two reasons,—1. Because of the form of the oath, which he calls foul and impious. And, 2. Because of the popish garments. The oath required him to swear by *the saints*, as well as by the name of God; which Hooper thought impious, because the Searcher of Hearts alone ought to be appealed to in an oath. The young king being convinced of this, struck out the words with his own pen.** But the scruples about the habits were not so easily got over. The king and council were inclined to dispense with them, as his majesty openly signified in the above letter to Cranmer: but Cranmer and Ridley were of another

* Heylin's Hist. of Refor. p. 65. † Strype's Parker, Appen. p. 41.

‡ Strype's Cranmer, p. 192. § Church Hist. b. vii. p. 402.

‖ Burnet's Refor. vol. iii. p. 199.—Fuller's Church Hist. b. vii. p. 402, 403.—King Edward, in his letter of nomination to Cranmer, dated Aug. 5, 1550, writes thus: "We, by the advice of our council, have called and chosen our right well-beloved and well-worthy Mr. John Hooper, professor of divinity, to be our Bishop of Gloucester; as well for his learning, deep judgment, and long study, both in the scriptures, and profane learning; as also for his good discretion, ready utterance, and honest life for that kind of vocation."—*Ibid.*

¶ Strype's Cranmer, p. 211.

** Burnet's Hist. of Refor. vol. iii. p. 203.

mind, and refused their allowance. Ridley was therefore nominated to a deputation with Hooper, with a view to bring him to a compliance; but this proved ineffectual. Hooper still remained unconvinced, and prayed to be excused from the old symbolizing popish garments. These garments, he observed, had no countenance in scripture or primitive antiquity: they were the inventions of antichrist, and introduced into the church in the most corrupt ages: they had been abused to idolatry, particularly in the pompous celebration of the mass: and to continue the use of them, was, in his opinion, to symbolize with antichrist, to mislead the people, and inconsistent with the simplicity of the christian religion.* He could appeal to the Searcher of Hearts, that it was not obstinacy, but the convictions of his conscience alone, which made him refuse these garments.†

Ridley's endeavours proving unsuccessful, Hooper was committed to the management of Cranmer, who, being unable to bring him to conformity, laid the affair before the council, and he was committed to the Fleet. Having remained in prison for several months, the matter was compromised, when he was released and consecrated.‡ He consented to put on the vestments at his consecration, when he preached before the king, and in his own cathedral; but was suffered to dispense with them at other times.§ How this business was adjusted, and with what degree of severity he was persecuted, is related by Mr. Fox, in the Latin edition of his "Acts and Monuments of the Martyrs." The passage, says Mr. Peirce, he hath left out in all his English editions, out of too great tenderness to the party. "Thus," says Mr. Fox, "ended this theological quarrel in the victory of the bishops, Hooper being forced to recant; or, to say the least, being constrained to appear once in public, attired after the manner of the bishops. Which, unless he had done, there are those who think the bishops would have endeavoured to take away his life: for his servant told me," adds the martyrologist, "that the Duke of Suffolk sent such word to Hooper, who was not himself ignorant of what they were doing."‖ Horrid barbarity! Who, before Hooper, was ever thrown into prison, and in danger of his life, merely

* Neal's Puritans, vol. i. p. 62. † Fuller's Church Hist. b. vii. p. 404.
‡ Strype's Cranmer, p. 211—215.—Baker's MS. Collec. vol. xviii. p. 269.
§ Burnet's Hist. of Refor. vol. ii. p. 166.
‖ Peirce's Vindication, part i. p. 30.

because he refused a bishopric? It was certainly some kind of excuse, that the bishops would not consecrate him contrary to law; but there can be no excuse for his imprisonment, and their conspiring to take away his life. When Hooper wished to be excused accepting the offered preferment upon the conditions of the ecclesiastical establishment, was there any law to constrain him, contrary to the convictions of his own conscience? Ridley, however, who was by far the most severe against Hooper, lived to change his opinions, as will appear hereafter.

Most of the reforming clergy were of Hooper's sentiments in this controversy. Several who had submitted to the habits in the late reign, now laid them aside: among whom were Bishops Latimer and Coverdale, Dr. Rowland Taylor, John Rogers, John Bradford, and John Philpot, all zealous nonconformists. They declaimed against them as mere popish and superstitious attire, and not fit for the ministers of the gospel.* Indeed, they were not so much as pressed upon the clergy in general, but mostly left as matters of indifference.†

During this reign, certain persons denominated anabaptists, having fled from the wars in Germany, and come to England, propagated their sentiments and made proselytes in this country. Complaints being brought against them to the council, Archbishop Cranmer, with several of the bishops and others, received a commission, April 12, 1550, "to examine and search after all anabaptists, heretics, or contemners of the common prayer." As they were able to discover such persons, they were to endeavour to reclaim them, and, after penance, to give them absolution; but all who continued obstinate, were to be excommunicated, imprisoned, and delivered over to the secular power. Several tradesmen in London being convened before the commissioners, abjured; but Joan Bocher, or Joan of Kent, was made a public example. She steadfastly maintained, "That Christ was not truly incarnate of the virgin, whose flesh being sinful, he could not partake of it; but the word, by the consent of the inward man of the virgin, took flesh of her."‡ These were her own words; not capable of doing much mischief, and, surely, undeserving any severe punishment. The poor woman could not reconcile the spotless purity of

* MS. Chronology, vol. i. p. 35. (30.)
† Burnet's Hist. of Refor. vol. iii. p. 310, 311.
‡ Burnet's Hist. of Refor. vol. ii. Collec. p. 168.

Christ's human nature, with his receiving flesh from a sinful creature; for which she was declared an obstinate heretic, and delivered over to the secular power to be burnt. The compassionate young king thought, that burning persons for their religious opinions savoured too much of that for which they censured the papists; therefore, when he could not prevail upon himself to sign the warrant for her execution, Cranmer, with his superior learning, was employed to persuade him. He argued from the practice of the Jewish church in stoning blasphemers; which *silenced*, rather than *satisfied* the king. He still looked upon it as cruel severity. And when at last he yielded to the archbishop's importunity, he told him, with tears in his eyes, "That if he did wrong, since it was in submission to his authority, he should answer for it to God." This is said to have struck the archbishop with much horror; yet he suffered the sentence to be executed.*

Besides those denominated anabaptists, there were also many others who administered the sacraments in other manner than was prescribed in the Book of Common Prayer. To prevent the number of these nonconformists from increasing, and to crush all who had already imbibed their sentiments, another commission was issued, empowering the archbishop and others to correct and punish them.† And in the year 1552, Cranmer and others received a third commission from the council, to examine a certain sect newly sprung up in Kent.‡ This was a sect of nonconformists, though their peculiar sentiments do not appear. Mr. Fox, in the Latin edition of his "Martyrs," observes, "That one Humphrey Middleton,§ with some others, had been kept prisoners in the last year of King Edward by the archbishop, and had been dreadfully teazed by him and the rest in commission, and were now just upon the point of being condemned; when in open court he said: *Well, reverend Sir, pass what sentence you think fit upon*

* Burnet's Hist. of Refor. vol. ii. p. 111, 112.—This female sufferer, according to Mr. Strype, "was a great reader of the scriptures, and formerly a great disperser of Tindal's New Testament; which book she dispersed in the court, and so became acquainted with certain women of quality. She used, for the greater secrecy, to tie the books with strings under her apparel, and so pass with them into the court." Thus she exposed her own life, in dangerous times, to bring others to a knowledge of God's holy word.—*Strype's Eccl. Memorials*, vol. ii. p. 214.

† Strype's Parker, p. 27. ‡ Strype's Cranmer, p. 291.

§ This person, a native of Ashford, in Kent, was afterwards burnt in the days of Queen Mary.—*Fox's Martyrs*, vol. iii. p. 313.

us; but that you may not say you were not forewarned, I testify that your own turn will be next. And accordingly it came to pass; for a little while after, King Edward died, when the prisoners were set at liberty, and the archbishop and bishops cast into prison."* The above severities, shewing the imperfect state of the English reformation, will be handed down to posterity, as monuments of lasting reproach to our famous reformers. Persecution, whoever may be the persecutors, deserves ever to appear in all its detestable and shocking features.

In the year 1553, upon the death of King Edward, his sister MARY coming to the crown, soon overturned the reformation, and restored the whole body of popery. The queen was a violent papist; yet she at first declared, "That though her conscience was settled in matters of religion, she was resolved not to compel others, only by the preaching of the word."† How far her majesty adhered to this sacred maxim, the numerous tragic scenes of her bloody reign, afford too strong a proof. She, within the same month, prohibited all preaching without her special license; and further declared, "That she would not compel her subjects to be of her religion, *till public order should be taken.*"‡ This was a clear intimation of the approaching storm. Many of the principal reformers were immediately cast into prison. Hooper was sent to the Fleet, and Cranmer and Latimer to the Tower, and above a thousand persons retired into foreign parts:§ among whom were five bishops, five deans, four archdeacons, and a great number of doctors in divinity, and celebrated preachers. In the number of worthy exiles were Coverdale, Turner, Sampson, Whitehead, Becon, Lever, Whittingham, and Fox, all afterwards famous in the days of Queen Elizabeth.‖ The two archbishops and most of the bishops were deprived of their sees. The most celebrated preachers in London were put under confinement, and no less than 12,000 of the clergy, for being married, were turned out of their livings; some of whom were deprived without conviction; some were never cited to appear; and many, being confined in prison, and unable to appear, were cited and deprived for non-appearance. In the mean time, the service and reformation of King Edward were abolished, and the old popish worship and ceremonies revived.¶

* Peirce's Vindication, part I. p. 35.
† Burnet's Hist. of Refor. vol. ii. p. 245. ‡ Ibid. § Ibid. p. 247, 250.
‖ Strype's Cranmer, p. 314. ¶ Burnet's Hist. of Refor. vol. ii. p. 276.

During this queen's reign, several hundred persons suffered death under the foul charge of heresy;* among whom were great numbers of pious and learned divines, all zealous for the reformation. Many of these divines being avowed nonconformists in the reign of King Edward, maintained their principles even at the stake. Mr. John Rogers, the protomartyr, peremptorily refused to wear the habits, unless the popish priests were enjoined to wear upon their sleeves, as a mark of distinction, a *chalice with an host.* The same may be observed of Mr. John Philpot and Mr. Tyms, two other eminent martyrs.† Bishop Latimer derided the garments; and when they pulled off the surplice at his degradation, he said, *Now I can make no more holy water.* In the articles against Bishop Farrar, it was objected, that he had vowed never to wear the *cap,* but that he came into his cathedral in his long gown and hat; which he did not deny, alleging that he did it to avoid superstition, and giving offence to the people.‡ When the popish vestments were put upon Dr. Taylor, at his degradation, he walked about with his hands by his sides, saying, "How say you, my lord, am I not a *godly fool?* How say you, my masters, if I were in Cheapside, should I not have boys enough to laugh at these *apish toys* and *toying trumpery?*" And it is observed, that when the surplice was pulled off, he said, *Now I am rid of a fool's coat.*§ The famous John Bradford excepted against the habits, and was ordained without them; and even Cranmer and Ridley, who, in the late reign had exercised great severity against Hooper and others, lived to see their mistakes, and to repent of their conduct. Cranmer being clothed in the habits, at his degradation, said, "All this needeth not. I had myself done with this years ago."‖ Ridley, when he refused to put on the surplice at his degradation, and they put it on by force, "vehemently inveighed against it, calling it *foolish* and *abominable,* and too *fond for a vice in a play.*"¶ And even during his confinement in prison, he wrote to Hooper, saying, "That

* Burnet reckons the number of those who suffered in the flames to be 284; and Mr. Strype, 288; but it is said there were no less than 800, during Queen Mary's bloody persecution.—*Ibid.* p. 364.—*Strype's Eccl. Mem.* vol. III. Appen. p. 291.

† Heylin's Hist. of Refor. part I. p. 93.

‡ Fox's Martyrs, vol. III. p. 168, 178.

§ Ibid. p. 143.

‖ It is observed that both Cranmer and Ridley intended to have procured an act for abolishing the habits, but were prevented.—*Peirce's Vindication,* part I. p. 44.

¶ Fox's Martyrs, vol. III. p. 427.

he was entirely knit to him, though in some circumstances of religion they had formerly jarred a little; wherein it was Hooper's wisdom, and his own simplicity, which had made the difference."*

All the severe persecution in this queen's reign, did not extinguish the light of the English reformation. Great numbers were driven, indeed, into exile, and multitudes suffered in the flames, yet many, who loved the gospel more than their lives, were enabled to endure the storm. Congregations were formed in various parts of the kingdom. There was a considerable congregation of these excellent christians, at Stoke, in Suffolk; with whom, on account of their number and unanimity, the bishops were for some time afraid to interfere. They constantly attended their private meetings, and never went to the parish church. An order was at length sent to the whole society, requiring them to receive the popish sacrament, or abide by the consequences. But the good people having assembled for the purpose of consultation, unanimously resolved not to comply. In about six months, the Bishop of Norwich sent his officers, strictly charging them to go to church on the following Lord's day, or, in case of failure, to appear before the commissary to give an account of their conduct. But having notice of this, they kept out of the way to avoid the summons. When they neither went to church, nor appeared before the commissary, the angry prelate suspended and excommunicated the whole congregation. And when officers were appointed to apprehend them, they left the town, and so escaped all the days of Queen Mary.†

The most considerable of these congregations, was that which met in and about London. Owing to the vigilance of their enemies, these people were obliged to assemble with the utmost secrecy; and though there were about 200 members, they remained for a considerable time undiscovered. Their meetings were held alternately in Aldgate, in Blackfriars, in Pudding-lane, in Thames-street, and in ships upon the river. Sometimes they assembled in the villages about London, especially at Islington, that they might the more easily elude the bishops' officers. To

* Prince's Chron. Hist. vol. i. p. 217.—Bishop Ridley was a famous disputant against the papists. He forced them to acknowledge, that Christ in his last supper, held himself in his hand, and afterwards eat himself.—*Granger's Biog. Hist.* vol. i. p. 159.

† Clark's Martyrologie, p. 515.

screen themselves from the notice of their persecutors, they often met in the night, and experienced many wonderful providential deliverances.* Their public devotions were conducted by the following ministers: Edmund Scambler, afterwards successively Bishop of Peterborough and Norwich, Mr. Fowler, Mr. John Rough, Mr. Augustine Birnher, Thomas Bentham, afterwards Bishop of Lichfield and Coventry, and Mr. John Pullain, afterwards an excellent puritan.†

During Mr. Rough's ministry among these people, he was apprehended, with Mr. Cuthbert Sympson and some others, at a house in Islington, where the church was about to assemble for prayer and preaching the word; and being taken before the council, after several examinations, he was sent to Newgate, and his case committed to the management of Bonner. The character of this prelate, whose hands were so deeply stained with innocent blood, needs no colouring in this place: the faithful pages of history will always hold it up to the execration of mankind. In his hands, Mr. Rough met with the most relentless cruelty. Not content with degrading him, and delivering him over to the secular power, the furious prelate flew upon him, and plucked the beard from his face. And, at length, after much cruel usage, he ended his life in the flames, in December, 1557.‡ Mr. Sympson, who was deacon of the church, was a pious, faithful, and zealous man, labouring incessantly to preserve the flock from the errors of popery, and to secure them from the dangers of persecution. At the time of his apprehension, the whole church was, indeed, in the utmost danger. It was Mr. Sympson's office to keep a book, containing the names of all the persons belonging to the congregation, which book he always carried to their private assemblies. But it was so ordered, by the good

* On one of these nocturnal occasions, being assembled in a house, by the side of the river, in Thames-street, they were discovered; and the house was so guarded, that their enemies were sure none could escape. But among them was a worthy mariner, who, seeing no other way of deliverance, got out at a back door; and swimming to a boat in the river, brought it; and having received all the good people into it, he made oars of his shoes, and conveyed them all away in safety.—Clark's Martyrologie, p. 313, 316.

† Ibid.—Strype's Annals, vol. i. p. 282.

‡ Fox's Martyrs, vol. iii. p. 722, 726.—Mr. Rough had been a celebrated preacher in Scotland, and also in England, in the reign of Edward VI. A sermon which he delivered in the parish church of St. Andrew, was made a great blessing to the celebrated Mr. John Knox, and proved the means of bringing him forth to engage in his public ministry.—Biog. Britan. vol. iv. p. 2863. Edit. 1747.

providence of God, that on the day of his apprehension, he left it with Mrs. Rough, the minister's wife.* Two or three days after this, he was sent to the Tower. During his confinement, because he would not discover the book, nor the names of the persons, he was cruelly racked three several times; and an arrow was tied between his two fore-fingers, and drawn out so violently as to cause the blood to gush forth; but all was without effect. He was then committed to Bonner, who bore this testimony concerning him before a number of spectators: "You see what a personable man this is; and for his patience, if he were not an heretic, I should much commend him. For he has been thrice racked in one day, and, in my house, he hath endured some sorrow; and yet I never saw his patience once moved." The relentless prelate, nevertheless, condemned him, ordering him first into the stocks in his coal-house, and from thence to Smithfield; where with Mr. Fox and Mr. Davenish, two others of the church taken at Islington, he ended his life in the flames.† Seven more of this church were burnt in Smithfield, six at Brentford, and others died in prison.‡

The numerous divines who fled from the persecution of Queen Mary, retired to Frankfort, Strasburgh, Zurich, Basil, Geneva, and other places; but they were most numerous at Frankfort. At this place it was, that a contest and division commenced, which gave rise to the PURITANS, and to that SEPARATION from the church of England which continues to this day. The exiles were in no place so happily settled as at Frankfort; where the senate gave them the use of a church, on condition that they should not vary from the French reformed church, either in doctrine or ceremonies. According to these conditions, they drew up a new liturgy, more agreeable to those of the foreign churches, omitting the responses and the litany, with many trifling ceremonies in the English prayer book, and declined the use of the surplice. They took possession

* A few nights before this, Mr. Rough had a remarkable dream. He thought he saw Mr. Sympson taken by two of the guard, and with the book above-mentioned. This giving him much trouble, he awoke, and related the dream to his wife. Afterwards, falling asleep, he again dreamt the same thing. Upon his awaking the second time, he determined to go immediately to Mr. Sympson, and put him upon his guard; but while he was getting ready, Mr. Sympson came to his house with the book, which he deposited with Mrs. Rough, as above related.—*Fox*, vol. iii. p. 726.

† Ibid. p. 726, 729.—Clark's Martyrologie, p. 497.

‡ Fox's Martyrs, vol. iii. p. 732, 734.

of the church, July 29, 1554; and having chosen a temporary minister and deacons, they sent to their brethren, who had fled to other places, inviting them to Frankfort, where they might hear God's word truly preached, the sacraments duly administered, and the requisite christian discipline properly exercised: privileges which could not be obtained in their own country.* The members of the congregation sent for Mr. John Knox from Geneva, Mr. James Haddon from Strasburgh, and Mr. Thomas Lever from Zurich, requesting them to take the oversight of them in the Lord.

The church at Frankfort being thus comfortably settled with pastors, deacons, and a liturgy, according to its own choice; Dr. Richard Cox, a man of a high spirit, coming to that city, with some of his friends, broke through the conditions of the new-formed church, and interrupted the public service by answering aloud after the minister. On the Lord's day following, one of the company, equally officious as himself, ascended the pulpit, and read the whole litany. Mr. Knox, upon this, taxed the authors of this disorder with a breach of the terms of their common agreement, and affirmed, that some things in the Book of Common Prayer were superstitious and impure. Dr. Cox reproved him for his censoriousness; and being admitted, with the rest of his company, to vote in the congregation, obtained a majority, prohibiting Mr. Knox from preaching any more.† But Mr. Knox's friends applied to the magistrates, who commanded them to unite with the *French* church both in doctrine and ceremonies, according to their original agreement. Dr. Cox and his party finding Knox's interest among the magistrates too strong, had recourse to an unworthy and unchristian method to get rid of him. This divine having published a book, while he was in England, entitled "An Admonition to Christians," in which he had said, "That the emperor was no less an enemy to Christ than Nero," these overbearing fellow-exiles basely availed themselves of this and some other expressions in the book, and accused him of high treason against the emperor. Upon this, the senate being tender of the emperor's honour, and unwilling to embroil themselves in these controversies, desired Mr. Knox, in a respectful manner, to depart from the city. So he left the place, March 25, 1555.

* Troubles at Frankeford, p. 1—3.

† Cox and his friends were admitted to vote in the congregation, through the particular solicitations of Mr. Knox.—*Ibid.* p. 33.

Upon Mr. Knox's departure, Cox's party having strengthened themselves by the addition of other exiles, petitioned the magistrates for the free use of King Edward's service-book; which they were pleased to grant. The old congregation was thus broken up by Dr. Cox and his friends, who now carried all before them. They chose new church-officers, taking no notice of the old ones, and set up the service-book without interruption. Among those who were driven from the peaceable and happy congregation, were Knox, Gilby, Goodman, Cole, Whittingham, and Fox, all celebrated nonconformists in the reign of Queen Elizabeth.* From the above account, it will sufficiently appear who were the aggressors. Bishop Burnet, with great injustice, says, "That Knox and his party certainly began the breach."†

Towards the close of this queen's unhappy reign, her government having sustained many losses, her spirits failed, her health declined, and, being seized with the dropsy, she died November 17, 1558, in the forty-third year of her age, having reigned a little more than five years and four months. Queen Mary was a princess of severe principles, and being wholly under the controul of her clergy, was ever forward to sanction all their cruelties. Her conscience was under the absolute direction of the pope and her confessor; who, to encourage her in the extirpation of heresy, and in all the cruelties inflicted upon protestants, gave her assurance, that she was doing God service. She was naturally of a melancholy and peevish temper; and her death was lamented only by her popish clergy.‡ Her reign was in every respect calamitous to the nation, and will be transmitted to posterity in characters of blood.

SECT. II.

From the Death of Queen Mary, to the Death of Queen Elizabeth.

THE accession of Queen ELIZABETH to the crown, gave new life to the Reformation. The news had no sooner reached the continent, than most of the worthy exiles with joy returned home; and those who had concealed themselves, during the late storm, came forth as men restored from the

* Troubles at Frankeford, p. 1—&c.
† Hist. of Refor. vol. ii. p. 339.
‡ Ibid. p. 369—371.

dead.* By the queen's royal proclamation, the public worship of God remained some time without alteration. All preaching was prohibited; and the people were charged to hear only the epistles and gospels for the day, the ten commandments, the litany, the Lord's prayer, and the creed, in English. No other prayers were to be read, nor other forms of worship to be observed, than those already appointed by law, till the meeting of parliament.†

The parliament being assembled, the two famous acts, entitled "The Act of Supremacy,"‡ and "The Act of Uniformity of Common Prayer," were passed. The former gave rise to a new ecclesiastical court, called *The Court of* HIGH COMMISSION, which, by the exercise of its unlimited power and authority, became the engine of inconceivable oppression to multitudes of the queen's best subjects. The latter attempted, indeed, to establish a perfect uniformity in public worship, but it could never be effected.§ During the whole of this reign, many of the best divines and others, were dissatisfied with the Book of Common Prayer, and with the rigorous imposition of it in divine worship. Some things contained in the book, they considered to be erroneous; others superstitious; and the greater part to be derived from the corrupt fountain of popery, and, therefore, could not with a good conscience observe the whole; on which account, they were treated by the prelates with the utmost severity. The principal debate in the first parliament of this queen's reign, was not whether popery or protestantism should be established; but whether they should carry on the reformation, so happily begun in the days of King Edward, to a greater degree of perfection, and abolish all the remains of superstition, idolatry, and

* It is observed, that when the exiles and others came forwards in public, a certain gentleman made suit to the queen, in behalf of *Matthew*, *Mark*, *Luke*, and *John*, who had long been imprisoned in a Latin translation, that they also might be restored to liberty, and walk abroad as formerly in the English tongue. To this petition her majesty immediately replied, "That he should first know the minds of the prisoners, who perhaps desired no such liberty as he requested."—*Heylin's Hist. of Refor.* p. 275.

† Burnet's Hist. of Refor. vol. ii. p. 378.—Strype's Annals, vol. i. p. 41—44. ‡ Ibid. p. 60.

§ This act was designed to establish a perfect and universal conformity, among the laity, as well as the clergy. It required "all persons diligently and faithfully, having no lawful or reasonable excuse, to resort to their parish church, every Sunday and all holidays, on pain of punishment by the *censures of the church*, and also on pain of forfeiting *twelve-pence* for every such offence, to be levied by way of distress."—*Burn's Eccl. Law*, vol. ii. p. 145. Edit, 1775.

popish innovations, which being still retained in the church, were stumbling blocks to many worthy subjects.*

In the year 1559, the queen published her *Injunctions*, consisting of upwards of *fifty* distinct articles. She commanded all her loving subjects obediently to receive, and truly to observe and keep them, according to their offices, degrees and estates, upon pain of suspension, deprivation, excommunication, and such other censures as to those who had ecclesiastical jurisdiction under her majesty, should seem meet.† Though in these injunctions the queen manifested some disapprobation of the Romish superstitions and idolatry, she was much inclined to retain images in churches, and thought they were useful in exciting devotion, and in drawing people to public worship. Her object was to unite the papists and protestants together.‡ She still retained a crucifix upon the altar, with lights burning before it, in her own chapel, when three bishops officiated, all in rich copes, before the idol.§ Instead of stripping religion of the numerous, pompous ceremonies with which it was incumbered, she was inclined rather to keep it as near as possible to the Romish ritual: and even some years after her accession, one of her chaplains having preached in defence of the *real presence*, she presented her public thanks to him, for his *pains* and *piety*.‖ She spoke with great bitterness against the marriage of the clergy, and repented having made married persons bishops.¶ Her majesty having appointed a committee of divines to review King Edward's liturgy, she commanded them to strike out all passages offensive to the pope, and to make the people easy about the corporeal presence of Christ in the sacrament.** The liturgy was, therefore, exceedingly well fitted to the approbation of the papists.†† The queen commanded, that the Lord's table should be placed in the form of an altar; that reverence should be made at the name of Jesus; that music should be retained in the churches; and that all the festivals should be observed as in times of popery.‡‡ The reformation of King Edward, therefore, instead of being carried forwards and perfected, was, according to Burnet, removed considerably backwards, partly

* MS. Remarks, p. 463. † Sparrow's Collec. p. 65—86.
‡ Burnet's Hist. of Refor. vol. ii. p. 397. § Ibid. vol. iii. p. 292.
‖ Heylin's Hist. of Refor. p. 124. Edit. 1670.
¶ Strype's Parker, p. 109.
** Burnet's Hist. of Refor. vol. ii. p. 392.
†† Heylin's Hist. of Pres. p. 259.
‡‡ Heylin's Hist. of Refor. p. 283. Edit. 1674.

from the queen's love of outward magnificence in religion, and partly in compliance with the papists.*

Many of our excellent reformers who had espoused the cause of nonconformity, in the days of King Edward, retained their principles, and acted upon them, during their exile in a foreign land, especially those who being driven from Frankfort, settled at Geneva and other places. Nor did they forget their principles upon the accession of Elizabeth. Having settled for several years among the best reformed churches in Europe, they examined more minutely the grand principles of the reformation, and returned home richly fraught with wisdom and knowledge. They wished to have the church purged of all its antichristian errors and superstitions, and to have its discipline, its government, and its ceremonies, as well as its doctrine, regulated by the standard of holy scripture. On the contrary, many of the bishops and clergy being too well affected to popery, opposed a thorough reformation, accounting that of King Edward sufficient, or more than sufficient, for the present church of England. Therefore, so early as in the year mentioned above, there were many warm debates betwixt the two contending parties.†

In addition to the oath of supremacy, a compliance with the act of uniformity, and an exact observance of the queen's injunctions, a public creed was drawn up by the bishops, entitled "A Declaration of certain principal Articles of Religion," which all clergymen were obliged to read publicly at their entrance upon their cures. These were, at this time, the terms of ministerial conformity. There was no dispute among the reformers, about the first and last of these qualifications, but they differed in some points about the other two. Many of the learned exiles and others, could not, with a good conscience, accept of livings according to the act of uniformity and the queen's injunctions. If the popish garments and ceremonies had been left indifferent, and some liberties allowed in the use of the common prayer, the contentions and divisions which afterwards followed, would no doubt have been prevented. But as the case then stood, it was almost miraculous that the reformation did not fall back to popery; and if some of the nonconforming divines had not in part complied, in hopes of the removal of these grievances at some future period, that would most probably have been the unhappy

* Burnet's Hist. of Refor. vol. iii. p. 305.
† Ibid. vol. ii. p. 407.—Baker's MS. Collec. vol. xxvii. p. 387.

consequence. Many churches were for a considerable time without ministers, and not a few mechanics, and persons altogether unlearned, were preferred, which brought much reproach upon the protestant cause; while others of the first rank for learning, piety and usefulness, were laid aside in silence. There was, indeed, very little preaching through the whole country.* The Bishop of Bangor writes, during this year, "that he had only two preachers in all his diocese."+ Indeed the bishops in general were not insensible of the calamity; but instead of opening the door a little wider, for the allowance of the more conscientious and zealous reformers, they admitted the meanest and most illiterate, who would come up to the terms of conformity.‡ And even at this early period, there were many of the clergy, who, though preferred to benefices, could not conform, but refused to observe the public service, and to wear the holy garments; at which the queen was exceedingly offended.§ Dr. Matthew Parker was this year consecrated Archbishop of Canterbury.

In the year 1562, sat the famous convocation, when "The Thirty-nine Articles of Religion," much the same as those of King Edward, were drawn up and subscribed by all the members then sitting, and required to be subscribed by all the clergy in the kingdom. The convocation proceeded next to consider the rites and ceremonies of the church, when Bishop Sandys presented a paper recommending the abolition of private baptism, and the crossing of the infant in the forehead, which, he said, was *needless* and *very superstitious*.‖ Another paper was, at the same time, presented to the house, with the following requests:—"That the psalms may be sung distinctly by the whole "congregation; and that organs may be laid aside.—That "none may baptize but ministers; and that they may leave "off the sign of the cross.—That in the administration of "the sacrament, the posture of *kneeling* may be left indif- "ferent.—That the use of copes and surplices may be "taken away; so that all ministers in their ministry use a "grave, comely, and long garment, as they commonly do "in preaching.—That ministers be not compelled to wear "such gowns and caps, as the enemies of Christ's gospel "have chosen for the special array of their priesthood.— "That the words in the thirty-third article, concerning the

* Biog. Britan. vol. v. p. 3297. Edit. 1747. + MS. Register, p. 886.
‡ Neal's Puritans, vol. i. p. 146.
§ Strype's Parker, p. 106. ‖ Strype's Annals, vol. i. p. 297.

"punishment of those who do not in all things conform to "the public order about ceremonies, may be mitigated.—"That all the saints' days, festivals, and holidays, bearing "the name of a creature, may be abrogated."—This paper was subscribed by one provost, five deans, twelve archdeacons, and fourteen proctors, many of whom were eminent for learning and ability; but their requests were rejected.*

In the above convocation, there was a great difference of sentiment among the learned reformers, which occasioned many warm debates upon points of great importance, especially upon this, "Whether it was most proper to retain the outward appearance of things, as near as possible to what had been practised in times of popery." While the one party maintained the affirmative, the other asserted, that this outward resemblance of the Romish church, would encourage the people in their former practices, nourish in them the old root of popery, and make them a more easy prey to their popish adversaries. Therefore they recommended that every thing might be removed as far as possible from the church of Rome.† In the conclusion, the contrary party prevailed: and the bishops, conceiving themselves empowered by the canons of this convocation, began to exercise their authority by requiring the clergy of their respective dioceses to subscribe to the liturgy, the ceremonies, and the discipline of the church; when such as refused, were branded with the odious name of PURITANS. This was a term of reproach given them by their enemies; because they wished to serve and worship God with greater *purity* than was allowed and established in the church of England.‡ All were stigmatized by this name, who distinguished themselves in the cause of *religious liberty*, and who could not in all points conform to the ecclesiastical establishment.

In the year 1564, Archbishop Parker, with the assistance of several of the bishops, published the *Advertisements*, with a view to secure a due conformity among ecclesiastical persons. By the first of these advertisements, all preachers throughout the province of Canterbury were at once disqualified; and by the last, they were required to subscribe, and promise not to preach or expound the scriptures, without a license from the bishop, which could not be obtained

* Strype's Annals, p. 298. vol. ii. Adden. p. 15.
† Burnet's Hist. of Refor. vol. iii. p. 302.
‡ Fuller's Church Hist. b. ix. p. 76.

without a protestation and promise under their hand of an absolute conformity to the ceremonies. No less than eight protestations were also required to be made and subscribed by all who should be admitted to any office or cure in the church.* Though the archbishop and his brethren at first met with some difficulties in carrying them into effect, (the queen refusing to sanction them,) yet afterwards, presuming upon her majesty's favour, they succeeded according to their wishes.† Upon the approach of these severities, Mr. Whittingham wrote a long and pressing letter to the Earl of Leicester, warmly urging him to interpose with the queen, to hinder their execution. In the conclusion of this most pathetic epistle, he says, "I need not appeal to the word of God, to the history of the primitive church, and to the just judgments of God poured out upon the nations for lack of true reformation. Judge ye betwixt us and our enemies. And if we seek the glory of God alone, the enjoyment of true christian liberty, the overthrow of all idolatry and superstition, and to win souls to Christ; I beseech your honour to pity our case, and use your utmost endeavours to secure our liberty."‡

Many of the clergy in both the universities, and in the country, but especially in the city of London, refused to wear the square cap, the tippet, and the surplice. "And it is marvellous," says Mr. Strype, "how much these habits were abhorred by many honest, well-meaning men; who styled them antichristian ceremonies, and by no means fit to be used in a true christian church."§ But Archbishop Parker and other high commissioners being resolved to reduce the church to one uniform order, cited many of the clergy before them, admonishing some, and threatening others. Among those who appeared, were Dr. Sampson, dean of Christ-church, Oxford, and Dr. Humphrey, president of Magdalen college, in the same university. They were divines of great renown throughout the kingdom, for learning, piety, and zeal for the reformation, but were cast into prison for nonconformity.‖ The famous Mr. Whitehead, with several others, was cited at the same

* Sparrow's Collec. p. 123—128.
† Strype's Parker, p. 151—161.
‡ See Art. Whittingham.
§ Strype's Parker, p. 151.
‖ It is proper here to observe, that throughout the Introduction, no authority will be given where the same things are treated more at large in the body of the work. Therefore, in order to examine the evidence of what the author has asserted, as well as a more circumstantial detail of facts, the reader, in all such instances, is directed to the respective articles.

time, and, refusing to subscribe, was immediately suspended. Mr. Becon, another celebrated reformer, being cited, and refusing to subscribe, was immediately sequestered and deprived. Mr. Allen was cited, and received the like censure. Many others were suspended and deprived, who, having wives and children, laboured under great poverty and want. Being driven from their ministerial employment, some, to procure a livelihood, betook themselves to trades, some to husbandry, and some went to sea.*

The principal reasons of these and other learned divines now refusing conformity, were—1. Because those things which the prelates required, were unsupported by scripture and primitive antiquity.—2. They were not received by other reformed churches.—And, 3. They savoured very much of the errors and superstitions of popery.† On these grounds, they disapproved of some things in the Book of Common Prayer, and forbore the use of the habits and ceremonies.

In the year 1565, the archbishop and his brethren in commission, not content with exercising all their own authority to its fullest extent, sought the favourable assistance of the council, and enforced an exact conformity to the ecclesiastical establishment with still greater rigour. They convened the London ministers before them; and when they appeared in court, Mr. Robert Cole, a clergyman,‡ being placed by the side of the commissioners in priestly apparel, they were addressed in these words:—"My masters, and ye ministers of London, the council's pleasure is, that strictly ye keep the unity of apparel, like this man who stands here canonically habited with a square cap, a scholar's gown, priest-like, a tippet, and, in the church, a linen surplice. Ye that will subscribe, write *Volo;* those that will not subscribe, write *Nolo.* Be brief: make no words." When some of the ministers offered to speak, they were immediately interrupted with the command, "*Peace, peace;* and *apparitor,* call over the churches: ye masters, answer presently under the *penalty of contempt.*"§ In the conclusion, sixty-one promised conformity, but *thirty-seven* absolutely refused, being, as the archbishop acknowledged, the best among them. These

* Strype's Grindal, p. 99. † MS. Remarks, p. 161.

‡ This Mr. Cole, for his subscription and conformity, was preferred by the archbishop to the benefice of Bow and Allhallows, London.—*Baker's MS. Collec.* vol. xxvii. p. 387.

§ Strype's Grindal, p. 98.—Annals, vol. i. p. 463.

were immediately suspended, and told, that if they did not conform within three months, they should be deprived of all their spiritual promotions.* Among those who received the ecclesiastical censure, was Mr. Crowley, who was afterwards deprived and imprisoned. Mr. Brokelsby was sequestered, and afterwards deprived, being the first who was thus censured for refusing to wear the surplice. Dr. Turner, dean of Wells, was sequestered and deprived for refusing to wear the surplice, and to use the Book of Common Prayer. The venerable Miles Coverdale was driven from his flock, and obliged to relinquish his benefice. In consequence of these proceedings, many of the churches in London were shut up, for want of ministers. "This," says the archbishop, "was no more than he foresaw before he began; and that when the queen put him upon doing what he had done, he told her, that these precise folks," as in contempt he calls them, "would offer their goods and bodies to prison, rather than they would relent."†

Notwithstanding these proceedings, the nonconformists greatly multiplied, and they were much esteemed and countenanced by persons of quality and influence. God raised them up many friends in both houses of parliament, and in her majesty's privy council: as, the Earls of Bedford, Warwick, and Leicester, Sir Francis Knollys, Sir William Cecil, and many others. All these were the constant friends of the puritans, and used their power and influence to obtain a further reformation.‡ Though in the latter they utterly failed of success, they often protected the persecuted ministers, or procured their release from suspension, deprivation, and imprisonment.

The principal persons for learning and piety, in the university of Cambridge, not only opposed the above severities, but refused conformity. The fellows and scholars of St. John's college, to the number of nearly *three hundred*, threw away their surplices with one consent; and many in other colleges followed their example.§ This, indeed, presently roused the zeal of the jealous archbishop. He looked upon Cambridge as becoming the very nursery of puritanism; and, therefore, to crush the evil in the bud, he warmly recommended the chancellor to enforce an exact conformity throughout that fountain of learning. In the mean time, the heads of colleges being dissatisfied with these proceedings, wrote a pressing letter to the chancellor,

* Strype's Parker, p. 211, 215.
† Ibid. p. 225.
‡ MS. Remarks, p. 111, 193.
§ Strype's Annals, vol. i. p. 441.

wishing him to put a stop to such severe measures. They observe that multitudes of pious and learned men thought in their consciences, that the use of the garments was utterly unlawful; and that the imposition of them upon all in the university, would compel these worthy persons to forsake the place, which would leave the university very destitute. Such an imposition of conformity, say they, will prove exceedingly detrimental to the preaching of the gospel, as well as to good learning.* The chancellor being a man of great prudence and circumspection, and loath to give offence by using severities, made some demur, with which the archbishop was displeased. Those who refused conformity reminded the chancellor, that they had cast away the ceremonies, not out of malice, for vain glory, an affection for popularity, contempt of laws, or any desire of innovation, but out of love to the truth. They could call the Searcher of Hearts to witness, that in what they had done, they had sought to enjoy peace of conscience, and the true worship of God. They prayed, therefore, that their consciences might not be brought into a state of most grievous bondage and exquisite torment, by being forced to observe the ceremonies.†

The proceedings of the prelates in censuring so many ministers of high reputation, was very afflictive to the foreign reformed churches. Therefore the famous Beza wrote a letter this year to Bishop Grindal, exposing the evils attending the imposition of conformity. He observes, that "if *they* do offend, who choose to leave their churches, rather than conform to rites and vestments against their consciences; a greater guilt is contracted by *those* who choose to spoil these flocks of able pastors, rather than suffer those pastors to make choice of their own apparel; or, choose to rob the people of the food of their souls, rather than suffer them to receive it otherwise than on their knees."‡ He observes also, that this intended conformity designed "to admit again, not only those garments which are the signs of *Baal's priests*, but also certain rites, which are degenerated into the worst of superstitions: as the signing with the cross, kneeling at the communion, and such like."§

The church of Scotland wrote, at the same time, a most

* Among those who subscribed this letter was even Dr. John Whitgift, afterwards the celebrated archbishop. This man was now a zealous friend of the nonconformists; but soon after as zealous a persecutor of them. —*Strype's Parker*, p. 194.

† Ibid. p. 192, 194, 196.

‡ Heylin's Hist. of Pres. p. 39.

§ Strype's Grindal, p. 113.

affectionate and pressing letter to the bishops and pastors of England, exposing the evil of persecution, and recommending peace among brethren. "We understand," say they, "that divers of our dearest brethren, among whom are some of the best learned in the realm, are deprived from the ecclesiastical function, and forbidden to preach, because their consciences will not suffer them to use such garments as idolaters in time of blindness, have used in their idolatry. We crave in the bowels of Jesus Christ, that christian charity may prevail among you. Ye cannot be ignorant how tender a thing the conscience of man is. If then the surplice, corner cap, and tippet, have been badges of idolatry, and used in the very act of idolatry, what hath the preacher of christian liberty, and the open rebuker of all superstition, to do with the dregs of that Romish beast? Our brethren who of conscience refuse that unprofitable apparel, do neither condemn, nor molest you, who use such vain trifles. If you should do the like to them, we doubt not that you will please God, and comfort the hearts of many, which are wounded by the present extremities. Our humble supplication is, that our brethren among you, who refuse the *Romish rags*, may find such favour of you prelates, as your Head and Master commandeth every one of his members to shew to all others. We expect to receive your gentleness, not only because you fear to offend God's majesty, by troubling your brethren with such vain trifles; but also because you will not refuse the humble request of us your brethren and fellow-preachers of Jesus Christ. We suppose you will esteem us to be of the number of those, who fight against the Romish antichrist, and travel for the advancement of the universal kingdom of Jesus Christ; before whom, we, and you, and your brethren, must soon give an account."*

Many of the puritans having, for the sake of peace, conformed as far as they possibly could, at length endeavoured, though under great discouragements, to obtain an accommodation. But the prelates proceeding with still greater severity against all who could not come up to the standard of conformity, made it too evidently appear, that they sought not their conformity, but their utter extir-

* This letter, dated Edinburg, Dec. 27, 1566, is entitled "The ministers and elders of the churches within the realme of Scotlande, to their brethren the bishops and pastours of Englande, who have renounced the Romane antichrist, and doe professe with them the Lord Jesus in sinceritie, desireth the perpetuall increase of the Holy Spirit."—*Parte of a Register*, p. 125—127.

pation. Having made application to certain persons of distinguished eminence, the business was laid before the parliament; and during this year, six bills were brought into the house of commons, to promote a further reformation of the church. They were warmly supported by many eminent statesmen, and one of them passed the house; but coming up to the lords, it met with some opposition; and by the superior power and influence of the bishops, it was cast out.*

Through the heavy oppressions of the prelates, many of the puritans, both ministers and others, withdrew from the national church, and set up their separate assemblies. They laid aside the ecclesiastical ceremonies and the Book of Common Prayer, and worshipped God in a way which to them appeared more agreeable to the word of God. The reason assigned for their separation was, "that the ceremonies of antichrist were so tied to the service of God, that no one might preach, or administer the sacraments without them, being compelled to observe these things by law." If the use of the habits and certain ceremonies had been left discretionary, both ministers and people would no doubt have been easy. This being denied, they entered into a serious consultation, when they came to this conclusion: "That, since they could not have the word of God preached, nor the sacraments administered, without *idolatrous gear;* and since there had been a separate congregation in London, and another at Geneva, in Queen Mary's time, which used a book and order of preaching, administration of the sacraments and discipline, which the great Mr. Calvin approved of, and which was freed from the superstitions of the English service; that therefore it was their duty in their present circumstances, to break off from the public churches, and to assemble as they had opportunity in private houses, or elsewhere, to worship God in a manner that might not offend their consciences."† This was about the year 1566, and was the æra of that SEPARATION from the church of England which continues to this day.

The chief leaders of the separation were Messrs. Coleman, Button, Halingham, Benson, and Hawkins, all, according to Fuller, active and zealous nonconformists, beneficed within the diocese of London.‡ Notwithstanding

* MS. Remarks, p. 463.
† Parte of a Register, p. 25.—Strype's Parker, p. 241, 242.
‡ Fuller's Church Hist. b. ix. p. 81.

the threatenings and severities of the prelates, they continued to meet in their private assemblies, as they found opportunity; and oftentimes assembled in the fields and the woods in the neighbourhood of London, to avoid the discovery of their watchful enemies.* But they ventured at length to appear more openly; and June 19, 1567, having agreed to have a sermon and the Lord's supper at Plumbers-hall in the city, they hired the place, as some one intimated, under pretence of a wedding. Here, the sheriffs and other officers discovered them, and broke up their meeting, when about one hundred were assembled; most of whom were taken into custody, and sent to Bridewell, the Compter, and other prisons. Having remained in prison nearly two years, and their patience and constancy being sufficiently tried, twenty-four men and seven women were released by an order from the council.†

The puritans of these times had many objections against the established church. They complained of the assumed superiority of bishops above presbyters.—They excepted against the numerous, pompous titles of ecclesiastical officers.—They complained of the exorbitant power and jurisdiction of the prelates.—They lamented the want of *godly discipline.*—They disliked some things in the public liturgy: as, the frequent repetition of the Lord's prayer, the responses, some things in the office of marriage, the burial of the dead, &c.—They disliked the reading of the apocryphal books, to the exclusion of some parts of canonical scripture.—They disallowed of the cathedral mode of worship.—They disapproved of the church festivals or holidays, as having no foundation in scripture.—They disapproved of pluralities, nonresidence, and lay patrons.—And they scrupled conformity to certain rites and ceremonies: as, the cross in baptism; the promises and vows; the use of sponsors, to the exclusion of parents; the custom of confirming children; kneeling at the Lord's supper; bowing at the name of Jesus; the ring in marriage; and the wearing of the surplice, with other ceremonies equally without foundation in scripture.‡

During the above year, the puritans felt the oppressions of the ruling ecclesiastics. Mr. Evans was convened before them and prosecuted, for keeping conventicles. Mr. Lawrence, a Suffolk divine of great eminence, was suspended for nonconformity; and Dr. Hardyman suffered deprivation.

* Heylin's Hist. of Pres. p. 259. † Strype's Grindal, p. 136.
‡ Neal's Puritans, vol. i. p. 209—213.

Mr. Stroud, minister of Yalding, in Kent, was cast into prison, excommunicated, deprived of his ministry, reduced to extreme poverty, and obliged to enter upon the employment of correcting the press for his support. Other puritans, denominated peaceable nonconformists, obtained for some time a connivance or toleration. These were Drs. Sampson, Humphrey, Wyburn, Penny and Coverdale, with Messrs. Fox, Lever, and Johnson.*

About the year 1570, other oppressions were inflicted upon certain London ministers: Mr. Crane and Mr. Bonham were both silenced and cast into prison for nonconformity. The former was afterwards for the same crime committed to Newgate; where, after languishing a long time under the hardships of the prison, he was delivered by death from all his afflictions. Mr. Axton, an excellent divine, for refusing the apparel, the cross in baptism, and kneeling at the Lord's supper, was convened before the Bishop of Lichfield and Coventry, and, after a long examination, was deprived and driven to seek his bread in a foreign land. The celebrated Mr. Cartwright, of Cambridge, was cited before Dr. Whitgift and others, when he was deprived of his public ministry, expelled from the university, and forced to depart out of the kingdom. Innumerable, indeed, were the hardships under which the puritans groaned. By the rigorous proceedings of the ruling prelates, the church was deprived of many of its brightest ornaments; and nearly all its faithful pastors were ejected; especially in Northamptonshire, Warwickshire, Leicestershire, Norfolk, and Suffolk.† While these ravages were made upon the church of Christ, several thousands of ministers of inferior character, such as common swearers, drunkards, gamesters, whoremongers, and massing priests, only because they were conformable, continued in their offices, enjoyed their livings, and obtained preferment. Most of the bishops having endured persecution and banishment in the days of Queen Mary, and being now exalted by promotion, honour, and wealth, forgot their former condition, and persecuted their brethren of the same faith, who could not come up to the standard of conformity.‡

At this period, there was considerable variety in the *kind* of bread used in the Lord's supper: some ministers, in conformity to the papists and the queen's injunctions, used the *wafer* bread; but others, in conformity to scripture

* Strype's Parker, p. 243.
† MS. Register, p. 147.
‡ Parte of a Register, p. 2—8.

and the convictions of their own minds, renounced the popish relict, and used the *loaf* bread. This gave great offence and much trouble to Archbishop Parker, who, with the assistance of Bishop Grindal, laboured much to bring all the clergy to an exact uniformity.*

The above proceedings having excited considerable alarm in the nation, some attempts were made in the parliament of 1571, to obtain a reformation of the ecclesiastical laws. The motion was warmly supported by some of the ablest statesmen; but was no sooner become the subject of public discussion, than the queen took great offence, and forbad the house to concern itself about such matters.† The commons ventured, however, to present a supplication to her majesty, in which they observe, that for want of true ecclesiastical discipline, there were great numbers of ministers of infamous lives, while those possessed of abilities for the sacred function were cast aside as useless. They complain of the great increase of popery, atheism and licentiousness, by which the protestant religion was in imminent danger. "And," say they, "being moved with pity towards so many thousands of your majesty's subjects, daily in danger of being lost for want of the food of the word, and true discipline; we, the commons in this present parliament assembled, are humbly bold to open the griefs, and to seek the salving of the sores of our country; and to beseech your majesty, seeing the same is of so great importance, that the parliament at this time may be so long continued, as that by good and godly laws, provision may be made for a reformation of these great and grievous wants and abuses, and by such other means as to your majesty shall seem meet, a perfect redress of the same may be obtained; by which the number of your majesty's faithful subjects will be increased, popery will be destroyed, the glory of God will be promoted, and your majesty's renown will be recommended to all posterity."‡ But the queen broke up the parliament without taking the least notice of the supplication.

These proceedings occasioned an act to pass during this parliament, requiring all ministers "to declare their assent to all the articles of religion, which *only* concern the confession of the true christian faith, and the doctrine of the sacraments." This was a great alleviation to the non-

* Strype's Parker, p. 308—310.
† D. Ewes's Journal, p. 157, 185.—Strype's Parker, p. 324.
‡ MS. Register, p. 92, 93.

conformists, when they all readily subscribed. But the bishops and clergy in convocation had the confidence, at the same time, to make new canons of discipline, by which they greatly increased the burdens of the puritans. They required subscription to *all* the articles, even those relating to the rites, ceremonies, order and policy of the church, as well as others, contrary to the above statute. The bishops called in all their licenses to preach, forbidding all ministers to preach without new ones. Most of the nonconformists claiming the liberty allowed them by the laws of the land, refused the canonical subscription, as a most grievous usurpation over their consciences; for which great numbers were turned out of their livings.* This led them to preach in other churches, or in private houses, without license, as they were able to procure an opportunity. But the queen hearing of this, immediately commanded the archbishop and other ecclesiastical commissioners not to suffer any minister to read, pray, preach, or administer either of the sacraments, in any church, chapel, or private place, without a license from her majesty, the archbishop, or the bishop of the diocese.†

These tyrannical measures, instead of bringing the puritans nearer the standard of conformity, drove them farther from the church. They could not with a good conscience, observe the new ecclesiastical impositions; and, therefore, the chief among them were cited to appear at Lambeth;‡ among whom were Drs. Sampson and Wyburn, and Messrs. Goodman, Lever, Walker, Goff, Deering, Field, Brown, and Johnson. These divines were ready to subscribe to the doctrines of faith and the sacraments, according to law, but excused themselves from doing more. Goodman was suspended, and constrained to sign a recantation. Lever quietly resigned his prebend in the church of Durham. Deering was long molested and suspended. Johnson suffered similar treatment. Dr. Willoughby was deprived for refusing the above canonical subscription.§ Mr. Gilby and Mr. Whittingham endured many troubles for their nonconformity.

These proceedings opened the eyes of the people; and the parliament in 1572, warmly espoused the cause of the distressed ministers. The queen and bishops having most shamefully abused their pretended spiritual power, two bills were brought into the house, in one of which the

* MS. Chronology, vol. i. p. 135. (1—2)
† Strype's Parker, p. 324, 325. ‡ Ibid, p. 326. § Ibid, p. 372.

hardships under which the puritans groaned, were intended to be redressed.* The bills passed smoothly through the commons, and were referred to a committee of both houses; which so alarmed the bishops, and gave such offence to the queen, that, two days after, she acquainted the commons, that it was her royal pleasure, that no bill relating to religion should henceforth be introduced into that house, till after the same had been considered and approved by the clergy; and she commanded the house to deliver up the two bills last read, touching rites and ceremonies.† With this high stretch of her majesty's prerogative, the commons quietly and tamely complied, and their efforts came to nothing.

In the mean time, the bishops stuck close to the canonical discipline; enforced conformity with the utmost rigour; and, according to the computation of Mr. Strype,‡ there were at least one hundred ministers deprived this year, for refusing subscription. The university of Cambridge was, indeed, become a nest of puritans. Dr. Browning and Mr. Brown, both fellows of Trinity college, were convened before the heads, and cast into prison for nonconformity. Mr. Clarke, fellow of Peter-house, and Mr. Millain, fellow of Christ's college, were expelled from their colleges, and banished from the university.§ But these severe proceedings had not the effect intended: for, instead of crushing the nonconformists, the more they were persecuted, the more they multiplied.

The puritans having in vain sought for a reformation from the queen and the bishops, resolved to apply to the parliament, and stand by the constitution. They published a treatise, presenting their grievances in one view. It was compiled by Mr. Field, assisted by Mr. Wilcocks, and revised by others. The work was entitled "An Admonition to the Parliament;" to which were annexed, Beza's letter to the Earl of Leicester, and Gaulter's to Bishop Parkhurst, upon the reformation of church discipline. It contains a platform of the church; the manners of electing ministers; with their several duties, and their equality in government.

* Strype's Parker, p. 394.

† D. Ewes's Journal, p. 207.—Strype's Annals, vol. ii. p. 125.

‡ Strype's Annals, vol. ii. p. 187.

§ In opposition to the above facts, Bishop Maddox insinuates that great favour and indulgence were shewn to the puritans, during this year; and refers to the words of Mr. Strype, saying, "That they were as *gently* treated as might be; no kind of brotherly persuasion omitted towards them; and most of them as yet kept their livings; though *one* or *two* were displaced." What degree of truth is contained in this statement, every one will easily judge.—*Maddox's Vindication*, p. 173.

It then exposes with some degree of sharpness the corruptions of the church, and the proceedings of the bishops. The admonition then concludes, by petitioning the houses, that discipline, more consonant to the word of God, and more agreeable to other reformed churches, may be established by law. Mr. Field and Mr. Wilcocks presented it themselves to the house, for which they were apprehended, and sent to Newgate, where they remained in close and miserable confinement at least fifteen months. While the authors were thus prosecuted, the book spread abroad, and soon passed through several editions.*

The leading puritans having presented their numerous petitions to the queen, the bishops, and the parliament, to little or no purpose, agreed to attempt to promote the desired reformation in a more private way. For this purpose, they erected a presbytery at Wandsworth, near London. The members of this association were Messrs. Smith, Crane, Field, Wilcocks, Standen, Jackson, Bonham, Saintloc, and Edmunds; to whom were afterwards joined Messrs. Travers, Clarke, Barber, Gardiner, Cheston, Crook, Egerton, and a number of respectable laymen. Eleven elders were chosen, and their offices described in a register, entitled "The Orders of Wandsworth." This was the first presbyterian church in England. Notwithstanding that all imaginable care was taken to keep their proceedings secret, the bishops' eyes were upon them, who gave immediate intelligence to the high commission; upon which the queen issued her royal proclamation for a more exact observance of the act of uniformity. And though the bishops knew of the presbytery, they could not discover its members, nor prevent others from being erected in other parts of the kingdom.†

While multitudes of the best preachers were utterly silenced, the church of England stood in the greatest need of their zealous and faithful labours. It was, indeed, in a most deplorable condition. The conformable clergy obtained all the benefices in their power, and resided upon none, utterly neglecting their cures: many of them alienated the church lands, made unreasonable leases, wasted the wood upon the lands, and granted reversions and advowsons for their own advantage. The churches fell greatly into decay, and became unfit for divine service. Among the laity there was very little devotion; and the Lord's day was

* For a circumstantial account of the controversy excited by the publication of the "Admonition," see Art. Thomas Cartwright.

† Fuller's Church Hist. b. ix. p. 103.—Neal's Puritans, vol. i. p. 266.

generally profaned. Many were mere heathens, epicures, or atheists, especially those about the court; and good men feared that some sore judgment hung over the nation.*

In the year 1573, the queen issued her royal proclamation, "strictly commanding all archbishops and bishops, all justices of assizes, and all others having authority, to put in execution the act of uniformity of common prayer, with all diligence and severity, neither favouring, nor dissembling with any one person, who doth neglect, despise, or seek to alter the godly orders and rites set forth in the said book." The proclamation requires further, "that all who shall be found nonconformable in the smallest matter, shall be immediately apprehended and cast into prison; all who shall forbear coming to the common prayer, and receiving the sacraments, according to the said book, shall be immediately presented and punished; and all who shall either in private houses, or in public assemblies, use any other rites of common prayer and administration of sacraments, or shall maintain in their houses any persons guilty of these things, shall be punished with the utmost severity."† This, from the *supreme governor* of the church, inspired the zealous prelates with new life and courage. They enforced subscription upon the clergy with great rigour. Though the forms of subscription varied in different dioceses, that which was most commonly imposed was the following: "I acknowledge the book of articles agreed upon by the clergy in the synod of 1563, and confirmed by the queen's majesty, to be sound and according to the word of God.— That the queen's majesty is the chief governor, next under Christ, of this church of England, as well in *ecclesiastical* as civil causes.—That in the Book of Common Prayer, there is nothing evil or repugnant to the word of God, but that it may well be used in this our christian church of England.—And that as the public preaching of the word in this church of England is sound and sincere, so the public order in the ministration of the sacraments is consonant to the word of God."‡

Upon the rigorous imposition of these forms, many ministers not being able with a good conscience to comply, were brought into great trouble. Messrs. Deering and Cartwright, together with Dr. Sampson and other excellent divines, endured much cruel usage for nonconformity.§ Dr. Wyburn, and Messrs. Brown, Johnson, Field, Wilcocks,

* Strype's Parker, p. 395. † Sparrow's Collec. p. 169, 170.
‡ Parte of a Register, p. 81. § Strype's Annals, vol. ii. p. 265—292.

Sparrow, and King, were deprived of their livings, and four of them committed to Newgate. They were told, that if they did not comply in a short time, they should be banished, though there was no law in existence to inflict any such punishment.* Mr. Johnson, who was fellow of King's college, Cambridge, and domestic chaplain to the Lord Keeper Bacon, was tried at Westminster-hall for nonconformity, and sent to the Gatehouse, where, through his cruel imprisonment, he soon after died. Several others, cast into prison at the same time, died under the pressures of their confinement. Mr. Bonham, Mr. Standen and Mr. Fenn, were committed to prison, where they remained a long time. Mr. Wake, rector of Great-Billing; Mr. Paget, minister of Oundle; Mr. Mosely, minister of Hardingstone; Mr. Gilderd, minister of Collingtree; and Mr. Dawson, minister of Weston-Favell, all in the diocese of Peterborough, were first suspended for three weeks, and then deprived of their livings. They were all useful preachers. Four of them were licensed by the university, as learned and religious divines, and three had been moderators in the religious exercises. Mr. Lowth, minister of Carlisle, was prosecuted in the high commission at York; while Mr. Sanderson and Dr. Crick, two learned and useful divines in Norfolk, fell into the hands of the high commissioners in the south, when the latter was deprived of his preferment. Many others in the diocese of Norwich refusing conformity, were prosecuted in the ecclesiastical courts.† And Mr. Aldrich, with many others in the university of Cambridge, received much unchristian usage from the governing ecclesiastics. At the same time, John Townley, esq. a layman, was committed to prison for nonconformity, when Dean Nowell, his near kinsman, presented a petition to the president of the north and the Archbishop of York, for his release.‡

The year 1574 was memorable for the suppression of the religious exercises, called *prophesyings*. Some of the bishops being persuaded of the usefulness of these exercises, discovered their unwillingness to put them down. This gave great offence to the queen, who addressed a letter to all the bishops in England, peremptorily commanding them to suppress them in their respective dioceses. Her majesty in this discovered a most despotic and tyrannical spirit. All the bishops and clergy in the nation must bow to her

* Strype's Parker, p. 412, 413. † Ibid. p. 451, 452.
‡ Baker's MS. Collec. vol. xxi. p. 382.

sovereign pleasure.* This was the royal lady who renounced the infallibility of the Pope of Rome. In these exercises, the clergy were divided into classes, and each class was under the direction of a moderator appointed by the bishop of the diocese. They were held once a fortnight, when a portion of scripture formed the subject of discussion. They were holden publicly in the churches; and besides exposing the errors of popery, they were of unspeakable service in promoting a knowledge of the scriptures among the people. But the jealous archbishop looked upon them as the nurseries of puritanism, calling them *vain prophesyings.*† They tended, in his opinion, to promote popularity, insubordination, and nonconformity. But the archbishop did not long survive. For he died May 17, 1575; when he was succeeded by Dr. Edmund Grindal, Archbishop of York. He was a prelate of rigid and cruel principles, and much concerned to establish an exact uniformity in outward things, to the neglect of more important matters.‡

During this year, a congregation of Dutch anabaptists was discovered, without Aldgate, London; *twenty-seven* of whom were apprehended and cast into prison, and four bearing fagots at Paul's cross, recanted their opinions. Eight were banished from the kingdom, and two were condemned to the flames, and burnt in Smithfield. The Dutch congregation in London interceded for their pardon, as did Mr. Fox, the martyrologist; but the queen remained inflexible, and the two poor men perfumed Smithfield with their ashes.§

The puritans, under all their hardships, had many able friends at court, who stood firm in the cause of religious liberty. Therefore a committee was this year appointed by parliament to draw up a bill "For the Reformation of Church Discipline." But, as before, the house most probably received a check for attempting to interfere in religious matters.‖

In the year 1576, many learned divines felt the vengeance of the ruling prelates. Mr. Harvy and Mr. Gawton, in

* Strype's Grindal, Appen. p. 85, 86. † Strype's Parker, p. 461.

‡ Though a late writer affirms that Archbishop Parker "was *prudent, gentle,* and *patient;*" Hume says "he was rigid in exacting conformity to the established worship, and in punishing, by fines or deprivation, all the puritanical clergymen, who attempted to innovate any thing in the habits, ceremonies, or liturgy of the church."—*Churton's Life of Nowell,* p. 113. —*Hume's Hist. of Eng.* vol. v. p. 188.

§ See Art. Fox. ‖ MS. Remarks, p. 463.

addition to many other troubles, were both suspended for nonconformity. As the storm approached, the ministers of Norfolk prepared for it, by presenting their humble supplication to the council, in which they express themselves as follows:—"As touching your letters wherein you say, that her majesty is fully bent to remove all those, who cannot be persuaded to conform themselves to all orders established, it grieveth our souls very much, considering what desolation is likely to come upon the poor flock of Christ, by being thus bereaved of many excellent pastors, who dare not yield to that conformity. Yet knowing that the hearts of princes are in the hands of God, we commit our cause, being God's own cause, unto him, waiting for a happy issue at his hands. In the mean time, we pour out our prayers before the throne of his mercy, to direct her majesty to promote his glory, lamenting our sins, and the sins of the land, as the reason of our prince being set against so godly a cause.

"As for ourselves, though we are willing to yield our bodies, goods, and lives to our sovereign prince, we dare not yield to this conformity, for fear of that terrible threatening of the Lord Jesus: 'Whosoever shall offend one of these little ones, it were better for him that a mill-stone were hanged about his neck, and that he were cast into the depth of the sea.' And though we have ever so much knowledge of christian liberty, we dare not cause our weak brother to perish, for whom Christ died. For in sinning against them, and wounding their consciences, we sin against Christ. We conclude with the apostle, 'Wherefore if meat (so we say of ceremonies) make my brother to offend, I will eat no flesh while the world standeth, lest I make my brother to offend.' Therefore we dare not yield to these ceremonies, because, so far from edifying and building up the church, they have rent it asunder, and torn it in pieces, to its great misery and ruin, as God knoweth; and unless some mitigation be granted, still greater misery and ruin will follow, by stopping the mouths of the servants of God.

"Although her majesty be incensed against us, as if we would obey no laws, we take the Lord of heaven and earth to witness, that we acknowledge, from the bottom of our hearts, her majesty to be our lawful queen, placed over us by God for our good; and we give God our most humble and hearty thanks for her happy government; and, both in public and private, we constantly pray for her prosperity.

We renounce all foreign power, and acknowledge her majesty's supremacy to be lawful and just. We detest all error and heresy. Yet we desire that her majesty will not think us disobedient, seeing we suffer ourselves to be displaced, rather than yield to some things required. Our bodies, and goods, and all we have, are in her majesty's hands; only our *souls we reserve to our God*, who alone is able to save us or condemn us.

"We humbly crave," say they, "that you will deal with her majesty, in our behalf. Let her majesty understand, that all laws commanding things which edify not, but are offensive, are contrary to the word of God. Let her further understand how dangerous a thing it is, to urge the observance of human ceremonies with greater severity, than the observance of the law of God. The word of God is in danger of being made of no effect, by the traditions of men. Though, in scripture, ministers are commanded to preach the word of God, this is now not half so strictly examined and enforced, as the observance of the ceremonies. Through the whole land it is manifest, that a minister who is conformable to the ceremonies, may continue on his charge undisturbed, though he cannot teach: so if he be ever so able to teach as God hath commanded, yet if he cannot conform to those ceremonies which men have devised and appointed, he must not continue in the ministry. This must needs be preferring the ordinance of man before the word of God."*

This supplication proving ineffectual, Messrs. John More, Richard Crick, George Leeds, Thomas Roberts, Vincent Goodwin, Richard Dowe, and John Mapes, all ministers in or near the city of Norwich, were suspended.† Mr. Thickpenny, a minister of good learning, and much beloved by his parishioners, was suspended for nonconformity. Mr. Greenham, a divine of a most excellent spirit, received the like treatment, because he could not in conscience subscribe and wear the habits, though he cautiously avoided speaking against them, lest he should give offence. Mr. Rockrey, a divine of great eminence at Cambridge, was twice expelled from the university for a similar offence. Mr. Field and Mr. Wilcocks having already suffered a long and painful imprisonment, were brought into fresh troubles. They were convened before Bishop Aylmer, who pronounced Mr. Field obstinate, for having taught children in

* MS. Register, p. 253—256. † Ibid. p. 285.

gentlemens' houses, contrary to the prohibition of the archbishop. Aylmer recommended, as their punishment, that they should both be sent into the most barbarous parts of the country, where they might be profitably employed in turning the people from the errors of popery. Mr. Whittingham, dean of Durham, a divine of distinguished eminence, was exercised with many troubles, which continued to the day of his death.

In the year 1579, Mr. Lawrence, already mentioned, was suspended by his diocesan. Though repeated intercessions were made for him, particularly by the lord treasurer, the bishop peremptorily refused to restore him, without a perfect conformity to all the rites and ceremonies. Mr. Merbury underwent a long examination before the high commission, when he was treated with much foul, abusive language. Bishop Aylmer, seldom sparing in bitter invectives, called him "a *very ass*, an *idiot*, and a *fool*." He was then sent to the Marshalsea, where he remained a prisoner several years. Aylmer, indeed, was not behind any of his brethren in the persecution of the puritans. This prelate, to enforce a due observance of the ecclesiastical orders, cited the London ministers before him no less than five times in one year. On these occasions, he made inquisition whether they truly and faithfully observed all things contained in the Book of Common Prayer; whether any preached without a license; and whether any kept private conventicles. In the visitation of his diocese, he inquired of ministers, churchwardens, and sworn-men, in every parish, whether there were any persons who refused to conform, to attend the church, or to receive the communion; and for what cause they refused. He required all ministers to wear the surplice, to keep to the exact order of public service, and to observe all the ceremonies without the slightest alteration. His lordship had no mercy on such as did not comply in every punctilio; and warmly declared, that he would surely and severely punish offenders, or, "I will lie," said he, "in the dust for it."*

This prelate had very little compassion in his nature, and apparently as little regard for the laws of the country, or the cries of the people for the word of God. There was a great scarcity of preachers in all parts of England; and even the city of London was now in a most lamentable state, as appears from their petition to parliament, in which

* Strype's Aylmer, p. 64, 65, 81—83.

are these words:—"There are in this city a great number of churches, but the one-half of them at the least are utterly unfurnished of preaching ministers, and are pestered with candlesticks not of gold, but of clay, with watchmen that have no eyes, and clouds that have no water: the other half, partly by means of nonresidents, which are very many; and partly through the poverty of many meanly qualified, there is scarcely the *tenth* man that makes conscience to wait upon his charge, whereby the Lord's sabbath is often wholly neglected, and for the most part miserably mangled; ignorance increaseth, and wickedness comes upon us like an armed man. Therefore we humbly on our knees beseech this honourable assembly, in the bowels and blood of Jesus Christ, to become humble suitors to her majesty, that we may have guides; that the bread of life may be brought home to us; that the pipes of water may be brought into our assemblies; that there may be food and refreshing for us, our poor wives and forlorn children: so shall the Lord have his due honour; you shall discharge good duty to her majesty; many languishing souls shall be comforted; atheism and heresy banished; her majesty have more faithful subjects; and you more hearty prayers for your prosperity in this life, and full happiness in the life to come."*

In the county of Cornwall there were one hundred and forty clergymen, scarcely any of whom could preach a sermon, and most of them were pluralists and nonresidents. The inhabitants of the county, in their supplication to the parliament, gave the following affecting description of their case:—"We have about one hundred and sixty churches, the greatest part of which are supplied by men who are guilty of the grossest sins; some fornicators, some adulterers, some felons, bearing the marks in their hands for the said offence; some drunkards, gamesters on the sabbath-day, &c. We have many nonresidents, who preach but once a quarter; so that between meal and meal the silly sheep may starve. We have some ministers who labour painfully and faithfully in the Lord's husbandry; but they are not suffered to attend their callings, because the mouths of papists, infidels, and filthy livers, are open against them, and the ears of those who are called *lords* over them, are sooner open to their accusations, though it be only for ceremonies, than to the others' answers. Nor is it safe for

* MS. Register, p. 302.

us to hear them; for though our own fountains are dried up, yet if we seek for the waters of life elsewhere, we are cited into the spiritual courts, reviled, and threatened with excommunication."* The ground of this scarcity was the violence of the high commission, and the narrow terms of conformity. Most of the old incumbents, says Dr. Keltridge, were disguised papists, more fit to sport with the timbrel and pipe, than to take into their hands the book of God.†

The common topic of conversation now was the Queen's marriage with the Duke of Anjou, a notorious papist.‡ All true protestants were displeased and under alarming apprehensions. The puritans in general protested against the match, dreading the consequence of having a *protestant body*, under a *popish head.* Mr. John Stubbs, a student of Lincoln's-inn, and a gentleman of excellent abilities, published a book, entitled "The Discoverie of the Gaping Gulph, whereinto England is like to be swallowed by another French marriage, if the Lord forbid not the banns, by letting her Majestie see the sin and punishment thereof." It no sooner came forth, than the queen issued her proclamation to suppress the book, and apprehend the author and printer. Stubbs the author, Singleton the printer, and Page the disperser, were apprehended, and sentenced to have their *right hands cut off*. Singleton was pardoned, but Stubbs and Page were brought to a scaffold erected at Westminster; where, with terrible formality, their right hands were cut off, by driving a cleaver through the wrist with a mallet; but as soon as Stubbs's *right hand* was cut off, he pulled off his hat with his *left*, and, to the great amazement of the spectators, exclaimed *God save the Queen*.§ He was then sent to the Tower, where he remained a long time; but afterwards proved himself a loyal subject, and a valiant and faithful commander in the wars in Ireland.

Many of the puritans being dissatisfied with the terms of conformity, and the episcopal ordination of the church of England, went to Antwerp and other places, where they received ordination according to the practice of the foreign reformed churches. Among these were Messrs. Cartwright, Fenner, Ashton, Travers, and Wright. The last, upon his return, became domestic chaplain to Lord Rich; but for saying, that "to keep the queen's birth-day as an

* MS. Register, p. 300. † Strype's Aylmer, p. 32.
‡ Strype's Annals, vol. ii. p. 566.
§ Kennet's Hist. of Eng. vol. ii. p. 487.

holiday, was to make her an *idol*," Bishop Aylmer committed him to the Fleet. Lord Rich, for attempting to vindicate him, was at the same time sent to the Marshalsea, and Mr. Dix to the Gatehouse.* Mr. Morley, a Norfolk minister, and Mr. Handson, preacher at Bury St. Edmunds, were both greatly molested, and suspended for nonconformity. The lord treasurer, with several other eminent persons, interceded with the bishop for the restoration of Mr. Handson, but all to no purpose. The angry prelate peremptorily declared, that he should not be restored, unless he would publicly acknowledge his fault, and enter into bonds for his good behaviour in future. Mr. Drewit was committed to Newgate, and Mr. Nash to the Marshalsea, where they remained a long time. Also, during this year, Mathew Hament, a poor plow-wright at Hethersett, near Norwich, being suspected of holding many unsound and dangerous opinions, was convened before the Bishop of Norwich, condemned as an heretic, and, May 20th, committed to the flames in the castle-ditch. As a preparative to this punishment, his ears were cut off on the 13th of the same month.† These proceedings were *too conformable* to those of the church of Rome.

Great numbers of pious and learned ministers were now indicted at the assizes, for omitting to use the surplice, the cross in baptism, the ring in marriage, or some part of the common prayer. They were ranked with the worst of felons, and exposed to public contempt, to the great dishonour of God, and injury of her majesty's subjects. Many persons of quality in the various counties of England, petitioned the lords of the council in behalf of the persecuted ministers. In the Suffolk petition are these words:— "The painful pastors and ministers of the word, by what justice we know not, are now of late brought to the bar at every assize; marshalled with the worst malefactors, indicted, arraigned, and condemned for matters, as we presume, of very slender moment: some for having holidays unbidden; some for singing the hymn *nunc dimittis* in the morning; some for turning the question in baptism from the infants to the godfathers, which is only *you*, for *thou*; some for leaving out the cross in baptism; some for leaving out the ring in marriage; whereunto," say they, "neither the law, nor the lawmakers, in our judgment, had ever any regard.‡

* Strype's Aylmer, p. 86. † Heylin's Hist. of Pres. p. 280, 281.
‡ Parte of a Register, p. 128.

But instead of relieving the suffering ministers, their burdens were greatly increased. In the year 1580, the parliament passed a law, entitled "An Act to retain the Queen's Subjects in their due Obedience," which enacted "That all persons who do not come to church or chapel, or other place where common prayer is said, according to the act of uniformity, shall forfeit *twenty pounds per month* to the queen, and suffer imprisonment till paid. Those who are absent for twelve months, shall, besides their former fine, be bound with two sufficient sureties in a bond of *two hundred pounds*, until they conform. And every *schoolmaster* who does not come to common prayer, shall forfeit *ten pounds a month*, be disabled from teaching school, and suffer a year's imprisonment."* This, says a learned churchman, was little better than making merchandize of souls.† The fine was, indeed, unmerciful, and the common people had nothing to expect but to rot in jails.

The legislature, by these violent measures, overshot the mark, and instead of crushing the puritans, or reconciling them to the church, they drove them farther from it. Men of integrity will not easily be beaten from their principles by canons, injunctions, subscriptions, fines, or imprisonment; much less will they esteem the church fighting with such weapons. Multitudes were by these methods driven to a total separation, and they became so far opposed to the persecuting church of England, as not to allow it to be a true church, nor its ministers true ministers. They renounced all communion with it, not only in the prayers and ceremonies, but in hearing the word and the sacraments. These were called BROWNISTS, from Robert Brown, at this time a preacher in the diocese of Norwich. The Brownists did not differ from the church of England in matters of faith; but were very rigid in points of discipline. They maintained the discipline of the church of England to be popish and antichristian, and all her ordinances to be invalid. They apprehended that, according to scripture, every church ought to be confined within a single congregation; and the choice of its officers, and the admission and exclusion of members, with all its other regulations, ought to be determined by the brotherhood. Many of the Brownists were great sufferers in their zeal for nonconformity: among these were Mr. Copping and Mr. Thacker, ministers in the county of Suffolk. After suffering imprisonment seven

* Burn's Eccl. Law, vol. ii. p. 146.
† Fuller's Church Hist. b. ix. p. 131.

years, for spreading Brown's books against the bishops and the established church, they were tried, condemned, and hanged at Bury St. Edmunds. At the same time, Mr. John Lewis, for denying the godhead of Christ, and, it is said, for holding other detestable heresies, was burnt at Norwich, September 17, 1583.*

Upon the death of Archbishop Grindal,† Dr. John Whitgift became Archbishop of Canterbury, and was confirmed September 23, 1583. The queen charged him "to restore the discipline of the church, and the uniformity established by law, which," says she, "through the connivance of some prelates, the obstinacy of the puritans, and the power of some noblemen, is *run out of square*."‡ Therefore, in obedience to her majesty's royal command, the new archbishop immediately published the following articles, and sent them to the bishops of his province, for their direction in the government of their dioceses:—"That all reading, preaching, catechising, and praying in any private family, where any are present besides the family, be utterly extinguished.—That none do preach or catechise except he also read the whole service, and administer the sacrament four times a year.—That all preachers, and others in ecclesiastical orders, do at all times wear the *habits* prescribed.—And that none be admitted to preach, or to execute any part of the ecclesiastical function, unless they be ordained according to the manner of the church of England; nor unless they subscribe the three following articles."

1. "That the queen hath, and ought to have, the sovereignty and rule over all manner of persons, born within her dominions, of what condition soever they be; and that none other power or potentate hath, or ought to have, any power, ecclesiastical or civil, within her realms or dominions.

2. "That the Book of Common Prayer, and of ordaining bishops, priests, and deacons, containeth in it *nothing contrary to the word of God*, but may be lawfully used;

* Parallel betwixt Phanatics, p. 11. Edit. 1661: from Stow.

† Grindal, in his latter days, was much inclined to favour the puritans, and was, with great difficulty, brought to punish them for their nonconformity. He had not sat long in the chair of Canterbury, before he was suspended and confined in his own house, for not suppressing the religious exercises called Prophesyings, which his conscience told him should have been encouraged and promoted. He continued under the tyrannical censure several years.—*Hume's Hist. of Eng.* vol. v. p. 188.—*Granger's Biog. Hist.* vol. i. p. 204.

‡ Kennet's Hist. of Eng. vol. ii. p. 494.

"and that he himself will use the same, and none other, in "public prayer and administration of the sacraments.

3. "That he alloweth the book of articles, agreed upon "in the convocation holden at London in 1562, and set "forth by her majesty's authority; and he believe all the "articles therein contained to be agreeable to the word "of God."*

These were called *Whitgift's* articles, because he was their principal author. Subscription to them was required for many years, without the warrant of any statute or canon whatsoever. By Whitgift's strict imposition of them upon all ministers, multitudes who refused to comply were suspended and deprived. They would most cordially have subscribed to the *first* and *third*, but could not in conscience subscribe, "That the Book of Common Prayer and Ordination contained *nothing contrary to the word of God*,"† These proceedings excited universal alarm, and great numbers of worthy ministers were brought under the ecclesiastical censure. Sixty-four ministers were suspended in the county of Norfolk, sixty in Suffolk,‡ thirty in Sussex, thirty-eight in Essex, twenty in Kent, and twenty-one in Lincolnshire. Among those in the county last mentioned, were Messrs. Charles Bingham, vicar of Croft, John Somerscales of Beseby, Joseph Gibson of Swaby, William Muming, vicar of Claxby, Reignald Grome of Thedilthorp

* Strype's Whitgift, p. 115, 116. † MS. Register, p. 513.

‡ The names of those suspended in Suffolk, were the following, forty-four of the last being suspended on one day;—Nicholas Bound, minister of Norton; Richard Grandish, A. M. rector of Bradfield; Lawrance Whitaker, A. B. rector of Bradfield; Richard Holden, A. B. rector of Testock; Gaulter Allen, B. D. of Rushbrook; Reignald Whitfield, A. M. of Barrow; Thomas Rogers of Horningsheath; Anthony Rowe of Hedgesset; Thomas Warren; William Cook; William Holden; Nicholas Bonnington, rector of Chettisham; John Tylmen, A. M. of Borgholt; Richard Dowe, A. M. vicar of Stratford; John Carter, A. M. vicar of Bramford; Martin Brige, A. M. vicar of Brettenham; Henry Sandes of Boxford; John Holden, rector of Bildeston; Thomas Cranshawe, A. M. rector of Boxted; Peter Cook, curate to Mr. Cranshawe; John Knewstubs, B. D. rector of Cockfield; William Hey, rector of Nedging; John Aulthroppe of Sudbury; Robert Ballard, A. B. rector of Clare: Lawrance Fairclough, vicar of Haverhil; John Ward; Nicholas Egleston, rector of Stradshill; William Turner, rector of Wratting-Parva; Robert Prick of Denham; Thomas Sutton, A. M. rector of Eriswell; Josias Hallington, Edmund Salmon, Thomas Jeffraye, Thomas Wattis, Mr. Phillips, Roger Nutle, Roger Geffrey, John Smith, John Forthe, Thomas Moore, William Browne, John Cooper, William Flemming, Robert Sweete, William Bentloc, John Smith, Thomas Hagas, Daniel Dennis, George Webb, William Bend, John English, Thomas Fowle, Robert Cotsford, Richard King, Mr. Lovell, Mr. Walsh, Mr. Pigge, Mr. Hill, Mr. Smith, and Dr. Crick.—*MS. Register*, p. 437.

St. Hellen, Mr. Sheppard, vicar of Bardney, Mr. Bradley of Torksey, Mr. Huddlestone of Saxilby, Mr. Rellet of Carlton in Moreland, Mr. Nelson of Skinnand, Mr. Hughe of Silk-Willoughby, Mr. Daniel of Ingolsby, Mr. Richard Holdsworth of Boothby, Mr. Thomas Fulbeck of Boultham, Mr. Anthony Hunt of West-Deeping, and Mr. Richard Allen of Ednam.* Great numbers in the diocese of Peterborough, in the city of London, and other parts of the kingdom, received the like ecclesiastical censure.

Multitudes of the best ministers and most laborious preachers in the nation, as the Earl of Leicester observes, were now deprived of their ministry.† The terrible storm fell upon Mr. Fenner and Mr. Wood, who were imprisoned twelve months, and suspended seven or eight years. Mr. Stroud was deprived of his ministry, and commanded to leave the country. He had so high a reputation, and was so universally beloved, that no less than *thirteen* petitions were presented to the archbishop for his restoration; but all to no purpose. Messrs. Underdown, Hopkinson, Norden, and Hely, together with Mr. Anthony Hobson, vicar of Leominster; Mr. John German, vicar of Buringham; Mr. Richard Whitaker, vicar of Almerby; Mr. William Clark, vicar of Langton; Mr. John Bingham, minister of Hadleigh, Mr. Turner, Mr. Star, Mr. Jackson, and many others, were all suspended at the same time.‡ Mr. Hill, minister at Bury St. Edmunds, for having omitted the cross in baptism, and making some trivial alteration in the vows, was suspended, several times indicted at the assizes, and committed to prison, where he continued a long time. The venerable Mr. Fenn was cited to Lambeth and suspended. Messrs. Hooke, Paget, and Oxenbridge, suffered the like ecclesiastical censure. Mr. Daniel Dyke, a most excellent divine, was twice suspended, deprived of his ministry, and driven out of the county. Mr. Benison was committed to the Gatehouse, where, to his unspeakable injury, he remained five years. Upon his application to the council, the lords were so moved with the reading of his case, that they wrote to Bishop Aylmer, signifying that he ought to make the good man some considerable recompence for his hard dealing. Dr. Browning was deprived of his fellowship at Cambridge, and forced from the university. Mr. Brayne, another learned divine at Cambridge, was cited to Lambeth, and, refusing the oath *ex officio*, was suspended. Many

* MS. Register, p. 696—712. † Ibid. 513. ‡ Ibid. p. 395.

others in the diocese of Ely were prosecuted for nonconformity. Also Messrs. Barber, Field, Egerton, and Rockrey, were all suspended, part of whom continued under the censure many years. Mr. Elliston of Preston, in Northamptonshire, was, for three years together, continually molested and cited before the prelates. During that period, he had ten journies to London, seven to Peterborough, one to Cambridge, and many to Leicester and Northampton. He was greatly impoverished, suspended from his ministry, and deprived of his living. Mr. Cawdrey, rector of Luffenham in Rutlandshire, a divine of good reputation, was suspended, deprived, cast into prison, degraded from the ministry, and, with a family of eight children, left to starve as a mere layman: also, during his troubles, which continued many years, he had *twenty-two* expensive journies to London. Mr. John Holden, rector of Bildeston, was suspended and excommunicated for not subscribing to Whitgift's articles.* Mr. Hopkins, vicar of Nazing, in Essex, was, for the same thing, deprived of his benefice. Mr. Whiting of Panfield, was twice suspended, and then deprived. Mr. Hawkdon, vicar of Fryon, was indicted at the assizes, suspended, and deprived of his living. Mr. Huckle of Eythorp-Roding, was suspended; and though the lords of the council applied to the bishop for his restoration, his grace positively refused. Mr. Cornwell of Markshall, was suspended, and openly reviled by the bishop, who called him *wretch,* and *beast,* and committed him to the custody of his pursuivant. Mr. Negus of Leigh, was suspended and deprived, for not promising to wear the surplice, though there was no surplice in the parish. Mr. Seridge of East Havingfield, was suspended and three times indicted at the assizes. Mr. Carew of Hatfield, being cited before the bishop, and refusing the oath *ex officio,* was suspended, deprived, and committed to the Fleet; and Mr. Allen, his patron, was committed at the same time. Mr. Gifford, vicar of Maldon, was twice suspended, and cast into prison, and his troubles continued several years. Mr. Morley of Ridgwell, having been molested several years, was indicted at the assizes, committed to prison, and obliged to enter into bonds not to preach any more within the diocese of London. Upwards of thirty other ministers in the county of Essex were suspended, deprived, or worse treated, by the inhuman proceedings of Bishop Aylmer,

* MS. Register, p. 586, 587.

for refusing to subscribe, wear the surplice, or some other trivial matter.* He, moreover, advised the heads of the university of Cambridge to call in all their licenses, and expel all who refused to wear the apparel, saying, "The folly that is bound up in the heart of a child, is to be expelled by the rod of discipline."† This cruel, persecuting prelate might, therefore, with truth say, "He was hated like a dog, and was called *the oppressor of the children of God*."‡

While the puritans were suffering the above extremities, there was the greatest scarcity of preachers in all parts of the kingdom. It appears from an impartial survey of all the counties of England, that there were only 2000 preachers, to serve nearly 10,000 parishes:§ and while many of the best and most useful preachers were silenced, there were multitudes of pluralists, nonresidents, and ministers, who could not preach. There were 416 ministers who could not preach in the county of Norfolk, 457 in Lincolnshire, and the same in other counties.‖ Numerous petitions were, at the same time, presented to parliament in favour of the suffering nonconformists; but by the opposition and influence of Whitgift and other prelates, they were rejected.¶ The lords of the council being much concerned for the persecuted ministers, wrote to Whitgift and Aylmer, saying, "That they had received complaints, that great numbers of *zealous* and *learned* preachers in various counties, especially in Essex, were suspended or deprived; that there was no preaching, prayers, or sacraments in the vacant places; that in some places, the persons appointed to succeed them, had neither good learning, nor good

* The names of these persecuted servants of Christ, were the following:—Messrs. Wyresdale of Maldon, Carr of Rayne, Tonstal of Totham, Piggot of Tilbury, Ward of Writtle, Dyke of Coggeshall, Northey of Colchester, Newman of Coggeshall, Taye of Pildon, Parker of Dedham, Farrar of Langham, Serls of Lexden, Lewis of St. Peter's, Colchester, Cock of St. Giles's, Colchester, Beaumont of Easthorpe, Redrige of Hutton, Chaplain of Hempsted, Calverwell of Felsted, Chapman of Dedham, Knevit, Mile-end, Colchester, Rogers of Wethersfield, Wilton of Aldham, Forth of Great-Glaston, Winkfield of Wicks, Dent of South-Southberry, Pain of Tolesbury, Barker of Prittlewell, Larking of Little-Waltham, Camillus Rusticus of Faagy, Howell of Paglesham, Maiburne of Great-Makering, Knight of Hempsted, and Chadwick of Danbury. These, says our author, are the painful ministers of Essex, of whom says the bishop, "You shall be *white* with me, or I will be *black* with you."—*MS. Register*, p. 684, 741, 742.

† Strype's Aylmer, p. 69.

‡ Ibid. p. 96.

§ MS. Register, p. 206.

‖ Ibid. p. 696.

¶ Strype's Whitgift, p. 186—188.

name; and that in other places, a great number of persons occupying cures, were notoriously unfit, some for lack of learning, and others chargeable with enormous faults; as, *drunkenness, filthiness of life, gaming at cards, haunting of ale-houses*, &c. against whom they heard of no proceedings."* The Lord Treasurer Burleigh, also, himself addressed the archbishop, saying, "I am sorry to trouble you so oft as I do, but I am more troubled myself, not only with many private petitions of ministers, recommended for persons of credit, and peaceable in their ministry, who are greatly troubled by your grace and your colleagues; but I am daily charged by counsellors and public persons, with neglect of my duty, in not staying your grace's vehement proceedings against ministers, whereby papists are encouraged, and the queen's safety endangered.—I have read over your *twenty-four* articles, formed in a *Romish style*, to examine all manner of ministers, and to be executed *ex officio nuro*. I think the Inquisition of Spain used not so many questions to comprehend and to trap their priests. Surely this judicial and canonical sifting of poor ministers, is not to edify or reform. This kind of proceeding is too much savouring of the *Romish Inquisition*, and is a device to *seek* for offenders, rather than to *reform* them."† But these applications were to no purpose: for, as Fuller observes, "This was the constant custom of Whitgift; if any lord or lady sued for favour to any nonconformist, he would profess how glad he was to serve them, and gratify their desires, assuring them for his part, that all possible kindness should be indulged to them, but he would remit nothing of his rigour. Thus he never *denied* any great man's desire, and yet never *granted* it; pleasing them for the present with general promises, but still kept to his own resolution; whereupon the nobility ceased making any further application to him, knowing them to be ineffectual."‡

The commons in parliament, at the same time, were not unmindful of the liberties of the subject. They presented a petition to the upper house, consisting of sixteen articles, with a view to further the reformation of the church, to remove the grievances of the puritans, and to promote an union of the conformists and nonconformists. But by the opposition of the bishops, nothing could be done.§ All that the puritans could obtain, was a kind of conference

* Fuller's Church Hist. b. ix. p. 151.

† Ibid. p. 155.

‡ Ibid. p. 218.

§ D. Ewes's Journal, p. 357—359.

betwixt the Archbishop and the Bishop of Winchester, on the one part; and Dr. Sparke and Mr. Travers, on the other, in the presence of the Earl of Leicester, Lord Gray, Sir Francis Walsingham, and some others. The conference was held at Lambeth, concerning things needful to be reformed in the Book of Common Prayer.*

In the year 1586, the persecution of the puritans went forwards with unabating fury. The celebrated Mr. Travers was silenced by Archbishop Whitgift. Mr. Udal was suspended and deprived of his living. Mr. Glover was convened before Whitgift, and cast into prison. Mr. Moore was cited before the high commission at York, where he endured many troubles. Mr. Hildersham, a most excellent divine, was suspended, and commanded to make a public recantation. Dr. Walward, a learned professor of divinity at Oxford, and Mr. Gillibrand, fellow of Magdalen college in the same university, were both cited before the high commission at Lambeth; when they were suspended, enjoined public recantations, and obliged to enter into bonds till they were performed. Mr. Gardiner was deprived and committed to Newgate by Bishop Aylmer, from whom he received most cruel usage. Mr. Wigginton, vicar of Sedburgh, was deprived of his living, and afterwards apprehended and carried before Whitgift; who, upon his refusal of the oath *ex officio*, committed him to prison, where he was treated with the utmost barbarity. The tyrannical archbishop also deprived him a second time, and degraded him from the ministry. Mr. Wigginton afterwards obtaining his release, returned home; and venturing to preach after his lordship's censure, he was apprehended and sent prisoner to Lancaster castle, where he remained a long time under very cruel usage. At the same time, about one hundred and forty of his people, for hearing him preach, were excommunicated. The zealous minister having at length obtained his liberty, was again apprehended and carried before Whitgift, who, for refusing the above oath, committed him to the Gatehouse, where he continued most probably till he consented to be banished. Mr. Settle, a Suffolk divine, was arraigned before the archbishop, who treated him with very reproachful language, calling him *ass, dolt, fool;* and after many threatenings, the angry prelate sent him to the Gatehouse, where he continued close prisoner

* See Art. Travers.

many years. Such were the proceedings of that archbishop who is said to have been eminently distinguished for his *mild* and *excellent* temper.*

The suffering puritans, during this year, presented a petition to the convocation, tending to promote a reconciliation betwixt the conformists and nonconformists, but most probably without the least effect.† They also made another effort to obtain a redress of their grievances from the parliament, by presenting an humble supplication to the house of commons; in which they say, "It pierces our hearts with grief to hear the cries of the people for the word of God. The bishops either preach not at all, or very seldom. And others abandon their flocks, contrary to the charge of Christ, *feed my sheep*. But great numbers of the best qualified for preaching, and of the most industrious in their spiritual function, are not suffered quietly to discharge their duties, but are followed with innumerable vexations, notwithstanding they are neither *heretics* nor *schismatics*, but keep within the pale of the church, and persuade others so to do, who would have departed from it. They fast and pray for the queen and the church, though they have been rebuked for it, and diversly punished by officers both civil and ecclesiastical. They are suspended and deprived of their ministry, and the fruits of their livings sequestered to others. This has continued many years; and last of all many of them are committed to prison, when some have been chained with *irons*, and continued in hard durance a long time.

"To bring about these severities, the bishops tender the suspected persons an oath *ex officio*, to answer all interrogatories to be put to them, though it be to accuse themselves; and when they have got a confession, they proceed upon it to punish them with all rigour, contrary to the laws of God and the land. Those who refused have been cast into prison, and commanded there to lie without bail, till they would yield. The grounds of these troubles are not *impiety*, *immorality*, *want of learning* or *diligence* in their ministerial work, but not being satisfied in the use of certain ceremonies and orders of the church of *Rome*, and for not being able to declare, that *every thing* in the Book of Common Prayer is *agreeable to the word of God*."‡ Two bills were at the same time brought into the house of commons, for the abolition of the old ecclesiastical laws,

* Paule's Life of Whitgift, p. 37.

† Parte of a Register, p. 323.

‡ MS. Register, p. 672.

and the old Book of Common Prayer, and for the establishment of a new one; but the queen being offended, forbad them to proceed.*

All the endeavours of the puritans proving ineffectual, and being wearied with repeated applications to their superiors, they began to despair of obtaining relief. Therefore, in one of their assemblies, they came to this conclusion: "That since the magistrates could not be induced to reform the discipline of the church, it was lawful, after waiting so many years, to act without them, and introduce a reformation in the best manner they could." They had their private classes or associations in Essex, Northamptonshire, Warwickshire, London, Cambridge and other places, when they consulted about the most proper means of promoting the desired object. And having revised their book, entitled "The Holy Discipline of the Church, described in the Word of God," it was subscribed by above *five hundred* ministers, all divines of good learning, and of unspotted lives.+

In the year 1587, Mr. Holmes, rector of Kenn, was driven from his flock and his living. Mr. Horrocks, vicar of Kildwick, in the West-Riding of Yorkshire, was convened before the high commission at York, committed to York castle, and enjoined a public recantation, for suffering Mr. Wilson, another puritan minister, to preach in his church, though it was his native place. Mr. Wilson was also convened, and cast into prison. After he had obtained his release, he was obliged to remove out of the archbishop's province; and going to London, he was called before Whitgift and suspended. Mr. Allison was twice suspended. Mr. Penry was summoned before the high commission and committed to prison. Mr. Johnson and Mr. Bainbrigg, both fellows in the university of Cambridge, and popular preachers, were cast into prison, where they continued a long time. Mr. Jewel was tried at the public assizes for nonconformity, and condemned to suffer five months' imprisonment. Mr. Wight was harassed for many years, when his study was broken open, searched, and his private papers carried away. Mr. Darrel and Mr. Moore were both cited before the high commission at Lambeth, when the former was deposed from his ministry, and committed close prisoner to the Gatehouse, and the latter close prisoner to the Clink, where they continued

* MS. Remarks, p. 465. + Neal's Puritans, vol. i. p. 423.

many years. Mr. Udal was summoned before the council, sent close prisoner to the Gatehouse, and not suffered to have *pen, ink*, or *paper*, or *any one to speak to him.* He was afterwards tried at the public assizes and condemned as a felon. Having received sentence of death, pardon was offered him if he would have recanted; but he continued firm to his principles, and died in the Marshalsea, as a martyr in the cause of religious liberty.

The proceedings of the high commission against the afflicted puritans, now exceeding all bounds, men of the greatest eminence began even to question the legality of the court. But the archbishop, to get over this difficulty, and remove the odium from himself, sent the principal nonconformists, especially those possessed of worldly estates, to be prosecuted in the star-chamber.* Indeed, several of the bishops, as well as many of the lords temporal, opposed these proceedings; and it appears from a list now before me, that upwards of one hundred and twenty of the house of commons, were not only averse to persecution, but zealous advocates for a reformation of the church, and the removal of those burdens under which the puritans groaned.† Therefore, in 1588, a bill against pluralities and nonresidence passed the commons, and was carried up to the lords; but by the determined opposition of the zealous prelates, it came to nothing.‡

The puritans still continued to hold their associations. Many divines, highly celebrated both for learning and piety, were leaders in their assemblies, and chosen moderators: as, Messrs. Knewstubs, Gifford, Rogers, Fenn and Cartwright.§ At one of these assemblies, held at Coventry, it was resolved, "That private baptism is unlawful.—That the sign of the cross ought not to be used in baptism.—That the faithful ought not to communicate with ignorant ministers.—That the calling of bishops is unlawful.—That it is not lawful to be ordained by them, nor to rest in their deprivation of any from the ministry.—And that

* Fuller's Church Hist. b. ix. p. 187.

† MS. Chronology, vol. ii. p. 417. (15.)

‡ During the debate upon this bill in the upper houses, when it was signified that the queen would confer with the bishops upon the points contained in the bill, the celebrated Lord Gray said, "he greatly wondered at her majesty choosing to confer with those who were enemies to the reformation; and added, that he wished the bishops might be served as they were in the days of Henry VIII. when they were all thrust out of doors."—*Strype's Annals*, vol. iii. p. 543.—*Fuller's Church Hist.* b. ix. p. 190.

§ Strype's Annals, vol. iii. p. 470, 471.

for the restoration of ecclesiastical discipline, it ought to be taught the people, as occasion shall serve.* Some of the more zealous nonconformists about this time, published Martin Mar-Prelate, and other satirical pamphlets.† They were designed to expose the blemishes of the established church, and the tyrannical proceedings of the bishops. They contained much truth, but were clothed in very offensive language. Many of the puritans were charged with being the authors: as, Udal, Penry, Throgmorton, and Wigginton; but the real authors were never known. However, to put a stop to these publications, the queen issued her royal proclamation, "For calling in all *schismatical* and seditious books, as tending to introduce monstrous and dangerous innovation, with the malicious purpose of dissolving the present prelacy and established church."‡

The flame of contention betwixt the conformists and nonconformists, broke out this year with redoubled fury, when Dr. Bancroft, afterwards Archbishop of Canterbury, ventured to assert, that the order of bishops was superior to that of presbyters, by divine appointment, and that the denial of it was *heresy*. This new doctrine§ was readily adopted by many, in favour of their high notions of episcopal ordination, and gave new fuel to the flame of controversy. They who embraced the sentiments of Bancroft, considered all ministers not episcopally ordained, as irregularly invested with the sacred office, as inferior to the *Romish* priests, and as mere laymen.‖

In the year 1590, the persecution of the puritans still raged with unabating fury. Many of the best divines were prosecuted with the utmost rigour in the high commission and the star-chamber. Mr. Hubbock and Mr. Kendal, two divines in great repute at Oxford, were cited before

* Fuller's Church Hist. b. ix. p. 194.

† The bishops having cried out loudly against Martin Mar-Prelate, it was prohibited that no person should presume to carry it about him, upon pain of punishment. This the queen declared in the presence of the Earl of Leicester, who, pulling the book out of his pocket, and shewing it the queen, said, "what then will become of me?" But it does not appear that any thing was done.—*Selection Harleim Miscel.* p. 157. Edit. 1793.

‡ Sparrow's Collec. p. 173.

§ The first English reformers admitted only two orders of church-officers, bishops and deacons, to be of divine appointment. They accounted a bishop and a presbyter to be only two names for the same office. But Bancroft, in his sermon at Paul's Cross, January 12, 1588, maintained, that the bishops of England were a distinct order from priests, and possessed a superiority over them, *jure divino*. Mr. Strype thinks that Bancroft published this *new* doctrine under the instructions of Whitgift.—*Strype's Whitgift*, p. 292.

‖ Mosheim's Eccl. Hist. vol. iv. p. 393.

Whitgift, and suspended. Mr. Hildersham was prosecuted a second time in the high commission, and again suspended. He was obliged to enter into bonds not to preach in any part of England; and when restored he was not allowed, for some time, to preach at any place south of the river Trent. The celebrated Mr. Cartwright, with many of his brethren, endured much severe persecution. This divine having been prosecuted for nonconformity, was driven into a foreign land, where he remained several years in a state of exile. Upon his return for the benefit of his health, he was immediately apprehended, and, though in a very languishing condition, was cast into prison. At length, having obtained his liberty, he was suspended by his diocesan, and convened before the high commission, when *thirty-one* articles were exhibited against him. But refusing the oath *ex officio*, to answer these articles, he was immediately committed to the Fleet, with his brethren, Messrs. Stephen Egerton, Humphrey Fenn, Daniel Wight, —— Farmer, Edward Lord, Edmund Snape, Andrew King, —— Rushbrooke, —— Wiggins, John Field, —— Royde, John Payne, William Proudlove, Melancton Jewel, &c.* Many others were summoned at the same time: as, Messrs. Henry Alvey, Thomas Edmunds, William Perkins, Edmund Littleton, John Johnson, Thomas Stone, Thomas Barber, Hercules Cleavely, and Andrew Nutter. These believing it to be their duty to take the oath, deposed many things relative to the associations, and thus became witnesses against their brethren; for which they were most probably released. But the others underwent many examinations; received much unkind treatment in the high commission and star-chamber; and they continued in prison several years. As this storm was gathering, Mr. Francis Kett, a man of some learning, and master of arts in one of the universities, was convened before the Bishop of Norwich; and for holding divers detestable opinions, as they are called, he was condemned and burnt near the city of Norwich.† Such was the outrageous persecution in the reign of Queen Elizabeth!

In the year 1592, the nonconformists had many bold and zealous advocates in both houses of parliament. Mr. Attorney Morrice, a man of distinguished eminence, moved the house of commons to enquire into the inquisition and other proceedings of the bishops, contrary to the honour

* Strype's Whitgift, p. 331—333.

† Parallel betwixt Phanatics, p. 11. Edit. 1661: from Stow.

of God, the laws of the realm, and the liberty of the subject; compelling learned and godly ministers upon their own oaths, to accuse themselves, and to deprive, degrade and imprison them upon this accusation.* He also offered two bills to the house; the one against the oath *ex officio*, the other against the illegal proceedings of the bishops, in which he was warmly supported by Sir Francis Knollys and other famous statesmen. But the queen, by her own arbitrary command, forbad the house to discuss ecclesiastical matters, and charged the speaker, upon his allegiance, not to read the bills.† Morrice was, at the same time, seized in the house, and carried prisoner to Tutbury castle, where he continued many years.

The parliament having tamely yielded its own liberties and those of the subject, to the tyrannical power of the queen, passed one of the most unjust and inhuman acts for oppression and cruelty, that was ever known in a protestant country. It is entitled "An Act for the Punishment of Persons obstinately refusing to come to Church;" and enacts, "that all persons above the age of sixteen, refusing to come to church; or persuading others to deny her majesty's authority in causes *ecclesiastical;* or dissuading them from coming to church; or being found present at any conventicle or meeting under pretence of religion; shall upon conviction be committed to prison without bail, till they shall conform and come to church." But in case such offenders should refuse to subscribe a most debasing recantation, it is further enacted, "That within three months, they shall ABJURE THE REALM and go into PERPETUAL BANISHMENT. And if they do not depart within the time appointed; or if they ever return without the queen's license, they shall SUFFER DEATH WITHOUT BENEFIT OF CLERGY."‡ The case of the nonconformists was by this act worse than that of felons. Herein the queen exceeded the tyranny of Henry VIII. For absolute as that monarch was, he contented himself with punishing those who *opposed* the established religion by some overt act; but by this new statute, the subjects were obliged, under the heaviest penalty, to make an *open profession* of the established religion, by a constant attendance on its public service."§

The oppression of this statute fell chiefly upon the Brownists, who renounced all communion with the national

* D. Ewes's Journal, p. 474. † MS. Remarks, p. 465.
‡ D. Ewes's Journal, p. 517.—Burn's Eccl. Law, vol. ii. p. 247, 248.
§ Warner's Hist. of Eng. vol. ii. p. 465.

church, and were now become very numerous.* There were several considerable persons at their head: as, Messrs. Smyth, Jacob, Ainsworth, Johnson, and Greenwood. Their London congregation being obliged to meet in different places, to hide itself from the bishops' officers, was at length discovered on a Lord's day at Islington, in the very place in which the protestant congregation met in the reign of Queen Mary; when about *fifty-six* were apprehended, and sent two by two to the different prisons about London, where many others had been long confined. The names of most of these persecuted servants of Christ, with the cruel oppressions they endured, are now before me. They suffered a long and miserable confinement; and under the barbarous usage they met with, many of them died in prison.† Mr. Roger Rippon, who died this year, is said to have been the last of *sixteen* or *seventeen* that were murdered in Newgate. Numerous families, as well as individuals, were driven into banishment, while many died in close imprisonment, and others suffered upon the gallows. Among the latter were Mr. Henry Barrow and Mr. John Greenwood. These persons having endured several years close confinement in the Fleet, were tried, condemned, and executed at Tyburn, giving the strongest testimony of their unfeigned piety towards God, and their unshaken loyalty to the queen. Also, Mr. John Penry, a pious and learned minister, was arraigned, condemned, and executed in a most cruel and barbarous manner. Mr. William Dennys was also executed on the same account, at Thetford in Norfolk.‡ These violent proceedings drove great numbers of the Brownists into Holland, where their leaders, Messrs. Smyth, Johnson, Ainsworth, Jacob, Robinson, and others, by leave of the states, erected churches according to their own views of the gospel, at Amsterdam, Arnheim, Middleburgh, and Leyden.

Several champions now appeared in defence of episcopacy: as, Drs. Bancroft, Bilcon, Bridges, Cosin, and Soam. These were answered by Bradshaw, Fenner,

* Sir Walter Raleigh declared in parliament, that in their various congregations, they were increased to the number of twenty thousand.—*D. Ewes's Journal*, p. 517.—*Townshend's Collections*, p. 76.

† Baker's MS. Collec. vol. xiv. p. 311. xv. 59—111.

‡ "These round dealings," says a reverend author, "did a little terrify the rest of the puritans, and checked the furiousness of the wiser sort. But having the Earls of Leicester, Warwick, and Shrewsbury, Lords North and Burleigh, Sir Francis Walsingham, and Sir Francis Knollys, with others of the nobility, for their honourable patrons, they resumed their courage."—*Peirce's Vindication*, part i. p. 151.—*Foulis's Hist. of Plots*, p. 61.

Morrice, and others; though the press was shut against the puritans. But Bancroft was their bitterest enemy. In his "Survey" and "Dangerous Positions," he wrote with much fierceness, misrepresentation, and abuse. He reproached the principles and practices of the puritans, as if they were enemies both to church and state, when they only sought, in the most peaceable manner, to promote a reformation of the ecclesiastical discipline and ceremonies, according to their views of the word of God.*

Towards the close of Queen Elizabeth's reign many severities were inflicted upon the nonconformists. Mr. William Smyth was apprehended and cast into prison. Mr. Smythurst was deprived of his living, and treated with great injustice by the high commission. Mr. Rudd was convened before the high commission, suspended, and forced to make a recantation. Mr. Aderster, a Lincolnshire divine, having endured many sufferings by suspension, deprivation, and other censures, in the high commission at Lambeth, was tried at the public assizes, when Judge Anderson treated him worse than a dog. Mr. Clarke, preacher to the society at Lincoln's-inn, London, and Mr. Philips, preacher at St. Saviour's, Southwark, were both summoned before the high commission; when the former was deprived, and the latter suspended and committed to the Gatehouse. Mr. Bradshaw, an excellent divine, was silenced by Archbishop Whitgift; and a great number of ministers in Norfolk were under suspension, and their people greatly oppressed in the ecclesiastical courts. Some, indeed, supposed that the puritans were now vanquished, and their number greatly diminished, by the rigorous execution of the penal laws.† This, however, is contrary to matter of fact. For in the beginning of the next reign, there were at least fifteen hundred ministers who avowed their nonconformity to the national church. The queen died March 24, 1603, having reigned upwards of forty-four years.

The puritans of these times were not without their failings, being men of like passions with their adversaries; yet, while they opposed the episcopal impositions and oppressions, if they had accomplished their wishes, there is cause to fear, that they would have imposed their own discipline. Their notions of civil and religious liberty were confused, and their principles and behaviour sometimes rigid; yet

* MS. Remarks, p. 461. † Fuller's Church Hist. b. ix. p. 233.

they were men eminent for piety, devotion, and zeal in the cause of Christ. The suspensions and deprivations of this long reign are said to amount to several thousands.* But, while the nonconformists were thus harassed, the church and the nation were in a most deplorable state. Great numbers of churches, in all parts of the country, were without ministers; and among those who professed to be ministers, about three thousand were mere readers, who could not preach at all. And under pretence of maintaining order and uniformity in the church, popery, immorality, and ungodliness were every where promoted: so that while the zealous prelates pretended to be building up the church of England, they were evidently undermining the church of God.†

Sect. III.

From the Death of Queen Elizabeth, to the Death of King James I.

King James was thirty-six years old when he came to the crown of England, having reigned in Scotland from his infancy. His majesty's behaviour in Scotland had raised too high the expectations of the puritans: they relied upon his education, his subscribing the covenant, his professed kindness for the suffering nonconformists, and his repeated declarations. He had declared in the general assembly at Edinburgh, with his hands lifted up to heaven, "That he praised God that he was born to be king of the purest kirk in the world. As for our neighbour kirk of England," said he, "their service is an evil-said mass in English. They want nothing of the mass but the liftings."‡ The king had given great offence to the English bishops, by saying, "that their order smelled vilely of popish pride; that they were a principal branch of the pope, bone of his bone, and flesh of his flesh; that the Book of Common Prayer was the English mass-book; and that the surplice, copes, and ceremonies were outward badges of popery."§ The expectations of the puritans were, therefore, highly

* Neal's Puritans, vol. i. p. 511.—The number of clergy suspended and deprived for nonconformity was, according to Hume, very great, and comprehended at one time *a third of all the ecclesiastics in the kingdom!!* —*Hist. of Eng.* vol. v. p. 337.

† MS. Remarks, p. 411.

‡ Calderwood's Hist. of Scotland, p. 256. § MS. Remarks, p. 535.

raised; and upon the king's accession, they took fresh courage, omitted some things in the public service, threw aside the surplice, and rejected the unprofitable ceremonies. During his majesty's progress to London, they presented their *millenary petition*, subscribed by above 1000 pious and able ministers, 750 of whom were out of twenty-five counties.* It is entitled "The humble Petition of the Ministers of the Church of England, desiring Reformation of certain ceremonies and abuses of the Church." They observe, "that they being more than 1000 ministers, groaning under the burden of human rites and ceremonies, with one consent, threw themselves at his royal feet, for a reformation in the church service, ministry, livings, and discipline."† But amidst all their hopes, many of them rejoiced with trembling; while James himself had, properly speaking, no other religion, than what flowed from a principle which he called *kingcraft*.‡

Indeed, this soon appeared at the Hampton-court conference. This conference, and the disputants on both sides, were appointed by his majesty. For the church, there were nine bishops and about the same number of dignitaries; but for the puritans, there were only four divines, Dr. Rainolds, Dr. Sparke, Mr. Chadderton, and Mr. Knewstubs. These divines having presented their request of a further reformation, in several particulars,§ towards the conclusion the king arose from his chair, and addressed Dr. Rainolds, saying, "If this be all your party have to say, I will make them conform, or I will hurry them out of the land, or else do worse." And to close the whole, he said, "I will have none of this arguing. Let them conform, and that quickly, or they shall hear of it."‖ Such was the royal logic of the new monarch! This conference, observes the judicious historian, was only a blind to introduce episcopacy into Scotland.¶ The conduct of the king, who bore down all before him, was highly gratifying to the dignified prelates. Besides other instances of palpable flattery, Archbishop Whitgift said, "He was verily persuaded the king spoke by the spirit of God."**

* Clark's Lives annexed to Martyr, p. 116.
† Fuller's Church Hist. b. x. p. 22.
‡ Warner's Hist. of Eng. vol. ii. p. 477.
§ See Art. Rainolds. ‖ Barlow's Sum of Conference, p. 170, 177.
¶ Rapin's Hist. of Eng. vol. ii. p. 162.
** Welwood's Memoirs, p. 21.—Bishop Bancroft, falling on his knees before the king, on this occasion, and with his eyes raised to him, said, "I protest my heart melteth for joy, that Almighty God, of his singular mercy, has given us such a king, as since Christ's time hath not been."—*Mosheim's Eccl. Hist.* vol. v. p. 386.

The above *mock* conference, as it is justly called, taught the puritans what to expect. The threatened storm soon overtook them. The persecuting prelates having received new life, presently renewed their tyrannical proceedings. Mr. Richard Rogers, of Wethersfield in Essex, a divine of incomparable worth, and six other ministers, were convened before the archbishop, and, refusing the oath *ex officio*, were all suspended. They were cited to appear before him a second time; but the archbishop died on the very day of their appearance. Whitgift, according to Fuller, was one of the worthiest men the church of England ever enjoyed.* Mr. Strype observes, that he was equal to both his predecessors, Parker and Grindal, in right godly and episcopal endowments; and that great wisdom, courage, and *gentleness* accompanied all his orders.† He was, however, an unfeeling and a relentless persecutor, and extravagantly fond of outward splendour, usually travelling with a most magnificent retinue.‡

Dr. Richard Bancroft having acquitted himself so much to the king's satisfaction, in the conference at Hampton-court, was thought the fittest person to succeed Whitgift in the chair of Canterbury.§ He trod in the steps of his predecessor in all the iniquities of persecution. He entered upon the work where Whitgift concluded, and immediately convened Mr. Rogers and his brethren before him. They endured continual molestations for a long time, having many expensive journies to London. Mr. Rogers was cited also before the Bishop of London, who protested "by the help of Jesus, that he would not leave one nonconformable minister in all his diocese;" but his death soon after put an end to his career. Mr. Baynes, the excellent lecturer at Cambridge, was silenced, and his lecture put down. Dr. Taylor was suspended from his ministry. Mr. Hilder-

* Church Hist. b. x. p. 25. † Life of Parker, Pref. p. 5.

‡ His train sometimes consisted of 1000 horse. The archbishop being once at Dover, attended by five hundred horse, one hundred of which were his own servants, many of them wearing chains of gold, a person of distinction then arriving from Rome, greatly wondered to see an English archbishop with so splendid a retinue. But seeing him the following sabbath in the cathedral of Canterbury, attended by the above magnificent train, with the dean, prebendaries, and preachers, in their surplices and scarlet hoods; and hearing the music of organs, cornets, and sacbuts, he was seized with admiration, and said, "That the people at Rome were led in blindness, being made to believe, that in England there was neither archbishop, nor bishop, nor cathedral, nor any ecclesiastical government; but that all were pulled down. But he protested, that unless it were in the *pope's chapel*, he never saw a more solemn sight, or heard a more heavenly sound."—*Paule's Life of Whitgift*, p. 104—106.

§ Granger's Biog. Hist. vol. i. p. 340.

sham was suspended a third time for nonconformity; and many others suffered the like extremity.

Numerous congregations being deprived of their zealous and faithful pastors, the distressed people presented a petition to the king, in behalf of their suffering ministers; which, because it was presented while his majesty was hunting, he was exceedingly displeased. The poor puritan ministers were now persecuted in every quarter, some of them being suspended, and others deprived of their livings.* And while the bishops were highly commended for suspending or depriving all who could not conform, Sir Richard Knightly, Sir Valentine Knightly, Sir Edward Montague, and some others, presented a petition to the king in behalf of the suffering ministers in Northamptonshire; for which they were summoned before the council, and told, that what they had done "tended to sedition, and was little less than treason."†

The king now issued two proclamations, intimating in the one, what regard he would have to the *tender consciences of the papists*; but in the other, that he would not allow the least indulgence to the *tender consciences of the puritans*.‡ In his majesty's long speech, at the opening of the first session of parliament, he said, "I acknowledge the Roman "church to be our *mother* church, although defiled with "some infirmities and corruptions;" and added, "I would "for my own part be content to meet them in the mid-"way;" but spoke with great indignation against the puritans.§ And many of the ministers still refusing to conform, the king issued another proclamation, dated July 10, 1604, allowing them to consider of their conformity till the end of November following: but in case of their refusal, he would have them all deprived, or banished out of the kingdom.‖

Most of the bishops and clergy in the convocation which sat with the above parliament, were very zealous against the puritans. Bishop Rudd was, indeed, a noble exception. He spoke much in their praise, and exposed the injustice and inhumanity of their persecutors. The book of canons passed both houses, and was afterwards ratified by the king's letters patent, under his great seal.¶ By these canons, new hardships were laid upon the oppressed puritans. Suspensions and deprivations were now thought not

* Winwood's Memorials, vol. ii. p. 36, 48. † Ibid. p. 49.
‡ Rapin's Hist. of Eng. vol. ii. p. 163. § Ibid. p. 165, 166.
‖ MS. Remarks, p. 563. ¶ Sparrow's Collec. p. 263.

to be a sufficient punishment for the sin of nonconformity. The puritans received the terrible sentence of excommunication, being turned out of the congregation, rendered incapable of sueing for their lawful debts, imprisoned for life, denied christian burial, and, as far as possible, *excluded from the kingdom of heaven.* Archbishop Bancroft, now at the head of all ecclesiastical affairs, enforced the observance of all the festivals of the church, the use of copes, surplices, caps, hoods, &c. and obliged the clergy to subscribe afresh to Whitgift's three articles, which, by canon xxxvi. they were to declare they did *willingly* and *from their hearts.* By these oppressive measures, four hundred ministers were suspended and cast out of their livings;* some of whom were excommunicated and cast into prison, while others, to preserve their consciences, were driven into a state of banishment.

Among the painful sufferers at this time, were Mr. Maunsel, minister of Yarmouth, and Mr. Lad, a merchant of the same place. For holding a supposed conventicle, they were cited before the high commission at Lambeth, and, refusing the oath *ex officio*, were cast into prison. When they were brought to the bar, Nicholas Fuller, esq. a bencher of Gray's-inn, and a learned man in his profession, was their counsel; who, for pleading their cause, was cast into prison, where he continued to the day of his death. Mr. Wotton and Mr. Cleaver, two learned and useful divines, were suspended for nonconformity. Mr. Rush, fellow of Christ's college, Cambridge, was convened and required to make a public recantation. Mr. Randall Bates, a pious and excellent preacher, was committed to the Gatehouse, where, after a long and miserable confinement, he died under the hardships of the prison. These severities drove many learned ministers and their followers out of the kingdom, when they retired to Amsterdam, Rotterdam, Leyden and other places. Among these were Dr. William Ames and Mr. Robert Parker, both divines of distinguished eminence.

Indeed, Archbishop Bancroft incessantly harassed and plagued the puritans, to bring them to an exact conformity. On account of his rigorous proceedings, great numbers

* Sion's Plea, p. 75.—MS. Remarks, p. 585.—Some of our high-church historians, it is acknowledged, have diminished the number to forty-five, others to forty-nine, evidently with a design to remove the odium from the persecuting prelates.—*Heylin's Hist. of Pres.* p. 376.—*Spotiswood's Hist. of Scotland*, p. 479. Edit. 1677.

resolved to transport themselves to Virginia, and settle in that uncivilized country, where they could enjoy the blessing of religious liberty. Some having departed for the new settlement, and the archbishop seeing many more ready for the voyage, obtained his majesty's proclamation, forbidding them to depart without the king's license. The arbitrary court was apprehensive this sect would in the end become too numerous and powerful in America.* The distressed puritans must not enjoy liberty of conscience at home, nor remove to another country, even among uncivilized pagans, where they could enjoy it.—The high commission, says Bishop Kennet, began now to swell into a grievance, of which the parliament complained. Every man must conform to the episcopal church, and quit his opinion or his safety. That court was the touch-stone, to try whether men were current. "This," he adds, "was the beginning of that mischief, which made such a bloody tincture in both kingdoms, as never will be got out of the *bishops' lawn sleeves*."†

The parliament, in 1610, was deeply concerned about these proceedings. In their petition to the king, they say, "That divers painful and learned pastors, who have long travelled in the work of the ministry, with good fruit and blessing of their labours, who were ready to subscribe to the true christian faith and doctrine of sacraments, for not conforming in some points of ceremony, and refusing the subscription directed by the late canons, have been removed from their ecclesiastical livings, being their freehold, and debarred from all means of maintenance, to the great grief of sundry of your majesty's well-affected subjects."‡ And in a memorable speech during this parliament, it was said, "The depriving, degrading, and imprisoning learned and godly ministers, whom God hath furnished with most heavenly graces, is the crying sin of the land, most provoking to God, and most grievous to the subjects."§ A bill was, therefore, introduced against pluralities and nonresidence; another against canonical subscription; a third against scandalous ministers; a fourth against the oath *ex officio*; and they all passed the commons.‖ An address was also presented to the king, entitled "An humble supplication for toleration and liberty to enjoy and

* Rapin's Hist. of Eng. vol. ii. p. 176.
† Kennet's Hist. of Eng. vol. ii. p. 681, 682.
‡ Calamy's Church and Dissenters, p. 131. § Ibid. p. 137.
‖ MS. Remarks, p. 629.

observe the ordinances of Jesus Christ in the ministration of his churches, in lieu of human constitutions." It was published by those who apprehended the church of England to be fast approaching towards the church of Rome.* But all these endeavours proved ineffectual to obtain a further reformation of the church.+ Archbishop Bancroft died November 10, 1610, and was succeeded by Dr. George Abbot, an avowed enemy to all the superstitions of popery.‡

King James, to shew his zeal against heresy, had now an opportunity of exercising it upon two of his own subjects; who, in the year 1611, were burnt alive for their heretical opinions. One was Bartholomew Legatt, a native of the county of Essex. He was a man of a bold spirit, a fluent tongue, well skilled in the scriptures, and of an unblameable conversation. He denied the divinity of Christ, and a plurality of persons in the Godhead. The king himself, and several of the bishops, conferred with him, and endeavoured to convince him of his errors.§ Having continued a long time prisoner in Newgate, he was at length brought before the king, many of the bishops, and many learned divines, in the consistory of St. Paul's; where he was declared a contumacious and obdurate heretic, and delivered over to the secular power. The king having signed a writ *de heretico comburendo* to the sheriffs of London, he was carried to Smithfield, March 18, and, before an immense number of spectators, was burnt to ashes. Pardon was offered him at the stake if he would have recanted, but he firmly refused.‖

Mr. Edward Whiteman of Burton-upon-Trent, was, at

* MS. Chronology, vol. ii. p. 619. (2.)

+ The puritans were now oppressed by every means that could be devised. Mrs. Venables, a lady of great liberality and exemplary piety, being deeply concerned for the numerous persecuted servants of Christ, bequeathed in her last will £5000, to be distributed among the suffering nonconformist ministers. This was no sooner known at court, than the money was seized, and given to such ministers as were conformable. Such was the fraud and barbarity of the times!!—*MS. Remarks*, p. 585.

‡ Bishop Kennet styles Archbishop Bancroft "a sturdy piece," and says, "he proceeded with *rigour*, *severity* and *wrath*, against the puritans."—*Kennet's Hist. of Eng.* vol. ii. p. 665.

§ The attempt of the king to convince Legatt having utterly failed, he arose in a passion from his chair, and, giving him a kick with his royal foot, said: "Away, base fellow, it shall never be said, that one stayeth in my presence, that hath never prayed to our Saviour for seven years."—*Fuller's Church Hist.* b. x. p. 62.

‖ He had a brother, called Thomas Legatt, who, at the same time, for holding certain heretical opinions, as they are called, was committed to Newgate, where he died under the pressures of his confinement.—*Jessop's Discovery of Anabaptists*, p. 77. Edit. 1623.

the same time, convicted of heresy by Dr. Neile, bishop of Coventry and Lichfield, and burnt at Lichfield, April 11. In the king's warrant for his execution, he is charged with no less than sixteen distinct heresies, among which are those of the Ebionites, Corinthians, Arians, and Anabaptists, and other heretical, execrable, and unheard-of opinions. Some of the opinions imputed to him savoured of vanity, superstition, and enthusiasm; and he was certainly an object more deserving of compassion than of punishment.* But, to gratify the wishes of his enemies, he must pass through the fire.—There was another condemned to be burnt for similar heresies; but the constancy of the above sufferers having greatly moved the pity of the spectators, he was left to linger out a miserable life in Newgate.†

Many of the puritans being driven into exile, continued a number of years in a foreign land. They raised congregations and formed christian churches, according to their views of the New Testament. Mr. John Robinson, pastor of the church at Leyden, first struck out the congregational or independent form of church government. Afterwards, about a hundred of his church transplanted themselves to America, and laid the foundation of the colony of New England. But some of the worthy exiles ventured at length to return home. Mr. Henry Jacob having espoused the sentiments of the independents, returned about the year 1616; and communicating to his friends his design of forming a separate church, like those in Holland, they, seeing no prospect of any reformation of the national church, signified their approbation. They spent a day in solemn devotion, to implore the divine blessing upon the undertaking; and having made an open confession of their faith in Christ, they joined hands, and convenanted with each other to walk together in all the ordinances of God, as far as he had already made known to them, or should hereafter make known to them. Mr. Jacob was chosen pastor by the suffrage of the brotherhood, and others to the office of deacons. This was the first INDEPENDENT church in England.

During this year, his majesty, by the advice of the bishops, issued his royal directions for a better conformity to the established church. He required "That all students who took their degrees, should subscribe to the thirty-sixth canon.—That all scholars should wear their scholastical

* Narration of the burning of Legatt and Whiteman, Edit. 1651.

† Fuller's Church Hist. b. x. p. 62—64.

habits.—That no one be allowed to preach without perfect conformity.—And that no preacher shall maintain any point of doctrine not allowed by the church of England."*

The distressed puritans felt the iron rod of their cruel persecutors in various parts of the country. Messrs. Ball, Nicholls, Paget, and many others, in the diocese of Chester, were often cited before the high commission, when attachments were issued to apprehend them, and commit them to prison. They were obliged to conceal themselves, and heavy fines were laid upon them for their nonappearance, and were aggravated from one court day to another; till their case was returned into the exchequer, when, to their unspeakable injury, they were obliged to compound. Mr. Bradshaw had his house searched by the bishops' pursuivants, and he was suspended. Mr. John Wilkinson was several times spoiled of his goods, and kept many years in prison by the furious prelates. Mr. Hildersham was suspended a fourth and a fifth time. He was afterwards summoned before the high commission, and, refusing the oath *ex officio*, committed first to the Fleet, then to the King's-bench, where he continued a long time. Having obtained his liberty, he was censured in the ecclesiastical court, upon the most glaring false witness, and fined £2,000, pronounced excommunicate, degraded from his ministry, ordered to be taken and cast into prison, required to make a public recantation in such form as the court should appoint, and condemned in costs of suit. His two friends, Mr. Dighton and Mr. Holt, being committed, one to the Fleet, the other to the Gatehouse, were fined £10,000 each, excommunicated, ordered to be publicly denounced, to make their submission in three different places, condemned in costs of suit, and sent back to prison. The learned Mr. John Selden, for publishing his "History of Tithes," was summoned before the high commission, and obliged to sign a recantation.†

To prevent the growth of puritanism, the king, in the year 1618, published his "Declaration for Sports on the Lord's-day," commonly called the Book of Sports. It was procured by the bishops, and all ministers were enjoined to approve of it, and read it in the public congregations; and those who refused were brought into the high commission,

* Heylin's Life of Laud, p. 72.

† Mr. Selden was justly denominated the glory of England for his uncommon learning. Archbishop Usher used to say, "I am not worthy to carry his books after him."

suspended and imprisoned. "It was designed," says Bishop Kennet, "as a trap to catch men of tender consciences, and as a means of promoting the ease, wealth and grandeur of the bishops."*

The king, at the opening of the parliament in 1620, made this solemn declaration: "*I mean,*" said he, "*not to compel any man's conscience; for I ever protested against it.*† But his majesty soon forgot his own declaration; and to increase the distress of the puritans, he set forth his directions to all the clergy, forbidding them to preach on the deep points of controversy betwixt the Arminians and Calvinists. The puritans had hitherto suffered only for refusing the ceremonies, but now their doctrine itself became an offence. Most Calvinists were now excluded from court preferments. The way to rise in the church, was to preach up the absolute power of the king, to declaim against the rigours of Calvinism, and to speak favourably of popery. Those who scrupled were neglected, and denominated *doctrinal puritans;* but having withstood all the arbitrary proceedings adopted both in church and state, they will be esteemed by posterity, as the glory of the English nation.‡

Many of the puritans now groaned under the oppressive measures of the prelates. Mr. Collins was cast into prison for nonconformity. Though he was not suffered to preach in the churches, he preached to the malefactors in prison, and there procured himself a subsistence by correcting the press.§ Mr. Knight of Pembroke college, Oxford, was cited up to London, and committed to the Gatehouse. Mr. Peck having catechised his family, and sung a psalm in his own house, when several of his neighbours were present, they were all required by Bishop Harsnet to do penance and recant. Those who refused were immediately excommunicated and condemned in heavy costs. The citizens of Norwich afterwards complained of this cruel oppression to parliament. The celebrated Mr. Dod was often cited before the bishops, and was four times suspended. Mr. Whately was convened before the high commission, and required to make a public recantation. Mr. Whiting was prosecuted by the Bishop of Norwich, and brought before the high commission, expecting to be deprived of considerable

* Several of the bishops, however, declared their opinion against the Book of Sports. And Archbishop Abbot being at Croydon the day on which it was ordered to be read in the churches, expressly forbad it to be read there.—*Kennet's Hist. of Eng.* vol. ii. p. 709.

† MS. Chronology, vol. ii. p. 667. (13.) ‡ Neal's Puritans, vol. ii. p. 128.

§ Wood's Athenæ Oxon. vol. ii. p. 194.

estates; but, happily, while the cause was pending, King James died, and the prosecution was dropped. The king finished his course March 27, 1625, not without suspicion of having been poisoned by the Duke of Buckingham.* He was a mere pedant, without judgment, courage, or steadiness, being the very scorn of the age. His reign was a continued course of mean practices.† He invaded the liberties of his subjects; endangered the religion of his country; was ever grasping at arbitrary power;‡ and, in a word, liberty of conscience was totally suppressed.§‖

Sect. IV.

From the Death of King James I. to the Death of King Charles I.

When King Charles came to the crown, he was at first thought favourable to puritanism. His tutor, and all his court, were puritanically inclined. Dr. Preston, one of the leading puritans, came in a coach to London with the King and the Duke of Buckingham, which gave great offence to the contrary party. His majesty was so overcharged with grief for the death of his father, that he wanted the comfort of so wise and great a man.¶ The puritans, however, soon found that no favour was to be expected. The unjust and inhuman proceedings of the council-table, the star-chamber, and the high commission, during this reign,

* Harris's Life of James I. p. 237. Edit. 1753.
† Burnet's Hist. of his Times, vol. i. p. 17.
‡ Bennet's-Mem. of Reformation, p. 147.
§ Hume's Hist. of Eng. vol. vi. p. 116.—‖ Bishop Laud observes of James, that the sweetness of his nature was scarcely to be paralleled, and little less than a miracle. Clemency, mercy, justice, and peace, were all eminent in him; and he was the most learned and religious prince that England ever knew. On the contrary, the learned Mosheim affirms, "that "as the desire of unlimited power and authority was the reigning passion "in the heart of this monarch, so all his measures, whether of a civil or "ecclesiastical nature, were calculated to answer the purposes of his "ambition. He was the bitterest enemy of the doctrine and discipline of "the puritans, to which he had been in his youth most warmly attached; "the most inflexible and ardent patron of the Arminians, in whose ruin "and condemnation in Holland he had been singularly instrumental; and "the most zealous defender of episcopal government, against which he had "more than once expressed himself in the strongest terms." Though he was no papist, he was certainly very much inclined to popery, and "was "excessively addicted to hunting and drinking."—*Breviate of Laud*, p. 5. —*Mosheim's Eccl. Hist.* vol. v. p. 385, 391, 392.—*Harris's Life of James I.* p. 45, 66.
¶ Burnet's Hist. of his Time, vol. i. p. 19.

are unparalleled. The two former were become courts of *law*, to determine matters of *right*; and courts of *revenue*, to bring money into the treasury. The *council-table*, by proclamations, enjoined upon the people what was not enjoined by law; and the *star-chamber* punished the disobedience of those proclamations by heavy fines and imprisonment. The exorbitances of this court were such, that there were very few persons of quality who did not suffer more or less, by the weight of its censures and judgments. And the *high commission* became justly odious, not only by meddling with things not within its cognizance, but by extending its sentences and judgments to a degree that was unjustifiable, and by treating the common law, and the professors of it, with great contempt. From an ecclesiastical court for the reformation of manners, it became a court of *revenue*, imposing heavy fines upon the subjects.*

These courts made strange havoc among the puritans, detaining them long in prison, without bringing them to trial, or acquainting them with the cause of their commitment. Their proceedings were, in some respects, worse than the *Romish Inquisition;* because they suspended, degraded, excommunicated, and imprisoned multitudes of learned and pious ministers, without the breach of any established law. While the heaviest penalties were inflicted upon the protestant nonconformists, the papists lived without molestation. Indeed, the king gave express orders "To forbear all manner of proceedings against Roman catholics, and that all pains and penalties to which they were liable, should cease."†

The Arminian tenets, warmly supported by Bishop Laud and his brethren, now began rapidly to gain ground. The points of controversy became so much the subject of public discussion, that the king issued his royal proclamation, threatening to proceed against all who should maintain any new opinions, contrary to the doctrines as by law established. Though this proclamation appeared to be in favour of the Calvinists, the execution of it being in the hands of Laud and his brethren, it was turned against them, and made use of to silence them; while it gave an uncontrouled liberty to the tongues and pens of the Arminians.‡ Many were, indeed, of opinion, that Bishops Laud and Neile procured this injunction on purpose to oppress the

* Clarendon's History, vol. i. p. 68, 69, 222, 283.
† Rushworth's Collections, vol. i. p. 173.
‡ Ibid. p. 416, 417.

Calvinists, who should venture to break it, while they should connive at the disobedience of the contrary party. It is certain, the Calvinists were prosecuted for disobeying the proclamation, while the Arminians were tolerated and countenanced.* The puritans, who wrote in defence of the received doctrines of the *thirty-nine* articles, were censured in the high commission, and their books suppressed; and when they ventured to preach or dispute upon those points, they were suspended, imprisoned, forced to recant, or banished to a foreign land.†

The king now usurped an arbitrary power, much more extensive than any of his predecessors. Henry VIII. did what he pleased by the use of parliament; but Charles evidently designed to rule *without* parliament.‡ To convince the people that it was their duty to submit to a monarch of such principles, the clergy were employed to preach up the doctrine of passive obedience and non-resistance. Dr. Manwaring preaching before his majesty, said, "The king is not bound to observe the laws of "the realm, concerning the subject's rights and liberties, "but that his royal will and pleasure, in imposing taxes "without consent of parliament, doth oblige the subject's "conscience on pain of eternal damnation."§

The church being governed by similar arbitrary and illegal methods, it was easy to foresee what the nonconformists had to expect. They were exceedingly harassed and persecuted in every corner of the land. In the year 1626, Mr. Brewer was censured in the high commission, and committed to prison, where he continued fourteen years. Mr. Smart, prebend of Durham, was many times convened before his ecclesiastical judges; then sent to the high commission at York, and kept a prisoner nine months. He was next sent to the high commission at Lambeth; then returned to York, fined £500, and ordered to recant; for refusing which, he was fined a second time, excommunicated, deprived, degraded, and committed to prison, where he remained eleven or twelve years, suffering

* Rapin's Hist. vol. ii. p. 258.

† Prynne's Canterburies Doome, p. 161.

‡ Rapin's Hist. vol. ii. p. 259.

§ Manwaring, for this sermon, was sentenced by the house of lords to pay a fine of a thousand pounds, to make a public submission at the bar of both houses, to be imprisoned during the pleasure of the lords, and declared incapable of holding any ecclesiastical dignity: nevertheless, he was so much a *court favourite*, he obtained the king's pardon, with a good benefice, and afterwards a bishopric.—*Ibid.*

immense damages. These severities were inflicted by the instigation of Laud, soon after made Bishop of London, and prime minister to his majesty.* This furious prelate was no sooner exalted, than he made strange havoc among the churches. Agreeable to the king's injunctions, many excellent lecturers were put down, and such as preached against Arminianism or the popish ceremonies, were suspended; among whom were Drs. Stoughton, Sibbs, Taylor, and Gouge, with Messrs. White of Dorchester, Rogers of Dedham, Rogers of Wethersfield, Hooker of Chelmsford, White of Knightsbridge, Archer, Edwards, Jones, Ward, Saunders, Salisbury, Foxley, William Martin, and James Gardiner.† Mr. Henry Burton was brought before the council-table, and the high commission. He was afterwards apprehended by a pursuivant, then suspended and committed to the Fleet. Mr. Nathaniel Bernard was suspended, excommunicated, fined £1,000, condemned in costs of suit, and committed to New Prison, where he was treated with great barbarity; and refusing to make a public recantation, after languishing a long time, he died through the rigour of his confinement. But the unparalleled cruelty of this prelate most appeared in the terrible sentence inflicted upon Dr. Alexander Leighton. He was seized by a warrant from the high commission; dragged before Bishop Laud; then, without examination, carried to Newgate, where he was treated a long time with unexampled barbarity. When brought to trial before that arbitrary court, the furious prelate desired the court to inflict the heaviest sentence that could be inflicted upon him. He was, therefore, condemned to be degraded from his ministry, to have his ears cut, his nose slit, to be branded in the face, whipped at a post, to stand in the pillory, to pay £10,000, and to suffer perpetual imprisonment. This horrible sentence being pronounced, Laud pulled off his hat; and holding up his hands, *gave thanks to God, who had given him the victory over his enemies.*‡

During these cruel proceedings, Mr. Palmer and Mr. Udney, two lecturers in Kent, were silenced. Mr. Angier was suspended.§ Mr. Huntley was grievously censured in the high commission, and committed to prison, where he continued a long time. Mr. John Workman was

* Prynne's Cant. Doome, p. 78. † Ibid. p. 362, 373.

‡ For an account of the barbarous execution of this shocking sentence, see Art. Leighton.

§ Calamy's Account, vol. ii. p. 395.

suspended, excommunicated, condemned in costs of suit, cast into prison, and obliged to make a public recantation at three different places. Mr. Crowder was committed close prisoner to Newgate for sixteen weeks, then deprived of his living, without there being any charge, witness, or other proof brought against him. Many others were prosecuted and deprived.* Bishop Land being made chancellor of Oxford, carried his severities to the university. He caused Mr. Hill to make a public recantation; Messrs. Ford, Thorne, and Hodges to be expelled from the university; the proctors to be deprived for receiving their appeal; and Drs. Prideaux and Wilkinson to be sharply admonished. Mr. William Hobbs, fellow of Trinity college, having preached against falling from grace; and Mr. Thomas Cook of Brasen-nose college, having in his Latin sermon used certain expressions against the Arminians, they were both enjoined public recantations. Dr. Prideaux, Dr. Burgess, Mr. White, Mr. Madye, with some others, suffered on the same account.†

By the unfeeling persecutions of the bishops, the puritans were driven from one diocese to another, and many of them obliged to leave the kingdom, and seek their bread in a foreign land. Messrs. Higginson, Skelton, Williams, Wilson, Wheelwright, Philips, Lathorp, Hooker, Stone, Cotton, with many others, fled to New England. Many of these divines, previous to their departure, were harassed, prosecuted, and cruelly censured by the ruling prelates.

The distressed puritans who remained at home, presented a petition to his majesty, in which they say, "We are not a little discouraged and deterred from preaching those saving doctrines of God's free grace in election and predestination which greatly confirm our faith of eternal salvation, and fervently kindle our love to God, as the seventeenth article expressly mentioneth. So we are brought into great strait, either of incurring God's heavy displeasure if we do not faithfully discharge our embassage, in declaring the whole council of God; or the danger of being censured as violaters of your majesty's acts, if we preach these constant doctrines of our church, and confute the opposite Pelagian and Arminian heresies, both boldly preached and printed without the least censure."‡ This

* Wharton's Troubles of Laud, vol. i. p. 519.

† Prynne's Cant. Doome, p. 173, 176.—Rushworth's Collec. vol. ii. p. 283.

‡ Prynne's Cant. Doome, p. 165.

appears, however, to have been followed with no good effect. By silencing so many learned and useful ministers, there was a great scarcity of preachers, and a famine of the word of God in every corner of the land; while ignorance, superstition, profaneness, and popery, every where increased.*

The sufferings of the people for want of the bread of life continually increasing, a number of ministers and gentlemen formed a scheme to promote preaching in the country, by setting up lectures in the different market towns. To defray the expence, a sum of money was raised by voluntary contribution, for purchasing such impropriations as were in the hands of the laity, the profits of which were to be divided into salaries of forty or fifty pounds a year, for the support of the lecturers. The money was deposited in the hands of the following persons, as FEOFFEES: Dr. George, Dr. Sibbs, Dr. Offspring, and Mr. Davenport, of the clergy; Ralph Eyre, Simon Brown, C. Sherland, and John White, esqrs.; and Messrs. John Gearing, Richard Davis, George Harwood, and Francis Bridges, citizens of London. Most people thought the design was very laudable, and wished them good success; but Bishop Laud looking upon the undertaking with an evil and a jealous eye, as if it was likely to become the great nursery of puritanism, applied to the king, and obtained an information against all the feoffees in the exchequer. The feoffment was, therefore, cancelled, their proceedings declared illegal, the impropriations already purchased, amounting to five or six thousand pounds, were confiscated to the king, and the feoffees themselves fined in the star-chamber.†

If the persecuted puritans at any time ventured to except against the proceedings of this fiery prelate, they were sure to feel his indignation. Mr. Hayden having spoken against them from the pulpit, was driven out of the diocese of Exeter, but afterwards apprehended by Bishop Harsnet, who took from him his horse, his money, and all his papers, and caused him to be shut up in close prison for thirteen weeks. His lordship then sent him to the high commission, when he was deprived, degraded, and fined, for having preached against superstitious decorations and images in churches. Mr. Hayden venturing afterwards to preach occasionally, was again apprehended by Bishop Laud,

* Prynne's Cent. Doome, p. 385. † Ibid. p. 385—387.

who sent him first to the Gatehouse, then to Bridewell, where he was whipped and kept to hard labour; then confined in a cold dark hole during the whole of winter, being chained to a post in the middle of the room, with irons on his hands and feet, having no other food than bread and water, and a pad of straw to lie on. Before his release, he was obliged to take an oath, and give bond, to preach no more, but depart from the kingdom, and never return. Henry Shirfield, esq. a bencher of Lincoln's-inn, and recorder of Salisbury, was tried in the star-chamber, for taking down some painted glass from one of the windows of St. Edmund's church, Salisbury. These pictures were extremely ridiculous and superstitious.* The taking down of the glass was agreed upon at a vestry, when six justices of the peace were present. Towards the close of his trial, Bishop Laud stood up, and moved the court, that Mr. Shirfield might be fined £1,000, removed from his recordership, committed to the Fleet till he paid the fine, and then bound to his good behaviour. The whole of this heavy sentence was inflicted upon him, excepting that the fine was mitigated to £500.†

In the year 1633, upon the death of Archbishop Abbot, Laud was made Archbishop of Canterbury; when he and several of his brethren renewed their zeal in the persecution of the puritans.‡ Numerous lecturers were silenced, and their lectures put down. Mr. Rathband and Mr. Blackerby, two most excellent divines, were often silenced, and driven from one place to another. Mr. John Budle, rector of Barnston, and Mr. Throgmorton, vicar of Mawling, were prosecuted in the high commission.§ Mr. Alder and Mr. Jessey were both silenced, the latter for not observing the ceremonies, and removing a crucifix.‖ Mr. John Vincent was continually harassed for nonconformity. He was so driven from place to place, that though he had many

* There were in this window seven pictures of *God the Father* in the form of little old men, in a blue and red coat, with a pouch by his side. One of them represented him creating the sun and moon with a pair of compasses; others as working upon the six days creation; and at last as sitting in an elbow chair at rest. Many of the people, upon their going in and out of the church, did reverence to this window, because, as they said, the Lord their God was there.—*Prynne's Cant. Doome*, p. 102.

† Ibid. p. 103.—Rushworth's Collec. vol. ii. p. 153—156.

‡ Archbishop Abbot, who succeeded Bancroft, is said to have imitated the *moderation* of Whitgift; and that Laud, who succeeded Abbot, imitated the *wrath* of Bancroft.—*Kennet's Hist. of Eng.* vol. ii. p. 665, note.

§ Wharton's Troubles of Laud, vol. i. p. 526—529.

‖ Calamy's Contin. vol. i. p. 46.

children, not two of them were born in the same county. Messrs. Angel, Buckley, Saunders, Bridges, Roberts, Erbery, Cradock, Newport, and others, were suspended, and some of them driven out of the country.* Mr. John Carter was censured by Bishop Wren, but death soon after delivered him from all his troubles. Messrs. Peters, Davenport, Nye,† and others, to escape the fury of the storm, fled to Holland. Mr. Peters, previous to his departure, was apprehended by Archbishop Laud, suspended, and committed for some time to New Prison. Many others were driven to New England, among whom were Messrs. Norton, Burr, Shepard, Sherman, and Nathaniel Ward, who was deprived and excommunicated by the archbishop.

During this year the king, by the recommendation of Laud, republished the "Book of Sports," for the encouragement of recreations and pastimes on the Lord's day. This opened a flood-gate to all manner of licentiousness, and became the instrument of unspeakable oppression to great numbers of his majesty's best subjects. The ruling prelates, though unauthorized by law, required the clergy to read it before the public congregation. This the puritans refused; for which they felt the iron rod of their tyrannical oppressors. Dr. Staunton, Mr. Chauncey, and Mr. Thomas, for refusing to read the book, were suspended.‡ Mr. Fairclough was often cited into the ecclesiastical courts. Mr. Tookie was turned out of his living. Mr. Cooper was suspended, and continued under the ecclesiastical censure seven years. Mr. Sanger was imprisoned at Salisbury. Mr. Moreland, rector of Hamsted-Marshall in Berkshire, was suspended and deprived of his living.§ Mr. Snelling was suspended, deprived, excommunicated, and cast into prison, where he continued till the meeting of the long parliament. Dr. Chambers was silenced, sequestered, and cast into prison.‖ Messrs. Culmer, Player, and Hieron being suspended, waited upon the archbishop, jointly requesting absolution from the unjust censure; when his grace said, "If you know not how to obey, I know not how to grant your favour," and dismissed them from his presence. Mr. Wilson was suspended from his office and benefice, and afterwards prosecuted in the high commission. Mr. Wroth and Mr. Erbery from Wales, Mr. Jones from

* Wharton's Troubles of Laud, vol. i. p. 532, 533.
† Calamy's Account, vol. ii. p. 29.
‡ Clark's Lives, last vol. part i. p. 162. § MS. Remarks, p. 903.
‖ Calamy's Account and Contin.

Gloucestershire, Mr. Whitfield of Ockham, Mr. Garth of Wovereh, Mr. Ward of Pepper-Harrow, Mr. Farrol of Purbright, Mr. Pegges of Weeford, and Mr. Thomas Valentine, minister of Chalfont St. Giles, with many others, were brought from various parts of the country, and prosecuted in the high commission.* Mr. Edmund Calamy, Mr. William Bridge, Mr. Thomas Allen, and about thirty other worthy ministers, for refusing to read the book and observe Bishop Wren's articles, were driven out of the diocese.† And Laud, at the same time, caused upwards of twenty ministers to be fined and expelled from their livings, for not bowing at the name of Jesus.‡

Towards the close of this year, William Prynne, esq. a member of Lincoln's-inn, having published a book, entitled "Histrio-mastix; or, the Play's Scourge," exposing the evil of plays, masquerades, &c. was sentenced to have his book burnt by the common hangman, to be put from the bar, to be for ever incapable of his profession, to be turned out of the society of Lincoln's-inn, to be degraded at Oxford, to stand in the pillory at Westminster and Cheapside, to lose both his ears, one in each place, to pay a fine of five thousand pounds, and to suffer perpetual imprisonment.§ Dr. Bastwick, a physician of Colchester, having published a book, entitled *Elenchus religionis, papisticæ*, with an appendix, called *Flagellum pontificis and episcoporum Latialium*, so greatly offended the prelates, by denying the divine right of bishops above that of presbyters, that by the high commission, he was discarded from his profession, excommunicated, fined one thousand pounds, and imprisoned till he should recant. And Mr. Burton having published two sermons against the late innovations, entitled "For God and the King," had his house and study broken open by a serjeant at arms, and his books and papers carried away. He was then suspended, and committed close prisoner to the Fleet, where he remained a long time.

These terrible proceedings made many conscientious nonconformists retire, with their families, to Holland and New England. Mr. Thomas Goodwin, Mr. Jeremiah Burroughs, Mr. William Bridge, Mr. Sydrach Sympson, Mr. Julines Herring, Mr. Samuel Ward, and many others, having

* Prynne's Cant. Doome, p. 149, 151, 382.
† Calamy's Account, vol. ii. p. 5, 476.
‡ Huntley's Prelates' Usurpations, p. 165.
§ Rushworth's Collec. vol. ii. p. 233.

endured the cruel oppressions of the prelates, went to Holland. Mr. Herring had been driven from his flock, and several times suspended. Mr. Ward had been suspended, required to recant, condemned in costs of suit, and cast into prison, where he had remained a long time. And Messrs. Mather, Bulkley, Hobert, Symes, Whitfield, Rogers, Partridge, Whiting, Knollys, and Chauncey, withdrew from the storm, and fled to New England. This was no rash adventure. They suffered many hardships by suspension and imprisonment, previous to their departure. Mr. Chauncey was twice prosecuted by the high commission, suspended from his ministry, cast into prison, condemned in costs of suit, and obliged to make a recantation.

While these fled from the storm, others continued to endure the painful conflict. Dr. Stoughton, rector of Aldermanbury, London; Mr. Andrew Moline, curate of St. Swithin's; Mr. John Goodwin, vicar of St. Stephen's, Colman-street; and Mr. Viner of St. Lawrence, Old Jewry, were prosecuted for breach of canons. Mr. Turner and Mr. Lindall, with some others, were censured in the high commission. Mr. John Wood, formerly censured in the high commission, and Mr. Sparrowhawke of St. Mary's, Woolnoth, were both suspended for preaching against bowing at the name of Jesus. Dr. Cornelius Burgess and Mr. Wharton suffered in the high commission. Mr. Matthews, rector of Penmayn, was suspended by his diocesan, for preaching against the observance of popish holidays.* Mr. Styles was prosecuted in the ecclesiastical court at York, for omitting the cross in baptism. Mr. Leigh, one of the prebendaries of Lichfield, was suspended for churching refractory women in private, for being averse to the good orders of the church, and for ordering the bell-man to give notice in open market of a sermon. Mr. Kendal of Tuddington, was suspended for preaching a sermon above an hour long, on a sabbath afternoon. Dr. Jenningson of Newcastle, was prosecuted in the high commission, and forced to quit the kingdom, to escape the fury of Laud. Mr. John Jemmet of Berwick, was apprehended by a pursuivant, suspended from the sacred function, and banished from the town, without any article or witness being brought against him; and above twenty other ministers were suspended for nonconformity.† Mr. John Evans was sent to the Gatehouse; Mr. John

* Wharton's Troubles of Laud, vol. i. p. 535—544.
† Prynne's Cant. Doome, p. 381, 382, 450.

Vicars was apprehended by a pursuivant, cast into prison, fined, and deprived of his living; and Mr. George Walker was prosecuted in the star-chamber, sequestered, and cast into prison, where he remained till the meeting of the long parliament.

Dr. Pierce, bishop of Bath and Wells, at the same time persecuted the nonconformists without mercy. He drove all the lecturers out of his diocese, and put down their lectures, as factions, and nurseries of puritanism. Upon a reflection on what he had done, he said, "I thank God, I have not one lecturer left in my diocese," hating the very name. He suspended Mr. Davenish of Bridgewater, for preaching a lecture in his own church on a market-day; and having absolved him upon his promise to preach no more, he said, *Go thy way, and sin no more, lest a worse thing befal thee.* He suspended Mr. Cornish for preaching a funeral sermon in the evening; and he questioned Mr. Thomas Erford for preaching on a revel-day, saying "his text was scandalous to the revel." He sharply reprimanded other ministers for explaining the questions and answers in the catechism, and said, "That was as bad as preaching." For this practice he enjoined Mr. Barret, rector of Barwick, to do public penance.* Dr. Conant, rector of Limington, received much molestation from this prelate.† Mr. Richard Allein, fifty years minister of Dichiat, endured great sufferings under him. And Dr. Chambers was silenced, sequestered, and cast into prison, being harassed several years.‡

Bishop Wren of Norwich, having ordered the communion tables in his diocese to be turned into altars, fencing them about with rails, many of the people, to avoid superstition and idolatry, refused to kneel before them. And though they presented themselves on their knees in the chancel, they were refused the communion; and afterwards, for not receiving it, they were excommunicated by this prelate.§ His lordship had no mercy on the puritans. He suspended, deprived, excommunicated,‖ or otherwise censured no less than *fifty* able and pious ministers, to the ruin of themselves, their wives, and their children. Among this

* Prynne's Cant. Doome, p. 377, 378.

† Palmer's Noncon. Mem. vol. i. p. 229.

‡ Calamy's Account, vol. ii. p. 580, 754.

§ Nalson's Collections, vol. ii. p. 399.

‖ A minister's son was excommunicated for only repeating the sermon of his father, who had been excommunicated.—*Rushworth's Collec. vol. iii.* p. 181.

number were Messrs. William Leigh, Richard Proud, Jonathan Burr, Matthew Browning, William Powell, Richard Raymund, John Carter, Robert Peck, William Bridge, William Green, Thomas Scott, Nicholas Beard, Robert Kent, Thomas Allen, John Allen, and John Ward.* Some of them spent their days in silence; others retired into foreign countries; but none were restored without a promise of conformity. This furious prelate, by these severities, drove upwards of three thousand persons to seek their bread in a foreign land.†

About the year 1637, many of the persecuted puritans, to obtain a refuge from the storm, retired to New England; among whom were Messrs. Fisk, Moxon, Newman, Peck, Ezekel Rogers, and Thomas Larkham.‡ Mr. Larkham was so followed by continued vexatious prosecutions, that he was a sufferer in almost all the courts in England. He was in the star-chamber and high commission at the same time. And, he said, he was so constantly hunted by hungry pursuivants, that at last, by the tyranny of the bishops, and the tenderness of his own conscience, he was forced into exile.§

While these ravages were made in the churches, numerous pious ministers and their flocks being torn asunder, if any attempted to separate from the national church, the jealous archbishop was sure to have his eye upon them. Mr. Lamb was accordingly prosecuted in the high commission, and cast into prison. He was confined in most of the jails about London. Mr. Wilson and Mr. Cornwall were committed to Maidstone jail. Many others were excommunicated and imprisoned by the archbishop.

This tyrannical arch-prelate suspended one Mr. Warren, a schoolmaster, for refusing conformity, and for reading only books on *divinity* among his scholars. Mr. Ephraim Hewet, minister of Wroxall in Warwickshire, was suspended by his diocesan, for keeping a fast in his parish, and not observing the ceremonies. Mr. Jeffryes was forced from his flock; and Mr. Wroth and Mr. Erbery were prosecuted, when the latter resigned his vicarage, and left the diocese in peace. Great numbers in Kent were excommunicated and cast into prison. About thirty of the London ministers

* Rushworth's Collec. vol. iii. p. 353.—Nalson's Collec. vol. ii. p. 400, 401.

† Prynne's Cant. Doome, p. 376.

‡ The number of ministers driven to New England by the hard dealings of the bishops, from the year 1620 to 1640, amounted to about ninety.—*MS. Remarks*, p. 919—921.

§ Calamy's Contin. vol. i. p. 330.

were convened before their diocesan; when many of them were suspended and excommunicated for refusing to receive the sacrament at the rails.* Mr. Miles Burket, vicar of Patteshall in Northamptonshire, was prosecuted in the high commission, for administering the sacrament without the rails, and for not bowing at the name of Jesus.+ Mr. Burton, Mr. Prynne, and Dr. Bastwick, already mentioned, having been long confined in prison, were prosecuted in the star-chamber, when they received the following dreadful sentence: —"Mr. Burton shall be deprived of his living, and degraded from his ministry, as Mr. Prynne and Dr. Bastwick had been already from their professions; they shall each be fined £5,000; they shall stand in the pillory at Westminster, and have their ears cut off; and because Prynne had lost his ears already, the remainder of the stumps shall be cut off, and he shall be stigmatized on both his cheeks with the letters S. L. for a *seditious libeller;* and they shall all three suffer perpetual imprisonment in the remotest parts of the kingdom."‡

The church of England and the governing prelates were now arrived at their highest power and splendour. The afflicted nonconformists, and those who favoured their cause,§ felt the relentless vengeance of the star-chamber and high commission. Dr. Williams, the excellent Bishop of Lincoln, was now removed from the court, and retired to his diocese. Here he connived at the nonconformists, and spoke with some keenness against the ceremonies. He once said, "That the puritans were the king's best subjects, and he was sure they would carry all at last." Laud being informed of this expression, caused an information to be lodged against him in the star-chamber, when, after suspension from all his offices and benefits in the high commission, he was fined £10,000 to the king, £1,000 to Sir John Mounson, and committed to the Tower during the king's pleasure. Being sent to the Tower, his library and all his goods were seized, and sold to pay the fine. His papers being seized, two letters were found written to him by Mr. Osbaldeston, chief

* Wharton's Troubles of Laud, vol. i. p. 546—557.

+ Prynne's Cant. Doome, p. 96.

‡ For a circumstantial account of the execution of this barbarous sentence, see Art. Henry Burton.

§ Many of those who favoured the cause of the nonconformists, paid great sums of money to obtain their release from the ecclesiastical censure. And Mr. John Packer, a gentleman of exemplary piety, charity, and zeal for a further reformation, was most liberal in supporting the silenced ministers; and he paid £1,000 for one of them to be released.—*MS. Chronology*, vol. iii. A.D. 1640, p. 44.

master of Westminster school, containing certain dark expressions,* on the ground of which he was condemned in the additional fine of £5,000 to the king, and £3,000 to the archbishop, and kept close prisoner in the Tower. Mr. Osbaldeston was fined £5,000 to the king, and £5,000 to the archbishop; to be deprived of all his spiritual promotions, to stand in the pillory before his own school, and have his ears nailed to it, and to be imprisoned during the king's pleasure. Mr. Osbaldeston being among the crowd in the court, when the sentence was pronounced, immediately went home, burnt some papers, and absconded, leaving a note on his desk in his study, with these words: "If the archbishop enquire for me, tell him I am gone beyond Canterbury." Mr. John Lilburne, afterwards a colonel in the army, for refusing to take an oath to answer all interrogatories concerning his importing and publishing seditious libels, was fined £5,000, and whipped through the streets from the Fleet to the pillory in Westminster. While in the pillory, he was gagged, then carried to the Fleet, and committed to close confinement, with irons on his hands and feet, where he remained betwixt two and three years, without any persons being allowed to see him.†

These terrible proceedings, without serving the interest of the church, awakened universal resentment against those in power. Many thousand families were driven to Holland, and many thousands to New England.‡ This so alarmed the king and the council, that a proclamation was issued, April 30, 1637, observing, "That great numbers of his majesty's subjects were yearly transported to New England, with their families and whole estates, *that they might be out of the reach of ecclesiastical authority*; his majesty therefore commands, that his officers of the several ports should suffer none to pass without license from the commissioners of the plantations, and a testimonial from their minister, of their conformity to the orders and discipline of the church." And to debar all *ministers*, it was ordered, "That whereas such ministers as are not conformable to the discipline and ceremonies of the church, do frequently transport themselves to the plantations, where they take liberty to nourish their factious and schismatical humours, to the hindrance of the

* These letters made mention of *a little great man*; and in another passage, the same person was denominated *a little urchin*. Such were the dark expressions which, by interpretation, were applied to Laud.

† Rushworth's Collec. vol. ii. p. 417, 803, 817.

‡ Sylvester's Life of Baxter, part i. p. 18.

good conformity and unity of the church; we therefore expressly command you, in his majesty's name, to suffer no clergyman to transport himself without a testimonial from the Archbishop of Canterbury and the Bishop of London."* The puritans must not be suffered to live peaceably at home, nor yet be allowed to take sanctuary in a foreign land. These unparalleled acts of cruel and tyrannical injustice in a protestant country, turned the hearts of tens of thousands to the cause of the puritans.

Notwithstanding the above prohibitions, multitudes went on board ships in disguise, and got over to the new plantations. There were, indeed, eight ships in the river Thames bound for New England, and filled with puritan families, among whom was OLIVER CROMWELL; who, seeing no end of the cruel oppressions in their native country, determined to spend the remainder of their days in America. But the council being informed of their design, issued an order "to stay those ships, and to put on shore all the provisions intended for the voyage." To prevent the same in future, the king prohibited all masters and owners of ships, from sending any ships with passengers to New England, without a special license from the privy council; "because," says he, "the people of New England are factious and unworthy our support."†

The puritans who remained at home still groaned under the merciless oppressions of the prelates. Mr. Obadiah Sedgwick was driven from his living and the people of his charge. Mr. Cox was summoned first before Bishop Hall, then Archbishop Laud. Mr. Simonds, rector of St. Martin's, Ironmonger-lane, London, and Mr. Daniel Votyer, rector of St. Peter's, West-cheap, were deprived, and forced to flee into Holland. Mr. Show was cited before Laud, and he fled to New England.‡ By the recommendation of Laud, Mr. Edward Moore, a student in the university of Oxford, was cast into prison, for the insignificant crime of wearing his hat in the town; and for his behaviour when reproved for his fault, he recommended him to be publicly whipped, and banished from the university.§ Mr. Bright was suspended for refusing to read the prayer against the Scots; and his brethren, the ministers of Kent, endured many troubles for the same crime. Mr. Barber was suspended and cast into prison, where he remained eleven months. Mr.

* Rushworth, vol. ii. p. 409, 410.
† Ibid. ‡ Wharton's Troubles of Laud, vol. i. p. 559—563.
§ Wharton's Troubles of Laud, vol. ii. p. 167.

Jessey and many others being assembled together for the purpose of fasting and prayer, were interrupted by the pursuivants, and sent to the Tower. Afterwards he was apprehended and several of his congregation, and committed to the Compter; but upon their application to the parliament, they were immediately released. Mr. Wilkinson was suspended, but restored by the house of commons.* Mr. Moreton, rector of Blisland in Cornwall, was driven from his living and his flock. Mr. Hughes and Mr. Todd were both silenced. Mr. Hieron was apprehended and prosecuted in the high commission, for very trivial matters.† By these proceedings of the bishops, many thousands of excellent christians and worthy subjects were ruined in their estates, and driven out of the country.‡

In the year 1640, the convocation continued to sit, after the parliament was dissolved. The canons adopted in this synod, entitled "Constitutions and Canons Ecclesiastical treated upon by the Archbishops of Canterbury and York, &c." are extremely superstitious and tyrannical. They required of all clergymen to swear "That they would never consent to the alteration of the present government of the church, by archbishops, bishops, deans, archdeacons, &c." And if any beneficed person should refuse this ridiculous and cruel oath, "he shall after one month be suspended from his office; after a second month, he shall be suspended from his office and benefice; and after a third month, he shall be deprived of all his ecclesiastical promotions."§ These canons were evidently designed to crush all the puritans at once; but they were soon virtually annulled.‖

November 3, 1640, the LONG PARLIAMENT first assembled, and continued sitting with some little interruption about *eighteen* years. The members of this parliament were *all members of the church of England*, and nearly all advocates for episcopal government.¶ The first week was spent in appointing committees, and receiving the numerous petitions from all parts of the kingdom, craving a redress of grievances both in church and state.** Numerous petitions were also

* Calamy's Contin. vol. i. p. 47, 91.

† Calamy's Account, vol. ii. p. 144, 162, 222, 797.

‡ Mather's Hist. of New Eng. b. iii. p. 136.

§ Sparrow's Collec. p. 359, 360.

‖ The above convocation, says Clarendon, gave subsidies, enjoined an oath, and did things, which, in the best of times, might have been questioned; and therefore, in the worst, were sure to be condemned.—*Hist. of Rebellion*, vol. i. p. 116.

¶ Clarendon's Hist. vol. i. p. 184. ** Whitlocke's Memorial, p. 36.

presented by the puritans who had been many years under close confinement; when the parliament favourably received them, released the prisoners, and voted them to receive considerable sums out of the estates of their persecutors, by way of damages. They released Dr. Leighton, who had been imprisoned ten years; Mr. Smart, eleven or twelve years; and Mr. Brewer, fourteen years. Also, Burton, Prynne, Bastwick, Walker, Lilburne, Bishop Williams, and many others, now obtained their liberty. The above canons were, at the same time, condemned in the house of commons, as being against the king's prerogative, the fundamental laws of the realm, the liberty and property of the subject, and as containing divers other things tending to sedition and dangerous consequence. For which several of the bishops were impeached of high crimes and misdemeanours.* The archbishop was impeached of *high treason*, and committed to the Tower.†

The *committee of accommodation* was appointed by the upper house, to consider of such innovations as were proper to be taken away. It consisted of ten earls, ten bishops, and ten barons. They also appointed a sub-committee of bishops and learned divines, to prepare matters for debate, Bishop Williams being chairman of both.‡ The result of their conference was drawn up for the debate of the committee, in a number of propositions and queries. But all attempts at an accommodation were blasted by the obstinacy of the bishops, and by the discovery of the plot for bringing the army up to London to dissolve the parliament. This widened the distance betwixt the king and the two houses, and broke up the committee, without bringing any thing to perfection. The moderation and mutual compliance of these divines, it is justly observed, might have saved the whole body of episcopacy, and prevented the civil war: but the court bishops expected no good from them, suspecting that the puritans would betray the church. Some hot

* Rushworth's Collec. vol. iv. p. 359.

† Prynne's Breviate of Laud, p. 23, 24.

‡ The names of these bishops and learned divines, were as follows:

Dr. Williams, bishop of Lincoln,	Dr. Richard Holdsworth,
Dr. Usher, archbishop of Armagh,	Dr. John Hacket,
Dr. Morton, bishop of Durham,	Dr. William Twisse,
Dr. Hall, bishop of Exeter,	Dr. Cornelius Burgess,
Dr. Samuel Ward,	Mr. John White,
Dr. John Prideaux,	Mr. Stephen Marshall,
Dr. Robert Sanderson,	Mr. Edmund Calamy,
Dr. Daniel Featley,	Mr. Thomas Hill.
Dr. Ralph Brownrigg,	*Fuller's Church Hist.* b. xi. p. 174.

spirits would abate nothing of the episcopal power or profit, but maintained, that to yield any thing was giving up the cause to the opposite party.*

In the year 1641, the parliament introduced two bills, one to abolish the high commission court, the other the star-chamber, both of which obtained the royal assent.† The former of these courts, observes Lord Clarendon, had assumed a disputable power of *imposing fines;* that it sometimes exceeded in the severity of its sentences; that it rendered itself very unpopular; and had managed its censures with more sharpness, and less *policy,* than the times would bear: but he declares he did not know that any *innocent* clergyman suffered by any of its ecclesiastical censures.‡ The abolition of these courts effectually clipped the wings of the persecuting prelates.

Numerous petitions being sent up from all quarters for preaching ministers, a committee of forty members of the house was appointed, called the *committee of preaching ministers,* to send ministers where there were vacancies, and provide for their maintenance.§ And there being many complaints of idle and licentious clergymen, another committee was appointed, called the *committee of scandalous ministers,* to examine these complaints.‖ A third committee was appointed, called the *committee of plundered ministers,* for the relief of such godly ministers as were driven from their cures, for adhering to the parliament.¶ Many pious and learned divines were members of these committees, who employed their abilities to the utmost for public usefulness.

Upon the presentation of numerous grievances from all

* Fuller's Church Hist. b. xi. p. 175.

† Scobell's Collections, part i. p. 9, 12.

‡ Clarendon's Hist. vol. i. p. 221, 222.—The high commission, says Hume, extended its jurisdiction over the whole kingdom, and over all orders of men; and every circumstance of its authority, and all its methods of proceeding, were contrary to the clearest principles of law and natural equity. The commissioners were impowered to administer the oath *ex officio,* by which a person was bound to answer all questions, and might thereby be obliged to accuse himself or his most intimate friend. The fines were discretionary, and often occasioned the total ruin of the offender, contrary to the established laws of the kingdom. This court was a real *Inquisition;* attended with all the *iniquities,* as well as *cruelties,* inseparable from that tribunal. It was armed, says Granger, with an *inquisitorial power,* to *force* any one to confess what he knew, and to punish him at *discretion.*—*Hume's Hist. of Eng.* vol. v. p. 189.—*Granger's Biog. Hist.* vol. i. p. 206.

§ Clarendon's Hist. vol. i. p. 295.

‖ Sylvester's Life of Baxter, part i. p. 19.

¶ Walker's Suf. Clergy, part i. p. 73.

parts of the kingdom, the parliament appointed a committee to draw out of them all, such kind of *remonstrance* as would give his majesty an impartial representation of the deplorable state of the nation. The remonstrance* was presented to the king, December 1, 1641; and enumerates the grievances, oppressions, and unbounded acts of the prerogative, since his majesty's accession: among which were "The suspension, deprivation, excommunication, and degradation of laborious, learned, and pious ministers.—The sharpness and severity of the high commission, assisted by the council-table, not much less grievous than the Romish inquisition.—The rigour of the bishops' courts in the country, whereby numbers of tradesmen have been impoverished, and driven to Holland and New England.—The advancement to ecclesiastical preferments, of those who were most officious in promoting superstition, and most virulent in railing against godliness and honesty.—The design of reconciling the church of England with that of Rome.—And the late *canons* and *oath* imposed upon the clergy, under the most grievous penalties."† But the king was displeased with the remonstrance; he published an answer to it, and issued his royal proclamation, requiring an exact conformity to the religion as by law established.‡

During the year 1642, the king and the parliament put themselves respectively in a posture of defence, and used those military precautions which soon led to all the horrors of a civil war, and deluged the land with blood. Both parties published their declarations, in justification of their own cause. The king set up his standard at Nottingham, where about 2,000 came to him; and greatly augmented his forces out of Shropshire, Worcestershire, and other counties. The parliament raised a gallant army under the command of the Earl of Essex. Many excellent divines became chaplains to the several regiments. Dr. Burgess and Mr. Marshall, to the general's own regiments; Mr. Obadiah Sedgwick, to Colonel Hollis's regiment; Dr. Downing, to Lord Roberts'; Mr. John Sedgwick, to the Earl of Stamford's; Dr. Spurstowe, to Mr. Hampden's; Mr. Perkins, to

* The debates in parliament about the remonstrance lasted from three o'clock in the afternoon, till ten next morning, which occasioned Sir B. R. to say, "It was the verdict of a starved jury." Oliver Cromwell told Lord Falkland, that if the remonstrance had been rejected, he would have sold all his estates next morning, and never have seen England any more.—*Whitlocke's Mem.* p. 49.—*Clarendon's Hist.* vol. i. p. 246, 247.

† Rushworth's Collec. vol. v. p. 438—Nalson's Collec. vol. ii. p. 694.

‡ Rushworth's Collec. vol. v. p. 456.

Colonel Goodwin's; Mr. Moore, to Lord Wharton's; Mr. Adoniram Byfield, to Sir Henry Cholmley's; Mr. Nalton, to Colonel Grentham's; Mr. Ashe, either to Lord Brook's or the Earl of Manchester's; and Mr. Morton, to Sir Arthur Hasilrigg's; with many more.*

The house of commons had already resolved, "That the Lord's day should be duly observed and sanctified; that all dancing and other sports, either before or after divine service, should be forborn and restrained; that the preaching of God's word be promoted in all parts of the kingdom; and that ministers be encouraged in this work."† May 5, 1643, the parliament issued an order, "That the Book of Sports shall be burnt by the common hangman, in Cheapside and other public places," which was done by direction of the sheriffs of London and Middlesex.‡ By an ordinance of both houses, it was appointed, "That no person shall henceforth on the Lord's day, use or be present at any wrestling, shooting, bowling, ringing of bells for pleasure, mask, wake, church-ale, games, dancing, sports, or other pastime, under the several penalties annexed." An ordinance also passed for removing all monuments of superstition and idolatry, commanding all altars and tables of stone to be demolished, communion tables to be removed from the east end of the church, the rails to be removed, the chancel to be levelled, tapers, candlesticks, basons, &c. to be removed from the communion tables; and all crosses, crucifixes, and images, to be taken away and defaced. And by another, it was appointed, "That all copes, surplices, superstitious vestments, roods, fonts, and organs, be utterly defaced."§

June 12, 1643, an ordinance passed both houses for calling the assembly of divines.‖ This assembly was not a convocation according to the diocesan modal, nor was it called by the votes of ministers according to the presbyterian way; but the parliament chose all the members themselves, merely with a view to obtain their opinion and advice, in settling the government, liturgy, and doctrine of the church. Their debates were confined to such things as the parliament proposed. Some counties had two members, and some only one. But to appear impartial, and

* Sylvester's Life of Baxter, part i. p. 42.

† Nalson's Collec. vol. ii. p. 482.

‡ An act of greater scorn, or greater insolency and disloyal impudence, says Dr. Heylin, was never offered to a sovereign and anointed Prince, than this severe usage of the Book of Sports.—*Hist. of Pres.* p. 465.

§ Scobell's Collec. part i. p. 53, 69.

‖ Ibid. p. 42.

give each party the liberty to speak, they chose many of the most learned episcopalians, as well as those of other denominations.* Lord Clarendon reproaches these pious and learned divines, of whom a list is given below,† by saying, "That some were infamous in their lives and conversation, and most of them of very mean parts, if not of scandalous ignorance, and of no other reputation than of malice to the

* Many of the episcopal divines, several of whom were bishops, did not attend.

† William Twisse, D.D. Newbury, prolocutor.
Corn. Burgess, D.D. Watford, } Assessors.
John White, Dorchester, } Assessors.
William Gonge, D.D. Blackfriars.
Robert Harris, B.D. Hanwell.
Tho. Gataker, B.D. Rotherhithe.
Oliver Bowles, B.D. Sutton.
Edward Reynolds, D.D. Bramston.
Jeremiah Whitaker, A.M. Stretton.
Anthony Tuckney, B.D. Boston.
John Arrowsmith, Lynn.
Simeon Ashe, St. Bride's.
Philip Nye, Kimbolton.
Jeremiah Burroughs, A.M. Stepney.
John Lightfoot, D.D. Ashly.
Stanley Gower, Brampton-Bryan.
Richard Heyricke, A.M. Manchester.
Thomas Case, London.
Thomas Temple, D.D. Battersea.
George Gipps, Aylesion.
Thomas Carter, Oxford.
Humphrey Chambers, B.D. Claverton.
Tho. Micklethwaite, Cherryburton.
John Gibbon, Waltham.
Christ. Tisdale, Uphurstborne.
John Phillips, Wrentham.
George Walker, B.D. London.
Edm. Calamy, B.D. Aldermanbury.
Joseph Caryl, A.M. Lincoln's-inn.
Lazarus Seaman, D.D. London.
Henry Wilkinson, B.D. Waddesdon.
Richard Vines, A.M. Calcot.
Nicholas Proffet, Marlborough.
Steph. Marshall, B.D. Finchingfield.
Joshua Hoyle, D.D. Dublin.
Thomas Wilson, A.M. Otham.
Thomas Hodges, B.D. Kensington.
Tho. Bayley, B.D. Maningford-Crucis.
Francis Taylor, A.M. Yalding.
Thomas Young, Stow-market.
Tho. Valentine, B.D. Chalfont St. Giles.
William Greenhill, Stepney.
Edward Peale, Compton.
John Green, Pencombe.
Andrew Perne, Wilby.
Samuel de la Place, French Church.
John de la March, French Church.
John Dury.
Philip Delme.
Sydrach Sympson, London.
John Langley, West-Tuderly.
Richard Cleyton, Showel.
Arthur Salwey, Severn Stoke.
John Ley, A.M. Budworth.
Charles Herle, A.M. Winwick, (prolocutor after Dr. Twisse.)
Herbert Palmer, B.D. Ashwell, (assessor after Mr. White.)
Daniel Cawdrey, A.M.
Henry Painter, B.D. Exeter.
Henry Scudder, Collingbourne.
Thomas Hill, D.D. Tichmarch.
William Reynor, B.D. Egham.
Thomas Goodwin, D.D. London.
William Spurstowe, D.D. Hampden.
Matthew Newcomen, Dedham.
John Conant, D.D. Limington.
Edmund Staunton, D.D. Kingston.
Anthony Burgess, Sutton-Coldfield.
William Rathband, Highgate.
Francis Cheynel, D.D. Petworth.
Henry Wilkinson, junior, B.D.
Obadiah Sedgwick, B.D. Coggeshall.
Edward Corbet, Merton coll. Oxford.
Samuel Gibson, Burley.
Thomas Coleman, A.M. Bliton.
Theod. Buckhurst, Overton-Watervile.
William Carter, London.
Peter Smith, D.D. Barkway.
John Maynard, A.M.
William Price, Covent-Garden.
John Wincop, D.D. St. Martin's.
William Bridge, A.M. Yarmouth.
Peter Sterry, London.
William Mew, B.D. Esington.
Benj. Pickering, East-Hoathly.
John Strickland, B.D. New Sarum.

church."* But Mr. Baxter, who knew them much better than his lordship, says, "They were men of eminent learning and godliness, ministerial abilities and fidelity. And the christian world, since the days of the apostles, has never had a synod of more excellent divines, than this synod, and the synod of Dort."† Many of the lords and commons were joined with the divines, to see that they did not go beyond their commission.‡ The assembly presented to the parliament the *confession of faith*, the *larger* and *shorter catechisms*, the *directory of public worship*, and their *humble advice concerning church government*. The "Assembly's Annotations," as it is commonly called, is unjustly ascribed to the assembly. The parliament employed the authors of that work, several of whom were members of this learned synod. The assembly first met July 1, 1643, in Henry the Seventh's chapel, and continued to meet several years.

Soon after the meeting of the assembly, a bond of union was agreed upon, entitled "A Solemn League and Covenant for Reformation, and Defence of Religion, the Honour and Happiness of the King, and the Peace and Safety of the three Kingdoms of England, Scotland and

Humphrey Hardwick.
Jasper Hickes, A.M. Lawrick.
John Bond, LL.D. Exeter.
Henry Hall, B.D. Norwich.
Thomas Ford, A.M.
Tho. Thorowgood, Massingham.
Peter Clark, A.M. Carnaby.
William Goad.
John Foxcroft, Gotham.
John Ward.
Richard Byfield, A.M.
Francis Woodcock, Cambridge.
J. Jackson, Cambridge.

The Commissioners for Scotland were,

Lord Maitland.
Alexander Henderson.
Samuel Rutterford.
George Gillespie.
Robert Baylie.

The Scribes were,

Henry Roborough. John Wallis. Adoniram Byfield.

* Clarendon's Hist. vol. i. p. 415.

† Sylvester's Life of Baxter, part i. p. 73.

‡ Algernon Earl of Northumb.
William Earl of Bedford.
Philip Earl of Pembroke.
William Earl of Salisbury.
Henry Earl of Holland.
Edward Earl of Manchester.
William Lord Viscount Say and Sele.
Edward Lord Viscount Conway.
Philip Lord Wharton.
Edward Lord Howard.
John Selden, esq.
Francis Rouse, esq.
Edmund Prideaux, esq.
Sir Henry Vane, senior, knt.
John Glyn, esq. recorder of London.
John White, esq.
Bulstrode Whitlocke, esq.
Humphrey Sallway, esq.
Oliver St. John, esq. king's solicitor.
Mr. Serjeant Wild.
Sir Benjamin Rudyard, knt.
John Pym, esq.
Sir John Clotworthy, knt.
John Maynard, esq.
Sir Henry Vane, junior, knt.
William Pierpoint, esq.
William Wheeler, esq.
Sir Thomas Barrington, knt.
Walter Young, esq.
Sir John Evelin, knt.

Ireland."* It was subscribed by both houses of parliament, the Scots commissioners, and the assembly of divines, in St. Margaret's church, Westminster; and afterwards required to be subscribed by all persons above the age of eighteen years.

In addition to the committees already mentioned, the parliament appointed *country committees*, in the different parts of the kingdom; and afterwards the *committee of sequestrations.* They were empowered to examine, and sequester, upon sufficient witness, such clergymen as were scandalous in their lives, ill-affected to the parliament, or fomenters of the unnatural war betwixt the king and parliament. Multitudes of the conformable clergy were cited before these committees, and such as were found guilty of notorious immorality, or an avowed hostility to the parliament, were deprived of their livings. Though it cannot be supposed in such times, that no innocent person unjustly suffered; yet, "many" says Fuller, "were cast out for their misdemeanours, and some of their offences were so foul, it is a shame to report them, crying to justice for punishment."† And, says Mr. Baxter, "in all the countries where he was "acquainted, *six to one at least*, if not *many more*, that "were sequestered by the committees, were by the oaths of "witnesses proved insufficient or scandalous, or especially "guilty of drunkenness and swearing. This I know," says he, "will displease the party, *but I am sure it is true.*"‡

In the year 1644, Archbishop Laud was brought to trial by the two houses of parliament, and being found guilty of high treason, was beheaded on Tower-hill. He was a prelate of imperious and bigotted principles, and rash and furious in his conduct, especially towards the puritans. His councils were high and arbitrary, tending to the ruin of the king and constitution. He obtained the ascendancy over his majesty's conscience and councils.§ Though he was no papist, he was much inclined to the popish impositions and superstitious rites, and to meet the church of Rome half way. While it was Laud's "chief object to maintain the outward splendour of the church, by daily increasing the number of pompous ceremonies and scan-

* Clarendon's Hist. vol. ii. p. 287.

† Fuller's Church Hist. b. xi. p. 207.

‡ Sylvester's Life of Baxter, part i. p. 74.

§ "Some of his majesty's ministers drove so fast," says Welwood, "that it was no wonder both the wheels and chariot were broken. And it was owing in a great part to the indiscreet zeal of a *mitred head*, (meaning Laud) who had got an ascendant over his master's *conscience* and *councils*, that both the *monarchy* and *hierarchy* owed afterwards their fall."—*Memoirs*, p. 37.

dalous innovations, he made many fair approaches towards Rome, in point of doctrine."* Under his primacy the church of England evidently assumed a very popish appearance. And, according to Hume, the court of Rome itself entertained hopes of regaining its authority in this island; and, in order to forward Laud's supposed good intentions, an offer was twice made him, in private, of a cardinal's hat, which he declined accepting. His answer was, as he observes himself, "that something dwelt within him which would not suffer his compliance, till Rome was other than it is."†

The London ministers having presented a petition to parliament, for a settlement of the ecclesiastical discipline and government, according to the directory of public worship, they had the thanks of the house; and a committee was appointed to confer with the assembly, and to ascertain how far tender consciences might be borne with, consistent with the peace of the kingdom and the word of God.‡ An ordinance soon passed to set aside the Book of Common Prayer, and to establish the directory.§ The presbyterians now gaining the ascendancy, discovered a strong propensity to grasp at the same arbitrary power, as that under which they had formerly and for a long time groaned. The parliament published two ordinances, one against the preaching of *unordained ministers*, the other against *blasphemy* and *heresy*, both of which became the engines of oppression and persecution. The latter, says Mr. Neal, is one of the most shocking laws I have met with in restraint of religious liberty, and shews, that the governing presbyterians would have made a terrible use of their power, had they been supported by the sword of the civil magistrate. Several ministers of puritan principles, became sufferers by these ordinances. Mr. Clarkson having embraced the sentiments of the antipædobaptists, was cast into prison, and required to recant, for the marvellous sin of *dipping*. Mr. Lamb, Mr. Denne, and Mr. Knollys, all of the same denomination, were apprehended and committed to prison. Mr.

* May's Hist. of Parliaments, p. 22—23.

† Prynne's Breviate of Laud, p. 18.—Hume's Hist of Eng. vol. vi. p. 209.—It is observed that a court lady, daughter of the Earl of Devonshire, having turned papist, was asked by Laud the reasons of her conversion. "It is chiefly," said she, "because I hate to travel in a crowd." The meaning of this expression being demanded, she replied, "I perceive your grace and many others are making haste to Rome; and, therefore, in order to prevent my being crowded, I have gone before you."—*Ibid.* p. 210.

‡ Whitlocke's Mem. p. 99.

§ Scobell's Collec. part i. p. 75, 97.

Knollys was afterwards prosecuted at the sessions, and sent prisoner to London. Mr. Oates was tried for his life, but acquitted. Mr. Biddle was cast into prison, where he remained seven years.

The civil war having now continued several years, introduced dreadful confusion and distress into every part of the kingdom. Numerous were the sufferers on both sides. But the parliament's army proving every where triumphant, the king himself was taken prisoner. During these commotions, the *rump* parliament passed a decree to establish a government without a king and house of lords, and so governed alone. They erected a high court of justice, brought the king to trial, condemned him, erected a scaffold before Whitehall, and there, before a large concourse of people, struck off his head, January 30, 1649. "The king had a mistaken principle, that kingly government in the state, could not stand without episcopal government in the church. Therefore, as the bishops flattered him by preaching up the sovereign prerogative, and inveighing against the puritans as factious and disloyal: so he protected them in their pomp and pride, and insolent practices against all the godly and sober people in the land."* "An *immoderate desire of power*, beyond what the constitution did allow of, was the rock on which he split."†

Sect. V.

From the Death of King Charles I. to the passing of the Act of Uniformity, in 1662.

The King being taken out of the way, Cromwell proposed a Commonwealth, till he laid a foundation for his own advancement. The parliament drew up a form of ENGAGEMENT, to be subscribed by all persons above eighteen years of age, in these words:—"I do promise to be true and faithful to the commonwealth as it is now established, without a king or house of lords." No man who refused this engagement could have the benefit of suing another at law, or hold any mastership in either university, or travel

* Memoirs of Col. Hutchinson, vol. i. p. 129, 130.

† Welwood's Memoirs, p. 87.—The puritan ministers of the presbyterian denomination in London being charged with bringing the king to the block, published a "Vindication" of themselves, declaring the falsehood of the charge, and protesting their abhorrence of the fact, and their unshaken loyalty to his majesty's person and just government.—*Calamy's Contin.* vol. ii. p. 737.

more than a certain number of miles from his own house.* Therefore, Mr. Vines, Mr. Blake, and many other puritan ministers, for refusing to subscribe, were turned out of their livings.

The terms of conformity were now less rigid than at any time since the commencement of the civil wars. The oppressive statutes of the parliament were relaxed or not acted upon, the covenant was laid aside, and no other civil qualification required of ministers, besides the engagement. Though the episcopal divines were forbidden to read the liturgy in form, they might frame their prayers as near it as they pleased; and upon this principle, many of them complied with the government. Numerous episcopal assemblies were connived at, where the liturgy was read, till they were found plotting against the government: nor would they have been denied an open toleration, if they would have given security for their peaceable behaviour, and not meddled with the affairs of government.†

Cromwell and his friends, indeed, gave it out, that they could not understand what right the magistrate had to use compulsion in matters of religion. They thought that all men ought to be left to the dictates of their own consciences, and that the civil magistrate could not interpose in any religious concerns, without ensnaring himself in the guilt of persecution.‡ Dr. George Bates, an eminent royalist, and an avowed enemy to Cromwell, observes, "That the protector indulged the use of the common prayer in families, and in private conventicles; and it cannot be denied, that churchmen had a great deal more favour and indulgence than under the parliament; which would never have been interrupted, had they not insulted the protector, and forfeited their liberty by their seditious practices and plottings against his person and government."§

December 16, 1653, Oliver Cromwell was installed Lord Protector of the Commonwealth of England, Scotland, and Ireland, when an Instrument of Government was adopted and subscribed. The thirty-seventh article observes, "that all who profess faith in God by Jesus Christ, shall be protected in their religion."‖ The parliament afterwards voted, that all should be tolerated, or indulged, who professed the fundamentals of christianity; and certain

* Sylvester's Life of Baxter, part i. p. 64.
† Neal's Puritans, vol. iv. p. 61.
‡ Sylvester's Life of Baxter, part ii. p. 193.
§ Neal's Puritans, vol. iv. p. 102.
‖ Whitlocke's Mem. p. 552—558.

learned divines were appointed to draw up the fundamentals to be presented to the house. Those who acted were Drs. Owen, Goodwin, and Cheynell, and Messrs. Marshall, Reyner, Nye, Sympson, Vines, Manton, Jacomb, and Baxter. Archbishop Usher was nominated, but declined his attendance.*

During the national confusions there were many persons denominated fifth monarchy-men, chiefly of the baptist persuasion. They were in immediate expectation of King Jesus, and of the commencement of his glorious, personal reign of a thousand years upon the earth. Though they were avowedly of commonwealth principles, they were extremely hostile to Cromwell's government.† Several of them having discovered considerable enmity and opposition against the protector, were apprehended and committed to prison; among whom were Mr. Rogers, Mr. Feake, and Mr. Vavasor Powell. On account of the rigorous laws still in force, they were kept in prison a long time, under the plea of mercy, and to save their lives.

The protector having discovered some inconvenience from the approbation of ministers being left wholly to the presbyterians, he contrived a middle way, by joining the various parties together, and committing the business to certain men of approved abilities and integrity, belonging to each denomination. For this purpose, an ordinance was passed, March 20, 1654, appointing thirty-eight commissioners to this office, commonly called TRYERS.‡ Another ordinance was also passed, "for ejecting scandalous, ignorant, and insufficient ministers and schoolmasters." It appointed certain lay-commissioners for every county, to be joined by ten or more of the best divines, as their assistants. They were required to call before them any public preacher, vicar, curate, or schoolmaster, reputed to be ignorant, scandalous, or insufficient.§

This ordinance, it must be acknowledged, bore hard upon some of the episcopal clergy; among whom were Dr. Pordage, charged with blasphemy and heresy; and Mr. Bushnal, charged with drunkenness, profanation of the sabbath, gaming, and disaffection to the government. For these crimes, they were both turned out of their livings.‖ Also, by the act for propagating the gospel in Wales, many ignorant and scandalous ministers were ejected, and others

* Sylvester's Life of Baxter, part ii. p. 197.

† Thurloe's State Papers, vol. i. p. 621, 641.

‡ Scobell's Collec. part ii. p. 279.

§ Ibid. p. 335, 340—347.

‖ Neal's Puritans, vol. iv. p. 112, 113.

put in their places. It is observed, that in a short time, there were one hundred and fifty good preachers in the thirteen Welch counties, most of whom preached three or four times a week.* But the generality of the ejected clergy did not preach at all, or were scandalous in their lives; and the commissioners affirm, that of the sixteen they turned out in Cardiganshire, only three of them were preachers, and those of very immoral character.†

The protector's health, through his excessive toils and fatigues, began at length to decline. And having nominated a successor, he died of a fever, September 3, 1658, aged fifty-nine years. Never was man more highly extolled, nor more basely vilified, according as men's interests led their judgments. "The royalists," says Mr. Baxter, "abhorred him as a most perfidious hypocrite, and the presbyterians thought him little better. He kept up his approbation of a godly life in the general, and of all that was good, except that which the interest of his sinful cause engaged him to be against. I perceived," our author adds, "that it was his design to do good in the main, and to promote the gospel and the interests of goodness, more than any had done before him."‡ His son Richard, according to his father's will, succeeded him. Numerous addresses were sent from all parts of the country, congratulating the new protector. He was of a calm and peaceable temper, but unfit to be at the helm in such boisterous times. Richard Cromwell finding the nation involved in difficulties, tamely resigned his high dignity and government, after enjoying it only eight months.

The nation being tired of changes, and now in danger of universal anarchy, soon discovered its uneasiness. General Monk, with his army, was called out of Scotland; and upon his arrival in London, he declared in favour of the king. A council of state was called; and having agreed to invite home the king, the question was put, "Whether they should call him in upon treaty and covenant, or entirely confide in him?" After some debate, it was resolved to trust him absolutely. The new parliament assembling, they unanimously voted the king home. He was sent for to Holland, when Mr. Calamy, Mr. Bowles, Dr. Manton, and some others, were deputed by the parliament and city to attend him. His majesty gave them such encouraging promises, as raised in some of them very high

* Whitlocke's Mem. p. 518.

† Neal's Puritans, vol. iv. p. 116.

‡ Sylvester's Life of Baxter, part i. p. 71, 98.

expectations. Upon the entrance of the king, May 29, 1660, as he passed through the city towards Westminster, the London ministers, by the hands of old Mr. Arthur Jackson, presented his majesty with a richly adorned bible; which he received, saying, "It shall be the rule of my government and my life."*

King CHARLES II. being now seated on the throne of his ancestors, the commencement of his reign was a continued jubilee. But from the period of his accession, he grasped at arbitrary power, and shewed but little inclination to depend upon parliaments.† "The restoration," says Burnet, "brought with it the throwing off the very professions of virtue and piety, and entertainments and drunkenness overrun the three kingdoms. The king had a good understanding; and knew well the state of affairs both at home and abroad. He had a softness of temper that charmed all who came near him, till they found out how little they could depend on good looks, kind words, and fair promises; in which he was liberal to an excess, because he intended nothing by them, but to get rid of importunities. He seemed to have no sense of religion. He was no atheist, but disguised his popery to the last."‡

Upon his majesty's accession, many of the puritans were in great hopes of favour. Besides the promises of men in power, they had an assurance from the king, in his declaration from Breda, "That he should grant liberty to tender consciences, and that no man should be questioned for a difference of opinion in matters of religion, who did not disturb the peace of the kingdom."§ Afterwards, the king having issued his declaration concerning ecclesiastical matters, dated October 25, 1660; and the London ministers having presented to him their address of thanks, his majesty returned them this answer: "Gentlemen, I will endeavour to give you all satisfaction, and to make you as happy as myself."‖ All this was, indeed, most encouraging. Their hopes were further cherished by ten of their number being made the king's chaplains, though none of them preached, except Dr. Reynolds, Dr. Spurstowe, Mr. Calamy, and Mr. Baxter, once each.¶ But all their hopes were soon blasted. Many hundreds of worthy ministers enjoying sequestered livings, were displaced soon after his majesty's return. The fellows and heads of colleges in the two universities, who

* Palmer's Noncon. Mem. vol. i. p. 20. † Welwood's Memoirs, p. 121.
‡ Burnet's Hist. of his Time, vol. i. p. 93.
§ Whitlocke's Mem. p. 702. ‖ Kennet's Chronicle, p. 315.
¶ Sylvester's Life of Baxter, part ii. p. 229.

had been ejected, were restored, and the others cast out.* Bishops being placed in most of the sees, and the hierarchy restored to its former splendour, though the presbyterians still flattered themselves with hopes of a comprehension, the independents and baptists sunk in despair.

Here was an end, says Mr. Neal, of those distracted times, which our historians have loaded with all the infamy and reproach that the wit of man could invent. The puritan ministers have been decried as ignorant mechanics, canting preachers, enemies to learning, and no better than public robbers. The common people have been stigmatized as *hypocrites*. Their looks, their dress, and behaviour, have been represented in the most odious colours; yet we may challenge these declaimers to produce any period since the reformation, wherein there was less open profaneness and impiety, and more of the spirit as well as appearance of religion. Better laws, he adds, were never made against vice, or more rigorously executed. Drunkenness, fornication, profane swearing, and every kind of debauchery, were justly deemed infamous, and universally discountenanced. The clergy were laborious to an excess, in preaching, praying, catechising, and visiting the sick. The magistrates were exact in suppressing all kinds of games, stage-plays, and abuses in public houses; and a play had not been acted in any theatre in England, for almost twenty years.†

But the court and bishops were now at ease. The doctrines of passive obedience and nonresistance were revived. And the puritans began to prepare for those persecutions which presently followed. Mr. Crofton, who had been very zealous for the king's restoration, for having written in favour of the covenant, was deprived of his living, and sent close prisoner to the Tower, where he was not permitted to have pen, ink, or paper.‡ Mr. Parsons, a noted royalist, was fined £200, and cast into prison, for nonconformity. The celebrated Mr. John Howe was committed to prison; and multitudes were sequestered and prosecuted in the ecclesiastical courts, for not wearing the surplice and observing the ceremonies. These were powerful indications of the approaching storm.

Upon Venner's insurrection,§ Mr. Knollys and many

* Kennet's Chronicle, p. 152, 153, 173, 221.

† Neal's Puritans, vol. iv. p. 269. ‡ Kennet's Chronicle, p. 501.

§ Mr. Thomas Venner, a wine-cooper, with about fifty of his admirers, being in expectation of a fifth universal monarchy, under the personal reign of *King Jesus* upon the earth, raised an insurrection in the city. But their mad scheme was frustrated. Many of them were killed in the contest; and Venner and some others were seized, tried, condemned, and executed. —*Burnet's Hist. of his Time*, vol. i. p. 160.

other innocent persons, were dragged to Newgate, where they continued eighteen weeks. The rebellion of Venner occasioned a royal proclamation, prohibiting all *anabaptists* and *other sectaries* from worshipping God in public, except at their parish churches. This unnatural edict was another signal for persecution. Mr. Biddle was tried at the public sessions, fined one hundred pounds, and cast into prison, where he soon after died. Mr. John James was seized in the pulpit, tried, condemned, and beheaded. His bowels were then burnt, and his body being quartered, was placed upon the four gates of the city of London, and his head first upon London bridge, then opposite his meeting-house in Bulstake-alley.

In order to crush the puritans in every corner of the land, and strike all nonconformists at once dumb, the famous "Act of Uniformity" was passed, requiring a perfect conformity to the Book of Common Prayer, and the rites and ceremonies of the church. This struck the nonconformists with universal consternation. The unmerciful act took place August 24, 1662, justly denominated the BLACK BARTHOLOMEW-DAY. By this act, "it is well known, that nearly "2,500 faithful ministers of the gospel were silenced. And "it is affirmed, upon a modest calculation, that it procured "the untimely death of 3,000 nonconformists, and the ruin "of 60,000 families."* And for what purpose were these cruelties inflicted? To establish an *uniformity* in all ecclesiastical matters. A charming word, indeed! for the thing itself is still wanting, even among those who promoted these tragic scenes. But this is the closing period of the present work. These barbarities are sufficiently delineated by our excellent historians.†

* Mather's Hist. of New England, b. iii. p. 4.—"The world," says Bishop Kennet, "has reason to admire not only the wisdom, but even the "*moderation* of this act, as being effectually made for ministerial confor-"mity alone, and leaving the people unable to complain of *any imposi-"tion!!*"—*Kennet's Hist. of Eng.* vol. iii. p. 243.

† Calamy's Account and Continuation, vol. iv.—And Palmer's Noncon. Mem. vol. iii.

THE

LIVES OF THE PURITANS.

John Bale, D. D.—This laborious and celebrated divine was born at Cove, near Dunwich, in Suffolk, November 21, 1495. His parents being in low circumstances, and incumbered with a large family, he was sent, at twelve years of age, to the monastery of Carmelites in Norwich; and from thence to Jesus College, Cambridge. He was educated in all the superstitions of the Romish church; but afterwards he became a most zealous and distinguished protestant. The account of this change in his sentiments is from his own pen, therefore we shall give it in his own words:—"I wandered," says he, "in utter ignorance and blindness of mind both there (at Norwich) and at Cambridge, having no tutor or patron; till, the word of God shining forth, the churches began to return to the pure fountain of true divinity. In which bright rising of the New Jerusalem, being not called by any monk or priest, but seriously stirred up by the illustrious the Lord Wentworth, as by that centurion who declared Christ to be the Son of God, I presently saw and acknowledged my own deformity; and immediately, through the divine goodness, I was removed from a barren mountain, to the flowery and fertile valley of the gospel, where I found all things built, not on the sand, but on a solid rock. Hence I made haste to deface the mark of wicked antichrist, and entirely threw off his yoke from me, that I might be partaker of the lot and liberty of the sons of God. And that I might never more serve so execrable a beast, I took to wife the faithful Dorothy, in obedience to that divine command, Let him that cannot contain, marry." Bishop Nicolson, with great injustice, insinuates, that a dislike of celibacy was the grand motive of Bale's conversion. "He was converted," says this writer, "by the procurement of Thomas Lord Wentworth;

though, in truth, his wife Dorothy seems to have had a great hand in that happy work."*

Bale no sooner experienced the power of converting grace, than he publicly professed his renunciation and abhorrence of popery. In one of his books, speaking of the idolatrous and superstitious worshippers in the Romish church, he pathetically adds: "Yea, I ask God mercy a thousand times; for I have been one of them myself."† Having felt the power of divine truth on his own mind, he conferred not with flesh and blood, but began, openly and fervently, to preach the pure gospel of Christ, in opposition to the ridiculous traditions and erroneous doctrines of the Romish church. This exposed him to the resentment and persecution of the ruling clergy; and for a sermon which he preached at Doncaster, in which he openly declared against the invocation of saints, he was dragged from the pulpit to the consistory of York, to appear before Archbishop Lee, when he was cast into prison. Nor did he meet with more humane treatment in the south. For a similar offence, he experienced similar usage from Stokesly, bishop of London. But by the interference of the celebrated Lord Cromwell, who had the highest opinion of him, and was then in high favour with King Henry VIII., he was delivered out of the hands of his enemies. Upon the death of this excellent nobleman, and the publication of the Six Articles, with the shocking persecution which immediately ensued, he could find no shelter from the storm, and was obliged to flee for safety. He retired into Germany, where he became intimate with Martin Luther and other distinguished reformers, and continued with them about eight years. While in a state of exile, he was not idle, but diligently employed in his own improvement, and in writing and publishing several learned books, chiefly against the popish superstitions.‡

After the death of King Henry, and the accession of Edward VI., Bale was invited home, and presented to the benefice of Bishopstoke in Hampshire. While in this situation, as well as when in exile, he wrote and published several books against the errors of popery. In the year 1550, he published a work, entitled "The Acts and unchaste Example of religious Votaries, gathered out of their own Legends and Chronicles." Mr. Strype calls it a *notable*

* Biog. Britan. vol. i. p. 532. Edit. 1778.

† Strype's Parker, p. 143.

‡ Fuller's Church Hist. b. ix. p. 68.—Abel Redivivus, p. 504—506.

book; and says, he designed to complete this history in *four* books, which should detect the foul lives and practices of the monastics, both men and women. He published the two first parts, which he dedicated to King Edward, and intimated that the other two should presently follow; but it is supposed they never came forth. He, at the same time, published "An Apology against a rank Papist, answering both him and the Doctors, that neither their Vows, nor yet their Priesthood, are of the Gospel, but of Antichrist." This was also dedicated to the king. The Apology begins thus: "A few months ago, by chance as I sat at supper, this question was moved unto me, by one who fervently loves God's verity, and mightily detesteth all falsehood and hypocrisy: Whether the vows expressed in the xxxth chapter of Numbers give any establishment to the vow of our priests now to live without wives of their own?" This piece was answered by a certain chaplain; and Bale published a reply. During the above year, he likewise published his "Image of both Churches," being an exposition of Revelation. Also, "A Dialogue or Communication to be had at table between two Children." And "A Confession of the Sinner, after the Sacred Scripture."* By these and similar productions of his pen, he so exposed the delusive superstitions and vile practices of the Romish church, as greatly to exasperate the party; and Bishop Gardiner, the cruel persecutor, complained of him to the lord protector, but most probably without success.†

During Bale's abode at Bishopstoke, where he lived retired from the world, he waited upon the king, who was then at Southampton. His majesty, who had been informed of his death, was greatly surprised and delighted to see him; and the bishopric of Ossory, in Ireland, being then vacant, he summoned his privy council, and appointed him to that see. Upon which the lords wrote the following letter to our author:

"To our very lovinge friende Doctour Bale. After our "heartye commendacyons. For as much as the kinges "majestie is minded in consideracyon of your learninge, "wysdome, and other vertuouse qualityes, to bestowe upon "yow the bishopricke of Ossorie in Irelande presently "voyde, we have thought mete both to give yow knowledge "thereof, and therewithall to lete you understande, that "his majestie wolde ye made your repayre hyther to the

* Strype's Eccl. Memorials, vol. ii. p. 263.

† Burnet's Hist. of Refor. vol. ii. p. 12.

"courte as soon as convenientley ye may, to thende that if "ye be enclined to embrace this charge, his highnesse may "at your comynge give such ordre for the farther pro-"cedings with yow herin, as shall be convenient. And "thus we bid yow hartely farewell. From Southampton, "the 16 daye of August 1552. Your lovinge frendes, W. "Winchestre, F. Bedford, H. Suffolke, W. Northampton, "T. Darcy, T. Cheine, F. Gate, W. Cecill."*

Bale, at first, refused the offered preferment, on account of his age, poverty, and ill health; but the king not admitting his excuses, he at length consented, and went soon after to London, where every thing relative to his election and confirmation was dispatched in a few days, without any expense to him. He was consecrated by the Archbishop of Dublin, assisted by the Bishops of Kildare and Down; and Hugh Goodacre, a particular friend of his, was, at the same time, consecrated Archbishop of Armagh. There was, however, some dispute about the form of consecration. Dr. Lockwood, dean of the church, desired the lord chancellor not to permit the form, in the Book of Common Prayer lately set forth by the parliament in England, to be used on this occasion, alledging that it would cause a tumult, and that it was not consented to by the parliament of Ireland. The lord chancellor proposed the case to the archbishop and the bishops, who agreed in opinion with the dean. Dr. Goodacre wished it might be otherwise, but was unwilling to enter into any disputation about it. But our author positively refused being consecrated according to the old popish form, alledging, that as England and Ireland were under one king, they were both bound to the observance of the same laws. Upon which, the lord chancellor ordered the ceremony to be performed according to the new book, and afterwards entertained the bishops at dinner.†

This celebrated divine having entered upon his new charge, did not become indolent, nor yet rise in worldly grandeur, but was constantly employed in his beloved work of preaching the gospel, labouring to the utmost of his power to draw the people from popery to Christ. He spent a great part of his income in the purchase of books, manuscripts, and records, for the purpose of publishing certain learned works which he had then in contemplation.

Upon the accession of Queen Mary, and the return of popery, Dr. Bale was again exposed to the resentment and

* Biog. Britan. vol. i. p. 532. † Ibid.

cruel persecution of his popish adversaries. All his endeavours to reform the manners of his diocese, to correct the lewd practices and debaucheries of the priests, to abolish the mass, and to establish the use of the new Book of Common Prayer set forth in England, were not only rendered abortive by the death of King Edward, and the accession of Mary, but exposed him so much to the fury of the papists, that his life was frequently in the utmost danger. At one time in particular, they murdered five of his domestics, who were making hay in a meadow near his house; and he would in all probability have shared the same fate, if the governor of Kilkenny had not seasonably interposed by sending a troop of soldiers to his protection. This, however, served only as a defence against the present outrage. It did not in the least allay the fury of his adversaries, who were implacably enraged against him for preaching the doctrines of the gospel. He could find no permanent security among them, and was obliged to flee for safety. He did not, indeed, withdraw from the storm till after his books and other moveable articles were seized, and he had received certain information, that the Romish priests were conspiring to take away his life.

Dr. Leland's reflections are not at all favourable to the memory of our prelate. After calling him the violent and acrimonious oppugner of popery, and relating his rigid and uncomplying conduct at his consecration, he adds: "That Bale insulted the prejudices of his flock without reserve, or caution. They were provoked; and not so restrained, or awed by the civil power, as to dissemble their resentments. During the short period of his residence in Ireland, he lived in a continual state of fear and persecution. On his first preaching the reformed doctrines, his clergy forsook him, or opposed him; and to such violence were the populace raised against him, that five of his domestics were slain before his face; and his own life saved only by the vigorous interposition of the civil magistrate. These outrages are pathetically related; but," he adds, "we are not informed what imprudencies provoked them, or what was the intemperate conduct which his adversaries retorted with such shocking barbarity."*

When Dr. Bale fled from the fury of his enemies, he went first to Dublin, where, for some time, he concealed himself. Afterwards, a favourable opportunity offering,

* Biog. Britan. vol. i. p. 535.

he endeavoured to make his escape in a small trading vessel, bound for Scotland, but was taken prisoner by the captain of a Dutch man of war, who rifled him of all his money, apparel and effects. This ship was driven by distress of weather into St. Ives in Cornwall, where our author was taken up on suspicion of treason. The accusation was brought against him by one Walter, an Irishman, and pilot of the Dutch ship, in hopes of obtaining a share of Bale's money, which was in the captain's hands. When our author was brought to his examination before one of the bailiffs of the town, he desired the bailiff to ask Walter, "How long he had known him? and what treason he had committed?" These interrogatories being proposed, Walter replied, that he had never seen him, nor ever heard of him, till he was brought into their ship. Then said the bailiff, "What treason have you known by this honest gentleman since? For I promise you he looks like an honest man." "Marry," said Walter, "he would have fled into Scotland." "Why," said the bailiff, "know you any impediment why he should not have gone into Scotland? If it be treason for a man, having business in Scotland, to go thither, it is more than I knew before." Walter was then so confounded, that he had nothing more to say. The captain and purser deposed in favour of Bale, assuring the bailiff that he was a very honest man, and that Walter was a vile fellow, deserving no credit. This they did, lest they should be deprived of the money and other articles which they had taken from our author.

Dr. Bale being honourably acquitted, the ship sailed, and, in a few days, arrived in Dover road, where he was again brought into danger by false accusation. One Martin, a Frenchman by birth, but now an English pirate, persuaded the Dutch captain and his crew, that Bale had been the principal instrument in pulling down the mass in England, and in keeping Dr. Gardiner, bishop of Winchester, a long time in the Tower; and that he had poisoned the king. With this information the captain and purser went ashore, carrying with them our author's episcopal seal, and two letters sent him from Conrad Gesner and Alexander Alesius, with commendations from Pellicanus, Pomeranus, Melancthon, and other celebrated reformers, who were desirous to become acquainted with the doctrines and antiquities of the English church. They also took from him the council's letter of his appointment to the bishopric of Ossory. All these things served to aggravate the charge. The episcopal seal was construed to be a counterfeiting of the king's seal; the two letters were heretical; and the council's letter a conspiracy against the queen. When the captain returned to the ship, it was proposed to send Bale to London; but, after some consultation, they resolved to send two persons, with information to the privy council. This determination, however, was relinquished, upon Bale's strong remonstrances to the captain, and offering to pay fifty pounds for his ransom, on his arrival in Holland.

He was carried into Zealand, and lodged in the house of one of the owners of the ship, who treated him with great civility and kindness. He had only twenty-six days allowed him for raising the money agreed upon for his ransom, and could not obtain the liberty of going abroad to find out his friends. In this state of perplexity and distress, he was sometimes threatened to be thrown into the common gaol, sometimes to be brought before the magistrates, sometimes to be left to the examination of the clergy, at other times to be sent to London, or to be delivered to the queen's ambassador at Brussels. At length his kind host interposed, and desired the captain to consider, how far he had exceeded the limits of his commission, in thus using a subject of England, with which nation they were at peace. This produced the desired effect, and the captain was willing to take *thirty* pounds for his ransom, as he should be able to pay it, and so discharged him.*

Dr. Bale having obtained his liberty, retired to Frankfort, where he and the other English exiles were favoured by the magistrates with the use of one of their churches. Having obtained so great a privilege, their next object was to agree to certain forms of worship: driven from their own country, and now comfortably settled in a foreign land, they thought it their duty to make certain improvements upon the reformation of King Edward. They entered, therefore, into a mutual and friendly consultation upon the subject, and agreed to the following things:—" Having perused the " English liturgy, it was concluded among them, That the " answering aloud after the minister should not be used; the " litany, surplice, and many other things also omitted, " because in the reformed churches abroad such things " would seem more than strange. It was further agreed " upon, that the minister, in the room of the English con-

* Biog. Britan. vol. i. p. 533.

" fession, should use another, both of more effect, and also " framed according to the state and time. And the same " ended, the people to sing a psalm in metre in a plain tune, " as was and is accustomed in the French, Dutch, Italian, " Spanish and Scottish churches: that done, the minister to " pray for the assistance of God's Holy Spirit, and to pro- " ceed to the sermon. After the sermon, a general prayer " for all estates, and for our country of England, was " devised: at the end of which prayer was joined the Lord's " prayer, and a rehearsal of the articles of belief; which " ended, the people to sing another psalm as afore. Then " the minister pronouncing this blessing, The peace of God, " &c. or some other of like effect, the people to depart. " And as touching the ministration of the sacraments, sundry " things were also by common consent omitted, as *supersti- " tious* and *superfluous*."*

Our learned and pious divine undoubtedly took an active part in the formation of the church at Frankfort. The pious exiles having comfortably settled their new congregation, entered into a friendly correspondence with their brethren who had settled at other places. In their letter addressed to the exiles at Strasburgh, signed by John Bale, William Whittingham, John Fox, and fourteen others, they conclude by saying: " We have a church freely granted to preach " God's word purely, to minister the sacraments sincerely, " and to execute discipline truly. And as touching our " book, we will practice it so far as God's word doth assure " it, and the state of this country permit."† They wrote also to their brethren who had fled to other places, signifying how comfortably they were settled, and inviting them to Frankfort. Upon the arrival of Dr. Cox ‡ and his friends,

* Troubles of Frankeford, p. 3. † Ibid. p. 20.

‡ Dr. Richard Cox had been preceptor and almoner to King Edward, and dean of Oxford and Westminster, but was now fled from the persecution of Queen Mary. He was a high churchman, a bigot to the English ceremonies, and of too imperious a disposition. On his return home, Queen Elizabeth made him Bishop of Ely, which he enjoyed to his death. He scrupled for some time to officiate in the royal chapel, on account of the queen's retaining the crucifix, with lights on the altar; and when he consented, it was, he said, with a *trembling conscience*. He was violent in his opposition against the puritans, as well in his own country, as at Frankfort. He wrote to Archbishop Parker, to go on vigorously in reclaiming or punishing them, and not be disheartened by the frowns of those court-favourites who protected them; assuring him, that he might expect the blessing of God on his pious labours. When the privy council interposed in favour of the puritans, and endeavoured to skreen them from punishment, he wrote a bold letter to the Lord Treasurer Burleigh; in which he warmly expostulated with the council, for meddling with the affairs of the church, which, he

who broke through the conditions of the new-formed church, interrupted the peace of the congregation, and, in effect, drove them from the city, they fled to other places. Dr. Bale retired to Basil in Switzerland, where he remained until the death of Queen Mary. The church at Basil was also exercised with contentions, of which our author, in a letter to one of his friends, gives a very deplorable account, severely censuring those who were of a contentious spirit.*

Though we have already mentioned Dr. Bale as an author, it will be proper to renew the subject. He published a celebrated work, containing the lives of the most eminent writers of Great Britain. It came out at three different times. He first published his "Summarium illustrium majoris Brytanniæ Scriptorum," Wesel, 1549. This was addressed to King Edward, and contained only *five centuries* of writers. Afterwards he added four more, and made several additions and corrections through the whole work. The book thus enlarged, was entitled "Scriptorum illustrium majoris Brytanniæ, quam nunc Angliam et Scotiam vacant, Catalogus; à Japheto per 3618 annos usque ad annum hunc Domini 1557," &c. It was completed and printed at Basil, while the author was in a state of exile. The writers, whose lives are contained in this celebrated work, are those of Great Britain, including England and Scotland. The work commences from Japhet, one of the sons of Noah, and is carried down through a series of 3618 years, to the year of our Lord 1557. It is collected from a great variety of authors: as, Barosus, Gennadius, Bede, Honorius, Boston of Bury, Frumentarius, Capgrave, Bostius, Burellus, Trithemius, Gesner, and our great antiquary John Leland. It consists of *nine* centuries, comprising the antiquity, origin, annals, places, successes, and the most remarkable actions, sayings, and writings of each author, in the whole of which a due regard is had to chronology; and with this particular view, "That the actions of the reprobate as well as the elect ministers of the church may historically and aptly correspond with the mysteries described in the Revelation, the stars, angels, horses, trumpets, thunderings, heads, horns, mountains, vials, and plagues, through every age of the same church." There are

said, ought to be left to the determination of the bishops. He, also, admonished their lordships to keep within their own sphere; and told them, that he would appeal to the queen, if they continued to interpose in matters not belonging to them.—*Wood's Athenæ Oxon.* vol. i. p. 161.—*Biog. Britan.* vol. iv. p. 398, 399.

* Strype's Eccl. Mem. vol. iii. p. 243. Appen. p. 107.

appendixes to many of the articles; also an account of such actions of the contemporary popes as are omitted by their flatterers, Carsulanus, Platina, and the like; together with the actions of the monks, particularly those of the mendicant order, who, he pretends, are meant by the *locusts* in Revelation ix. 3, 7. To the appendixes is added a perpetual succession both of the holy fathers and the antichrists of the church, with instances from the histories of various nations and countries; in order to expose their adulteries, debaucheries, strifes, seditions, sects, deceits, poisonings, murders, treasons, and innumerable impostures. The book is dedicated to Otho Henry, Prince Palatine of the Rhine, Duke of both Bavarias, and Elector of the Roman Empire; dated from Basil in September, 1557. Our learned divine was, therefore, laboriously employed while in a foreign land.

In the month of February, 1559, he published a new edition of this celebrated work, with the addition of *five* more centuries, making in all *fourteen;* to which is prefixed an account of the writers before the deluge and the birth of Christ, with a description of England from Paulus Jovius, George Lilly, John Leland, Andrew Althamerus, and others. This impression is dedicated to Count Zkradin and Dr. Paul Scalechius of Lika.*

On the accession of Queen Elizabeth, Dr. Bale returned to England, but not to his bishopric in Ireland. The queen, during her minority, and while exercised with troubles under her sister Mary, shewed the highest respect for him, and even honoured him by sending him a book which she had translated into French. It was too manifest, however, that she afterwards drew her affections from him: but whether this was on account of the puritanical principles which he imbibed while abroad, or from some other cause, we do not undertake to determine. During the few years that he lived under her majesty's government, he contented himself with a prebend in the church of Canterbury, where he continued the rest of his days, still refusing to accept of his bishopric. "One may wonder," says Fuller, "that being so learned a man, who had done and suffered so much for religion, higher promotion was not forced upon him; seeing about the beginning of Queen Elizabeth's reign, bishoprics went about begging able men to receive them."†

It ought to be recollected, that many of the pious

* Biog. Britan. vol. i. p. 533, 534.
† Fuller's Worthies, part iii. p. 61.

reformers, while in a state of exile, and living among foreign protestants, were led to examine more minutely the grand principles of the reformation; and they acted upon those principles, as we have already observed, while dwelling in a foreign land. Nor did they forget their principles on their return to their native country. Notwithstanding their want of success, they constantly endeavoured, as the times would permit, to obtain a more pure reformation of the English church. This was the case with Dr. Bale, and was undoubtedly the reason of his refusing to accept his former preferment. Though it does not appear that he gave his reasons for this refusal; yet it is evident, says our author, that, while he was a zealous opposer of the Romish superstitions, he was a leading person among the nonconformists, and was against the use of the English rites and ceremonies: he opposed the divine institution of bishops, and was a zealous advocate for the discipline of the foreign reformed churches. It was a settled principle with him, that the government of the church by bishops, did not exist till the beginning of the seventh century. These are his own words:—"In the year 607, the church "began to be ruled by the policy and government of "bishops, which government was especially devised and "invented by the monks."* From the above facts, Dr. Bale, with great justice, stands first on the list of our *puritan* worthies. He was summoned to assist in the consecration of Archbishop Parker, but refused to attend, no doubt on account of his puritanical principles.† He died at Canterbury in the month of November, 1563, aged sixty-eight years; and his remains were interred in the cathedral at that place.‡ Several of our historians are greatly mistaken in both the time and place of his death.§

The character of no man has been more variously represented than that of our author, as will appear from the different testimonies concerning him. Bishop Montague censures him for his unjustifiable freedom in speaking and writing; yet he thinks him of credit and weight in many things. Valerius Andreas calls him an impious wretch and a wicked apostate; but at the same time allows him his merit as a writer. Vossius charges him with disingenuity in his accounts of ancient writers. But of all the authors, who have censured Bale, no one has fallen upon him with

* MS. Chronology, vol. i. p. 49. (2.) † Strype's Parker, p. 54.
‡ Biog. Britan. vol. i. p. 534.
§ Lupton's Modern Divines, p. 201.—Fuller's Worthies, part iii. p. 61.

greater severity than his follower John Pits. The following are some of those invenomed arrows which he has shot at him:—"This writer," says he, "did not so much enlarge Leland's catalogue, as corrupt it in a monstrous manner. For he has stuffed it full of lies and calumnies, and spoiled Leland's work, by his own barbarous style. He says many things worthy, indeed, of the mind and mouth of an heretic, but absolutely void of all civility and moral honesty, some things plainly unworthy of a christian ear.—If we except his slanders against men, and his blasphemies against God, the poor wretch has nothing of his own, which deserves our notice.—I hoped to have found at least some gem of antiquity in that dunghill: but more unlucky than Esop's cock, I was disappointed in my expectation." He brands him with the name of *Baal*, and calls him an apostate Carmelite monk, and a married priest. Such are the foul accusations brought against our divine, by this bigotted papist. Wharton charges Bale with paying very little regard to truth, provided he could increase the number of enemies to the Romish church; and adds, that, for the most part, he settled the chronology of the English writers with his eyes shut. Bishop Nicolson says: "The ground-plot of his famous work was borrowed from Leland; and the chief of his own superstructure is malicious and bitter invectives against the papists."*

It will be proper on the contrary to observe, that Gesner denominates Bale "a writer of the greatest diligence;" and Bishop Godwin gives him the character of a laborious inquirer into the British antiquities. Dr. Lawrence Humphrey says, that Vergerius, Platina, and Luther, have discovered many errors and frauds of the papists; but that Bale hath detected them all. Valentine Henry Vogler says, "it will be less matter of wonder, that Bale inveighs with so much asperity against the power of the pope, when it is considered that England was more grievously oppressed, by the tyranny of the holy see, than any other kingdom. Though he rendered himself so odious to the papists, his very enemies could not help praising his Catalogue of English writers."†

It is generally allowed that Bale's sufferings from the popish party, is some apology for his severe treatment of them: He wrote with all the warmth of one who had escaped the flames. Granger observes, that his intemperate

* Biog. Britan. vol. i. p. 535. † Ibid. p. 534.

zeal often carries him beyond the bounds of decency and candour, in his accounts of the papists. Anthony Wood styles him "the foul-mouthed Bale;"* but, the above writer adds, some of his foul language translated into English, would appear to be of the same import with many expressions used by that writer himself.† Perhaps some allowance ought to be made not only for his resentment of what he had suffered, but for the age in which he lived. It would be doing him great injustice, to form our ideas of him from the *popish* authors, many of whom were exceedingly exasperated against him, on account of the vehemence with which he had attacked the errors and superstitions of the papal see.

Dr. Bale's writings are prohibited by the church of Rome, among those of the first class of *heretical* books. The *Index Expurgatorius*, published at Madrid in 1667, calls him a most impudent and scurrilous writer against the see of Rome, the Mass, the Eucharist, and one that is perpetually breathing out poison; for which, it forbids the reading of his works for ever.‡ His writings were numerous, a list of which, according to the subjects, is given below: the exact titles cannot now be ascertained.

His WORKS, while he was a papist.—1. A Bundle of Things worth knowing.—2. The Writers from Elias.—3. The Writers from Berthold. —4. Additions to Trithemius.—5. German Collections.—6. French Collections.—7. English Collections.—8. Divers Writings of divers learned Men.—9. A Catalogue of Generals.—10. The Spiritual War. —11. The Castle of Peace.—12. Sermons for Children.—13. To the Synod of Hull.—14. An Answer to certain Questions.—15. Addition to Palaonydorus.—16. The History of Patronage.—17. The Story of Simon the Englishman.—18. The Story of Francus Senensis.—19. The Story of St. Brocard.—20. A Commentary on Mantuan's Preface to his Fasti.

He wrote the following after he renounced popery:—1. The Heliades of the English.—2. Notes on the three Tomes of Walden.—3. On his Bundle of Tares.—4. On Polydore de Rerum Inventionibus.—5. On Textor's Officina.—6. On Capgrave's Catalogue.—7. On Barnes's Lives of the Popes.—8. The Acts of the Popes of Rome.—9. A Translation of Thorp's Examination.—10. The Life of John Baptist. —11. Of John Baptist's Preaching.§—12. Of Christ's Temptation.—

* Wood's Athenæ, vol. i. p. 60.

† Granger's Biog. Hist. vol. i. p. 139, 140.

‡ Biog. Britan. vol. i. p. 535.

§ The title of this piece is, "A Comedy, or Interlude, of Johan Baptyst's Preachynge in the Wildernesse; opening the Crafts of Hypocrytes," and is printed in the "Harleian Miscellany." "There was a time," says Mr. Granger, "when the lamentable comedies of Bale were acted with applause. He tells us, in the account of his vocation to the bishopric of Ossory, that his comedy of John Baptist's Preaching, and his

13. Two Comedies of Christ's Baptism and Temptations.—14. A Comedy of Christ at twelve years old.—15. A Comedy of the Raising of Lazarus.—16. A Comedy of the High Priest's Council.—17. A Comedy of Simon the Leper.—18. A Comedy of the Lord's Supper, and the Washing of the Disciples Feet.—19. Two Comedies (or rather Tragedies) of Christ's Passion.—20. Two Comedies of Christ's Burial and Resurrection.—21 A Poem of God's Promises.—22. Against those that pervert God's Word.—23. Of the Corrupting of God's Laws.—24. Against Carpers and Traducers.—25. A Defence of King John.—26. Of King Henry's two Marriages.—27. Of Popish Sects.—28. Of Popish Treacheries.—29. Of Thomas Becket's Impostures.—30. The Image of Love.—31. Pamachius's Tragedies, translated into English.—32. Christian Sonnets.—33. A Commentary on St. John's Apocalypse.—34. A Locupletation of the Apocalypse.—35. Wickliffe's War with the Papists.—36. Sir John Oldcastle's Trials.—37. An Apology for Barnes.—38. A Defence of Grey against Smith.—39. John Lambert's Confession.—40. Anne Askew's Martyrdom.—41. Of Luther's Decease.—42. The Bishops Alcoran.—43. The Man of Sin.—44. The Mystery of Iniquity.—45. Against Anti-Christs, or False Christs.—46. Against Baal's Priests, or Baalamites.—47. Against the Clergy's Single Life.—48. A Dispatch of Popish Vows and Priesthood.—49. The Acts of English Votaries, in two parts.—50. Of Heretics indeed.—51. Against the Popish Mass.—52. The Drunkard's Mass.—53. Against Popish Persuasions.—54. Against Bonner's Articles.—55. Certain Dialogues.—56. To Elizabeth the King's Daughter.—57. Against Customary Swearing.—58. On Mantuan of Death.—59. A Week before God.—60. Of his Calling to a Bishopric.*—61. Of Leland's Journal, or an Abridgement of Leland, with Additions.—62. A Translation of Sebald Heyden's Apology against Salve Regina.—63. A Translation of Gardiner's Oration of true Obedience, and Bonner's Epistle before it, with a Preface to it, Notes on it, and an Epilogue to the Reader.—But his most capital work was his Lives of the Writers, already noticed.—Bale's Collectanea is preserved among the Cottonean Manuscripts, and now deposited in the British Museum.

John Pullain, B. D.—This zealous reformer was born in Yorkshire, in the year 1517, and educated first in New college, then in Christ's college, Oxford. He was a famous preacher, and a celebrated reformer, in the days of King Edward VI. He became rector of St. Peter's, Cornhill, London, in the year 1552, but suffered deprivation in 1555.† Upon the commencement of Queen Mary's bloody persecution, he did not immediately flee, but endured the storm for some

Tragedy of God's Promises, were acted by young men at the market-cross of Kilkenny, upon a Sunday. Surely this tragedy must be as extraordinary a composition, in its kind, as his comedies."—*Granger's Biog. Hist.* vol. i. p. 139.

* This work is entitled "The Vocacyon of Johan Bale to the Bishopric of Ossorie in Irelande, his persecutions in the same, and finall Delyverance."

† Newcourt's Repert. Eccl. vol. i. p. 92.

time. Having no prospect of enjoying his public ministry, and being deeply concerned for his persecuted countrymen, he continued to labour in private as he found an opportunity. He preached and administered the Lord's supper, about a year, to the protestant congregation, which assembled in private places, in and about the city of London.*

The persecution of the protestants becoming, at length, extremely hot, and Mr. Pullain finding himself most probably in danger of the fire, he fled into a foreign land, and became an exile at Geneva; where he became a member of the English congregation, and abode during the remainder of the bloody queen's reign. The news of the queen's death, and of the accession of Queen Elizabeth, gladdened the hearts of all the worthy exiles. On this occasion, Mr. Pullain united with his brethren at Geneva, in their letter of congratulation, addressed to their fellow-exiles at Arrau, Basil, Strasburgh, Frankfort, and other places.† Upon the reception of the joyful news, he immediately prepared to return home; and was no sooner arrived in his native country, than he resumed his zealous ministerial labours. But he had not continued long in his beloved work, before he received a sudden check. For the new queen having issued her royal proclamation prohibiting all preaching, till all the affairs of the church were finally settled, this worthy servant of Christ was taken into custody at Colchester, and sent prisoner up to London. His crime was that of preaching when prohibited by the queen; but our historian does not say what further prosecution he underwent.‡

Towards the close of the year 1559, Mr. Pullain became rector of Capford in Essex, which he kept to his death.§ About the same time, he was made Archdeacon of Colchester. He sat in the famous convocation of 1562, and subscribed the articles of religion.‖ He was an avowed enemy to all popery and superstition; and, therefore, was much grieved at the imperfect state in which the reformation rested, and the severe proceedings of the prelates which immediately followed. He was ever anxious to have the church purged of all its corruptions and antichristian ceremonies, and for its discipline and government, as well as its

* Fox's Martyrs, vol. iii. p. 525.—Strype's Annals, vol. i. p. 292.
† Troubles at Frankeford, p. 160—162.
‡ Strype's Annals, vol. i. p. 44.
§ Newcourt's Repert. Eccl. vol. ii. p. 192.
‖ Strype's Annals, vol. i. p. 289.

doctrine, to be regulated by the word of God alone. These things made so deep an impression upon his mind, as brought a complaint upon his body, of which he died in the month of July, 1565, aged forty-eight years. He was a truly pious man, a constant preacher, a learned divine, a thorough puritan, and an admired English and Latin poet.* He published "A Tract against the Arians," and several translations of the works of other learned men.

John Hardyman, D. D.—He was educated at Cambridge, where he took his degrees; and was made preacher at St. Martin's church, Ironmonger-lane, London, in the reign of Henry VIII., when he came forwards openly and boldly in the cause of the reformation. He preached publicly, "That confession to priests, was confusion; that the ceremonies of the church being the superstitious inventions of men, ought to be abhorred; that to esteem any internal virtue in the sacrament, was mischievous and robbing God of his glóry; and that faith in Christ, without any other sacrament, was sufficient for justification;" for which, in the year 1541, he was presented and most probably deprived.† The Oxford historian, with his usual bitterness against the puritans, says, that he ran with the mutable times of Henry VIII., Edward VI., Queen Mary, and Queen Elizabeth. However, the above account of his suffering persecution for the avowal of his principles, shews that this account is not altogether correct. Though it does not appear whether he ever changed his sentiments, it is certain that upon the accession of Elizabeth, he was still a zealous protestant, and still desirous to carry forwards the reformation. In the year 1560, the queen appointed him one of the twelve prebendaries of Westminster; and about the same time, he became famous for his puritanical principles, and distinguished himself in the cause of the reformation. He was not, indeed, like too many of the clergy, who rested in the reformation of King Edward, or even in that which fell short of it; but laboured to carry on the work to perfection. He wished, with the rest of the puritanical reformers, to have the church thoroughly purged of all the remnants of antichrist. But his zeal for nonconformity presently exposed him to the resentment and persecution of the ruling prelates; and in the year 1567, he was summoned

* MS. Chronology, vol. i. p. 135. (6.)
† Fox's Martyrs, vol. ii. p. 450.

before the high commission, and deprived of his benefice. He is charged with breaking down the altars, and defacing the ancient utensils and ornaments belonging to the church of Westminster;* but with what degree of justice we are unable to ascertain.

MILES COVERDALE, D. D.—This celebrated puritan was born in Yorkshire, in the year 1486, and educated in the university of Cambridge. Being brought up in the popish religion, he became an Augustine monk at the place of his education, where Dr. Barnes was prior, who was afterwards burnt for pretended heresy. He took his doctor's degree at Tubingen, in Germany, and was incorporated in the same at Cambridge. At an early period in the reign of Henry VIII., he cast off the shackles of popery, and became a zealous and an avowed protestant. When the king quarrelled with the pope, and renounced the authority of Rome, he is said to have been one of the first who preached the gospel in its purity, and wholly devoted himself to promote the reformed religion.† In the year 1528, he preached at Burnsted in Essex, when he declared openly against the popish mass, the worship of images, and auricular confession. He maintained that contrition for sin, betwixt God and a man's own conscience, was sufficient of itself, without any confession to a priest. His zealous and faithful labours at this place were not in vain: It is preserved on authentic record, that he was the honoured instrument of turning one Thomas Topley, afterwards a martyr, from the superstitions and errors of popery, to the true protestant faith.‡

Coverdale having espoused the same opinions as Dr. Barnes, and finding himself in danger of the fire, fled, not long after the above period, beyond sea, and lived for some time in Holland, where he chiefly applied himself to the study and translation of the holy scriptures.§ In the year 1529, the famous Mr. William Tindal having finished his translation of the Pentateuch, wished to have it printed at Hamburgh; but in crossing the sea, the ship was wrecked, when he lost all his money and papers: and so had to begin the work afresh. Upon his arrival at Hamburgh, his friend Coverdale, who was waiting for him, assisted him in writing

* Wood's Athenæ Oxon. vol. i. p. 692.
† Clark's Lives annexed to Martyrologie, p. 3.
‡ Fox's Martyrs, vol. ii. p. 267.
§ Lewis's Hist. of Translations, p. 23. Edit. 1731.

a new translation.* In the year 1535, (some by mistake say 1532,) Tindal and Coverdale translated and published the whole Bible, the first that was ever printed in the English language. It was printed at Hamburgh, by Grafton and Whitchurch, when Mr. John Rogers, afterwards the proto-martyr, corrected the press. This first English translation was called *Matthew's* Bible, a fictitious name, and was dedicated by Coverdale to King Henry.† The form of dedication is preserved by Mr. Strype;‡ in which our reverend author expressed himself in the following manner:

"Unto the moost victorious prynce and our moost gra-"cyous soverygne lorde Kynge HENRY eyghth, kynge of "Englande and of Fraunce, lorde of Irelande, &c. defen-"dour of the fayth; and under God the chefe and suppreme "heade of the church of Englande. The ryght and just "administracyon of the lawes that God gave unto Moses and "Josua: the testimonye of faythfulness that God gave to "David: the plenteous abundaunce of wysdome that God "gave unto Solomon: the lucky and prosperous age with "the multiplicacyon of sede which God gave to Abraham "and Sara his wyfe, be given unto you, moost gracyous "prynce, with your dearest just wyfe and moost vertuous "pryncesse Quene Jane. Amen.

"Your graces humble subjecte and daylye oratour,

"MYLES COVERDALE."

In this dedication he tells his majesty, that the blind bishop of Rome no more knew what he did when he gave this title, *Defender of the Faith*, than the Jewish bishop Caiaphas when he taught, that it was better to put Christ to death, than that all the people should perish: that the pope gave him this title, only because his highness suffered his bishops to burn God's word, and to persecute the lovers and ministers of it; whereas, he openly declared, that by the righteous administration of his majesty, the faith ought to be so defended, that God's word, the mother of faith, should have its free course through all christendom, but especially in these realms: and that his majesty should, indeed, *defend the faith;* yea, even the true faith of *Christ*, not dreams, not fables, not heresy, not papistical inventions, but the uncorrupt faith of God's most holy word, to set forth which, his highness, with his most honourable council, applied all study and endeavour.

* Fox's Martyrs, vol. ii, p. 303.
† Ibid. p. 434.
‡ Annals, vol. ii. Appen. p. 43.

He next observes to his majesty, that as the word of God is the only truth that driveth away all error, and discovereth all juggling and deceit; therefore, is the Balaam of Rome so loath to have the scriptures known in the mother-tongue, lest by kings and princes becoming acquainted with them, they should again claim and challenge their due authority, which hath been falsely usurped for many years; and lest the people, being taught by the word of God, should renounce their feigned obedience to him and his disguised apostles, and observe the true obedience commanded by God's own mouth, and not embrace his painted religion.

As to the present translation, Coverdale observes here, and in his epistle to the reader, that it was neither his labour nor desire to have this work put into *his* hand, but that being *instantly required* to undertake it, and the Holy Ghost moving other men to be at the cost thereof, he was the more bold to take it in hand. He considered how great pity it was, that the English should want such a translation so long, and called to his remembrance the adversity of those, who were not only endowed with right knowledge, but would, with all their hearts, have performed that which they had begun, if no impediment had been in the way. Therefore, as he was desired, he took the more upon him, as he said, to set forth this *special translation*, not as a reprover or despiser of other mens' labours, but lowly and faithfully following his interpreters, and that under correction. Of these, he said, he made use of *five* different ones, who had translated the scriptures, not only into Latin, but also into Dutch. He made this declaration, that he had neither wrested nor altered so much as one word, for the maintenance of any manner of sect, but had with a clear conscience, purely and faithfully translated out of the foregoing interpreters, having only the manifest scriptures before his eyes.

This translation was divided into six tomes or parts, and Coverdale prefixed to every book the contents of the several chapters, and not to the particular chapters, which was done afterwards. It is adorned throughout with wooden cuts, and in the margin are scripture references. In the last page it is said, "Prynted in the yeare of our Lorde M.D.XXXV. and fynished the fourth day of October." This Bible was reprinted in 1550, and again in 1553.*

In the year 1537, the Bible was published a second time in English, entitled "The Bible, which is all the Holy

* Lewis's Hist. of Translations, p. 23—25.

Scripture, in which are contayned the Olde and Newe Testament, truelye and purelye translated into English." The translators were Tindal and Coverdale. John Rogers is said to have had a share in it; but this appears incorrect. From the end of the Chronicles to the end of the Apocrypha was Coverdale's, and the rest was Tindal's. This was called "The Great Bible,"* but it did not come forth till after Tindal's death.†

The New Testament was afterwards printed in Latin and English in quarto, with the following title: "The Newe Testament both in Latine and Englishe eche correspondent to the other after the vulgare Text communely called St. Jerome's. Faithfully translated by Johan Hollybushe anno M.CCCCC.XXXVIII." This was Coverdale's translation, which he gave Hollybushe leave to print. It was dedicated "To the moost noble, moost gracious, and "our moost dradde soveraigne lord Kynge HENRY the "eyght, kynge of England and of Fraunce, defender of "Christ's true fayth, and under GOD the chefe and supreme "heade of the church of Englande, Irelande, &c." In the dedication, he tells his majesty, "that oon of the chiefest causes why he did now with moost humble obedience dedicate and offre thys translation of the New Testament unto his moost royall majesty, was his highnesse's so lovingly and favourably taking his infancy and rudeness in dedicating the whole Bible in Englysh to his most noble Grace."

This translation, as Coverdale says, was *sinistrally printed* and *negligently corrected.* He, therefore, the next year, 1539, published another edition in 8vo., which he dedicated "To the right honourable Lorde Cromwell lorde "prevye seale, vicegerent to the kynge's hyghnesse concer- "nynge all his jurisdiccion ecclesiasticall within the realme "of Englande."‡

In the year 1538, Lord Cromwell procured letters from

* Lewis's Hist. of Translations, p. 26.—Strype's Cranmer, p. 82.

† William Tindal, deservedly styled "The Apostle of England," was the first who translated the New Testament into English, from the original Greek. This translation was printed at Antwerp, in 1526; when Bishop Tonstal and Sir Thomas Moore purchased all the impression, and burnt them at Paul's cross. The sale of this impression enabled the translator to print a larger, and more correct edition. Tindal was burnt for an heretic at Wilford, near Brussels, in 1536, crying at the stake, "Lord, open the King of England's eyes."—*Fox's Martyrs*, vol. ii. p. 301—305.—*Strype's Cranmer*, p. 81.

‡ Lewis's Hist. of Translations, p. 27, 28.

Henry VIII. to the King of France, soliciting his license and allowance for printing the English Bible in the university of Paris, since it could be done there to much greater advantage than in England. The King of France granting the privilege, the work was immediately undertaken; and as Coverdale was a person eminently qualified for the office, he was appointed to superintend the press. He also compared the former translations with the original Hebrew and Greek, making the requisite alterations and amendments. When the work was nearly completed, the printer was convened before the tribunal of the Inquisition, and charged with heresy. Coverdale and others were sent for; but, aware of the approaching storm, they fled for their lives, and left their Bibles behind them, to the number of two thousand five hundred. Thus, he narrowly escaped the rack, the fire, or some equally cruel torture.

As the heretical translator could not be found, the Bibles were all seized, and committed to the care of one Lieutenant Criminal, to be burnt at Paris; but instead of casting the whole of them to the flames, he, through covetousness, sold four great fats full of them to an haberdasher, as waste paper, of whom they were afterwards purchased. All the rest were publicly burnt at Paris. Afterwards Lord Cromwell * went himself to Paris, when he procured the printing-press, and brought the servants of the printer to London, where the remaining part of the Bible was printed, though not without much opposition from the bishops.†

The first publication of the Bible in English roused the malice and ill-will of the bigotted prelates. Their anger and jealousy being awakened, they laid their complaints before the king; who, in compliance with their suggestions, ordered all the copies to be called in, and promised them a new translation. And when the translation in 1537, called Coverdale's translation, came forth, the bishops told Henry,

* Thomas Lord Cromwell was the son of a blacksmith at Putney, and some time served as a soldier in Italy, under the Duke of Bourbon. He was afterwards secretary to Cardinal Wolsey; and recommended himself to Henry VIII. by discovering that the clergy were privately absolved from their oath to him, and sworn anew to the pope. This discovery furnished the king with a pretence for the suppression of monasteries, in which Cromwell was a principal instrument. The king, whose mercies were cruel, raised him to a most envied pitch of honour and preferment, a little before his fall. He first amused him with an agreeable prospect, and then pushed him down a precipice. Cromwell, as vicegerent, had the precedence of all great officers of state; but lost his head July 28, 1540.—*Granger's Biog. Hist.* vol. i. p. 86.

† Fox's Martyrs, vol. ii. p. 434, 435,—Lewis's Hist. of Trans. p. 29.

that there were many faults in it. His majesty asked them whether it contained any heresies; and when the bishops said they had found none, the king replied, "Then in the name of God let it go abroad among the people."*

Coverdale's immense labours in publishing the various translations of the scriptures, exposed him to the wrath of the English bishops, by whom he was most severely persecuted for his pains. The angry prelates hunted him from place to place, which obliged him to flee from the storm, and continue many years in a foreign land. While in a state of exile, he printed the Bible, and sent it to be sold in England, by which means he obtained a comfortable support. This, however, could not long be concealed from the jealous eye of the Bishop of London; who no sooner found what Coverdale was doing, than he inquired where the Bibles were sold, and bought them all up: supposing by this means he should be able to suppress their circulation. But God so ordered it, contrary to the prelate's expectations, that the merchant of whom the Bibles were purchased, sent the money to Coverdale; whereby he was enabled to print more, and send them over to England.† This, indeed, roused the fury of the angry prelates, who, by their outstretched arms, reached him even in Holland; and to escape their potent malice, he was obliged to retire into Germany. He settled under the palsgrave of the Rhiene, where he found much favour. Here, upon his first settlement, he taught school for a subsistence. But having afterwards learned the Dutch language, the Prince Elector Palatine conferred upon him the benefice of Burghsaber, where his faithful ministry and holy life were made a blessing to the people. During his continuance in this situation, he was maintained partly by his benefice, and partly by Lord Cromwell, his liberal and worthy benefactor.‡

Upon the accession of Edward VI. the tyrannical cruelties of King Henry began immediately to relax; the prison

* Strype's Cranmer, p. 444.—Burnet's Hist. Abridged, vol. iii. p. 31.

† Clark's Lives, p. 3.

‡ Coverdale was almoner to Queen Katharine Parr, the last wife of Henry VIII., and a great friend to the reformation. In the month of September 1548, he officiated at her funeral, and preached a sermon on the occasion; in which he declared, "That there shulde none there thinke, "saye, or spread abrode, that the offeringe which was there don anye thing "to proffyth the deade, but for the poore onlye; and also the lights which "were carried and strode abowte the corps, were for the honnour of the "person, and for none other intente nor purpose; and so wente throughe "with his sermonde, and made a godlye prayer," &c.—*Biographia Britan.* vol. iv. p. 310, 311. Edit. 1778.

doors were set open; and those who had been driven into a state of exile, returned home. Among the last, was Dr. Miles Coverdale. Not long after his return, he became chaplain to Lord Russel, in his expedition to suppress the insurrection in Devonshire. For his excellent labours and behaviour on this occasion, he was highly extolled by the famous Peter Martyr.* In the year 1551, he, though a married man, was made Bishop of Exeter, being promoted "on account of his extraordinary knowledge in divinity, and his unblemished character." His consecration was performed at Lambeth, by Archbishop Cranmer.† The following is King Edward's letter patent nominating him to the bishopric:

"The king to all to whom the presents shall come "greeting. Whereas the bishopric of Exon is without a "bishop, and is destitute of a fit pastor, by the free resig-"nation of John late bishop of that place, and doth by "right belong to our collation and donation. We willing "to collate another fit person to the bishopric aforesaid, "and judging our well-beloved Miles Coverdale, professor "of divinity, for his signal learning in the scriptures, and "for his most approved manners, wherewith he is endowed, "to be a fit man for the place and office aforesaid. Know "ye, therefore, that we of our special grace, and certain "knowledge, and mere motion, have conferred, given, and "granted, and by these presents do confer, give, and grant, "to the aforesaid Miles Coverdale, the said bishopric of "Exeter: and we translate the same Miles to the bishopric "of Exon, and we nominate, ordain, and constitute by these "presents, the same Miles, Bishop of Exon, and of Exeter "diocese; to have and to hold, execute and enjoy the said "bishopric of Exon to the same Miles, during his natural "life."‡

The diocese of Exeter, on account of the late insurrection, and the prevalence of popery, was in a most lamentable state; and some wise, courageous, and excellent preacher, was extremely necessary for that situation. Therefore Coverdale was judged a most fit person to be invested with the above charge. Archbishop Cranmer had the highest opinion of him; was intimately acquainted with him; and was ever ready to do him acts of kindness.§ Though

* Burnet's Hist. Abridged, vol. iii. p. 148.
† Clark's Lives, p. 3.—Burnet's Hist. of Refor. vol. ii. p. 166.
‡ Huntley's Prelates' Usurpations, p. 122.
§ Strype's Cranmer, p. 266, 267.

Coverdale had submitted to wear the habits, in the late reign, he now, with many other celebrated divines, laid them aside.*

At this early period, there were many persons in the kingdom, who, besides the papists, were nonconformable to the established church. They refused to have their children baptized, and differed in some points of doctrine from the national creed. These, out of reproach, were denominated anabaptists. Also, there were many others who administered the sacraments in other manner than as prescribed by the Book of Common Prayer, set forth by public authority. Therefore to prevent these persons from propagating their opinions, and to bring them to conformity, a commission was issued to thirty-one persons, empowering them to correct and punish these nonconformists. Among those in the commission were Cranmer, Latimer, Parker, and Coverdale; but it does not appear whether any of the nonconformists were prosecuted by them.† Coverdale being ever celebrated for peace and moderation, would undoubtedly disapprove of all such measures.

This excellent divine, while he was Bishop of Exeter, conducted himself in a manner worthy of his high office. Like a true primitive bishop, he was a constant preacher, and much given to hospitality. He was sober and temperate in all things, holy and blameless, friendly to good men, liberal to the poor, courteous to all, void of pride, clothed with humility, abhorring covetousness and every scene of vice. His house was a little church, in which was exercised all virtue and godliness. He suffered no one to abide under his roof, who could not give some satisfactory account of his faith and hope, and whose life did not correspond with his profession. He was not, however, without his enemies. Because he was a constant and faithful preacher of the gospel, an avowed enemy to all superstition and popery, and a most upright worthy man, his adversaries sought to have him disgraced: sometimes by secret backbiting; sometimes by open raillery; and sometimes by false accusation. Indeed, their malice is said to have been carried to so great a length, that they endeavoured at last to poison him; but through the good providence of God, their snares were broken, and he was delivered out of their hands.‡

Coverdale having continued in the episcopal office

* Neal's Puritans, vol. i. p. 65.
† Strype's Parker, p. 27.
‡ Clark's Lives, p. 4.

betwixt two and three years, it pleased God to remove, by death, the excellent King Edward. Upon the accession of his sister Mary, the face of religion was soon changed; great numbers of the most worthy preachers in the kingdom were immediately silenced; and this good bishop, together with many others, was cast into prison.* During the confinement of Coverdale and the other protestant bishops, they drew up and subscribed their confession of faith. This confession, with the names of those who subscribed it, is still preserved, but too long for our insertion.† The malice of the papists designed Coverdale for the fire; but the Lord most wonderfully preserved and delivered him. During his imprisonment, the King of Denmark, with whom he had become acquainted when he was in Germany, became his honoured friend, warmly espoused his cause, and wrote several letters to Queen Mary, earnestly soliciting his release.‡ By the king's continued importunity, yet as a very great favour, he was permitted to go into banishment. Burnet, by mistake, calls him a Dane; and observes, that on this account some allowance was made for him, and a passport was granted him, with two of his servants, to go to Denmark.§ He retired first to his kind friend, the King of Denmark; then to Wezel in Westphalia; and afterwards he went into Germany, to his worthy patron the Elector of the Rhiene, by whom he was cordially received, and restored to his former benefice of Burghsaber.‖ Here he continued a zealous and laborious preacher, and a careful shepherd over the flock of Christ, all the remaining days of Queen Mary.

Coverdale and several of his brethren, during their exile, published a new translation of the Bible, commonly called the *Geneva* Bible. The translators of this Bible were Coverdale, Goodman, Gilby, Whittingham, Sampson, Cole, Knox, Bodliegh, and Pullain, all celebrated puritans. They first published the New Testament in 1557. This was the first that was ever printed with numerical verses. The whole Bible, with marginal notes, was printed in

* The two archbishops, Cranmer and Holgate, with the bishops, Ridley, Poinet, Scory, Coverdale, Taylor, Harvey, Bird, Bush, Hooper, Farrer, and Barlow, and twelve thousand clergymen, were all silenced at this time, and many of them were cast into prison.—*Burnet's Hist. of Refor.* vol. ii. p. 276.

† Fox's Martyrs, vol. iii. p. 15, 82, 83.

‡ These letters are still preserved.—*Ibid.* p. 149—151.

§ Hist. of Refor. vol. iii. p. 239.

‖ Troubles at Frankeford, p. 158.

1560, and dedicated to Queen Elizabeth. The translators say, "They were employed in the work night and day, with fear and trembling; and they protest from their consciences, and call God to witness, that in every point and word, they have faithfully rendered the text, to the best of their knowledge." But the marginal notes giving some offence, it was not suffered to be printed in England till after the death of Archbishop Parker; when it was printed in 1576, and soon passed through twenty or thirty editions.* This translation of the Bible has been lately published, under the title of "The Reformers' Bible."

During the rage of persecution in the reign of Queen Mary, every effort was made for the suppression of the reformation, and the re-establishment of popery. The frauds, and impositions, and superstitions of the latter being ashamed of an examination, the people were not allowed to read the writings of protestants. Therefore, in the year 1555, her majesty issued her royal proclamation for suppressing the books of the reformers. Among the works enumerated in this proclamation, were those of Luther, Calvin, Latimer, Hooper, Cranmer, and Coverdale.†

Soon after the accession of Queen Elizabeth, Dr. Coverdale again returned to his native country. His bishopric was reserved for him, and he was repeatedly urged to accept it; but on account of the popish habits and ceremonies retained in the church, he modestly refused. He assisted in the consecration of Archbishop Parker, in Lambeth chapel, December 17, 1559. The ceremony was performed in a plain manner, by the imposition of hands and prayer. Coverdale, on this occasion, wore only a *plain black gown;* and because he could not with a good conscience come up to the terms of conformity, he was neglected, and for some time had no preferment.‡ He had the plague in the year 1563, but afterwards recovered. He was commonly called *Father* Coverdale. But on account of the neglect with which he was treated, and the reproach which it brought upon the ruling prelates, Grindal, bishop of London, said, "Surely it is not well that he, who was in Christ before any of us, should be now in his age without stay of living. I cannot herein excuse us bishops." Grindal therefore in the above year, gave him the living of St.

* Strype's Parker, p. 205, 206.—Neal's Puritans, vol. ii. p. 88.

† Fox's Martyrs, vol. iii. p. 226.

‡ Strype's Parker, p. 58—60.—Annals, vol. i. p. 366.—Neal's Puritans, vol. i. p. 165.

Magnus, at the Bridge-foot. But he being old and poor, petitioned Secretary Cecil and others, to be released from paying the first fruits, amounting to upwards of sixty pounds, adding, "If poor old Miles might be thus provided for, he should think this enough and as good as a feast." This favour was granted.*

Coverdale continued in the undisturbed exercise of his ministry a little more than two years;† but not coming up to the terms of conformity, he was driven from his flock, and obliged to relinquish his benefice.‡ Though he was laden with old age and infirmities, he did not relinquish his beloved work. He still continued preaching as he found an opportunity, without the habits; and multitudes flocked to hear him. They used to send to his house on a Saturday, inquiring where he was to preach on the following sabbath, and were sure to follow him. This, however, giving offence to the ruling prelates, the good old man was, at length, obliged to tell his friends, that he durst not any more inform them of his preaching, through fear of offending his superiors.§ He, nevertheless, continued preaching as long as he was able; and died a most comfortable and happy death, January 20, 1568, aged eighty-one years. He was a man of most exemplary piety, an indefatigable student, a great scholar, a celebrated preacher, a peaceable nonconformist, and much admired and followed by the puritans; but the Act of Uniformity brought down his grey hairs with sorrow to the grave. His remains were honourably interred in the chancel of St. Bartholomew's church, behind the Exchange, London; when vast crowds of people attended the funeral procession. A monumental inscription was afterwards erected to his memory, of which the following is a translation:‖

In Memory
of the most reverend Father,
Miles Coverdale,
who died, aged eighty years.
This Tomb
contains the mortal Remains of Coverdale,
who having finished his labours,
now lies at rest.
He was once the most faithful
and worthy *Bishop* of Exeter,
a man remarkable for the uprightness of his life.

* Strype's Grindal, p. 91.—Parker, p. 148, 149.—Annals, vol. i. p. 367.
† Newcourt's Repert. Eccl. vol. i. p. 398.
‡ Strype's Parker, p. 149.
§ Parte of a Register, p. 25.
‖ Stow's Survey of London, b. ii. p. 122.

He lived to exceed the age of eighty years,
having several times
been unjustly sent into banishment;
and after being tossed about, and
exposed to the various
hardships of life,
the Earth kindly received him into
her bosom.

His Works.—1. The Christen Rule or State of all the Worlde from the highest to the lowest: and how every Man shulde lyve to please God in his Callynge, 1547.—2. The Christen State of Matrimonye, wherein Husbands and Wyfes maye lerne to keepe House together with Love, 1547.—3. A Christen Exhortation to customable Swearers. What a ryght and lawfull Othe is: when, and before whom it oughte to be, 1547.—4. The Maner of sayenge Grace, or gyvyng Thankes to God, after the Doctrine of Holy Scrypture, 1547.—5. The old Fayth: an evident Probacion out of the Holy Scrypture, that Christen Fayth (which is the ryghte, true, olde, and undoubted Fayth) hath endured sins the beginyng of the Worlde, 1547.—6. A faythful and true Prognostication upon the year M.CCCC.XLIX. and perpetualy after to the Worlde's Ende, gathered out of the Prophecies and Scryptures of God, by the Experience and Practice of hys Workes, very comfortable for all Christen Hertes.—7. A Spiritual Almanacke, wherein every Christen Man and Woman may see what they oughte daylye to do, or leave undone.—8. A Confutation of John Standish. —9. A Discourse on the Holy Sacraments.—10. A Concordance to the New Testament.—11. A Christian Catechism.—12. Several Translations from Bullinger, Luther, and others.—The version of the Psalms in the Book of Common Prayer, is taken from Coverdale's Bible.*

William Turner, M. D.—This distinguished person was born at Morpeth in Northumberland, and educated in the university of Cambridge, where he became famous for his knowledge in philosophy, physic, and divinity. He was a most learned and pious nonconformist, an avowed enemy to all the abominations of popery, and a most zealous promoter of the reformation. Beholding the deplorable ignorance of the people, and the great scarcity of useful preachers in every part of the kingdom, he renounced all thoughts of preferment, though he had the most flattering prospects, and became a zealous and constant preacher, in cities, towns, and villages, through most parts of the country. As he could not with a good conscience, submit to the ceremonies required in the ordination of ministers, he generously employed his talents in preaching the gospel *without* ordination. Having continued in these ministerial

* Churton's Life of Nowell, p. 394. note.

labours for some time, he at length settled at Oxford, where he enjoyed the advantage of learned men and books. There he continued preaching, not without hopes of gaining learned men to espouse the reformation, till he was cast into prison; and after close confinement for a considerable time, he was banished from the country. Such was the effect of bigotry and popish cruelty!

During his banishment, he travelled into Italy; and at Ferrara, being much admired for his great learning, he was created doctor of physic. Towards the close of the reign of Henry VIII. he lived at Cologne and other places in Germany. In the reign of Edward VI. he returned home, when he was greatly esteemed among our pious and learned reformers. Upon his return he was made prebendary of York, canon of Windsor, and dean of Wells, and incorporated doctor of physic at Oxford. Having obtained a license to preach, he renewed his former ministerial exercises; and, at the same time, practised physic among the nobility and gentry, and was chosen both chaplain* and physician to the Duke of Somerset, lord protector. Upon the accession of Queen Mary, and the commencement of her bloody persecution, he fled from the storm, and retired first into Germany, then to Rome, and afterwards settled, with others of his fellow exiles, at Basil in Switzerland.† Upon the accession of Queen Elizabeth, he returned a second time to his native country, when he was restored to his deanery, being highly esteemed both as a physician and divine, but especially on account of his numerous learned writings.‡

He was author of a work, entitled "A New Herbal," the first original work on the subject in the English language, and afterwards the foundation of Gerard's celebrated work on the same subject.§ It is said, the first publisher of an original Herbal in our tongue, Dr. William Turner, informs us, that botany, or the knowledge of simpling, was fallen into such neglect, that in King Henry's reign, he found not a physician in the university of Cambridge, who could inform him of the Greek, Latin, or English names of any plants he produced, as he gathered them to compile

* Strype's Annals, vol. i. p. 136.

† Bishop Ridley, during his imprisonment, writing to Grindal, then an exile at Frankfort, made the most affectionate and honourable mention of Turner, Lever, Sampson, and other worthy exiles.—*Fox's Martyrs*, vol. iii. p. 374.

‡ Wood's Athenæ Oxon. vol. i. p. 120, 121.

§ Strype's Cranmer, p. 274.

his first Latin skeleton of his Herbal. The learned Dr. John Kaius, enumerating the celebrated men who have written on this subject, asks, "And who shall forget the most worthy Dr. William Turner? whose learned acts I leave to the witty commendations, and immortal praise, of Conradus Gesnerus. Yet his book of herbs will always grow green, and never wither, as long as Dioscorides is had in mind among us mortal wits."* He wrote with great zeal and strength of argument against the superstitions and errors of popery. It is observed, that in his book entitled "The Hunting of the Romish Fox," he has "unanswerably proved, that those who labour to advance and bring in the canon law, labour to advance and usher in the pope."†

September 10, 1559, Dr. Turner preached the sermon at Paul's cross; and, as he was a person universally beloved, and a most popular preacher, his audience, consisting of courtiers, citizens, and people from the country, was uncommonly large.‡ He was a decided nonconformist, and refused subscription and the habits. Mr. Strype observes, that in the year 1565, he enjoined a common adulterer to do open penance in the *priest's square cap*, and thus discovered his contempt of the clerical garments. For this flagrant crime, Archbishop Parker complained of him to Secretary Cecil. And, as our historian adds, he used to call the bishops, *white coates and tippet gentlemen.* He also contemned their office, by asking, "Who gave them more authority over me, than I over them, either to forbid me preaching, or to deprive me, unless they have received it from their holy father the pope?" This was certainly bold language for those times of severity. But without attempting to vindicate the claim here expressed, or inquiring from whom their authority was derived, their lordships ventured to exercise this authority upon Dr. Turner, and caused him, with many of his brethren, to feel the weight of their outstretched arms. For upon his refusal to wear the surplice, and use the Book of Common Prayer, he was sequestered and deprived, with nearly forty other London ministers.§

It has been generally, but improperly supposed, says Mr. Middleton, that Mr. Cartwright was the first noted dissenter from the etsablished church. Dr. Turner, dean of Wells,

* Biog. Britan. vol. iii. p. 2, 6. Edit. 1778.
† Huntley's Prelates, p. 39.
‡ Strype's Annals, vol. i. p. 186.
§ Strype's Parker, p. 151.—Neal's Hist. of New Eng. vol. i. p. 50.

says he, about the year 1563, seems to have been the first, or one of the first, after the church of England was settled, who opposed both its episcopacy and ceremonies, and made some disturbance about them. This Turner, adds the pious but mistaken author, was a very intemperate and indiscreet man, as appears from an anecdote recorded of him, wherein he manifested his rude treatment of a bishop, whom he had invited to dine with him.*

That Dr. Turner was opposed to the episcopacy and ceremonies of the church, was never doubted; but that he was a disturber of the peace, was never proved. And whether he was a very intemperate and indiscreet man, will best appear from the anecdote itself, which was the following: the doctor having invited a bishop to dine with him, and having a very sagacious dog, was desirous to put a joke upon his lordship. Therefore, while they were at dinner, he called his dog, and told him that the bishop perspired very much. The dog then immediately flew upon his lordship, snatched off his cornered cap, and ran with it to his master.†

This celebrated divine having spent his life in active and vigorous endeavours to promote the reformation of the church, and the welfare of the state; and having suffered imprisonment and banishment from the hands of the papists, and deprivation from his fellow protestants, he died full of years, July 7, 1568. His remains were interred in the chancel of St. Olave's church, Hart-street, London, where a monumental inscription was erected to his memory, of which the following is a translation:‡

In Memory
of that famous, learned and holy man,
William Turner, Dean of Wells,
a most skilful Physician and Divine,
in which professions
he served the Church and the Commonwealth,
with the greatest diligence and success,
for thirty years.
Against the implacable enemies of both,
but especially against the Roman Antichrist,
he fought bravely
as a good Soldier of Jesus Christ.
When worn out with age and labours,
he laid down his body
in hope of a blessed resurrection.

* Middleton's Biographia Evangelica, vol. ii. p. 326. Edit. 1780.

† Strype's Parker, p. 152.

‡ Ward's Gresham Professors, p. 130.—An imperfect account of this inscription is given in Stow's "Survey of London," b. ii. p. 28.

Jane Turner erected this monument
to the Memory
of her beloved and pious husband.
By the power of Christ
they both overcame the world and the flesh,
and now they triumph for ever.

Turner, an honour to the healing art,
And in religion he was truly great;
But envious death has snatched him from our eyes;
We suffer loss, but Turner gains the prize.
He died July 7, 1568.

The Oxford historian, with an evident design to blacken his memory, says, he was conceited of his own worth, hot-headed, a busy body, and much addicted to the opinions of Luther, always refusing the use of the ceremonies.* Fuller denominates him a most excellent Latinist, Grecian, orator, and poet, and a most learned and zealous protestant.† Mr. Strype styles him an eminent preacher, and says, he was greatly befriended by Sir John Cheke and Sir William Cecil.‡ He had a son called Peter, who became doctor of physic, a member of parliament in 1584, and a most zealous man in the cause of religion and his country. He died May 27, 1614, when his remains were interred in the chancel of the above church. Dr. William Turner was a celebrated writer, especially against the papists.

His Works.—1. The Hunting of the Romish Fox, which more than seven years hath been hid among the Bishops of England, after that the King's Highness had commanded him (Turner) to be driven out of the Realm, 1543.—2. Avium præcipaurum, quarum apud Plinum & Aristotelum mentio est, brevis & succincta historia, 1544.—3. The Rescuing of the Romish Fox; otherwise called the Examination of the Hunter, devised by Stephen Gardiner, Doctor and Defender of the Pope's Canon Law, and his ungodly Ceremonies, 1545.—4. The Hunting the Romish Wolf, 154..—5. A Dialogue, wherein is contained the Examination of the Masse, and of that kind of Priesthood which is ordained to say Masse, 1549.—6. A new Herbal, wherein are contained the names of Herbs in Greek, Latin, English, Dutch, French, and in the Apothecaries and Herbaries, with their properties, 1551.—7. A Preservative, or Triacle against the Poyson of Pelagius, 1551.—8. A new Book of Spiritual Physick for divers Diseases of the Nobilitie and Gentlemen of England, 1555.—9. The Hunting of the Fox and the Wolf, because they did make Havock of the Sheep of Jesus Christ, 156..—10. A Book of the Natures and Properties, as well of the Bathes of England, as of other Bathes in Germany and Italy, 1562.—11. A Treatise of the Bath at Barth in England, 1562.—12. Of the Nature of all Waters, 1562.—13. The

* Wood's Athenæ, vol. i. p. 129. † Worthies, part ii. p. 206.
‡ Strype's Cranmer, p. 274.

Nature of Wines commonly used in England, with a Confutation of them that hold, that Rhenish and other small Wines ought not to be drunken, either of them that have the Stone, the Rume, or other Diseases, 1568.—14. The Nature and Virtue of Triacle, 1568. —15. The rare Treasure of English Baths, 1587.—16. Arguments against the Popish Ceremonies.*—He translated into English, "A Comparison between the Old Learning and the New," 1538.—And "The Palsgraves Catechism," 1572.

ROBERT HAWKINS.—This zealous puritan was beneficed in London, but endured many troubles for nonconformity. In the year 1566, conformity to the habits and ceremonies being enforced with great rigour, especially in London and its vicinity, and many of the nonconformable ministers being silenced, and their friends treated with great severity, they came at length to a determination to form themselves into a separate congregation; and they assembled together privately, in various places in the city, as they found opportunity. It is observed from Mr. Strype, that the refusers of the orders of the church, who by this time were commonly called puritans, were now grown into two factions. The one was of a more quiet and peaceable demeanour, who indeed would not use the habits, nor subscribe to the ceremonies, as kneeling at the sacrament, the cross in baptism, the ring in marriage; but held the communion of the church, and willingly and devoutly joined in the common prayer. There was another sort, who disliked the whole *constitution* of the church, charging it with many gross remainders of popery, and that it was still full of antichristian corruptions, and not to be tolerated. These separated themselves into private assemblies, meeting together not in churches, but in private houses, where they had ministers of their own. They rejected wholly the Book of Common Prayer, and used a book of prayers framed at Geneva for the congregation of English exiles lately sojourning there. This book had been revised and allowed by Calvin and the rest of the Geneva divines. At these private assemblies, they had not only prayers and sermons, but the Lord's supper likewise sometimes administered. This gave great offence to the queen, who issued her letters to the ecclesiastical commissioners, to this effect: "That they should move these nonconformists by gentle means to conformity, or else for their first punishment to lose their

* The author has seen a MS. copy of this work, but is not certain whether it was ever published.

freedom of the city, and afterwards to suffer what should follow."*

Mr. Hawkins was a leading person among these separatists, and an active and a zealous preacher. Several other ministers were members of the congregation. Having kept their assemblies for some time more privately, to elude the notice of the bishop's officers, they at length ventured to come forth more publicly; and June 19, 1567, they agreed to have a sermon and the Lord's supper at Plumbers-hall, which they hired for the day, as some one gave it out, under pretence of a wedding. Here the sheriffs of London discovered them, and broke up their meeting, when about one hundred were assembled together. Most of them were taken into custody, and sent to the Compter. These were the first puritans who accounted it unlawful to hold communion with the church of England, and who totally separated from it. They did not separate, however, till after their ministers were silenced; and they appear to have been the first who were cast into prison, in the reign of Queen Elizabeth, for not coming to their parish churches, and for holding conventicles. They deserved more humane treatment, especially when it is recollected, that they only imitated the worthy protestants a few years before, in the time of Queen Mary; who, to the great hazard of their lives, assembled in private places; and some of them were, indeed, the same persons. They were harassed and persecuted, while the papists continued unmolested.†

The day after their imprisonment in the Compter, Mr. Hawkins, and Messrs. William White, Thomas Bowland, John Smith, William Nixson, James Ireland, and Richard Morecraft, were brought before Bishop Grindal, Dean Goodman, Archdeacon Watts, the lord mayor, and other commissioners. The bishop charged them with absenting themselves from the parish churches, and with setting up separate assemblies for prayer, preaching, and administering the sacrament. He told them, that by these proceedings, they condemned the church of England, which was well reformed according to the word of God, and those martyrs who shed their blood for it.‡ To this charge, Mr. Hawkins replied in the name of the rest, as follows; and would have said more, but was interrupted.

Hawkins. We condemn them not. We only stand to the truth of God's word.

* Biographia Britan. vol. iv. p. 2432. Edit. 1747.

† MS. Remarks, p. 213. ‡ Parte of a Register, p. 23, 24.

Bishop. Have you not the gospel truly preached, and the sacraments duly ministered, and good order preserved; though we differ from other churches in indifferent ceremonies, which the prince has power to command for the sake of order? What say you, Smith, as you seem the *ancientest?*

Smith. Indeed, my lord, we thank God for reformation; and that is the thing we desire, according to God's word.

White. I beseech you, let me answer.

Bishop. Nay, White, hold your peace. You shall be heard anon.

Nixson. I beseech you, let me answer a word or two.

Bishop. Nixson, you are a busy fellow. I know your words. You are full of talk. I know from whence you came.

Hawkins. I would be glad to answer.

Bishop. Smith, you shall answer.

Smith. So long, indeed, as we might have the word freely preached, and the sacraments administered without the use of *idolatrous gear*, we never assembled in private houses. But when all our preachers, who could not subscribe to your apparel and your laws, were displaced; so that we could not hear any of them in the church for the space of seven or eight weeks, excepting father Coverdale, who at length durst not make known unto us where he preached; and then we were troubled in your courts from day to day, for not coming to our parish churches; we considered among ourselves what we should do. We remembered that there was a congregation of us in this city, in the days of Queen Mary; and a congregation at Geneva, which used a book and order of preaching, ministering the sacraments and discipline, most agreeable to the word of God. This book is allowed by the godly and learned Mr. Calvin, and the other preachers at Geneva, which book and order we now hold. And if you can, by the word of God, reprove this book, or any thing that we hold, we will yield to you, and do open penance at Paul's cross; but if not, we will, by the grace of God, stand to it.

Bishop. This is no answer.

Smith. Would you have me go back from better to worse? I would as soon go to *mass* as to some churches, and particularly to my own parish church; for the minister is a very *papist*.

Dean. He counteth the service and reformation in the days of King Edward, as evil as the mass.

Bishop. Because he knoweth one that is evil, he findeth fault with all. You may go to other places.

White. If it were tried, there would be found a great company of papists in this city, whom you allow to be ministers, and thrust out the godly.

Bishop. Can you accuse any of them of false doctrine?

Nixson. Yes, I can accuse one of false doctrine, who is even now in this house. Let him come forth, and answer to the doctrine which he preached upon John x.*

Dean. You would take away the authority of the prince, and the liberty of christians.

Bishop. Yes, and you suffer justly.

Hawkins. It does not belong to the prince, nor to the liberty of christians, to use and defend that which appertaineth to papistry and idolatry, as appears from Deuteronomy vii. and other parts of scripture.

Dean. When do you hear us maintain such things in our preaching?

Hawkins. Though you do not defend them in your preaching, you do it by your deeds, and your laws. You preach Christ to be a prophet and priest, but not to be a king; nor will you suffer him to reign in his church *alone*, by the sceptre of his word; but the *pope's canon law*, and the *will of the prince*, must be preferred before the word and ordinance of God.

Dean. You speak irreverently of the prince, before the magistrates. You were not required to speak, and therefore might hold your peace.

Hawkins. You will suffer us to make our defence, seeing you persecute us.

Bishop. What is so preferred?

Nixson. Your laws, your copes, and your surplices; because you will suffer none to preach, except they wear them, and subscribe.

Bishop. No! what say you of Sampson and Lever, and others? Do not they preach?

White. Though they preach, you have deprived and forbidden them; and though you suffer them, the law stands in force against them. But for what cause you will not suffer others, whom you cannot reprove by the word of God, I know not.

* This was one Bedall, then present, who immediately held down his head, but said nothing. The bishop and other commissioners, at the same time, looked upon one another, as if they knew not what to do, but proceeded no further.—*Parts of a Register*, p. 26.

Bishop. They will not preach among you.

White. Your doings are the cause.

Hawkins. And they will not join with you. One of them told me, "he had rather be torn in a hundred pieces, than communicate with you." We neither hold nor allow any thing that is not contained in the word of God. But if you think we do not hold the truth, shew unto us, and we will renounce it.

Smith. And if you cannot, we pray you, let us not be thus used.

Dean. You are not obedient to the authority of the prince.

White. Yes, we are. For we resist not, but suffer whatsoever authority is pleased to lay upon us.

Bishop. Thieves likewise suffer, when the laws are laid upon them.

White. What a comparison is this! They suffer for evil doing, and you punish us for serving God according to his word.

Nixson. The prince, as well as ourselves, must be ruled by the word of God: as we read, 1 Kings xii., that the king should teach only the word of God.

Bishop. What! should the king teach the word of God? Lie not.

Nixson. It means that both king and people should obey the word of God.

Bishop. It is indeed true, that princes must obey the word of God only. But obedience consisteth of three points.—1. That which God commandeth may not be left undone.—2. That which God forbiddeth may not be done. —3. That which God hath neither commanded nor forbidden, and consisteth in things *indifferent*: such things princes have authority to appoint and command.

Prisoners. Prove that. Where find you that?

Bishop. I have talked with many persons, and yet I never saw any behave themselves so irreverently before magistrates.

White. I beseech you, let me speak a word or two.

Bishop. White, stay a little. You shall speak anon.

Hawkins. Kings have their rule and commandment, Deut. xvii., not to decline from the word of God, to the right hand or the left, notwithstanding your distinction.

Smith. How can you prove those things to be *indifferent*, which are *abominable*.

Bishop. You mean our caps and tippets, which, you say, came from Rome.

Ireland. They belong to the papists, therefore throw them to them.

Watts. You would have us use nothing that the papists used. Then should we use no churches, seeing the papists used them.

Hawkins. Churches are necessary to keep our bodies from the rain; but *copes* and *surplices* are superstitious and idolatrous.

White. Christ did cast the buyers and sellers, and their wares, out of the temple, yet was not the temple overthrown.

Bishop. Things not forbidden of God, may be used for the sake of order and obedience. This is according to the judgment of the learned Bullinger. We, therefore, desire you to be conformable.

Smith. What if I can shew you Bullinger against Bullinger, in this thing?

Bishop. I think you cannot, Smith.

Smith. Yes, that I can.

Bishop. Though we differ from other reformed churches, in rites and ceremonies, we agree with them in the substance of doctrine.

Hawkins. Yes, but we should follow the truth in all things. Christ saith, "Go ye, therefore, and teach all nations, baptizing them in the name of the Father, and of the Son, and of the Holy Ghost; teaching them to observe *all things whatsoever I have commanded you.*" But you have brought the gospel and its ordinances into bondage to the ceremonies of antichrist; and you defend idolatry and papistry. You have mingled your own inventions with every ordinance of Christ. How do you address godfathers and godmothers in baptism?

Watts. Oh! a wise reason.

Bishop. How say you of the church at Geneva? They communicate with wafer cakes, which you are so much against.

Nixson. Yes, but they do not compel any to receive it so and in no other way.

Bishop. Yes, in their parish churches.

White. The English congregation, while residing there, did minister the sacrament with loaf bread.

Bishop. Because they were of another language.

White. It is good to follow the best example. But we must follow them only as they follow Christ.

Dean. All the learned men in Europe are against you.

Watts. You will believe no man.

Smith. Yes, we reverence the learned at Geneva, and

in all other places. Yet we build not our faith and religion upon them.

Bishop. Will you be judged by the learned at Geneva? They are against you.

Hawkins. We will be judged by the word of God, which shall judge us all at the last day, and is, therefore, sufficient to judge us *now*. But how can they be against us, seeing they know not of our doings?

Bishop. Here is a letter from Geneva; and they are against you and your doings, in going from us. They tremble at your cause.

Hawkins. The place is against you. For they tremble at your case, and the case of the prince; because, by your severities, you drive us to a separation against our wills.

Bishop. Then you enter into judgment against us.

Hawkins. No; we judge not. But we know the letter well enough; for we have it in our houses. It maketh nothing against us.

Bishop. We grant it doth not. Yet they account the apparel, in its own nature, indifferent, and not impious and wicked; and, therefore, counsel preachers not to give up their functions, or leave their flocks, for these things.

Hawkins. But it is said, in the same letter, "that ministers should give up their ministry, rather than be compelled to subscribe unto the allowance of such things."

Nixson. Let us answer to your first question.

Bishop. Say on, Nixson.

Nixson. We do not refuse you for preaching the word of God; but because you have tied the ceremonies of antichrist to your ministry, and set them before it, seeing no man may preach or minister the sacraments without them. Before you used this compulsion, all was quiet.

Bishop. So you are against things indifferent, which for the sake of order and obedience may be borne with.

Mayor. Well, good people, I wish you would wisely consider these things, and be obedient to the queen's good laws; that you may live quietly, and have liberty. I am sorry that you are troubled; but I am an officer under my prince, and therefore blame not me. The queen hath not established these garments and other things, for the sake of any holiness in them, only for civil order and comeliness; and because she would have ministers known from other men, as aldermen are known by their tippets, judges by their red gowns, and noblemen's servants by their liveries. Therefore, you will do well to take heed and obey.

Hawkins. Philip Melancthon, upon Romans xiv. hath these words: "When the opinion of *holiness*, or *merit*, or *necessity*, is put to things indifferent, they darken the light of the gospel, and ought always to be taken away."

Bishop. These things are not commanded as *necessary* in the church.

Hawkins. You have made them necessary, and that many a poor man doth feel.

Nixson. As you say, my lord, that the alderman is known by his tippet, even as by this apparel were the mass-priests known from other men.

Dean. What a great matter you make of it!

Hawkins. The apostle Paul would not be like the false apostles in any such things; therefore the apostle is against you.

Bishop. There were good men and good martyrs, who, in the days of King Edward, did wear these things. Do you condemn them?

Nixson. We condemn them not. We would go forward to perfection. The best of them who maintained the habits, did recant at their death: as did Dr. Ridley, bishop of London, and Dr. Taylor. Ridley did acknowledge his fault to Hooper, and when they would have put the apparel upon him, he said it was *abominable* and too fond for a vice in a play.*

Bishop. Do you find that in the Book of Martyrs?

Hawkins. It may be shewed from the book of the "Monuments of the Church," that many who were burned in the time of Queen Mary, died for standing against popery, as we do now.

Bishop. I have said mass. I am sorry for it.

Ireland. But you go still like one of the mass-priests.

Bishop. You saw me wear a cope or surplice in St. Paul's. I had rather minister without them, only for the sake of order and obedience to my prince.

Nixson. Your garments, as they are now used, are accursed.

Bishop. Where do you find them forbidden in scripture?

Nixson. Where is the mass forbidden in the scriptures?

Bishop. The mass is forbidden in scripture thus:—It was thought meritorious. It took away free justification. It

* What is here observed relative to the worthy reformers, is abundantly confirmed by the concurrent testimony of our historians. *Fox's Acts and Monuments of Martyrs*, vol. iii. p. 143, 168, 172, 427.—*Heylin's Hist. of Refor.* part i. p. 93.—*Prince's Chron. Hist.* vol. i. p. 217.

was made an idol: and idolatry is forbidden in the scriptures.

Hawkins. By the same argument, I will prove your garments to be forbidden in the scriptures. In Psalm cxxxviii. it is said, that "God hath magnified his word above all his name." And 2 Cor. x. it is said, "The weapons of our warfare are not carnal, but mighty through God to the pulling down of strong holds; casting down imaginations, and every high thing that exalteth itself against the knowledge of God, and bringeth into captivity every thought to the obedience of Christ." But you have brought the word of God into captivity to the *pope's garments* and his *canon law*. Therefore they are forbidden in the scriptures. "And," says Christ, "that which is highly esteemed amongst men, is abomination in the sight of God." Luke xvi.

White. Reprove what we hold, and prove what you would have us to observe, by the scriptures, and we will yield to you. But if you cannot do this, why do you persecute us.

Bishop. You are not obedient to the prince.

Dean. Doth not St. Peter say, "Be obedient unto every ordinance of man?"

White. Yes, so far as their ordinances are according to the will of God.

Nixson. It hath always been the practice of popish bishops, when they could not defend their cause by scripture, to make the mayor and aldermen their servants and butchers, to execute punishment. But you, my lord, seeing you have heard and seen our cause, will take good advertisement concerning the same.

Mayor. How irreverently you speak before my lords and us, in making such a comparison!

Bishop. Have we not a godly prince? Or, is she evil?

White. What the answer to that question is, the fruits do shew.

Bowland. Yes, the servants of God are persecuted under her.

Bishop. Mark this, my lord.

Hawkins. The prophet may answer this question. "Have all the workers of iniquity no knowledge, who eat up my people as they eat bread?"

Dean. Do we hold any heresy? Do we deny any article of faith? Do we maintain purgatory or pilgrimage? No;

we hold the reformation that was promoted in the days of King Edward.

White. You build much upon the time of King Edward. And though it was the best time of reformation, all was confined to one prescript order of service, patched together out of the popish mattins, even-song, and mass-book; and no dicipline, according to the word of God, might be brought into the church.

Nixson. Yet they never made a law, that none should preach, nor administer the sacraments, without the garments, as you have done.

Hawkins. It can never be proved, that the ceremonies of antichrist, and the pope's canon law, are clean to christians. For the apostle saith, there is no fellowship between Christ and Belial, and light and darkness.

Dean. All the learned are against you.

White. I delivered a book to Justice Harris, containing the order which we hold. Reprove the same by the word of God, and we will renounce it altogether.

Bishop. We cannot reprove it. But to gather yourselves together disorderly, and to trouble the quiet of the realm, against the will of the prince, we like not.

White. We hold nothing that is not warranted by the word of God.

Hawkins. That which we do, we do in obedience to the command of God. "Now, I beseech you, brethren, *mark* them which cause divisions and offences, contrary to the doctrine which ye have learned, and *avoid* them."

Dean. Yes; but what you hold is disorderly, and against the authority of the prince.

Hawkins. That which is according to the word of God is truth, whoever holds it; unless you make the truth of God subject to the authority of the prince. It were better for us never to have been born, than to suffer the word of God to be defaced by the pleasure of princes.

Bishop. All the learned are against you. Will you be tried by them?

White. We will be tried by the word of God, by which we shall all be judged at the last day.

Dean. But who will you have to be judge of the word of God?

Hawkins. That was the cavil of the papists, in the time of Queen Mary. I have myself heard them say, when the truth was defended by the word of God, "Who shall judge of the word of God? The catholic church must be judge."

White. We will be tried by the best reformed churches. The church of Scotland hath the word truly preached, the sacraments truly ministered, and discipline according to the word of God: these are the marks by which a true church is known.

Dean. We have a gracious prince.

Prisoners. May God preserve her majesty and council.

White. That which God commandeth, ought to be done; and that which God forbiddeth, ought not to be done.

Bishop. Yes; and so say I.

White. It is manifest that what God commandeth to be done, is left undone; and what God forbiddeth, is done by authority. God says, "Six days shalt thou labour, and do all that thou hast to do: but the seventh day is the sabbath of the Lord thy God." But the law of the prince saith, "Thou shalt not labour six days, but shalt keep the popish holy-days."—Christ commandeth discipline to be used in his church, Matt. xviii., and it was practised by the apostles: but in the church of England, that is set aside, and none used but the popish discipline. And Christ saith, "If any man shall add unto those things which he has revealed, God shall add unto him the plagues that are written in his book: and if any man shall take away from the words of his book, God shall take away his part out of the book of life, and out of the holy city." Rev. xxii. How will you avoid this?

Bishop. Why, is it not well to hear a good sermon or two on the holy-days?

White. We are not against that. But what shall we do when the sermons are ended? If we do any work, we are commanded to appear in your courts.

Bishop. You may be well employed in serving God.

White. So we are, when we are at our work, as God commandeth.

Dean. Then you would have no sermons, nor prayers, all the week.

White. I think he is no christian who does not pray and serve God every day in the week.

Nixson. You can suffer bear-baiting, bowling, and other games, both on the sabbath and your holy-days, without any trouble for it.

Dean. Then you would have no holy-days, because the papists have used them?

White. We ought to do what God commandeth.

Dean. Then you must not use the Lord's prayer, because the papists used it; and many other prayers, because the papists used them. You would have nothing but the word of God. Are all the psalms which you sing the word of God?

White. Is every word delivered in a good sermon the word of God?

Dean. No.

White. But every word and thing *agreeing* with the word of God, is as the word of God.

Bishop. There hath been no heretic, but he hath challenged the word of God to defend himself.

White. What is that to us? If you know any heresy that we hold, charge us with it.

Bishop. Holy-days may be well used.

Hawkins. Bishop Hooper, in his Commentary upon the Commandments, saith, "that holy-days are the leaven of antichrist."*

In the conclusion, the prisoners not yielding to the conformity required, were sent to Bridewell, where they, with their brethren, and several women, were kept in confinement two years. During this period, the famous Mr. Thomas Lever had a conference with them, and, by their desire, wrote them a letter to comfort and encourage them under their present trials, giving his opinion of those things for which they suffered. In this letter, dated December 5, 1568, he declares, that by the grace of God, he was determined never to wear the *square cap* and *surplice*, nor kneel at the communion, because it was a symbolizing with popery. Yet he would not condemn those who should observe these things.† The celebrated Mr. John Knox wrote, also, a most affectionate and faithful letter to certain prisoners confined for nonconformity; urging them to hear the ministers who preached sound doctrine, though they conformed to the habits and ceremonies of the church. This letter, written about the same time, was most probably addressed to the same persons.‡

The patience and constancy of Mr. Hawkins and the rest of the prisoners, being at length sufficiently tried, an order at the motion of Bishop Grindal, was sent from the lords of the council to release them. Therefore, in the month of April, 1569, after admonition to behave themselves better

* Parte of a Register, p. 24—37.

† MS. Register, p. 18, 19.

‡ Ibid. p. 20, 21.

in future, *twenty-four men*, and *seven women*, were discharged.* Bishop Maddox insinuates that these persons were guilty of *disloyalty;* and adds, "that it was no wonder they "were not more respectful to the queen, since their whole

* The names of the men were, Robert Hawkins, John Smith, John Roper, James Ireland, William Nixson, Walter Hinkesman, Thomas Bowland, George Waddy, William Turner, John Nash, James Adderton, Thomas Lidford, Richard Langton, Alexander Lacy, John Leonard, Robert Tod, Roger Hawksworth, Robert Sparrow, Richard King, Christopher Coleman, John Benson, John Bolton, Robert Gates, and William White.† Several of them had been beneficed ministers in the church, the rest were religious and worthy laymen, but all sufferers in the same cause. Among the latter was Mr. William White, a substantial citizen of London, whom Fuller, by mistake, calls a minister. He was oftentimes fined and tossed from one prison to another, contrary to law and justice, only for not going to his own parish church. Having been examined before the Bishop of London, he wrote his lordship a most bold and excellent letter, now before me, dated December 19, 1569; in the conclusion of which, he subscribes himself, "Yours in the Lord to command, *William White*, who joineth with you "in every speck of truth, but utterly detesteth whole antichrist, head, "body, and tail, never to join with you, or any, in the least joint thereof; "nor in any ordinance of man, contrary to the word of God."‡ An abstract of this letter is preserved by Mr. Neal.§

January 18, 1573, Mr. White appeared before the commissioners, who treated him neither as men, nor as christians. He was examined in the presence of the Lord Chief Justice, the Master of the Rolls, the Master of the Requests, the Dean of Westminster, the Sheriff of London, the Clerk of the Peace, and Mr. Gerard. Some others having been dispatched, Mr. White was brought forth, whom his lordship accosted as follows:—

L. C. J. Who is this?

White. White, if it please your honour.

L. C. J. White! as black as the devil.

White. Not so, my lord, one of God's children.

L. C. J. By whom were you released?

White. By the commissioners, I suppose.

L. C. J. That is well, indeed, if we shall commit, and others set at liberty!

White. They did no more than they might do.

L. C. J. By which of the commissioners were you delivered?

White. I know not. There were the hands of four or five commissioners set to the warrant.

L. C. J. But who were they?

White. I suppose Sir Walter ——— and my Lord Mayor were two of them.

Master of Requests. How were you delivered?

White. Upon sureties.

M. Requests. How long is it since you were delivered?

White. Since the birth-day of our Lord.

L. C. J. How often, during this time, have you been at your parish church?

White. I could not go to any church, being myself, with sureties, bound to be a true prisoner in my own house.

L. C. J. Oh! you were glad of that.

White. Not so, my lord; for if I had been at liberty, I would have frequented the place of public preaching and prayer.

† Strype's Grindal, p. 136. ‡ MS. Register, p. 22—25.

§ Hist. of Puritans, vol. i. p. 220.

"scheme of church government appears to be calculated for "the overthrow of monarchy."* We are at a loss to say whether this calumny discovers greater ignorance or bigotry. The twofold charge is asserted without the least shadow of

Gerard. When were you bound to appear?

White. At any time, I suppose, when I should be called.

Gerard. You are now called: you must then answer.

White. I acknowledge it, and am here to answer.

L. C. J. Why will you not come to your parish church?

White. My lord, I did use to frequent my parish church before my troubles, and procured several godly men to preach there, as well as other places of preaching and prayer; and since my troubles, I have not frequented any private assemblies, but, as I have had liberty, have gone to my parish church. Therefore, they who have presented me, have done it out of malice; for if any of the things can be proved against me, or that I hold all things common, your lordship may dismiss me from hence to the gallows.

Gerard. You have not usually frequented your *own* church.

White. I allow I have more used other places, where I was better edified.

Gerard. Then your presentation is in part true.

White. Not so, if it please you; for I am presented for not coming at *all* to my parish church.

Gerard. Will you then come to prayers when there is no sermon?

White. I crave the liberty of a subject. But if I do not publicly frequent both preaching, prayer, and the sacraments, deal with me accordingly.

Master of the Rolls. You must answer yes or no.

White. You know my mind, how that I would avoid those things which are a grief to me, an offence to others, and disturb the quiet state of the church.

Dean. You disobey the queen's laws.

White. Not so, if it please you.

Dean. What fault do you find in the common prayer?

White. Let them answer to whom it appertains; for being in prison almost a whole year about these matters, I was indicted upon a statute relating to that book; and before I came to liberty, almost outlawed, as your worship Mr. Gerard knoweth.

M. Requests. What scripture have you to ground your conscience upon against these garments?

White. The whole scriptures are for destroying idolatry, and every thing belonging unto it.

M. Requests. These things never served to idolatry.

White. Shough! they are the same as those which heretofore were used for that purpose.

M. Requests. Where are they forbidden in scripture?

White. In Deuteronomy and other places, the Israelites are commanded, not only to destroy the altars, groves, and images, with all thereto belonging, but also to abolish the very *names*. And God by Isaiah commandeth us not to pollute ourselves with the garments of the image, but to cast them away as a *menstruous clout*.

M. Rolls. These are no part of idolatry, but are commanded by the prince for civil order; and if you will not be ordered you shew yourself disobedient to the laws.

White. I would not willingly disobey any law, only I would avoid those things which are not warranted by the word of God.

* Maddox's Vindication, p. 210.

evidence, excepting what might arise in his lordship's episcopal imagination. Mr. Hawkins and several others had been beneficed ministers in London, but were now silenced and persecuted for nonconformity. The rest were

M. Requests. You disobey the queen's laws; for these things are commanded by act of parliament.

Dean. Nay, you disobey God; for God commandeth you to obey your prince. Therefore in disobeying her in these things, you disobey God.

White. I do not avoid those things of contempt, but of conscience. In all other things I am an obedient subject.

L. C. J. The queen's majesty was overseen not to make thee of her council, to make laws and orders for religion.

White. Not so, my lord. I am to obey laws warranted by God's word.

L. C. J. Do the queen's laws command any thing against God's word?

White. I do not say so, my lord.

L. C. J. Yes, marry, you do; and there I will hold you.

White. Only God and his laws are absolutely perfect. All men and their laws may err.

L. C. J. This is one of Shaw's darlings. I tell thee what, I will not say any thing of affection, for I know thee not, saving by this occasion; thou art the wickedest, and most contemptuous person, that has come before me, since I sat in this commission.

White. Not so, my Lord; my conscience doth witness otherwise.

M. Requests. What if the queen should command to wear a grey frize gown, would you then come to church?

White. That were more tolerable, than that God's ministers should wear the habit of his enemies.

L. C. J. How if she should command them to wear a fool's coat and a cock's comb?

White. That were unseemly, my lord, for God's ministers.

Dean. You will not be obedient to the queen's commands.

White. I am, and will be, obedient.

M. Requests. Yes, you say so. But how are you obedient, when you will not do what she commandeth?

White. I would only avoid those things that have no warrant in the word of God, that are neither decent nor edifying, but flatly the contrary, and condemned by the foreign reformed churches.

M. Requests. Do the church and pews edify? And because the papists used these, will you, therefore, cast them away?

White. The church and pews, and such things, are both necessary and profitable.

Gerard. White, you were released, thinking you would be conformable, but you are worse than ever.

White. Not so, if it please you.

L. C. J. He would have no laws.

White. If there were no laws, I would live like a christian, and do no wrong, though I received wrong.

L. C. J. Thou art a rebel.

White. Not so, my lord; a true subject.

L. C. J. Yea, I swear by God, thou art a very rebel; for thou wouldst draw thy sword, and lift up thy hand against thy prince, if time served.

White. My lord, I thank God, my heart standeth right towards God and my prince; and God will not condemn, though your honour hath so judged.

L. C. J. Take him away.

worthy, religious persons, but great sufferers in the same cause. These proceedings against zealous protestants, of pious and sober lives, excited the compassion of all unprejudiced beholders, and brought many over to their interests. It was, indeed, a great grief to the prelates, to see persons

White. I would speak a word, which I am sure will offend, and yet I must speak it. I heard the name of God taken in vain. If I had done it, it had been a greater offence than that which I stand here for.

Gerard. White, White, you do not behave yourself well.

White. I pray your worship, shew me wherein, and I will beg your pardon and amend it.

L. C. J. I may swear in a matter of charity.

White. There is no such occasion now.

Gerard. White, you do much misuse yourself.

White. If I do, I am sorry for it.

M. Requests. There is none here but pitieth thee.

White. If it be so, I praise God for it. But because it is said, that at my last being before you, I denied the supremacy of my prince, I desire your honours and worships, with all that be present, to bear witness, that I acknowledge her majesty the chief governor, next under Christ, over all persons and causes within her dominions, and to this I will subscribe. I acknowledge the Book of Articles, and the Book of Common Prayer, as far as they agree with the word of God. I acknowledge the substance of the doctrine and sacraments of the church to be sound and sincere; and so I do of rites and orders, as far as they agree with the word of God.

Dean. Are not all things in the Articles and the Book of Common Prayer, taken out of the word of God?

White. Though they were; yet being done by man, I may not give them the same warrant as the writings of the Holy Ghost.

Dean. You will not then allow of sermons.

White. We are commanded to search the scriptures, and to try the spirits; therefore, we must allow of sermons as they agree with the scriptures.

L. C. J. Take him away.

White. I would to the Lord Jesus, that my two years' imprisonment might be a means of having these matters fairly decided by the word of God, and the judgment of other reformed churches.

L. C. J. You shall be committed, I warrant you.

White. Pray, my lord, let me have justice. I am unjustly prosecuted. I desire a copy of my presentment.

L. C. J. You shall have your head from your shoulders. Have him to the Gatehouse.

White. I pray you to commit me to some prison in London, that I may be near my house.

L. C. J. No, sir, you shall go thither.

White. I have paid fines and fees in other prisons; send me not where I must pay them again.

L. C. J. Yes, marry shall you. That is your glory.

M. Requests. It will cost you *twenty pounds*, I warrant you, before you come out.

White. God's will be done.

The good man was then carried to the Gatehouse; but how long he remained in a state of confinement, we are not able to learn. These severe proceedings, instead of crushing, greatly promoted the cause of puritanism. The sword of persecution was always found a bad argument to convince men of understanding and conscience.—*MS. Register*, p. 176—178.

going off from the first establishment of the protestant religion, concluding the service book to be unlawful, and the ecclesiastical state antichristian; and labouring to set up another kind of church government and discipline. But who drove them to these extremities? Why were not a few amendments made in the liturgy, by which conscientious persons might have been made easy; or, even liberty given them to worship God in their own way? How far these proceedings were justifiable by the laws of God, or consistent with that universal rule of conduct given by Jesus Christ, *Whatsoever ye would that men should do to you, do ye even so to them*, is left with the impartial reader to determine.

Andrew Kingsmill, LL.B.—This excellent person was born at Sidmanton in Hampshire, in the year 1538, educated in Corpus Christi college, Oxford, and elected fellow of All Souls college in the same university, in 1558. He studied the civil law, in the knowledge of which he made considerable proficiency. But while he was thus employed, he did not forget to seek first the kingdom of God and his righteousness. He discovered the warmest desires for a knowledge of the mysteries of the gospel, and for the attainment of which, he paid the closest application. He would receive nothing for truth, till he found the testimony of scripture for its support. By a constant and close attention to the word of God, its sacred pages became familiar to him; and, indeed, he so addicted himself to search and recite the holy scriptures, that he could readily repeat by heart, and in the Greek language, the whole of the epistles to the Romans and Galatians, the first epistle of John, and many other parts of the sacred volume.*

Mr. Kingsmill did not so much esteem the preferment and profit, to which he might easily have attained by the profession of the law, as the comfortable assurance and blessed hope of eternal life, and to be useful in preaching the gospel to his fellow creatures. He, therefore, relinquished the law, entered the sacred function, and became an admired preacher in the university of Oxford. For some time after the accession of Queen Elizabeth, there were only three preachers in this university, Dr. Humphrey, Dr. Sampson, and Mr. Kingsmill, all puritans. But upon

* Wood's Athenæ Oxon. vol. i. p. 125.

the rigorous imposition of conformity, Dr. Sampson being already deprived of his deanery, Mr. Kingsmill withdrew from the storm. He was averse to all severity in the imposition of habits and ceremonies; and being fixed in his nonconformity, he wrote a long letter to Archbishop Parker, against urging a conformity to the papists in habits, ceremonies, and other things equally superstitious.*

Upon Mr. Kingsmill's departure from the kingdom, he resolved to take up his abode among the best reformed churches, both for doctrine and discipline, that he could meet with in a foreign land. During the first three years, he settled at Geneva, where he was highly esteemed by persons eminent for learning and piety. Afterwards, he removed to Lausanne, where he died in the month of September, 1569, aged thirty-one years. Though he was a zealous puritan, and an avowed nonconformist, seeing he was a man of such great worth, and universally beloved, Wood found himself obliged to give him an excellent character. Accordingly, he says he was too good for this world, and left behind him a most excellent pattern of piety, devotion, and every other amiable virtue.†

His Works.—1. A View of Man's Estate, wherein the great Mercy of God in Man's free Justification is shewed, 1574.—2. An excellent and comfortable Treatise for all such as are in any manner of way either troubled in Mind or afflicted in Body, 1578.—3. Godly Advice touching Marriage, 1580.—4. A godly and learned Exhortation to bear patiently all Afflictions of the Gospel of Jesus Christ.—5. A Conference between a godly learned Christian and an afflicted Conscience, concerning a Conflict had with Satan.—7. A Sermon on John iii. 16.

Christopher Coleman was a zealous puritan, and one of the preachers to the congregation of separatists in London. In the year 1567, he was apprehended, with the rest of his brethren, at Plumbers-hall, and cast into prison, where he remained a long time. This heavy sentence was inflicted upon him, for separating from the established church, and holding private meetings for divine worship, when he could not in conscience conform to the church of England.‡ Having at length obtained his release, he wrote a letter, in the year 1569, to Secretary Cecil, earnestly urging him to employ his interest to promote a further

* Wood's Athenæ Oxon. vol. i. p. 126.—Strype's Parker, p. 157.
† Athenæ Oxon. vol. i. p. 126.
‡ See Art. Robert Hawkins.

reformation of the church. He is denominated from this letter a man of good intentions, but of little learning.* Mr. Coleman and his brethren, Messrs. Benson, Button, and Hallingham, are said to have been more ardently zealous in the cause of the reformation than any others; and it is observed, that they condemned the discipline of the church; the calling of the bishops, and the public liturgy, as savouring too much of the church of Rome; that they would allow of nothing in the public worship of God, besides what was expressly laid down in the holy scriptures; and that though the queen had commanded them to be *laid by the heels*, it is incredible how the number of their followers increased in all parts of the kingdom.†

William Axton was a truly pious man, a steady nonconformist, and a learned divine. He was some years rector of Moreton Corbet in Shropshire;‡ where Sir Robert Corbet, who was his great and worthy friend, protected him for some time from the severities of the prelates.§ Though under the wing of so excellent a patron, he found protection only for a season, and was brought into trouble for nonconformity. About the year 1570, he was cited before Dr. Bentham, bishop of Lichfield and Coventry, when he underwent several examinations for refusing the *apparel*, the *cross* in baptism, and *kneeling* at the sacrament. Upon his appearance, he debated these points with the bishop and his officers, with great freedom and courage. These examinations, now before me, though at considerable length, are here presented to the curious reader. Mr. Axton being brought before his ecclesiastical judges, the bishop thus addresed him:

Bishop. Though we allow you, Mr. Axton, to assign your reasons, you shall not be unanswered. Therefore set forth your reasons, and we will consider them.

Axton. If there be any odds in the disputation, it is on your side. For you are many, and I am but one, and have no equal judge or moderator; but I am content to set down my reasons, and leave them to God and your own con-

* Strype's Annals, vol. i. p. 568—570.

† Heylin's Hist. of Pres. p. 257, 258.

‡ Mr. Neal, by mistake, says Leicestershire.—*Hist. of Puritans*, vol. i. p. 238.

§ Sir Robert was a constant friend to the persecuted nonconformists, and often sheltered them from the tyrannical oppressions of the bishops.—*MS. Chronology*, vol. ii. p. 373. (14.)

sciences.—As the priesthood of Christ or of Aaron, and even their very garments, were most honourable: so the priesthood of antichrist, and even the very garments, as the cope and surplice, is most detestable.

B. Then you will condemn as unlawful, whatsoever the papists used in their idolatrous service.

A. Some things have been abused by idolaters, and yet are necessary and profitable in the service of God. Other things they have abused, which are neither necessary nor profitable. The former are to be retained, and the latter to be refused. The surplice hath been used by the priests of antichrist, and hath no necessary nor profitable use in the service of God, any more than any other thing used in idolatrous worship; therefore the surplice ought not to be used.

B. The surplice hath a *necessary* use.

A. If it have, you sin in omitting it at any time. In this you condemn the reformed churches abroad, for excluding a thing so necessary.

B. It is necessary, because the prince hath commanded it.

A. Indeed, it is so necessarily commanded, that without the use of it, a minister must not preach, nor administer the sacraments, however great are his learning, his gifts, and his godliness. This is a most wicked necessity.

B. But it is comely in the church of God.

A. What comeliness is it for the minister of Christ, to wear the rags of antichrist? If this be comely, then the velvet and golden copes, for the same reason, are more comely. But this is not the comeliness of the gospel.

B. You are not a judge whether the surplice be comely.

A. The apostle saith to all christians, "Try the spirits, whether they be of God." Is it then unlawful for a christian, and a minister of Christ, to judge of a ceremony of man's invention? The reformed churches have judged the surplice to be uncomely for the ministers of Christ. Luther, Calvin, Beza, Peter Martyr, and many others, have disallowed the use of it. And most learned men now in England, who use the surplice, wish with all their hearts, it were taken away. Yea, I think this is your opinion also. Ridley said "it was more fit for a player on the stage, than for a minister of God in his church."

B. We will not allow that the surplice is the garment of antichrist.

A. That which was consecrated by antichrist, and constantly worn by the priests of antichrist, in their idolatrous service, was one of the garments of antichrist. But the surplice was consecrated by antichrist, and constantly worn by the priests of antichrist in their idolatrous service. Therefore, the surplice is a garment of antichrist.

B. But this surplice which we use, was never used by idolatrous priests.

A. Then you confess that their surplices may not be used by us. Yet in many churches in England, the massing surplices and copes have been used, and are still used; which, by your own confession, are accursed and abominable. But when we speak of the surplice, we do not mean this or that surplice, but surplices in general.

Barker. How do you prove that?

A. When the king of Judah came to Damascus, and there saw a brazen altar, he sent the pattern of it to Jerusalem, commanding the high priest to make one like unto it, and set it up in the temple of God. This was as great a sin, as if he had set up the very same altar which he saw at Damascus; therefore, though we have not the very same surplice, we have one made like unto it, even as like that at Damascus as it can be made.

B. Then we will have it made shorter or longer than theirs, or wider or narrower.*

A. That is a poor shift. You know, that nearly all the surplices in England are like the papists' surplices.

B. I have a cup like the papists' calice, and is it unlawful for me to use it?

A. Your cup is not used in the service of God, nor is it convenient for that purpose. But supposing it were both convenient and useful in the supper of the Lord, it cannot be compared with the surplice, which is neither convenient nor useful.

B. We have appointed the surplice for another end, than the papists did.

A. You cannot appoint it to any good end. According to what you now plead, you may bring into the church

* The profound reasoning of the reverend prelate, reminds us of an anecdote we have met with concerning a pious minister, who, in the reign of Queen Elizabeth, was urged by his ordinary to wear the surplice; but who, in addition to other reasons, alleged, that the surplice offered him to put on, was the *very same* surplice as the mass-priest had used. The bishop admitted the excuse, and commanded another to be made; and when it was taken to the church, the minister took it up, and thus addressed the people present:—"Good people," said he, "the bishop himself confessed, that the former *massing* surplice was not to be worn by a minister of the gospel; but judge you if this be as like that, as one eye is like another? Let this, therefore, go after the other:" and so he cast it away.—*Ames' Fresh Suit*, part ii. p. 435.

of God, nearly all the trash of popery, their candles, their torches, their banners, their oil in baptism, and nearly all other things pertaining to antichrist.

B. Yes; and why not, if it please the prince, seeing they are things in their own nature indifferent.

A. I beseech you in the Lord, mind what you say. Shall we again bring tapers into the church of God, and oil into the sacrament of baptism?

B. Yes; and why not? Is not oil one of the sacraments in the church of God? Why do you speak so contemptuously of oil?

A. It is no contempt to exclude oil, milk, salt, or any such thing, from the sacrament. And why do you call oil a sacrament, seeing it is neither a sacrament, nor any sign of a sacrament?

B. Though it be no sacrament now, it was in the time of the apostles.

A. To speak properly, it never was a sacrament, the nature and use of which is to remember and seal unto us the mercies of God in Christ Jesus.

B. This is talk. You do not allege the scriptures.

A. You cannot drink the cup of the Lord, and the cup of devils; and ye cannot partake of the table of the Lord, and the table of devils. Meats, drinks, and apparel, are all of the same nature; therefore, being consecrated to idolatry, they are condemned. So it is said, "Ye shall also defile the covering of the graven images of silver, and the ornament of the molten image of gold: Thou shalt cast them away as a menstruous cloth; thou shalt say unto it, get thee hence. And whether ye eat or drink, or whatsoever ye do, do all to the glory of God." But the surplice, and the wearing of it, is not for the glory of God, therefore not to be worn.

B. The surplice is for the glory of God.

A. That which promotes the glory of the papists, does not promote the glory of God; but the wearing of the surplice promotes the glory and triumph of the papists, and, therefore, not to be worn.

B. I deny your argument.

A. It is a syllogism.

B. You are full of your syllogisms.

A. Our reason is the gift of God, and the right use of it is to find out the truth.

B. But a syllogism may be false. Let us proceed to your second argument.

A. I will allege one reason more. We ought to be without offence to the Jew, to the Gentile, and to the church of God. But our wearing the surplice is an offence to the Jew, and the Gentile, (meaning the papists) and the church of God. Therefore we ought not to wear the surplice.

B. How will you be an offence to the papists by wearing the surplice?

A. By offence, the apostle does not mean to *grieve*, but to be an occasion to another to *sin*. But if I wear the surplice, I shall be an occasion or encouragement to the papists to sin. Therefore I may not wear it.

B. How will you be an offence to the church of God? You perhaps may be to three or four; but you must regard the greater part.

A. I should be an offence to the greater part, and the lesser part, and all the church of God.

B. How do you prove that?

A. I should be an offence to the lesser part, being those who are effectually called, because their souls are exceedingly grieved with those who do wear it. And to the greater part, being such as are beginning to dislike popery, and follow true religion; who, by wearing it, would be ready to give up their zeal, and return to popery.

B. You must teach them to hate popery, though you wear the surplice.

A. If I teach them one thing, and I myself do the contrary, how will they believe me? You know most people look more at our doings, than our doctrine.—Hitherto I have given my reasons against wearing the surplice; if you have any reasons to shew why I *should* wear it, let me hear a few of the best.

Barker. That which doth not offend in its institution, matter, form, or use, is not to be refused. But the surplice doth not offend in its institution, matter, form, or use. Therefore it may not be refused.

A. Your reasoning is not good. You must first prove that the surplice has not been abused, and is not offensive, then will you conclude better.

Walton. If nothing may be used in the church, that has been abused to idolatry, then the pulpits, and even the churches, of the papists, may not be used.

A. This, in effect, hath been already answered. Prove that the surplice is as useful as the pulpit and the church, and you will do something.

Chancellor. Then you deny that the prince hath any authority to command things indifferent.

A. You have said more than I have done all day. Your unjust charge is contrary to what I have said. I wonder you can charge me so falsely to my face.

B. You run to your former distinction.

A. It is not my distinction, but Tertullian's; and it is that distinction which you will never be able to condemn. I trust I have now confirmed the truth, and shewed sufficient reason why I may not wear the surplice, there being no reason why I should.

B. No, indeed! your reasons are no reasons.

A. They are such as have not yet been answered, and I am persuaded, will not be answered. I am not afraid that all these things should be made known, that the learned may judge.

C. Yes, you would have them in print, would you not?

A. I thought of no such thing. But, as a witness for the truth, I am not ashamed that these things should undergo the examination of the learned and the godly.*

The second conference was about the use and signification of the *cross* in baptism. Upon Mr. Axton's appearance before the bishop and others, being required to deliver his opinion, he spoke as follows:

A. Nothing may be added to the institution of Christ: as, *I have received of the Lord, that which also I delivered unto you.* But the cross in baptism is an addition to the institution of Christ. Therefore the cross in baptism is unlawful.

B. The necessary parts of the sacrament are to be retained; but whether the water be poured upon the child's forehead, or it be marked with a cross, being ceremonial, is left to the determination of the church.

A. If you produce as good warrant from the word, for the crossing of the child, as I can for the washing of it, then I will grant that the church has authority so to determine. But such warrant cannot be produced. Besides, we have just reason to leave out the cross, because papists abuse it to superstition and idolatry, and in itself it is entirely useless.

C. Do you then say it is a sin to make any cross?

A. It is no sin in the carpenter, the mason, or the mathe-

* MS. Register, p. 26—37.

matician, making crosses, any more than it is in his making lines and angles.

B. You would take away the liberty of the church, to establish or alter these things.

A. The church is the spouse, and hath no authority to introduce any thing that will dishonour Jesus Christ, her true husband.

B. Hath not the church liberty to use the font, or the bason, or both?

A. The church may use that which is necessary, to hold the water for baptism, as becometh the institution of Christ.

B. But I can shew you that matters of greater importance were altered by the apostles themselves.

A. What are they?

B. That they might not baptize in the name of the Father, the Son, and the Holy Ghost.

A. Do you mean that the apostles did not always baptize in the name of the Father, the Son, and the Holy Ghost?

B. Yes; and I can shew you that they did not always use that form of words.—"For," it is said, "as yet the Holy Ghost was come upon none of them, only they were baptized in the name of the Lord Jesus. And he commanded them to be baptized in the name of the Lord."

A. Because they were baptized in the name of the Lord Jesus, does that prove they were not baptized in the name of the Father, the Son, and the Holy Ghost? How can you from this, charge the apostles with altering the institution of their Master; they baptized in the name of the Lord Jesus; therefore, you say, they did not baptize in the name of the Father, the Son, and the Holy Ghost. Because one part of the action is mentioned, does that prove they did not attend to the other parts?

C. You may not take such advantage of my lord.

B. I did not say, that the apostles did not baptize in the name of the Father, the Son, and the Holy Ghost; but that it was probable they did not.

A. Yes, you said you could shew this; and you have not shewn it to be certain, or even probable.

B. The cross, you say, is no part of baptism: only an addition to the sacrament. What say you then of the signification of the cross?

A. To use such signs, tokens, or instructions in the service of God, which are only the inventions of men, is the fancy of papists. And they draw us not unto the spiritual service of God, but from it.

B. But the cross is used as a token only, that we should not be ashamed of the cross of Christ.

W. And is it not lawful to be taught not to be ashamed of Christ?

A. Yes; but we may not teach by unlawful means. Where doth the word of God warrant us, that making a cross, signifies that we should not be ashamed of Christ?

W. Would you then take all symbolical signs out of the church of God?

B. The church hath authority to ordain all symbolical signs, that are useful in the church. Therefore the church hath authority to ordain the cross in baptism.

A. This is only begging the question. You are as far from the mark as ever.

B. Is not the cross a symbolical sign, that is useful in the church of God?

A. That is the point in dispute, and yet remains to be proved.

B. What scriptures have you against the cross?

A. In the second commandment, we are forbidden to use in the service of God, "The likeness of any thing." But the cross in baptism is the likeness of something: Therefore the cross in baptism is forbidden, and may not be used.

C. May we not then make the likeness of any thing?

A. The commandment meaneth, that we should make no likeness of any thing for a religious purpose. We may not make the likeness of any thing in heaven or earth, for a religious purpose. But the cross in baptism is the likeness of something in heaven or earth, and appointed for a religious purpose. Therefore we may not make the cross in baptism. The making of the cross, because for a religious purpose, is here forbidden.

Barker. The cross in baptism is not forbidden in the *first* commandment.

A. I did not say it was. It is sufficient that it is forbidden in the *second.*

Barker. But the same thing is meant in them both.

A. You confound the first and second commandments, and, like the papists, make them to be the same. I must say, this is great ignorance.

Barker. I am not so ignorant as you suppose.

A. Your own words do betray you.

B. You are too captious. He shall reason you out of it.

Barker. The making of the cross in baptism is not forbidden in all the prophets; and, therefore, not in the commandment.

A. You had better first prove, that the cross is not forbidden in all the prophets. Your reasoning is not good.

C. If God have bestowed better gifts upon you, than upon others, you must thank him for it; but not contemn other mens' gifts.

A. God forbid that I should contemn the gifts of God in any man.

B. What say you about kneeling at the communion?

A. Jesus Christ and his apostles received the communion sitting, and why may we not imitate them?

Barker. Jesus Christ, with his apostles, celebrated the communion sitting, because he had immediately before, celebrated the passover sitting.

A. After the celebration of the passover, Christ *arose* and washed the feet of his disciples. Then it is said, he did again *sit down* to celebrate the communion; which shews, that he preferred doing it *sitting*, rather than in any other posture.*

B. Mr. Axton, I have other questions to propose to you. What think you of the calling of bishops, or of my calling?

A. I am not ignorant of the danger I may fall into, by answering your question. Yet I am not compelled to answer it, not being accused of any crime.

B. Yes, I may compel you to answer upon your oath.

A. But I may choose whether I will answer you upon my oath.

B. I may urge you with your own speeches, which you delivered the last time you were before me.

A. What I then spoke to the glory of God, that will I also speak now.

* The learned Beza, in his letter to Bishop Grindal, said, "If you have rejected the doctrine of transubstantiation, and the practice of adoring the host, why do you symbolize with popery, and seem to hold both by kneeling at the sacrament? Kneeling had never been thought of, had it not been for transubstantiation." Grindal replied, that though the sacrament was to be received kneeling, yet the rubric accompanied the service book, and informed the people, that no adoration of the elements was intended. "O! I understand you," said Beza, "there was a certain *great lord*, who repaired his house, and, having finished it, left before his gate, a great stone, for which he had no occasion. This stone caused many people in the dark to stumble and fall. Complaint was made to his lordship, and many a humble petition was presented, praying for the removal of the stone; but he remained long obstinate. At length, he condescended to order a *lanthorn* to be hung over it. My lord, said one, if you would be pleased to rid yourself of further solicitation, and to quiet all parties, order the stone and the candle to be both removed."—*Robinson's Claude*, vol. ii. p. 77.

B. You then said, that every minister of God is a bishop, and to be a bishop is only to be a minister of God. You said also, that no bishop in England had authority to excommunicate.

A. I said so, indeed; and proved what I said by the word of God. I am not bound to bring myself into danger; but because I am persuaded it will advance God's glory, I will speak, be the consequence what it will. I trust in the Holy Spirit, that I shall be willing to die in defence of the truth.

B. Then what say you of my calling?

A. You are not lawfully called to be a bishop, according to the word of God.

B. I thought so: But why?

A. For three reasons,—1. Because you were not ordained by the consent of the eldership.

B. But I had the hands of three or four bishops.

A. That is not the eldership St. Paul speaks of, 1 Tim. iv. 14.

B. By what eldership were you ordained? Was it not by a bishop?

A. I had, indeed, the laying on of the hands of one of the bishops of England, but that was the least part of my calling.

B. What calling had you more?

A. I having exercised and expounded the word several times in an orderly assembly of ten ministers, they joined in prayer; and being required to speak their consciences, they declared upon the trial they had of me, that they were persuaded I might become a profitable labourer in the house of God. After this I received the laying on of the hand of the bishop.

B. But you had not the laying on of the hands of those preachers.

A. No: I had the substance, but wanted the accident; and in this, I beseech the Lord to be merciful unto me. For the laying on of hands, as it is the *word*, so it is agreeable to the mighty action of ordaining the ministers of God.

A. Then your ordination is imperfect as well as mine.

A. Mine is imperfect for want of the accident: the Lord be merciful to me for it. And yours is imperfect for want of the substance.

B. What is your second reason?

A. Because you are not ordained bishop over any *one flock*,

Nay, you are not a pastor to any one congregation, contrary to 1 Pet. v. 2. and Acts xiv. 23., "Feed the flock." From which it is manifest there should be a bishop and elders in every congregation.

B. What is a congregation?

A. Not a whole diocese, but such a number of people as ordinarily assemble in one place, to hear the word of God.

B. What if you had a parish six or seven miles long, where many could not come to hear you once in a quarter of a year?

A. I would not be pastor of such a flock.

B. What is your third reason?

A. Because you are not chosen by the people. Acts xiv. 23.

C. How came you to be parson of Moreton Corbet?

A. I am no *parson.*

C. Are you then vicar?

A. No: I am no vicar. I abhor those names as antichristian. I am pastor of the congregation there.

C. Are you neither parson nor vicar? How hold you the living?

A. I receive those temporal things of the people, because, being their pastor, I minister to them spiritual things.

C. If you be neither parson nor vicar, you must receive no profit.

A. Do you mean in good faith what you say?

C. Yes, if you will be neither parson nor vicar, there is good cause why another should.

B. You must understand, that all livings in the church are given to ministers as parsons and vicars, and not as pastors and ministers.

A. I am sure the names of parsons and vicars were not given by Jesus Christ, but by antichrist.

B. How were you chosen pastor?

A. By the free election of the people, according to the word of God.

B. Why, did not the patron place you there?

A. The patron allowed the people the free choice of their minister; and after I had preached about six weeks by way of probation, I was chosen by one consent of them all, and a sermon was preached by one of my brethren, setting forth the mutual duties of pastor and people.

B. May the bishops of England ordain ministers?

A. You ought not to do it in the manner you do, without the consent of the eldership, without sufficient proof of their qualifications, and without ordaining them to some particular congregation.

C. How do you like my lord's book of articles.

A. Some of the articles approach near to the institution of the apostles, but the best of them appear to be very little practised.

B. I admit none to the ministry but those who have a recommendation from some nobleman or gentleman.

A. You had need beware of breaking the institution of God. This door being opened, will admit thieves and robbers. The Lord give you a sound conscience to keep hirelings out of the church of God.

B. Well, Mr. Axton, you must yield in some things to me, and I will yield in some things to you. I will not trouble you about the cross in baptism, if you will sometimes wear the surplice.

A. I cannot consent to wear the surplice: it is against my conscience. I trust, by the help of God, I shall never put on that sleeve which is the mark of the beast.

B. Will you leave your flock for the surplice?

A. Nay: Will you persecute me from my flock for the surplice? I love my flock in Jesus Christ, and had rather have my right arm cut off than be removed from them.

B. Well, I will not deprive you at this time.

A. I beseech you consider what you do in removing me from my flock, seeing I am not come in at the window, nor by simony, but according to the institution of Jesus Christ.*

The second day's conference concluded as above, when Mr. Axton was taken away, the bishop requiring his future attendance. Accordingly, upon his appearance at the time appointed, he underwent a third examination concerning the use of instrumental music in the public worship of God, and obedience to the queen's laws, with some other things. Being questioned about the use of organs in public worship, he replied as follows:

A. They are Jewish, and not to be used in christian congregations.

Bickley. Did not David command organs and cymbals to be used?

A. That command was ceremonial, and is abrogated.

Bickley. You will then abrogate singing in the church, because David and the Jews sung.

A. Piping with instruments is abolished.

Bickley. How do you prove that?

A. Because our joy in public worship must be more

* MS. Register, p. 27—50.

spiritual than that of the Jews; and it is said, that in the time of the gospel, all shall sing praises unto God.

Bickley. The organs are used before the prince.

A. That does not prove them to be lawful.

Bickley. The organs are used before the prince, and therefore they are lawful. The argument is good.

A. Do you then reason, that the cross in churches is lawful, because it used to stand before the prince?

Bickley. As it stood before the prince, it might have been lawfully used.

A. From what you say, tapers, and lights, and nearly all the trash of popery, may still be lawfully used.

Bickley. If you had the cross on which Christ died, would you say it was of no use?

A. After the crucifixion of Christ, as well as before, the cross on which he died was the same as any other piece of wood.

B. But, in refusing the surplice, you are disloyal to the queen, and shew your contempt of her laws.

A. In charging me with disloyalty, you do me great injury; and especially when you call me and my brethren traitors, and say, that we are more troublesome subjects than papists.

B. I say the same still. The papists are afraid to stir; but you are presumptuous, and disquiet the state more than papists.

A. If I, or any others who fear God, speak the truth, doth this disquiet the state? The papists for twelve years have been plotting treason against the queen and the gospel, yet this doth not grieve you. But I protest in the presence of God and you all, that I am a true and faithful subject to her majesty. I pray daily, both in public and private, for her safety, for her long and prosperous reign, and for the overthrow of all her enemies, especially the papists. I do profess myself an enemy to her enemies, and a friend to her friends. If, therefore, you have any conscience, cease to charge me with disloyalty to my prince.

B. Seeing you refuse to wear the surplice, which her majesty hath commanded, you do in effect deny her to be supreme governess in all causes ecclesiastical and temporal.

A. I do so far admit her majesty's supremacy, that if there be any error among the governors of the church, she has power to reform it: but I do not admit her to be an ecclesiastical elder, or church governor.

B. Yes, but she is, and hath full power and authority all

manner of ways. Indeed, she doth not administer the sacraments and preach, but leaveth those things to us. But if she were a man, as she is a woman, why might she not preach the word, as well as ourselves?

A. Might she preach the word of God, if she were a man? Then she might also administer the sacraments.

B. That does not follow. For you know Paul preached, but did not baptize.

A. Paul confesseth that he did baptize, though he was sent especially to preach.

B. Did not Moses teach the people, and yet he was a civil governor.

A. The calling of Moses was extraordinary. Remember the king of Judah, how he would have sacrificed in the temple of God. Take heed how you confound those offices which God hath distinguished.

B. You see how he runneth.

Bickley. He speaketh very confidently and rashly.

B. This is his arrogant spirit.

Sale. Why should you refuse the surplice, seeing the queen hath commanded it?

Bickley. The queen hath authority to command all things indifferent.

A. If those things be decent, tend to edification, and promote God's glory; but the surplice does none of these.

Bickley. Has not the church liberty to command the surplice to be used, as well as any other garment?

A. No: because the surplice hath been abused, and is still abused, by the papists, in their superstition and idolatry.

Bickley. I deny your reasons.

A. I prove what I said thus: God will not allow his church to borrow ceremonies from idolators, or to imitate them in their ceremonies, as is evident from Ezekiel xliv. But the papists are idolators. Therefore, God will not allow us to borrow our ceremonies, as garments and other things, from the papists.

Bickley. How do you prove that out of Ezekiel?

A. I prove it thus: The Egyptian priests used to shave their heads; but God commanded his priests should not shave. The Egyptian priests used to drink wine: but God commanded his priests, that when they did sacrifice, they should not drink wine. And the Egyptian priests wore linen garments before the people: but God commanded that his priests should not sanctify the people with their garments.

B. God commanded the contrary. Do you not remember the garments of Aaron?

A. I do remember them. But if you would wear the garments of Aaron, you must attend to the other ceremonies of Aaron's priesthood.

B. Shew your place in Ezekiel. There is no such place. You are deceived.

A. I will thank you for a Bible.

B. You should have brought your own books with you. You see, I have brought my books.

A. And have you not a Bible among them? I pray you let me have a Bible.

B. Let him have the Hebrew Bible.

A. I pray you, let me have the Hebrew Bible.

Bickley. Then let us hear you read the place.

A. The place is this: "And when they go forth into the outer court, even into the outer court of the people, they shall put off their garments wherein they ministered, and lay them in the holy chambers, and they shall put on other garments; and they shall not sanctify the people with their garments."*

Here the dispute broke off. And notwithstanding all his entreaties and supplications, though the bishop† acknowledged him to be a divine of good learning, a strong memory, and well qualified for the pulpit, the good man was deprived of his living, and driven to seek his bread

* MS. Register, p. 50—56.

† Bishop Bentham complied with popery in the reign of Henry VIII., but afterwards repented. Upon the accession of Queen Mary, being perpetual fellow of Magdalen college, Oxford, he was required to correct the junior scholars for their absence from the popish worship, but refused, saying, "He had indeed but too much repented of his compliance with the popish religion already; and he esteemed it unjust to punish that in others, which he himself would willingly and knowingly do." He was one of the preachers to the protestant congregation which assembled in private places, during this queen's reign; and it is said, "that by his encouragement and constant preaching, the protestants did not only stand to their former principle, but were resolved to suffer whatever could be laid upon them, rather than forfeit a good conscience." He witnessed the sufferings of many of the martyrs; and notwithstanding the cruel proclamation, "that no man should either pray for or speak to them, or once say *God bless them*," Bentham seeing the fire set to some of them, turned his eyes to the people, and said, "We know they are the people of God; and therefore we cannot choose but wish them well, and say *God strengthen them*:" and so he boldly cried out, "Almighty God, for Christ's sake, strengthen them!" upon which all the people with one accord, cried, *Amen*, *Amen*; the noise of which was so great, from the vast crowd of people, that the officers knew not whom to seize, or against whom to bring their accusations. Bentham would have done well to have remembered these things when he became a lord bishop, and a persecutor of his fellow protestants.—*Biographia Britan.* vol. ii. p. 208. Edit. 1778.

in a foreign land. But, surely, such proceedings were unworthy of a protestant prelate, and too obvious an imitation of the popish severities. Do we find any such proceedings in the first ages of the church of Christ? "I am sure," says the learned Dr. Stillingfleet, "it is contrary to the primitive practice, and the moderation then used, to suspend or deprive men of their ministerial functions, for not consenting to habits, gestures, and the like."*

THOMAS BECON.—This celebrated divine was born in Suffolk, and educated in the university of Cambridge. He afterwards became chaplain to Archbishop Cranmer, and a zealous advocate for the reformation, even from its very commencement in the reign of King Henry VIII. He endured many troubles from the persecuting prelates; and in the year 1544, was apprehended, with Mr. Robert Wisdome, another excellent reformer, by the cruel Bishop Bonner, when he was obliged to make a public recantation at Paul's cross, and burn his books.† Having obtained his release, he travelled for future safety towards the north, and settled at Alsop in the Dale, in the Peak of Derbyshire, where he taught school for his subsistence. At this place, Mr. Alsop, a pious gentleman, and an avowed friend to the reformation, shewed him much civility, and afforded him seasonable relief.

The severity of the times not suffering the zealous and faithful servants of the Lord to abide long in any one place, Mr. Becon was obliged to move into Staffordshire, where he was kindly entertained in the house of Mr. John Old, a man eminently distinguished for charity and piety. Mr. Wisdome, mentioned above, was also entertained with him. Mr. Becon, in his treatise, entitled "The Jewel of Joy," published in the reign of King Edward, gives this character of Mr. Old: "He was to me and Wisdome, as Jason was to Paul and Silas: he received us joyfully into his house, and liberally, for the Lord's sake, ministered to our necessities. And as he began, so did he continue a right hearty friend, and dearly loving brother, so long as we remained in the country.‡ Here, as in his former situation, he educated children in good literature and sound christian doctrine, continuing, at the same time, in a close application to his studies. Afterwards, he removed into Leicestershire,

* Conformist's Plea, p. 14. Edit. 1681. From "Irenicum."
† Fox's Martyrs, vol. ii. p. 45. ‡ Strype's Cranmer, p. 276, 277.

where he was for some time hospitably entertained by the Marquis of Dorset. Here he contracted a familiar acquaintance with Mr. John Aylmer, afterwards the famous bishop of London, whom he calls his countryman.* He next removed into Warwickshire, where he still occupied the office of tutor to gentlemens' sons. Upon this last removal, to his great joy, he met with his old friend, the famous Hugh Latimer; who, about twenty years before, while they were at Cambridge, had been instrumental in bringing him to the knowledge of the gospel.

During the reign of Henry VIII. the city of Canterbury was more hostile to the reformation than most other places; therefore, upon the accession of King Edward, Archbishop Cranmer placed in that city six of the most distinguished preachers for learning and piety; among whom was Mr. Becon. The others were Nicholas Ridley, afterwards bishop of London and martyr, Lancelot Ridley, Richard Turner, Richard Beasely, and John Joseph. The ministry of these learned divines proved a great blessing to the place, and, by their labours, many persons were brought to embrace the gospel.† Also, during the reign of the above excellent prince, Mr. Becon, justly denominated a worthy and reverend divine, became chaplain to the protector Somerset, and was made professor of divinity in the university of Oxford, where he gained much reputation.‡ But upon the accession of Queen Mary, he was apprehended in London, with Mr. Veron and Mr. John Bradford, and committed to the Tower. Here he remained above seven months in close confinement, meeting with most cruel usage; and having been made rector of St. Stephen, Walbrook, London, in 1547, he was deprived of both his office and benefit.§

It was, indeed, nearly miraculous that this zealous reformer escaped the fire. While many of his brethren, and even those committed with him to the Tower, suffered at the stake, a kind providence constantly watched over him, and at length delivered him from the rage of all his enemies. During the reign of King Henry and former part of Queen Mary, Mr. Becon, to conceal himself from his malicious foes, who narrowly watched for his life, went by the name of Theodore Bazil, and in the proclamation of the king, in 1546, as well as that of the queen, in 1555, he

* Strype's Aylmer, p. 7.
† Strype's Cranmer, p. 161, 423.
‡ Churton's Life of Nowell, p. 21.—Lupton's Divines, p. 331.
§ Strype's Cranmer, p. 423.—Newcourt's Repert. Eccl. vol. i. p. 540.

is specified by that name.* At length, having been driven from one situation to another, and finding no place of safety in his own country, he fled into a foreign land, and became an exile in Germany. During his abode on the continent, he wrote an excellent letter to his godly brethren at home; in which, besides declaring the cause of those calamities now come upon England, he earnestly directed them to the mercy and faithfulness of God, for a redress of all their grievances. This letter was read in the private religious meetings of his persecuted countrymen, to their great edification and benefit. He wrote, also, an epistle to the popish priests, wherein he made a just and an important difference betwixt the Lord's supper, and the popish mass, denominating the latter a *wicked idol.*†

Mr. Becon remained in exile till the accession of Queen Elizabeth, when he returned to his native country, and became a most faithful and zealous labourer in the vineyard of Christ. Having obtained distinguished reputation, he was soon preferred to several ecclesiastical benefices. He is said to have been designed for one of the chief preferments then vacant.‡ In the year 1560, he became rector of Buckland in Hertfordshire, but most probably did not hold it long. About the same time, he was preferred to a prebend in the church of Canterbury; and in 1563, he became rector of St. Dionis Back-church, London. This last he held to his death.§

In the year 1564, when conformity was rigorously imposed upon the London clergy, Mr. Becon, with many of his puritan brethren, was cited before Archbishop Parker at Lambeth, and refusing to subscribe, he was immediately sequestered and deprived; though it is said, he afterwards complied, and was preferred.‖ It does not, however, appear what preferment he obtained. During the same year, he revised and republished most of his numerous and excellent writings in three volumes folio, dedicating them to all the bishops and archbishops of the realm. The clergy were in general at this time in a state of deplorable ignorance. Mr. Becon was deeply affected with their situation, and extremely anxious to render them all the assistance in his power. Therefore, in the year 1566, he published a book, entitled "A new Postil, containing most godly and learned Sermons,

* MS. Chronology, vol. i. p. 221. (3 | 3.)

† Strype's Cranmer, p. 357, 358.

‡ Churton's Life of Nowell, p. 40.

§ Strype's Parker, p. 72, 180.—Newcourt's Repert. Eccl. vol. i. p. 330, 814.

‖ Strype's Grindal, p. 98.

to be read in the Church throughout the Year; lately set forth unto the great Profit, not only of all Curates and Spiritual Ministers, but also of all Godly and Faithful Readers." Mr. Strype stiles him a famed preacher and writer, and the book a very useful work, containing honest, plain sermons upon the gospels, for all the Sundays in the year, to be read by the curates of congregations. The preface, dated from Canterbury, July 16, 1566, is addressed "to his fellow labourers in the Lord's harvest, the ministers and preachers of God's most holy word;" in which he earnestly exhorts them to the discharge of their important duties. To this Postil he added two prayers, one at some length, the other shorter, either of which was to be said before sermon, according to the minister's discretion: also a third prayer, to be repeated after sermon. These prayers and sermons were drawn up for the use of ministers who were not able to compose prayers and sermons, and for the further instruction of the people in sound and wholesome doctrine.* Bishop Parkhurst published verses in commendation of Mr. Becon and his excellent writings.† During the above year, he preached the sermon at Paul's cross; and such was his great fame, and such his favour among persons of distinction, that the lord mayor for that year presented a petition to Archbishop Parker, entreating his grace to prevail upon him to preach one of the sermons at the Spittle the following Easter.‡

Our historians are divided in their opinion concerning the time of Mr. Becon's death. Newcourt observes that he died previous to September 26, 1567; and Lupton says he died in 1570.§ He was a divine of great learning and piety, a constant preacher, a great sufferer in the cause of Christ, and an avowed enemy to pluralities, nonresidence, and all the relics of popery,‖ being ever zealous for the reformation of the church. He was a man of a peaceable spirit, always adverse to the imposition of ceremonies, and an avowed nonconformist, both in principle and practice. Mr. Strype justly denominates him famous for his great learning, his frequent preaching, his excellent writings, and manifold sufferings in the reigns of King Henry, King Edward, Queen Mary, and Queen Elizabeth.¶ One Mr. Thomas

* Strype's Parker, p. 228. † Lupton's Modern Divines, p. 332.
‡ Strype's Cranmer, p. 424.
§ Repert. Eccl. vol. i. p. 330.—Hist. of Divines, p. 332.
‖ MS. Chronology, vol. i. p. 48.
¶ Strype's Cranmer, p. 423.—Parker, p. 130.

Becon was of St. John's college, Cambridge, public orator and proctor in the university, and an active leading man, most probably in the cause of nonconformity, by which he is said to have incurred the displeasure of the chancellor, formerly his patron and great admirer. This was undoubtedly the same person.* He was author of numerous books, many of which were designed to expose the superstitions and errors of popery, and to encourage his fellow christians under persecution; and his labour of love was signally useful. He wrote against the superstitious practice of bowing at the name of Jesus, as did several other puritans after him. According to Mr. Lupton, the following appears to be the most correct list of his numerous learned writings that can now be obtained:

His Works.—1. News from Heaven.—2. A Banquet of Christ's Birth.—3. A Quadragesimal Feast.—4. A Method of Praying.—5. A Bundle or Posey of Flowers.—6. An Invective against Swearing.—7. Discipline for a Christian Soldier.—8. David's Harp.—9. The Government of Virtue.—10. A short Catechism.—11. A Book of Matrimony.—12. A Christian's New-Year's Gift.—13. A Jewel of Mirth.—14. Principles of the Christian Religion.—15. A Treatise of Fasting.—16. The Castle of Comfort.—17. The Soul's Solace.—18. The Tower of the Faithful.—19. The Christian Knight.—20. Homilies against Whoredom.—21. The Flowers of Prayers.—22. A sweet Box of Prayers.—23. The Sick Man's Medicine.—24. A Dialogue of Christ's Nativity.—25. An Invective against Idolatry.—26. An Epistle to the distressed Servants of God.—27. A Supplication to God for the Restoration of his Word.—28. The Rising of the Popish Mass.†—29. Common-places of Scripture.—30. A Comparison betwixt the Lord's Supper and the Papal Mass.—31. Articles of Religion confirmed by the Authority of the Fathers.—32. The monstrous Wages of the Roman Priests.—33. Romish Relics.—34. The Difference betwixt God's Word and Human Inventions.—35. Acts of Christ and Antichrist, with their Lives and Doctrine.—36. Chronicles of Christ.—37. An Abridgement of the New Testament.—38. Questions of the Holy Scripture.—39. The glorious Triumph of God's Word.—40. The Praise of Death.—41. Postils upon all the Sundays' Gospels.—42. A Disputation upon the Lord's Supper.

Gilbert Alcock was an excellent minister of puritan principles, but silenced, with many of his brethren, for nonconformity. April 3, 1571, he presented a supplication to the convocation, in behalf of himself and his suffering brethren,

* Baker's MS. Collection, vol. i. p. 193.

† This excellent work was reprinted in the time of Archbishop Laud; but upon the complaint of a popish priest, his grace commanded it to be suppressed, and threatened the printer with a prosecution. Such was the spirit and inclination of this *protestant* prelate.—*Canterburies Doome*, p. 516.

earnestly soliciting the house to consider their case, and redress their grievances. In this supplication, now before me, he spoke with considerable freedom and boldness, concerning the corruptions of the church. He expressed himself as follows:—"The ceremonies now retained in the church, and urged upon the consciences of christians, occasion the blind to stumble and fall, the obstinate to become more hard-hearted, Christ's messengers are persecuted, the holy sacrament is profaned, God dishonoured, the truth despised, christian duty broken, and the hearts of many are sorely vexed: they cause papists and wicked men to rejoice in superstition, error, idolatry, and wickedness: they set friends at variance, and provoke the curse of God. *Woe unto him by whom the offence cometh.*

"The godfathers and godmothers, who promise to do so much for the child, are the pope's kindred; and, by his canon law, like priests, are forbidden to marry. It is holden that kneeling in the public sacrament, is more reverent, more religious, and more honourable to God; and thus they make themselves wiser than Jesus Christ, who sat with his disciples at the last supper. Matt. xxvi. *In vain do ye worship me, teaching for doctrines the commandments of men.*

"If a minister preach true doctrine and live virtuously, yet omit the least ceremony for conscience sake, he is immediately indicted, deprived, cast into prison, and his goods wasted and destroyed; he is kept from his wife and children, and at last excommunicated, even though the articles brought against him be ever so false.* How heavy these ceremonies lie upon the consciences of christians; and what difference there is between them, and those for which the people of God have been, and are still, so much persecuted, judge ye, as ye expect to be judged in the day of judgment. Those who observe your ceremonies, though they be idolaters, common swearers, adulterers, or much worse, live without punishment, and have many friends. We, therefore, beseech your fatherhoods to pity our case, to take these stumbling-blocks from us, that we may live quiet and peaceable lives, to the honour of our God."† The convocation were, however, of another mind; and, instead of lessening their burdens, very much increased them.

* Bishop Maddox has endeavoured to invalidate this statement of Mr. Alcock, but completely failed in the attempt. He has produced additional evidence of the extreme severities inflicted upon the oppressed puritans.—*Vindication*, p. 335, 336.

† MS. Register, p. 90—92.

DAVID WHITEHEAD, B. D.—This famous divine, greatly celebrated for learning, piety, and moderation, was educated at Oxford, and chaplain to Queen Anne Bullen. Archbishop Cranmer says, "he was endowed with good knowledge, special honesty, fervent zeal, and politic wisdom;" for which, in the year 1552, he nominated him as the fittest person to become Archbishop of Armagh. The nomination, however, did not succeed; for another was chosen to the place.* In the beginning of the bloody persecution of Queen Mary, he fled from the storm, and retired to Frankfort, where he was chosen pastor to the English congregation. Here he was held in high esteem by his fellow exiles. He discovered his great wisdom and moderation, and answered the objections of Mr. Horne, relative to church discipline, and the worship of God, and used his utmost endeavours to compose the differences among his brethren.†

Upon the accession of Queen Elizabeth, Mr. Whitehead returned home; and, the same year, was appointed, together with Drs. Parker, Bill, May, Cox, Grindal, Pilkington, and Sir Thomas Smith, to review King Edward's liturgy. The same liturgy was published the following year. This was the third edition of the English liturgy ever published, the two former editions having come forth in the reign of King Edward.‡ In the year 1559, he was appointed one of the public disputants against the popish bishops. The subjects of disputation were,—1. "Whether it was not against the word of God, and the custom of the ancient church, to use, in the common prayers and administration of the sacraments, a tongue unknown to the people.—2. Whether every church hath authority to appoint, change, and take away, ceremonies and ecclesiastical rites; so the same were done to edification.—And 3, whether it could be proved by the word of God, that in the mass there was a propitiatory sacrifice for the quick and the dead." The other disputants on the side of the protestants, were, Dr. Story, bishop of Chichester, Dr. Cox, Mr. Grindal, Mr. Horne, Mr. Sandys, Mr. Gest, Mr. Aylmer, and Mr. Jewel; most or all of whom afterwards became bishops, and some of them archbishops.§ On this occasion, Mr. Whitehead had a fine opportunity of displaying his great learning, piety, and moderation; and he shewed himself to be so profound a divine, that the

* Strype's Cranmer, p. 274—278.
† Troubles at Frankeford, p. 52, 122—144.
‡ Strype's Annals, vol. i. p. 52. § Fox's Martyrs, vol. iii. p. 822.

queen offered him the archbishopric of Canterbury. This he declined, as some thought, from a desire of privacy; but as others thought, from a disaffection to the ecclesiastical discipline. The mastership of the Savoy, which he might have accepted without subscription, was also offered him about the same time; but he would accept of no preferment in the church, as it then stood. Refusing to embrace these offered promotions, he excused himself to the queen, by saying, he could live plentifully by the preaching of the gospel without any preferment.* While others exerted themselves to *obtain* dignified titles and worldly emolument, he was content with *deserving* them. Accordingly, he went up and down like an apostle, preaching the word where it was most wanted; and spent his life in celibacy, which gained him the greater reputation in the eye of the queen, who was never fond of married priests. It is observed, that Mr. Whitehead coming one day to the queen, her majesty said to him, "I like thee the better, Whitehead, because thou livest unmarried." "In troth, Madam," replied Mr. Whitehead, "I like you the worse for the same cause."†

In the year 1564, Mr. Whitehead shared the same fate with many of his brethren. He was cited before the ecclesiastical commissioners, and suffered deprivation, for nonconformity to the rites and ceremonies of the church.‡ Though it does not appear how long he remained under the ecclesiastical censure, Bishop Maddox is greatly mistaken, when he asserts, "that Mr. Whitehead always continued preaching, that he approved the constitution of the church, and died a member of the church of England."§ The celebrated Lord Bacon observes, that though he was much esteemed by Queen Elizabeth, he was not preferred, because he was *against* the government of the bishops.‖ During his deprivation, he most probably united with the other nonconformist divines, in presenting to Archbishop Parker, a paper of reasons for refusing the apparel. This excellent paper, now before me, is entitled "Reasons grounded upon the Scriptures, whereby we are persuaded not to admit the use of the outward apparel, and ministering garments of the pope's church."¶ Mr. Whitehead died in the year 1571. According to Wood, he was a great scholar, and a

* Fuller's Worthies, part ii. p. 12. † Ibid.
‡ Strype's Grindal, p. 98. § Vindication of the Church, p. 337.
‖ Bacon's Works, vol. ii. p. 419. Edit. 1803.
¶ MS. Register, p. 57—60.

most excellent professor of divinity.* In the opinion of Fuller, he was a man of great learning, a deep divine, and a rare example of moderation and self-denial.† It is observed of Coverdale, Turner, and Whitehead, three worthy puritans, "That they were the most ancient preachers of the gospel, and the most ancient fathers of this our country; and that from their pens, as well as their mouths, most of Queen Elizabeth's divines and bishops first received the light of the gospel."‡ Mr. Whitehead was author of "Lections and Homilies on St. Paul's Epistles," and probably some other works.

Mr. MILLAIN was fellow of Christ's college, Cambridge, and one of the preachers to the university. He maintained liberty of conscience, and publicly avowed his sentiments. Being thoroughly dissatisfied with the corruptions in the church, he openly declared his opinion of them, as things worthy of censure. In the year 1572, having delivered a sermon in St. Mary's church, he was convened before the vice-chancellor Dr. Bying, and the heads of colleges, when he was charged with having delivered the following opinions:—1. "That the ordering and making of ministers as used in the church of England, is an horrible confusion, and contrary to the word of God.—2. That ignorant and unpreaching ministers are no ministers.—3. That such as are not called by some particular congregation, are no ministers.—4. That able and sufficient ministers are rejected from the sacred function.—5. That the clergy of England deface and pull down the church, by maintaining both adultery and idolatry.—6. That to command saints' eves to be observed, is idolatry.—7. That to command saints' days to be kept as days of fasting, is abominable idolatry."—When he was examined upon these points, he confessed the whole, declaring that what he had delivered was according to the word of God. Refusing, therefore, to revoke these dangerous errors, as they are called, he was expelled from his college, and driven from the university.§

WILLIAM BONHAM was a zealous nonconformist, and a considerable sufferer under the oppressions of the perse-

* Wood's Athenæ Oxon. vol. i. p. 135, 136.
† Fuller's Worthies, part ii. p. 12. ‡ Strype's Cranmer, p. 274.
§ Strype's Whitgift, p. 46, 49. Appen. p. 16.

cuting prelates. In the year 1569, he and Mr. Nicholas Crane, another puritan minister, were licensed to preach by Bishop Grindal. Their licenses are said to have been granted on condition that they should avoid all conventicles, and all things contrary to the order established in this kingdom. Accordingly, they made the following promise, signed with their own hands:—"I do faithfully "promise, that I will not, any time hereafter, use any "public preaching, or open reading, or expounding of the "scriptures; nor cause, neither be present at, any private "assemblies of prayer or expounding of the scriptures, or "ministering the communion in any house, or other place, "contrary to the state of religion now by public authority "established, or contrary to the laws of this realm of Eng- "land. Neither will I inveigh against any rites or cere- "monies used or received by common authority within "this realm."* Such were the conditions on which these divines entered the sacred function! But, surely, if the church of England, so lately separated from the church of Rome, had come immediately from heaven, and been as infallible as its natural parent, the mother church, pretended, it would have been too wisely constructed to require such tyrannical promises of the Lord's servants.

The two divines were afterwards apprehended and cast into prison for nonconformity, where they remained more than twelve months, and then they were released. But persisting in the same practice, and not keeping to the exact order established in the church of England, Mr. Bonham was again committed to prison, and Mr. Crane was silenced from preaching within the diocese of London; but it does not appear how long they continued under these ecclesiastical oppressions.†

Mr. Bonham was a zealous man in the cause of the reformation. Being concerned for the restoration of a purer ecclesiastical discipline, he, in 1572, united with his brethren in the formation of the presbyterian church at Wandsworth in Surrey.‡ Our divine was afterwards called to endure fresh trials. Mr. Bonham and Mr. Nicholas Standen, another puritan minister, were brought under the tyrannical power of the high commission, and cast into prison for nonconformity. After having continued under confinement a long time, and being deeply afflicted with the sickness of

* Strype's Grindal, p. 156.
† Ibid. p. 153—155.—MS. Chronology, vol. ii. p. 405. (6.)
‡ Fuller's Church Hist. b. ix. p. 103.

the prison, they presented their petitions to the lords of the council, to which their lordships paid immediate attention. They accordingly addressed a letter to Archbishop Parker and other commissioners, signifying that they should be glad to assist them in any *lawful* cause against such as refused conformity; yet they did not like men to be so long detained without having their casue examined, and desire them to proceed in such cases more speedily in future. They entreat them to examine the cause of the two complainants, and, in case they should be found so sick that they could not continue in prison without inconvenience, to suffer them to be bailed till their cause should be ended.*

This effort of the council seems to have been without any good effect. Undismayed, however, by the first repulse, they made a second application, but in a style much more peremptory. They addressed another letter to the archbishop alone, signifying, that, for good considerations, it was her majesty's pleasure that Bonham and Standen, committed by his lordship for breach of conformity, should be set at liberty, upon warning to observe the laws in their public ministry in future, or else to abstain from it.+

Mr. Strype observes, that, during the above year, these two divines were accused of being concerned in Undertree's sham plot, and committed to prison; but, upon examination, they were found innocent, and were both acquitted and released by order of council.‡

Robert Johnson was fellow of King's college, Cambridge, and domestic chaplain to Lord Keeper Bacon. He preached and administered the sacrament in his lordship's family at Gorambury, and was statedly employed in the ministry at St. Alban's. In July, 1571, he was brought into trouble for nonconformity. He was cited before Archbishop Parker, and the Bishops of Winchester and Ely, at Lambeth. Upon his appearance, he was threatened to be silenced if he would not subscribe. Accordingly, not being satisfied in every point contained in the articles proposed to him, and refusing subscription, he was immediately suspended. Afterwards, he sent the following humble letter to the commissioners, earnestly desiring to be restored to his

* Baker's MS. Collec. vol. xxi. p. 384. + Ibid. p. 385.
‡ Strype's Parker, p. 466.

ministry. This letter was dated from the lord keeper's house, Gorambury, near St. Albans, August 14, 1571.

"Whereas July 4th," says he, "being before your lordships, to answer to your three articles, I did forbear to subscribe to the first, viz. 'That the Book of Common Prayer is agreeable to the word of God,' because it seemed to me to contain a license of administering baptism by women, a thing forbidden by the word of God. And being suspended and sequestered, I have abstained from preaching and administering the sacrament, and thereby, my lord, and his family, have suffered the want of those most necessary and comfortable religious privileges. Therefore, my duty to his lordship's household, and to that part of the church from which I receive some maintenance, move me with all due humility and submission, to beseech you that I may be restored to my former liberty.

"And concerning the articles, I trust this will suffice and fully answer your intention, that, by this my letter, subscribed with my own hand, I do promise and declare, that I did not mean to vary from the ordinary book of service, in my ministry. Neither to inveigh against it by public speech, wittingly, or maliciously; but to move the auditory to hold the truth in matters of faith and sound religious practice, and to live for ever in the fear of God. And I think that the contents of the service book, then expressly mentioned, and according to the exposition then given to me, are not defective, nor expressly contrary to the word of God; and that the imperfections thereof, may, for the sake of unity and charity, be suffered, till God grant a more perfect reformation: for which, every man, according to his particular vocation, ought diligently to labour.

"As to the second article, 'That the apparel of ministers is not wicked, and directly against the word of God; and being appointed by the prince only for the sake of policy, obedience, and order, it may be used;' yet is it not generally expedient, nor edifying.

"And as to the third, 'That the articles of religion, which only concern the confession of the true christian faith, and the doctrine of the sacrament, comprised in a book, entitled Articles agreed upon by the Archbishops and Bishops of both Provinces, and the whole Clergy, in the convocation holden in London, in the year of our Lord 1562,' and every of them, contain true and godly christian doctrine.

"And because I perceived it to be offensive to his grace

the archbishop, that I hold by the favour of the lord keeper, a prebend in Norwich, I now inform you, that I mean to relinquish it the next half year following. Trusting, that upon the receipt of this my humble submission, you will release me, and grant me a new license to preach. And so committing your lordships, in all your godly and zealous undertakings, to the direction and blessing of Almighty God. Subscribing myself your lordships' most humble petitioner "ROBERT JOHNSON."*

What effect this letter produced, we are not able to learn; but it probably failed to answer the end proposed. We find, however, in the year 1573, that Mr. Johnson was brought into further trouble. He was convened before the Bishop of Lincoln, and required to subscribe to the three curious articles following:

1. "I am content hereafter, in my open sermons and public preaching, to forbear to impugn the articles of religion agreed upon in the Synod at London, in 1562, or any of them.

2. "Neither will I speak against the state of the church of England, now allowed by the laws of this realm; nor against the Book of Common Prayer, or any thing contained therein.

3. "Neither will I say or sing, or cause, procure, or maintain any other to say or sing, any common or open prayer, or minister any sacrament, otherwise, or in any other manner or form, than is mentioned in the said book, till further order be taken by public authority."

Mr. Johnson refusing subscription, answered as follows:—"Whether these articles be such as I ought in duty to subscribe, and whether for refusing this subscription, I deserve to be openly declared a forsaker of the church, and the flock committed to my care, and whether it be matter for which I ought to be defamed, I refer to your worship's consideration, upon the following reasons:

"I take it for granted, that there are faults, and such as ought to be reformed, both in the government of the church, and in the Book of Common Prayer, upon which I reason thus. Either there is, or there is not, a reformation intended by those in authority. If there be a reformation intended, then it is good that the people's minds be prepared the more willingly to receive it when it comes, and to persuade them

* Strype's Parker, p. 327, 328.

by sound reason and the authority of scripture, before they are compelled by law to obey. This preparation of the people to obey, is necessary, lest they be compelled to obey they know not what. Therefore, that the people may the more willingly, and without murmuring, agree to a reformation, and praise the Lord for the same, it is necessary they should first know the *defects* in the church, which need reformation. But if no reformation be intended, it is proper the people should understand how much the church stands in need of it, that they may pray unto God to stir up those who are in authority to promote it; and, no doubt, the Lord will the sooner hear their prayers. So that, whether a reformation be intended, or not intended, the church of God should be told of its corruptions, that the people may the more willingly praise God when they are taken away, and the more earnestly pray unto him until they be taken away. This is one reason why ministers should not bind themselves to conceal the faults and corruptions remaining in the church.

"Another reason is, that seeing there are many preachers who maintain that the government of the church is perfectly good, and that the Prayer Book needs no amendment; and as these preachers have license to preach where they please, they may preach these things to that flock over which God hath made me overseer; if I should consent and subscribe, that, in such a case, I will not speak, I cannot see how I could acquit myself before God. Therefore, the fear of this evil, in these days of peril and confusion, is another reason for not giving either the promise of my word, or the subscription of my hand, to hold my peace against the government of the church, and every thing contained in the Book of Common Prayer.

"Also, in the Book of Common Prayer, there is a manifest abuse of scripture: as in the ordination of ministers, it is said, *Receive the Holy Ghost.* Corrupt prayers: as in confirmation, "Almighty God, who hast vouchsafed to regenerate these thy servants, by water and the *Holy Ghost*, and *hast given them the forgiveness of all their sins.*" These and many such faults in the book, are such, that a preacher ought not to promise and subscribe, that he will *never speak any thing against them.* There are, likewise, many things in the government of the church: as the court of faculties, the high commission court, dispensations for nonresidence, and many others, against which I cannot oblige myself that I will *never speak.*" This answer, with much more to the same purpose, Mr. Johnson delivered August 6, 1573, subscribed with his own hand.*

We do not, indeed, find what immediately followed his refusing to subscribe; whether he was dismissed, and allowed to go on in his ministry, or sent to prison. Most probably he was released; for he afterwards became minister of St. Clement's church, London. Here, however, he enjoyed but little repose; for towards the close of December, in the above year, he and some others were committed close prisoners to the Gatehouse, for nonconformity.† February 2d, following, Mr. Johnson being still in prison, wrote a letter to Dr. Sandys, bishop of London, whom he styles "superintendant of popish corruptions in the diocese of London." In this letter, he reminds his lordship of some of the existing evils, especially that of professed christians persecuting one another. "There is," says he, "persecution enough. Some are imprisoned, and are in danger of losing, not only their liberty, but also their lives, being compelled to remain in filthy jails, more unwholesome than dunghills, and more stinking than pig-styes. Others are persecuted in their minds, by being enforced to subscribe to those things against which every good man's conscience makes a stand, and every godly man disallows. It is a great evil for a man to lose or spend his property in prison; it is a greater, to lose his reputation; it is greater still, to lose his liberty; but it is greatest of all, to be greatly distressed and disquieted in his conscience. Take heed, therefore, lest you get your name enrolled amongst the number of persecutors. Let not worldly policy prevail more than true divinity. Let not man cause you to do that which God has forbidden. Let not the commission draw you further than God's word will allow. Let not your honour here on earth, cause you to do that which is against the honour of God. Let not your palace make you forget the temple of Christ.

"The present persecution is among brethren, not only of one nation, but of one profession: those who persecute, and those who are persecuted, believing in one God, professing one Christ, embracing one religion, receiving one gospel, communicating in one sacrament, and having one hope of salvation. Dissention in a kingdom, discord in a nation, controversy among neighbours, and contention among brethren, are more to be feared than any of them among enemies. You say, you are our chief pastor, we desire

* Parte of a Register, p. 94—100. † Baker's MS. Collec. vol. xxxii. p. 440.

food: you say, you are our doctor, we desire to be taught. This is the best way to win us, and the best for you to use. The laws and authority of *men*, should not set aside the laws and authority of *God*. The popish logic of slander and imprisonment will not prevail at last. The Fleet, the Gate-house, the White-lion, the King's-bench, and Newgate, are weak arguments to convince the conscience."*

Upon the 20th day of the same month, Mr. Johnson was brought to trial before his judges, and examined at Westminster-hall, in the presence of the queen's commissioners, the bishop of London, the dean of Westminster, the lord chief justice, and others. He was accused of marrying without the *ring*, and of baptizing without the *cross*, which he did for a time; but upon complaint against him, he begun again to use them. He was accused, also, of a misdemeanour, as it is called; because when he was once administering the sacrament, the wine falling short, he sent for more, but did not consecrate it afresh, accounting the former consecration sufficient for what was applied to the same use, at the same time. The examination which he underwent at his trial, was as follows:

Johnson. If it please your honours, may I not submit myself, and declare the truth of things as they were done?

Lord Chief Justice. Yes, you may.

J. I stand here indicted for three points. The first is, that I have not repeated the words of the institution; or, as they commonly call it, I did not consecrate the wine, when I delivered it to the communicants.—Secondly, that I have not married with the ring.—Thirdly, that I have not used the cross in the administration of baptism, and have left out the whole sentence for that purpose.†—Unto these charges, I answer, that respecting the *contempt*, as expressed in the indictment, I plead, *not guilty*. And as to the first of those charges, I answer under my protestation, that at no time, in celebrating the communion, have I omitted any prayer or words of the institution, which the book prescribeth, but have used them in as full and ample a manner

* Parte of a Register, p. 101—105.

† In Mr. Johnson's indictment, he was charged with having solemnized matrimony, between one Leonard Morris and Agnes Miles, without using the ring. And having baptized a male child that he did not know, he did not make the sign of the cross on its forehead, nor use the following words: "We receive this child into the congregation of Christ's flock, and do sign "him with the sign of the cross," as contained in the Book of Common Prayer; "And that he did the same voluntarily, and in contempt of the "queen and her laws, and against the peace of the realm."—*MS. Register*, p. 199.

as they are appointed. Only upon a certain occasion, when the wine failed, I sent for more, which I delivered to the people, using the words appointed in the book to be used in the delivery of the sacrament, not again repeating the words of the institution: partly, because, as I take it, being an entire action and one supper, the words of the institution at first delivered were sufficient; and partly, because, in the Book of Common Prayer, there is no order appointed to which I could refer the case. And as to the second, I answer that once or twice, I did not use the ring. For looking into the mass-book, I found the words with which the papists *hallow* the ring; and because this seemed to me no less derogatory to the death of Christ, than holy bread and holy water, I thought as other persons had omitted those, I might omit this.

Commissioner. There is no such thing in the Book of Common Prayer.

Dean. He speaketh of the mass-book.

Bishop. Then you compare the mass-book and the common prayer book, and make the one as bad as the other.

J. My lord, I make no such comparison. But after I was complained of to my ordinary, Dr. Watts, archdeacon of Middlesex, who reprehended me, I used the ring, as I have good and sufficient witness. Since, therefore, I did in this default correct myself, I refer myself to your honour's discretion, whether I have herein stubbornly and contemptuously broken the law.—As to the third charge, I answer, that I have omitted to make the sign of the cross, but not of contempt. But seeing I have already suffered seven weeks imprisonment, with the loss of my place and living, I beseech you, be indifferent judges, whether this be not sufficient for so small a crime.

Mr. Gerard. You were not sent to prison for that, but for your irreverent behaviour.

J. I trust, sir, I did not behave myself more irreverently than I do now. Whereas the indictment is, that I omitted the whole prayer, "We receive this child," &c. This is false; for I never administered baptism without using that prayer, though I omitted making the sign of the cross.

B. Those two are but trifles. The chief is the consecration of the sacrament. For, as it had not the word, it was no sacrament, and so the people were mocked.

J. My lord, I did not mock the people; for it was a sacrament.

D. St. Augustin saith, "That the word must be added to

the element, to make a sacrament." You lacked the word; therefore, it was no sacrament.

J. I had the word.

B. How had you the word, when you confess that you recited not the institution?

J. I had recited the institution before, and that was sufficient.

D. Yea, for that bread and wine that was present; but when you sent for more bread or wine, you should again have rehearsed the words of the institution.

J. The book appointed no such thing.

B. Yes, sir, the book saith, you shall have sufficient bread and wine, and then the prayer of the institution must be recited. Now, as you had not sufficient, you should, therefore, have repeated the institution.

J. There is no such caveat, nor proviso, appointed in the book.

B. But that is the meaning of the book.

J. Men may make what meaning they please; but I refer myself to the book, whether or not it be so appointed.

D. You are not forbidden to use the repetition.

J. Neither am I commanded.

D. I will prove this to be the meaning of the book. For it is said in the prayer, "these creatures of bread and wine:" so that the book hath respect to the bread and wine there present, and not to any other. Therefore, if there be any more brought, it must be consecrated afresh, by the words of the institution.

J. I pray you tell me one thing. Are the words of the institution spoken for the bread, or for the receivers?

D. For both.

J. I deny that. For the evangelist declares, that Christ said unto his *disciples*, to teach them for what end and purpose they should take the bread.

D. Then the word is of no force.

J. I deny that. The word is necessary to the substance of the sacrament. But this is not the question: we both confess this. Herein is the controversy, whether it be necessary for the institution to be repeated, seeing it is but one and the same action, and the same communicants as before, for whom the words are spoken. If it had not been the same supper, or if the communicants had been changed, it would have been necessary to rehearse the institution.

B. You like yourself very well, and you are stubborn

and arrogant. I have before heard of your stubborn heart, but now I perceive it.

J. My lord, who he is that liketh himself so well, and is so stubborn and arrogant, that Lord, who trieth the hearts of all, must judge.

B. Why, you being unlearned, stand stubbornly against us all, and so no learning will satisfy you.

J. I would fain understand with what words Christ did consecrate.

Dr. Wilson. With this word, *benedixit*.

J. Be it so. But we know not the words with which Christ did *benedicere*. Therefore, we must consecrate with we know not what.

L. C. J. Ah! Johnson. Is this your submission?

J. I must needs defend my own innocence.

G. Johnson, you in a manner confess as much as you are charged with. For you confess, that when the words of the institution were recited, you had no wine.

J. I do not confess that. I had both bread and wine.

G. But you had not that wine.

J. No.

G. Therefore it was not consecrated.

J. The words before repeated were sufficient for the consecration.

D. Then, with those words you consecrated all the wine in the tavern.

J. No, sir, it was the wine that was brought from the tavern to the church, and of a common wine, was appointed to be a sacramental wine, to represent Christ's blood; and this is consecration.

D. Why then, with you, the word is of no force.

J. It is not of force to bring any holiness to the sacrament. I trust you do not think that the word maketh the bread any holier when used in the sacrament.

W. Yes, it is holy bread.

B. It is a holy sacrament.

J. That I confess. But holiness is in the use and end, not in the substance. For otherwise you would make a magical enchantment of it, and not a consecration. Dr. Cranmer, in his book on the sacrament, saith, "There cometh no holiness to the bread by consecration."

G. If thou wert well served, thou wouldst be used like a magician.

J. Whatever your judgment may be, I stand or fall to my own Lord.

B. You know not what harm you have done, by defending an error before this company, bringing them so into doubt, that they know not which way to take.

J. My lord, I defend no error. I maintain the truth.

D. Nay, you maintain a *horrible heresy*.

Bromley. Yea, if you were well served, you should *fry a faggot*.

J. As you say that I maintain a heresy, I pray you shew me by what commandment I am bound to the precise words of the institution.

D. As the word in baptism is, "I baptize thee in the name of the Father, the Son, and the Holy Ghost:" so the word in the Lord's supper is the rehearsal of the institution.

J. Bullinger was of another mind; for he saith, "The consecration of sacraments is not by the nature, will, command, or precept of Christ, nor from the authority of any other."

D. Where doth he say this?

J. Sermon vi. decad 5.

D. You falsify his words.

J. No, I cite them right. And the churches of Geneva and Scotland consecrate with other words, without using the words of the institution, except in preaching.

D. You slander those churches, as appeareth from their own words, which I have here in a book.

J. I have not slandered those famous churches. Let their liturgy witness. And as to that book, there is nothing in it which I do not believe. But I pray you, my lord of London, answer me one question. Must consecration be performed before the delivery of the elements, or after?

B. I will not answer it.

J. It is only a question. I pray you answer it.

B. Answer it thyself.

D. It shall be answered. The consecration must go before; for Christ gave a sacrament, which could not be without the word. Consecration, therefore, must go before.

J. But Christ spake the word after the distribution. For he first gave them the bread, and then said, "Take, eat, this is my body."

D. And what then?

J. Then, according to what you say, Christ did not consecrate aright.

D. You defend a horrible heresy: for you reject the word,

J. I do not reject the word, but would understand what the word meaneth.

D. It meaneth the institution of Christ.

J. All writers do not so understand it. Some by the word, understand the promises, as Musculus, Bullinger, Peter Martyr, and Calvin.

D. The word is not the promise.

J. These learned men so take it. Herein I am content to refer myself to the judgment of the learned.

L. C. J. Here is my lord of London, a prelate of the realm, and a bishop, and this gentleman, Mr. Dean; dost thou think they are not learned?

J. I neither despise, nor deprave their learning. But as to the words of the institution, I say, they are to be considered, either as they are expressly set down by the evangelist; or, as other words are used equivalent to them, declaring the sum and substance of them, and, in either case, the institution is whole and sound. Consecration may be taken either according to the consecration of the papists, who say, "This is my body, and this is my blood;" or, as the best writers in our time, take it for the rehearsal of the promises and thanksgiving to be enjoined; and whichsoever of these two be accepted, seeing I used the words of delivery, there was sufficient consecration.

L. C. J. Let us make an end of it. Charge the jury.—The witnesses were then called and sworn, some of whom were known papists, and others had done penance for the foulest crimes, against whom no exception would be taken; and Mr. Johnson being by their verdict found guilty, was condemned to one year's imprisonment, and immediately sent back to the Gatehouse.*

The hard treatment Mr. Johnson received from Bishop Sandys, and the other commissioners, as appears in the above examination; with the heavy sentence pronounced upon him, after having endured some close and severe imprisonment already, were, surely, more than proportionate to any crime with which he was charged, even supposing he had been guilty. Indeed, whether the principal thing with which he was charged was good or evil, was matter of mere opinion, and a point much to be disputed. But right or wrong, he must be punished.

During the execution of the heavy sentence, and about two weeks after his trial, Mr. Johnson wrote a letter to

* Parte of a Register, p. 105—111.

Bishop Sandys, dated March 7, 1574, in which he earnestly pleads for more kind treatment. He thus observes, "Our Saviour saith, *Blessed are the merciful, for they shall obtain mercy:* And the apostle, *He shall have judgment without mercy, that hath shewed no mercy.* I wonder what mercy you, and the rest of the commissioners, hope for, and what judgment you look for, seeing for trifles and of no weight, nay of no truth, as I doubt not you are persuaded in your own consciences, you not only mock and molest men, deprave and deprive them, but to their great poverty and utter ruin, and without any bowels of mercy, you condemn them to long imprisonment. Where hath God given any such commandment? Where hath Christ given any such precedent? Where did the apostles put any such thing in practice? If you say, that we hold errors, are schismatics, and promote sects; then do you the part of a teacher, to reform our errors, to reduce schismatics to unity, and to dissuade sectaries from dissention. Your office and function, your name and title, your degree and profession, your knowledge and religion, yea the apostles, Jesus Christ, and God himself, requireth this at your hands. You know who saith, *If a man be overtaken in a fault, ye which are spiritual, restore such a one in the spirit of meekness.* Compare your doctrine in time past, and your doings now, and see how they agree. We may say as the prophet said: *The Lord God of your fathers was wroth with Judah, and he hath delivered them into your hand, and you have persecuted them in a rage that reacheth up to heaven.*

"If to imprison and famish men, be the proper way to instruct the ignorant and reduce the obstinate, where is the office and work of a shepherd, to seek that which was lost, and bring home that which went astray? We beseech you, therefore, to gather something out of the Old and New Testament, that you may reduce those who go astray, and heal that which is bruised and broken. And I pray you, let us feel some of your charitable relief, to preserve us from death, under this hard usage; especially as you have been the chief cause of my trouble, I desire you to be some part of my comfort. Let pity requite spite, and mercy recompence malice. Thus beseeching God, that you may proceed faithfully in all the duties of a bishop, I commend you to Jesus Christ, the great Shepherd and Bishop of souls.

"Robert Johnson."*

* Parte of a Register, p. 117, 118.

Mr. Johnson, at the same time, presented a petition to the queen or council, desiring to be restored to his former liberty of preaching, from which he was restrained by the foregoing heavy sentence. This petition, together with a letter from the court, dated Greenwich, March 19, 1573, were sent to the Archbishop of Canterbury and the Bishop of London, pressing them to take the case into consideration, and take such order therein as should appear most convenient. The council also sent another letter to the Bishop of London, dated Greenwich, May 16, 1574, signifying that their lordships were given to understand, that Mr. Johnson, committed to the Gatehouse for nonconformity, was very sick and likely to die, unless he might enjoy more open air. Therefore they commanded his grace to give order for the poor afflicted man to be bailed, and upon sureties to be removed to his own house, but not to depart thence without further order.*

All these efforts were, however, without any good effect. The relentless prelate continued inflexible. Mr. Johnson experienced neither his lenity, nor his charity, nor any other favour: for the good man died soon after, a prisoner in the Gatehouse, through the cruelty of his imprisonment, and his extreme poverty and want.† Herein, surely, his inhuman persecutors would be highly gratified. Bishop Sandys, who was at the head of these proceedings, is said to have been "a man very eminent for his learning, probity, and prudence;"‡ but, surely, it may be questioned whether he exercised these excellent qualifications on the present occasion. This is even admitted by his partial biographer: for he observes, that during the above period, the *good* bishop proceeded so vigorously against the puritans, that his doings brought *public reproach* on his name and reputation.§

Mr. Johnson wrote a letter, a little before his death, to the Dean of Westminster, another zealous promoter of his persecution. This letter is still preserved.‖ Mr. Strype charges Mr. Johnson as a false accuser, and, in 1609, as reviling the puritans. But the fact of his being dead several years before either of these events are said to have taken place, at once acquits him of the twofold charge. Some other person of the same name, who was a rigid churchman, we believe to have been guilty of those crimes.¶

* Baker's MS. Collec. vol. xxi. p. 383, 384.
† Parte of a Register, p. 111, 118.
‡ Le Neve's Lives, vol. i. part ii. p. 69. § Ibid. p. 31.
‖ Parte of a Register, p. 112—116. ¶ Strype's Parker, p. 328, 329.

Richard Taverner, A. M.—This distinguished person was born at Brisley in Norfolk, in the year 1505, and educated first in Bennet college, Cambridge, then in the university of Oxford. The famous Cardinal Wolsey having founded a new college at the latter place,* furnished it with all the best scholars in the nation; among whom were Taverner, Tindal, Frith, Goodman, and many others. Here Mr. Taverner and his brethren were soon called to the trial of their faith. They were men of good learning and grave judgments, and Mr. Taverner was famous for his knowledge of music; but conferring together about the corruptions of the church, they were presently accused to the cardinal, and cast into prison. They were confined in a deep cell under the college, where salt fish was wont to be preserved; so that by the filthiness and infection of the place, several of them soon lost their lives. Mr. Taverner, however, escaped the fatal malady. Though he was accused of hiding one Mr. Clark's books under the boards of his school, the cardinal, on account of his music, exempted him, saying, "He is only a musician;" and so he was released.† He had a good knowledge of the Greek language, philosophy, and divinity; but about this time he removed or was expelled from the university, and became a student at the inns of court. Here, when he read any thing in the law, he made his quotations in Greek. In the year 1534, he was taken under the patronage of Lord Cromwell, principal secretary to Henry VIII.; by whose recommendation the king afterwards made him one of the clerks of the signet. This place he kept till the accession of Queen Mary, having been held in high esteem by King Henry, Edward VI., and the Duke of Somerset, the lord protector.

In the year 1539, he published "A Recognition or Correction of the Bible after the best Exemplars." It was printed in folio, dedicated to the king, and allowed to be publicly read in the churches. But upon the fall of Lord Cromwell, in 1540, the bishops causing the printers of the Bible in English to be cast into prison and punished, Mr. Taverner, as the reward of his labours, was sent to the

* Cardinal Wolsey possessed, for some years, all that power and grandeur which could be enjoyed by the greatest favourite, and most absolute minister, under an arbitrary prince. He exercised as absolute a power in the church, as he had done in the state. His abilities were equal to his great offices, but these were by no means equal to his ambition. He was the only man that ever had the ascendancy of Henry VIII., but afterwards fell into disgrace.—*Granger's Biog. Hist.* vol. i. p. 92.

† Fox's Martyrs, vol. ii. p. 209, 251.

Tower. Here, however, he did not continue long; for, having fully acquitted himself before his judges, he was soon after released, and restored to his place and the king's favour. He was about this time, a member of parliament, and held in high esteem by men of piety and worth. Upon King Henry's coming to the parliament house in 1545, and exhorting the members to charity, unity, and concord, he published a translation of Erasmus, entitled "An Introduction to Christian concord and unitie in matters of Religion."

In the year 1552, Mr. Taverner, though he was not ordained, obtained a special license subscribed by King Edward, to preach in any part of his dominions; and he did not fail to make use of the liberty granted him. He preached from place to place through the kingdom; also at court before the king, and in other public places, wearing a velvet bonnet or round cap, a damask gown, and a chain of gold about his neck; in which habit, he sometimes preached in St. Mary's church, Oxford, in the days of Queen Elizabeth. When Queen Mary came to the crown, he retired to his country house called Norbiton-hall, in Surrey, where he continued during the whole of her reign. Upon the accession of Elizabeth, he presented her majesty with a congratulatory epistle in Latin, for which she exceedingly respected him, placed great confidence in him, and, besides offering him the degree of knighthood, put him into the commission of peace for the county of Oxford. Here numerous concerns were entrusted to him, and, in 1569, he was made high sheriff of the county. Notwithstanding his high station, he did not relinquish his ministerial labours, but continued preaching as he found opportunity. While he was in the office of high sheriff, he appeared in St. Mary's pulpit, with his gold chain about his neck, and his sword by his side, and preached to the scholars, beginning his sermon with the following words:—"Arriving at the mount "of St. Mary's, in the stony* stage where I now stand, I "have brought you some fine biskets, baked in the oven of "charity, and carefully conserved for the chickins of the "church, the sparrows of the spirit, and the sweet swallows "of salvation."† This way of preaching was then mostly fashionable, and commended by the generality of scholars

* Wood says the pulpit of St. Mary's was then of fine carved stone; but it was taken away in 1654, when Dr. John Owen was vice-chancellor, and a pulpit of wood set up in its place.—*Athenæ Oxon.* vol. i. p. 144. note.

† Fuller's Church Hist. b. ix. p. 65.

in those times. This celebrated reformer and zealous nonconformist to the church of England, laid down his head in peace, July 14, 1575, aged seventy years. He died at his manor-house, at Wood-Eaton, in Oxfordshire, and his remains were interred with great funeral solemnity, in the chancel of the church at that place.*

His Works.—1. The Sum or Pith of the 150 Psalmes of David, reduced into a forme of Prayers and Meditations, with other certaine godly Orisons, 1539.—2. Correction of the Bible, already mentioned. —3. The Epistles and Gospels, with a brief Postill upon the same, from Advent to Low Sunday, drawn forth by divers learned men for the singular commoditie of all good Christian Persons, and namely of Priests and Curates, 1540.—4. The Epistles and Gospels, with a brief Postill upon the same, from after Easter till Advent, 1540.—5. Fruite of Faith, containing all the Prayers of the holy Fathers, Patriarks, Prophets, Judges, Kings, renowned Men, and Women, in the Old and New Testament, 1582.—6. Various Poems in Latin and English, and several Translations of the works of other learned men.

R. Harvey was a zealous and learned minister in the city of Norwich, a divine of puritanical principles, and brought into troubles for his nonconformity. Having spoken against the pompous titles, and the government of bishops, and other ecclesiastical officers, he was summoned, May 13, 1576, to appear before his diocesan at Norwich. Upon his appearance before his lordship, he was immediately suspended; when the dean, who pronounced the sentence, behaved himself towards Mr. Harvey, not as a judge, but a most angry tyrant.†

Mr. Harvey having received the ecclesiastical censure, and conceiving himself to have been hardly used, wrote a letter to the Bishop of Norwich, in which he addressed his lordship with considerable freedom and boldness. The substance of this letter is as follows:—"I am moved in conscience," says he, "to address you in this way, that I may give a further account of my behaviour. I think you may see, if you shut not your eyes, how the man of sin, I mean the pope of Rome, hath so perverted and corrupted the doctrine of Christ, that not one free spot of it now remaineth. In like manner, touching the discipline and government of the church, although our Saviour, who is the only king of his church, sate in the seat of judgment, with the crown of life on his head, and the sceptre of righteousness in his hand;

* Wood's Athenæ Oxon. vol. i. p. 143—145.

† Strype's Annals, vol. ii. p. 448, 449.—Parte of a Register, p. 389.

that man of sin plucked him from his throne, and placed himself upon it, having on his head the mitre of death, and in his hand the sword of cruelty and blood. These things I hope you know.

"We find in the scriptures of truth, that when Christ ruled and reigned in his church, his officers were bishops or pastors, and elders and deacons. But when the pope set aside this government, he appointed new governors in the church, as cardinals, archbishops, lord-bishops, deans, chancellors, commissioners, and many others. The doctrine and government of the church being thus thrown down, it pleased the Lord in his time to shew us favour. By means of our good prince, he hath purged the doctrines of our church from the errors of popery; and was ready to have restored unto us true discipline, if it had not been prevented by our own slackness and unthankfulness. But you prelates turn the edge of the sword against us, and stand in the way to keep us from the tree of life. The government of the church is much the same as it was under popery. The pope's officers, you know, still bear rule; and, therefore, the reins of government are not in the hands of Christ, but in the hands of antichrist. And though you hide yourselves under the shadow of the prince, saying, that she created you and your authority; you perversely attempt to deceive the world, and you miserably abuse the name and goodness of our prince. For how long were your names and offices in full force before our prince was born? How then will you make her authority the origin of your jurisdiction?

"Moreover, as Jesus Christ is the only lawgiver in his church, and as he alone has power and authority to appoint its officers, if any king or prince in the world appoint any other officers in the church, than those which Christ hath already allowed and appointed, we will lay down our necks upon the block, rather than consent to them. Wherefore, do not so often object to us the name of our prince; for you use it as a cloak to cover your cursed enterprizes. Have you not thrust out those who preached the word of God sincerely and faithfully? Have you not plucked out those preachers whom God fixed in his church? And do you think that this plea, *I did but execute the law,* will excuse you before the High Judge."* It does not appear what effect this bold address had on the mind of the reverend

* Parte of a Register, p. 365—370.

prelate; nor whether the good man ever procured his restoration.

Mr. Harvey appears to have written "A Treatise of the Church and Kingdom of Christ," a copy of which is still preserved, though most probably it was never published.* The Oxford historian gives a very curious account of one Mr. Richard Harvey, who lived about the same time, but he does not appear to have been the same person.† One Mr. Richard Harvey of Pembroke-hall, Cambridge, took his degrees in Arts in 1581 and 1585. This was probably the same person as that last mentioned.‡

Edward Deering, B. D.—This learned and distinguished puritan was descended from a very ancient and worthy family at Surrenden-Dering, in Kent; and having been carefully brought up in religion, and the rudiments of sound learning, completed his education in Christ's college, Cambridge. Here he made amazing progress in valuable knowledge, and became an eminently popular preacher. He was fellow of the house, was chosen proctor in 1566, and Lady Margaret's preacher the year following.§ This, indeed, was not sufficient to protect him from the fury and persecution of the prelates.

In the year 1571, being cited before Archbishop Parker and other commissioners, he was charged with certain assertions, which, it is said, he maintained and subscribed before them. These assertions were the following: "That breaking the laws of civil government is, in its own nature, no sin, but only on account of scandal.—That Christ's descent into hell relates only to the force and efficacy of his passion; but that neither his body, nor his soul, went to that place.—That it is lawful to take oaths, when the forms are written or printed, to determine the sense of the imposer; but to make use of the book, as a circumstance of solemnity, is a sacrilegious addition.—That the clerical garments, which are derived from popery, are full of offence, and appear to me directly against the truth."‖ It does not appear, however, what punishment was inflicted upon him for these assertions.

* MS. Register, p. 533—554.
† Wood's Athenæ Oxon. vol. i. p. 173, 174.
‡ Baker's MS. Collec. vol. ii. p. 381.
§ MS. Chronology, vol. i. p. 262. (2.)
‖ Strype's Parker, p. 326.—Baker's MS. Collec. vol. xxxvi. p. 337.

Mr. Deering was domestic chaplain to the unfortunate Duke of Norfolk, (who, in the above year, lost his head on Tower-hill,) and was tutor to his children. In this situation, he conducted himself with great propriety, and much to the satisfaction of his noble patron.* When the duke was imprisoned for his treasonable connections with the Queen of Scots, Mr. Deering thus addressed him: "You once earnestly professed the gospel; but now dissimulation, ambition, and hypocrisy hath bewitched you. You know how many times I dissuaded you from your wicked servants, your popish friends, and your adulterous woman. Alas! my lord, your high calling hath so bridled my words, that I could not speak to you as I would: my words were too soft to heal so old a disease."†

In the year 1572, he became lecturer at St. Paul's, London; where, on account of his great learning, ready utterance, and uncommon boldness, he was amazingly followed. This being grievous to certain ecclesiastical persons, it was deemed most proper to silence him. This was accordingly done the very next year. Our historian intimates, that he was a great enemy to the order of bishops. This was, indeed, the case with most of the puritans. They generally looked upon the episcopal office, as appointed in the church, to be equally a popish invention, and contrary to its original design, according to the New Testament. He further informs us, that Mr. Deering was intimately acquainted with the Lord Treasurer Burleigh, with whom he often interceded, in behalf of the suffering nonconformists.‡

While he was lecturer of St. Paul's, he was charged with having spoken certain things, which, by interpretation, were said to reflect upon the magistrate, and tend to break the peace of the church. Therefore, by an order from the council, his lecture was put down. Persons were appointed to watch him continually, to take advantage of what he delivered; and when he was brought under examination for delivering certain things offensive to the ruling powers, he utterly denied that he had said any such thing, and declared that the charges were mere slanders. Indeed, upon his appearance before the attorney-general and the bishop of London, the bishop frankly acknowledged that he could not accuse him.§ What a pity then was it, that so excellent a preacher as he is denominated, who had so large a

* Strype's Annals, vol. ii. p. 130.
† MS. Chronology, vol. i. p. 262. (2.)
‡ Strype's Annals, vol. ii. p. 190. § Ibid. p. 269.

congregation, and when such preachers were much wanted, should be put to silence!

In September this year, he wrote to the treasurer, requesting that he might no more appear before the council, but be judged by the bishops themselves, at any time and place they should appoint. In order to the restoration of his lecture, he requested that judgment might not be deferred; that he might be charged with some impropriety, either in his words or actions; and that upon the knowledge of which, his honour might himself be able to judge what he deserved. He beseeched his lordship to inquire into his character, and examine his actions, till he could find only two persons who had heard him speak evil: but if such evidence of his ill behaviour could not be obtained, he intreated him to become his friend. He urged further, that his lordship would either believe his own judgment, having himself sometimes heard him, or the report of multitudes, who were his constant hearers. And if his lecture might not be restored, as he was persuaded it was his duty to seek the good of souls, he earnestly prayed that he might have liberty to preach in some other place.

Though the treasurer was undoubtedly willing and desirous to serve him, he obtained no redress; but was cited to appear before the court of the star-chamber, when several articles were exhibited against him. But before his appearance to answer these articles, he wrote a long letter to Burleigh, dated November 1, 1573, in which he addressed him with great spirit and freedom, concerning his own case, and several important points of controversy. This letter was as follows:

"Grace and peace from God the Father, &c.

"Bear with me, I beseech your honour, though I trouble "you; and let the cause of my grief be the discharge of my "boldness. It behoveth me to discharge myself from "slander, lest the gospel should be reproached in me. And "it behoveth you to obey this commandment, *Receive no "accusation against a preacher without good and sufficient "witness*. I know, my lord, you will not do it. I have "good evidence of your equity in this behalf. Yet I am "bold to put you in mind of the word of Christ, which you "cannot possibly too often remember. I ask no more than "what is due to me, even from her majesty's seat of govern-"ment and justice. If I have done evil, let me be punished; "if not, let me be eased of undeserved blame. I crave no "partiality, but seek to answer, and to make you (including "the other lords of the council) judges of my cause; before "whose presence I ought to fear, and the steps of whose "feet I humbly reverence. If, before your honours, I "should be convinced of these pretended crimes, with what "shame should I hide my face all the days of my life! "Where were the rejoicing that I have in God, in all things "that he hath wrought by me? Where were their comfort, "who have so desirously heard me? Where were the good "opinion of many, and all the good-will you have shewed "me? I am not so ignorant, that I see not this. Therefore "persuade yourself, that I am on sure ground. Trial shall "teach your eyes and ears the truth. And to persuade your "heart, I give unto you my faith, I cannot accuse myself "of any thought of my mind, in which I have not honoured "the magistrate, or word of my mouth, in which I have not "regarded the peace of the church. And I thank God, "who of his unspeakable mercy, hath kept for me this con-"science against the day of trouble.

"If you muse now, how these slanders have risen, you "may easily know, that the malice of satan is great against "the ministry of the gospel. I know I have given no "cause, more than I have confessed; and with what words "I have spoken, I desire to be judged by the hearers. And "so much the more bold I now speak to you, because my "lord of London, of late told me, before Mr. Attorney "and Mr. Solicitor, that he could not accuse me of any "such thing. As I was glad to hear this discharge, so I "should have been much more glad, if, upon so free a con-"fession, he would favourably have restored me to my "lecture. Though it be somewhat strange to punish a "man before he offend, lest hereafter he should offend; yet "I am contented with it, and leave it unto them, who "should be as much grieved as myself to see so great a con-"gregation dispersed."

Mr. Deering next proceeds to prove the *lordship* and *civil* government of bishops to be unlawful, and contrary to scripture. "The lordship and civil government of bishops," says he, "is utterly unlawful. The kingdom of Christ is "a spiritual government only. But the government of the "church is a part of the kingdom of Christ. Therefore, "the government of the church is only a *spiritual* govern-"ment. What the kingdom of Christ is, and what "government he hath established in it, learn not of me, but "of God himself. What can be plainer than the words of "Christ? *My kingdom is not of this world?* How plainly "doth St. Paul say, *The weapons of our warfare are not* "*carnal?* Let him, therefore, who is the King of kings, "have the pre-eminence of government. And let him, "whose dominion is the kingdom of heaven, have the sword "and the sceptre that is not fleshly. Let not a vile pope, in "the name of Christ, erect a new kingdom, which Christ "never knew: a kingdom of this world, which, in the "ministry of the gospel, he hath condemned. This kind of "rule hath set all out of order, and in confusion, mingled "heaven and earth together.—As the minister hath nothing "to do with the temporal sword, so it much less becometh "him to be called *lord*. The reason is plain from scripture. "Ministers are called *fishers of men*, *labourers* in the harvest, "*callers* to the marriage, *servants* of the people, *workmen*, "*stewards*, *builders*, *planters*, &c. In all of which, they are "removed from a *lordship* over the people. And again, "they are called fellow-elders, fellow-helpers, fellow-"workmen, fellow-soldiers, fellow-servants, fellow-travel-"lers, &c. In which names, they are forbidden *lordship* "over their brethren. And, surely, it must be great rashness "to refuse so many names, which God hath given us, and "take another, which importeth dominion over others. Can "we doubt then in the question of *lordship?* We appeal to "Christ, and the words of his mouth, to decide the contro-"versy. The disciples had this contention, as well as "ourselves. They strove much, who should be highest; "against which strife, our Saviour Christ pronounceth this "sentence, *He that is greatest among you, let him be as the* "*least. And whosoever of you will be the chief, shall be* "*servant of all.* This is a brief account of the superiority "in the ministry. And this shall for ever determine the "controversy, though all the wisdom in the world reply to "the contrary. If a *lord bishop* find his titles given him "here, let him rejoice in his portion. If he have them not "hence, he shall not have them from us: we will not so "dishonour him who hath given the sentence."

Afterwards, speaking of bishops in the primitive church, and those in modern times, he makes the following distinctions: "The bishops and ministers *then*, were one in degree: "*now* they are divers.—There were many bishops in one "town: now there is but one in a whole country.—No "bishop's authority was more than in one city: now it is in "many shires.—The bishops then used no bodily punish-"ments: now they imprison, fine, &c.—Those bishops "could not excommunicate, nor absolve, of their own "authority: now they may.—Then, without consent, they "could make no ministers: now they do.—They could "confirm no children in other parishes: they do now in "many shires.—Then they had no living of the church, but "only in one congregation: now they have.—Then they "had neither officials, nor commissaries, nor chancellors, "under them.—Then they dealt in no *civil* government, by "any established authority.—Then they had no right in "alienating any parsonage, to give it in lease.—Then they "had the church where they served the cure, even as those "whom we now call *parish ministers*."—This bold and excellent letter contains many other interesting particulars, too numerous for our insertion.* Upon the appearance of Mr. Deering in the star-chamber, the following charges were brought against him: "That he had spoken against *godfathers* and *godmothers*.—That he had asserted that the statute of providing for the poor was not competent to the object.—That he had said, he could provide for them in a better way, by committing them to be kept by the rich.—That, at a public dinner, he took off his cap, and said, 'Now I will prophesy, *Matthew Parker* is the last archbishop that shall ever sit in that seat:' and that Mr. Cartwright said, *Accipio omen*."

To acquit himself of these charges, he presented an address, November 28th, to the lords of the council, who constituted the above court. In this address, he proves his innocence, and establishes his own reputation. He says here, "Against godfathers and godmothers, save only the name, I spake nothing.—That I said the statute of provision for the poor was not competent to the object, or any such words, I utterly deny: I commended the statute.—That I said I could provide for the poor, I utterly deny, as words which I never spake, and thoughts which were never yet in my heart. And if I had spoken any such thing, I had spoken wickedly, and accordingly deserved punishment. And thus much I profess and protest, before the seat of justice, where I dare not lie.—In the last place, I am charged with taking off my cap, and saying, 'Now I will prophesy, Matthew Parker is the last archbishop that shall ever sit in that seat: and that Mr. Cartwright said, *Accipio omen*.' To this I answer, that I have confessed what I said; and here I send it, witnessed by the hands of those who heard it. I put off no cap, nor spake of any prophesy."†

* Strype's Annals, vol. ii. p. 270—279.
† Ibid. Appendix, p. 55—58.

However before Mr. Deering could be restored to his beloved ministerial work, the bishop or the archbishop required him to acknowledge and subscribe to the four following articles:—"1. I acknowledge the Book of Articles, agreed upon by the clergy in the Synod of 1563, and confirmed by the queen's majesty, to be sound, and according to the word of God."

In reply to this, he excepted against the article of the consecration of bishops and archbishops, as contained in the said book. "To what purpose," says he, "is this article put in? What reason is there to make all subscribe unto it? Who dare make so bold an addition to the word of God, as to warrant these consecrations to be tied unto it? Let him allow of it, who hath the profit of it: and he that liketh it not, let him have no bishopric. I would, therefore, gladly make this exception. Also, the article touching homilies, to which, because they are made by man, I dare not give my absolute warrant, that they are, in all things, according to the word of God. And when I set my hand unto it, I must needs avow that which I know not. I would, therefore, make this addition, *As far as I know.*"

"2. That the queen's majesty is the chief governor, next under Christ, of the church of England, as well in ecclesiastical, as civil causes."—"The second article," says he, "I freely acknowledge."

"3. That in the Book of Common Prayer, there is nothing evil, or repugnant to the word of God; but that it may be well used in this our church of England."

To this he excepts, "That in the book, there are many phrases and hard speeches, which require a favourable exposition. There are many things, though well meant, when first appointed, which were certainly ill devised, being first used by papists. And, therefore, being still kept in the Prayer Book, they are offensive.—That day in which there is no communion, certain prayers are to be said after the offertory. What this offertory is, and what it meaneth, I cannot tell. And to account our prayers as offertories, I dare not warrant that it is according to the word of God.—In this book, we are commonly called by the name of *priests;* which name, besides importing a popish sacrificer, and so is sacrilegious, cannot possibly be given to us, and to our Saviour also.—On Christmas-day, we say, 'Thou hast given us thy Son *this day*, to be born of a virgin.' The same words we use all the week after, as if Christ had been born anew every day in the week. If it be said, *this is but a trifle*, the more loath I am to subscribe, that it is according to the word of God.—In one of the prayers, we say, 'Grant us that, which, for our unworthiness, we dare not ask.' These words cannot be excused. They fight directly against our faith. We must come boldly to the throne of grace, and doubt not of obtaining mercy, in whatever God has promised. These and such other things, thus standing in the prayer book, make many fearful of subscribing, that *every part* of it is according to the word of God."

"4. That, as the public preaching of the word, in the church of England, is sound and sincere; so the public order, in the ministration of the sacraments, is consonant to the word of God."

Upon this he observes, "How can I tell, that all preaching in England is sound and sincere, when I hear not all preachers? And sometimes those whom I do hear, preach neither soundly, nor sincerely: but this is the fault of man. —And that the public order, in the ministration of the sacraments, is according to God's word, I cannot simply confess. There is an order how women may baptize. All reformed churches have condemned this, and how can I allow it? All learned men write against the questions and crossings in baptism; and why should I, with my hand, condemn all their doings? The wafer cake in many churches, is thought intolerable; and our own act of parliament for avoiding superstition, hath appointed other bread: what then if I should dislike it?

"Another reason why I cannot subscribe both to this article and the first, is the one contradicting the other. In the first I must subscribe to all the homilies: in this, to all the ceremonies; and yet our homilies condemn many of our ceremonies. In the homilies it is said, 'That the costly and manifold furniture of vestments lately used in the church, is Jewish, and maketh us the more willingly, in such apparel to become Jewish.' If I subscribe to this, how can I subscribe to the ceremonies used in cathedral churches, where the priests, deacon, and subdeacon, are in copes and vestments? In the homilies, it is said, 'That piping, singing, chanting, playing on organs, &c. greatly displease God, and filthily defile his holy temple.' If I must subscribe to this, then I must not subscribe to the contrary, even that all our ceremonies are good, and acording to the word of God. How can I say, that our doctrine, our sacraments, our prayers, our ceremonies, our orders, even that all is according to the word of God? A person having a conscience, or no conscience, must needs be tried here: and blessed is he that is not offended. See, I beseech you, what wrong I sustain, if I be urged to this subscription. While any law bound me to wear the cap and surplice, I wore both. When I was at liberty, surely I would not wear them for devotion. I never persuaded any to refuse them, nor am I charged with ever preaching against them. Thus, according to my promise, I have set down how far I would yield in these articles which your worship sent me. If I seem curious, or to stand upon little points, conscience, it should be remembered, is very tender, and will not yield contrary to its persuasion of the truth. I have sent you these articles, subscribed with mine own hand, and sealed with my heart; even in the presence of God; whom I humbly beseech, for Christ's sake, to give peace unto his church, that her ministers may rejoice, and her subjects be glad. I conclude, desiring God to make you rich in all grace, to his honour and glory. December 16, 1573."* Here we see the evil of requiring subscription to articles and creeds of human composition. To yield in such a case as this, would rack the conscience of every honest man.

Twenty other articles were, about the same time, presented to Mr. Deering in the star-chamber; to each of which, he gave a particular answer. These articles were designed, says Mr. Strype, to make exact inquiry into his principles and opinions, concerning the church, its usages, practices, and clergy, and the queen's authority; and he might, with truth, have added, that it assumed all the appearance of a tyrannical and cruel inquisition. Mr. Deering, in the preface to his answers to these articles, thus expressed himself:—"I most humbly beseech your honours, to remember my former protestation, that I have never spoken against the book of prayers; and in my book in print, I have spoken openly for the allowance of it. I resort to common prayers; and sometimes, being requested, I say the prayers as prescribed. If I be now urged to speak what I think, as before an inquisition, there being no law of God requiring me to accuse myself, I beseech your honours, let my answer witness my humble duty and obedience, rather than be prejudicial and hurtful to me. This I most humbly crave; and under the persuasion of your favour, I will answer boldly, as I am required." These articles, which so

* Parte of a Register, p. 81—85.

much discover the spirit of the times, and the answers which Mr. Deering presented to the court, though at some length, we here present to the curious and inquisitive reader. They were the following:

Article 1. Is the book entitled "The Book of Common Service," allowed by public authority in this realm, to be allowed in the church of God, by God's word, or not?

Answer. The similitude of this book, to that form of prayer used by the papists, leads me to think it declineth from those laws, Deut. vii. 25., xii. 30., xviii. 9. Also, its great inconvenience in encouraging unlearned and indolent ministers to conclude, that the mere *reading* of the service is sufficient. These are some of the reasons why I cannot subscribe, that all the book is allowable by the word of God. Some other things, the bishops themselves confess to be faulty.

2. Are the articles set down by the clergy in Synod, and allowed by public authority, according to God's word, or not?

I confess, as I am persuaded, that the articles of faith are good. I think the same of the articles about traditions, an oath before a judge, the civil magistrate, the doctrine of the homilies, &c. But that which relates to the consecration of archbishops and bishops, I can by no means confess as godly, and according to the word of God.

3. Are we tied in all things, by God's word, to the order and usage of the apostles and primitive church, or not?

No doubt we are bound to whatsoever was the usual order of the apostles. When St. Paul had said to Timothy, "Thou hast fully known my doctrine, manner of life, purpose," &c. &c. he adds, *continue in the things which thou hast learned.* And he chargeth the Philippians, *Those things which ye have both learned and received, and heard and seen in me, do.*

4. Is there any right ministry, or ecclesiastical government, at this time, in the church of England, or not?

If, by right, you mean such a calling as the word of God requireth: as, 1 Tim. iii. 2., Acts i. 23., xiv. 23., 1 Tim. iv. 14., I am sure you will confess it is not right. If you mean a right ministration of the doctrine and sacraments, I humbly confess, that no man ought to separate himself from the church. Concerning government, see the seventh article.

5. May nothing be in the church, either concerning cere-

monies, or government, but that only which the Lord in his word, commandeth?

Such ceremonies as do not necessarily appertain to the gospel of Christ, may be changed; observing always that which St. Paul hath commanded, Phil. iv. 8., 1 Cor. xiv. 26.

6. Ought every particular church or parish in England, of necessity, and by the order of God's word, to have its own pastor, elder, and deacons, chosen by the people of that parish; and they only to have the whole government of that particular church, in matters ecclesiastical?

Wherever this government hath been, the choice hath been by certain persons, with the allowance of the people, so far as I ever read. But what is most requisite at the present time, I leave to those whom God hath set in authority.

7. Should there be an equality among all the ministers of this realm, as well in government and jurisdiction, as in the ministration of the word and sacraments?

That all ministers are called to the preaching of the word, and the ministration of the sacraments, no man, I think, will deny. Touching government or governors, the Holy Ghost calleth them fellow-ministers, fellow-elders, fellow-officers, fellow-soldiers, fellow-labourers, fellow-servants: and St. Peter expressly forbids them being *lords over God's heritage.* St. John evidently condemneth the lordly dominion of Diotrephes, in commanding and excommunicating by his own authority. Our Lord himself, refused to exercise any lordly dominion; and when his disciples strove for superiority, he expressly forbad them, and reproved them for aspiring after it. Though ministers are worthy of double honour, singular love, great reverence, and all humble duty, I dare, by no means, make them *lords* in the ministry, nor give to any one of them authority above the rest.

8. Are the patrimonies of the church, such as bishops' lands, the lands belonging to cathedral churches, the glebe lands, and tithes, by right, and God's word, to be taken from them?

Render unto Cæsar, the things which are Cæsar's; and unto God, the things that are God's, is a rule always binding. Every prince who feareth the King of kings, must make sufficient provision for the ministry, then for the poor, then for schools and the universities, in such a degree as may supply the wants of the ministry; without which the spoil of the church is most unnatural sacrilege.

9. Are the ministers of this realm, of whatsoever calling, now in place, lawful ministers; and their administration, and ecclesiastical actions, lawful and effectual?

This article, so far as I can see, is the same as the fourth.

10. Is it not convenient at a marriage, to have the communion, and the newly married persons to communicate; and, at a funeral, to have a sermon?

I would have communions at such times as the church appoints. On those days, if there be a marriage, it is meet that the parties communicate. As to the funeral sermons, they may be used. Yet, if there be any inconvenience, by hurting or offending the church, they ought to be omitted.

11. Is it lawful for any man to preach, besides he who is a pastor; and may a pastor preach out of his own flock without a license?

None may preach but a pastor, and he, on just occasion, being requested, may preach out of his own flock. But, surely, if he have no license to preach, he hath no license to be a pastor.

12. Is it better and more agreeable to God's word, and more for the profit of God's church, that a prescribed order of common prayer be used, or that every minister pray publicly, as his own spirit shall direct him?

An ordinary prayer is very necessary, that it may be familiar to the people: but, as every parish will have its occasions and necessities, so it is necessary, that the minister be able to pray in the congregation, according to the necessities of the people.

13. Are the children of parents, who are perfect papists, to be baptized? And are infants within God's covenant, and have they faith?

If parents are obstinate, and perfect papists, wanting nothing of the spiritual wickedness of antichrist, and are so accounted by the church, their children are not to be admitted to this sacrament, though we exclude them not from the election of God: but if the parents be not cast out of the church, we may admit the children; yet not as having that faith which cometh by hearing, but as being within the covenant: *I am their God, and the God of their children.*

14. May any ecclesiastical persons have more ecclesiastical livings than one?*

For one man to have many parsonages, where he cannot possibly reside, is great wickedness. And seeing Christ hath purchased his church with his own blood, whosoever enjoys several livings, considers very little the words of St. Paul: *Take heed unto all the flock, over which the Holy Ghost hath made you overseers, to feed the church of God.* I, therefore, humbly beseech your honours, to have this carefully reformed.

15. May one be a minister, who has no particular flock assigned him? And may an ecclesiastical person be exercised, also, in a *civil* function?

A minister can no more be without a charge, than a king without a kingdom. *No man that warreth entangleth himself with the affairs of this life.* And I am sure whatsoever person seeketh after civil offices, wanteth that love which should most abound. Our Saviour refused to be judge in the division of lands. Yet I judge not him, who, on special occasions, seeketh to do good to others.

16. Are all the commandments of God needful for salvation?

All the commandments are necessary for all men in all places, and are ever to be observed. And as Christ was minister, not of earthly things, but heavenly; so the observance of all his commandments is necessary to salvation; and the breach of the least of them, if imputed to us, hath the just recompence of eternal death.

17. Has the Queen of England authority over the ecclesiastical state, and in ecclesiastical matters, as well as civil?

Let every soul be subject to the higher powers, whether he be an apostle, or evangelist, or prophet, or whatsoever he be. This subjection is not against his calling. Princes have full authority over all ecclesiastical and civil persons, and equally over both, to punish offenders, and to praise well-doers. Only this is the difference in the sovereignty over both. The commonwealth cannot be without the magistrate; but if all magistrates fall from the church, we must still hold this article, "I believe in the catholic church." For Christ, and not the christian magistrate, is the life and head of the church. In the commonwealth,

* What could the commissioners design by proposing this question? Did they imagine it was a crime to speak against pluralities, the great plague of the christian church, and at which even papists blush?

the prince maketh and repealeth laws, as appears most for the safety of the state, and the benefit of the people; but in the church, there is only ONE LAWGIVER, even JESUS CHRIST.

18. Is the Queen of England the chief governor under Christ, over the whole church and state ecclesiastical in this realm, or but a member of it? And may the church of England be established without the magistrate?

This is answered under the seventeenth article.

19. Is the Queen of England bound to observe the judicial laws of Moses, in the punishment and pardon of criminal offences?

We are sure that the law of Moses, was, to the people of Israel, an absolute and a most perfect rule of justice; so that all laws ought to be made according to its equity. Yet, to decide on all particular cases, dare I not. It belongeth to the Lord to say, I will pardon, or I will destroy.

20. May the Queen of England, of herself, and by her own authority, assign and appoint civil officers?

I never knew a man who doubted this article. And sure I am, that her majesty, in her wisdom, may do as she thinketh best.*

These were the articles proposed to Mr. Deering in the star-chamber, and this was the substance of those answers which he presented to the court in writing. In these answers, says Mr. Strype, he made *very ill* reflections upon the reformation and religion of the established church.† Whether this remark be consistent with christian liberality, or even common justice, every reader will easily judge. What could be the design of the commissioners in proposing such inquiries? Some of them relating wholly to matters of state, seem designed to ensnare him. Others were evidently intended to draw him either to approve, or to censure, the corruptions of the church. And in general, it is extremely manifest, that they were put to him, to rack his conscience, and to get something out of him; to make him an offender by his own confession. "For my part," says Mr. Peirce, "when I consider the abominable tyranny of all such proceedings, and the barbarous wickedness of sifting the secrets of mens' hearts, about those matters, of which perhaps they never spoke any thing in their lives; I heartily bless my God that he did not cast my lot in those days, but reserved me for times of greater equity and freedom."‡

* Parte of a Register, p. 73—80.—Strype's Annals, vol. ii. p. 280, 281.
† Strype's Parker, p. 452. ‡ Peirce's Vindication, part i. p. 81.

During Mr. Deering's suspension, the Bishop of London, out of good nature, it is said, interceded with the treasurer, to procure the consent of the council for his liberty to preach again at St. Paul's; upon these conditions, that he taught sound doctrine, exhorted to virtue, dissuaded from vice, and meddled not with matters of order and policy, but left them to the magistrate: and, he said, he believed Mr. Deering would be brought so to do. He thought these gentle dealings the best, for the present, and would quiet the minds of the people. He thought a soft plaster, in such a case, much better than a corrosive. But the treasurer, we are informed, disliked the advice, and sharply reproved the bishop for giving it. At length, however, he prevailed; got Mr. Deering's suspension taken off, and, notwithstanding his puritanical answers to the above articles, procured his restoration to his lecture.*

The lords of the council having restored him to his beloved work of preaching, the archbishop and several of the bishops were much offended. Dr. Cox, bishop of Ely, wrote a warm letter to the treasurer, signifying his great disapprobation of the conduct of the council in restoring him, even as a man sound in the faith, and by their own authority, without consulting *spiritual* men, whose business it was to determine in such cases: and that they ought not to have determined a matter relating to religion without the assistance of those who belonged to the ecclesiastical function. Mr. Deering was, indeed, restored in consequence of the answers he gave to the articles, which articles, it seems, were collected out of Mr. Cartwright's book against Whitgift. Though Bishop Cox said his answers were *fond* and *untrue*, the lords of the council thought otherwise, and were satisfied with them. The bishop urged, that in these matters they ought to have consulted the judgment of learned divines, adding, "In all godly assemblies, *priests* have usually been called, as in parliaments and privy councils." And in the warmth of his zeal, he seemed inclined to move the queen's majesty to oppose and recall the decree of the council: but he trusted that the treasurer would, in his *wisdom* and *godly* zeal, undertake to do it himself.† Our author further adds, that when Mr. Deering and three of his brethren were first cited into the star-chamber, the Bishop of London remained silent, for which the queen afterwards bitterly rebuked him.‡

* Strype's Parker, p. 426. † Ibid. p. 426, 427.

‡ Queen Elizabeth was a lady of a proud and imperious spirit; and

Although Mr. Deering was again allowed to preach, his troubles were not ended. The Bishop of London, by whose influence he had been restored, appeared soon to repent of what he had done. When he waited upon the bishop, informing him that the council, by their letters, had restored him to his lecture, his grace said he would see the letters, or he should not preach, and added, "That unless he preached more soberly and discreetly than before, he would silence him again." Mr. Deering replied, "If you do forbid me, I think I shall obey." His obedience was, indeed, soon brought to the test; for the bishop silenced him presently after. He brought complaints against him in the star-chamber, and urged the treasurer to procure an order from the queen to put down his lecture. He wrote also to the Earl of Leicester, signifying how much he disliked Mr. Deering's continuance. This was going the right way to work, and he was sure of success. Accordingly, the business was brought before her majesty, who commanded him to be silenced; and a warrant being sent to the bishop for this purpose, he was again suspended.*

In the year 1574, the famous Dr. Thomas Sampson being laden with old age and infirmities, was desirous of Mr. Deering succeeding him in his lecture at Whittington-college, London, for which there was a stipend of ten pounds a year. The company of cloth-workers had the power of nomination, and the archbishop had the allowance. Dr. Sampson had no doubt of the company's approbation, but doubted the favour of the archbishop. And, indeed, his doubts were not without foundation; for his grace being moved to allow of Mr. Deering, in case he should be nominated by the company, he utterly refused. Dr. Sampson, however, wrote to Burleigh, the treasurer, earnestly intreating him, in this case, to use his influence with the archbishop. In this letter, he observed, that though the archbishop did not himself like to take pains in the congregation, he should

usually carried things with a very high hand, expecting all to bow to her will and pleasure. This arbitrary temper she exercised over her own clergy, as well as others. Dr. Nowell, dean of St. Paul's, and one of the queen's chaplains, having spoken less reverently of the sign of the cross, in a sermon preached before her majesty, she called aloud to him from her closet window, commanding him to retire from that ungodly digression, and return to his text.—On another occasion, Elizabeth and the Earl of Essex not exactly agreeing in a point of political prudence, this sovereign lady was so exceedingly provoked, that she gave him a box on the ear, and bid him "go and be hanged."—*Heylin's Hist. of Refor.* p. 124. Edit. 1610.—*Rapin's Hist.* vol. ii. p. 149.

* Strype's Parker, p. 428.

not hinder or forbid others, who were both able and willing. He could say of Mr. Deering, that his grace of Canterbury could find no fault with him, either in his doctrine or his life. Also, that it was no great promotion, but a place in which, by the labours of Mr. Deering, he doubted not that her majesty's subjects would be much profited. It was all to no purpose. The archbishop remembered his former nonconformity, but especially his puritanical answers to the articles in the star-chamber; and, therefore, remained inflexible, and would not admit him.*

At length, Mr. Deering being worn out by hard labours and manifold troubles, fell sick; and perceiving his dissolution to approach, he said to his friends, "The good Lord pardon my great negligence, that, while I had time, I used not his precious gifts more for the advancement of his glory, as I might have done: yet I bless God, that I have not abused those gifts to ambition and vain studies. When I am dead, my enemies will be reconciled to me; excepting such as knew me not, or such as have in them no sense of the truth. I have faithfully, and with a good conscience, served the Lord my God, and my prince." A brother minister standing by him, said, "It is a great blessing to you, that you shall depart in peace, and be taken from many troubles, which your brethren shall behold and suffer." To whom he replied, "If the Lord hath appointed that his saints shall sup together in heaven, why do I not go to them? But if there be any doubt or hesitation resting on my spirit, the Lord reveal the truth unto me." Having for some time lain still, a friend who attended him, said, that he hoped his mind had been employed in holy meditation; to whom he thus replied: "A poor wretch and a miserable man that I am, the least of all saints, the chief of all sinners! yet I trust in Christ my Saviour. Yet a little while, and we shall see our hope. The end of the world is coming upon us; and we shall quickly receive the end of our hope, which we have so much looked for. Afflictions, diseases, sickness, and grief, are only parts of that portion which God hath allotted us in this world. It is not enough to continue some time in his ways; we must persevere in the fear of the Lord to the end of our days. For in a moment we shall be taken away. Take heed, therefore, that you do not make sport of the word of God, nor lightly esteem so great a treasure.

* Strype's Parker, p. 469, 470.

Blessed are they who, while they have tongues, use them to God's glory."

As the hour of his dissolution approached, being raised up in bed, his friends desired him to say something to their edification and comfort. The sun shining in his face, he thus addressed them: "As there is only one sun in the world, so there is only one righteousness, and one communion of saints. If I were the most excellent creature in the world, equal in righteousness to Abraham, Isaac, and Jacob, yet would I confess myself to be a sinner, and that I expected salvation in the righteousness of Jesus Christ alone: for we all stand in need of the grace of God. As for my death, I bless God, I find and feel so much comfort and joy in my soul, that if I were put to my choice, whether to die or live, I would a thousand times rather choose death than life, if it was the holy will of God." He died soon after, June 26, 1576.*

Fuller denominates Mr. Deering a pious man, a painful preacher, and an eminent divine; but disaffected to bishops and ceremonies.† Mr. Strype says, he was disliked by the bishops, and some other great personages, as a man vain and full of fancies, because he would tell them of their common swearing and covetousness. He would not associate with persecutors; and was much grieved when the benefice of a great parish was given to an unpreaching minister. Yet, says he, it was Mr. Deering's common fault *to tell lies*.‡ Does not this look like a slander? What did the excellent Dr. Sampson say of him, as already noticed, who knew him well? Surely, if this had been his common fault, having so many enemies constantly and narrowly watching him, his sin would have found him out. Granger gives a very different account of him. "The happy death," says he, "of this truly religious man, was suitable to the purity and integrity of his life."§ He is classed with the other learned writers and fellows of Christ's college, Cambridge.‖

Mr. Deering was a man of great learning, and a fine orator; but in his sermon before the queen, February 25, 1569, he had the boldness to say, "If you have sometimes said (meaning in the days of her sister Mary,) *tanquam ovis*, as a sheep appointed to be slain; take heed you hear not

* Account annexed to Mr. Deering's Lects. on Heb.—Fuller's Abel Redivivus, p. 341, 342.

† Fuller's Church Hist. b. ix. p. 109.

‡ Strype's Parker, p. 381, 429.

§ Granger's Biog. Hist. vol. i. p. 215.

‖ Fuller's Hist. of Cam. p. 92.

now of the prophet, *tanquam indomica juvenca*, as an untamed and unruly heifer."* For this, he was forbidden preaching any more at court; and surely, says Fuller, "the queen still retained much of her former disposition, *as a sheep*, in not inflicting a greater punishment, for so public a reproof.†

Mr. Clark relates the following anecdote, shewing the amiableness of his truly christian spirit. Mr. Deering being once at a public dinner, a gallant young man sat on the opposite side the table, who, besides other vain discourse, broke out into profane swearing; for which Mr. Deering gravely and sharply reproved him. The young man taking this as an affront, immediately threw a glass of beer in his face. Mr. Deering took no notice of the insult, but wiped his face, and continued eating as before. The young gentleman presently renewed his profane conversation; and Mr. Deering reproved him as before; upon which, but with more rage and violence, he flung another glass of beer in his face. Mr. Deering continued unmoved, still shewing his zeal for the glory of God, by bearing the insult with christian meekness and humble silence. This so astonished the young gentleman, that he rose from the table, fell on his knees, and asked Mr. Deering's pardon; and declared, that if any of the company offered him similar insults, he would stab them with his sword.‡ Here was practically verified, the New Testament maxim, "Be not overcome of evil, but overcome evil with good."

His Works.—1. A Sermon at the Tower of London, 1569.—2. A sparing Restraint of many lavish Untruths, which Master D. Harding doth challenge in the first Article of my L. of Salisburies Reply, 1569.—3. Certaine godly and comfortable Letters, full of Christian Consolation, 1571.—4. Twenty-seven Lectures, or Readings, upon part of the Epistle to the Hebreues, 1576.—5. A Sermon preached before the Queen's Majesty, the 25th day of February, 1569, from Psalm lxxviii. 70., 1584.—6. A briefe and necessarie Catechisme, or Instruction very needful to be known to all Householders.—All these were collected and published in one volume, in 4to., 1597.

Thomas Aldrich, A. M.—He was son of John Aldrich, who was twice chosen mayor of the city of Norwich, and member of several parliaments for that city. His father being a public character, introduced him to public notice,

* Sermon before the Queen, Feb. 25, 1569.
† Fuller's Church Hist. b. ix. p. 109.
‡ Clark's Examples, p. 500. Edit. 1671.

and obtained his preferment to several ecclesiastical benefices. He was made archdeacon of Sudbury, prebendary of Westminster, master of Bennet college, Cambridge, proctor of the university, and rector of Hadleigh in Suffolk.* About the same time, he became chaplain to Archbishop Parker, and was appointed one of the commissioners for visiting and reforming the papists in the county of Norfolk.† Notwithstanding all these worldly allurements, together with a flattering prospect of much higher advancement, he espoused the cause of the despised puritans; became a zealous nonconformist, and one of their leaders in the university of Cambridge.

It is observed, that, May 20, 1571, Mr. Aldrich preached at Thetford, in Norfolk: May 21st, he preached at Wymondham: May 22d, he preached at Matshall: May 24th, he preached in St. Clement's church, Norwich: and the next Lord's day, May 27th, he preached in the Greenyard, before the mayor and citizens. He was, therefore, no indolent labourer in the Lord's vineyard.‡

Mr. Aldrich being master of the above college, and refusing, from a scrupulous conscience, to take the degrees required of those in that office, was brought into many troubles, and at length, to avoid expulsion, resigned his mastership of the college. Many other grievous complaints are said to have been brought against him, most probably about his nonconformity. In one of these complaints, he is said to have called the archbishop "the pope of Lambeth and Bennet college." Dr. Whitgift, at this time one of the heads of the university, took an active part in these severities. This was in the year 1573; but some time previous to these troubles, Mr. Aldrich voluntarily resigned his prebend at Westminster.§ It is, indeed, acknowledged, that as he objected taking the degrees, upon the ground of a scrupulous conscience, the treatment he met with was *rather too severe*.‖

The author last cited, however, brings many foul accusations against him. He observes, that Mr. Aldrich was charged, not only with refusing to qualify for his office, but with evil government of his college, in neglecting its exercises and discipline; with things prejudicial to its temporal interests; and with various other things, to the number of twenty. And the troubles of the college did not

* Blomefield's Hist. of Norfolk, vol. ii. p. 468.
† Newcourt's Repert. Eccl. vol. i. p. 925.
‡ Strype's Parker, p. 254. § Ibid. p. 429—433.—Whitgift, p. 49.
‖ Master's Hist. of C. C. C. p. 112. Edit. 1753.

end with his resignation. For the masters and fellows, says he, were afterwards under the necessity of appealing to Chancery, to oblige him to account for several sums of money which he had received, and had not paid; to restore many writings, the private seal of the master, and some other things; and to discharge the various debts which he had contracted. These, however, were not recovered till after his death, which happened in the year 1576.* These are certainly very heavy charges! But how far he was guilty, is not easy now to ascertain. He was a man well versed in the learned languages, also in the French and Italian.† The Oxford historian says, that he was deprived of his prebend for notorious nonconformity; but, upon his repentance and reconciliation, that he was admitted to another prebend, in 1576, the year in which he died.‡ It is not easy to reconcile this with the account given above from Mr. Strype.

Thomas Lever, B. D.—This celebrated divine was born of respectable parents at Little Lever in Lancashire, and educated in the university of Cambridge. After taking his degrees, he was chosen fellow, then master of St. John's college; in which office he succeeded Dr. William Bill, and was the seventh master of the house.§ He was a famous disputant, a celebrated scholar, and remarkably zealous in the advancement of true religion.‖ He was ordained both priest and deacon, in the year 1550, by Bishop Ridley, afterwards martyr in the Marian persecution, and was a most eloquent and popular preacher to the close of the reign of King Edward.¶ This learned prelate had a very high opinion of him, and esteemed him famous for his bold and plain preaching. Speaking of the preaching of Latimer, Bradford, Knox, and Lever, he said: "They ripped so deeply in the galled backs of the great men at court, to have purged them of the filthy matter festered in their hearts; as, insatiable covetousness, filthy carnality, voluptuousness, intolerable pride, and ungodly loathsomeness to hear poor mens' cases and God's word; that they could never abide them above all others."** Afterwards,

* Master's Hist. of C. C. C. p. 111, 112.
† Strype's Parker, p. 289. ‡ Wood's Athenæ Oxon. vol. i. p. 725.
§ Baker's MS. Collec. vol. i. p. 146.
‖ Strype's Cranmer, p. 163.
¶ Baker's MS. Collec. vol. i. p. 146. ** Strype's Parker, p. 211.

when Ridley was cast into prison, and not long before he was committed to the flames, he wrote a letter to his friend Grindal, then in exile, in which he made affectionate and honourable mention of Mr. Lever, as one of the persecuted servants of Christ.*

In the above year he preached two sermons, the one at Paul's cross,† the other before the king, which, it is said, would in that day have spoiled any man's preferment. As he delivered several things on these occasions, illustrating the history of the time, and particularly shewing the state of learning, the way of living, and the course of study, as well as the manner of preaching, in those days, we shall take notice of one or two passages; which serve also to describe the author in his spirit and address. Having spoken in commendation of King Henry's bounty, in giving £200 annually, towards the exhibition of five learned men, to read and teach divinity, law, physic, Greek and Hebrew, and of his munificence in founding Trinity college, and other bounties, he proceeds as follows:

" Howbeit, all they that have knowen the universitye of " Cambryge, sense that tyme that it dyd fyrst begynne to " receive these greate and manyefolde benefytes from the " kynges magstye, at youre handes, have juste occasion " to suspecte that you have decyved boeth the kynge and " universitie, to enryche yourselves. For before that you " dyd begynne to be the disposers of the kynges lyberalitye " towards learnynge and poverty, ther was in houses be- " longynge unto the universitye of Cambryge two hundred " students of dyvynytye, many verye well learned: whyche " be nowe all clene gone, house and name; younge towarde " scholers, and old fatherlye doctors, not one of them " lefte. One hundred also of an other sorte, that havynge " rich frendes or beying benefyced men dyd lyve of theym- " selves in ottels and innes, be eyther gon awaye, or elles " fayne to crepe into colleges, and put poore men from " bare lyvynges. Those bothe be all gone, and a small " number of poore godly dylygent students now remaynynge " only in colleges be not able to tary, and contynue " their studye in the universitye, for lacke of exhibition " and healpe. There be dyverse ther which ryse dayly " betwixt foure and fyve of the clocke in the mornynge;

* Fox's Martyrs, vol. iii. p. 347.

† Paul's cross was a pulpit, in the form of a cross, which stood nearly in the middle of St. Paul's church-yard, where the first reformers used frequently to preach unto the people.

"and from fyve untill syxe of the clocke, use common "prayer, wyth an exhortation of God's worde, in a common "chappell; and from sixe unto ten of the clocke, use ever "eyther private study or common lectures. At tenne of "the clocke they go to dynner, where as they be contente "wyth a penye pyece of biefe amongest foure, havynge "a fewe porage made of the brothe of the same byefe, "wythe salte and otemel, and nothynge els.

"After thys slender dinner, they be either teachinge or "learnynge untyll fyve of the clocke in the evening, "whenas they have a supper not much better than theyr "diner. Immedyatelye after the wyche, they go eyther to "reasonynge in problemes or unto some other studye, untyl "it be nyne or tenne of the clocke; and there beynge "wythout fyre, are fayne to walke or runne up and downe "halfe an houre, to gette a heate on their feete, when they "go to bed."*

Notwithstanding the heavy pressures under which the university, and particularly St. John's college, groaned, of which Mr. Lever complains in his sermons, occasioned by the hungry courtiers invading the ecclesiastical preferments; yet his college greatly flourished, as well in religion as in sound learning. The reformation in no place gained more ground, or was maintained with greater zeal, than in this college, and under the worthy example and just government of this master. This was manifest in the day of trial; when he, with twenty-four of his fellows, quitted their places and preferments, to preserve their own consciences.†

Mr. Lever was a zealous advocate for the reformation, as well as genuine piety. He held a correspondence with his numerous friends; and among his letters, the following, which contains information not unworthy of notice, is given as a specimen of his sentiments and address. It is addressed to the learned Roger Ascham; and though there is no year mentioned, it appears from the contents to have been written November 13, 1551, and about the time when he was preferred to the mastership of his college.‡

"To Roger Ascham.

"My salutation in Christ. I have received your letters "written unto me. As concerning a privilege to be pro- "cured for you, so that the reading of Greek in Cambridge "might be free from *Celibatus*, and such acts as the fellows

* Baker's MS. Collec. vol. i. p. 147, 148. † Ibid. p. 149, 150.
‡ Ibid. vol. xxxii. p. 496, 497.

"of the house be bound unto. I have also shewed Mr. "Cheek your request, and have as yet no answer from him. "Your letters of news written to all the fellows of St. "John's, are as yet reserved there, and come not as yet "unto my sight. As touching the imprisonment of the "Duke of Somerset and his wife, the Earl of Arundel, the "Earl Paget, Lord Gray and others, that be lately put "into the Tower, other men that know more than I do "may write unto you better than I can. The bishoprics of "Lincoln, Rochester and Chichester, be as yet void, and "appointed as yet certainly to no man for as much as I know. "Mr. Horne is dean of Durham, Dr. Redman is deceased, "and Dr. Bill by the king is appointed master of Trinity "college, Cambridge, and I to succeed him in the master-"ship of St. John's. Dr. Redman being in a consumption "did look certainly for death, and did ever talk of religion "as one who had clean forsaken the world, and look and "desire to be with God. I will shew you part of such talk "as Mr. Young of Cambridge did hear of Dr. Redman "himself, and did shew unto me afterwards. First, Dr. "Redman being desired to answer to questions of religion "his judgment, did say, that he would answer betwixt God "and his conscience, without any worldly respect. Then "being demanded what he thought of the see of Rome, he "said, it was the *sink of iniquity:* but do not you also think "that we have a *stinking pump* in the *church of England?* "To the demand of *purgatory*, he said, there was no such pur-"gatory as the schoolmen do imagine; but when Christ shall "come surrounded with fire from heaven, then all meeting "him shall there be purged, as I think, said he, and as "many authors do take it. And to make the *mass* a "sacrifice for the dead, is to be plain against Christ. And "to the proposition, *faith only justifieth*, he answered, that "was a comfortable and sweet doctrine, being rightly under-"stood of a true and lively faith, and that no works could "deserve salvation; no, not the works of grace in a man "that is justified. When he was asked what he thought of "*transubstantiation*, he said, he had studied that matter "these twelve years, and did find that Tertullian, Irenæus "and Origen, did plainly write contrary to it, and in the other "ancient writers it was not taught nor maintained. There-"fore, in the schoolmen, he thought he should have found "plain and sufficient matter for it; but in them there was "no good ground, but all was imaginations and gross errors. "Concerning the presence, he said, that Christ was in the "sacrament really and corporally, as Mr. Young told me; "and yet being asked whether that was Christ's body which "we see the priest lift up, he said that Christ's body "could neither be lifted up, nor down; and carrying it "about to be honoured, he said, was an evil abuse. Also, "he said, that evil men do not receive Christ's body, but "the sacrament thereof. He advised Mr. Young to study "the scriptures, and to beware of men. He said also that "the book which my lord of Canterbury last set forth "of this matter, is a wonderful book, and willed Mr. "Young to read it with diligence. Mr. Young said to me, "that whereas he was aforetime as ready and willing to "have died for the transubstantiation of the sacrament, as "for Christ's incarnation; he is now purposed to take "deliberation, and to study after a more indifferent sort, to "ground his judgment better than upon a common consent "of many that have borne the name of Christ. I trust that "not only Mr. Young, but many others are drawn from "their obstinacy unto more indifferency, by Dr. Redman's "communication.

"If I be master of St. John's college, I shall be desirous "to have you at home, and not unwilling that you should "have and enjoy any privilege that may encourage you to "a better knowledge of the Greek tongue.* Since I wrote "last, there be dead of your acquaintance Dr. Neveyear, "Dr. Redman, and Dr. Bell the physician. All other your "friends and acquaintance are in good health. When you "talk with God in meditation and prayer remember me. "Consider; be vigilant; pray, pray, pray. Scribbled at "London, 13 November.

"Faithfully yours,

"THOMAS LEVER."

On the death of King Edward, and the return of popery and persecution, Mr. Lever withdrew from the storm, fled beyond sea, and was involved in the troubles at Frankfort. It does not, however, appear that he took any active part in

* Roger Ascham, to whom this epistle was addressed, was one of the brightest geniuses and politest scholars of his age. He was public orator of the university of Cambridge, and Latin secretary to Edward VI., Queen Mary, and Queen Elizabeth, the last of whom he taught to write a fine hand, and instructed in the Greek and Latin languages, of which he was a consummate master. His letters are valuable both for style and matter, and are almost the only classical work of the kind written by an Englishman; yet with all his learning and refinement, he was extravagantly fond of archery, dicing and cockfighting.—*Wood's Athenæ Oxon.* vol. i. p. 695. *Granger's Biog. Hist.* vol. i. p. 276.

those disgraceful broils, but was invited thither to be one of the pastors of the church, and a judicious mediator between the contending parties. Herein his worthy service utterly failed. He also visited the learned protestants at Strasburgh, Basil, Zurich, Berne, Lausanne, and Geneva; among whom he discovered great learning, sound doctrine, and godly discipline, especially in Bullinger and Calvin; as he wrote to his intimate friend Mr. John Bradford, then in confinement previous to his martyrdom.* While Mr. Lever was in a state of exile, he lived chiefly at Arrau in Switzerland, where he was chosen pastor to the English church. The members of this church, under his pastoral care, are said to have lived together in godly quietness among themselves, and in great favour with the people among whom they were planted. Upon the arrival of news of the queen's death, and a prospect of better days in his own country, he united with his brethren at Arrau, in addressing a most affectionate letter of congratulation to their brethren in exile at Geneva.†

On the accession of Queen Elizabeth, Mr. Lever returned home, but not to the mastership of his college, having brought with him, it is said, "that unhappy tincture which disqualified him for his preferment."‡ This was his nonconformity. Having acted upon the genuine protestant principles, in matters of ceremony and discipline, while in a foreign land, he wished to act upon them now he was returned to his native country, and was desirous that the reformation might be carried on towards perfection.

He was a celebrated preacher at court, and was often called to preach before the queen. He had so much influence over her majesty, that he dissuaded her from assuming the title of *Supreme Head;* for which, though he did it with great temper, he was severely censured by persons of another spirit.§ It was this which gave the first and great offence to the ruling courtiers. Though they had heard him with great attention in the days of King Edward, they would not amend their lives under Queen Elizabeth, nor would many of them attend upon his ministry. He entered upon the married state soon after his return from exile, and sooner than he could do it with safety. His marriage, as well as his puritanical principles, appears to

* Troubles at Frankeford, p. 30.—Strype's Annals, vol. i. p. 131.
† Troubles at Frankeford, p. 159, 164.
‡ Baker's MS. Collec. vol i. p. 150.
§ Strype's Annals, vol. i. p. 132.

have been some hinderance to his return to the mastership of his college.*

In the year 1561, according to Mr. Strype, he was preferred to a prebend in the church of Durham, and to the mastership of Sherborn hospital, near Durham; the former of which, he says, in one place, he supposes Mr. Lever was deprived of for nonconformity, and in another, that he resigned it in the year 1571.† In addition to this information, he tells us that upon Mr. Lever's return from exile, he obtained no other preferment besides that of the mastership of the above hospital, which he kept to his death: yet he mentions him as Archdeacon of Coventry, and in this capacity, sat in the convocation of 1562, and subscribed the Articles of Religion.‡ It is extremely difficult, not to say impossible, to reconcile these accounts of the learned and voluminous historian. By another writer, he is said to have been collated to the mastership of the above hospital, January 28, 1562; and, the year following, to his prebend in the church of Durham; both of which, he supposes Mr. Lever held by connivance from Bishop Pilkington, who had formerly been one of the fellows in the university.§

Archbishop Parker having pressed conformity to the habits and ceremonies, sequestered and deprived many learned and faithful ministers. This was a great affliction to the Lord's servants. They were exceedingly tempted and tried. The sorrow of most ministers was, indeed, very great; and they murmured, saying, "We are killed in our souls, by this pollution of the bishops. We cannot perform our ministry in the singleness of our hearts. We abide in extreme misery, our wives, and our children, by the proceedings of the bishops, who oppose us, and place ignorant ministers in our places."‖ Mr. Lever, therefore, addressed an excellent letter to the Earl of Leicester and Sir William Cecil, dated February 24, 1565, in which he exposes the extreme hardships under which the puritans laboured, by the imposition of the habits and ceremonies; and earnestly solicits them to use their utmost endeavours to procure some favour for his silenced brethren, who had been lawfully admitted into the ministry, and had always

* Baker's MS. Collec. vol. i. p. 152.
† Strype's Annals, vol. i. p. 133.—Parker, p. 325.
‡ Strype's Annals, vol. i. p. 290. vol. ii. Appen. p. 15.
§ Baker's MS. Collec. vol. i. p. 150.
‖ Ibid. vol. xxvii. p. 388, 389.

faithfully preached the gospel. In this letter, he expressed himself as follows:*

"Wherefore in the universities and elsewhere," says he, "no standing but sinking doth appear; when, as the office and living of a minister shall be taken from him, who, once lawfully admitted, hath ever since diligently preached, because he now refuseth prescription of men in apparel; and the name, living, and office of a minister of God's word, allowed to him who neither *can* nor *will* preach, except as a mere form.—Now there is notable papistry in England and Scotland proved and proclaimed by the preaching of the gospel, to be idolatry and treason, and how much idolatry and treason is yet nourished in the hearts of many, God knoweth; and how the old stumbling-blocks are set up in many things and many places, especially the crucifix in England, and the mass in Scotland, before the faces of the highest, is daily seen by idolaters and traitors with rejoicing and hope; and by christian and obedient subjects with sorrow of heart and fear of the state.

"If, in the ministry and ministers of God's word, the sharpness of salt by doctrine to mortify affections, be rejected, and ceremonial service, with flattery to feed affections, be retained, then doth Christ threaten such treading under foot, as no power nor policy can withstand.

"Now, therefore, my prayer unto God, and writing to your honours, is, that authority in England, and especially you may for sincere religion refuse worldly pleasure and gains. You ought not to allow any such corruptions among protestants, being God's servants, as to make papists to rejoice and hope for a day, being God's enemies: but rather cause such abolishing of inward papistry, and outward monuments of the same, as should cause idolatrous traitors to grieve, and faithful subjects to be glad: such casting forth of the unsavoury ministry and ministers, as might make only such as have the savouryness of doctrine and edification to be allowed to that office, seeing such ministry only may preserve princes, and priests, and people from casting and treading under foot: and so not deceiving and leaving the godly in distress, to perish with the ungodly; but ever travelling to deliver, defend and help the godly, till by God's providence and promise they be delivered and preserved from all danger, and in continuance and increase of

* Baker's MS. Collec. vol. xxi. p. 559—561.—Strype's Parker, Appen. 77.

godly honour; which God for his mercy in Christ grant unto the queen's majesty, unto you and all other of her honourable council, amen. By yours at commandment, faithfully in Christ,

"Thomas Lever."

Mr. Lever was a person greatly beloved, especially by persons of learning and real worth; but the above letter was most probably without its desired effect. He was a most learned and popular preacher at court; and though he was a decided nonconformist, he obtained a connivance for some time. In the year 1566, when many excellent minsters were silenced for refusing the habits and ceremonies, he is said to have been still allowed to preach;* but the year following, he was deprived of his prebend in the church of Durham.†

There were at this period numerous puritans confined in the various prisons about London, for refusing conformity to the established church; when Mr. Lever wrote a letter, dated December 5, 1568, to those who were confined in Bridewell. In this excellent letter, he first endeavours to comfort the prisoners under their manifold afflictions; then declares that though the popish garments were not in themselves unclean, he was resolved, by the grace of God, never to wear the *square cap* and *surplice;* "because," says he, "they tend neither to decency nor edification, but to offence, dissention, and division in the church of Christ." He would, therefore, use his utmost endeavours to get them abolished; and adds, "that he would not kneel at the communion, because it would be symbolizing with popery, and would look too much like the adoration of the host."‡ Though he was a fixed nonconformist, he was a man of a peaceable spirit, and of great moderation, and constantly opposed to a total separation from the church.

These excellent qualifications could not screen him from the persecutions of the times: for he was not only deprived of his prebend, as observed above, but, in June 1571, he was convened before Archbishop Parker and others of the high commission at Lambeth. What prosecution he underwent on this occasion, we are unable fully to ascertain, only our historian by mistake observes, that he resigned, or was deprived of, his prebend.§

* Strype's Parker, p. 223. † Baker's MS. Collec. vol. i. p. 151.
‡ MS. Register, p. 18, 19.
§ Strype's Parker, p. 325.—Grindal, p. 170.

Mr. Lever was a person of great usefulness. He spent great pains in promoting the welfare of his hospital, not only by preaching and other religious exercises, but by recovering its temporal privileges. On account of the corrupt management of its estates, which were rented by several persons one of another, its pecuniary income was very much reduced, and even almost lost: but by his zealous and vigorous efforts, it was effectually recovered. His endeavours in this business reflect much honour on his character.* In this situation he spent the latter part of life in great reputation and usefulness, and died in the month of July, 1577. His remains were interred in the chapel belonging to the hospital, and over his grave was the following plain monumental inscription erected to his memory:†

THOMAS LEVER,
preacher to King EDWARD VI.
He died in July,
1577.

A few weeks previous to his death, Mr. Lever received a letter from the Bishop of Coventry and Lichfield, dated June 18, 1577, requiring him, in her majesty's name, to put down the prophesyings within his archdeaconry.‡ Had he lived a little longer, he would in all probability have felt the severities of persecution from the new Bishop of Durham, as was the case with his brother Whittingham; but God took him away from the evil to come. Fuller says, that whatever preferment in the church he pleased, courted his acceptance; but is greatly mistaken concerning the time and place of his death.§ Mr. Strype denominates him a man of distinguished eminence for piety, learning, and preaching the gospel.‖ Mr. Gilpin says, he was a man of excellent parts, considerable learning, and very exemplary piety; that, in the days of King Edward, he was esteemed an excellent and bold preacher; and that he was the intimate friend of the celebrated Bernard Gilpin.¶ Mr. Baker has favoured us with the following account of him: "Preaching," says this writer, "was indeed his talent, which, as it was thought fit to be made the only ingredient in his character, so he continued in it to the last, even after

* Strype's Annals, vol. ii. p. 513, 514.
† Ibid.—Baker's MS. Collec. vol. i. p. 151.
‡ MS. Register, p. 284. § Fuller's Worthies, part ii. p. 284.
‖ Strype's Parker, p. 211.
¶ Gilpin's Life of Bernard Gilpin, p. 249. Edit. 1780.

he was deprived. Thus much may be gathered from the printed Register, that will give a very authentic character of the man. From the passage, it appears, that he was a useful preacher, and permitted to preach after his deprivation; that he was inoffensive in his temper; and that no sufferings could provoke him. In the days of King Edward, when others were striving for preferment, no man was more vehement, or more galling in his sermons, against the waste of church revenues, and other prevailing corruptions of the court; which occasioned Bishop Ridley to rank him with Latimer and Knox. He was a man of as much natural probity and blunt native honesty as his college ever bred: a man without guile and artifice; who never made suit to any patron, or for any preferment; one that had the spirit of Hugh Latimer. No one can read his sermons without imagining he has something before him of Latimer or Luther. Though his sermons are bold and daring, and full of rebuke, it was his preaching that got him his preferment. His rebuking the courtiers made them afraid of him, and procured him reverence from the king. He was one of the best masters of his college, as well as one of the best of men the college ever bred."* He was succeeded in the mastership of his hospital by his brother, Mr. Ralph Lever, another puritan divine. Mr. Henry Lever, his grandson, and Mr. Robert Lever, his great-grandson, were both ejected by the act of uniformity in 1662.†

His Works.—1. Sermon on Rom. xiii. 1—7., 1550.—2. A Sermon preached the thyrd Sondaye in Lente before the Kynges Majestie, on John vi. 5—14., 1550.—3. A Sermon preached at Paul's Cross, the 14th day of December, on 1 Cor. iv. 1., 1550.—4. The right Way from the Danger of Sin and Vengeance in this wicked World, unto godly Wealth and Salvation in Christ, 1575.—5. A Commentary on the Lord's Prayer.—6. The Path-way to Christ.

Francis Merbury was minister at Northampton, and brought into many troubles for nonconformity, being several times cast into prison. November 5, 1578, he was convened before the high commission; when he underwent the following examination before Bishop Aylmer, Sir Owen Hopton, Dr. Lewis, Mr. Recorder, and Archdeacon Mullins, in the consistory of St. Paul's, London:

* Baker's MS. Collec. vol. i. p. 146, 152.
† Palmer's Noncon. Mem. vol. iii. p. 58, 78.

Bishop. Merbury, where have you been since your last enlargement?

Merbury. At Northampton.

B. You were especially forbidden to go to that place. For there you did all the harm.

M. I was not, neither in justice may be inhibited from that place. Neither have I done harm there, but good.

B. As you say, sir.

M. Not so. I refer myself to the judgment of God's church at that place.

B. The last time, you found more favour than you deserved, and more than you shall find hereafter; and yet you vaunted that you had rattled the Bishop of Peterborough, and in like manner you would treat me.

M. If your ears be open to every sycophant, you will have slanders enow: but for proof, bring forth mine accusers. For if bare words will serve your purpose, you may as well accuse me of high treason.

B. Well, sir, what have you to say against my lord of Peterborough, or me?

M. Nothing; but God save you both.

B. Nothing! Why, you were wont to bark much of dumb dogs. Are you now weary of it?

M. I came not to accuse, but to defend. Yet because you urge me for advantage, I say, that the bishops of London and Peterborough, and all the bishops in England, are guilty of the death of as many souls, as have perished by the ignorance of the ministers of their making, whom they *knew* to be unable.

B. Whom such have I made?

M. I accuse you not particularly, because I know not your state. If you have, you must bear the condemnation.

B. Thy proposition is false. If it were in Cambridge, it would be hissed out of the schools.

M. Then you had need hire hissers.

B. If I, finding one well qualified with learning, admit him, and he afterwards play the truant, and become ignorant, and by his ignorance slay souls, am I guilty of their death?

M. This is another question. I distinguish and speak of them which never were able.

B. Distinguish! thou knowest not a distinction. What is a distinction?

M. It is the severing of things which appear to be the same.

B. Nay, that is *differentia.**

M. *Different, quæ non sunt ambigua;* but we distinguish those things only which are ambiguous: as, you differ not from the Bishop of London; but I may distinguish between you and the Bishop of London, because you are a man though you were without a bishopric.

B. Here is a tale of a tub. How many predicaments are there?

M. I answer you according to your question, if I say there are enow of seven. Why do you ask me questions so impertinent?

B. How many predicables be there? Where didst thou learn logic?

M. The last time you spoke of good behaviour; but this is something else. I am no logician.

Recorder. Merbury, use my lord more reverently. He is a peer of the realm. I perceive your words are puffed up with pride.

M. I speak only the truth. I reverence him so far as he is reverend; and I pray God to teach him to die.

B. Thou speakest of making ministers. The Bishop of Peterborough was never more overseen in his life than when he admitted thee to be a preacher in Northampton.

M. Like enough so, in some sense. I pray God those scales may fall from his eyes.

B. Thou art a very ass; thou art mad; thou art courageous; nay, thou art impudent. By my troth, I think he is mad: he careth for nobody.

M. Sir, I take exception against swearing judges. I praise God I am not mad, but sorry to see you so much out of temper.

B. Did you ever hear one more impudent.

M. It is not impudency, I trust, to answer for myself.

B. Nay, I know thou art courageous; thou art foolhardy.

M. Though I fear not you, yet I fear the Lord.

R. Is he learned?

B. Learned! He hath an arrogant spirit. He can scarce construe Cato, I think.

M. Sir, you do not punish me because I am unlearned. Howbeit, I understand both Greek and Latin. Make trial of me, to prove your disgrace.

* What ridiculous trifling was this! Yet this is the prelate whom Mr. Strype extols on account of his great learning, and deep knowledge of divinity.—*Strype's Aylmer*, p. 255.

B. Thou takest upon thee to be a preacher, but there is nothing in thee. Thou art a *very ass*, an *idiot*, and a *fool.*[*]

M. I humbly beseech you, sir, have patience, and give this people a better example. Through the Lord, I am what I am. I submit the trial of my sufficiency to the judgment of the learned. But this wandering speech is not logical.

Hopton. Mr. Merbury, how do you prove all the bishops in England, to be guilty of the death of as many souls as have perished, by the ignorance of the unable ministers which they have made?

M. If they ordain unmeet or unable ministers, they give unto them imposition of hands *too hastily*, to do which, the apostle saith, they are partakers of other mens' sins.

B. The Greek word importeth nothing but the examination of their lives.

M. It is general enough to include both; and it is before set down in the Epistle as a positive law. "A bishop (a word formerly used in a more general sense) must be apt to teach;" and, according to the apostle, if he be not so approved to your conscience, you communicate with his sins.

B. What sins are those, I pray thee?

M. Soul-murder.

B. How dost thou prove that?

M. The words of the prophet are, "My people are destroyed for lack of knowledge." And who should teach them knowledge?

B. Knowledge! Have they not the homilies and the catechism? It is more, methinks, than they will learn.

M. Yes, or their parish priest either, to any purpose, in many places.

B. Why then, by thy saying, it seems they have too much of this already.

M. And too little of the other.

B. What other?

M. I mean preaching. What can an ignorant minister see in those things more than a book-learned parishioner?

B. O! thou wouldst have all preaching. Are not the homilies sermons?

M. God giveth his own blessing to his own appointed means, which is preaching, not reading.

[*] Such was the language from a lord bishop, whom Mr. Strype highly commends as an *exact logician*, and a man of *universal learning!*—*Strype's Aylmer*, p. 240.

B. Mark you what his words insinuate. He condemneth reading in churches; and seemeth to affirm, that they are all damned, whose minister is not a preacher. You see what he is.

Dr. Lewis. By St. Mary, these be pernicious errors. Sir, what say you of them?

M. Mr. Doctor, I allow of the reading of the scriptures in the church; for Christ read Esaias in the temple, and expounded what he read. I am no judge. God hath extraordinary supplies, when he takes away the ordinary means; but it is good for us not to tempt God, but thankfully to use his ordinary means.

L. Go to the purpose. If I present a man to my lord, whom I take to be a true man, and he prove a thief, am I guilty of his theft? Neither is the bishop guilty of the faults of ministers, of whom there is good hope when he maketh them.

M. Sir, you argue *a paribus*, but your reason holdeth not.

L. Why?

M. You may try him who would be a spiritual thief before you trust him: but you cannot try the other till he have stolen something.

L. What trial would you have more than this: he is a honest man, and in time likely to prove learned?

M. Then, in the mean time, the people perish. You will not commit your sucking child to a dry nurse, be she ever so honest.

L. A good life is a good sermon; and such ministers slay no souls, though they be not so exquisite.

M. To teach by example only, is good in a matron whom silence best becometh; but the apostle telleth Titus, that "ministers must be able by sound doctrine, both to exhort and to convince the gainsayers."

B. This fellow would have a preacher in every parish church!

M. So would St. Paul.

B. Where wouldst thou have them?

M. In Cambridge, in Oxford, in the inns of court, yea, and some in prison, if more were wanted. We doing our part, the Lord would do his.

B. I thought where thou wouldst be. But where is the living for them?

M. A man might cut a large thong out of your hide, and that of the other prelates, and it would never be missed.

B. Go thou on to contrive. Thou shalt orderly dispose of our livings.

M. That is more than you can do yourselves. If rich livings be the fault, they are to blame who have too much. Whatever be the cause, the church feeleth the smart.

Mullins. Sir, in the beginning of her majesty's reign, there was a defect of able men; and the church was constrained to take such as it could get, upon the recommendation of noblemen.

M. I speak of later times. As for noblemen, they are no sureties for us; and as to the defect, it cannot wholly dispense with the word. A minister must be able to teach.

Mull. Then you would have a preacher, or none at all; and so the church would be unserved.

M. It would be better to have nothing, than that which God would not have.

B. How dost thou prove that God would not have them, when we can get no better?

M. Doth he not say, "Because thou hast rejected knowledge, I will also reject thee, that thou shalt be no priest unto me?"

B. Thou are an overthwart, proud, puritan knave.* Thou wilt go to Northampton; and thou wilt have thine own sayings till thou die. But thou shalt repent.

M. I am no puritan. I beseech you to be good to me. I have been twice in prison already; but I know not why.

B. Where was he before?

Keeper of the Gatehouse. With me, my lord.

B. Have him to the Marshalsea. There he shall cope with the papists.

M. I must go where it pleaseth God. But remember God's judgments. You do me open wrong. I pray God forgive you.†

Mr. Merbury was then carried to the Marshalsea; but how long he remained in prison we are not able to learn. Notwithstanding the cruelty with which the good man was treated, he was not a person of severe principles, but acted with great moderation; and afterwards, with liberty of interpretation, became much more conformable.‡ A minister of the same name was afterwards

* This prelate was much accustomed to use foul language. He called Bishop Bonner, because he was remarkably corpulent, "My Lord Lubber of London."—*Strype's Aylmer*, p. 275.

† Parte of a Register, p. 381—386. ‡ Baxter's Second Plea, p. 41.

beneficed in the city of London; but whether he was the same person appears rather doubtful.*

William Whittingham, A. M.—This excellent divine was born in the city of Chester, in the year 1524, and educated in Brazen-nose college, Oxford. In 1545, he became fellow of All-Souls college. Afterwards, being accounted one of the best scholars in the university, he was translated to Christ-church, then founded by Henry VIII. In the year 1550, he travelled into France, Germany, and Italy, and returned towards the close of the reign of Edward VI. Upon the accession of Queen Mary, and the commencement of her bloody persecution, he fled from the storm, and retired to Frankfort, where he settled among the first of the English exiles. Here he was the first who took the charge of the congregation, but afterwards resigned to Mr. John Knox. Mr. Whittingham and his brethren having comfortably settled their church at Frankfort, invited their brethren, who had taken refuge in other places, to come to them, and participate of their comforts: but on the arrival of Dr. Cox and his friends, instead of union and comfort, they were soon deeply involved in discord and contention; and many of them, in a short were time, obliged to leave the place. Our historian observes, that when "Dr. Cox and others with him came to Frankfort, they began to break that order which was agreed upon: first, by answering aloud after the minister, contrary to the determination of the church; and being admonished thereof by the seniors of the congregation, he, with the rest who came with him, made answer, that they would do as they had done in England, and that they would have the *face* of the English church. And the Sunday following, one of his company, without the consent and knowledge of the congregation, got up suddenly into the pulpit, read the litany, and Dr. Cox with his company answered aloud, whereby the determination of the church was broken."† These imperious exiles having, by very ungenerous and unchristian methods, procured the use of the church, Mr. Whittingham said, he did not doubt that it was lawful for him and others to join themselves to some other church. But Dr. Cox sought *that it might not be suffered.* Then Mr. Whittingham observed, that it would be great cruelty to force men, contrary to their consciences,

* Newcourt's Repert. Eccl. vol. i. p. 406, 422, 519.
† Troubles at Frankeford, p. 31.

to obey all their disorderly proceedings; and offered, if the magistrate would be pleased to give them the hearing, to dispute the matter against all the contrary party, and prove, that the order which they sought to establish, ought not to take place in any reformed church. In this they were expressly prohibited, and even forbidden meddling any more in the business. They ventured, however, to offer, as their last refuge, to refer the whole matter to four arbitrators, two on each side; that it might appear who was faulty, and they might vindicate themselves from the charge of schism: but the proposal was rejected; and after this unkind and unchristian treatment, they left the place.* Mr. Whittingham being, in effect, driven from Frankfort, went to Geneva, where he was invited to become pastor to the English church. He refused, at first, to accept the charge; but, by the earnest persuasion of John Calvin, he complied with their invitation, and was ordained by the laying on of the hands of the presbytery. During his abode at Geneva, he was employed with several other learned divines, in publishing a new translation of the Bible. This was afterwards called the Geneva Translation, a particular account of which is given in another place.†

Soon after the accession of Queen Elizabeth, Mr. Whittingham returned home; and presently after his arrival, was nominated to accompany the Earl of Bedford on his mission to the court of France. Upon his return from France, he accompanied the Earl of Warwick, in his defence of Newhaven against the French. There he was a preacher for some time; and, as Wood observes, though he was ready in his ministerial function, he dissuaded his hearers against conformity, and the observance of the rites and ceremonies of the English church. Yet, such was the high esteem which this excellent earl had for him, that, about 1563, he was the means of procuring from the queen, his preferment to the deanery of Durham.‡ He was a very learned and popular preacher; and in September 1563, he preached before the queen.§ During this year, the ruling prelates proceeded to a more rigorous imposition of the clerical habits; therefore, Mr. Whittingham wrote a most pressing letter to the Earl of Leicester, intreating him to use his interest to prevent it. In this letter, he expressed him-

* Troubles at Frankeford, p. 38—51.
† See Art. Coverdale.
‡ Wood's Athenæ Oxon. vol. i. p. 153.—Strype's Annals, vol. i. p. 327.
§ Strype's Parker, p. 135.

self with considerable freedom, upon the painful subject; the substance of which was as follows:*

"I understand," says he, "they are about to compel us, contrary to our consciences, to wear the popish apparel, or deprive us of our ministry and livings. Yet when I consider the weighty charge enjoined upon us by Almighty God, and the exact account we have to give of the right use and faithful dispensation of his mysteries, I cannot doubt which to choose. He that would prove the use of the apparel to be a thing indifferent, and may be imposed, must prove that it tendeth to God's glory; that it agreeth with his word; that it edifieth his church; and that it maintaineth christian liberty. But if it wanteth these things, then is it not indifferent, but hurtful. And how can God's glory be advanced by those garments which antichristian superstition has invented to maintain and beautify idolatry? What agreement can the superstitious inventions of men, have with the pure word of God? What edification can there be, when the Spirit of God is grieved, the children of God discouraged, wicked papists confirmed, and a door open for such popish traditions and antichristian impiety? And can that be called true christian liberty, where a yoke is laid on the necks of the disciples; where the conscience is clogged with impositions; where faithful preachers are threatened with deprivation; where the regular dispensation of the word of God is interrupted; where congregations are robbed of their learned and godly pastors; and where the holy sacraments are made subject to superstitious and idolatrous vestments?

"Your lordship will thus see, that to use the ornaments and manners of the wicked, is to approve of their doctrine. God forbid, that we, by wearing the popish attire, as a thing merely indifferent, should seem to consent to their superstitious errors. The ancient fathers with one consent, acknowledge that all agreement with idolatry, is so far from being indifferent, that it is exceedingly pernicious. Some will say, that the apparel is not designed to set forth popery, but for good policy. Will it then be deemed good policy, to deck the spouse of Christ with the ornaments of the Babylonish strumpet, or to force her faithful pastors to be decorated like superstitious papists? God would not permit his people of old, to retain any of the Gentile manners for

* Strype's Parker, Appen. p. 43—47.

the sake of policy, but expressly forbad their imitation of them, and commanded them to destroy all the appurtenances of idolatry and superstition. And, in the time of the gospel, our Lord did not think it good policy, either to wear the pharisaical robes himself, or to suffer any of his disciples to do it; but condemned it as altogether superstitious. When I consider that Jereboam maintained his calves in Dan and Bethel, under the plausible name of policy, it makes me tremble to see the popish ornaments set forth under the same pretence. For if policy may serve as a cloak to superstition and papistry, then crowns and crosses, oil and cream, images and candles, palms and beads, with most of the other branches of antichrist, may again be introduced.

"It is well known, that when Hezekiah, Josiah, and other famous princes, promoted the reformation of religion according to the word of God, they compelled not the ministers of God to wear the apparel of Baal's priests, but utterly destroyed all their vestments. Hezekiah commanded all the *appendages* of superstition and idolatry, to be carried out of the Temple, and to be cast into Kedron. Josiah burnt all the vestments and other things belonging to Baal and his priests, not in Jerusalem, but out of the city. All this was done according to the word of the Lord, who commanded that not only the idols, but all things pertaining to them, should be abhorred and rejected. And if we compel the servants of Christ, to conform unto the papists, I greatly fear we shall return again to popery.

"Our case, my lord, will be deplorable, if such compulsion should be used against us, while so much lenity is used towards the papists. How many papists enjoy their liberty and livings, who have neither sworn obedience to the queen's majesty, nor discharged their duty to their miserable flocks! These men laugh and triumph to see us treated thus, and are not ashamed of boasting, that they hope the rest of popery will soon return. My noble lord, pity the disconsolate churches. Hear the cries and groans of many thousands of God's poor children, hungering and thirsting after spiritual food. I need not appeal to the word of God, to the history of the primitive church, to the just judgments of God poured out upon the nations for lack of true reformation. Judge ye betwixt us and our enemies. And if we seek the glory of God alone, the enjoyment of true christian liberty, the overthrow of all idolatry and superstition, and to win souls to Christ; I beseech your honour to pity our case, and use your utmost endeavours to secure unto us our liberty."*

What effect this generous letter produced, we are not able to learn. Mr. Whittingham was a man of an excellent character and admirable abilities. This was well known at court. Therefore, some time after his settlement at Durham, Secretary Cecil being made lord treasurer, he was nominated to the secretary's place; and, says Wood, if he had sought after this office, and made interest with his noble friend, the Earl of Leicester, he might have obtained

* Bishop Pilkington of Durham wrote a letter, at the same time, to the same noble person; in which he addressed him as follows:—"Consider, I "beseech your honour, how that all countries, which have reformed "religion, have cast away the popish apparel with the pope; and yet we, "who would be taken for the best, contend to keep it as a holy relic. "Mark, also, how many ministers there be here in all countries, who are "so zealous, not only to forsake the wicked doctrine of popery, but ready "to leave the ministry and their livings, rather than be like the popish "teachers of such superstitions, either in apparel or behaviour. This "realm has such scarcity of teachers, that if so many worthy men should "be cast out of the ministry, for such small matters, many places would be "destitute of preachers; and it would give an incurable offence to all the "favourers of God's truth, in other countries. Shall we make that so "precious, which other reformed churches esteem as vile? God forbid. "If we forsake popery as wicked, how shall we say their apparel "becomes saints and professors of true holiness? St. Paul bids us refrain "from all *outward shew* of evil; but, surely, in keeping this popish "apparel, we forbear not an outward shew of *much evil*, if popery be "judged evil. How christian peace shall be kept in this church, when so "many, for such small things, shall be thrust from their ministry and "livings, it passes my simple wit to conceive. We must not so subtilly "dispute what christian liberty would suffer us to do, but what is most "meet and edifying for christian charity, and promoting true religion. "But, surely, how popish apparel should edify, or set forth the gospel "of Jesus Christ, cannot be seen of the multitude. How much it rejoices "the adversaries, when they see what we borrow of them, and contend for, "as things necessary. The bishops wearing their white rockets began first "by Sisinius, an heretic bishop of the Novatians; and these other have the "like foundation. They have so long continued and pleased popery, "which is beggarly patched up of all sorts of ceremonies, that they could "never be rooted out since, even from many professors of the truth. "Though things may be borne with for christian liberty's sake for a time, "in hope to win the weak; yet, when liberty is turned to necessity, it is "evil, and no longer liberty; and that which was for winning the weak, is "become the confirming of the froward. Paul used circumcision for a "time as of liberty; but when it was urged of necessity, he would not "bend unto it. Bucer, when he was asked why he did not wear the "*square cap*, made answer, *because my head is not square*. God be merciful to us, and grant us uprightly to seek his honour with all simplicity "and earnestness." This prelate, who had been an exile in the days of Queen Mary, was a man of great learning, piety, and moderation, and a constant friend to the persecuted puritans.—*Strype's Parker*, Appen. p. 40, 41.

it; but he was not in the least anxious for court preferment.* During the severities inflicted upon the nonconformists, in the former part of Queen Elizabeth's reign, when good men were obliged to conform, or be deprived of their livings and ministry, it is said that Mr. Whittingham at first refused, but afterwards subscribed.† And in the year 1571, by the instigation of Archbishop Parker, he was cited before Grindal, archbishop of York; but the particular cause of his citation, or what prosecution he underwent, at least at that time, does not appear.‡

While Grindal lived, who, towards the close of life, connived at the nonconformists, Mr. Whittingham and his brethren in the province of York, were not much interrupted; but Dr. Sandys was no sooner made archbishop, than he was brought into troubles, from which the stroke of death alone could deliver him. In the year 1577, the new archbishop resolved to visit the whole of his province, and to begin with Durham, where Dean Whittingham had obtained a distinguished reputation, but had been ordained only according to the reformed church at Geneva, and not according to the English service book. The accusations brought against him contained *thirty-five* articles, and *forty-nine* interrogatories; but the principal charge was his Geneva ordination. Mr. Whittingham refused to answer the charge, but stood by the rites of the church of Durham, and denied the archbishop's power of visitation in that church, upon which his grace was pleased to excommunicate him. Mr. Whittingham then appealed to the queen, who directed a commission to the archbishop, Henry Earl of Huntington, lord president of the north, and Dr. Hutton, dean of York, to hear and determine the validity of his ordination, and to inquire into the other misdemeanours contained in the articles. The president was a zealous favourer of the puritans, and Dr. Hutton was of Whittingham's principles, and boldly declared, "That Mr. Whittingham was ordained in a better sort than even the archbishop himself." The commission, therefore, came to nothing.§

Sandys being sorely vexed at this disappointment, as well as Whittingham's calling in question his right of visitation, obtained another commission directed to himself, the Bishop

* Wood's Athenæ Oxon. vol. i. p. 153.
† Strype's Grindal, p. 98.
‡ Ibid. p. 170.—Strype's Parker, p. 326.
§ Strype's Annals, vol. ii. p. 481, 519—521.

of Durham, the Lord President, the Chancellor of the Diocese, and some others in whom he could confide, to visit the church of Durham. The chief design of this was to deprive Mr. Whittingham, as a mere layman. Upon his appearance before the commissioners, he produced a certificate under the hands of eight persons, signifying the manner of his ordination, in these words:—"It pleased God, by the "suffrages of the whole congregation (at Geneva) orderly "to choose to Mr. W. Whittingham, unto the office of "preaching the word of God and ministering the sacra-"ments; and he was admitted minister, and so published, "with such other ceremonies as are there used and accus-"tomed."* It was then objected, that there was no mention made of bishops or superintendants, nor of any external solemnities, nor even of imposition of hands. Mr. Whittingham replied, that the testimonial specified in general the ceremonies of that church, and that he was able to prove his vocation to be the same as all other ministers of Geneva. Upon this the lord president said, "I cannot in conscience agree to deprive him for that cause alone. This," he added, "would be ill taken by all the godly and learned, both at home and abroad, that we allow of *popish massing priests* in our ministry, and disallow of ministers made in a reformed church." The commission was, therefore, adjourned, and never renewed.†

The archbishop's proceedings against Mr. Whittingham, were evidently invidious; and they greatly sunk his reputation, both in town and country. His calling Whittingham's ordination in question was expressly contrary to the statute of 13 Eliz. by which, says Mr. Strype, "The ordination of foreign reformed churches was made valid; and those who had no other orders, were made of like capacity with others, to enjoy any place of ministry in England."‡ Indeed, the Oxford historian says, Mr. Whittingham did good service to his country, not only against the popish rebels in the north, but in repelling the Archbishop of York, from visiting the church of Durham. Yet he denominates him a lukewarm conformist, an enemy to the habits and ceremonies, and an active promoter of the Geneva doctrine and discipline; and he brings many severe charges against him, styling them works of *impiety*. He caused several stone coffins, belonging to the priors, and laid in the cathedral of Durham, to be taken up, and appointed them

* Strype's Annals, vol. ii. p. 523. † Ibid. p. 524. ‡ Ibid.

to be used as troughs for horses and swine, and their covers to pave his own house. He defaced all the brazen pictures and imagery work, and used the stones to build a washing-house for himself. The two *holy water* stones of fine marble, very artificially engraven, with hollow bosses very curiously wrought, he took away, and employed them to steep beef and salt fish in. He caused the image of St. Cuthbert, and other ancient monuments, to be defaced. And the truth is, he could not endure any thing that appertained to a monastic life.* How far Mr. Whittingham was concerned in these *works of impiety*, it is not in our power to ascertain; and how far he is censurable for these things, is left with the reader to determine.

With an evident design to reproach his memory, Dr. Bancroft says, that Mr. Whittingham, with the rest of his Geneva accomplices, urged all states to take arms, and reform religion themselves by force, rather than suffer such idolatry and superstition to remain in the land.† And a late writer, with the same ill design, observes, "that when he returned from exile, he imported with him, much of the leaven of Geneva."‡

He was, however, a truly pious man, opposed to all superstition, an excellent preacher, and an ornament to religion and learning. He died while the cause of his deprivation, for not being ordained according to the rites of the English church, was depending, June 10, 1579, in the sixty-fifth year of his age. Wood informs us, though without the smallest evidence, that he *unwillingly submitted to the stroke of death.*§ His remains were interred in the cathedral at Durham.

This learned divine wrote prefaces to the works of several learned men; as, Mr. Goodman's book, entitled "How superior powers ought to be obeyed," &c. He published the translations of several learned works, and he turned part of the Psalms of David into metre. These are still used in the church of England. Those which he did, have W. W. prefixed to them, among which is Psalm cxix.; as may be seen in the Common Prayer Book.‖

* Wood's Athenæ Oxon. vol. i. p. 154.

† Bancroft's Dangerous Positions, p. 62. Edit. 1640.

‡ Churton's Life of Nowell, p. 114.

§ Athenæ, p. 155.

‖ The other persons concerned in turning the Psalms into metre, were Messrs. Thomas Sternhold, John Hopkins, and Thomas Norton, all eminent in their day, and zealous in promoting the reformation of the church. The parts which they performed have the initials of their names prefixed to them, as may be seen in the Common Prayer Book.—*Wood's Athenæ*, vol. i. p. 62, 63, 153.

Mr. LAWRANCE was a man of great piety, an admired preacher, and incumbent in the county of Suffolk. He discovered great modesty, was unblameable in his life, sound in doctrine, and a laborious and constant preacher. He was first employed in the ministry in the above county, about the year 1561, where he continued to labour about six years with great acceptance and usefulness. But in the year 1567, he was silenced by Archbishop Parker's visitors for nonconformity. The good man having received the ecclesiastical censure, several persons of quality in that county, who knew his excellent character and great worth, wrote a letter to the archbishop, earnestly soliciting his restoration. This letter, dated October 27, 1567, was as follows:

"Our humble commendations and duties remembered to your grace. Great necessity doth occasion us to write to you for one Mr. Lawrance, lately a preacher; of whose great modesty, unblameable life, and sound doctrine, we have good experience, having with great diligence been well exercised among us these five or six years. He commonly preached twice every Lord's day, and many times on the working days, without ever receiving any thing. His enemies cannot accuse him of any thing worthy of reproach, as we testified to your grace's visitors, and desired them that he might still continue his preaching; for we knew very well that we should have great need of him. Now we see it more evident. For there is not one preacher within a circuit of *twenty miles*, in which circuit he was wont to preach.

"Thus we have thought good to certify your grace of the necessity of our country, and diligence and good behaviour of the man; trusting that your grace will either restore him again, or send us some other in his room; which we most earnestly desire. Commending the same to Almighty God, and praying that he may preserve your grace. Your grace's to command,

"ROBERT WINGFIELD, THOMAS PEITON,
WILLIAM HOPTON, THOMAS COLBY,
ROBERT HOPTON, THOMAS PLAYLESS."*
WILLIAM CAVENDISH,

Though it does not appear what success attended their application, nor yet how long Mr. Lawrance remained

* MS. Register, p. 889, 890.

under the ecclesiastical censure, he was afterwards restored to his beloved ministry.

This, however, was not the end of his troubles: for in the year 1579, he was again suspended by the Bishop of Norwich, for not observing all the ecclesiastical rites and ceremonies. Upon his suspension, his people soon experienced the loss of his excellent labours. Mr. Calthrop, a gentleman of distinguished eminence in the county, and the lord treasurer Burleigh, therefore, applied to the bishop for his restoration. But his grace observed, that what he had done in suspending him, was by virtue of the queen's orders, requiring him to allow no ministers to preach who were not in all things perfectly conformable to the rites and ceremonies of the church. Mr. Calthrop urged the great want there was of such excellent preachers as Mr. Lawrance, for whose fitness for the work of the ministry he would undertake to obtain the testimonial of the chief gentlemen in the county. But all was unavailable: the good man still remained under the episcopal censure.*

Mr. Lawrance was greatly beloved by persons of a religious character throughout the county where he lived, and his suspension was the cause of much sorrow and grief to all who knew him. Therefore, in the month of April, 1580, the above worthy persons made a second application to the bishop, but with no better success. The bishop remained inflexible, and declared that unless the treasurer commanded him, he would not restore Mr. Lawrance without perfect conformity. So he still continued under suspension.†

JOHN HANDSON was curate of St. James's church, Bury St. Edmunds, in Suffolk, and brought into trouble for nonconformity. He refused to wear the surplice, not only in time of divine service, but even in the administration of the sacrament; saying, that by law he thought himself not bound to wear it. He was examined by the chancellor to the Bishop of Norwich; but it does not appear what penalties were then inflicted upon him. This was in the year 1573.‡ In 1581, he was again brought into trouble by his diocesan, Dr. Freke, who suspended him for nonconformity. The bishop gave an account of this affair, in a letter to the treasurer, dated April 19th, this year.

* Strype's Annals, vol. ii. p. 585, 586. † Ibid. p. 660.
‡ Strype's Parker, p. 452.

Mr. Handson having continued for some time under the episcopal censure, the treasurer, after due examination of the case, wrote to the bishop in reply to his letter, desiring that the good man might be restored to his ministry. At the same time, Sir Robert Jermin, Lord North, and some others, wrote to his grace, requesting the same favour. Sir Robert, in his letter, said, "That his lordship had examined Mr. Handson's case at length, but, in his opinion, very indiscreetly, in many of the principal points; that they knew his ministry to have been very profitable to great numbers; that they who sought to remove him, were adversaries, rather than friends to the truth; that, as to faith and manners, he was ever held a sound teacher; that in these indifferent things (meaning the matters of conformity) he had never laboured much; and that, from these considerations, he requested the bishop would allow him the free exercise of his ministry." But the angry prelate stood resolute, and declared peremptorily, that he never would, unless Mr. Handson would publicly acknowledge his fault, and enter into bonds for his good behaviour in future. Other applications were made to the bishop, to take off his suspension; but whether he ever became so favourably disposed, we have not been able to learn.*

Robert Wright.—He lived fourteen years in the university of Cambridge, was a very learned man, and tutor to the Earl of Essex, both in school learning and at the university. Being dissatisfied with episcopal ordination, he went to Antwerp, where he was ordained by the laying on of the hands of the presbytery. Upon his return to England, Lord Rich of Rochford, in Essex, made him his domestic chaplain; and he constantly preached and administered the sacrament in his lordship's chapel, but in no other place, seeing the bishop utterly refused him a license. He was an admired preacher; and, for his great seriousness and piety, was universally beloved by the clergy in the county. While his noble patron lived, he protected him from danger; but this excellent lord was no sooner dead, than Dr. Aylmer, bishop of London, laid hands on him; and for saying, "That to keep the queen's birth-day as an *holiday*, is to make her an *idol*," he was committed to the Gatehouse, where he continued a long time.†

* Strype's Annals, vol. iii. p. 15, 21. † Strype's Aylmer, p. 83—87.

Having lain in prison several months, he petitioned the bishop to be brought to trial, or admitted to bail. But all the answer he could obtain of his grace, was, that he *deserved to lie in prison seven years.* This very hard usage, together with Mr. Wright's open and undisguised honesty and piety, moved the compassion of his keeper; and, his poor wife being in child-bed and in great distress, he gave him leave, with the private allowance of the secretary of state, to make her a visit at Rochford, upon his parole. But it so happened, that Dr. Ford, the civilian, met him on the road, and acquainted the bishop with his escape; who, falling into a violent passion, sent immediately for the keeper, and demanded his prisoner. The keeper pleaded the great compassion of the case; but all was unavailable. For the bishop threatened to complain of him to the queen, and have him turned out of his place. Mr. Wright, having received information of his keeper's danger, returned immediately to his prison, and wrote as follows to the lord treasurer in his behalf:—"Oh! my lord," says he, "I most humbly crave your lordship's favour, that I may be delivered from such unpitiful minds; and especially, that your lordship will stand a good lord to my *keeper*, that he may not be discouraged from favouring those who profess true religion." This was written in May, 1582. The keeper was therefore pardoned.*

The bishop, however, was resolved to have full satisfaction of the prisoner; and, bringing him before the high commission, he was examined upon certain articles concerning the Book of Common Prayer; the rites and ceremonies; praying for the queen and church; and the established form of ordaining ministers. He was, moreover, charged with preaching without a license, and with being a mere *layman.* To which he replied, "that he thought the Book of Common Prayer, upon the whole, was good and godly, but could not answer for every particular. That as to rites and ceremonies, he thought that his resorting to churches where they were used, was a sufficient proof, that he did not utterly condemn them. That he prayed for the queen, and for all the ministers of God's word; consequently, for archbishops, bishops, &c. That he was only a private chaplain, and knew of no law that required a license for such a place. But he could not acknowledge, that he was a mere

* Strype's Annals, vol. iii. p. 123, 124.

layman, having preached seven years in the university with a license, and being since that time regularly ordained, by the laying on of the hands of the presbytery at Antwerp."

The bishop having charged Mr. Wright with saying, "That the election of ministers ought to be by their flocks," he acknowledged the charge, and supposed it was no error; adding, "That he was himself thus chosen by his flock at Rochford; that in his opinion, every minister was a *bishop*, though not a *lord* bishop; and that his grace of London, must be of the same opinion; because when he was last before him, he rebuked Mr. White for striking one of his parishioners, alleging that text, *A bishop must be no striker*; which had been impertinent, if Mr. White, who was only a minister, had not been a *bishop*." When he was charged with saying, "That the ministers who only used the common prayer, were *dumb dogs*;" he said, "the phrase, though used in scripture, has very seldom been in my mouth, on any occasion whatever. But it can never be proved, that I ever called any man, especially any preacher, by that name. Yet a man who is professedly the pastor of a flock, and does not preach at all, may, according to the design of the prophet, deserve the name of dumb dog."

Aylmer also charged him with saying, "There were no lawful ministers in the church of England; and that those who are called ministers, are thieves and murderers." To this, Mr. Wright said, "I will be content to be condemned, if I bring not two hundred godly, preaching ministers, as witnesses against this accusation. I do as certainly believe, that there are lawful ministers in England, as that there is a sun in the sky. In Essex, I can bring twenty godly ministers, all preachers, who will testify that they love me, and have cause to think that I love and reverence them. I preached seven years in the university of Cambridge with approbation, and have a testimonial under the hands and seals of the master and fellows of Christ's college, being all ministers, of my good behaviour."*

This excellent divine having been a considerable time in the Gatehouse, in September, 1582, became willing to subscribe to the allowance of the ministry of the church of England, and the Book of Common Prayer. Yet Bishop Aylmer required his friends to be bound in a *good round sum*, that henceforth he should never preach, nor act, contrary to the same. Upon these conditions, his grace was

* Strype's Annals, vol. iii. Appen. p. 38—43.

not unwilling to grant him favour, if the queen approved of it.* It is, indeed, very doubtful whether the favour was ever obtained; for the unmerciful proceedings of the above prelate against the puritans, were almost unparalleled.†

Bernard Gilpin, B. D.—This celebrated person was born of an ancient and honourable family, at Kentmire in Westmoreland, in the year 1517, and educated in Queen's college, Oxford. He made the closest application to his studies, and uncommon progress in useful learning. Having determined to apply himself to divinity, he made the scriptures his principal study; and with a view to his better acquaintance with them, he resolved by the greatest industry to gain a thorough knowledge of the Greek and Hebrew languages. He had not been long thus employed before he was noticed as a young man of excellent parts and considerable learning; and became exceedingly admired and beloved for the sweetness of his disposition, and the politeness of his manners. At the usual term, he took his degrees in Arts, and was elected fellow of his college. His reputation was, indeed, so great, that he was chosen to supply the college newly founded by Cardinal Wolsey.‡

* Strype's Aylmer, p. 87.

† The zeal and assiduity of Bishop Aylmer in defence of the church of England, is said to have recommended him to the particular favour of Queen Elizabeth. Though in the early part of his life he declaimed against the wealth and splendour of bishops, and spoke with vehemence against their *lordly dignity* and *civil authority*, and was an avowed advocate of what was afterwards called *puritanism*; yet, as he rose in ecclesiastical preferment and worldly grandeur, he changed his opinions, and became the most violent in the opposite sentiments. And notwithstanding he is styled a person of extraordinary wisdom, a *worthy* prelate, and a blessing to the church; he was certainly one of the most unfeeling and cruel persecutors, of which the pages of history afford sufficient proof. He was preceptor to Lady Jane Grey; and, on the accession of Queen Mary, he went into exile. His escape was very remarkable. Being a *little* man, the merchant of the ship in which he made his escape, put him into a *wine butt*, with a partition in the middle; so that he was inclosed in one end of the cask, while the *searchers* drank wine drawn out of the other.—He was a man of great courage, and had one of his own teeth drawn, to encourage Queen Elizabeth to submit to a similar operation. When he wished to rouse the attention of his audience while he was preaching, he usually took his Hebrew Bible out of his pocket, and read them a few verses, and then resumed his discourse. He was remarkably fond of bowls, even on the Lord's-day, when he commonly used very unbecoming language, to the great reproach of his character.—*Strype's Aylmer*, p. 215—292.—*Wood's Athenæ*, vol. i. p. 611.—*Biog. Britan.* vol. i. p. 384—391. Edit. 1778.—*Granger's Biog. Hist.* vol. i. p. 208.

‡ The following memoir of Mr. Gilpin is chiefly collected from the "British Biography," vol. iii. p. 98—.

Mr. Gilpin having been trained up in the popish religion, still continued a steady son of that church; and in defence of popery, had held a disputation with John Hooper, afterwards bishop of Worcester, and the famous martyr. This was in the reign of Henry VIII.; but upon the accession of King Edward, Peter Martyr being sent to Oxford, delivered public lectures upon divinity in a strain to which that university had been little accustomed. He attacked the Romish doctrines in a manner that alarmed the popish party; which induced them to unite, and make as strong an opposition as they were able. Mr. Gilpin having gained considerable reputation in the university, the popish party were exceedingly solicitous to engage him in a public defence of their cause, and made the most pressing applications for this purpose. But they found his zeal much cooler than their own. Indeed, he was not satisfied with the cause of the reformers, having never had a sufficient opportunity of acquainting himself with their principles: but, on the other hand, he had never been a bigotted papist; and had discovered, in his dispute with Hooper, that several of the Romish doctrines were not so well supported by scripture, as he had before supposed. While his mind was thus unsettled, he thought himself ill qualified to defend either side by public disputation. His inclination was to stand by as an unprejudiced observer; and to embrace the truth, whether he found it among papists or protestants. By much importunity, however, he at length yielded, and the next day appeared in public against Peter Martyr.*

Mr. Gilpin being thus drawn into the controversy against his inclination, was determined to make it as useful as possible to himself. By bringing his old opinions to the test, he hoped that he should be enabled to discover whether they were justly founded, or he had hitherto been involved in error. He resolved, therefore, to lay aside as much as possible, the temper of a caviller; and to follow truth, from which he was determined nothing should make him swerve. Having commenced the dispute, he soon found the arguments of his adversary too strong for him. They came so forcibly authorized by the testimony of scripture, that he

* Dr. Peter Martyr, a celebrated reformer, was born in Florence, and invited to England by the Protector Somerset and Archbishop Cranmer. In the year 1548, he was made regius professor of divinity at Oxford, and, in 1550, installed canon of Christ-church. His numerous works, which are in Latin, consist chiefly of commentaries on the scriptures, and pieces on controversy. On the accession of Queen Mary, and the commencement of persecution, he desired to withdraw, and died at Zurich, November 12, 1562.—*Granger's Biog. Hist.* vol. i. p. 141.

could not help frankly acknowledging they were of a very different nature from the wire-drawn proofs and strained interpretations, in which he had hitherto acquiesced. The disputation, therefore, was soon over. Mr. Gilpin had too much honesty to defend suspected opinions. He yielded to the force of truth; and owned publicly, that he could not maintain what he undertook to defend; and therefore determined to enter no more upon controversy, till he had gained that full information which he was anxious to obtain.*

Mr. Gilpin being thus staggered by his opponent's arguments, the first step he took, after imploring divine assistance, was to commit to paper, the substance of the dispute. Also, he resolved to enter into a strict examination of the whole, but especially those points in which he had found himself the most closely pressed. At the same time, he began with great assiduity to examine the scriptures, and the writings of the fathers, with a particular view to the controversy betwixt protestants and papists. The first result of his inquiries, cooled his zeal for popery, and gave him a more favourable opinion of the doctrines of the reformation. In this unsettled state of mind, he communicated his thoughts to his friends, and particularly to Tonstal, bishop of Durham, who was his mother's uncle, and his great friend. The advice he received induced him to examine the scriptures and the fathers with still greater attention; and at last he became thoroughly convinced, that there were numerous sore abuses and corruptions in the church of Rome, and that a reformation was highly necessary.

As an academic life affords the greatest leisure for study, Mr. Gilpin was resolved still to continue wholly employed in the pursuit of knowledge. He had too just a sense of the ministerial work, to rush upon it hastily, or to be unacquainted with the qualifications requisite to the discharge of it; and too mean an opinion of himself, to think he was yet possessed of them. He thought more learning was necessary in that controversial age, than he had yet acquired. And his chief argument with his friends, who were continually urging him to leave the university, was, that he was not yet sufficiently instructed in religion himself

* Peter Martyr was much concerned for Mr. Gilpin's welfare, and used to say, he cared not much for his other adversaries; but for Gilpin, who spoke and acted like a man of integrity, he was much troubled. He therefore often prayed that God would convince him of his error, and convert him to the truth; which the Lord was pleased afterwards to do.—*Fuller's Abel Redivivus*, p. 358.

to teach others. The christian ministry, said he, was an arduous work, especially in those times; and protestantism could not suffer more than by the rawness and inexperience of its teachers. These thoughts continued to attend him at Oxford till the thirty-fifth year of his age. About this time, the vicarage of Norton, in the diocese of Durham, becoming void, his friends, with some difficulty, prevailed upon him to accept it. Accordingly, he was presented to this living in November, 1552. But before he entered upon his important charge, he was appointed to preach before King Edward at Greenwich.

Mr. Gilpin was resolved on this occasion to censure the prevailing avarice and corruptions with honest freedom, and ordered his sermon accordingly. He began by first addressing the clergy. He was sorry, said he, to observe amongst them so manifest a neglect of their function. To *get benefices*, not to take care of their flocks, was their great object. Half of them were pluralists, or nonresidents, and such could never fulfil their charge. He was shocked, he said, to hear them quote human laws against the word of God. If such laws did exist, they were the remains of popery, and ought to be repealed. For while mens' consciences would permit them to hold as many livings as they could get, and discharge none, it was impossible the gospel could have any considerable success.

From the clergy he turned to the court; and observing the king was absent, he was obliged to introduce that part of his sermon, by saying, it grieved him to see those absent, who, for example's sake, ought to have been present. He had also heard other preachers remark, that it was common for them to be absent. Business might, perhaps, be their excuse; but he could not believe that serving God would ever hinder business. If he could, he said, he would make them hear in their chambers. However, he would speak to their seats, not doubting that what he said would be carried to them.—"You, great prince," said he, "are appointed by God to be the governor of this land; let me then here call upon you in behalf of your people. It is in your power to redress them; and if you do not, the neglect must be accounted for. Take away dispensations for pluralities and nonresidence, and oblige every pastor to hold only one benefice; and, as far as you can, make every one do his duty. Your grace's eye to look through the realm, would do more good than a thousand preachers. The land is full of idle pastors. And how can it be otherwise, while the nobility, and patrons of livings, put in just who will allow them to take out most profit? It would be good, if your grace would send out surveyors, to see how benefices are bestowed. It is no wonder that your people are continually rising up in rebellion, when they have no instructors to teach them their duty. If some remedies be not applied to these evils, we are in danger of falling into more ignorance, superstition, and idolatry, than we ever were in while under the Bishop of Rome. This must, indeed, be the case, if some proper methods be not taken to prevent it; for benefices are every where so plundered and robbed by patrons, that in a little time no one will bring up his children to the church. It is amazing to see how the universities are diminished within these few years. And I must tell your grace, that all these evils will be laid to your charge, if you do not exert yourself to prevent them. For my part, I will do my duty: I will tell your grace what corruptions and abuses prevail, and pray to God that he will direct your heart to amend them."

He next addressed the nobility and magistrates. He told them, that they all received their honours, their powers, and their authority, from God, who expected they would make a proper use of such gifts; and would certainly call them to an account for the abuse of them. But he saw so much ambitious striving for these things at court, that he was afraid they did not all consider them in their true light. He observed, that the spirit of avarice was crept in among them; that the country cried out against their extortions; and that when the poor came to seek for justice in London, the great men would not see them; but their servants must first be bribed. Oh! said he, with what glad hearts and clear consciences might noblemen go to rest, after having spent the day in hearing the complaints of the poor, and redressing their wrongs. For want of this, he said, they were obliged to seek their right among lawyers, who quickly devoured every thing they had, and thousands every term were obliged to return worse than they came.—"Then," said he, "let me call upon you magistrates, and put you in mind, that if the people are debtors to you for obedience, you are debtors to them for protection. If you deny this, they must suffer; but God will assuredly espouse their cause against you. And now, if we search for the root of all these evils, what is it but avarice? This it is that maketh the bad nobleman, the bad magistrate, the bad pastor, the bad lawyer."—Having thus freely addressed his audience, he concluded his sermon with a warm exhortation, that all would consider these things, and that such as found themselves faulty would amend their lives.*

Such was the manner in which Mr. Gilpin entered on the work of the ministry; and such was the sense he had of the sincerity and faithfulness necessary to the proper discharge of it. Whatever appeared to be his duty, appeared also to be his interest; and he was never swayed by hope or fear. He considered himself in some degree chargeable with those vices of which he had the knowledge, if he failed to rebuke them. His plain dealing on this occasion was therefore well taken, and recommended him to the notice of many persons of the first rank. And Sir William Cecil presented him a general license for preaching.

Soon after this, he repaired to his parish, and with becoming seriousness entered upon the duties of his function. Though he failed not occasionally to use the king's license in other parts of the country, he considered his own parish as requiring his principal labours. He chiefly preached on practical subjects; and seldom touched on points of controversy, lest by attempting to instruct, he should only mislead. Though he was fully resolved against popery, he did not see protestantism in its clearest light; and was scarcely settled in some of his religious opinions. Hence by degrees he became extremely diffident, which gave him great uneasiness. He thought he had engaged too soon in the work of the ministry; that he ought not to rest in giving his hearers merely moral instructions; and that, as the country was overspread with popish errors, he did ill in pretending to be a teacher of religion, if he were unable to oppose those errors.

These thoughts made deeper impressions upon his mind every day; and being at length extremely unhappy, he wrote to Bishop Tonstal, then in the Tower, giving him an account of his situation. The venerable prelate advised Gilpin to provide a *trusty curate* for his parish, and to spend a year or two in Germany, France, and Holland; by which means he might have an opportunity of conversing with men celebrated for learning, both papists and protestants. Mr. Gilpin having long earnestly desired a conference with learned men abroad, was much pleased with the advice. And as to the expense, Tonstal observed, that his living would do something towards his maintenance, and

* This sermon is published with Carleton and Gilpin's Life of Bernard Gilpin, and is the only thing he ever published.

he would make up all deficiencies. This, however, did not remove the difficulty from his mind. Mr. Gilpin's views of the pastoral office were so correct, that he thought no excuse could justify nonresidence for so considerable a time as he intended to be abroad. He, therefore, could not think of supporting himself with any part of the income of his living. Yet he was resolved to go abroad; and if he stayed only a short time, he would rely on the frugal management of the little money he possessed, and leave the rest to the bishop's generosity. He accordingly resigned his living, and set out for London, to receive his last orders from the bishop, and to embark for the continent.

The account of his resignation got to London before himself; and Tonstal, anxious for his kinsman to thrive in the world, was much concerned about it. "Here are your friends," said his grace, "endeavouring to provide for you, and you are taking every method to frustrate their endeavours. But be warned; by these courses you will presently bring yourself to a morsel of bread." Mr. Gilpin begged the bishop would attribute what he had done to a scrupulous conscience, which would not permit him to act otherwise. "Conscience!" replied the bishop, "why, you might have had a dispensation." "Will my dispensation," answered Gilpin, "restrain the tempter, in my absence, from endeavouring to corrupt the people committed to my care? Alas! I fear it would be but an ill excuse for the harm done to my flock, if I should say, when God shall call me to an account of my stewardship, that I was absent by dispensation." This reply put the bishop a little out of humour. But after his temper cooled, this instance of Mr. Gilpin's integrity raised him still higher in the prelate's esteem. Nevertheless, Tonstal would frequently chide him for his qualms of conscience, as he called them; and often told him, that if he did not look better to his own interest, he "would certainly die a beggar."

Before his departure, the bishop entrusted him with his Treatise on the Eucharist, in manuscript, desiring him to inspect the printing of it at Paris. Upon his arrival in Holland, he travelled to Mechlin, to see his brother George, there prosecuting his studies. Afterwards, he went to Louvain, resolving there to abide. He made frequent excursions to Antwerp, Ghent, Brussels, and other places, where he usually spent a few weeks with persons of reputation, both papists and protestants. But Louvain being the principal place for students in divinity, was his chief residence. Here some of the most celebrated divines on both sides of the question resided; and the most important topics in divinity were discussed with great freedom.

Mr. Gilpin's first business was to get himself introduced to men eminent for learning; to whom his own address and attainments were no mean recommendation, and supplied the place of long acquaintance. He attended upon all public readings and disputations. He committed every thing material to writing; re-examined all his own opinions; proposed his doubts to friends in private; and, in every respect, made the best use of his time. Hereby, he began to obtain more correct views of the doctrines of the reformation; he saw things in a clearer and stronger light, and felt great satisfaction in the change he had made.

While he was thus prosecuting his studies, and making considerable improvement in useful knowledge, he was suddenly alarmed, together with numerous other protestants in those parts, by the melancholy news of the death of King Edward, and the accession of Queen Mary. This news, however, was attended with one favourable circumstance, which was, the release of Bishop Tonstal from the Tower, and his restoration to his bishopric. Soon after, Tonstal finding a rich living vacant in his diocese, made the offer of it to Mr. Gilpin; supposing that by this time he might have got over his former scruples. But Mr. Gilpin still continued inflexible in his resolution not to accept any benefice without discharging the duties of it. He, therefore, gave the bishop his reasons for not accepting his kind offer, in the following letter, dated from Louvain, November 22, 1554:

"Right honourable and singular good lord, my duty "remembered in most humble manner. Pleaseth it your "lordship to be informed, that of late my brother wrote to "me, that in any wise I must meet him at Mechlin; for he "must debate with me urgent affairs, such as could not be "dispatched by writing. When we met, I perceived it "was nothing else but to see if he could persuade me to "take a benefice, and continue in study at the university; "which if I had known to be the cause of his sending for "me, I should not have needed to interrupt my study to "meet him. For I have so long debated that matter with "learned men, especially with the holy prophets, and most "ancient and godly writers since Christ's time, that I trust "so long as I have to live, never to burden my conscience "with having a benefice, and lying from it. My brother "said, that your lordship had written to him, that you "would gladly bestow one on me; and that your lordship "thought, and so did other of my friends, of which he "was one, that I was much too scrupulous in that point. "Whereunto I always say, if I be too scrupulous, as I "cannot think that I am, the matter is such, that I had "rather my conscience were a great deal too strait, than a "a little too large. For I am seriously persuaded, that I "shall never offend God by refusing to have a benefice, "and lie from it, so long as I judge not evil of others; "which, I trust, I shall not; but rather pray God daily, "that all who have cures may discharge their office in his "sight, as may tend most to his glory and the profit of his "church. He replied against me, that your lordship would "give me no benefice, but what you would see discharged "in my absence, as well or better than I could discharge it "myself. Whereunto I answered, that I would be sorry, "if I thought not that there were many thousands in "England, more able to discharge a cure than I find myself. "And therefore I desire they may take both the care and "the profits also; that they may be able to feed both the "body and the soul, as I think all pastors are bounden. "As for me, I can never persuade myself to take the *profit*, "and another take the *pains:* for if he should teach and "preach as faithfully as ever St. Austin did, yet I should "not think myself discharged. And if I should strain my "conscience herein, I strive with it to remain here, or in any "other university, the unquietness of it would not suffer "me to profit in my study at all.

"I am here, at this present, I thank God, very well "placed for study among a company of learned men, joining "to the friers minors; having free access at all times to a "notable library among the friers, men both well learned "and studious. I have entered acquaintance with divers "the best learned in the town; and for my part was never "more desirous to learn in all my life than at present. "Wherefore, I am bold, knowing your lordship's singular "good will towards me, to open my mind thus rudely and "plainly unto your goodness, most humbly beseeching you "to suffer me to live without charge, that I may study "quietly.

"And whereas I know well your lordship is careful how "I should live, if God should call your lordship, being "now aged, I desire you will not let that care trouble you. "For if I had no other shift, I could get a lectureship, I "know, shortly, either in this university, or at least in some "abbey hereby; where I should not lose any time; and this "kind of life, if God be pleased, I desire before any "benefice. And thus I pray Christ always to have your "lordship in blessed keeping. By your lordship's humble "scholar and chaplain,

"BERNARD GILPIN."

The bishop was not offended with this letter. The unaffected piety which it discovered disarmed all resentment, and led him rather to admire a behaviour, in which the motives of conscience shewed themselves so much superior to those of interest. "Which of our modern "gaping rooks," exclaims Bishop Carleton, "could endeavour with greater industry to *obtain* a benefice, than this "man did to *avoid* one!" Mr. Gilpin having got over this affair, continued some time longer at Louvain, daily improving in religious knowledge. And having remained about two years, he went to Paris; where his first care was the printing of Tonstal's book, which he performed entirely to the bishop's satisfaction, and received his thanks for it.

Mr. Gilpin having spent three years on the continent, was fully satisfied in all his former scruples. He was firmly convinced of the errors and evil tendency of popery; and of the truth and importance of the doctrines of the reformation. Therefore, in the year 1556, he returned to England, though the persecutions of Queen Mary were carrying on with unabating fury. Tonstal received his kinsman with great kindness; and soon after his arrival, gave him the archdeaconry of Durham, to which the rectory of Easington was annexed. He immediately repaired to his parish, where he preached with great boldness against the vices, errors, and corruptions of the times; also, by virtue of his office as archdeacon, he took great pains to reform the manners of the clergy. His free and open reproofs soon roused the malice of proud ecclesiastics, who used every method in their power to remove so inconvenient a person. It soon became their popular clamour, that he was an enemy to the church; a scandalizer of the clergy; a preacher of damnable doctrines; and that if he was spared much longer, religion must suffer from the heresies he was daily propagating.* Indeed, a charge of heresy, consisting of

* Mr. Gilpin, in a letter to his brother, makes the following observation:—"After I entered upon the parsonage of Easington, and began to "preach," says he, "I soon procured many mighty and grievous adversaries; for that I preached against pluralities and nonresidence. Some said,

thirteen articles, was soon drawn up against him; and he was accused in form before the Bishop of Durham. But the bishop, who was much acquainted with the world, easily found a method of dismissing the cause, so as to protect his nephew, without endangering himself. The malice of his enemies, however, could not rest; and they created him so much trouble, and on account of the extreme fatigue of keeping both his places, he begged leave of the bishop to resign either the archdeaconry or his parish. But the bishop observing that the income of the former was not a sufficient support without the latter, and that he was unwilling they should be separated, Mr. Gilpin therefore resigned them both.

The bishop soon after presented him to the rectory of Houghton-le-Spring, in the county of Durham. The living was valuable; but the duties of it were proportionably laborious. The parish contained no less than fourteen villages; and the instruction of the people having been so exceedingly neglected, popery was arrived to its full growth of superstition. Scarcely any traces of true christianity were indeed left. Nay, what little remained, was even popery itself corrupted. Here all its idle ceremonies were carried to a greater extent than in most other places, and were looked upon as the very essentials of religion. And how these barbarous people were excluded from all means of better information, appears from hence, that through the neglect of the bishops and the justices of peace, King Edward's proclamations for a change of worship, had not been even heard of, in that part of the kingdom, at the time of his death. Such was the condition of the parish of Houghton, when first committed to the care of Mr. Gilpin. He was grieved to see ignorance and vice so lamentably prevail; but he did not despair. He implored the assistance and blessing of God, and was much encouraged. The people crowded about him, and heard him with great attention. They perceived him to be a very different teacher from those to whom they had been accustomed.

After the acceptance of Houghton, Tonstal urged him to accept of a stall in the cathedral of Durham; telling him, that there did not exist the same objection against this as against the archdeaconry, it being altogether a sinecure;

"all who preached that doctrine became heretics soon after. Others found "great fault, for that I preached repentance and salvation by Christ; "and did not make whole sermons, as they did, about transubstantiation, "purgatory, holy-water, images, prayers to saints, and such like."

and that he could have no reasonable pretence for refusing it. But Mr. Gilpin resolving not to accept it, told the bishop, that by his bounty he had already more wealth, than he was afraid, he could give a good account of. He, therefore, begged that he might not have any additional charge; but that his lordship would bestow his preferment on some one who stood in greater need of it.

Mr. Gilpin now lived retired, and gave no immediate offence to the clergy. The experience he had of their temper, made him more cautious not to offend them. He was, indeed, more cautious than he afterwards approved. For in future life he often taxed his behaviour, at this period, with weakness and cowardice. But all the caution he could use availed nothing. He was soon formally accused a second time before the Bishop of Durham; who again found means to protect him. The malice of his enemies, however, succeeded in part. From this time, Tonstal's favour towards him visibly declined; and to shew his dislike of heresy, and of his kinsman's conduct, he struck him out of his will, though he had before made him his executor. The loss gave Mr. Gilpin very little uneasiness. His heart was not set upon the things of this world. It was no less than he expected, nor more than he had provided for. He was, indeed, sorry to see the bishop disgusted; and would have given up any thing, except his conscience, to have satisfied him. But a good conscience, he was assured, was the best friend in the world; and he was resolved not to part with that, to please any man upon earth.

His enemies, in the mean time, were not silenced. They were so exceedingly enraged by their second failure, that they caused *thirty-two* articles, expressed in the strongest terms, to be exhibited against him, before Bonner, bishop of London. Here they went the right way to work. Bonner was a man exactly suited to their purpose, nature having formed him for an inquisitor. The fierce zealot at once took fire, extolled so laudable a concern for religion, and promised that the heretic should be at the stake in a fortnight. Mr. Gilpin, who was no stranger to the *burning* zeal of the Bishop of London, received the account with great composure, and immediately prepared for martyrdom. Laying his hand on the shoulder of a favourite domestic, he said, "At length they have prevailed against me. I am "accused to the Bishop of London, from whom there will "be no escaping. God forgive their malice, and give me "strength to undergo the trial." He then ordered his servant to provide a long garment, in which he might go decently to the stake, and desired it might be got ready with all expedition; "for I know not," said he, "how "soon I may have occasion for it."* As soon as he was apprehended, he set out for London, in expectation of the fire and faggot. But on his journey to the metropolis, we are informed, that he broke his leg, which unavoidably detained him some time on the road. The persons conducting him, took occasion from this disaster maliciously to retort upon him a frequent observation of his, viz. "That nothing happens to us but what is intended for our good." And when they asked him whether he thought his broken leg was so intended, he meekly replied, that he had no doubt of it. And, indeed, so it soon appeared in the strictest sense. For before he was able to travel, Queen Mary died, and he was set at liberty. Thus he again escaped out of the hands of his enemies.

Mr. Gilpin having obtained this providential deliverance, returned to Houghton through crowds of people, expressing the utmost joy, and blessing God for his happy release. The following year he lost his friend and relation Bishop Tonstal;† but soon procured himself other friends. Upon the deprivation of the popish bishops, the Earl of Bedford recommended him to the patronage of Queen Elizabeth, who offered him the bishopric of Carlisle; and according to Wood, he was much pressed to accept it.‡ The Bishop of Worcester, his near relation, wrote to him expressly for this purpose, and warmly urged him to accept the offer, declaring that no man was more fit for such kind of preferment.§ After all, Mr. Gilpin modestly refused. No arguments could induce him to act contrary to the dictates of his conscience. The accounts given us by Bishop Nicolson and Dr. Heylin of Mr. Gilpin's behaviour on this occasion, are extremely disingenuous: they both ascribe it to his lucrative motives. The former intimates that the good man knew what he was about, when he refused to part with the rectory of Houghton for the bishopric of Carlisle: the latter supposes that all his

* Biog. Britan. vol. vii. Sup. p. 72.

† Bishop Tonstal was one of the politest scholars of the age, and a man of the most amiable character. He published a book, entitled *De Arte Supputandi*, which was the first book of arithmetic ever printed in England, and passed through many editions.—*Granger*, vol. i. p. 95.

‡ Athenæ Oxon. vol. i. p. 593.

§ Fuller's Church Hist. b. ix. p. 63.

scruples would have vanished, might he have had the old temporalities undiminished. Both these writers seem to have been very little acquainted with Mr. Gilpin's character. He considered his income in no other light, than that of a fund to be managed for the public good. The bishop's insinuation, therefore, is contradicted by every action in Mr. Gilpin's life: and Dr. Heylin's is most notoriously false, for the bishopric was offered him with the old temporalities undiminished.*

It is certain that Mr. Gilpin was reckoned among the nonconformists of his time; and though he had several reasons for rejecting the offered preferment, that which prevailed most with him, was his disaffection to some points of conformity.† It was his fixed opinion, that no human invention should take place in the church, instead of a divine institution. The excellent Bishop Pilkington, who succeeded Tonstal at Durham, connived at his nonconformity; and excused him from subscription, the use of the habits, and a strict observance of the ceremonies.‡ But the bishop could screen him only for a season. For upon the controversy about the habits, about the year 1566, he was deprived for nonconformity; § but it is extremely probable he did not continue long under the ecclesiastical censure. The year after he was offered and nominated to the bishopric of Carlisle, he was offered the provostship of Queen's college, Oxford; but this he declined also. His heart was set on ministerial usefulness, not ecclesiastical preferment.

Mr. Gilpin continued many years at Houghton without further molestation, discharging all the duties of his function in a most exemplary manner. When he first undertook the care of souls, it was his settled maxim to do all the good in his power; and accordingly his whole conduct was one direct line towards this point. His first object was to gain the affections of his people. Yet he used no servile compliances: his means, as well as his ends, were good. His behaviour was free without levity, obliging without meanness, and insinuating without art. He condescended to the weak, bore with the passionate, and complied with the scrupulous. Hereby he convinced them how much he loved them; and thus gained their high esteem. He was unwearied in the instruction of those

* Biog. Britan. vol. vii. Sup. p. 72.

† MS. Remarks, p. 117. ‡ Neal's Puritans, vol. i. p. 245.

§ Calamy's Account, vol. i. Pref.

under his care. He was not satisfied with the advice he gave them in public, but taught them from house to house; and disposed his people to come to him with their doubts and difficulties. And even the reproofs which he gave, evidently proceeding from friendship, and given with gentleness, very seldom gave offence. Thus, with unceasing assiduity, he was employed in admonishing the vicious, and encouraging the well-disposed. And in a few years, by the blessing of God upon his endeavours, a greater change was effected throughout his parish, than could have been expected.

Mr. Gilpin continued to discharge the duties of his ministerial function in the most conscientious and laborious manner. Notwithstanding all his painful industry, and the large scope of labour in his own parish, he thought the sphere of his exertions were too confined. *It grieved his righteous soul* to behold in all the surrounding parishes so much ignorance, superstition, and vice, occasioned by the shameful neglect of the clergy. The ignorance and public vices in that part of the country, were very remarkable. This appears from the injunctions of Archbishop Grindal in 1570; among which were the following:—"That no "pedlar shall be admitted to sell his wares in the church "porch in divine service.—That parish clerks shall be able "to read.—That no lords of misrule, or summer lords and "ladies, or any disguised persons, morrice-dancers or "others, shall come irreverently into the church, or play "any unseemly parts with scoffs, jests, wanton gestures, "or ribbald talk, in the time of divine service."* Such was the deplorable condition of the people. Therefore, to supply as far as he was able, what was manifestly wanting in others, he used regularly every year to visit the most neglected parishes in Northumberland, Westmoreland, Cumberland, and Yorkshire: and that his own people might not suffer, he was at the expense of keeping an assistant. Even in those wild parts of the country, he never wanted an audience; and was the means under God of rousing many to a sense of religion, and the great importance of their salvation.

There is a tract of country on the borders of Northumberland, called Reads-dale and Tyne-dale; which, of all other places in the north, were the most barbarous. It was inhabited by a kind of desperate banditti, who lived chiefly

* Biog. Britan. vol. vii. Sup. p. 73.

by plunder. In this wretched part of the country, where no one would even travel if he could avoid it, Mr. Gilpin never failed to spend some part of the year, labouring for the good of their souls. He had fixed places for preaching, and punctually attended. If he came where there was a church, he made use of it; but if there were none, he used to preach in barns, or any other large buildings, where great crowds of people were sure to attend. In these itinerating excursions, his labours were always very great, and he often endured the most amazing hardships.

This excellent servant of Christ sometimes gave incontestible evidence of his firmness in reproving the vices of the greatest as well as the poorest. Having at one time made the requisite preparations for his journey to Readsdale and Tyne-dale, he received a message from Dr. Barns, bishop of Durham, appointing him to preach a visitation sermon on the following sabbath. He therefore acquainted the bishop with his engagements, and the obligation he was under to fulfil them, begging his lordship at that time to excuse him. As the bishop returned no answer, he concluded that he was satisfied, and set out on his journey. But, upon his return, he was greatly surprised to find himself suspended. After some time, he received an order to meet the bishop and many of the clergy, when the bishop ordered Mr. Gilpin to preach before them. He pleaded his suspension, and that he was unprepared; but the bishop immediately took off his suspension, and would admit of no excuse. Mr. Gilpin then went up into the pulpit, and preached upon the high charge of a christian bishop. In the sermon, after exposing the corruptions of the clergy, he boldly addressed the bishop in these words:—"Let not "your lordship say, that these crimes have been committed "by others, without your knowledge; for whatever either "yourself shall do in person, or suffer through your con-"nivance to be done by others, is wholly your own. "Therefore, in the presence of God, angels, and men, I "pronounce you to be the author of all these evils. Yea, "and in that strict day of general account, I will be a "witness to testify against you, that all these things have "come to your knowledge by my means; and all these "men shall bear witness thereof, who have heard me speak "to you this day."

This great freedom alarmed all who wished well to Mr. Gilpin. They said, the bishop had now got that advantage over him which his enemies had long sought to obtain. And when they expostulated with him, he said, "Be not afraid. The Lord God ruleth over all. If God may be glorified, and his truth propagated, God's will be done concerning me." Thus he assured them, that if his discourse answered the purpose he intended, he was regardless what might befall himself. Upon his going to the bishop, to pay his compliments before he went home, the bishop said, "Sir, I purpose to wait upon you home myself;" and so accompanied him to his house. As soon as Mr. Gilpin had conducted him into the parlour, the bishop suddenly turned round, and seizing him by the hand, said, "Father Gilpin, "I acknowledge you are fitter to be the Bishop of Durham, "than I am to be the parson of your church. I ask "forgiveness of past injuries. Forgive me, father. I know "you have enemies; but while I live Bishop of Durham, "be secure: none of them shall cause you any further "trouble."*

The benevolence and hospitality of Mr. Gilpin were the admiration of all the country. Strangers and travellers found a cheerful reception at his house. All were welcome that came: and every sabbath, from Michaelmas to Easter, he expected to see all his parishioners and their families. For their reception, he had three tables well covered: the first for gentlemen, the second for husbandmen and farmers, and the third for the labouring poor. This kind of hospitality he never omitted, even when losses or scarcity rendered its continuance rather difficult. He thought it was his duty; and that was a deciding motive. Even when he was from home, the poor were fed, and strangers entertained, as usual. Every Thursday throughout the year, a very large quantity of meat was dressed wholly for the poor; and every day they had as much broth as they wanted. Twenty-four of the poorest were his constant pensioners. Four times in the year a dinner was provided for the poor in general, when they received a certain quantity of corn and a sum of money; and at Christmas they had always an ox divided among them. Whenever he heard of any persons in distress, whether in his own parish or any other, he was sure to relieve them. As he walked abroad, he frequently brought home with him poor people, and sent them away clothed as well as fed. He took great pains to acquaint himself with the circumstances of his neighbours, that the modesty of sufferers might not prevent their relief. But the money best

* Wood says, that Bishop Barns was a constant favourer of puritanism. —*Athenæ Oxon.* vol. i. p. 607.

laid out, in his opinion, was that which encouraged industry. He took great pleasure in making up the losses of those who were laborious. If a poor man had lost a beast, he would send him another in its room: or if the farmers had at any time a bad harvest, he would make them an abatement in their tithes. Thus, as far as he was able, he took the misfortunes of his parish upon himself, and, like a true shepherd, exposed himself for his flock.

In the distant places where he preached, as well as in his own neighbourhood, his generosity and benevolence were continually manifested, particularly in the parts of Northumberland where he preached. Upon the public road, he never passed an opportunity of doing good. He was often known to take off his cloak, and give it to a poor traveller. "When he began a journey to those distant places," it is said, "he would have ten pounds in his purse; and at his coming home, would be twenty nobles in debt, which he would always pay within a fortnight after."

Among the many instances of Mr. Gilpin's uncommon benevolence, was the erection and endowment of a public grammar school. His school was no sooner opened, than it began to flourish; and there was so great a resort of young people to it, that in a little time the town could not accommodate them. For the sake of convenience, however, he fitted up his own house, where he had seldom fewer than twenty or thirty children. The greater part of these were poor children, whom he not only educated, but clothed and maintained. He was also at the expense of boarding many poor children in the town. He sent many of his scholars to the university, and devoted sixty pounds a year to their support during their continuance there. The common allowance for each scholar was ten pounds annually; which to a sober youth was at that time a sufficient support. And he not only procured able teachers for his school, but took a very active part himself in the constant inspection of it. To increase the number of his scholars, one method which he used was rather singular. Whenever he met with a poor boy upon the road, he would make trial of his abilities by asking him questions; and if he was pleased with him, would provide for his education. Among those educated at his school, and sent to the university, were Dr. George Carleton, afterwards bishop of Chichester, who published Mr. Gilpin's life; Dr. Henry Airay, and the celebrated Mr. Hugh Broughton.

Towards the close of life, Mr. Gilpin went through his

laborious exercises with great difficulty. By extreme fatigue for many years, his constitution was worn down, and his health much impaired. He thus expressed himself in a letter to a friend: "To sustain all these travels and troubles, I have a very weak body, subject to many diseases; by the motions whereof, I am daily warned to remember death. My greatest grief of all is, that my memory is quite decayed: my sight faileth; my hearing faileth; with other ailments, more than I can well express." While he was thus struggling with old age and an impaired constitution, as he was one day crossing the market-place at Durham, an ox ran at him, and pushed him down with such violence, that it was thought it would have occasioned his death. Though he survived the shock and bruises he received, he was long confined to his house, and continued lame as long as he lived.

During his last sickness, he made known his apprehensions to his friends, and spoke of death with happy composure of mind. A few days previous to his departure, he requested that his friends, acquaintance, and dependents, might be called into his chamber; and being raised in his bed, he delivered to each of them the pathetic exhortation of a dying man. His remaining hours were employed in prayer, and broken conversation with select friends, speaking often of the sweet consolations of the gospel. He finished his laborious life, and entered upon his rest, March 4, 1583, aged sixty-six years.

Such was the end of Mr. Bernard Gilpin, whose learning, piety, charity, labours, and usefulness, were almost unbounded. He possessed a quick imagination, a strong memory, and a solid judgment; and greatly excelled in the knowledge of languages, history, and divinity. He was so laborious for the good of souls, that he was usually called the NORTHERN APOSTLE; and he was so universally benevolent to the necessitous, that he was commonly styled the FATHER OF THE POOR. He was a thorough puritan in principle, and a most conscientious nonconformist in practice, but against separation. Being full of faith and good works, he was accounted a saint by his very enemies; and was at last gathered in as a shock of corn fully ripe. By his last will and testament, he left half of his property to the poor of Houghton, and the other half to a number of poor scholars at the university.*

* Wood's Athenæ Oxon. vol. i. p. 703.

Mr. Gilpin, from the earliest period, was inclined to serious thoughtfulness. This was discovered by the following circumstance. A begging friar coming on a Saturday evening to his father's house, was received, according to the custom of those times, in a very hospitable manner. The friar made too free with the bounty set before him, and became thoroughly intoxicated. The next morning, however, he ordered the bell to toll for public worship; and from the pulpit, expressed himself with great vehemence against the debauchery of the times, but particularly against drunkenness. Young Gilpin, then a child on his mother's lap, seemed for some time exceedingly affected by the friar's discourse; and at length, with the utmost indignation, cried out: "Oh, mamma, do you hear how this fellow "dares speak against drunkenness, and was drunk himself "last night!"

The disinterested pains which Mr. Gilpin took among the barbarous people in the north, and the great kindness he manifested towards them, excited in them the warmest gratitude and esteem. One instance is related, shewing how greatly he was revered. Being once on his journey to Reads-dale and Tyne-dale, by the carelessness of his servant, he had his horses stolen. The news quickly spread through the country, and every one expressed the highest indignation against it. While the thief was rejoicing over his prize, he found, by the report of the country, whose horses he had stolen; and being exceedingly terrified at what he had done, he instantly came trembling back, confessed the fact, returned the horses, and declared he believed the devil would have seized him immediately, if he had taken them off, when he found they belonged to Mr. Gilpin.

The hospitality of this excellent person was not confined in its objects. Strangers and travellers found the kindest entertainment in his house. And even their beasts were so well taken care of, that it was humorously said, "If a horse was turned out in any part of the country, he would immediately make his way to the rectory of Houghton."—The following instance of his benevolent spirit, is preserved. As he was one day returning from a journey, he saw several persons crowding together in a field; and supposing some disaster had happened, he rode up to them, and found that one of the horses in a team had suddenly dropped down, and was dead. The owner bemoaning the greatness of his loss, Mr. Gilpin said, "Honest man, be not discouraged; I'll let you have that horse of mine," pointing at his servant's." "Ah! master," replied the countryman, "my pocket will not reach such a beast as that." "Come, come," said Mr. Gilpin, "take him, take him; and when I demand the money, then shalt thou pay me;" and so gave him his horse.

The celebrated Lord Burleigh being once sent into Scotland, embraced the opportunity on his return to visit his old acquaintance at Houghton. His visit was without previous notice; yet the economy of Mr. Gilpin's house was not easily disconcerted. He received his noble guest with so much true politeness, and treated him and his whole retinue in so affluent and generous a manner, that the treasurer would often afterwards say, "he could hardly have expected more at Lambeth." During his stay, he took great pains to acquaint himself with the order and regularity of the house, which gave him uncommon pleasure and satisfaction. This noble lord, at parting, embraced his much respected friend with all the warmth of affection, and told him, he had heard great things in his commendation, but he had now seen what far exceeded all that he had heard. "If Mr. Gilpin," added he, "I can "ever be of any service to you at court or elsewhere, use "me with all freedom, as one on whom you may depend." When he had got upon Rainton-hill, which rises about a mile from Houghton, and commands the vale, he turned his horse to take one more view of the place, and having fixed his eye upon it for some time, he broke out into this exclamation: "There is the enjoyment of life indeed! "Who can blame that man for refusing a bishopric? What "doth he want, to make him greater, or happier, or more "useful to mankind?"*

Dr. Richard Gilpin, an excellent and useful divine, ejected by the Act of Uniformity in 1662; and Mr. William Gilpin, author of "The Lives of eminent Reformers," were both descendants of Mr. Gilpin's family.†

JOHN COPPING.—This unhappy man was minister near Bury St. Edmunds, a zealous puritan of the Brownist persuasion, and a most painful sufferer for nonconformity. In the year 1576, he was brought into trouble by the commis-

* Biog. Britan. vol. vii. Sup. p. 75.

† Palmer's Noncon. Mem. vol. i. p. 388.—Granger's Biog. Hist. vol. i. p. 163.

sary of the Bishop of Norwich, and committed to prison at Bury. He is said to have maintained the following opinions: "That unpreaching ministers were dumb dogs.—That whoever keeps saints' days, is an idolater.—That the queen, who had sworn to keep God's law, and set forth God's glory, as appointed in the scriptures, and did not perform it, was perjured." And it is added, that for the space of six months, he had refused to have his own child baptized; "because," he said, "none should baptize his child who did not preach;" and that when it was baptized, he would have neither godfathers nor godmothers. These were the great crimes alleged against him! Mr. Copping having for these offences remained in prison two years, and still refusing to conform; December 1, 1578, he underwent an examination before Justice Andrews, when the above *false* and *malicious opinions*, as they are called, were proved against him.* The good man continuing steadfast to his principles, and still refusing to sacrifice a good conscience on the altar of conformity, was sent back to prison, where he remained nearly five years longer. What shocking barbarity was this! Here Mr. Elias Thacker, another Brownist minister, was his fellow prisoner. The two prisoners having suffered this long and painful confinement, were indicted, tried, and condemned for spreading certain books, said to be seditiously penned by Robert Brown against the Book of Common Prayer. The sedition charged upon Brown's book, was, that it subverted the constitution of the established church, and acknowledged her majesty's supremacy only in *civil* matters, not in matters *ecclesiastical*. The judges took hold of this to aggravate their offence to the queen, after they had passed sentence upon them, on the statute of 23 Eliz. against seditious libels, and for refusing the oath of supremacy. Having received the sentence of death, they were both hanged at Bury, in the month of June, 1583. Such, indeed, was the resentment, and even the madness, of the persecutors of these two servants of Christ, that, previous to their death, all Brown's books that could be found, were collected together, and burnt before their eyes.† Under all these barbarities, the two champions for nonconformity continued immoveable to the last, and died sound in the faith, and of holy and unblemished lives. But, to hang men for spreading a book written against the church

* Strype's Annals, vol. ii. p. 532, 533.

† Ibid. vol. iii. p. 186.

only, appeared extremely hard, especially at the very time when Brown himself was pardoned and set at liberty.

Thomas Underdown was minister of St. Mary's church in Lewes, in the county of Sussex, but was brought into trouble for nonconformity. By a special warrant from Dr. Longworth, visitor to Archbishop Whitgift, dated November 18, 1583, he was summoned to appear in the ecclesiastical court at Lewes.* Upon his appearance in the court, he was immediately required to subscribe to Whitgift's three articles. He signified his readiness to subscribe to the *first* and *third* of those articles, but, hesitating about the *second*, he was immediately suspended. At the same time, Mr. William Hopkinson, vicar of Salehurst, Mr. Samuel Norden, minister of Hamsey, Mr. Thomas Hely, minister of Warbleton, with many others in the same county, were cited and suspended, for refusing subscription, though their refusal was not out of contempt, but because to them some things appeared doubtful.†

These ministers having received the ecclesiastical censure, ventured to lay their case at the feet of the archbishop. They appeared before his grace at Lambeth, December 5th, in the same year; when they entered upon the following conference:

Underdown. We are become suitors to your lordship, out of the diocese of Chichester, being urged thereunto by the hard dealing of Dr. Longworth; who hath suspended us from the exercise of our functions, for not subscribing to certain articles, pretended to be sent by your lordship; and to request your favour to be released from the same.

* Dr. Longworth sent the following warrant or citation to all the ministers within the archdeaconry of Lewes, requiring them to appear before him:—"These are to command you in her majesty's name, to "appear personally in St. Michael's church in Lewes, the 20th day of this "present November, between the hours of eight and ten o'clock in the "forenoon, then and there to perform all such duties and injunctions, as I "am to impose upon you, from the Archbishop's grace of Canterbury, as "appeareth by a special letter directed to me in that behalf. Fail you "not hereof, upon pain of the law which will necessarily ensue upon the "default which you shall commit in these premises. From Lewes, "November 18, 1583.

"Signed your loving friend,

"John Longworth."

MS. Register, p. 396.

† Ibid. p. 395, 396.—Strype's Whitgift, p. 128, 129.

Archbishop. I am so far from releasing you from your suspensions, that I declare it to have been orderly done; and I approve and justify the same, and shall further proceed against you unless you subscribe.

U. My lord, we have subscribed to the first and third articles, but desired respite for the second. And though we have used the Book of Common Prayer, so far as concerned our ministry, we cannot with a good conscience, subscribe to every particular in that book.

A. If you use that to which you will not subscribe, you dissemble. And how much respite would you have, after the exercise of twenty-five years?

U. Every thing in the book doth not pertain to our ministry; and in some things we are left to our liberty; but this subscription bindeth us to give our full consent to the whole, and thus abridgeth us of the liberty which the book alloweth.

A. What do you dislike in the Book of Common Prayer?

U. We do not say *dislike*, my lord; but there are many things *doubtful*, and about which we are not yet resolved.

A. What are the points doubtful, which you wish to have resolved? I will endeavour to satisfy you, if you will be satisfied.

U. We desire to know what book your lordship would have us to subscribe unto. For there are many copies, which differ in many points of great weight; and those which have been printed last, have most declined to superstition.

A. I mean the book which is now used for divine service and administration of the sacraments in the church of England.

U. That is not the book established by law, according to 1 Eliz., but differeth in more points from the book of 5 Edward VI. than the law of the land alloweth.

A. And what is the difference?

U. They differ in the following points and some others: The kalenders are not the same; the first lessons on all saints' days are appointed out of the apocrypha: the kalender appoints the saints' eves to be observed by fasting: it putteth in the popish saints: it prescribeth a number of holy-days: and it omitteth the advertisement after the communion, to avoid the popish adoration in kneeling at the sacrament.

A. The kalenders are not of the substance of the book.

U. They form a principal part of the book, and have a

chief interest in the directions there given: and the statute calleth it a part.

A. What other doubts have you which you wish to be resolved?

U. The book prescribeth certain parts of the apocrypha to be read in public worship, which contain gross errors, both in doctrine and practice; and leaveth out some parts of canonical scripture.

A. All the apocrypha is not appointed to be read, but those parts which are most edifying. And the ancient fathers permitted them to be read in the church.

U. Not some detached parts only, my lord, but whole books are appointed.

A. What errors in doctrine and practice do they contain?

U. Raphael maketh a lie, Tobit v. 15.

A. If this be a lie, then the angels lied to Abraham, by seeming to have bodies and to eat, when they had no bodies and did not eat: And Christ, when he seemed to intend going farther than Emmaus: And God, when he destroyed not Ninevah.

U. The cases are not alike.—Again, the devil is said to have loved Sara, Tobit vi. 16., which is fabulous.

A. Is it strange to you that the devil should love men and women? Do you think the devil doth not love?

U. In Ecclesiasticus xlvi. 20. it is said, that Samuel preached after he was dead.

A. It is controverted whether this were Samuel or some evil spirit.

U. What writers are of this opinion?

A. What point of faith is it to believe it was Samuel?

U. A principal point, my lord; for Rev. xiv. 13. it is said, that the souls of the righteous are in the hands of God, and rest from their labours; which is not true, if they be at the call of a witch or sorcerer, to do those things which while they lived, they would not have done.

A. Cannot the Lord dispense with them, and allow them to come, being called?

U. He dispenseth with things according to his word. And, surely, he would not condemn such abominations, and encourage them.

A. It is no matter whether we believe the one or the other. What is your next error? Are there any other faults in the apocrypha?

U. There are many others, which at this time we remember not.

A. Is there any other reason why you will not subscribe to the Book of Common Prayer?

U. Yes, my lord, there are many others. For if we subscribe to the book, we must subscribe to the massing apparel: as copes, vestments, tunicle, &c.

A. Whatever you are discharged from by any article or injunction, you are not required to subscribe unto it in the book.

U. Who then shall interpret how far our subscription shall extend?

A. That will I and the other bishops do, who know best what the book and subscription meaneth.

U. But, my lord, we dare not subscribe without protestation.

A. I will have no protestation. You are not called to rule in this church of England; and you shall not rule, but obey. And unless you subscribe, you shall have no place in the ministry. Is there any other thing which hindereth your subscription?

U. The rubric requireth that after the reading of the Nicene creed, an homily shall be read, either one already set forth by public authority, or hereafter to be set forth; and we think it is absurd to subscribe to the use of things not yet published.

A. You need not trouble yourself about that. Have you any thing else?

U. If we subscribe, we must subscribe to private baptism, and the baptism of women, directly contrary to the word of God.

A. Though baptism were unlawfully performed, yet being once performed, it is not to be repeated; and seeing it has the seal of the prince, it may not be condemned, though not performed by an ordinary minister.

U. We acknowledge the necessity of baptism, and that he who administereth it, does not make the sacrament better; yet from the words of Christ, "Go teach and baptize," it appears that he who administers this sacrament should be a minister of the word.

A. Whosoever shall say it is of the substance of the sacrament, that he who baptizeth must be a minister, I will proceed against him as an *heretic*. I say, moreover, it is not lawful for women to baptize; yet if they do baptize, their baptism is valid, and ought not to be set aside.

U. Seeing the sacrament is not saving, but the seal of God's promises, there is no need of them to baptize.

A. If I had a child dying without baptism, I should be doubtful of its salvation.

U. We think, my lord, that it is not the *want* of baptism, but the *contempt* of it, and that not of his friends, but the person himself, that doth condemn. Yet we believe and teach the lawfulness and necessity of childrens' baptism, and that it ought to be performed by ministers.

A. The book doth not speak of women; and it is called *private* because of the place, not the persons.

U. The circumstances of it can admit of no other sense. For it may be administered when there is not time to say the Lord's prayer.

A. There may not be so much time after the minister is come.

U. We know that the baptism of a certain nobleman by the midwife was allowed and defended by the Book of Common Prayer.

A. You should have complained of this abuse, that the parties might have been punished.

U. Your lordship knoweth the opinion of most persons upon this point, and that they practise accordingly.

A. It is not the fault of the book, if in this case it be misunderstood.

U. The practice was condemned in the convocation, when your lordship was prolocutor.

A. True: and you are to take away the superstition attached to it, by preaching against it.—Have you any other thing to mention?

U. We object against private communion.

A. Strange, indeed! Do you not think it lawful for two to communicate alone? If there were only two persons together in time of persecution, or in a wilderness, or in the world, would you have them not to communicate?

U. Such communion, if the church were there, would not be private. But we live in a time of gospel light and peace; therefore, the communion which your lordship defendeth, savours too much of the popish housel.

A. The minister is not compelled to do it, but only suffered if he will.

U. But if we subscribe, we must subscribe unto this as a convenient order appointed by the book. We have many other things; but we fear to be tedious. There are many others who are suspended, and are waiting your lordship's pleasure.

A. Why did they not all come? I would have endeavoured to satisfy them. You seem to be sober and discreet men. I would not have you depend on any vain fancies; but be ruled and enjoy your places, which, without this subscription, you shall not hold.

U. If our ministry have been useful to souls, we thank God for it; and we desire to keep our places, if it may be done with peace of conscience.

Hely. If we may subscribe with a good conscience, it is what we desire. But, my lord, if we subscribe to the book, do we not subscribe to the translation of the Bible, which the book appointeth to be read? That translation is faulty and incorrect in many places.

A. Mention some place.

H. In the Psalms.*

The first day's conference thus broke off; but by order of the archbishop, they all attended the next morning; when they appeared before the archbishop, the bishops of London, Salisbury, and Rochester, and the dean of Westminster. The archbishop having rehearsed the substance of what had passed the preceding day, with some enlargement upon the *devil's loving women*, the Bishop of London spoke as follows:

Bishop. If you had read either divinity or philosophy, it would not be strange to you that the devil should love women.

U. My lord, we have not learned any such divinity.

A. You must subscribe, It will be much to your advantage.

Hopkinson. We cannot subscribe, my lord, without protestation. And we have not so far examined every point, that we can subscribe at present, therefore we desire longer respite.

B. What respite would you have, after the use of the book twenty-five years? If you be not skilful in the knowledge of it, in so long a time, it seems as if you had not used it much.

Hopk. There are many things in the book which belong not to us, or to our ministry, therefore we desire favour in this subscription.

A. You shall subscribe or you shall enjoy no place in the ministry. And because you are the first who have been thus far proceeded against, in this case, you shall be made an example to all others.

* MS. Register, p. 397—401.

Hopk. If your lordship will deal thus hardly with us, we must give up our places.

A. If you do give them up, I can furnish them with as sufficient men as you are, and yet conformable.

B. Rochester. There are many learned men who are now in want of livings. These will fill up their places.

A. You of Sussex have been accounted very disorderly and contentious; and her majesty hath been informed of you; and I mean to proceed strictly with you.

U. My lord, the ministers of Sussex have been as well ordered as any in the kingdom, until one Shales came among them, and broached certain points of popery and heresy, which hath been the cause of all those troubles.

A. It would have been a wonder, if you had not been quiet, seeing you have all done as you pleased, without the least controul: the devil will be quiet so long. Why do you not accuse the man? and you shall see how I will deal with him.

B. Roches. What were his points of popery and heresy?

U. My lord hath been informed of these things already.

A. I remember you found fault yesterday with holy-days.

B. Have we not as good reason to maintain the holy-days established by law, as you have to make them when you please?

Hopk. We make no holy-days.

B. What do you else, when you call the people together unto sermons on working-days?

Hopk. When we have sermons, the people go to work before sermon, and return to work after sermon, as on other days: but to do this on the holy-days, they might be presented and punished, as hath been lately witnessed.

A. I see whence you have most of your doubts. Mr. Cartwright and I might have been better employed, especially he, who began the contest.* If you have any more doubts, propose them now, seeing there are so many of the bishops to answer them.

H. In the rubric before confirmation, salvation is ascribed to baptism. For whosoever is baptized, is said to be undoubtedly saved.

A. Is there any such thing in the book?

H. Yes, my lord, those are the words.

* This statement is incorrect. Mr. Cartwright did not begin the contest; but Whitgift himself engaged first in the controversy.—See Art. Cartwright.

A. Let us see the book.

Hartwell. They are the last words of the rubric.

A. The meaning of the book is to exclude the popish opinion of confirmation, as if it were as necessary as baptism. Therefore, those who have been baptized have all outward things necessary to salvation, even without confirmation.

H. The words may be taken in another sense, and, therefore, may not be subscribed without some deliberation.

Dean. I wonder you do not subscribe, seeing there is nothing in the second article which is not in the third, and you are willing to subscribe the third.

U. We have subscribed to the third already; and seeing all things contained in the second are contained in the third, we desire you to be satisfied with that subscription.

B. Not so.

Norden. How do your lordships understand these words, "Receive the Holy Ghost, for the office of a priest?"

A. Not imperatively, but optatively; and this speech is much the same as that other, "I baptize thee," &c.

B. We cannot give the Holy Ghost.

B. Roches. Do you not think, that when we use these words, we do communicate something?

U. I think not, my lord. For persons return from you no better furnished, than when they came unto you, if we may form our opinion from their practice.

A. We hope you are now resolved, and will now subscribe. You are unlearned, and only boys in comparison of us, who studied divinity before most of you were born.

U. We acknowledge our youth, my lord, and have no high opinion of our learning. Yet we hold ourselves sufficiently learned to know and teach Jesus Christ, as the way of salvation.

Hopk. If we subscribe under such interpretations, our subscription may become dangerous to us hereafter, when no interpretation may be allowed; therefore, we desire some protestation.

A. I will admit no protestation.

Dean. Come, Mr. Hopkinson, subscribe. My lord will favour you much, and help you against your adversaries.

Hopk. We must be better advised, Mr. Dean.

A. Go into the garden, or elsewhere, and consider of this matter, and return here again.

These divines having retired for some time, after consultation among themselves, they returned and consented to subscribe, on condition that their subscription should not be required to any thing against the word of God, or contrary to the analogy of faith; and that it should not be extended to any thing not already contained in the Book of Common Prayer. Also, to avoid all cavilling, Mr. Underdown protested, that the book of consecration did not belong to them, and that they could not subscribe to it; yet he acknowledged the ministry of the church to be lawful. To these conditions the archbishop and bishops agreed; and the ministers accordingly subscribed. Afterwards, Mr. Underdown having requested that the cross in baptism might not be urged, the conversation was briefly renewed, as follows:

A. You must use the cross, or the statute will reach you.

Hopk. Because it is intended as a significant sign, and is a new mystery in the church, we take it to be contrary to the second commandment.

A. Remember, it is required in the rubric.

N. It seemeth hard that the child must be asked whether it believe, and will be baptized.

A. The child is not asked, but the godfathers.

N. The godfathers and godmothers are several; therefore, if this were the meaning of the book, the number should be altered.

U. There are in our county many more of our brethren suspended for not subscribing. We beseech you that they may enjoy the same benefit, if they will subscribe as we have done.

A. I am content.

B. Roches. Are there any more who have refused?

U. Yes, my lord; there are above *twenty* in all.

B. Are there so many in your county?

German. There are some who have subscribed, and are greatly troubled in mind for what they have done. What do you think they had best do?

A. Let them come to me, and I hope to satisfy them.*

In the conclusion of the above conference, Mr. Underdown and his brethren were dismissed, when they returned home; and December 11th, being assembled in open court at Lewes, they were publicly released from their suspensions, where the business ended.

* MS. Register, p. 401—406.

Mr. SANDERSON was minister at Lynn in Norfolk, and troubled for his nonconformity. In the year 1573, he was charged, together with the people of the town, with having impugned the Book of Common Prayer. This was, indeed, a sad crime in those days.* February 8th, in that year, the following articles were exhibited against him in the ecclesiastical court:

1. "That he had called the curate of the place, a *dumb dog*, and a *camelion priest*.

2. "That he said the curate would not say the morning prayer, but would bid the popish holy-days, and say the popish service (meaning the common prayer) for those days.

3. "That, January 17th, he declared in the pulpit, that they who formerly employed their labours, and their goods, for the benefit of their poor and afflicted brethren, were now become judges over them; they sat in judgment upon them; and, like the Galatians, had received another gospel.

4. "That he exhorted the people to pray unto God, to change the heart of the queen's majesty, that she might set forth true doctrine and worship.

5. "That he said the apostle Paul would have contention for the truth, rather than suffer any inconvenience to enter into the church of God.

6. "That, January 24th, he said, that if either bishops, deans, or any others, or even an angel from heaven, preached any other doctrine than that which he then preached, they should hold him accursed, and not believe him.

7. "That he called the appointed holy-days, Jewish ceremonies; and the churching of women, Jewish purifications; and said, that many persons made the queen's laws their divinity.

8. "That, February 7th, he said in his sermon, that unpreaching and scandalous ministers were one principal occasion of the present dearth."†

Upon the examination of Mr. Sanderson, though we do not find what penalty was inflicted upon him, one Francis Shaxton, an alderman of the place, accused him of having delivered these opinions and assertions in two of his sermons, and even said he heard them, when, in fact, he was in London at the very time when the sermons were preached.

* "On Christmas-day last," says the Bishop of Norwich, in his letter to Archbishop Parker, "some of the aldermen went to church in their scarlets, and some would not; some opened their shops, and some shut them up; some eat flesh on that day, and others eat fish." Surely, then, it was high time to punish these rebellious people!—*Strype's Parker*, p. 452.

† MS. Register, p. 191.

In the year 1583, Mr. Sanderson's name is among those of the Norfolk divines, being upwards of sixty in all, who were not resolved to subscribe to Whitgift's three articles.*

John Hill was minister at Bury St. Edmunds, and, for omitting the cross in baptism, and making some trivial alteration in the vows, was suspended by the high commission. Not long after receiving the ecclesiastical censure, he was indicted at the assizes for the same thing. Upon his appearance at the bar, having heard his indictment read, he pleaded *guilty*. Then said Judge Anderson, before whom he appeared, what can you say that you should not suffer one year's imprisonment ?† Mr. Hill replied, "the law hath provided that I should not be punished, seeing I have been already suspended for the same matter, by the commissary." Upon this, the judge gave him liberty to produce his testimonial under the hand and seal of the commissary, at the next assizes. Accordingly, at the next assizes, his testimonial was produced and read in open court, when his discharge as founded thereon according to law being pleaded by his counsel, he was openly acquitted and dismissed.

Notwithstanding his public acquittance in open court, at the Lent assizes in 1583, the good man was summoned again by the same judge, and for the same crime. When he appeared at the bar, and heard the charges brought against himself, he greatly marvelled, seeing he had been already discharged of the same things. He was obliged to attend upon the court many times, when being known to be a divine of puritan principles, nothing more was done than he was always bound to appear at the next assize. At length, however, the judge charged him with having complained of their hard usage. And, surely, he had great reason for so doing. To this charge Mr. Hill replied, "I have

* MS. Register, p. 436.

† Sir Edmund Anderson, lord chief justice of the common pleas, was a most furious and cruel persecutor of the puritans. He sat in judgment upon Mary, Queen of Scots, in October, 1586; and the next year presided at the trial of Secretary Davison, in the star-chamber, for signing the warrant for the execution of that princess. His decision on that nice point was, "That he had done *justum, non juste;* he had done what was right in an "unlawful manner, otherwise he thought him no bad man." "This was excellent logic," says Granger, "for finding an innocent man guilty. But upon the queen's *order*, and *no-order*, he was obliged to find him guilty, upon pain of being deprived of his office."—*Biog. Hist.* vol. i. p. 235.

spoken no untruth of your honours." Anderson then shewed him the copy of a supplication, demanding whether he had not set his hand to it; and Mr. Hill answering that he thought he had, the angry judge said, "we shewed you favour before in accepting your plea, but we will shew you no more." Mr. Hill then replied, "I hope your lordships will not revoke what you have done, seeing you have discharged me of this matter already." The judge then answered, "that which we did, we did out of favour to you." Here the business closed, and Mr. Hill was sent to prison, being charged with no other crime than that of which the same judge had acquitted him. He continued in prison a long time; but whether he was ever restored to his ministry, is very doubtful.*

Nicholas Brown, B.D.—This learned divine was fellow of Trinity college, Cambridge, and one of the preachers to the university, but dissatisfied with the discipline of the national church. In the year 1573, he was brought into trouble for two sermons which he preached in the university. For the erroneous and dangerous doctrines supposed to be contained in these sermons, he was several times called before the heads of colleges, and, after repeated examination, was kept for some time in a state of confinement. Dr. Whitgift, afterwards the famous archbishop, was a leading person in these severe proceedings.

Upon Mr. Brown's appearance before his learned judges, he was required to retract his dangerous positions; which, at first, he utterly refused; but afterwards, it is said, he complied. These dangerous positions were contained in the two following articles: "That in his two sermons, he uttered doctrine and reasons tending to infringe the order and manner of creating and electing ministers, and the regimen now used in the church of England.—And that no priests made in the time of popery ought to have any function in the church of England, except they be called afresh."† These doctrines, said to have been delivered in his sermons, contain all the crimes with which he was accused even by his enemies. He was, therefore, required to make the following recantation, in the place, and before the congregation, where he had delivered the sermons:

"Whereas, I preaching in this place, the Sunday before

* MS. Register, p. 314. † Strype's Parker, p. 391, 392.

"Christmas, and January 25, last past, was noted to have "preached offensively; speaking as well against the manner "and form of making and ordering of ministers and deacons "in the church of England, as by law established: also, "against such priests as were made in the time of King "Henry and Queen Mary, saying that they were not to be "admitted into the ministry without a new calling. I now "let you understand, that I never meant so. For I do here "acknowledge and openly protest, that the manner and "form of ordering ministers and deacons in the church of "England, now established, is lawful and to be allowed. "Also, that the priests made in the time of King Henry and "Queen Mary, now allowed, and now exercising any "function in the church, are lawful ministers of the word "and sacraments, without any new ordering, otherwise than "is prescribed by the laws of this realm."*

Mr. Brown refused to comply with the above tyrannical requisition. He would not defile his conscience by doing that which was contrary to the convictions of his own mind. He considered it to be his duty to obey God, rather than men, though they were the spiritual rulers of an ecclesiastical establishment. He was, therefore, detained in prison a considerable time, but afterwards obtained his release. Notwithstanding this, his troubles were not over. After his deliverance from prison, he was repeatedly convened before the vice-chancellor and heads of colleges. On one of these occasions, the vice-chancellor commanded him to deliver another sermon in St. Mary's church, on a particular day, and at the usual hour of public service, requiring him to read openly and distinctly a paper, which the vice-chancellor should deliver to him. He also charged him "to accomplish the same humbly and charitably, without any *flouting*, *girding*, *twisting*, or *overthwarting* any man, and without using any words or gesture tending to the discredit of any person, or to the stirring up or maintaining of any contention or dissention."† That which the learned ecclesiastic delivered to him, and commanded him to read before the public congregation, was a kind of revocation of his opinions; but he remained inflexible, and would not comply with the tyrannical imposition.‡

On account of the cruelty with which he was treated, he presented his distressing case to Lord Burleigh, the chancellor, who warmly espoused his cause, and sent a letter to

* Strype's Parker, p. 391, 392.—Baker's MS. Collec. vol. iv. p. 55, 56.
† Ibid. vol. iii. p. 395, 396. ‡ Ibid. p. 399, 400.

the vice-chancellor, dated June 26, 1573, in which his lordship wrote as follows:—"Mr. Brown was with me," says he, "five or six days past, to entreat me, that by my means to you and others, he might forbear the execution of a certain order by you as vice-chancellor prescribed, to *pronounce a certain declaratory sentence*, in a sermon to be made by him now at the commencement. In which matter I had no disposition to deal; yet by the importunity of his sorrowful petition, and purpose not to offend in any such cause wherewith he hath been charged, I did with my pen write suddenly a few lines, to shew my inclination to have him favoured, and so dismissed him. Since which time, he is this day returned to me with a letter from Sir Thomas Smith, the queen's majesty's principal secretary, whereby you shall see how I am entreated to procure more favour for him. And yet without hearing you and others, who best know his cause, I dare not precisely require any alteration of your orders, but do recommend the party, who hath a good report, to be as favourably ordered, as he may find his repair to me hath in some measure relieved him, without hurting the public cause of good order."*

This pacific address from the treasurer proved ineffectual. The tyrannical vice-chancellor and his reverend colleagues refused to observe the generous instructions of the chancellor. Mr. Brown still remained under their ecclesiastical oppressions; and on account of the cruel usage he met with, he again laid his distressing case before Burleigh, July 6, 1573; but whether with any better success, we have not been able to learn.†

The year following, a puritan divine of the same name, and no doubt the same person, was concerned in Undertree's sham plot, when many letters were forged in his name. After examination, his innocence, with that of his brethren, was made openly and perfectly manifest.‡ Upon Mr. Brown's removal from the university, he became minister at Norton in Suffolk, where he was afterwards molested for nonconformity. For, in the year 1583, on the publication of Whitgift's three articles, he refused subscription, and, with many others, was immediately suspended. How long he continued under the ecclesiastical censure, or whether he was ever restored, we are unable to ascertain.§

* Strype's Parker, vol. xxix. p. 371, 372.
† Ibid. vol. iv. p. 56.
‡ Ibid. p. 466.
§ MS. Register, p. 436, 437.

RICHARD CRICK, D.D.—He was chaplain to the Bishop of Norwich, and much commended for his learning and sobriety. In the year 1573, he preached at Paul's cross; and having in his sermon commended Mr. Cartwright's reply to Whitgift, a special messenger was sent from Archbishop Parker to apprehend him. Though at that time he escaped the snare, he afterwards fell into the hands of the high commissioners, by whom he was deprived of his preferment in the church at Norwich.*

Dr. Crick being silenced, and many of his brethren in the same diocese, they united in presenting a supplication to the council, that they might be restored to their beloved ministry, and allowed again to preach the glad tidings of the gospel. This supplication was dated September 25, 1576; a further account of which is given in another place.† Afterwards, he and many of his brethren, being the silenced ministers in that diocese, presented their humble submission, to their diocesan, dated August 21, 1578. In this submission, they request to be restored to their ministry, promising to subscribe to the articles of faith and the doctrine of the sacraments, according to the laws of the realm. They profess, at the same time, that the ceremonies and government of the church are so far to be allowed, that no man ought to withdraw from hearing the word and receiving the holy sacraments, on account of them. They also offer to the bishop, their reasons for refusing to subscribe, requesting to have their difficulties removed, without which they could never subscribe in the manner required.‡ This excellent divine, therefore, remained a long time under deprivation. Though he was afterwards restored to his ministry, yet, upon the publication of Whitgift's three articles, he was again suspended, with many others, for refusing subscription.§

ANTHONY GILBY.—This pious and zealous nonconformist was born in Lincolnshire, and educated in Christ's college, Cambridge, where he obtained a most exact knowledge of the Latin, Greek, and Hebrew languages. He constantly laboured to promote a further reformation; and having published his sentiments of the habits, ceremonies, and corruptions in the church, more openly than many of

* Strype's Parker, p. 421, 427.
† See Art. John More.
‡ Ibid.
§ MS. Register, p. 437.

his brethren, he is represented by some of our historians, as a fiery and furious opposer of the discipline in the church of England.*

Upon the accession of Queen Mary, and the commencement of her bloody persecution, he became an exile in a foreign land. He was among the first who retired to Frankfort, where he was deeply involved in the troubles occasioned by the officious interference of Dr. Cox and his party. When the order of church discipline, highly esteemed by many, was presented to the whole congregation, and rejected by the zealous episcopalians, "Mr. Gilby, with a godly grief, as was openly manifest, kneeled down before them; and with tears in his eyes, besought them to promote the desired reformation, solemnly protesting, that, in this matter, they sought not themselves, but the glory of God only: adding, that he wished the very hand which he then held up, might be struck off, if godly peace and unity could thereby be promoted."† Such was his truly generous spirit; and such his fervent zeal for the peace and unity of the church! Upon the unkind usage at Frankfort, Mr. Gilby removed to Geneva. Afterwards, he united with his brethren in writing a letter to those who still remained at Frankfort, defending the lawfulness of their departure, against the slanderous reports of those who stigmatized them as schismatics. This letter, signed by eighteen persons, among whom was the famous Mr. John Fox, breathes a most condescending, humble, and healing spirit.‡ During Mr. Gilby's abode at Geneva, he assisted Coverdale, Sampson, and other learned divines, in the translation of the Bible.§

After the accession of Queen Elizabeth, our divine returned from exile, and was greatly admired and beloved by all who sought a thorough reformation of the English church. He is, indeed, exceedingly reproached by several of our bigotted historians. Dr. Bancroft says, that Mr. Gilby, with the rest of the Geneva accomplices, urged all states by degrees, to take up arms, and reform religion themselves by force, rather than suffer so much idolatry and superstition to remain in the land.‖ Another peevish writer, with an evident design to blacken his memory, says, "That in obedience to John Calvin, the supreme head of Geneva,

* Fuller's Worthies, part ii. p. 167.
† Troubles at Frankeford, p. 30.
‡ Ibid. p. 47.
§ See Art. Coverdale.
‖ Bancroft's Dangerous Positions, p. 62. Edit. 1640.

doth his dear subject and disciple Anthony Gilby, and others of that fraternity, shoot their wild-fire against the statutes of England; by which they shew their schism and madness, more than their christian prudence."* This is wholly the language of misrepresentation and abuse.

Notwithstanding these calumnies, Mr. Gilby enjoyed the favour of several of the nobility, men of excellent character and high reputation. The Earl of Huntington, who was his constant friend and patron, presented him to the vicarage of Ashby-de-la-Zouch in Leicestershire; where, through the blessing of God on his ministry, he was made exceedingly useful. Here he obtained a distinguished reputation, when the worthy earl used to style him *Father Gilby.*† Bishop Hall, who probably had some acquaintance with him, denominates him "a reverend and famous divine;"‡ and he is said to have lived at Ashby "as great as a bishop." He was highly esteemed by some of the learned prelates, as well as many of the most celebrated divines of the age, with whom he held a friendly correspondence. The following is the copy of a letter, which he received from the Bishop of Lichfield and Coventry:§

"To my loving friend and brother in Christ, Mr. Gilby,
"at Ashby.

"With my hearty commendations to you Mr. Gilby. I "received your letter but now and heretofore, to the which "I proposed to have made some answer by this time; but "either lack of convenient messenger, or some other present "business, have stayed; and, therefore, these are in few "words to signify to you, that such reports as you have "heard of me, touching Stretton, were untrue, (I thank "Almighty God) and so saying to my brother. Augustin "added these words, that I marvelled much if you did "judge as you wrote. Notwithstanding, I was not dis-"pleased with your writing, but accepted the same as "friendly and lovingly as I can any man's writing.

"It is plain that many enormities remain uncorrected, "either for lack of knowledge thereof, or else through the "corruption of mine officers, or otherwise through negli-"gence or forgetfulness of myself; yet when I have proof "of them, I either call the offenders myself, or charge mine

* Foulis' Hist. of Plots, p. 36.
† Nichols's Hist. of Leicestershire, vol. ii. p. 626.
‡ Life of Bp. Hall prefixed to his Works.
§ Baker's MS. Collec. vol. xxxii. p. 434.

"officers with the same. Concerning that evil man, Sir "William Radish, I engage to have him called as soon as "I can, to answer his doings and such sayings as ———. "Touching the person of Stretton, I will do that which "lieth in me to displace, for the which I have given charge "divers times to mine officers. I would not have my "brother Dawberry to do any thing touching the same; for "the matter will not pass through at Lichfield. I will then "send you word, and use your counsel. And thus omitting "all other matters, till we shall have occasion to meet "together, I commit you and good Mrs. Gilby (whose "health and happiness I wish) to the goodness of Almighty "God; this 12 day of Nov. 1565. At Eccleshall-castle.

"Your loving friend and brother in Christ,

"THOMAS COVEN. and LICHFIELD."

The above letter, justly deemed a curiosity, shews at once the great intimacy and familiarity which subsisted betwixt Mr. Gilby and the bishop, and the high esteem and respect in which our divine was held by his learned diocesan. Mr. Gilby was a celebrated scholar, and a most profound and pious divine, and admirably qualified for the translation of the holy scriptures. The famous Dr. Lawrence Humphrey, with whom he held a frequent correspondence, had the highest opinion of him. Several of the doctor's letters to Mr. Gilby are now before me, one of which, though very short, it will be proper here to insert; which is as follows:*

"To his worshipful and good friend Mr. Ant. Gilby.

"Salutation in Christ Jesus. Albeit your days are evil "and your time short; yet I pray you be occupied in the "gift which God has betowed upon you, in translating the "prophets, and conjoin somewhat also out of the Rabbins "or Chaldee Paraphrast, that may be a testimony of your "industry, and an help for your son. We must do what we "may, and what we cannot must leave to God. The Lord "be merciful to us. Commend me to your good wife. "Oxon. March 5.

"Yours in the Lord,

"LAWRENCE HUMPHREY."

This letter appears to have been addressed to our divine towards the close of life, but there is no particular year

* Baker's MS. Collec. vol. xxxii. p. 431.

specified in the date. Several other letters from Dr. Thomas Sampson, Mr. Thomas Wilcocks, and other celebrated divines, addressed to Mr. Gilby, are now before me. Such of them as are particularly illustrative of the history of the times, will be found inserted in their proper places.

The high respect in which Mr. Gilby was held, was no screen against the persecution of the tyrannizing ecclesiastics. Therefore, in the year 1571, Archbishop Parker binding the clergy to a more exact conformity, by wearing the habits and observing the ceremonies, commanded Archbishop Grindal of York, to prosecute him for nonconformity. But Grindal, who, towards the close of life, was averse to all severe measures, signified to his brother of Canterbury, that as Mr. Gilby dwelt in Leicestershire, and out of his province, he could not proceed against him; and so referred his case to the commissioners in the south. Hence it is extremely probable that he was now summoned, with several other learned divines, before Parker and his colleagues at Lambeth; but of this we have no certain information.* It appears, however, pretty evident, that he was silenced from his public ministry, either at this, or at some other time.†

Mr. Gilby, according to Fuller, stands first on the list of learned writers, who received their education in Christ's college, Cambridge.‡ He was author of a work, entitled "A Viewe of Antichrist, his Lawes and Ceremonies in our English Church unreformed," 1570. The first part of this humorous piece is called "The Book of the Generation of Antichrist the Pope, the revealed Child of Perdition and his Successors;" and is so singular and curious, that, for the satisfaction of the inquisitive reader, the substance of it is here transcribed. The ecclesiastical genealogy is expressed as follows:

The devil begat darkness. Darkness begat ignorance. Ignorance begat error and his brethren. Error begat free-will and self-love. Free-will begat merit. Merit begat forgetfulness of the grace of God. Forgetfulness of the grace of God, begat transgression. Transgression begat mistrust. Mistrust begat satisfaction. Satisfaction begat the sacrifice of the mass. Sacrifice of the mass begat popish priesthood. Popish priesthood begat superstition.

* Strype's Parker, p. 320.—Grindal, p. 170.
† Nichols's Defence, p. 21. Edit. 1740.
‡ Fuller's Hist. of Cam. p. 92.

Superstition begat hypocrisy the king. Hypocrisy the king begat lucre. Lucre begat purgatory. Purgatory begat the foundation of pensions, and the patrimony of the church. Pensions and patrimony begat the mammon of iniquity. Mammon begat abundance. Abundance begat fulness. Fulness begat cruelty. Cruelty begat dominion in ruling. Dominion begat ambition. Ambition begat simony. And simony begat the POPE, and his brethren the cardinals, with all their successors, abbots, priors, archbishops, lord-bishops, archdeacons, deans, chancellors, commissaries, officials, and proctors, with the rest of the viperous brood.

The pope begat the mystery of iniquity. The mystery of iniquity begat divine sophistry. Divine sophistry begat rejection of the holy scriptures. Rejection of the holy scriptures begat tyranny. Tyranny begat murder of the saints. Murder begat despising of God. Despising of God begat dispensation of offences. Dispensation begat license for sin. License for sin begat abomination. Abomination begat confusion in matters of religion. Confusion brought forth travail of the spirit. Travail of the spirit brought forth matter of disputation for the truth; by which that desolator, antichrist the pope, hath been revealed, and all other antichrists shall in due time be revealed. And they are antichrists, who make laws for the church, contrary to the truth, and deprive, imprison, and banish the members of Christ, both preachers and others, refusing obedience thereunto.—Most of the points in this curious genealogy, are supported by an appropriate portion of scripture.* Though Mr. Toplady styles the author, "a very acrimonious puritan;" yet he adds, "that as far as matters of mere doctrine were concerned, it is in perfect harmony with the creed of the church of England."†

As Mr. Gilby was a zealous opposer of the ecclesiastical corruptions, and constantly desirous to obtain a more pure reformation, he could not escape the severe animadversion of the contrary party. For having said, "that the habits and ceremonies used in the church of England, were carnal, beggarly, antichristian elements," Dr. Nichols has treated him with much scurrility and abuse. But, surely, if the apostle might call the Jewish ceremonies *carnal*, when God himself had appointed them; why might not Mr. Gilby say

* Parte of a Register, p. 56, 57.
† Toplady's Historic Proof, vol. ii. p. 356.

the same of the popish ceremonies, which he never appointed? If the one called Jewish ceremonies, *weak* and *beggarly elements*; why might not the other call the popish ceremonies, *beggarly* and *antichristian pomps*? The celebrated Bishop Ridley, once a zealous defender of the ceremonies, when the surplice was forced upon him, bitterly inveighed against it, calling it *foolish*, *abominable*, and *not fit for a player on the stage.* The excellent Bishop Jewel called the garments, *relics of popery*. Why then is Mr. Gilby so bitterly censured for saying, they were *popish fopperies*, *Romish relics*, *rags of antichrist*, and *dregs of disguised popery*?* Mr. Gilby publicly declared, adds the above writer, "that if he was *suffered to preach* some time longer, being so conceited of his popular eloquence, he would shake the very foundations of the English church."† Whether he was, indeed, thus conceited of his own superior eloquence, and whether he ever made any such declaration, it is not now very easy to ascertain. If Dr. Nichols had any authority for what he has asserted, he would certainly have done his own cause no injury, but have conferred a favour upon the public, by bringing it forwards. However, admitting the twofold charge, it reflects no great degree of honour upon the rulers of the church, that so eloquent, learned, pious and useful a divine, should be condemned to silence.

This worthy servant of Christ appears to have lived to a very great age, but we cannot learn the particular time of his death. The last of the letters addressed to him, that we have seen, is one from Dr. Sampson, dated March 8, 1584; when he must have been living.‡

His Works.—1. An Answer to the Devilish Detection of Stephen Gardiner, Bishop of Winchester, 1547.—2. A Commentary on the Prophet Micah, 1551.—3. An Admonition to England and Scotland, to call them to Repentance for their Declension and Apostacy from the Truth, 1557.—4. A Viewe of Antichrist, &c. already mentioned. —5. A Godly and Zealous Letter written to Master Coverdale, M. Turner, M. Sampson, M. Doctor Humphrey, Mr. Lever, M. Crowley, and others that labour to roote out the Weedes of Poperie, 1570.—6. A pleasant Dialogue between a Soldier of Berwick and an English Captain, wherein are largely handled and laid open such Reasons as are brought for Maintenance of Popish Traditions in our English Church.

* Peirce's Vindication, part ii. p. 8, 9.
† Nichols's Defence, p. 21. Edit. 1740.
‡ Baker's MS. Collec. vol. xxxii. p. 443.

John Edwin was a man of great learning and piety, a zealous and constant preacher, and many years vicar of Wandsworth in Surrey, but was prosecuted for nonconformity. He was cited before the Bishop of Winchester; and, upon his appearance, April 30, 1584, he underwent the following examination:

Bishop. Where do you dwell?

Edwin. At Wandsworth in Surrey.

B. Where were you brought up?

E. For the most part at Wandsworth.

B. What in no school!

E. Never in any public school, only some time at Rochester. I have lived at Wandsworth forty-two years, and have been vicar of Wandsworth twenty-five years, during which time, I thank God, I have not been idle.

B. Where were you made minister?

E. I was made minister when Dr. Parker was created Archbishop of Canterbury, by the Bishop of Bangor, who, by the command of the archbishop, made me minister in Bow-church, London.

B. Do you use to catechize? and how do you perform it?

E. I catechize every Lord's day before evening prayer, and in the midst of evening prayer.

B. Have you not subscribed?

E. No.

B. Why not?

E. My Lord, I perceive that you wish us to signify our allowance of the Book of Common Prayer. There is no cause why I should be called in question for this matter; for I use the book, and do not refuse it, and I speak not against it. These are manifest proofs that I allow of it.

B. Many of you who say so, will not confess what you have done, neither what you will do. Therefore you must subscribe.

E. I consider it a greater allowance to *use* a thing, than to *subscribe* unto it.

B. So you think and say it is unreasonable and unlawful to require you to subscribe.

E. Do you gather this, my lord, from what I have said?

B. No.

E. Then all is well.

B. But you must subscribe, or shew some cause why you will not.

E. My lord, if no excuse will serve, but I must subscribe,

or shew some cause why I refuse, I will shew your lordship three reasons: As, 1. There are some things in the Book of Common Prayer *against* the word of God, and, therefore, *repugnant* to the word of God.—2. My next reason—

B. Nay, stop; let us talk of the first.

E. I like your order well. And to prove what I have said, I refer you to the words of the rubric, before the office of confirmation, where it is said, "That no man shall think any detriment will come to children by deferring their confirmation; he shall know for *truth*, that it is *certain by God's word*, that children being baptized have *all things necessary to salvation*, and be *undoubtedly saved*."

B. You must not take it as the words import.

E. No, my lord! Is it not your pleasure that we should subscribe to the things in the book? Or, is it your pleasure that we should subscribe to your interpretation of those things?

B. You must subscribe to the *sense* of what is contained in the book.

E. If we must subscribe to the sense, then must you amend your article. For your article, to which you require us to subscribe, saith, that there is nothing in the Book of Common Prayer repugnant to the word of God.

B. If you were to subscribe to the gospel, would you subscribe to the words, or the sense?

E. I would subscribe to the words——*

B. You lie.

E. My lord, I beseech you let us have good words. I say again, we must subscribe both to the *words* and to the *sense*.

B. But I say nay. For where Christ saith, "I am the door," will you subscribe to the words?

E. My lord, mistake me not. I say we must subscribe to the sense and the words; and where the words are figurative, we must subscribe to the sense. But when the words and sense are the same, and without any figure, then we must subscribe to both.

B. What think you of the words of Christ, "My father is the husbandman," and, "the word was made flesh?"

E. If you compare Gen. i. with the words going before those you have mentioned, you will see that we must subscribe to the *sense* of the words.

* Here, as Mr. Edwin attempted to proceed, his grace suddenly and passionately interrupted him.

B. "The word was made flesh:" I am sure you will not say, the Godhead of Christ was made flesh.

E. No, my lord, and I am as sure you will not say, that the manhood of Christ was made flesh, without his Godhead. But, my lord, allow me to prove my assertion.

B. Tell me, what is the English of *verbum*?

E. I can prove out of the Greek, the Hebrew, and the Syriac, that the word *verbum*, as near as it can be rendered in English, signifieth *a thing*. Allow me to prove my assertion.

B. I confess we must subscribe both to sense and words.

E. Then in this we are agreed.

B. In the place you cited from the book, the meaning is, that those who are baptized, and therewith receive the grace of that sacrament, being of the number of the elect, are undoubtedly saved.

E. I beseech your lordship to read the words of the book, and let it be seen how you can give it that interpretation. But I wish to mention a second reason, and that is the administration of the communion to an individual person in private. How doth this agree with the word of God, and with the word *communion*?

B. The doctrine contained in the sacrament, belongeth to wise and learned men to determine. You had best exercise yourself in catechizing, and let this alone.

E. My lord, you must bear with me. For I think God requireth it at our hands, that we learn and teach all things revealed in his holy word.

B. In some parts of Saxony, there are various articles of religion prohibited from being taught; and we ought to be content and thankful for the liberty we enjoy.

E. I cannot, without tears, remember the marvellous benefits we enjoy by the freedom of the gospel, which I pray God may never be interrupted. I must, also, call to mind, and I do also remember, the innumerable comforts and benefits we enjoy under the government of our most gracious Queen Elizabeth, whom, I beseech God, long to continue and bless. But are these sufficient reasons for us to yield to any thing against the word of God?

B. The communion in private is a *single* communion.

E. How can the words *single* and *communion* be made to agree?

B. I do not say they can.

E. Why then do you join them together?

B. In the time of Justin Martyr, being two hundred years after Christ, the sacrament, in time of persecution, was carried from house to house, because the people dare not come together. And on one occasion, the sacrament was sent by a boy to a sick man, who earnestly desired to receive it.

E. But, my lord, your bringing forward the example of primitive christians is to no purpose. Our question is, whether the Book of Common Prayer containeth any thing repugnant to the word of God. And, my lord, I think no good man will deny that the two places I have mentioned are repugnant to the word of God.

B. What! do you condemn all who have subscribed? Do you say they have all acted wickedly?

E. You misunderstand my words. What I speak, I speak with consideration, and I know what I say.

B. What o'clock is it?

E. We have not yet done. I told you I had *three* reasons.

B. I have had more ado with you than all the rest.

E. You have not yet finished with me. As I said, I have three reasons; and I trust you will hear them before you proceed against me.

B. What are your other reasons?

E. If you will promise that we shall examine them, I will mention them; but if not, it is unnecessary.

B. I had rather persuade many learned men than you.

E. I speak not of learning, but of conscience; and my conscience, without persuasion, will not yield. Hitherto in my ministry, I have enjoyed a good conscience, founded upon the word of God; and, my lord, with as good a conscience, by the help of God, will I be removed from it, or I will not be removed.*

Here the examination broke off, and the good man departed most probably under suspension or deprivation. His two other reasons for refusing to subscribe, which he designed to have mentioned, were, "That in the Book of Common Prayer, there are some things contrary to the *laws of the realm*.—And that there are some things which maintain and encourage some of the *grossest errors* and *heresies of popery*."†

* MS. Register, p. 576—579. † Ibid.

Edward Brayne was a learned divine of Cambridge, and greatly harassed for refusing subscription to Whitgift's three articles, accounting them contrary to scripture and the dictates of his own conscience. Having received two canonical admonitions, he united with his brethren in the diocese of Ely, in writing the following peaceable letter to the archbishop, dated March 12, 1584:—"Whereas two canonical admonitions are already passed upon us, for refusing to subscribe to things, some of which we know not, and others we greatly doubt. We are, therefore, bold to offer our humble supplication unto you, as well as crave your lordship's favour that a longer space of time may be granted us, endeavouring and praying daily with our whole hearts for the peace of the church. Wherefore, if it shall please your lordship, we wish either to be freed from all subscription, excepting to her majesty's authority, and the articles of religion, as by law required, or to give us so long a time, that we may sufficiently consider the subject, and be persuaded that we ought to subscribe; or if, at length, we cannot subscribe, to submit ourselves to suffer punishment, for the peace of the church. In the mean time, we condemn not those who have subscribed, and we desire that they may not condemn us. Thus if it shall please Almighty God to move your lordship to have compassion on our troubled consciences, we shall praise God and manifest our thankfulness to you."*

It does not, however, appear that this letter had any good effect on the mind and conduct of this severe prelate. His grace remained inflexible. Therefore, May 24, 1584, Mr. Brayne and his brethren presented a supplication to the lords of the council; in which they protest their aversion to popery, and their inviolable loyalty to the queen, having already sworn obedience to her authority, and subscribed the articles of religion, and were ready to do the same again, if required. That they abhorred all error, heresy, and schism, and made use of the Book of Common Prayer, and endeavoured both in doctrine and conversation, to maintain a conscience void of offence towards God and men. And that being commanded to subscribe to many things not required by law, they humbly crave their lordships to accept of the following reasons for their refusal, and to be a means of releasing them from the subscription required:

* MS. Register, p. 333, 334.

"Some things," say they, "appear to us repugnant to the word of God; as the allowance of an unlearned ministry, reading the apocrypha in the service of God, private baptism, and the government of the church. And to us many things appear very doubtful, some of which it is impossible for us to practice with a good conscience. Yet, as we judge not others in the practice of them; so we desire that we may not be judged by them, but left to our liberty in not subscribing. There are other things to the use of which we have subscribed, because they are tolerated for a time, and imposed upon us by the laws of the church; yet we see not how they agree with the word of God, and cannot approve of them. But if we offend against any law of the church or statute, we humbly crave such favour and clemency as is not contrary to law; but if this cannot be obtained, we submit ourselves to the censures of the law, still avowing our peaceableness both in church and state.

"We, therefore, must humbly on our knees, beseech your honours, that we may be freed from the subscription now urged upon us; or have so much time allowed us to examine and consider the case, as your wisdoms shall think fit; or we must give up our places for the peace of the church. For we most humbly confess before God and the elect angels, that to subscribe as now required, we should act contrary to the doctrines of faith and repentance which we have taught among the people of our charge: We should subscribe to some things *against* our consciences, to many things with a *doubtful* conscience, and most of all with an *ignorant* conscience; from all such dealing the Lord ever preserve us. We commend to your wise consideration the indignity and reproach which is likely to be cast upon us and our ministry, being accounted disloyal and seditious against her majesty; but we much more commend to you our doubtful, fearful, and distressed consciences, and the miserable state of our poor and distressed people hungering after the word of life, who, when they are deprived of us, almost despair of having a learned and godly ministry. If they might have better than ourselves, we should rejoice, and be much more content. We bless the Lord, that the people of our charges are free from heresies and seditions, and most of them from gross crimes, and all, so far as we know, are faithful subjects, and many of them are known and approved christians. But what may befall them when they are left as sheep without a shepherd, we leave to your honoured wisdoms to judge.

"We have only to add our humble apology for now soliciting the favour of your honours. We have forborne applying to you as long as we possibly could, and perhaps till it is too late, as three canonical admonitions have already passed upon us, and our deprivation is threatened; which sentence, two of us have already tasted. We have used means by our right worshipful and some of her majesty's justices, with the Archbishop of Canterbury, who have used their earnest suit for us with the archbishop, both by their letters and private conference; but hitherto to no purpose. Such dealing may seem favourable to them who treat us thus, but to us it seemeth very hard. Our release from this hard dealing by your kind favour, will provoke us to pray for your honours' present peace and prosperity, and that when you have done with all things here, you may receive the crown of glory."*

Notwithstanding this supplication, or their letter to the archbishop, in the month of July this year, Mr. Brayne was cited to appear before his grace and other high commissioners at Lambeth. Having attended several times according to appointment, and being required to take the oath *ex officio*, to answer the interrogatories of the court, he refused, unless he might first see them, and write down his answers with his own hand. His grace refusing to grant him the favour, immediately gave his canonical admonitions, *once, twice, thrice;* and caused him to be registered for contempt, and suspended from his ministry. "But," says the good man, "God knoweth how far contempt was from my heart, and, I trust, my words and behaviour will witness the same."† But guilty or not guilty, the tyrannical archbishop cut him off from all public usefulness in the church of God.

Mr. Brayne being silenced from his beloved work, wrote a very appropriate letter, dated July 6th, to the Lord Treasurer Burleigh, giving him an account of the hard treatment he had met with. In this letter, he earnestly solicited the treasurer's kind favour and interference; but whether it proved the means of procuring his restoration, appears extremely doubtful.‡ The treasurer, indeed, used his utmost endeavours. He applied to the archbishop, signifying

* MS. Register, p. 455—457.
† Strype's Whitgift, p. 163. ‡ Ibid. p. 164.

his dissatisfaction with his lordship's urging ministers, by his method of examination, to accuse themselves; and then to punish them upon their own confessions. He further observed, "that he would not call his proceedings *captious*, but they were scarcely *charitable*. That he would not offend his grace; and was content that he and the Bishop of London, might use Mr. Brayne as their wisdoms should think fit. But when by examining him, it was only meant to sift him with *twenty-four* articles, he had cause to pity the poor man."* Such was the wisdom, the boldness, and the sympathy of this celebrated statesman; but his generous efforts appear to have been without effect.†

Barnaby Benison was minister in London, a divine of good learning, and suspended and imprisoned for several years, by Bishop Aylmer, on pretence of some irregularity in his marriage. The bishop charged him with being married in an afternoon, and in the presence of two or three hundred people, by Mr. Field, a nonconformist. For this singular crime, in the year 1579, he was committed to the Gatehouse, where he continued till towards the close of the year 1584. Mr. Strype, with a design to blacken his memory, observes, "that he studied for some time at Geneva; and upon his return to England, was fraught with innovation and disobedience." He undoubtedly was dis-

* Strype's Whitgift, p. 160.

† Lord Burleigh was a decided friend to the persecuted puritans, and often screened them from the inhuman proceedings of the prelates, or procured their release from bonds and imprisonment. On account of his great abilities, indefatigable application, amazing capacity for business, and immoveable integrity, he is deservedly placed at the head of our English statesmen. His capacity for business appears from the following passage in his life:—"Besides all business in council, or other weighty causes, and "such as were answered by word of mouth, there was not a day in term "wherein he received not threescore, fourscore, or a hundred petitions, "which he commonly read that night, and gave every man an answer the "next morning as he went to the hall. Hence the excellence of his "memory was greatly admired; for when any of these petitioners told "him their names, or what countrymen they were, he presently entered "into the merit of his request, and having discussed it, gave him his "answer." This was his practice towards persons in all circumstances. He would answer the *poorest*, as well as others, from his own mouth. When at any time he was forced to keep his chamber, or his bed, he ordered that poor suitors should send in their petitions sealed; and upon every petition he caused his answer to be written, and subscribed it with his own hand. "He was prayed for by the poor, honoured by the rich, feared by the "bad, and loved by the good."——*Biog. Britan.* vol. iii. p. 391. Edit. 1778.

obedient to the tyrannical proceedings of the bishops. Our author adds, "that he fixed his station in London, refused to go to church, gathered conventicles, and sought to promote schism and confusion in the city. That the bishop finding in him unspeakable disobedience, and he refusing the oath usually tendered by the high commission, (meaning the oath *ex officio*, by which he would have become his own accuser,) was committed to prison. And," our learned historian asks, "what could the bishop have done less?"*

It is not very difficult to find out many things, which his lordship might not have done less than this, even admitting that Mr. Benison was deserving of punishment. Four or five years' confinement in prison is a penalty of no small magnitude, and appears greatly disproportionate to any crime with which he was charged. And, indeed, Mr. Strype himself intimates as much, in the very next words: "But," says he, "it seems the bishop overshot himself, and did not proceed so *circumspectly* in the imprisonment of him for so long a time. For Mr. Benison's cause being brought before the lords of the council, the bishop was judged to have dealt *too hardly* with him; for which, therefore, he received a reprimand."†

Mr. Benison having suffered so long a confinement in prison, applied both to the queen and council; and in the statement of his own case, he declares concerning his marriage, the irregularity of which was the crime alleged against him, "That he had invited only forty persons to the solemnity, and only thirty attended: that he was married in the morning, and according to law: that when the bishop sent for him, charging him with sedition, he cleared himself to his lordship's satisfaction; but that after he went home, he gave a private order under his own hand for him to be apprehended and sent to the Gatehouse; and that he was there shut up in a dungeon eight days, without knowing the cause of his imprisonment." Moreover, when Mr. Benison was first apprehended and carried to prison, he was plundered of a great part of his household furniture; his valuable library was utterly spoiled and taken away, and he suffered great losses in various other ways.‡ Dr. Hammond, and his faithful friend Mr. John Fox, who were

* Strype's Aylmer, p. 209, 210.

† Ibid.

‡ Ibid. p. 211, 212.

both at the wedding, and witnessed the whole proceeding, went to the bishop, and assured him, that he was faultless in those things charged against him. But his lordship remained inflexible, and would not release him without such bonds for his good behaviour and future appearance, as the prisoner was unable to procure. Mr. Benison, in his letter to the queen and council, concludes in the following moving language:*

"Thus I continue," says he, "separated from my wife before I had been married two weeks, to the great trouble of her friends and relations, and to the staggering of the patient obedience of my wife. For since my imprisonment, his lordship has been endeavouring to separate us, whom God, in the open presence of his people, has joined together. Wherefore, I most humbly beseech your godly honours, for the everlasting love of God, and for the pity you take upon God's true protestants and his poor people, to be a means that my pitiful cry may be heard, and my just cause with some credit be cleared, to the honour of God and her majesty, whom for ever I esteem more than all the bishop's blessings or bitter cursings: and that I, being now half dead, may recover again to get a poor living with the little learning which God has given me, to his glory, to the discharge of some part of my duty, and to the profit of my country." This was Mr. Benison's impartial statement of his own case; upon the reception of which, the lords of the council were so moved, that they sent the bishop the following letter:†

"Hampton-court, November 14, 1584.

"Whereas, Barnaby Benison, minister, has given us to "understand, the great hinderance he has received by your "hard dealing with him, and his long imprisonment, for "which if he should bring his action against you of *false* "*imprisonment*, he would *by law recover damages*, which "would touch your lordship's credit. We have, therefore, "thought fit to require your lordship to use some consi-"deration towards him, in giving him a reasonable sum of "money to repay the wrong you have done unto him, "and to supply the hinderance he hath incurred by your "hard dealings with him. Therefore, praying your "lordship to deal with the poor man, that he may have "occasion to turn his complaint into a good report unto

* MS. Register, p. 591. † Ibid, p. 589.

"us of your charitable dealing. We bid you farewell.
"Signed,

"Bromley, Chan. "Wil. Burghley, "Amb. Warwick, "Fr. Bedford, "Robert Leicester, "Charles Howard, Francis Knolles, James Croft, Walter Mildmay, Christ. Hatton, Fr. Walsingham."

Upon the bishop's reception of the above letter, he returned this answer:—"I beseech your lordships to "consider, that it is a rare example thus to press a *bishop*, "for his zealous service to the queen and the peace of the "church, especially as the man was found worthy to be "committed for refusing to go to church, and other instances "of nonconformity, to say nothing of his contemptuous "behaviour towards me. Nevertheless, since it pleaseth "your lordships to require some reasonable sum of money, "I pray you consider my *poor estate* and great charges, "together with the *great vaunt* the man will make of his "conquest over a *bishop*. I hope, therefore, your lordships "will be favourable to me, and refer it to myself, either to "bestow upon him some small benefice, or otherwise to help "him as opportunity offers. Or if this shall not satisfy the "man, or not content your lordships, leave him to the trial "of the law, which, I hope, will not be so plain for him as "he taketh it. Surely, my lords, this and the like must "greatly discourage me in this poor service of mine in the "commission; wherein, if I seem remiss, I pray you impute "it to the troubles and infirmities of old age."*

The manner in which the bishop answered the accusations against him, is a sufficient evidence that his conduct could not be defended. What reparation Mr. Benison obtained for the injurious treatment he received, or whether any, does not appear. But he was certainly too wise to go to law with a bishop of the high commission court, who having but little conscience, exercised much cruelty; and who, notwithstanding his *poor estates* and *great charges*, left behind him at his death several very large estates, properties out upon mortgage, and above sixteen thousand pounds in money.† These were immense riches in those days. Mr. Strype‡ represents Aylmer's ill treatment of Mr. Benison as

* MS. Register, p. 589.
† Strype's Aylmer, p. 172, 194.—Neal's Puritans, vol. i. p. 284.
‡ Strype's Aylmer, p. 205.

the *slander of his enemies;* as if his lordship had dealt with him only according to his *deserts;* but what degree of justice there is in this representation, the foregoing statement of facts will best determine.

WILLIAM NEGUS was minister at Leigh in Essex, but suspended by Bishop Aylmer in the year 1584. Mr. Negus gives us the following account of this ecclesiastical censure:—"The cause of my suspension," says he, "was this: being convened before the bishop at Waltham, and he demanding whether I had worn the surplice since my coming to Leigh, my answer was, that I had it not, so I had not refused it. There was none offered me, nor was there a surplice in the parish. He then inquired whether I would wear it, when there was one provided. My answer was, that I desired his favour to proceed in my ministry, until a surplice was procured; and that he knew my unwillingness to wear it. He was not satisfied with this answer, but urged me to say that I *would*, or that I *would not* wear it. But I abiding by my former answer, and desiring that I might be accepted, he thus concluded: 'Seeing you will not promise to wear it, we suspend you until you do promise.'"* The good man was thus silenced for refusing to wear the clerical garment.

Having received the episcopal censure, twenty-eight of his parishioners, who subscribed themselves his *hungry sheep now without a shepherd*, signed a most affectionate and pressing letter, earnestly beseeching him to wear the surplice. Though they wished that the linen garment were utterly abolished, they anxiously desired him, for the sake of their advantage, to conform. But he found it impossible, with a good conscience, to wear that garment in the public worship of God, which to him appeared wholly founded in superstition, and the very badge of antichrist; and so he quietly submitted to be deprived.†

JOHN STROUD was minister first at Yalding, then at Cranbrook in Kent. He was a man of good learning, most exemplary piety, peaceable behaviour, and a faithful, laborious, and very useful preacher; but was repeatedly persecuted for nonconformity. He entered upon his troubles

* MS. Register, p. 568. † Ibid.

about the year 1567. Having had in his possession the Book of Ecclesiastical Discipline, he was cited before the chancellor to the Bishop of Rochester; and confessing the fact, that such a book had been in his hands, the chancellor said, "it contains treason, rebellion, and heresy," and immediately committed him to prison. Mr. Stroud observing that he hoped he was not deserving of such hard usage, wished to give sufficient security, but his offer was utterly disregarded. Upon his release from prison, he was forbidden to preach, and even to teach children, within the parish of Yalding or elsewhere, and commanded to depart out of the diocese in forty days. This unfeeling and inhuman sentence was sent to the churchwardens of Yalding, with a strict command to see it fully executed. But an impartial statement of his case being laid before the Archbishop of Canterbury, the cruel sentence was in part reversed. By the license, and under the seal, of the archbishop, he obtained liberty to continue a twelvemonth; when he returned to Yalding, hoping to proceed in his ministry without further molestation.

His liberty, however, was of very short continuance. For in a few months, he was cited, with several others, to appear at Rochester; and the citation was ordered to be read publicly in the church at Yalding. Upon his appearance in the court, the churchwardens were first called and examined. The chief article of their examination was, "whether any child or children had been baptized in their parish, when the order prescribed and appointed in the Book of Common Prayer was not in all points observed; and whose children they were, who were godfathers and godmothers, and whether they answered according to the form required in the said book?" But the churchwardens were too wise to accuse their own minister, and they were all dismissed.

Afterwards, both minister and churchwardens were again brought into the bishop's court, at Rochester. The churchwardens were first examined as before; and in addition to the former interrogatory, their examination was extended to the following articles:—"Whether any one preached at Yalding without a license?—Whether any preached who were forbidden, and commanded to leave the diocese?—Whether any such preachers have any unlawful or suspected books, leading to the contempt or derogation of the Book of Common Prayer, or of any orders, rites, or ceremonies of the church, as by law established? or who hath in any public meeting or private conventicle set forth any such books, or any doctrine therein contained?—And whether they knew or had heard, that Mr. Stroud had observed or done any of the things above named?"

Mr. Stroud being next called, and required to take the oath *ex officio*, to answer the inquiries of the court, he refused till he knew those inquiries. The following interrogatories were then read to him:—"Have you now, or have you had in time past, any printing-press and letters, and where are they?—Have you printed any contentious or rebellious books, and when, and where, and how long since, and what is become of them?—Have you any suspected or unlawful books leading to the contempt of the Book of Common Prayer?"—Mr. Stroud refused to answer these interrogatories, which were evidently designed to make him accuse himself, and told the chancellor that these things belonged to her majesty's commissioners, and not to him. Upon this, the angry and cruel chancellor pronounced upon him the sentence of excommunication, which he commanded to be publicly announced in the church of Yalding.* He, also, received the sentence of deprivation from the bishop.

The good man being thus cast out of the church, and reduced to extreme poverty, was obliged to condescend to the low office of correcting the press, and of publishing books to obtain a livelihood. But even in this occupation, he was not suffered to enjoy quietness. For, having published Mr. Cartwright's Reply to Whitgift, he was summoned, November 25, 1573, before the Bishop of London and other high commissioners, when he underwent the following examination:

Mr. Stroud being asked what became of Cartwright's books after they were printed, said he delivered thirty-four of them to the Bishop of London; but the rest were dispersed abroad. And being asked how he dared to print them a second time, seeing the queen's proclamation was against him, he said they were printed before the queen's proclamation came out, or he would not have printed them; upon which, the bishop thus addressed him:

Bishop. Are Mr. Cartwright's books good and lawful, or not? And will you defend them?

Stroud. As there is no book without its faults, the book of God excepted; so will I not affirm that this book is altogether without faults; but to defend it I will not. He

* MS. Register, p. 191—194.

is of age to defend himself. And as for the book, I think your lordship will not utterly condemn it.

B. I confess there is something in it godly. It is a very evil book that hath no good thing in it. But I say the book is wicked, and is the cause of error and dissention in the church.

Catlin. Wilt thou condemn the Book of Common Prayer? Is it antichristian?

S. For these five years, I have not served in any church; but when I have attended, I have resorted to common prayer, which, if I had condemned it, I would not have done. Yet if I should allow of all things in our ministry, I should allow of those things which his lordship has denied. For he said, in his sermon at Paul's cross, "that there were certain evils in our ministry."

B. Indeed, I said there were. Yet ought they not to be removed by private, but by public authority.

S. That is granted. But are those things to be removed?

B. Though they may be removed, they are such things as cannot offend the church; and every true christian ought to bear with them until they be removed.

S. I have borne with them, or I should not have resorted to the church, as I have done.

B. Have you been a minister, and now given it up? Every one laying his hand to the plough, ought not to look back, without some special cause.

S. About five or six years since, I was called before my ordinary, who told me I must subscribe, or lose my living, and be discharged from the ministry. Accordingly, I refusing to subscribe, he deprived me of my ministry.

C. Wilt thou receive the communion according to the order prescribed in the Book of Common Prayer?

S. I have never refused to receive it according to the word of God; and where I have resorted, I have received it more than six times in the year.

Goodman. Name one church where thou hast received the communion.

S. You seek to injure me.

G. Nay; we seek to save thee.

S. I have refused to attend upon idle shepherds; and, as you said they were dumb dogs, there can be no good received from them. Therefore, I beseech you to endeavour to get them removed.

G. Why, every member of the church of Christ is a sinner.

B. Shall we then receive no communion?

Dyer. What sayest thou of the order of baptism? Wilt thou have thy child baptized according to the order prescribed in the Book of Common Prayer?

S. I have no child to baptize.

D. Dost thou condemn the order of the sacrament of the Lord's supper, the order of churching women, the burial service, or the ceremonies of the church?

S. If I had condemned them, I would not have resorted to the church, as I have done.

B. Thou wilt then agree to these three things:—1. "That thou hast offended against the law in printing Cartwright's book.—2. That Cartwright's book is neither godly, nor lawful.—3. That thou dost not condemn the Book of Common Prayer, but wilt receive the sacrament of the Lord's supper, according to the order prescribed."

S. I say as I have said before, if I had condemned the Book of Common Prayer, I would not have resorted to the church, as I have done.

Garret. But wilt thou subscribe?

S. I will.*

Upon Mr. Stroud's submission to subscribe, he returned to his beloved exercise, and became minister at Cranbrook. But his troubles were not ended. For, upon the translation of Whitgift to the see of Canterbury, his nonconformity exposed him to the displeasure of the new archbishop, who deprived him of his ministry, and commanded him to leave the country. But the good man was so universally beloved, that multitudes of persons in Kent signed petitions to the archbishop, earnestly soliciting his continuance. In one of these petitions, they address his lordship as follows:

"We know, most reverend father, that Mr. Stroud has been several times beaten and whipt with the untrue reports of slanderous tongues, and accused of crimes whereof he has most clearly acquitted himself. Most of us have heard him preach Christ truly, and rebuke sin boldly, and have seen him hitherto apply to his calling faithfully, and live among us most peaceably: so that, by his diligence and doctrine, not only has our youth been instructed, and ourselves have been confirmed in true religion and learning; but we are daily allured by his holy conversation and example, to a christian life, and the exercises of charity. And no one of us, most reverend father, hath hitherto heard

* MS. Register, p. 194—195.

from his own mouth, nor by the credible relation of others, that he has publicly in his sermons, or privately in conversation, taught unsound doctrine, or opposed the discipline, about which, alas! there is now so great a controversy. And as he hath given a faithful promise to forbear handling any questions concerning the policy of the church; so we think in our consciences, he has hitherto performed it.

"In consideration of these things; and that our country may not be deprived of so excellent a labourer in the Lord's harvest; that the enemies of God's truth, the papists, may not have cause of joy and triumph; and that the man himself may not be thus discouraged and wounded to the heart, in receiving condemnation without examination: We, therefore, most humbly beseech your grace, for the poor man's sake, for your own sake, and for the Lord's sake, either to take judicial knowledge of his cause, that he may be confronted by his adversaries; or, of your great wisdom and goodness, to restore him to his liberty of preaching the gospel among us. So we shall heartily thank God, and shall continually pray for you."*

Besides the above petition, signed by many worthy persons, another was signed by *twenty-four ministers* and others; a third by George Ely, vicar of Tenderden, and his parishioners; a fourth by Thomas Bathurst, minister of Staplehurst, and his parishioners; a fifth by William Walter, vicar of Gouldhurst, and parishioners; a sixth by Matthias Water, minister of Frittenden, and parishioners; a seventh by Anthony Francis, minister of Lamberhurst, and parishioners; an eighth by Alexander Love, minister of Rolvenden, and parishioners; a ninth by Christopher Vinebrook, minister of Helcorne, and parishioners; a tenth by Matthew Walton, curate of Benenden, and parishioners; an eleventh by William Cocks, minister of Marden, and parishioners; a twelfth by William Vicar, minister of Tisehurst, and parishioners; and a thirteenth by William Hopkinson, minister of Salehurst, and his parishioners.†

So high a reputation had Mr. Stroud among persons of true piety, and holy zeal for the protestant religion. All these petitions, signed by numerous persons respectable both for learning and piety, were presented to Whitgift; but whether they proved the happy means of procuring his lordship's favour, is extremely doubtful. Mr. Stroud was a man of most exemplary piety, and universally beloved,

* MS. Register, p. 196, 197. † Ibid.

and a most excellent and peaceable divine, but continually molested and vexed in the ecclesiastical courts.

John Browning, D. D.—This learned divine was senior fellow of Trinity college, Cambridge, and afterwards domestic chaplain to the Earl of Bedford, but was deprived of his fellowship for his puritanical opinions. Having delivered a sermon in St. Mary's church, in which were contained certain heretical opinions, as they were called, he was convened, February 1, 1572, before the heads of colleges, and commanded to abstain from preaching, till he should be purged from his dangerous heresy. Under these circumstances, he looked upon it to be his duty to obey God, rather than men, and therefore refused to obey their command, and still continued in his beloved work of preaching; on which account he was cast into prison for contempt. Whatever were the pretended charges of his enemies, his principal crime was his nonconformity.*

Dr. Browning having remained for some time in prison, was at length released, upon giving bond of two hundred marks, and obtaining two sureties bound in forty pounds each, for his appearance to answer such charges as should be alleged against him, and to abstain from preaching till further leave should be granted.† Being called before his spiritual judges, they resolved, "that if the said John Browning shall from time to time appear and answer, when and wheresoever he shall be lawfully called within the realm of England, to all such matters as shall be objected unto him, touching certain words uttered by him in two sermons, for which he hath been convened before the said vice-chancellor, until he shall be lawfully discharged; and also shall abstain from preaching, until he shall be permitted or called by the said vice-chancellor, or his deputy, or successors: And further, shall behave himself quietly and peaceably towards the queen's majesty, and all her subjects, and especially within the university of Cambridge, that then the recognizance to be void and of no effect, or else to stand and remain in its full power and strength."‡ The day following, Dr. Bying, the vice-chancellor, sent a statement of his crimes, with an account of the above proceedings, to Lord Burleigh the chancellor.§

* Baker's MS. Collec. vol. iv. p. 55.
† Strype's Parker, p. 390.—Whitgift, p. 46.—Annals, vol. ii. p. 189.
‡ Baker's MS. Collec. vol. iii. p. 392. § Ibid. vol. iv. p. 55.

Dr. Browning himself, after his release from prison, appeared before the chancellor, subscribed a submission with his own hand, and was so far acquitted that he was sent back to the university, and the vice-chancellor and heads were urged to re-admit him to his former office and preferment. But this will best appear in Burleigh's own words, addressed to the vice-chancellor and heads, which were as follows:—"Having received from you a declaration of two errors committed by this bearer, John Browning, in his sermons, one of them containing matter of heresy, and the other tending to sedition, I have caused him to be further examined hereupon, in the presence of Sir Thomas Smith, her majesty's principal secretary; and finding as well by the relation of Mr. Secretary, as by his own confession subscribed with his hand, that he utterly abhorreth them both, and affirmeth that he hath been much mistaken in the same, I thought it best, for preserving the university's reputation, and for the reverence of the church of God, wherein he is a minister, to suppress the memory and notice of the said errors, especially that which may be drawn to an interpretation that he should be justly thought seditious and offensive. Therefore, my advice is, that you should receive him again into his place; and if he shall willingly acknowledge before you the same doctrine, and misliking of the foresaid errors, whereof I mean to send you his confession under his hand, and then he may continue quietly among you."*

Though he returned to his office in the college, and to his public ministerial exercise, his troubles were not over. Having taken his doctor's degree at Oxford, two years earlier than he ought to have done, brought upon him many fresh trials. For this singular offence, which some deemed a mere trifle, and others accounted a very grievous crime, he was deprived of his fellowship, and in effect expelled from the university. This oppressive sentence was inflicted upon him in a most clandestine and illegal manner by Dr. Still, and even above four years after taking his degree at Oxford. This was done a long time after Dr. Still had signified his approbation of his taking the degree, by allowing him to deliver public lectures in the chapel, according to the statute of the university, and by allowing him to be incorporated in the same degree at Cambridge. He also confirmed to Dr. Browning his fellowship and place in the

* Baker's MS. Collec. vol. xxix. p. 368.

college, not only by suffering him quietly and peaceably to enjoy it, with all the privileges thereof, for more than three years, but also elected him by his own voice to be senior bursar of the college, and to be vice-master for two years by two separate elections.*

Moreover, Dr. Still's conduct was in many particulars most shameful. He proceeded against Dr. Browning with great injustice and inhumanity. Not content with illegally depriving him of his office and benefice, he would not suffer him to dine in the hall of the college, nor any one to eat or drink with him. When Dr. Browning kept his chamber in the college, this inveterate enemy would not permit any of his friends or acquaintance to come to him, or converse with him; and those of his friends who had any private intercourse with him, he strictly examined by threatenings and oaths to confess what had passed, with a view to accuse them from their own mouths. He also complained in this case to a foreign judge, expressly contrary to the statute of the college. And though he caused the name of Dr. Browning to be struck out of the buttery, he commenced an action of £300 against him, merely on supposition that he had done the same by him. He, moreover, procured a restraint of Dr. Browning's liberty, by watching him and keeping him in his chamber for some time as in a prison. Not satisfied with these tyrannical proceedings, he assaulted Dr. Browning's lodgings in a most violent manner, and broke open his doors, and dragged him out of his chamber, to the great injury of his body; notwithstanding the Earl of Bedford by his letters had previously required all proceedings against him to be stayed, till the cause should be heard. To finish the business, this cruel oppressor of the Lord's servants prohibited Dr. Browning's pupils, servants and friends, from coming near him, or bringing him any thing to eat or drink, intending to starve him to death.†

During these rigorous and illegal proceedings, the Earl of Bedford, as intimated above,‡ wrote to the Chancellor Burleigh, desiring his lordship not to give his consent to the sentence pronounced upon Dr. Browning, till after he had heard both parties. He spoke, at the same time, in high commendation of his character; that he had good

* Baker's MS. Collec. vol. iv. p. 45, 46. † Ibid.

‡ Francis Earl of Bedford was a celebrated statesman, and a constant friend to the persecuted puritans. At his death he left twenty pounds to be given to a number of pious ministers, for preaching twenty sermons at Cheney, Woburn and Melshburn.—*MS. Chronology*, vol. ii. p. 373. (22.)

experience of his sound doctrine, his useful preaching, and exemplary conversation, saying, that his deprivation was *hard dealing*.* If his deprivation of his fellowship was hard dealing, what must all the other proceedings have been? These troubles came upon him in the year 1584: but we do not find that this persecuted servant of Christ obtained any relief.

Stephen Turner was minister of Arlington in Sussex, but much troubled for nonconformity. About the year 1584, being convened before his ecclesiastical judges, and required to subscribe to Whitgift's three articles, he refused, saying, that he was willing to subscribe as far as the laws of the realm required. With an evident design to ensnare his conscience, or accuse him upon his own confession, he was asked whether the Book of Common Prayer contained any thing contrary to the word of God; when he observed, that he was not bound by law to answer such an inquiry. Also, when he was asked whether he would use the form of prayers and administration of the sacraments, as prescribed, and no other, he replied, that he did not consider himself bound by law to answer. He was then suspended from his ministry.† Having remained a considerable time under the ecclesiastical censure, he sent the following certificate to certain persons of quality: "These may certify your honours, that I, Stephen Turner, minister of Arlington in Sussex, have been suspended from my charge this year and a quarter, for refusing to subscribe, no other matter being laid to my charge."‡

John Ward was a celebrated puritan divine, and many years the laborious minister of Haverhil in Suffolk. Afterwards, he appears to have become minister of Writtle, near Chelmsford, in Essex; but, about the year 1584, he was suspended by Bishop Aylmer, for not wearing the surplice. On account of his nonconformity, though he was a most excellent and peaceable man, Aylmer drove him from one place to another, by which means he was exceedingly harassed, and not suffered to continue long in any one situation.§

* Strype's Parker, 391. † MS. Register, p. 569.
‡ MS. Chronology, vol. ii. p. 419. (1.1.)
§ MS. Register, p. 584, 742.

He subscribed the "Book of Discipline,"* and united with his brethren in their endeavours to promote the desired reformation of the church, meeting with them in their private associations.† This persecuted servant of Christ died at Haverhil, where his remains were interred. Upon his grave was a monumental inscription erected to his memory, of which Fuller gives the following translation: ‡

Grant some of knowledge greater store,
More learned some in teaching;
Yet few in life did lighten more,
None thundered more in preaching.

Mr. Ward was an excellent divine, of whom the famous Dr. William Whitaker had the highest opinion, and used to say, "Give me John Ward for a text."§ Mr. Richard Rogers, the worthy puritan minister of Wethersfield in Essex, married his widow. Mr. Ward had four sons in the ministry. Samuel and Nathaniel were puritan divines of distinguished eminence. Mr. Ward, the ejected nonconformist, was most probably his son.‖

Edmund Rockrey, B. D.—He was fellow of Queen's college, Cambridge, and a person distinguished for learning and abilities, but was brought into many troubles on account of his nonconformity. He was a man of great reputation, and, in the year 1569, was chosen one of the proctors of the university.¶ The year following, he was convened before the ruling ecclesiastics, and required to enter into a bond of forty pounds, to appear from time to time before the vice-chancellor or his deputy, until such matters should be determined and ended as were and should be laid against him. After appearing several times before the vice-chancellor, Dr. Whitgift, and the heads of colleges, it was decreed, "that he should remain, continue, and quietly keep his chamber as a true prisoner, till the matters objected against him should be ended."**

It appears very probable that he continued under con-

* Neal's Puritans, vol. i. p. 423.
† Baker's MS. Collec. vol. xv. p. 79.
‡ Fuller's Worthies, part iii. p. 70. § Firmin's Real Christian, Pref.
‖ Palmer's Noncon. Mem. vol. iii. p. 284.
¶ Fuller's Hist. of Cam. p. 141.
** Baker's MS. Collec. vol. iii. p. 377, 378.

finement a long time: for towards the close of the year 1571, he was again several times brought before the vice-chancellor and heads of colleges; when "Dr. Whitgift willed him to acknowledge and confess his fault, and openly to revoke his rashness in the same place, and before the same company, where he had given the offence;" and in the conclusion, he was required to make the following public recantation:

"For as much as on Sunday, being the 26th of November, in this place before you, I disorderly stood up, "(after that Dr. Chadderton, having commandment from "the vice-chancellor, had given warning that we should "not speak against such statutes as the queen's majesty had "sent to the university,) and spoke words tending to the "complaining of such things as were then by our master "spoken, to the discrediting of some about the queen's "majesty; saying, that godly princes might be deceived by "hypocrites and flatterers, as David was by Shebna, or "such like; and to the derogation of the said statutes, and "condemnation of some of them, saying, that they tended "to the impairing of the liberty and privileges of the "university, and that some of them were directly against "God's word. I therefore acknowledge my rashness and "indiscreetness in so doing, and am heartily sorry for them, "desiring you to think as it becometh dutiful subjects to "think of the queen's majesty, her counsellors and laws, and "reverently obey the same, as I for my part intend to do, "God willing, to the uttermost of my power. In witness "whereof, I have subscribed this confession with my own "hand, and deliver the same here in your presence, to "our master, to be by him also delivered to Mr. Vice-"chancellor."*

From the above, we see the crimes with which Mr. Rockrey was charged, together with the proceedings of these ruling ecclesiastics. He seems to have refused making this recantation. He would not defile his conscience, by subscribing that which appeared to him contrary to truth, as well as a tyrannical invasion of christian liberty. Though he was several times summoned before his superiors, it is probable, our author adds, that he still continued in the same mind.†

Mr. Rockrey scrupled wearing the habits, for which, during the above troubles, he was deprived of his fellowship,

* Baker's MS. Collec. vol. iii. p. 382, 383. † Ibid. p. 384.

and in effect, expelled from the university. Lord Burleigh, the chancellor, procured his restoration, with a dispensation from wearing the habits for a twelvemonth, at the expiration of which, he was admonished three times by the master of the college, to conform himself in wearing the apparel. But he could not with a good conscience comply, and, therefore, was finally expelled, as an example to keep others in a state of obedience.* He was one of the prebendaries of Rochester, where he was justly esteemed an admired and popular preacher; but, about the year 1584, was suspended from his ministerial function, and continued under the ecclesiastical censure many years.†

H. Gray was a puritanical minister in Cambridge, and one of the preachers to the university. He delivered a sermon in St. Mary's church, January 8, 1586, in which he was charged with asserting the following opinions:—"That the church of England doth maintain Jewish music, contrary to the word of God, which alone ought to sound in his church.—That it is contrary to the same word, to use in sermons the testimonies of doctors and profane writers.—That to play at dice or cards is to crucify Christ.—That there are in this church *dumb dogs*, Jereboam's priests, and Chemarins, that have place at the upper end of the altar, which by the word should have no place in the church.—That it is thought there be some among us who send over news to Rome and Rheims, and would have us all murdered.—That whoever would, might fill his hand, and be minister among us, as in the time of Jereboam; whereby it cometh to pass that some go about the country to offer their service for ten pounds a year and a *canvas doublet*.—And that we celebrate the joyful time of the nativity throughout the land as atheists and epicures."‡

For these assertions, alleged against him, he appears to have been called before the ruling ecclesiastics, when he gave the following answers to the various accusations:—"Concerning music, I had no set treatise against it, but only I made this simile, that set music and its curious notes is an imitation of the Jewish music; and because it is not understood, it may delight, but not *edify:* so affected and curious eloquence, which the people cannot understand, may affect and delight the outward sense, but it cannot enter

* Strype's Annals, vol. ii. p. 434. † MS. Register, p. 265, 585.
‡ Baker's MS. Collec. vol. xxx. p. 294.

and descend into the heart.—Concerning citing of fathers and profane authors, I did not teach that it was simply unlawful; but when we are to teach the simple people, and to instruct and build the conscience, we are not to stuff our sermons with authorities of fathers or sentences of profane writers.—Concerning carding and dicing, I spake only against the unlawful use of it, and shewed the abuse of the celebration of the nativity.—I said that we have dumb dogs, and some such as were once Chemarins, when I did not, neither was it my purpose to, enter any question whether they might, or might not, lawfully be ministers.—I said, it is thought there be some among us, who are not of us, who lurk here to spy out what is done, that they may give notice to Rome; and they lie among us, that they may point out and set forth which of us should first go to the fire, when the days of mourning for Jacob should come: where I desire that my meaning may be thus interpreted, that I did not notice particulars, but spake only upon the probable suspicion, to stir us up to be diligent in searching whether there be any papists among us, who are the Lord's and her majesty's enemies.—I said, for want of restraint, every man may fill his hand, and consecrate himself, alluding to 2 Chron. xiii. I would have this to be considered, that in citing or alluding to any place, every word is not to be observed, but the drift and purpose for which it is alleged. —I said, that we have some ministers who are not worthy to stand in the belfrey, but they sit at the end of the altar. I protest this to have been my meaning, that those who were altogether unfit for the ministry, did supply the places of those who ought to have been learned ministers."*

These were Mr. Gray's answers to the foregoing accusations. But it does not appear what prosecution was entered against him.

Robert Moore was rector of Guisely in Yorkshire, and prosecuted for nonconformity. January 9, 1586, he was cited before the Archbishop of York and other high commissioners, when *twenty* charges were exhibited and aggravated against him; but he so judiciously answered them, and so fully proved his own innocence, that he was acquitted by law. Upon the complete failure of the prosecution, the angry archbishop charged Mr. Moore with

* Baker's MS. Collec. vol. xxx. p. 295.

having said that he *could not preach*, calling him an *old doating fool*. This Mr. Moore denied upon his oath. When they failed in the proof of this charge also, his lordship was more angry than before; and seeing they could procure no evidence for any of their accusations, the good man was dismissed, and appointed to appear the week following.

January 16th, Mr. Moore appeared before the archbishop and nine other commissioners, when he was again charged with the same crimes, and they said that now they could prove him guilty. To this he replied, that as he had already cleared himself of all charges, except that of refusing to observe in all points the Book of Common Prayer, which he did not out of contempt, but from conscience; so, notwithstanding the malice of his enemies, he still stood on sure ground, and no honest man could prove him guilty. Upon this, he was immediately threatened with imprisonment and utter ruin, if they should proceed against him according to law. In the conclusion, he was obliged to enter into a bond of a hundred pounds to observe the Book of Common Prayer, and was then dismissed.

The archbishop and his colleagues were aware of the disgrace that would necessarily fall upon their own heads, if Mr. Moore should escape without submission. Therefore, they cited him a third time; and upon his appearance, presented him with the form of a recantation, requiring him, as the condition of obtaining their favour, to confess and read the same publicly in his own church. But he absolutely refused to purchase his liberty at so dear a rate, declaring that he would be cast into prison, and even put to death, rather than thus dishonour the Lord by lying against the Holy Ghost and his own conscience. He was, therefore, again dismissed; but two of his servants were committed to prison.*

From the examination of Mr. Higgins, churchwarden of Guisely, before the above commissioners, January 10, 1586, which is now before me, Mr. Moore is evidently acquitted of the principal charges alleged against him. The uprightness of his deportment, and the purity of his character, were thus made manifest, even in the face of his enemies. He was a zealous, faithful, and laborious minister, spending his strength and his long life for the salvation of souls.†

It is observed of our divine, that he survived most of his

* MS. Register, p. 787. † Ibid. p. 789—790.

brethren, having lived to a great age. He baptized a child after he entered upon the benefice of Guiseley, and afterwards buried the same person threescore years of age, being rector of the place *sixty-three* years. He built the present stately parsonage house there.*

Edward Gellibrand.—This learned and pious divine was fellow of Magdalen college, Oxford, and a person of distinguished eminence among the puritans in that university. He was much concerned for a further reformation of the church, and ever zealous in promoting the desired object. The letters from the classis in London and other places, were commonly addressed to him, and, by the appointment of the brethren, he usually answered them. January 12, 1585, he wrote a letter to Mr. John Field, signifying how he had consulted several colleges about church discipline, and a further reformation; and that many were disposed to favour it, but were afraid to testify any thing under their hands, lest it should bring them into trouble. This letter, which, in the opinion of Dr. Bancroft, tended to promote sedition, was the following:—"I have," says Mr. Gellibrand, "already entered into the matters whereof "you write, and dealt with three or four of several colleges, "concerning those among whom they live. I find that "men are very dangerous in this point, generally savouring "reformation; but when it comes to the particular point, "some have not yet considered of those things for which "others in the church are so much troubled. Others are "afraid to testify any thing with their hands, lest it should "breed danger before the time. And many favour the "cause of reformation, but they are not ministers, but "young students, of whom there is good hope, if it be not "cut off by violent dealing before the time. As I hear of "you, so I mean to go forward, where there is any hope; "and to learn the number, and certify you thereof." The candid reader will easily judge how far this letter tended to promote sedition, being merely designed to effect by the most peaceable means, a more pure reformation of the church.† He united with many of his brethren in subscribing the "Book of Discipline."‡

April 7, 1586, Mr. Gellibrand was cited before Archbishop

* Thoresby's Vicaria Leodiensis, p. 65.
† Bancroft's Dangerous Positions, p. 74, 75.
‡ Neal's Puritans, vol. i. p. 423.

Whitgift, Bishop Cooper of Winchester, Bishop Piers of Salisbury, and other high commissioners. When he was called before their lordships, and the charges alleged against him had been read, the reverend archbishop thus addressed him:—"You have spoken against the ecclesiastical state and governors, as confirmed and established by the laws of this land. You have inveighed against the swelling titles of bishops and archbishops. You are full of pride and arrogancy, and the spirit of pride hath possessed you. And you have preached against the Bishop of Winchester, by which you have discouraged men from doing good to the church." Then said the Bishop of Winchester, "If you had read any of the ancient fathers, or ecclesiastical histories, you could not have been ignorant, that the office of archbishops was from the time of the apostles, though the name be not found in the scriptures. Other churches do not condemn ours, as we do not theirs. This discipline which you dream of, may peradventure be convenient for Geneva, or some such free city, which hath half a dozen villages joining to it; but not for a kingdom. You are a child, yea, a babe."

Mr. Gellibrand, craving leave to answer for himself, replied to these accusations, and said, "Concerning preaching against the Bishop of Winchester, I am guiltless. I was not present at his sermon, nor did I hear of his sermon till after I had preached, according to my oath already taken." And being charged with speaking against the consecration of bishops and archbishops, he replied, "My words were uttered simply as the occasion offered from a note of Beza on Heb. ii. 10. And concerning my exhortation to those who suffer persecution for the sake of Christ, it was necessarily deduced from my text, in which the sufferings of christians are called the sufferings of Christ." Then said Dr. Cosin, "Such ifs are intolerable under the government of so gracious a prince. And it is a most grievous thing that you have made discipline a part of the gospel."

The archbishop next charged him with having made a comparison between Jesuits, and nonresidents, saying, "You make nonresidents worse than Jesuits, and in this comparison there is neither truth, nor charity, nor honesty, nor christianity. I myself have been one of those whom you call nonresidents, and have done more good by preaching, partly in my own cure, and partly in other mens', than you will do as long as you live. The church hath not been built by you, nor such as you; but by those whom you call nonresidents!!" Upon Mr. Gellibrand's attempting to answer, he was interrupted, and not allowed to proceed. And when Dr. Cosin charged him with speaking against the laws of the land, he replied, "I have long been of this opinion, and so have many others, that nonresidents are allowed by law."

Mr. Gellibrand being charged with seducing her majesty's subjects, and with bringing the archbishop and bishops into contempt, which, it was said, gave much encouragement to papists; he replied, "I never entered upon any discourse about the government of the church, but delivered the true sense of the scriptures." When he was urged to a further consideration of the charges brought against him, and to submit to the court, he was carried out, until the commissioners determined what punishment should be inflicted upon him. After some consultation, he was called in, when the archbishop thus addressed him:—"You deserve not only to be sequestered from your ministry, but to be expelled from your house, banished from the university, and cast into prison; and all this we could inflict upon you; but we will not deal thus with you, if you will revoke your errors, and give satisfaction for your offences." The good man was, therefore, suspended from his ministry, obliged to enter into a bond of a hundred pounds, either to revoke his errors in such form as their lordships should appoint, or to make his appearance at Lambeth at any time by them to be determined, when they would further proceed against him.* But it does not appear whether he recanted, or was brought under additional hardships by the relentless prelates.

Edward Glover was a nonconformist to the church of England, as well in doctrine, as in ceremonies. He appears to have mixed faith and works in the article of justification, and to have denied the doctrine of predestination; for which, in the year 1586, he, together with some others, was apprehended by Archbishop Whitgift, and cast into prison. These persons, denominated "a poor handful of free-will men," it is said, could not assemble in a private conventicle, without attracting the rod of ecclesiastical censure, and suffering by means of the archbishop, the rigorous penalty of imprisonment. But whatever were their character and

* MS. Register, p. 801—803.

opinions, they were so far excusable to the Lord Treasurer Burleigh, that he warmly espoused their cause, and wrote a letter to the archbishop in their favour.* In all probability, says Mr. Toplady, Burleigh's humane application to the primate, in behalf of these theological delinquents, procured them a gaol-delivery, and set the free-will men corporally free. This he conjectures from the letter of thanks, which Mr. Glover afterwards wrote to the treasurer. Mr. Glover, says he, lays all the cause of his and his brethren's imprisonment, on their dissenting from Luther's doctrine of justification without works, and from Calvin's doctrine of unconditional predestination; and loudly complains of the "iniquity and tyranny" of their prosecutors: which included a tacit fling at the archbishop himself. Had they not just cause to complain both of iniquity and tyranny? And was not the archbishop the very person who exercised this cruel oppression? Without approving of their sentiments, it may be asked, what greater right had he to cast them into prison, merely for difference of religious opinions, than they had to cast him into prison, for the same cause? His lordship having the sword in his own hands, will afford no satisfactory answer to this question. But our author further observes, "the bishops had just as much regard for the free-will men, as St. Paul had for the viper he shook into the fire."† This representation, which contains too much truth, will remain a stigma upon their character, and a reproach to their memory, as long as men are disposed to examine the impartial records of history.

John Walward, D. D.—He was professor of divinity at Oxford, and a man of great learning, but involved in much trouble for nonconformity. He was summoned before the high commission, April 7, 1586, and appeared before Archbishop Whitgift, Bishop Aylmer, the Bishops of Winchester and Sarum, and other commissioners, at Lambeth. And for having taught, that the order of the Jewish synagogue and eldership, was adopted into the christian church, by Jesus Christ and his apostles; and asserting that the same was designed as a perpetual modal of church government, he was enjoined a public recantation, and suspended from his public exercises in the university, till it should be performed. As the whole of this

* Strype's Annals, vol. iii. p. 431.
† Toplady's Historic Proof, vol. ii. p. 201, 202.

affair, attested by the hand of Abraham Hartwell, notary public, is now before me, it will be proper to transcribe it.

The above commissioners decreed, "That the said John Walward shall, upon some Sunday in the afternoon, deliver a sermon in the parish church of Alhallows in Oxford, wherein he shall not in any way, either covertly or openly, impugn any part of the government ecclesiastical now received and used in the church of England; but shall stir up all his hearers to unity, peace, obedience, and the good liking of the laws, orders, and present government of this church; and shall, also, in such his sermon publicly and distinctly read, without any addition, diminution, or alteration, the form of words following, signifying that he is so enjoined by authority for his demerits." Then follows the form of his recantation, expressed in these words:

"Whereas I, John Walward, the 22d of February last, "preaching in this place, amongst other things, did utter, "'That the order of a Jewish synagogue governed by an "eldership, which I untruly affirmed to be still observed in "Germany and Spain, was established by Jesus Christ and "his apostles to continue for ever, to admonish, to suspend, "to interdict, and to excommunicate in every congregation: "that the same was practised by the apostles, and long after "in the better times of the church: that those who are put "in authority, according to the laws of this land, by the "bishops and other ecclesiastical persons, to see such "censures executed, are not sufficiently warranted thereto, "but are in danger of God's heavy judgment; therefore, "the pastor of the congregation where the offender dwelleth, "hath an interest, and ought to have a dealing therein.' "And, whereas, I did then also affirm matter to the de-"praving of the office of archdeacons, and the canons agreed "upon in the last convocation, and confirmed by her "majesty's authority: and did avouch a necessary, sub-"stantial, and unalterable platform of government and dis-"cipline to have been left by Christ, for hearing, ordering, "and determining all cases and causes of censure, which I "then said ought of necessity to be by the ministry and "presbytery of the congregation where the offender "dwelleth, to the impeaching of her majesty's authority "in causes ecclesiastical, to the discredit of the present "government of the church of England wherein I live, to "the breach of the unity and peace of it, and to an ill "example and offence to others. And further, whereas I "promised after my said sermon, if I might be suffered to "continue my divinity lecture, I would not meddle in any "matters tending to the disturbance of the peace and unity "of the church, or just offence of any. I did, notwith- "standing, shew myself the same man I was before, by "bitter and factious speeches, and complaining that I was "thus treated, as I thought, without just desert. I do here, "therefore, in the sight of God, and you, my brethren, "frankly acknowledge, my unadvised dealing herein, and "my oversight in the former points, heartily desiring you "all to be satisfied with this my unfeigned and humble "submission."*

When Dr. Walward appeared before his ecclesiastical judges, he was obliged to enter into a bond of one hundred pounds to make this debasing public recantation; and in case he failed to perform it according to the order and form prescribed, he should not only forfeit his hundred pounds, but within four days appear again at Lambeth, to receive such censure as his case might deserve. For the better execution of the above decrees, a letter was addressed to the vice-chancellor of Oxford, requiring and authorizing him to see that they should in all points be duly executed; and in case of Walward's failure in complying with them, to bring him again before the high commission at Lambeth.† This learned divine was thus debased by the tyrannical prelates! He was compelled to sacrifice the right of private judgment, and the liberty of conscience, at the shrine of their usurped power and authority.

John Gardiner was the laborious minister of Malden in Essex, but deprived of his ministry, and most cruelly treated. His sufferings would have moved the compassion of any man, excepting Aylmer, bishop of London. The bishop committed him to Newgate for matters scandalously laid to his charge seven years before, of which he had even been cleared by a regular course of law. He requested his lordship, that he might be bailed; and if he was found guilty, that he might have punishment without mercy. The account of his barbarous usage is given in a supplication which Mr. Gardiner sent to the bishop, dated September 7, 1586; in which he expressed himself as follows:§

* MS. Register, p. 800. † Ibid. p. 801. § Ibid. p. 752.

"To the Right Reverend Father in God the Lord Bishop
"of London.

"My duty in humble-wise remembered, my lord. I am "cast into Newgate by your lordship, for a matter which "about seven years past, was slanderously raised against "me. I was by course of law cleared, and the Lord God "who searcheth the hearts, before whom you and I shall "shortly appear, doth know, and him I call to witness, "that I was and am falsely accused. I have been extremely "sick in prison. I thank God, I am amended, but am yet "so ill, that the physicians say my infection from the prison "will be very dangerous. I have a poor wife and five "children, who are in a lamentable case. I had six at the "beginning of my imprisonment; but by reason of my "sickness in prison, and my wife being constrained to "attend upon me, one of my children, for want of some-"body to oversee them, was drowned in a tub of wort, "being two years and a half old. If your lordship have no "compassion on me, yet take pity upon the widow and "fatherless, (for in that state are now my wife and poor "infants) whose tears are before the Lord. I crave only "to be bailed; and if I am found guilty of any breach of "law, let me have extremity without any favour. Your "lordship's to command in Christ.

"JOHN GARDINER."

It does not appear how long Mr. Gardiner remained in prison, nor what other punishment he endured. He was a member of the presbyterian church erected at Wandsworth in Surrey; and he united with his brethren in subscribing the "Book of Discipline."*

NICHOLAS STANDEN was educated in the university of Cambridge; he became rector of St. Magaret-Pattens, London; but was deprived, it is supposed, for nonconformity, in 1568.† He was a learned and religious man, an orthodox divine, and ever zealous for a reformation of the church; often meeting with his brethren to promote the desired object. About the year 1570, he was chaplain to the Earl of Warwick, in his expedition against the rebels in the north.‡ In 1572, he was a member of the presby-

* Fuller's Church Hist. b. ix. p. 103.—Neal's Puritans, vol. i. p. 423.
† Newcourt's Repert. Eccl. vol. i. p. 409.
‡ MS. Chronology, vol. ii. p. 373. (8.)

terian church erected at Wandsworth in Surrey.* About two years after this, he was accused of being concerned in Undertree's sham plot; and with Mr. Bonham, another puritan minister, was cast into prison: but upon their examination, being found innocent, they were both acquitted, and released by order of the council.† Mr. Standen and Mr. Bonham were convened before the high commission for nonconformity, and committed to prison, where they remained a long time. After having endured a shameful confinement, together with the sickness of the prison, they were released by order of the queen, as will appear more at large in another place.‡

Mr. Standen, with other nonconformable ministers, wrote an answer to this question, "Whether the ministers, for certain ceremonies laid upon them under pretence of policy only, may forsake their ministry?" Upon this question, he gives his opinion with great freedom, particularly against the use of the cross in baptism. He proves with great clearness, that the use of the cross in that ordinance, is wholly founded in superstition; that it can answer no good purpose whatever, but oftentimes a bad one; and consequently, that it ought to be laid aside.§ This divine being always anxious to obtain better regulations in the church, united with his brethren about the year 1586, in subscribing the "Book of Discipline."‖

John Field, A. M.—This excellent divine was a great sufferer in the cause of nonconformity. There having been several persons of the same name, has rendered it rather difficult to distinguish them; yet this Mr. John Field appears to have been fellow of Lincoln college, Oxford. Wood intimates, that he was afterwards a famous preacher at St. Giles, Cripplegate, London; but this is rather doubtful.** It is certain, however, that he was the excellent minister of Aldermary church, in the city.

The puritans having in vain sought for a further reformation from the queen and the bishops, resolved in future to apply to the parliament, and stand by the constitution. Accordingly, they made all the interest in their power among the members, and compiled a treatise, setting forth

* Fuller's Church Hist. b. ix. p. 103. † Strype's Parker, p. 466.
‡ See Art. Bonham.
§ MS. Chronology, vol. ii. p. 373, (8.)—Parte of a Register, p. 409.
‖ Neal's Puritans, vol. i. p. 423. ** Athenæ Oxon. vol. i. p. 188.

their numerous grievances in one view. This was drawn up by Mr. Field, assisted by Mr. Thomas Wilcocks, and was revised by several of the brethren. The work was entitled "An Admonition to the Parliament;" with Beza's letter to the Earl of Leicester, and Gualter's to Bishop Parkhurst, for reformation of church discipline, annexed. It contains the platform of a church; the manner of electing ministers; with their several duties, and their equality in government. It then exposes, with some sharp language, the corruptions of the hierarchy, and the tyrannical proceedings of the bishops. The Admonition concludes with a petition to both houses, that discipline, more consonant to the word of God, and agreeable to the foreign reformed churches, may be *established by law.* Their attempt to procure an *establishment* of their own opinions, Mr. Peirce justly observes, was the greatest fault in the book, or in any of the attempts which the puritans made. With unanswerable evidence they exposed the corruptions of the established ecclesiastical government, and particularly the persecution and tyranny by which it was upheld. But I fear, says he, could they have obtained their desire of the parliament, the *platform* which they proposed, must have been established by some persecuting laws; which I cannot find that Christ ever appointed his ministers to use for the advancement of his kingdom. All compulsion, and all enforcing of ecclesiastical discipline, by civil penalties, is quite contrary to the spirit of christianity.* Mr. Field and Mr. Wilcocks presented the Admonition themselves to the parliament; for which, July 7, 1572, they were sent to prison; and after examination, they were, by the instigation of the bishops, committed to Newgate.† Upon this, the book, already printed, was suffered to go abroad, and it passed through no less than four editions in about two years, notwithstanding all the vigilant endeavours of the bishops to suppress it.‡

The two prisoners were indicted, and sentenced to suffer imprisonment one whole year, which they did accordingly. After having suffered confinement some months in a most loathsome prison, by which their health was greatly impaired, they petitioned their noble friend, the Earl of Leicester, to procure their removal to some other prison, where they should meet with better usage. Their wives and children also presented a petition to the same

* Peirce's Vindication, part i. p. 84, 85. † MS. Register, p. 118.
‡ Strype's Parker, p. 347.

nobleman, earnestly desiring him to move the queen to discharge them from prison, on account of their great sufferings, and their extreme poverty and want. But these two petitions were without effect.* The prisoners still remained in close confinement, enduring many extreme hardships; and though they were committed to prison three months previous to receiving the sentence, and remained in prison twelve months after conviction, according to the cruel tenor of the sentence, they could not, even at the expiration of that period, obtain their liberty. Under these afflictive circumstances, they presented the following petition to the lords of the council:

"Whereas, right honourable lords, your poor and daily "orators, John Field and Thomas Wilcocks, being indicted "before the lord mayor and court of aldermen, in the city "of London, upon a statute of the first year of her majesty's "most happy and gracious reign, entitled 'An Act for the "Uniformity of Common Prayer,' &c. were adjudged to "suffer imprisonment by the space of one whole year, which "they have already fully endured, according to the effect "of the said statute. And now being given to understand, "that they cannot be discharged otherwise than by a special "order from your good lordships, they most humbly, and "for Jesus Christ's sake, pray and beseech your honours, "to take pity of their great poverty and extreme necessity, "now come upon them and their poor wives and children, "through their so long imprisonment. And that in your "accustomed clemency, so graciously and continually "extended towards all her majesty's subjects, you will also "vouchsafe, in compassion to their great misery, take order "for their enlargement. And as in duty they are bound, "so they and theirs will daily pour out their hearty prayers "to Almighty God, for his merciful favour, and most "gracious protection, to be extended to your lordships for "ever, Amen."†

During their imprisonment, they also petitioned the Earl of Leicester, humbly entreating him to be a means of forwarding their petition to the council. In this petition, they express themselves thus:—"This in all humility "sheweth unto your honour, that your poor and faithful "orators, John Field and Thomas Wilcocks, upon October "2, 1572, by virtue of a certain statute made the first year "of her majesty's reign, were convicted and committed to

* MS. Register, p. 118. † Ibid. p. 117.

" prison, there to continue for the space of one whole year, " and have now endured patiently all that time, besides a " quarter of a year before conviction, to their great charge " and utter undoing. May it, therefore, please your honour, " for the tender mercies of God, and in consideration of " them, their poor wives and children, to be a means with " the rest of her majesty's most honourable privy council, " to whom they have exhibited their most humble supplica- " tion that they may be released and discharged, and as much " as in your honour lieth, to promote and further the same. " So they shall be greatly comforted, after this their tedious " and long imprisonment; and they will not be unmindful " to pray for your lordship's great and continued pros- " perity."* It does not, however, appear whether they were released, or still detained in a state of confinement.

During the imprisonment of these two divines, Dr. Whitgift published his " Answer to the Admonition," in which he brought many severe charges against its authors: as, " That they were disturbers of good order; enemies to the state; and as holding many dangerous heresies." To these slanderous charges, they wrote a reply, entitled " A brief Confession of Faith, written by the Authors of the first Admonition to the Parliament, to testify their Persuasion in the Faith, against the uncharitable Surmises and Suspicions of Dr. Whitgift, uttered in his *Answer to their Admonition*, in Defence both of themselves and their Brethren." This Confession was written from Newgate, dated September 4, 1572, and contains a very judicious and comprehensive statement of their religious opinions, upon the principal doctrines of the gospel.†

In the month of September this year, Archbishop Parker sent one of his chaplains to confer with the two prisoners in Newgate, most probably with a view to convince them of their supposed errors, and bring them to a recantation. During this conference, they acknowledged themselves to be the authors of the Admonition, saying, " We wrote a book in parliament time, which should be a time of speaking and writing freely, justly craving redress and reformation of

* MS. Register, p. 118.

† Upon the holy scriptures, they say, " We hold that they alone ought " to be preached, and the whole of them preached, and nothing kept back; " and that it is not lawful for men, or for angels, to add any thing thereto, " or take any thing therefrom. And we affirm, that no antiquity, custom, " interpretation, or opinion of men, no, nor statute or ordinance of any " pope, council, parliament, or prince, may be set against the word of " God."—*Ibid.* p. 119—132.

many abuses, for which we are so uncourteously treated." A particular account of this conference is given in another place.*

There being no prospect of any further reformation of the church by the legislature, some of the leading puritans agreed to attempt it in a more private way. For this purpose, they erected a presbytery at Wandsworth in Surrey; which, being seated on the banks of the Thames, was convenient for the brethren in London. Among the members of this society was one Mr. Field, lecturer of Wandsworth, and undoubtedly this painful sufferer for nonconformity. The formation of this presbytery is said to have been in the year 1572; in which case, it must not have been in the month of November, as some have supposed, but previous to the month of July; for on the seventh of July, this year, Mr. Field and Mr. Wilcocks were committed to prison, and remained in close confinement, at least till towards the close of 1573.

Mr. Strype observes, that while these sufferers for conscience were closely confined in Newgate, they were frequently visited by their brethren, Drs. Fulke and Humphrey, and Messrs. Wyburn, Cartwright, Deering, Lever, Crowley, Johnson, and Brown. And upon their appearance before the council, they were told, that unless they could obtain the queen's pardon, they must be banished from their country, for the singular crime of disliking the Book of Common Prayer;† though at that time there was no law in existence requiring such punishment. Whether they ever sought to her majesty for pardon, we are not able to learn; only in 1574, Mr. Field, we find, was minister of Aldermary church, London.‡ Though he was released from prison, his troubles were not over. In the year 1577, he was cited before Bishop Aylmer, who pronounced him *obstinate*, for having taught children in gentlemens' houses, contrary to the prohibitions of the archbishop. Bishop Aylmer, therefore, recommended that both Mr. Field and Mr. Wilcocks might be sent into the most barbarous parts of Staffordshire, Shropshire, Lancashire, or other places, where, his lordship observed, they might be profitably employed in reclaiming people from the ignorance and errors of popery.§

What the bishop recommended was undoubtedly a more

* See Art. Wilcocks. † Strype's Parker, p. 413.
‡ MS. Register, p. 285. § Strype's Aylmer, p. 55, 56.

moderate kind of punishment than close confinement from one year to another, in a filthy, cold prison; and was, indeed, exceedingly moderate for a prelate of his tyrannical principles. Accordingly, Mr. Field was silenced or separated from the people of his charge. The parishioners of Aldermary, at the same time, used every effort in their power to procure his restoration. They applied to the Archbishop, as well as to the Bishop of London, but without success. They also presented two supplications to the Earl of Leicester, being one of the council, to be a means of promoting his restoration.

These supplications are now before me, in one of which they expressed themselves as follows:—"We, in most "humble-wise, beseech your honour, that whereas of late "we did to our comfort enjoy, one Mr. Field to be our "preacher, who laboured painfully amongst us for the "space of four years, in preaching the word of God, and "catechizing our youth, teaching obedience both to God "and our prince, and keeping us in good order. Whereas "since his restraint and inhibition, we are left as scattered "sheep upon the mountains, and have none ordinarily to "break unto us the bread of life, than which a greater evil "cannot come upon us. Hearing that God of his great "goodness hath made you the honoured instrument of "restoring many, we, your humble suppliants, beseech "you, even for the cause of God, to be a means also for us. "We feel persuaded that, if the matter be fairly examined, "there will be no cause found in him why he should "be sequestered from us. For we are able to witness to "your honour, even in the presence of Him who seeth all "hearts, that to our knowledge he ever behaved himself "wisely and faithfully, as became a true minister of Jesus "Christ. The things urged against him were never hindered, "impugned, or any way resisted by him, but were duly "kept and observed. And seeing that which he received "was out of our purses, without any burden upon the "church whatever, we cannot help feeling ourselves hardly "treated, that without cause he should be taken from us. "We have used what means we could with the Archbishop "and Bishop of London; but as we could learn of them no "cause of his sequestration, so we could receive no favour-"able answer for his restoration. We beseech your honour, "therefore, in behalf of ourselves, our wives, our children, "and our servants, so to stand forth our good lord in this "our necessary and holy suit, as that by your means, he "may be again restored: So shall many hearts be made "glad; and we shall evermore pray for your honour's long "and happy state. Your honour's poor suppliants ever to "command, of the parish of Aldermary, in London."*

How long Mr. Field continued under the ecclesiastical censure, or whether he was ever restored to his charge at Aldermary, appears extremely doubtful.

The next account we meet with of this excellent divine, is, that in 1582, he was engaged, with several other learned men, in a disputation with certain papists in the Tower; but our information is so extremely scanty, that he is only said to have taken an active part in those learned disputations,† and to have collected and published an account of them, after it had undergone the examination of the persons who engaged. In 1584, we find him brought into other troubles, when he was suspended by the Bishop of London. The cause of his suspension was, his admitting an assembly of ministers at his house, among whom were several Scotch divines. These divines being disaffected to the hierarchy, the assembly was declared to be an unlawful conventicle. Mr. Field was, therefore, suspended from his ministry, for entertaining them, and the rest were deprived for refusing subscription.‡ How long he continued under suspension, and whether he was ever restored, is very uncertain. He died in February, 1587, when his remains were interred in Cripplegate church, London. Mr. Field, a short time before his death, united with his brethren in subscribing the "Book of Discipline."§

His Works.—1. Prayers and Meditations for the use of private Families, 1581.—2. A Caveat for Parsons Howlet, concerning his untimelye Flighte, and Scriching in the clear Day Lighte of the Gospel, necessarie for him, and all the rest of that darke Brood, and uncleane Cage of Papists, 1581.—3. Exposition of the Symbol of the Apostles, 1581.—4. A godly Exhortation, by occasion of a late Judgment of God at Paris Garden, 1583.—He published Translations of many of Calvin's Sermons, and the productions of other learned men.

John Huckle was pastor of the church at Aythorp Roding in Essex, but prosecuted by Bishop Aylmer, for nonconformity. Mr. Strype is pleased to stigmatize him as a busy body, an enemy to the peace of the church, a

* MS. Register, p. 285.

† Strype's Annals, vol. ii. p. 647.—Life of Parker, p. 219.—Churton's Life of Nowell, p. 278.

‡ MS. Register, p. 460, 568, 569.

§ Neal's Puritans, vol. i. p. 423.

transgressor of its orders, an impugner of the common prayer, a gatherer of night-conventicles, and a busy disputer against the Athanasian creed; and, therefore, to reclaim him from his dangerous errors, the bishop suspended him from his ministry.*

Upon his suspension, Mr. Huckle laid his case before the lords of the council, and procured the following letter, dated from Greenwich, May 4, 1584, addressed to the bishop:†

"Our hearty commendations to your lordship.

"The bearer, John Huckle, minister of the word of God, "hath been here before us, who, with his confession of faith "and solemn protestation, doth seem to detest Arianism, and "every other the like heresy with which he may be charged; "and offereth to subscribe Athanasius's creed, and to testify "to the world, by any other means, his sincere and unfeigned belief of the doctrine contained in the same. And "so far as we can find, he is a man clear and sound in "religion, and no other matter, according to our knowledge, "can be proved against him. We, therefore, see no cause "why he should be any longer suspended from the exercise "of his ministry; and we pray your lordship, that you will "now, upon his recognition, revoke your suspension, and "treat him with all convenient favour; whereby he may be "the better encouraged, and the more able to discharge the "duty belonging to him. And so we bid your lordship "hearty farewell. Your very loving friends,

"William Burghley, Ed. Warwick,
"Fr. Knolles, Fr. Walsingham,
"Charles Howard, Hen. Sydney."

Such was the opinion and commendation of these distinguished persons, but the bishop was of another mind; and, notwithstanding Mr. Huckle's protestation and readiness to subscribe, the hard-hearted prelate refused to restore him. This appears from his lordship's answer to the council's letter; wherein he says, "If I should restore him, I could not answer for it before God, her majesty, my own conscience, nor the church of God."‡ Such was the sentiment of this relentless prelate! He was unwilling to rescind his own determination, though recommended so to do by the greatest persons in the land; therefore, Mr. Huckle, with many others, who fell into the hands of this lordly ecclesiastic, remained under suspension, at least for several

* Strype's Aylmer, p. 108. † MS. Register, p. 584. ‡ Ibid.

years; and whether he was ever restored, is extremely doubtful. In the year 1587, he was among the suspended ministers of Essex, who, to obtain some redress of their grievances, presented a supplication to parliament, an account of which is given in another place.*

John Fox, A. M.—This celebrated man, usually denominated the English Martyrologist, was born of respectable parents at Boston in Lincolnshire, in the year 1517. His father dying when he was young, and his mother marrying again, he came under the guardianship of his father-in-law. At the age of sixteen, he was sent to Brazen-nose college, Oxford; and afterwards he became fellow of Magdalen college, in the same university. In the days of his youth, he discovered a genius and taste for poetry, and wrote several Latin comedies, upon subjects taken from the scriptures.

For some time after his going to the university, Mr. Fox was strongly attached to the superstitions and errors of popery. He was not only zealous for the Romish church, and strictly moral in his life, but rejected the doctrine of justification by faith in the imputed righteousness of Christ, and concluded himself to be sufficiently safe by trusting in the imaginary merit of his own self-denial, penances, almsdeeds, and compliance with the ceremonies of the church. Afterwards, by the blessing of God upon his studies, he was delivered from this self-righteousness, and led to submit himself to the righteousness of Jesus Christ. And by his indefatigable researches into ecclesiastical history, together with the writings of the fathers, but especially by his thorough acquaintance with the holy scriptures, he was convinced of the immense distance to which the church of Rome had departed from the faith, and spirit, and practice of the gospel.

In order to make himself a more competent judge of the controversy, which now began to be warmly discussed betwixt protestants and papists, he searched all the ancient and modern histories of the church with indefatigable assiduity. His labours to find out the truth were indeed so great, that, before he was thirty years of age, he read all the Greek and Latin fathers, all the schoolmen, and the decrees of councils, and made considerable progress in other

* See Art. George Gifford.

branches of useful knowledge. During this close application, he avoided all kinds of company, and betook himself to the most solitary retirement, often spending whole nights in his study. At length, from this strict and severe application, having forsaken his old popish friends, and from the dubious manner in which he spoke, when he was obliged to give his opinion on religious subjects, but, above all, from his sparing attendance on the public worship of the national church, in which he had been remarkably strict, he was suspected of alienation from her constitution and ceremonies, and of being infected with heresy.

Mr. Fox having found the truth, soon became bold and courageous in the profession of it, even in those dark times of popery. He chose rather to suffer affliction with the people of God in the cause of truth, than enjoy the pleasures of sin for a season. Being deeply impressed with the declaration of our Lord, "Whosoever is ashamed of me, and of my words, in this adulterous and sinful generation, of him shall the Son of man be ashamed, when he cometh in the glory of his Father, with his holy angels;" he determined to venture the loss of all things for the sake of Christ; and, therefore, openly professed himself a protestant. This he had no sooner done, than he was publicly accused of heresy, and expelled from the college. His adversaries, indeed, thought they dealt favourably in suffering him to escape with his life. This was in the year 1545.* Wood, by mistake, says, he resigned his fellowship, and left the university, to avoid expulsion.†

Mr. Fox being expelled from the university, lost the favour of his friends and relations. As he was convicted of heresy, they thought it unsafe, and were therefore unwilling, to countenance or protect him. His father-in-law, in particular, seized this opportunity of withholding from him the estate which his own father had left him. While he was thus forsaken and oppressed, God, in the hour of extremity, raised up an unexpected friend and patron, in Sir Thomas Lucy of Warwickshire. This worthy person took him into his house, and made him tutor to his children. Here he found a comfortable asylum from the storm of persecution. While in this situation, he married a citizen's daughter of Coventry, but still continued in Sir Thomas's family till his pupils were grown up. Afterwards,

* Life of Mr. Fox prefixed to his "Acts and Monuments of the Martyrs."

† Athenæ Oxon. vol. i. p. 186.

with some difficulty, he procured entertainment sometimes at the house of his father-in-law, and sometimes at the house of his wife's father in Coventry, till a little before the death of King Henry VIII., when he removed to London.

For a considerable time after his removal to the metropolis, having no employment, nor yet any preferment, he was again reduced to extreme want. However, by the kind providence of God, he was at length relieved, in the following remarkable manner: As he was sitting one day in St. Paul's church, his countenance being pale, his eyes hollow, and like a ghastly, dying man, a person, whom he never remembered to have seen before, came and sat down by him, and accosting him with much familiarity, put a sum of money into his hand, saying, "Be of good comfort, Mr. Fox. Take care of yourself, and use all means to preserve your life. For, depend upon it, God will, in a few days, give you a better prospect, and more certain means of subsistence." Though he could never learn from whom he received this seasonable relief, within three days of that memorable event, he was taken into the family of the Duchess of Richmond, to be tutor to the Earl of Surrey's children, whose education was committed to her care.*

Mr. Fox continued in this honourable family, at Ryegate in Surrey, during part of the reign of Henry VIII., the whole of Edward VI., and part of Queen Mary's. Bishop Gardiner, a most bloody persecutor, in whose diocese he found so comfortable and safe a retreat, would have brought him to the stake, had he not been protected by the Duke of Norfolk, who had been one of his pupils. Mr. Fox, it is said, was the first person who ventured to preach the gospel at Ryegate; and with deep concern, Gardiner beheld the heir to one of the noblest families in England, trained up, under his influence, to the protestant religion. This prelate formed various designs against the safety of Mr. Fox; and sought by numerous stratagems, to effect his ruin. The good man, who was less suspicious of the bishop, than the bishop was of him, was obliged, at length, to quit his native country, and seek refuge in a foreign land. The duke, who loved and revered him as a father, sheltered him from the storm as long as he was able; and when Mr. Fox was obliged to flee for safety, he took care to provide him with every comfortable accommodation for the voyage.

* Life of Mr. Fox.

He set sail from Ipswich, accompanied by his wife, and some other persons, who left the country on a similar account. The vessel had no sooner got to sea, than a tremendous storm arose, which obliged them to return to port next day. Having with great difficulty reached the land, Mr. Fox was saluted with indubitable information, that Bishop Gardiner had issued warrants for apprehending him, and that the most diligent search had been made for him, during his absence at sea. He, therefore, prevailed upon the master of the ship to put to sea again, though the attempt was extremely dangerous; and in two days, they arrived at Newport in Flanders. Thus, by the kind providence of God, he a second time, narrowly escaped the fire.*

After his arrival in Flanders, Mr. Fox travelled to Antwerp, then to Frankfort in Germany; where he was involved in the troubles excited by the officious and unkind proceedings of Dr. Cox and his party.† The first settlers at Frankfort being driven from the place, Mr. Fox removed to Basil in Switzerland, to which city many of his fellow exiles accompanied him. Basil was then one of the most famous places in Europe, for printing; and many of the English refugees, who retired thither, procured their subsistence by revising and correcting the press. By this employment, Mr. Fox maintained himself and his family. Also, at Basil, he laid the plan of his "Acts and Monuments of the Martyrs," which he afterwards, with immense labour, finished in his own country. Mr. Strype is, however, very incorrect when he intimates that our author published his first book while he was in a state of exile.‡

Having mentioned the above celebrated work, commonly called Fox's "Book of Martyrs," it will be proper to give some account of this fruit of his Herculean labour. We have already observed that the author directed his attention to this work, during his residence at Basil; but he reserved the greatest part of it till his return to his native country, that he might procure the authority and testimony of more witnesses. It appears from the author's own notes, that he was eleven years in compiling this great work; and in this, as well as in some others of his labours, Mr. Fox was favoured with the particular assistance of several distinguished persons. Among these were Mr. John Aylmer,

* Life of Mr. Fox.
† Troubles at Frankeford, p. 30, 47, 50.
‡ Strype's Cranmer, p. 358.

afterwards Bishop of London;[*] Mr. Edmund Grindal, afterwards Archbishop of Canterbury; and Mr. Thomas Norton, afterwards a celebrated lawyer, member of parliament, and a noted puritan, who married the only daughter of Archbishop Cranmer. From the last of these, our author is said to have derived the greatest assistance.[†] It also appears that Grindal, besides his constant counsel and advice in the course of the work, supplied our author with numerous materials, which, when he had digested and methodized them, were of great use to him. During Grindal's exile, he established a correspondence in England for this purpose, by which means, accounts of most of the acts and sufferings of those who were persecuted in Queen Mary's reign, came to his hands; and it is said to have been owing to Grindal's strict and tender regard to truth, that the work was so long in hand; for he rejected all common reports and relations that were carried over, till more satisfactory evidence could be procured. It was by his advice, that Mr. Fox at first printed separately the acts of some particular persons, of whom any sure and authentic memoirs came to hand, till materials for a more complete history of the martyrs, with their persecutions and sufferings, could be obtained. In pursuance of this advice, Mr. Fox published at Basil, various histories of the English bishops and divines, in single pieces, soon after their respective persecutions and martyrdoms.

Mr. Fox at first undertook to publish his laborious work in Latin; but by the advice of Grindal, it was printed in Latin and English, for more general usefulness. It was published in London in 1563, in one thick volume folio, with this title, "Actes and Monuments of these latter perillous days touching matters of the Churche, wherein are comprehended and described the great persecutions and horrible troubles that have been wrought and practised by the Romish prelates speciallye in this realme of England and Scotland, from the yeare of our Lorde a thousand unto the time now present," &c. A fourth edition was printed in London in 1583, in two volumes folio, and it was reprinted in 1632, in three volumes folio. The ninth edition was printed in London in 1684, in three volumes folio, with copper cuts, the former editions having only wooden ones.[‡]

* Strype's Aylmer, p. 11.

† MS. Chronology, vol. i. p. 243 (2), 243 (3.)

‡ Biog. Britan. vol. iii. p. 2022, 2023. Edit. 1747.—Wood's Athenæ Oxon. vol. i. p. 187.

To this edition there is frequent reference in the present volume.

Several writers have laboured to deprecate the memory of Mr. Fox, by insinuating that his History of the Martyrs contained many misrepresentations and falsehoods. Dr. Collier, who embraces all opportunities to lessen his reputation and undervalue his work, accuses him of disingenuity and ill nature, and says, he ought to be read with great caution. He tells us, that a vein of satire and coarse language runs through his martyrology, and instances the case of the cruel Bishop Gardiner, whom he styles "an insensible ass, who had no feeling of God's spirit in the matter of justification."* He charges Mr. Fox with other improprieties and inconsistencies, and adds, "I cannot perceive the martyrologist had any right to Elijah's sarcasm. His zeal without doubt was too much imbittered. He was plainly ridden by his passion, and pushed by disaffection, towards profaneness."† It is readily acknowledged, that Mr. Fox sometimes discovers too warm a temper; and it was almost impossible it should be otherwise, considering the circumstances under which he wrote, and those cruel proceedings which he has handed down to posterity. This was too common among our zealous reformers, who, it must be confessed, were sometimes hurried forwards to lengths by no means jutifiable.

Wood observes, "that as Mr. Fox hath taken a great deal of pains in his work, and shewed sometimes much judgment in it; so hath he committed many errors therein, by trusting to the relations of poor simple people, and in making such martyrs as were living after the first edition of his book came forth, though afterwards by him excused and omitted."‡ Admitting all this, what does it prove? It is very justly observed, that as to private stories, Mr. Fox and his friends used the utmost diligence and care, that no falsehood might be obtruded on the reader, and were ever ready to correct any mistakes that might happen.§ Though he might be misinformed in several parts of his intelligence; yet these he corrected, as they came to his knowledge. Indeed, these were inconveniences which must attend the compiling of so large a body of modern history, as Mr. Fox's chiefly was. No man is likely to receive, from

* Collier's Eccl. Hist. vol. ii. p. 45, 233. † Ibid. p. 43, 375, 586.
‡ Wood's Athenæ, vol. i. p. 187.
§ Biog. Britan. vol. iii. p. 2024. Edit. 1747.

various hands, so large a mass of information, and all be found perfect truth, and when digested to be found without the least trait of error. What is the weight of all the objections offered in contempt of the Foxian martyrs, to overthrow so solid and immoveable a fabric? It is compiled of so many undeniable evidences of popish barbarity, that its reputation will remain unsullied to the latest period of time. The Acts and Monuments of the Martyrs have long been, they still remain, and will always continue, substantial pillars of the protestant church; of more force than many more volumes of bare arguments, to withstand the tide of popery; and, like a Pharos, should be lighted up in every age, as a warning to all posterity.*

The indefatigable Strype passes the following encomium on the work:—"Mr. Fox," says he, "hath done such exquisite service to the protestant cause, in shewing from abundance of ancient books, records, registers, and choice manuscripts, the encroachments of popes and papelins, and the stout oppositions that were made by learned and good men in all ages, and in all countries, against them; especially under King Henry and Queen Mary in England. He hath preserved the memoirs of those holy men and women, those bishops and divines, together with their histories, acts, sufferings and deaths, willingly undergone for the sake of Christ and his gospel, and for refusing to comply with the popish doctrines and superstitions. And Mr. Fox must not pass without the commendation of a most painful searcher into records, archives, and repositories of original acts, and letters of state, and a great collector of manuscripts. The world is infinitely indebted to him for abundance of extracts thence, and communicated in these volumes. And as he hath been found most diligent, so most strictly true and faithful in his transcriptions."†

No book ever gave so deep a wound to the errors, superstitions, and persecutions of popery; on which account the talents, virtues, and labours of Mr. Fox rendered him a fit object of papal malice and enmity. No man could be more hated and calumniated than he was by his enemies. His name, together with some others, was inserted at Rome in a "bede-roll," or list of persons who were appointed to be dispatched; and the particular mode of his death, as by

* Biog. Britan. vol. ii. p. 556. Edit. 1778.
† Strype's Annals, vol. i. p. 239, 241.

burning or hanging, pointed out, when the design of invading and over-running England should be accomplished.* By order of Queen Elizabeth, Mr. Fox's History of the Martyrs was placed in the common halls of archbishops, bishops, deans, archdeacons, and heads of colleges, and in all churches and chapels throughout the kingdom.†

On the accession of Queen Elizabeth, our learned divine returned from exile, and was cordially received and courteously entertained by his noble pupil, the Duke of Norfolk;‡ who maintained him at his house, and settled a pension upon him at his death. Afterwards, in 1572, when this unhappy duke was beheaded on Tower-hill, for his treasonable connections with the Queen of Scots, Mr. Fox and Dr. Nowell, dean of St. Paul's, attended him upon the scaffold.§

Mr. Fox lived many years highly esteemed and favoured by persons of quality. Bishops Grindal, Parkhurst, Pilkington, and Aylmer; also Sir Francis Walsingham, Sir Francis Drake, Sir Thomas Gresham, and many others, were his powerful friends. By their influence, they would have raised him to the highest preferment; but, as he could not subscribe, and disapproved of some of the ceremonies, he modestly declined their offers. Indeed, he was offered almost any preferment he pleased, but was more happy in declining them, excepting a prebend in the church of Salisbury.‖

For the space of three years after his return from exile, Mr. Fox had no preferment whatever: and in a letter to his friend Dr. Lawrence Humphrey, he says, "I still "wear the same clothes, and remain in the same sordid con-"dition that England received me in, when I first came "from Germany: nor do I change my degree or order, "which is that of the *mendicants*, or, if you will, of the

* Churton's Life of Nowell, p. 271, 272.

† Mr. Fox's Acts and Monuments of the Martyrs, and Bishop Jewel's Reply to Harding, continued to be thus honoured till the time of Archbishop Laud. This domineering prelate no sooner understood that the learned authors maintained, "That the communion table ought to stand among the people in the body of the church, and not altar-wise, at one end of it," than he was displeased, and ordered their books to be taken out of the churches.—*Wood's Athenæ*, vol. i. p. 187.—*Prynne's Cant. Doome*, p. 88.

‡ Strype's Annals, vol. i. p. 132.

§ Churton's Life of Nowell, p. 208.

‖ Wood's Athenæ Oxon. vol. i. p. 186.

"*friars preachers*."* Thus did this grave and learned divine pleasantly reproach the ingratitude of the times. He continued without the least preferment till the year 1563, when Secretary Cecil procured him the above prebend; which, with some difficulty, he kept to his death. This was all the preferment he ever obtained.

In the year 1564, the Bishop of London having preached the Emperor Ferdinand's funeral sermon, in the cathedral of St. Paul's, it was ordered to be printed, and to be translated into Latin, "by the ready and elegant pen of John Fox."† During the same year, Archbishop Parker attempted to force the clergy into a conformity to the established church; for which purpose he summoned all the London ministers to appear at Lambeth, when they were examined upon the following question: "Will you promise conformity to the apparel by law established, and testify the same by the subscription of your hands?" Those who refused were immediately suspended, and after three months, deprived of their livings.‡ To prepare the way, Mr. Fox was summoned first, that the reputation of his great piety, might give the greater countenance to their proceedings. When they called him to subscribe, he took his Greek Testament out of his pocket, and said, *To this I will subscribe.* And when the commissioners required him to subscribe the canons, he refused, saying, "I have nothing in the church but a prebend in Salisbury, and much good may it do you, if you take it from me."§ His ecclesiastical judges, however, had not sufficient courage to deprive so celebrated a divine, who held up the ashes of Smithfield before their eyes. It ought here to be observed, that Mr. Strype is guilty of *a twofold mistake*, when he says, that, in 1566, Mr. Fox had no ecclesiastical living; and that though he was no approver of the habits, he was not summoned before the ecclesiastical commissioners.‖

Though Mr. Fox refused subscription and conformity to certain ecclesiastical ceremonies, he behaved with great moderation, and disapproved of the warmth of the more

* The remains of popish superstition were so prevalent in the church of England, especially among the ruling prelates in the time of Queen Elizabeth, that for many years, the *eating of flesh* was prohibited, during the weeks of Lent; yet, in certain cases, dispensations were granted. Accordingly, Mr. Fox being a man of a weak and sickly constitution, this favour was conferred upon him by Archbishop Parker!!—*Strype's Parker*, p.112, 178.

† Churton's Life of Nowell, p. 106. ‡ Strype's Grindal, p. 98.

§ Fuller's Church Hist. b. ix. p. 76.—Heylin's Hist. of Refor. p. 337.

‖ Strype's Parker, p. 223.

rigid and zealous puritans. And while be expressed his dislike of separation, he was exceedingly grieved about those things which gave the occasion.* Speaking of Blumfield, a wicked persecutor of the pious Mr. Harelson, for not wearing the surplice, he said, "It is a pity that such baits "of popery are left to the enemies, to take christians in. "God take them away from us, or us from them. For God "knoweth they are the cause of much blindness and strife "among men."†

At the above period, Mr. Fox presented a Latin panegyric to the queen, for having granted indulgence to several nonconformist divines. But in the year 1575, he addressed her majesty on a very different occasion. During this year a most severe persecution was raised against the anabaptists in London, ten of whom were condemned, eight ordered to be banished, and two to be executed. Mr. Fox, therefore, wrote an excellent Latin letter to the queen, in which he observes, "That to punish with the flames, the bodies of those who err rather from ignorance, than obstinacy, is cruel, and more like the church of Rome, than the mildness of the gospel. I do not write thus," says he, "from any bias to the indulgence of error; but to save the lives of men, being myself a man; and in hope that the offending parties may have an opportunity to repent, and retract their mistakes." He then earnestly entreats that the fires of Smithfield might not be rekindled; but that some milder punishment might be inflicted upon them, to prevent, if possible, the destruction of their souls, as well as their bodies.‡ But his remonstrances were ineffectual. The queen remained inflexible; and though she constantly called him *Father Fox*, she gave him a flat denial, as to saving their lives, unless they would recant their dangerous errors. They both refusing to recant, were burnt in Smithfield, July 22, 1575; to the great and lasting disgrace of the reign and character of Queen Elizabeth.§

* Fuller's Church Hist. b. ix. p. 106.—Strype's Parker, p. 223, 224.
† Baxter's Second Plea, p. 56.
‡ Fuller's Church Hist. b. ix. p. 104, 105.
§ On Easter Sunday in this year, a congregation of Dutch anabaptists was discovered, without Aldgate, London; when twenty-seven persons were apprehended and cast into prison, four of whom, bearing fagots at Paul's cross, recanted their dangerous opinions. The two who were executed were John Wielmaker and Hendrick Ter Woort; or, as some of our historians call them, John Paterson and Henry Terwoordt. Previous to their execution, they suffered sixteen weeks imprisonment. The Dutch congregation in London made earnest intercession to the lords of the council, to obtain their pardon; but all to no purpose. The two unhappy

Mr. Fox was a man of great humanity and uncommon liberality. He was a most laborious student, and remarkably abstemious; and a most learned, pious, and judicious divine, and ever opposed to all methods of severity in matters of religion. But as he was a nonconformist, he was shamefully neglected. "Although the richest mitre in England," says Fuller, "would have counted itself preferred by being placed upon his head, he contented himself with a prebend of Salisbury. And while proud persons stretched out their plumes in ostentation, he used their vanity for his shelter; and was more pleased to *have* worth, than to have others *take notice* of it. And how learnedly he wrote, how constantly he preached, how piously he lived, and how cheerfully he died, may be seen at large in his life prefixed to his book."* And even Wood denominates him a person of good natural endowments, a sagacious searcher into antiquity, incomparably charitable, and of an exemplary life and conversation, but a severe Calvinist, and a bitter enemy to popery.†

This celebrated man, having spent his life in the most laborious study, and in promoting the cause of Christ and the interests of true religion, resigned his spirit to God, April 18, 1587, in the seventieth year of his age. His death was greatly lamented; and his mortal part was interred in the chancel of St. Giles's church, Cripplegate, London; where, against the south wall, was a monumental inscription erected by his son,‡ of which the following is a translation:

In memory of JOHN FOX,
the most faithful Martyrologist of our English Church,
a most diligent searcher into historical antiquities,
a most strong bulwark
and fighter for Evangelical Truth;
who hath revived the Marian Martyrs
as so many Phœnixes,
from the dust of oblivion,
is this monument erected,
in grief and affection,
by his eldest son SAMUEL FOX.
He died April 18, An. Dom. 1587,
in his seventieth year.

men must perfume Smithfield with their ashes. It is, however, extremely surprising that Fuller attempts to palliate, and even to justify, the cruel barbarity exercised upon these unhappy men.—*Strype's Annals*, vol. ii. p. 380.—*Brandt's Hist. of Refor.* vol. i. p. 315. Edit. 1720.—*Fuller's Church Hist.* b. ix. p. 105.

* Fuller's Abel Redivius, p. 381. † Athenæ Oxon. vol. i. p. 188.

‡ Stow's Survey of London, b. iii. p. 83.

Mr. Fox, during his residence at Basil, preaching to his fellow exiles, confidently declared in his sermon, "Now is the time for your return to England, and I bring you the news by the command of God." For these words he was sharply reproved by some of his brethren; but, remarkable as it may appear, they afterwards found that Queen Mary died the very day preceding the delivery of this sermon, and so a way was open for their return home.*

It was Mr. Fox who had the memorable interview with Mrs. Honiwood, often related by historians. This pious lady was under most distressing doubts and fears about the salvation of her soul, and her sorrow became so grievous, that she sunk in despair. This so affected her bodily health, that she appeared to be in a deep consumption, and even on the very brink of death, for about twenty years. In vain did the ablest physicians administer their medical assistance; and in vain did the ablest ministers preach comfort to her soul. At length, Mr. Fox was sent for; who, on his arrival, found her in a most distressed and languishing condition. He prayed with her, and reminded her of the faithfulness of God's promises, and of the sufferings of Christ for her soul. But all he could say appeared ineffectual. Not in the least discouraged, he still proceeded in his discourse, and said, "You will not only recover of your bodily disease, but also live to an exceeding great age; and which is yet better, you are interested in Christ, and will go to heaven when you die." She, looking earnestly at him as he spake these words, with great emotion, answered, "Impossible; I am as surely damned, as this glass will break," and immediately dashed a Venice glass, which she had in her hand, with great violence to the ground; but the glass received not the smallest injury. The event, indeed, proved according to the words of Mr. Fox. Though Mrs. Honiwood was then sixty years old, she recovered from her sickness, and lived the rest of her days, being upwards of thirty years, in much peace and comfort.†

* Fuller's Abel Red. p. 380.—Clark's Marrow of Eccl. Hist. p. 793.

† Mrs. Honiwood, in the days of Queen Mary, used to visit the prisons, and to comfort and relieve the confessors. She was present at the burning of Mr. John Bradford in Smithfield, and was resolved to see the end of his sufferings. But the press of the people was so great, that her shoes were trodden off her feet; and she was obliged to go barefoot from Smithfield to St. Martin's, before she could procure a new pair for money. This excellent lady had three hundred and sixty-seven children lawfully descended from her: sixteen from her own body, one hundred and fourteen grandchildren, two hundred and twenty-eight great-grandchildren, and nine

Mr. Fox was uncommonly liberal to the poor and distressed, and never refused giving to any who asked for Jesus's sake. Being once asked whether he remembered a certain poor man whom he used to relieve, he said, "Yes, I remember him, and I forget lords and ladies to remember such."—As Mr. Fox was going one day from the house of the Bishop of London, he found many people begging at the gate; and having no money, he immediately returned to the bishop and borrowed five pounds, which he distributed among the poor people. After some time, the bishop asking him for the money, Mr. Fox said, "I have laid it out for you, and have paid it where you owed it, to the poor that lay at your gate;" when his lordship thanked him for what he had done.*

As Mr. Fox was going one day along the streets in London, a woman of his acquaintance met him; and as they discoursed together, she pulled out her Bible, and with too much forwardness, told him she was going to hear a sermon; upon which, he said to her, "If you will be advised by me, go home again." But, said she, then when shall I go to church? To which he immediately replied, "When you tell no body of it."†

Mr. Fox, it is said, used to wear a strait cap, covering his head and ears; and over that, a deepish crowned, shallow-brimmed, slouched hat. His portrait is taken with his hat on, and is supposed to have been the first English engraving with a hat.‡

His Works.—1. De Christo Triumphante, 1551.—2. De censura seu excommunicatione ecclesiastica, 1551.—3. Tables of Grammar, 1552.—4. Commentarii rerum in Ecclesia gestarum, 1554.—5. Articuli, seu Aphorismi aliquot Johannis Wiclevi &c., 1554.—6. Collectania quædam ex Reginaldi Pecocki Episc. &c., 1554.—7. Opistographia ad Oxonienses, 1554.—8. Locorum communicam Logicalium tituli & ordinationes &c., 1557.—9. Probationes & Resolutiones de re & mataria sacramenti Eucharistici, 1563.—10. De Christi crucifixo, 1571.—11. De Oliva Evangelica, 1587.—12. Concerning Man's Election to Salvation, 1581.—13. Certain Notes of Election, 1581.—14. De Christo gratis justificante, contra Jesuitas, 1583.—15. Disputatio contra Jesuitas & eorum argumenta, 1585.—

great-great-grandchildren. She lived a most pious life, and died a most christian death, May 11, 1620, in the ninety-third year of her age. Her remains were interred in Markshall church in Essex, where there was a monumental inscription erected to her memory.—*Fuller's Worthies*, part ii. p. 85.

* Fuller's Abel Redivivus, p. 382.

† Clarke's Marrow of Eccl. Hist. p. 796.

‡ Peck's Desiderata Curiosa, vol. i. l. xv. p. 9.

16. Eicasmi, seu Meditationes in Apocal. S. Johannis, 1587.—17. Papa Confutatus.—18. A brief Exhortation, to be read in the time of God's Visitation.—He published several translations of the works of other learned men: but his most celebrated work is his "History of the Acts and Monuments of the Martyrs," commonly called "The Book of Martyrs."

JOHN WILSON was born in the parish of Kildwick in Yorkshire, and ordained deacon according to the order of the church of England; when he obtained a license from the Archbishop of York to preach at Skipton, in the same county. He was a pious, faithful, and useful preacher, but endured much severe usage for nonconformity. Archbishop Sandys receiving complaints against him, sent his pursuivant with all haste to apprehend him, and bring him before the high commission. Upon his appearance before their lordships, and inquiring what charges were alleged against him, he was told that he must obtain two sureties to be bound in two hundred pounds for his future appearance. Accordingly, he obtained the securities demanded, and, January 9, 1587, appeared again before the archbishop and other commissioners at Bishopsthorp, when he underwent the following examination:

Archbishop. You are brought before us for certain disorders, contempts, and disobedience, by you committed, to which you must answer as they shall be objected against you.

Dean. You must answer as truly as if you were sworn.

A. He must be sworn, and answer upon his oath. Hold him a book, and let him take the oath.

Wilson. If the law require me to be sworn, I am contented. But I think it doth not compel a man to accuse himself; and I hope I shall not be urged to do more than the law requireth.

A. If you refuse to be sworn, answer as you will; but be sure, if I prove any thing against you which you deny, you shall smart for it.

W. Let me have the law, and spare not. But because I mean to deny no truth objected against me, whether I be sworn or not, I am, therefore, contented to answer upon my oath. (He then took the oath.)

A. Read the first article against him.

Fathergill. You have taken upon you to execute the office of a minister for the space of three years, without any warrant so to do.

W. I know not what law maketh known the minister's duty. I must, therefore, be informed of this, before I can answer.

A. Tell him.

Hudson. It is to say service, to preach the word, to minister the sacraments, to marry, and to bury the dead.

W. I have not done all these things without the law.

A. What warrant of law have you?

W. I have the orders for the office of a deacon, according to law.

A. Shew unto us your orders. (Here Mr. Wilson produced his orders, which was read by the dean, but nothing was observed.)

W. Write, Mr. Proctor, that I am deacon, according to law.

A. What say you of your preaching? At what churches have you preached?

W. At all the churches near Kildwick.* Mr. Proctor, record this.

A. You must always have that refuge to fly to.

W. My lord, I am sworn. There may be more, though I do not remember them. I dare not upon mine oath set down an uncertain thing as certain; therefore, I say, these are all, *so far as I recollect.*

A. What authority then had you to preach?

W. I had your grace's authority in writing.

A. That was only upon condition that the people would receive you, and be willing to hear you.

W. I know not what was the condition. I followed the direction under the hand of Mr. Cock, in which I am sure no such thing was expressed.

Cock. My lord, I wrote that it was your grace's pleasure that he should preach at Skipton, until your return from London, if he behaved himself according to law.

A. I ordered you to write no such thing, unless the people would receive him willingly, as Mr. Palmer said they would.

C. My lord, they are ill-natured people, and would willingly receive none.

A. You have said service without surplice, and not according to the Book of Common Prayer.

W. That is not true.

A. You have not used the surplice in reading the service.

* Here Mr. Wilson, by request of the archbishop, named, as far as he could recollect, all the churches in which he had preached.

W. I have no pastoral charge. I said service only in the absence of the pastor, which was very seldom; and, on those occasions, I thought I was not bound to use it.

A. You say not the service according to the book.

W. I do.

H. You use a prayer of your own at the beginning.

W. That is not true, Mr. Proctor.

A. Let me know the order you have observed.

W. I first read one of the portions of scripture appointed, and then exhorted the people to the confession of their sins. That being done, I read some of the Psalms, after that two chapters, and then the sermon.

A. Then you say not according to the book.

W. Yes, my lord, that which I read is according to the book.

A. But you omit many things.

W. And so I may according to law, especially when there is preaching, or any more profitable exercise.

A. More profitable exercise! that is, your *talking*.

W. I am sure that preaching is more profitable than reading. And I am sure your lordship will not deny, that my *talking*, being out of the word of God, is more profitable than *saying service*.

A. Nay, you have your tongue at your will. What is the next article?

F. When you should say the epistle and gospel, according to the book, you will not call them the epistle and gospel, but the *portion of scripture*.

A. Have you never administered the sacraments?

W. No.

H. Did you never christen?

W. Some few times, though very seldom.

A. Did you use the sign of the cross?

W. No, my lord, I said the words, but did not use the cross.

A. Did you say, "I sign thee with the sign of the cross?"

W. No.

A. Tell me then what words you used.

W. "We receive this child into the congregation of Christ's flock, that hereafter he shall not be ashamed to confess the faith of Christ crucified upon the cross."

H. Did you never minister the communion?

W. No.

H. What, neither the bread, nor the cup?

[illegible] Yes, I have ministered the cup by the appointment [illegible], being warranted in this by law.

A. Did you ever receive the communion?

W. Yes, my lord.

A. Where?

W. At Kildwick.

A. At whose hands?

W. At the hands of the pastor.

A. When?

W. At the last communion, if I remember right.

A. You must ever take this advantage.

W. My lord, seeing I answer upon mine oath, you should not think the worse of me, because I am so careful not to speak wrong, or that which is not true.

H. You do not bury the dead according to the book.

W. I do.

H. You do not meet the corpse at the church-stile, and walk before it into the church.

W. Though I have sometimes done this, the book doth not bind me to do any such thing.

H. You do not read the prayers and places of scripture appointed.

W. I do.

H. You omit the prayers.

W. Sometimes I do, and sometimes I do not.

A. What is the next article?

F. You have gone from your own ordinary, without his consent, and have received orders from another bishop.

W. My own ordinary giveth no orders; but if his consent be his dimissary, I had his consent.

A. If you have his dimissary, shew it us.

W. See, it is here, my lord.

A. What is the next article?

F. You have taken upon you to say service without any authority by license or toleration from your ordinary.

W. I have all the authority which the orders of a deacon can give; and I hope that is sufficient to say the service.

F. You confess yourself that you were born in Kildwick parish.

W. Yes.

F. Do you acknowledge yourself to belong to this diocese, and submit yourself to the authority of your diocesan?

W. I acknowledge all this.

A. You have a haughty and a proud spirit.

W. I confess, my lord, I am not free from any one sin; but I hope that sin hath not so great a power over me as you represent.

A. Nay, you care not for mine authority.

W. My lord, I reverence your authority.

Swinborn. That is not likely, Mr. Wilson, seeing you have so much disobeyed.

W. And that disobedience is no likely argument to disprove my reverence of his authority. If your argument were good, few subjects would be found who reverence even the queen's authority.

A. You can speak for yourself I warrant you. But what say you of your calling? The scripture mentions only the offices of apostles, prophets, evangelists, pastors, and doctors. Which of these then have you?

W. The office of a doctor or teacher.

A. Where do you exercise it?

W. At Kildwick.

A. Who called you?

W. The minister and the people of that place earnestly entreated me to teach and instruct them.

A. Tush! that is nothing.

W. But it hath been something in time past.

A. Lo! this fellow would have ministers to be elected by consent of the people!

W. My lord, the word of God is plain enough upon that point, and this you know well enough yourself. Your grace made this sufficiently manifest in refusing me to be at Skipton, unless the people would consent to receive me.

A. That I did, because I would not intrude you upon them.

W. Then it follows, that you think *intrusion* is not the right calling; and on the contrary, that the right calling is by the consent or choice of the people.

A. There is no end to your talk.

W. Yes, my lord, but I had the license of your own word for that place.

A. That is true; but it was a donor.

W. And when the donor came, I stayed.

A. Yes, but you have preached there since that time.

W. I have, indeed, preached there once; which, I hope, is not so great a crime, but that your grace will deal favourably with me, and thus cause me the more to revere and esteem you.*

Mr. Wilson's first examination being concluded, the good man was taken away and sent to prison, where he remained

* MS. Register, p. 782—784.

for some time. At length, he was brought to a second examination at Bishopsthorp, when the archbishop opened the business by affirming, that Mr. Wilson had been guilty of the most wilful disobedience, and malicious contempt. His lordship used very opprobrious language, as if he had been arraigned for treason or rebellion, exulting, at the same time, in his own favourable dealing with him. Also, he declared that before Mr. Wilson should be discharged, he should confess both in open court, and publicly in the church, how greatly he had offended; to which Mr. Wilson made the following reply:

W. My lord, I hope you will find it more difficult to prove me guilty of those odious crimes which you say I am guilty of, than to charge me with them. And as to your favour, when I find it, I shall acknowledge it. Hitherto I have felt nothing but extremity, bringing my ministry into open disgrace, and my person into public reproach.

A. You see the stubbornness of this fellow. I purposed to have discharged him, the second day of his imprisonment, and would have done it, if he had sued for it. And though he hath now been a week in prison, the pride of his heart would not let him once sue for his liberty.

W. It was neither my pride, nor my stubbornness, as you uncharitably misrepresent, and slanderously magnify against me; but my ignorance of the prisoner's duty, that I did not su, to your grace for liberty.

A. We shall never make an end, if we babble with him thus. Will you yield to the conditions?*

W. My lord, I beseech you consider those conditions with impartiality, and, I hope, your grace will not urge me. My imprisonment will greatly injure my ministry, and bring reproach upon my person; but to do open penance before the people, will be worse than all. Therefore, I beseech your lordship not to reward one evil, by inflicting another which is much greater.

A. These are only your imaginations. Tell us plainly: Will you subscribe the bond?

W. My lord, I must take all the care in my power to preserve my ministry from the contempt of the wicked. And seeing how much harm it would be likely to do to the church of God, I cannot in any wise subscribe unto it.

* The conditions here referred to, and afterwards often mentioned, were, that he should confess before the archbishop, and publicly in the church where he had preached, the great offence he had committed, and enter into a bond to fulfil the same.

A. See again the stubbornness of this arrogant fool! But I tell thee, thou may and shalt subscribe unto it.

W. And I answer, that, by the help of God, I neither may, nor ever will, subscribe unto it. Such unmerciful and cruel dealings are too bad among professing christians. The Lord grant me patience, and I shall be satisfied.

A. I always thought what a stir we should have with him. But thou persuadest people to meetings and private conventicles.

W. My lord, you now remind me of a duty which I have hitherto neglected; but by the grace of God I will remember it hereafter, and will exhort the people of God to meet together, and to edify and comfort one another with what they have learned. And this, by the help of God, I mean to do; though I hear that for so doing, one of the Lord's servants is committed a close prisoner.

A. Will you then defend his doings to be lawful?

W. I will defend the lawfulness of God's people meeting together, to confer upon the points of religion or the doctrines taught them out of the word of God, to sing psalms, and to pray together. I hear of no other things for which he was committed. And I am sure your grace will not deny these things to be lawful.

A. But he gathered *night-assemblies*, contrary to law. Will you defend them also?

W. Certain religious householders requested him and others to meet at night in their houses. Shall we then say that he collected night-assemblies? I do defend by the word of God, that to meet together for the above purposes, whether in the night or the day, is lawful. Yet I would have persons to satisfy the law of the realm, as much as they can with a good conscience.

A. If we follow him thus, we shall never come to an end. Will you subscribe the bond?

W. I have answered that already. I refuse not to do any thing that is lawful. If you can prove out of the word of God, that I may do it with a good conscience, I am ready to yield; otherwise I cannot, and I will not, subscribe. I will be bound, however, to leave your province in a fortnight.

S. You had then better go out of his grace's province to make your submission.

W. That is more than I say, Mr. Swinborn: but I would rather go out of his province and twenty others;

yea, out of the world, and this soul out of this body, than I would subscribe to that submission.

A. I hear that in prison thou hast great liberty, and that thou lovest it. It is that which maketh thee so bold and stubborn, but I will remove thee thence.

W. I have no cause to complain of my keeper. And as to my liberty, it is confined within the walls of the castle. I know not how you would have me handled, unless you would have me into the lower prison, where you would soon have my skin for your fees: But you can do nothing, except it be given you from above.

A. I tell thee plainly, that if thou wilt not yield, I will remove thee to Hull jail, and afterwards to other places.

W. My lord, the word of God will strengthen and comfort me, more than your threatenings can hurt me or make me afraid. I care not for all your prisons. Remove me where you please. God will strengthen me against all your extremities. I will not yield so long as I live, and so long as the word of God persuades me to the contrary.

A. Thou art an *arrogant puritan*.

W. Gross errors and slanderous abuses have been cast upon the godly in all ages. Your charges against me are uncharitable and unjust.

A. Thou art a rebel, an enemy to her majesty, and an underminer of the state.

W. These speeches savour not of the spirit of God. I am as true a subject, and as good a friend to her majesty and the state, according to my ability, as you are.

A. I tell thee, the queen said, that these puritans are greater enemies to her than the papists.

W. What just cause she had so to say, all the world knoweth; and the Lord will one day judge the numerous traitorous conspiracies that have been detected. When did any, who are slanderously called puritans, give the least cause of any such suspicion? Their lives and writings testify to all the world, how far they are from such things. Therefore, they who charge them with these things, have the greater sin.

A. If we suffer thee to prattle, thy tongue will never cease. Therefore, that we may make an end of it, I counsel thee to admit the conditions proposed.

W. If your grace will shew me the least warrant from the word of God, I am ready to submit. Though you call my answers by what name you please, they are not deserving of your reproach.

A. Will you yield to the conditions?

W. My mind is so well settled already, that I can see no reason to alter it. Therefore, I cannot yield to the conditions.

A. Perhaps you think it is very hard dealing to be tied to *read* it. Will you then yield, if we give you liberty to use your own words?

W. I strive not about the *manner*, but the *matter;* and I utterly refuse to do any such thing, either in my own words or any others.

A. What! surely you can say two words, even that you have preached without license. In so doing, you shall have my favour more than you think of.

W. My lord, let me have your favour only according to my behaviour in a good and just cause; but the word of God will persuade more than either your threatenings or promises. So while I see the word of God favouring me in the present case, I will never yield to speak two words, nor even one word, to any such purpose.

A. Choose then for yourself, whether you will be excommunicated out of my diocese, or return to prison, or yield to the conditions required.

W. My lord, I hope that christian charity and brotherly dealing will not bring me into any of those extremities.

A. No! but you shall observe one of them.*

Mr. Wilson's second examination being thus concluded, he was immediately sent back to prison. After confinement for some time, by the appointment of the archbishop, he appeared before the commissioners at the dean's house in the city of York, his grace being absent. Upon the commencement of his third examination, a new bond was produced, in which he was required not to exercise any part of his ministry within the archbishop's province, without further license; nor, during his silence, allowed to come within Kildwick church, the place of his ordinary labours. This being read, he was addressed as follows:

D. Mr. Wilson, what say you of this?

W. I say it is marvellously strange dealing, that one extremity must drive out another. Excommunication from Kildwick church must drive out the public confession before required. Will you neither suffer me to preach

* MS. Register, p. 784—786.

there, nor to hear others? This is very hard dealing. God willing, I will never yield unto it.

D. Do as you please. Do as you please.

W. I was born and brought up in that parish, and I am bound to attend there by the laws of the realm. Do you then sit here to execute the law, and will you bind me to act contrary to the law?

Palmer. Erase it, erase it, for shame! It is a thing never before heard of, that a man should be bound from attending at his own parish church.

Proctor. I will put this in its place, "that he shall never come there to preach."

W. Will you put in that, Mr. Proctor? Will you first exclude me from his whole province, and then exclude me from that particular place?

D. What else have you for him to do?

P. He must confess that before us, which he would not acknowledge publicly in the church.

D. Then read it unto him.

W. I will confess these things neither publicly, nor privately. But if you allow me, I will separate those things which are true, from those which are false.

D. Give him the paper.

He then took the paper, and told them what was true, and what was false. This being done, and the good man having bound himself to preach no more in the archbishop's province, he was released, ascribing honour and praise to God for his merciful deliverance.*

Mr. Wilson having obtained his liberty, though excluded from all usefulness in the province of York, went to London, and, during the same year, frequently preached at Alhallows in Thames-street. Also, by the allowance of the minister of St. Michael's, Cornhill, he delivered a sermon there; for which Bishop Aylmer silenced him the very next day, and summoned him, and the church-wardens of Alhallows, to appear before him the Saturday following. Mr. Wilson not seeing the bishop's officer when he left the information at his lodgings; nor knowing what warrant he had for what he did, refused to appear. But one of the church-wardens appeared, when, though the bishop was not present, Dr. Stanhope pronounced upon them both the sentence of excommunication; upon the one for not appearing, and upon the other for suffering Mr. Wilson to

* MS. Register, p. 784—786.

preach without a license. This excellent minister was thus exercised with tribulations in the south, as well as in the north.

At length, our divine finding that the high commissioners, with Aylmer and Whitgift at their head, were anxious to apprehend him; that they had issued several warrants for this purpose; that a printed order was sent to all the churches in London and its vicinity, that none should preach without a license; and that his name, with several others, was particularly mentioned,* he wisely concealed himself for a season, and retired into the north. Towards the close of the year, he returned to London; and after his arrival, Mr. Glover and Mr. Weblin, two of his cordial friends living in the parish of Alhallows, waited upon Archbishop Whitgift at Lambeth, soliciting his favour in behalf of Mr. Wilson. They had no sooner mentioned his name, than his lordship asked, "What that factious fellow who intruded himself into the church in Cornhill, and there delivered a seditious sermon?" "Yes," said Mr. Glover, "that is the man; but he hopeth to clear himself of all faction, intrusion, and sedition." "Let him then come to me any day after tomorrow," said the archbishop, "and I will say more about him." Therefore, December 1st, Mr. Wilson and his friends

* The worthy divines whose names accompanied this order, were Mr. Wilson, Mr. Davison, Mr. Barber, Mr. Wigginton, Mr. Gifford, Mr. Carew, and some others. The order itself, dated August 16, 1587, being descriptive of the spirit of the times, was the following:—"Whereas sundry "ministers, preachers, have lately come into the city of London and "the suburbs; some of them not being ministers, some having no sufficient warrant for their calling; and others having been detected in "the country, have taken upon them to preach publicly in the city, to the "great infamy of their calling: and some of them in their preaching, "have stirred up the people to innovation, rather than sought the peace of "the church. These are, therefore, in her majesty's name, by virtue of "her high commission for causes ecclesiastical to us and others directed, "strictly to enjoin, command, and charge, all parsons, vicars, curates, and "church-wardens, of all churches in the city of London and the suburbs "thereof, as well in places exempt as not exempt, that neither they nor "any of them, do suffer any to preach in their churches, or to read any "lectures, they not being in their own cures; but only such whose licenses "they shall first have seen and read, and whom they shall find to be "licensed thereto, either by the queen's majesty, or by one of the universities, or by the Lord Archbishop of Canterbury, or the Bishop of "London, for the time being. And that this may be published, and take "the better effect, we will that a true copy thereof shall be taken and "delivered to every curate and church-warden of all the churches aforesaid. Signed,

"John Canterbury, Ed. Stanhope,
"John London, Ric. Cosins."
"Val. Dale,

MS. Register, p. 835.

waited upon his grace at Lambeth; and upon their appearance, after asking Mr. Wilson his name, where he was born, and where educated, the archbishop thus addressed him:

Archbishop. Did not you intrude yourself into a church in Cornhill, and there preach a seditious sermon?

Wilson. That I preached there is certainly true; but there was nothing seditious. And as to intrusion, I will prove upon the oath of honest men, that I had the minister's consent, both before and after I came into the church.

A. Did you not then intrude yourself?

W. I will prove, I say, upon the oath of honest men, that it is an impudent falsehood.

A. Say you so. I did not know this before.

W. It is malice that hath propagated these things.

A. But why did you not remain in your own country?

W. Because I cannot and may not place myself where I please, much less in mine own country; for I must go where I am called, and be placed where the Lord shall appoint.

A. If you will then be placed here, you must subscribe to certain articles.

W. I will subscribe to any thing that is lawful.

A. Do you mean any thing according to law?

W. Surely, I dare very well say so. But I meant the law of God, which is the only rule of conscience.

A. You must subscribe to those articles.

W. I must first see them, and then I can answer you.

A. There is good reason why you should see them; and therefore I refer you to my lord of London. If he will allow you, I will not disallow you. But you Londoners, (speaking to Mr. Glover and Mr. Weblin) are so much given to novelty, that if there be one man more new than others, him you will have.

Glover. Surely, my lord, we cannot be justly accused of novelty. For we have had neither new nor old at our church since I knew the place, having now only a drunken reader, who can do us no good.

A. Well, you know my mind about this matter.

Stanhope. You must be sworn.

W. To what must I be sworn.

S. You shall know that afterwards.

W. No, by your leave, sir, I will see the articles before I take any oath.

S. No, you may not see them till you are sworn.

W. I will not swear till I see them. It is hard dealing

to make men swear to they know not what. You may ask me things which it is not lawful for me to make known.

S. What are those things?

W. It is against the law of the land, that a man should be sworn to accuse himself. And by this oath, you may urge me to disclose the secret things of my heart, or the secrets of my friends, both of which are unnatural and unlawful. Such dealing is intolerable and cruel. Let me see the articles; and if I may lawfully answer them, I will do it upon my oath.

S. Let him then see the articles.

W. Setting aside all circumstantial questions, I will answer these articles upon my oath.

S. Well, all other matters shall be set aside.

W. I will make a true answer to these articles, so help me God.*

S. I can tell you, Mr. Wilson, if you mean to preach here, you must also minister the communion, at least thrice every year.

W. There is one to do that in the place already.

S. That is no matter. You must join him in that action, to shew that you do not divide your ministry.

W. My ministry shall be to preach the word only.

S. The laws of the realm allow of no such ministry.

W. But the laws of God do.

S. But I am set to examine the laws of the realm.

W. And I am set to maintain the laws of God, and to declare the truth of them.

S. It must be as I tell you. And that is not all: you must subscribe to certain articles.

W. What are those articles?

S. I think they are here. Read them, and tell me what you think of them.

W. I think it is unlawful to subscribe to them.

S. What is there you dislike?

W. Many things, and the *second* article altogether.

S. Shew me this at large.

* These articles, *nineteen* in number, consist of certain things professedly collected from his sermon at Cornhill. They are said to have been his expressions, and are mostly against pluralities, nonresidents, and idle, ungodly, and nonpreaching ministers. In one of them he is charged with having said of such ministers, "They eat up the sins of the people." And in another, "That by the word of God, it is necessary that every congregation should have a preaching minister." This is a specimen of the treasonable charges brought against Mr. Wilson; but the whole, together with his answers, is too long to be inserted.—*MS. Register*, p. 820—821.

W. I fear you seek some advantage against me.

S. I promise you, that you shall have no hurt for any thing you may speak here.

W. I dislike private baptism by laymen or women.

S. You know my lord of Canterbury denies that the book alloweth any such thing.

W. It is too plain to be denied. And though he do deny it, he alloweth that if a woman or any private person perform the action, it is a sacrament, and is not to be renewed by the minister. Where there no other things, this is sufficient to keep me from subscribing.

S. But if you may have favour in that point, will you yield to the rest?

W. I wish they were such things, that I could yield to them.

S. What else then do you dislike.

W. The book of making bishops and ministers.

S. Why so?

W. Because I find no such thing done by one man, and in that manner, in the word of God.

S. Then I can say nothing to you.

W. But I could say something to you, sir, if you would patiently hear me.

S. What is that? Say what you please.

W. If you can shew me any statute, now in force in England, which requireth me to subscribe to the Book of Common Prayer, to the book of making bishops and ministers, and to the whole book of articles; I will promise before you and these people, that I will subscribe. But if I offer my hand to subscribe, as far as any statute doth require, why is the offer not admitted? or by what law can it be rejected?

S. There is a statute which *alloweth* these things. This, I think you will not deny.

W. I do not deny it. But where is the statute which *commandeth* subscription to them?

S. The bishops have a commission from her majesty, to deal in these matters according to their own *discretion.*

W. But neither their commission, nor their discretion, may oppose the discreet laws made by her majesty and parliament. If they do, I dare boldly say, that they abuse her majesty, her subjects, and their own commission.

S. Take heed what you say. You must yield to this subscription, or you cannot be admitted. Besides, you are no proper minister, and were never authorized to preach.

W. That is a slander. For I am a deacon, and was licensed to preach by the present Archbishop of York.

S. What think you of the titles of *grace*, *lord*, and others of the same kind?

W. I think the law doth require them.

S. Do you take them to be lawful?

W. Yes, they are lawful, if you mean according to law.*

Here the conversation closed, when Mr. Wilson was suspended, and admonished to appear before the Bishop of London and other commissioners, on the Tuesday following. This was the unkind usage he met with, though at the beginning of the conference, he was promised that no evil should befall him for what he might say. The reader will here see how little such persons were to be trusted. However, according to appointment, the good man appeared before the bishop, Dr. Stanhope, Dr. Walker, Mr. Mullins, and others. When he was called, his lordship said nothing, but left the management of the case wholly to the other commissioners, when his former opponent thus addressed him:

S. Mr. Wilson, you remember certain articles exhibited against you, as collected out of your sermon preached at St. Michael's in Cornhill. You also confessed that you were not a minister, but a deacon, and licensed to preach by the present Archbishop of York, and not by my lord of London.

W. I remember these things well, and many others.

Mullins. It was not necessary that all things should be set down.

W. Neither was it necessary he should mention only those things, when I spoke many others.

S. Well, sir, you remember I did suspend you from preaching, which sentence, by the judgment of the court, must stand. As for other matters, Dr. Walker and Mr. Mullins will attend unto them next term.

W. It is hard dealing to keep a man so long in suspense, and for so small a matter. I am chargeable either to myself, or friends, or both. I have been almost a month in town already, and now I must be put off so long a time. This is more than christian charity would do. Therefore, I pray you, sir, that I may have a more speedy dispatch.

S. You may apply to them, and they will perhaps make greater haste in this matter. (Mr. Mullins having read the charges against Mr. Wilson, thus addressed him:)

* MS. Register, p. 828—832.

M. What are these things? Who is the accuser? And who is accused?

W. Who is the accuser, I know not; but they say they are articles objected against me.

M. Who troubleth us with such things? There is no accuser; and no man accused. There is no man or thing particularly mentioned, but all is expressed in general terms. What can we do with such things?

W. I cannot tell. But I suffer the greater wrong, being carried up and down, and tossed to and fro, for nothing.

M. Who began this matter? And who bade you follow it?

W. Who began it, I know not. But I am appointed to desire you to make an end of it. I have been much troubled in your courts; and my friends have been much charged in paying money, I cannot tell for what.

M. I wish their money was in their bellies.

W. I wish rather it was in their purses. But, I pray you, sir, let the case be ended.

M. I have other business to mind.

W. If my case be of so small a moment, you may soon finish it. I pray you, therefore, let charity move you to make an end of it, that I may be no more troubled about it.

Walker. The more we consider your case, the worse we find it. There are such words and sayings as become a railer, rather than a sober preacher.

W. The words and sayings are not mine, but the malicious accuser's, who set them down thus to make me the more odious.

Walk. Why then do you confess them to be yours, in your answer?

W. I do not confess the *words*, but the substance of the matter. For the register would not take down my answers in mine own words, but would write them as they are there.

Walk. I tell thee they are full of bitterness, malice, and slander.

W. Sir, I came for your certificate to make an end of it, as you promised me.

Walk. I tell thee, thou shalt have none of our certificate. The register shall have it, and not shew it thee till the next term.

W. That is very hard dealing.

Walk. What sayest thou? Do we do thee any wrong?

W. Yes, sir, even you.

Walk. What sayest thou, boy? Thou hast neither learning, nor manners in thee.

W. I have no less for what you say. And as to manners, you have no great cause to find fault.

Walk. Thou art an ass; thou art a dolt; thou art a beardless boy. Thou hast neither learning, nor humanity in thee.

W. Your words, sir, do not make me worse. We must and do bear these things at your hands, and have never requited you with the like.

Mr. Wilson having received the above abusive language, was obliged to depart without the examination of his case, and without obtaining his certificate, though his ecclesiastical judges had promised to give it him. He waited upon them repeatedly for the same purpose, but with no better success; and it appears extremely doubtful whether he ever obtained it, or whether he was ever restored to his ministry.*

JOHN ELLISTON was a most diligent and pious minister, beneficed at Preston in Northamptonshire, where he laboured much to reform his parish, by frequent preaching and catechizing. But he endured manifold troubles for his nonconformity. His enemies being inclined to popery, brought complaints against him to the chancellor of Peterborough, that he did not wear the surplice, read the litany, nor use the cross in baptism. He was, therefore, indicted at the assizes; but after his case was heard before the judge, he was dismissed. Mr. Elliston having left an account of his various troubles, let us hear him speak for himself.

"Having been pastor of Preston," says he, "about ten weeks, and being desirous to instruct the people according to my ability, some of my parishioners, persons much inclined towards popery, complained of me to Dr. Ellis, the chancellor, and the case was heard before the judge at the assizes, when I was charged with not wearing the surplice, not reading the litany, and not using the cross in baptism; but was acquitted and dismissed. After this, they exhibited a charge against me to Dr. Scambler, bishop of Peterborough, consisting of *sixteen* articles. Upon my appearance before the bishop, February 10, 1584, he asked me whether I would subscribe; but when I refused, he treated me with much abusive language.

"The first article charged against me, was, that I did not wear the surplice.—I said, I did not refuse it, and so denied the charge.

* MS. Register, p. 832—834.

"The second article was, that I did not use the cross in baptism. And when the bishop asked me why I did not, I replied, that I did not use it, because it was not required in the word of God. At this he scoffed, saying, neither is it required what kind of boots you shall wear. I replied, that my boots were not offensive, and what kind I shall wear is at my discretion, and therefore lawful; but God hath set down the holy sacraments in his word, and not left the ordering to our discretion. He then abused me as before.

"In the next place, when he asked me why I catechized all persons, both old and young, I replied, that I had the charge of all, and must, therefore, instruct all. When he said that old people should not be catechized, and that they did not stand in need of it, I desired him to promote, and not to hinder good things.

"Another charge was, that I omitted the litany on sabbath days. When I replied, that I preached on sabbath days, he said, that whether I preached or not, the litany must be read. When he asked why I kept persons from the communion, I answered, because they would not submit to be examined. He then said, that I should admit them, if they could say the Lord's prayer and ten commandments.

"There were many other articles charged against me," says Mr. Elliston, "to each of which I answered as the occasion served. At my departure, he suspended me, saying, I should not remain in his diocese if I would not subscribe. I said, if I do not remain in your diocese, the earth is the Lord's, and he hath a place for me to live in; and so I departed.

"March 6th following, he cited me, and several other ministers, to appear before him, and required us to subscribe. And May 30th he cited me a third time; but not having sufficient warning, he deprived me before I could appear before him. I, therefore, appealed against his unjust sentence, and told him that he did not deal with me with uprightness, though I wished to discharge my duties with a good conscience; and that he treated others with great kindness, if they would only subscribe, though they had neither learning nor honesty. But if you go about to discredit us, you will gain no credit to yourself. After this I had four journies to Peterborough; and though it was at least thirty-six miles from the place where I lived, I went seven times in little more than one year.

"April 6th I went to London for an inhibition; and upon my return, I went again to Peterborough, to have it served on the bishop. And on ascension-day, Archbishop Whitgift cited me to appear before him, who, by this means, sought to prevent me from prosecuting my appeal. When I appeared before the archbishop, he urged me to subscribe, but I refused. He then said, he had matter against me in the high commission; and I was therefore examined, but obtained leave to return home till the next term. But before the next term, the archbishop sent his pursuivant for me. This was my third journey to London.

"When I appeared before his grace, two articles were brought against me. 1. 'That at morning prayer on Whit-sunday, I did only read two psalms and two chapters, and then preached. And, 2. That preaching out of the second psalm, and railing against my enemies, I affirmed, that they would all be damned, who troubled me.' But when they heard my answers to those articles, I was dismissed; though the fees of the pursuivant, and other expenses, were very considerable. After this I was called up to London several times, and appeared sometimes before the Archbishop, and sometimes before the Bishop of London.

"These my troubles," says the good man, "endured almost three years, during which time, I had ten journies to London, seven to Peterborough, many to Leicester and Northampton, and one to Cambridge."* By the expense unavoidably attending so many journies, Mr. Elliston was almost ruined. He was also a long time deprived of his living. He was a zealous and peaceable nonconformist, and, in the year 1587, was a member in the classis at Daventry, and often attended the associations of the puritans. A minister of the same name was preferred to the rectory of Chignal-Smeby in Essex, in the year 1597, but resigned it by death previous to September 20, 1617; when the next incumbent entered upon the benefice. We are not able to learn whether this was the same person.†

Robert Crowley, A. M.—This distinguished person was born in Gloucestershire,‡ and educated in Magdalen college, Oxford. In the year 1542, having been at the university eight years, he was elected probationer fellow. Upon the accession of King Edward, he removed to London, and was for some time a printer and bookseller, and preached occasionally as opportunity offered. He was a

* MS. Register, p. 579—592. † Newcourt's Repert. Eccl. vol. ii. p. 139.

‡ Fuller says he was born in Northamptonshire.—*Worthies*, pt. ii. p. 290.

man of excellent parts and eminent piety, and received ordination from Bishop Ridley, afterwards the famous martyr.* Upon the accession of Queen Mary, he withdrew from the storm, and fled to Frankfort, where he was involved in the troubles occasioned by Dr. Cox and his party. His name, together with the names of many of his brethren, is annexed to "The Form of Discipline reformed and confirmed by the Church and Magistrates of that city."†

Upon the death of Queen Mary, and the accession of her sister Elizabeth, Mr. Crowley returned from exile, and obtained some preferment in the church. In the year 1563, he had the prebend of Mora, of which, however, he was deprived in 1565; most probably for nonconformity. In 1566, he became vicar of St. Giles's, near Cripplegate, London, where he was much followed and respected. In 1576, he was collated to the vicarage of St. Lawrence Jewry, in the city, which, however, he did not hold long; for the living became void in 1578.‡ It appears also, that soon after his return from exile, he became archdeacon of Hereford. He sat in the convocation of 1562, and subscribed the articles, together with the paper of requests then presented to the house, desiring a further reformation of the church.§ He was a learned and popular preacher; therefore, October 15, 1559, he was nominated to preach the sermon at Paul's cross.

Early in the reign of Queen Elizabeth, one Campneys, a turbulent and abusive pelagian, sought to disturb the peace of the church, by publishing a book against the received doctrine of predestination, though he had not the courage to affix his name to it. This virulent publication was answered by Mr. Crowley and Mr. John Veron, one of the queen's chaplains, and both the learned replies were approved and licensed by public authority.‖

Soon after the accession of Queen Elizabeth, her majesty was greatly offended with many of the clergy, especially those in the city of London, for refusing to wear the square cap, the tippet, and the surplice. "And it is marvellous," says Mr. Strype, "how much these habits were abhorred by many honest, well-meaning men, accounting them the relics of antichrist, and that they ought not to be used in the church of Christ. Mr. Crowley called them *conjuring*

* Wood's Athenæ, vol. i. p. 190.—Strype's Parker, p. 218.
† Troubles at Frankeford, p. 114.
‡ Newcourt's Repert. Eccl. vol. i. p. 181.
§ Strype's Annals, vol. i. p. 290. vol. ii. Adden. to Appen. p. 15.
‖ Toplady's Historic Proof, vol. ii. p. 184, 185.

garments of popery, and would not, therefore, be persuaded to wear them."* Previous to the year 1566, this worthy servant of Christ was suspended; and though the cause of his suspension is not mentioned, it was, undoubtedly, his nonconformity to those rites and ceremonies which he accounted popish, superstitious, and unlawful.

During the same year he was involved in other troubles. For in the month of April, seeing a corpse coming to be buried at his church, attended by clerks in their surplices singing before it, he threatened to shut the church-doors against them; but the singing-men resisted, being resolved to go through with their work, till the alderman's deputy threatened to put them in the stocks for breaking the peace. Upon this, they slunk away. But complaint was made to Archbishop Parker and other commissioners, and Mr. Crowley was summoned to appear before them. Accordingly, April 4th, he appeared before the Archbishop, the Bishop of London, and the rest of their colleagues. During his examination, says our author, there fell from his lips several *fond paradoxes*, tending to anabaptism. These fond paradoxes, as he is pleased to call them, were the following: When speaking of a call to the ministry, he said, "A man may have a motion in his conscience to preach, without any external call. And, as *pastor*, he would resist the surplice-men." When the commissioners asked him whether he would resist a minister thus sent to him, (meaning in his surplice) he said, "That till he was deprived, his conscience would move him so to do." These are his fond paradoxes, said to be of so dangerous a tendency! When the archbishop discharged him from his flock and his parish, he refused to be deprived contrary to law, saying, "he would be committed to prison, rather than suffer a *wolf* to come to his flock." The good man was, therefore, deprived of his living, separated from his flock, and committed to prison. Also, the alderman's deputy mentioned above, for taking his part against the surplice-men, was obliged to enter into a bond of a hundred pounds, to be ready when called. "So gentle," says Mr. "Strype, was our archbishop in his censure of so great a fault!"†

How long Mr. Crowley remained a prisoner, we have not been able to learn. Certain it is, that he continued under

* Strype's Parker, p. 151. † Ibid. p. 213.

confinement some time. The mild archbishop informed the secretary how he had dealt with him, and that he could not have treated him otherwise, considering his behaviour, and especially his saying, that he would not suffer the wolf to come to his flock. By the *wolf*, Mr. Crowley appears to have meant a minister in a surplice; and this expression seems to have been a very material part of the crime for which he was censured. The Lord's day following his deprivation and commitment, the archbishop sent Mr. Bickley, his chaplain, to preach in his place.

In the year 1582, Mr. Crowley was very diligent in disputing with certain popish priests, confined in the Tower, under sentence of death. With one of them, named Kirby, he took much pains, and laboured to the utmost of his power, to convince him of his error, in maintaining the lawfulness of the pope's deposing princes. He attended them to the place of execution, where he used all his endeavours to convince Kirby of the absurdity of those principles for which he was about to suffer. He urged from Rom. xiii. and John xix., that, as princes receive their authority from God alone, they could not be deposed by any other power. When Kirby asked whether a prince guilty of turcism, atheism, or infidelity, might not be deposed, it is said, that Mr. Crowley and the rest of the ministers answered very learnedly in the negative. On this occasion, our divine observed, "That if a prince fall into any such errors, he is indeed punishable. But by whom? Not by any earthly prince; but by that heavenly prince, who gave him his authority; and who, seeing him abuse it, will, in justice, correct him for so doing."*

Mr. Crowley was a man of a most holy and exemplary life, a pious, learned, and laborious preacher, and much beloved by his people.† Mr. Strype denominates him a learned and zealous man, possessing great parts and eminent piety.‡ Wood says, that he lived to a considerable age, and spent his life chiefly in labouring to propagate and settle the protestant religion.§ He was a most learned and laborious writer, as appears from his numerous works, many of which were written against the errors of popery. He died June 18, 1588, and his remains were interred in the chancel of St. Giles's church, where he had been vicar. The following

* Strype's Parker, p. 219. † MS. *penes me.*
‡ Strype's Annals, vol. i. p. 136.—Life of Parker, p. 219.
§ Wood's Athenæ Oxon. vol. i. p. 191.

monumental inscription, engraven on a brass plate, was afterwards erected to his memory :*

Here lieth the body
of ROBERT CROWLEY, clerk,
late vicar of this parish,
who departed this life the 18 day of June,
in the year 1588.

His WORKS.—1. The Supper of the Lord after the true meaning of the Sixth of John, and the xi of the 1 Epistle to the Corinthians. And incidentally in the Exposition of the Supper, is confuted the Letter of Mr. Thomas More against Joh. Frith, 1533.—2. Confutation of Nicholas Shaxton, Bishop of Sarum, his Recantation of 13 Articles at the Burning of Mrs. Anne Askew, 1546.—3. Explicatio petetoria (ad Parliamentum) adversus expilatores plebis, published in English in 1548.—4. Confutation of Miles Hoggard's wicked Ballad made in Defence of Transubstantiation of the Sacrament, 1548.—5. The Voice of the last Trumpet blown by the seventh Angel, containing twelve Lessons, 1549.—6. Translation of the Psalms of David, 1549.—7. The Litany with Hymns, 1549.—8. David's Psalms turned into Metre, 1549.—9. The Visions of Pierce Plowman, 1550.—10. Pleasure and Pain, Heaven and Hell. Remember these four and all shall be well, 1550.—11. Way to Wealth, wherein is plainly a most present Remedy for Sedition, 1550.—12. One and thirty Epigrams, wherein are briefly touched so many Abuses, that may, and ought to, be put away, 1550.—13. An Apologie of those English Preachers and Writers, which Cerberus the Three-headed Dog of Hell, chargeth with false Doctrine under the name of Predestination, 1566.—14. Of the Signes and Tokens of the latter Day, 1567.—15. A Setting open of the subtle Sophistry of Tho. Watson, D. D. which he used in his two Sermons preached before Qu. Mary, in Lent 1553, concerning the real Presence in the Sacrament, 1569.†—16. Sermon in the Chappell at Gilde-hall in London, 29 Sept. 1574, before the Lord Mayor and the whole state of the Citie, on Psalme cxxxix. 21, &c., 1575.—17. Answer to Tho. Pound in six Reasons, wherein he sheweth that the Scriptures must be judged by the Church, 1581.—18. Brief Discourse concerning those four usual Notes whereby Christ's Catholick Church is known, 1581.—19. Replication to that lewd Answer which Frier Joh. Francis (of the Minimies order in Nigeon, near Paris) hath made to a Letter that his Mother caused to be sent to him out of England, 1586.—20. Deliberate Aunsweare to a Papist, proving that Papists are Antichristian Schismatics, and that Religious Protestants are indeed true Catholicks, 1587.—21. The Schoole of Vertue and Book of good Nurture, teaching Children and Youths their Duties, 1588.—22. Dialogue between Lent and Libertie, wherein is declared that Lent is a meer Invention of Man.

* Stow's Survey of London, b. iii. p. 83.

† Mr. Strype says, that these sermons being very much admired, and preventing many from embracing the protestant religion, ought to have been answered much sooner.—*Strype's Annals*, vol. i. p. 540.

NICHOLAS CRANE was educated at Cambridge, a divine of great learning, and a zealous nonconformist. He was minister of Roehampton in Surrey, but falling under the displeasure of the prelates, he was more than once cast into prison, and at last he died in Newgate, for nonconformity. In the year 1569, Mr. Crane, and Mr. William Bonham, were licensed to preach by Bishop Grindal. Their licenses are said to have been granted upon condition that they should avoid all conventicles, and all other things contrary to the order established in this kingdom.

Afterwards, the two divines were apprehended and cast into prison for nonconformity, where they remained more than twelve months, and were then released. But persisting in their nonconformity, and not keeping to the exact order established in the church of England, Mr. Crane was silenced from preaching within the diocese of London, and Mr. Bonham was again committed to prison;* but it does not appear how long they continued under the ecclesiastical censure.†

Mr. Crane was a leading man among the nonconformists of his time, and, in the year 1572, united with his brethren in the erection of the presbyterian church at Wandsworth in Surrey.‡ His exceptions against subscription to the Book of Common Prayer, are still on record. They were delivered most probably upon his appearance before the ecclesiastical commissioners, and were chiefly the following:—"He excepted against reading the apocryphal books in public worship, to the exclusion of some parts of canonical scripture:—Against that part of the ordination service, *receive the Holy Ghost, &c.*:—Against the interrogatories in baptism proposed to infants who cannot give any answer:—Against the cross in baptism, which has been often used to superstitious purposes:—Against private baptism, which the Book of Common Prayer allows to be administered by persons not ordained:—Against the gospel appointed to be read the sabbath after Easter, which is taken from the mass book, and is manifestly untrue when compared with scripture. He concludes by observing, that if these and some other things equally erroneous, were reformed, it would please Almighty God; the ministers of Christ would be more firmly united against their common enemy, the papists; many of God's ministers and people now weeping,

* See Art. Bonham.

† Strype's Grindal, p. 153—155.—MS. Chronology, vol. ii. p. 405. (6.)

‡ Fuller's Church Hist. b. ix. p. 103.

would rejoice; many able students would be encouraged to enter the ministry; and the religion of Jesus Christ would more extensively prevail."*

In the year 1583, Mr. Crane, with nine other learned divines of Cambridge, wrote to Mr. Thomas Cartwright, warmly recommending him to publish an answer to the Rhemist Translation of the New Testament.† Afterwards, he was cast into prison for refusing conformity to the established church. He subscribed the petition presented to the lord treasurer, and signed by about *sixty protestant nonconformists*, then confined in the various prisons in and about London.‡ Mr. Strype has placed this petition in the year 1592: but it should have been earlier. Mr. Crane died in Newgate, in the year 1588,§ where many of his suffering brethren shared the same fate.‖

Lawrence Humphrey, D.D.—This celebrated puritan was born at Newport-Pagnel in Buckinghamshire, about the year 1527, and educated first in the university of Cambridge, then in Magdalen college, Oxford, where, in 1549, he became perpetual fellow, and was chosen reader of Greek in 1552. Having applied himself closely to theological studies, he entered, about the same time, into the sacred function. He remained at Oxford, some time after the accession of Queen Mary and the commencement of her severities; but, at length, by the permission of the president, vice-president, and others of his college, was allowed to go abroad. "In the opinion of all," says the Oxford historian, "he was much commended for his life and con-

* Parte of a Register, p. 119—124. † See Art. Cartwright.

‡ An abstract of this most moving petition is given in another place.—See *Art. John Greenwood.*

§ Account prefixed to "Parte of a Register."

‖ Great numbers perished in the various prisons where they were long confined and most cruelly used. Among the rest, was one Mr. Roger Rippon; who, dying in Newgate, his fellow prisoners put the following inscription upon his coffin:

"This is the corpse of Roger Rippon, a servant of Christ, and her "majesty's faithful subject; who is the last of sixteen or seventeen which "that great enemy of God, the Archbishop of Canterbury, with his high "commissioners, have murdered in Newgate within these five years, "manifestly for the testimony of Jesus Christ. His soul is now with the "Lord; and his blood crieth for speedy vengeance against that great "enemy of the saints, and against Mr. Richard Young, (a justice of the "peace in London) who in this and many the like points, hath abused his "power, for the upholding of the Romish antichrist, prelacy, and priest-"hood. He died A. D. 1592."—*Strype's Annals*, vol. iv. p. 133.

versation, and for his wit and learning; and was permitted, for the benefit of his studies, to travel one year into foreign parts, on condition that he kept himself from such places as were suspected to be heretical, or favourers of heresy, and that he refrained himself from the company of those who are, or have been, authors of heresy or heretical opinions." Having thus obtained liberty to leave the country, he went to Zurich, where he joined the English protestant exiles, and, not returning at the end of the year, was deprived of his fellowship.* During his exile, we find his name subscribed to a letter from the exiles at Zurich, to their brethren at Frankfort. This letter is dated October 23, 1554.†

Upon the accession of Queen Elizabeth, Humphrey returned home. But having held a correspondence with the learned divines at Geneva, during his absence, he is said to have returned to England, so much the *Calvinian*, both in doctrine and worship, that the best that could be said of him was, that he was a moderate and conscientious nonconformist. Upon his return he was immediately restored to his fellowship, and, by her majesty, nominated queen's professor of divinity in the university of Oxford, being accounted the fittest person in the kingdom for that office. He soon after took his degrees in divinity, and was elected president of Magdalen college, though not without much opposition from the popish party.‡ In this situation, many persons, afterwards famed for their celebrity, were brought up under him; among whom was the famous Sir Thomas Bodley.§

In the following account of this celebrated divine, we shall have frequent occasion to mention his worthy and intimate friend, the famous Dr. Thomas Sampson. They were persons of great reputation, especially in Oxford, and were highly distinguished for their learning, piety, and zeal in promoting true religion. But their learning, piety, and zeal, were no sufficient screen from the prosecution of the high commission,

* Wood's Athenæ Oxon. vol. i. p. 195.
† Troubles at Frankeford, p. 10—12.
‡ Wood's Athenæ, vol. i. p. 195.
§ Sir Thomas Bodley was celebrated as a statesman, and as a man of letters; but incomparably more, in the ample provision he has made for literature, in which he stands unrivalled. In 1599, he opened his library, called the Bodleian Library, at Oxford, which will perpetuate his memory as long as books shall endure. He drew up the statutes of the library; wrote the memoirs of his own life; and died Jan. 28, 1613.—*Ibid.* p. 326, 327.—*Granger's Biog. Hist.* vol. i. p. 233, 271.

for refusing to wear the popish habits. Accordingly, March 3, 1564, both Humphrey and Sampson, with four other divines, were cited before Archbishop Parker and his colleagues, at Lambeth. Upon their appearance, the archbishop urged the opinions of foreign divines: as, Peter Martyr and Martin Bucer, with the view of bringing them to conformity. This, indeed, proved ineffectual; for their judgments remained unconvinced. They requested that they might be dismissed, and return to their usual exercises at Oxford; but this the archbishop refused, intending to bring them before the council. After attendance for some time, they prepared a supplication, in a very elegant, but submissive style, which they presented to the Archbishop, the Bishops of London, Winchester, Ely, and Lincoln, and other commissioners.

In this supplication, they protested before God, how great a grief it was to them, that there should be any dissention about so small a matter as *woollen* and *linen*, as they styled the cap and surplice. But it comforted them, that, under Christ, the captain of salvation, they all professed the same gospel, and the same faith; and that in the matter of habits, each party followed the dictates of their own minds, where there was often room for liberty, and always for charity. They alleged the authorities of Augustin, Socrates, and Theodoret, to shew that in their times, there was a variety of rites and observances in the churches, yet unity and concord. They had many and powerful reasons for this address: as, "That their consciences were tender, and ought not to be grieved.—That they were not turbulent, nor obstinate, nor did they study novelty, nor refuse to be convinced, nor attempt to disturb the peace of the church.—That they were certain, that things in themselves indifferent, did not always appear indifferent, even to persons of a tender conscience.—And that the law for restoring the ceremonies of the *Romish* church, was connected with bondage and superstition." They also added, "Because these things do not seem so to you, you are not to be condemned by us; and because they do seem so to us, we ought not to be condemned by you." They beseech their lordships, therefore, that if there be any fellowship in Christ, they would follow the direction of divine inspiration, about things in their own nature indifferent, "that every one might be persuaded in his own mind."*

They wrote, also, to the Earl of Leicester, but all to no

* Strype's Parker, p. 162, 163.

purpose. They could not procure their release; but were obliged to continue their attendance. The commissioners themselves were very much divided in their opinions. Some wished to have their reasons answered, and the habits enforced: others were for a connivance. But the archbishop, who was at the head of the commission, would abate nothing. For April 29th, he peremptorily declared in open court, "That they should conform to wear the square cap and no hats, in their long gowns; to wear the surplice with non-regent's hoods in the choirs, according to ancient custom; and to communicate kneeling, with wafer bread; or immediately part with their preferment." To this they replied, that their consciences would not suffer them to comply, whatever might be the consequences.* Upon this, they were still kept under confinement; but the storm fell chiefly upon Dr. Sampson.†

In one of their examinations, during this year, the archbishop put the following questions to them, to which they gave the answers subjoined.

Question. Is the surplice a thing evil and wicked, or is it indifferent?

Answer. Though the surplice in substance be indifferent, yet in the present circumstance it is not, being of the same nature as the garment of an harlot, or the apparel of idolatry; for which God, by the prophet, threatens to visit the people.

Q. If it be not indifferent, for what cause?

A. Because things consecrated to idolatry are not indifferent.

Q. May the bishop detesting popery, enjoin the surplice to be worn, and enforce his injunctions?

A. It may be said to such a one, in the words of Tertullian, "If thou hatest the pomp and pageantry of the devil, whatsoever of it thou meddlest with, is idolatry." Which, if he believe, he will not enforce.

Q. Is the cope a thing indifferent, being prescribed by law for decency and reverence, and not in respect of superstition or holiness?

A. Decency is not promoted by a *cope*, which was devised to deface the sacrament. St. Jerome says, "That the gold, ordained by God for the reverence and decency of the Jewish temple, is not fit to be admitted to beautify the church of Christ;" and if so, how much less *copes* brought

* Strype's Parker, p. 164. † See Art. Sampson.

in by papists, and continued in their service as proper ornaments of their religion.

Q. May any thing that is indifferent be enjoined as godly, for the use of the common prayer and sacraments?

A. If it be merely indifferent, as *time*, *place*, and such necessary circumstances of divine worship, for which there may be ground brought from scripture, we think it may.

Q. May the civil magistrate constitute by law, an abstinence from meats on certain days?

A. If it be sufficiently guarded against superstition, he may appoint it, due regard being had to persons and times.

Q. May a law be enacted to make a difference in the apparel of ministers from laymen?

A. Whether such prescription to a minister of the gospel of Christ be lawful, may be doubted; because no such thing is decreed in the New Testament. Nor did the primitive church appoint any such thing, but chose rather to have their ministers distinguished from the laity by their *doctrine*, not by their *vestments*.

Q. Ought the ministers going in popish apparel, to be condemned for so doing?

A. We judge no man. To his own master he standeth or falleth.

Q. Ought such preachers to be reformed or restrained, or not?

A. Irenæus will not have brethren restrained from brotherly communion, for diversity in ceremonies, provided there be unity of faith and charity; and it is desirable to have the like charitable permission among us.

To these answers, they subjoined several additional arguments against wearing and imposing the habits: as, "Apparel ought not to be worn, as meat ought not to be eaten; but according to St. Paul, meat offered to idols ought not to be eaten, therefore popish apparel ought not to be worn.—We ought not to give offence in matters of mere indifference; therefore the bishops who are of this opinion, ought not to enforce the habits.—Popish garments have many superstitious mystical significations, for which they are consecrated; we ought, therefore, to lay them aside.—Some suppose our ministrations are not valid, or acceptable to God, unless performed in the apparel; we apprehend it, therefore, highly necessary to undeceive the people.—Things indifferent ought not to be made necessary, because then their nature is changed, and we lose our liberty.—And if we are bound to wear popish apparel when commanded, we may be obliged to have shaven crowns, and to make use of oil, spittle, cream, and all other papistical additions to the ordinances of Christ."*

Humphrey and Sampson having thus openly and fully delivered their opinions, a pacific proposition was drawn up, which they both subscribed, with the reserve of the apostle, *All things are lawful, but all things are not expedient. All things are lawful, but all things edify not.* Upon this, it seems, they were both released. Dr. Humphrey, about the same time, wrote a very excellent letter to the queen, in which he addressed her majesty as follows:— "Kings being kindled with zeal for the house of God, "have removed all the relics of superstition; so that no "token thereof remained. This form and pattern of "reformation is then perfect, when there is no blemish in "the face, and when, in religion and ceremonies, nothing "is taken from the enemies of the truth. You know, that in "things indifferent, especially those which are in contro-"versy, it is lawful for every man, without prejudice to "others, to have his full persuasion, and that the con-"science ought not in any case to be bound. That the "matter which we handle is agreeable to religion and "equity, I think there is no man that doubteth. Seeing, "therefore, the thing which we request is honest, and "that which is commanded is doubtful; and they who make "the request, are your most loving and obedient subjects, "and ministers of the word, why should your mercy, O "queen! which is usually open for all, be shut up from "us? You being the prince will not give place to your "subjects; yet being *merciful*, you may spare them who "are in misery. You will not disannul a public decree; "yet you may mitigate it. You cannot abolish a law; "yet you may grant a toleration. It is not meet you "should follow every man's affections; yet it is most right "and convenient, that the mind and conscience be not "forced.

"We do not go about, O most gracious queen, to bear "rule, who ought to be subjects; but we would that *reason*, "the queen of queens, should rule, and that the humble "entreaty of the ministers of Christ, might obtain that which "religion commandeth. Wherefore, O most noble prince, "I do in most humble sort, request and earnestly desire, "that your majesty would seriously and attentively consider

* Strype's Parker, p. 166—171.

"the majesty of the glorious gospel, the equity of the cause, "the small number of workmen, the greatness of the "harvest, the multitude of tares, the grievousness of the "punishment, the lightness of the fault, the sighs of the "good, the triumphs of the wicked, and the mischiefs of "the times."* By using these urgent endeavours, and having many friends at court, he, at length, obtained a connivance and a toleration.

Dr. Humphrey having procured his liberty, the Bishop of Winchester presented to him a small living, in the diocese of Salisbury, but Bishop Jewel, his professed friend, and intimate acquaintance, refused to admit him; and protested he never would admit him, till he obtained some good assurance of his conformity.† Jewel's great objection against admitting him, was his nonconformity; upon which, said he, "God is not the author of *confusion*, but of *peace;* and diversity in the worship of God, is *deformity*, and a sufficient cause of deprivation." Dr. Humphrey, in a letter to the bishop, dated December 20, 1565, replied, "That his lordship's objection had but little ground to rest upon.—That he never was the author of *confusion.*—That he had ever lived in peace and concord with his brethren, and in due obedience to his superiors, and, by the grace of God, was still resolved so to do.—And that if diversity in outward ceremonies be *deformity*, if it be any confusion, if it be a sufficient cause of deprivation, if conformity be a necessary part of the ministry; if all this came not from the *pope*," said he, "and if it existed before popery, then I am much deceived. But whatever he called it, whether order or disorder, it was of very little consequence. He assured his lordship, that he did not mean to innovate, nor to violate their ecclesiastical ordinances." Though he had obtained the patronage of his grace of Winchester, and the favour of the archbishop, and the benefice was only very small, Jewel seems to have remained inflexible;‡ for it does not appear that he was admitted.§

* Baker's MS. Collec. vol. vi. p. 353, 354.

† MS. Register, p. 873.—Strype's Annals, vol. i. p. 421.

‡ Strype's Parker, p. 185, 186.

§ Though Bishop Jewel was a zealous churchman, he was of a different spirit from many of his brethren. In a letter dated May 22, 1559, he wrote, "that the Queen (Elizabeth) refused to be called *Head of the Church;* and adds, that title could not be justly given to any mortal, it being due only to Christ; and that such titles had been so much abused by antichrist, that they ought not to be any longer continued."—*Simpson's Plea for Religion*, p. 146. Edit. 1810.

Upon the publication of the advertisements, for enforcing a more strict conformity, Dr. Humphrey wrote to Secretary Cecil, earnestly desiring him to use all his influence towards stopping their execution. In this letter, dated April 23, 1566, he says, "I am sorry that the old sore is broken out again, to the calamity of many, and to the wonder and sorrow of all. The cause is not so good, in my poor opinion, as it is represented. The trouble is greater than we imagine. The inhibition of preaching, how strange and lamentable! The cries of numbers awaken the pity of God and man. The book of advertisements contains many things, which, on many accounts, are much disliked by wise men. The execution of it, which has hitherto been vehement, has greatly agitated and spoiled all. I humbly request you to be a means with the queen's majesty, to put a stop to the execution of it, and that the book may sleep in silence. The people in these days, require other kind of advertisements. We stand in need of unity and concord; but these advertisements have produced greater *variety* and *discord* than was ever known before. To your wisdom and goodness, I refer all."*

About the same time, he wrote a very warm and affectionate letter to the bishops, boldly expostulating with them about their corrupt and unchristian proceedings. He says, "The gospel requireth Christ to be openly preached, professed, and glorified; but, alas! a man qualified with inward gifts, for want of outward shews in matters of ceremony, is punished: and a man only outwardly conformable, and inwardly unfurnished, is exalted. The preacher, for his labour, is beaten; the unpreaching prelate offending, goes free. The learned man without his cap, is afflicted: the man with his cap is not touched. Is not this a direct breach of God's laws? Is not this the way of the pharisees? Is not this to wash the outside of the cup, and leave the inside uncleansed? Is not this to prefer mint and annis, to faith, and judgment, and mercy? Is not this preferring man's traditions before the ordinance of God? Is not this a sore disorder in the school of Christ?—Charity, my lords, would first have taught us, equity would first have spared us, brotherly-kindness would have warned us, pity would have pardoned us, if we had been found transgressors. God is my witness, that I think honourably of your lordships, esteeming you as brethren, reverencing you as lords and

* Strype's Parker, p. 217.

masters of the congregation. Alas then! why have you not some good opinion of us? Why do you trust known adversaries, and distrust your brethren? We confess one faith of Jesus; we preach one doctrine; we acknowledge one ruler upon earth: in all these things we are of your judgment. Shall we be used thus then for the sake of a surplice? Shall brethren persecute brethren for a forked cap, devised for singularity by our enemy? Shall we fight for the *pope's coat*, now that his head and his body are banished out of the land? Shall the labourers, for lack of this furniture, lack their wages, and the church their preaching? Shall we not teach? Shall we not exercise our talents as God hath commanded? My lords, before this take place, consider the cause of the church; the triumphs of antichrist; the laughter of satan; and the sighing, sorrowing, and misery of your fellow-creatures."*

In July 1566, Dr. Humphrey and Dr. Sampson wrote to Bullinger at Zurich, giving him a particular account of their opinions and nonconformity. "We do not think," say they, "that prescribing the habits is merely a civil thing. And how can that habit be thought decent, which was brought in to dress up the theatrical pomp of popery? The papists glory in this our imitation of them. We approve of rules to promote order, but this ought not to be applied to those things which destroy the peace of the church, and which are neither necessary, nor useful; and that tend not to any edification, but only to recommend those forms which most persons abhor. The papists glory in this, that these habits were brought in by them; for the proof of which, they vouch Otho's constitutions and the Roman pontifical.

"In King Edward's time, the surplice was not universally used, nor pressed upon the clergy, and the copes then taken away, are now restored. This is not to extirpate popery, but to plant it again; and instead of going forwards in the work of reformation, is going backwards. We do not make religion to consist in habits; but only oppose those who do. We hate contention, and are ever ready to enter into a friendly conference about this matter. We do not desert our churches, and leave them exposed to wolves, but, to our great grief, are driven from them. And we leave our brethren (meaning those who conformed) to stand or fall to their own master, and desire the same favourable

* Ames's Fresh Suit, part ii. p. 269—272.

forbearance from them. All that is pretended is, that the habits are not *unlawful*. But they ought not to be taken from our enemies.

"We are far," say they, "from any design of making a schism, or of quarrelling. We will not condemn things indifferent, as unlawful. We wish the occasion of the contention removed, and the remembrance of it for ever buried. They who condemn the papal pride, cannot like tyranny in a free church. The doctrine of our church is now pure, and why should there be any defect in our worship? Why should we borrow any thing from popery? Why should we not agree in rites, as well as in doctrine, with the other reformed churches? We have a good opinion of our bishops, and bear with their state and pomp. We once bore the same cross with them, and preached the same Christ with them; why then are we now turned out of our benefices, and some cast into prison, only about the habits? We pray that God may quiet these dissentions, and send forth more labourers into his vineyard."*

"But the dispute," say they, "is not about the cap and surplice. There are other grievances which ought to be redressed, or dispensed with: as music and organs in divine worship.—The sponsors in baptism answering in the name of the child.—The cross in baptism.—Kneeling at the sacrament, and the use of unleavened bread.—The want of discipline in the church.—The marriage of the clergy is not legitimate, but their children are looked upon as bastards.—Marriage is not to be performed without a *ring*.—Women are not to be churched without a veil.—The court of faculties; pluralities; licenses for nonresidences, for eating flesh in Lent, &c.—Ministers have not free liberty to preach, without subscribing to the use and approbation of all the ceremonies."†

During the above year, Queen Elizabeth paid her pompous visit to the university of Oxford, on which occasion our author distinguished himself in a public disputation before her majesty. Every day the queen was entertained with academical exercises of different kinds; in which the wits of the ablest men in that age, were stretched to the utmost, to merit the applause of so illustrious an audience. The queen, together with her train of courtiers, was present at a divinity act, in which Dr. Humphrey was defendant; and Drs. Godwin, Westphaling, Overton, Calfchill, and

* Burnet's Hist. of Refor. vol. iii. p. 310—312.
† Ibid. Records, p. 335.

Peirce, were opponents. Bishop Jewel acted on this occasion, as moderator. At the conclusion, her majesty delivered a speech in praise of the learned disputants.*

This learned divine was, at length, favoured with a toleration for about ten or eleven years; and about 1576, he consented to wear the habits. Wood says, in the year 1570, but Mr. Strype, 1576, he was made dean of Gloucester; and in 1580, he was removed from the deanery of Gloucester, to that of Winchester. This he kept to his death.† He was particularly intimate with the Lord Treasurer Burleigh, who, even before he consented to wear the habits, moved the queen to prefer him to a bishopric: but, as Burleigh informed him, his nonconformity seemed to be the chief impediment in the way.‡ The Earl of Leicester, in his letter to the university of Cambridge, dated March 26, 1567, makes very honourable mention of him, and most warmly recommends him to the office of vice-chancellor of that university; "who," says he, "is every way a right worthy man."§ Dr. Humphrey was intimate with Mr. Gilby, a celebrated puritan, at Ashby-de-la-Zouch in Leicestershire, with whom he held a friendly correspondence. Some of his letters to this venerable divine are now before me, addressed "to his worshipful and well beloved friend Mr. Anthony Gilby, at Ashby;" in one of which he writes as follows:‖

"My salvation in Christ Jesus.

"I thank you for your good counsel. I would I were "as well able as I am willing. Though many brethren and "nobles also wish; yet we must pray that God may open "the queen's majesty's ears to hear of a reformation; for "there is the stay. And openly to publish such admoni-"tions as are abroad, I like not; for in some parts and "terms, they are too broad and overshoot themselves. A "book, indeed, I gave as a present of mine office and "cognizance of the university, a Greek Testament, with "mine additions or collections, to stir up her majesty to "peruse the book, and to reform the church, by it, in cer-"tain sentences. I have there declared, and in a word or "two using orations, the copy whereof I send you. The "Lord Jesus bless you and yours. Oxon. Jan. 17, 1572.

"Yours, L. HUMPHREY."

* Biog. Britan. vol. iv. p. 2230. Edit. 1747.

† Wood's Athenæ Oxon. vol. i. p. 195.—Strype's Annals, vol. ii. p. 451.

‡ Ibid. vol. i. p. 430.

§ Baker's MS. Collec. vol. xvii. p. 256.

‖ Ibid. vol. xxxii. p. 431.

As Dr. Humphrey was many years president of Magdalen college, Oxford, public professor of divinity in the university, and several times vice-chancellor; so the Oxford historian, who denominates him the standard-bearer of the nonconformists, says, that he stocked his college with such a generation of nonconformists, as could not be rooted out of it many years after his death; and that he sowed in the divinity schools, such seeds of *Calvinism*, and such hatred of *popery*, as if nothing but divine truth was to be found in the one, and nothing but abominations in the other. Nevertheless, he adds, Humphrey was a great and general scholar, an able linguist, and a deep divine; and who, for the excellency of his style, the exactness of his method, and the solidity of his matter, was superior to most theologians in his day. Archbishop Matthews said, "Dr. Humphrey hath read more fathers, than Campian the Jesuit ever saw; devoured more than he ever tasted; and taught more than he ever heard or read."* He had the honour of seeing many of his pupils become bishops, while he, who was every way their superior, was denied any considerable preferment, on account of his puritanical principles. At length, after a life of much labour and hard study, he died in the month of February, 1589, aged sixty-three years. Fuller styles him a moderate and conscientious nonconformist, and says, that at his death, he bequeathed a considerable quantity of gold to Magdalen college.† Granger says, he was one of the greatest divines, and most general scholars, of his age; and that when Queen Elizabeth visited the university, he and Bishop Jewel entertained her majesty with a public theological disputation.‡ The remains of Dr. Humphrey were interred in the inner chapel belonging to Magdalen college, where a monumental inscription was erected to his memory, of which the following is a translation:§

Sacred to the MEMORY
of LAWRENCE HUMPHREY, D. D.
twenty-eight years Regius Professor
and Governor of this College.
His eldest daughter,
JUSTINIA DORMER,
erected this monument to the memory
of her venerable Father.
He died in February, 1589,
aged 63.

* Wood's Athenæ Oxon. vol. i. p. 195, 196.
† Fuller's Church Hist. b. ix. p. 234.
‡ Granger's Biog. Hist. vol. i. p. 211.
§ Wood's Hist. et Antiq. lib. ii. p. 203.

His Works.—1. Epistola de Græcis literis, & Homeri lectione & imitatione, ad Præsidem, &c., 1558.—2. De Religione Conversatione & Reformatione deque Primatus Regum, 1559.—3. De Ratione Interpretandi Authores, 1559.—4. Optimates sive de Nobilitate, ejusque antiqua origine, natura, officiis, disciplina, &c., 1560.*—5. Orationes Woodstochiæ habitæ ad illustress. R. Eliz., 1572.—6. De Vita et Morte Johannis Juelli: Ejusq; veræ Doctrinæ Defensio, cum Refutatione quorundam Objectorum, Hardingi, Sanderi, &c., 1573.—7. De fermento vitando: conscio in Matt. xvi. Marc. viii. Luc. xii., 1582.—8. Jesuitismi pars prima, 1582.—9. Jesuitismi pars secunda, 1584.—10. Apologelica Epistola ad Academiæ Oxoniensis Chancellarium, 1585.—11. Seven Sermons against Treason, 1588.—12. Conscio in die Cinerum.—Many of these articles were translated and published in English.

Thomas Sampson, D. D.—This celebrated divine was born about the year 1517, and educated in the university of Oxford. Afterwards he studied at the Temple, became a zealous protestant, a distinguished preacher, and instrumental in the conversion of John Bradford, the famous martyr. He married the niece of old Bishop Latimer. He was ordained by Archbishop Cranmer and Bishop Ridley, who, at his request, dispensed with the habits. He was highly esteemed by these two reverend prelates. He was preacher in the army of Lord Russel, in his expedition against the Scots. In the year 1551, he became rector of Allhallows, Bread-street, London; the year following he was preferred to the deanery of Winchester; and he continued a famous preacher to the death of King Edward.† Upon the accession of Queen Mary, he concealed himself for some time. During this period, he and Mr. Richard Chambers, another zealous protestant, collected money in London, for the support and encouragement of poor scholars in the two universities. But it was no sooner discovered, than they were both obliged to flee for their lives. For, August 16, 1554, Mr. Bradford, Mr. Becon, and Mr. Veron, were apprehended and committed to the Tower; and Sampson was to have been committed the same day, and was even sought after for this purpose, in the house in which Mr.

* Mr. Strype highly commends this work, both for the excellency of its matter, and the elegancy of its style. In this work, the author, speaking of astrology, says, "This science above the rest was so snatched at, so "beloved, and even devoured by most persons of fashion, that they needed "no incitements to it, but a bridle rather; not to be set on, but rather "taken off from it. And that many had so trusted to this, that they almost "distrusted God."—*Strype's Cranmer*, p. 356.—*Biog. Britan.* vol. iii. p. 487. Edit. 1778.

† Strype's Cranmer, p. 192, 292.—Troubles at Frankeford, p. 168.

Bradford was taken. Because he could not be found, the Bishop of Winchester fumed exceedingly, as was usually the case with angry prelates.* Thus, having narrowly escaped the fire, he fled to Strasburgh, where he was much esteemed by the learned Tremelius.† He was intimately acquainted with most of the learned exiles, and particularly John Jewel, afterwards the celebrated Bishop of Salisbury. By the joint advice of Dr. Sampson, Dr. Edwin Sandys, and Mr. Richard Chambers, Jewel was induced soon after his arrival on the continent, to make a public confession of his sorrow, for his late subscription in favour of popery.‡ Sampson, during his exile, was concerned in writing and publishing the Geneva Translation of the Bible.§

Upon the accession of Queen Elizabeth, our learned divine returned home. While on his journey, being informed that a bishopric was designed for him, he wrote to Peter Martyr for his opinion and advice, whether it was lawful to swear "that the queen was supreme head of the church under Christ." He thought that Christ was the *only* supreme head of the church, and that no account of any inferior head was to be found in scripture. He thought, also, that the want of discipline in the church of England, rendered it impossible for a bishop to perform his duty. The method of electing bishops, appeared to him, totally different from the primitive institution: the consent of neither clergy, nor people, being so much as asked. The superstitious dress of bishops seemed to him very unbecoming. He wrote to his learned friend, not that he expected a bishopric would be offered him; but he prayed to God that it might not. He resolved to apply himself to preaching the gospel, and to avoid having any share in the government of the church, till he saw a thorough reformation, both in doctrine and discipline.

Upon the reception of Peter Martyr's answer, Sampson replied, January 6, 1560, saying, "We are under sad apprehensions, concerning which, we desire an interest in your prayers. We are afraid lest the truth of religion, in England, should either be overturned, or very much darkened. Things still stick with me. I can have neither ingress, nor egress. God knows how glad I should be to have an egress. Let others be bishops, I desire only to be

* Fox's Martyrs, vol. iii. p. 76.
† Wood's Athenæ Oxon. vol. i. p. 192.
‡ Biog. Britan. vol. iv. p. 2759. Edit. 1747.
§ See Art. Coverdale.

a preacher, and no bishop. There is yet a general prohibition of preaching; and still a crucifix on the altar at court, with lights burning before it. And though, by the queen's order, images are removed out of the churches all over the kingdom, yet the people rejoice to see that this is still kept in the queen's chapel.* Three bishops officiate at the altar: one as priest, another as deacon, and a third as sub-deacon, all in rich copes before the idol: and there is sacrament without any sermon. Injunctions are sent to preachers not to use freedom in reproving vice." He then asks Martyr, Bullinger, and Bernardin, what they thought of these things; and whether, if similar injunctions were sent to all churches, the clergy ought to obey, or suffer deprivation rather than comply.

May 13th he wrote again, signifying that a bishopric had been offered him, but he had refused to accept it; for which, he desired Peter Martyr not to censure him, till he became acquainted with the whole matter. He rejoiced that Parkhurst† was made Bishop of Norwich. And Norwich, it seems, was the bishopric offered to him.‡ This illustrious divine, therefore, refused the offered preferment, because he was thoroughly dissatisfied with the episcopal office, the popish habits, and the superstitious ceremonies.

During the three first years of Queen Elizabeth's reign, Dr. Sampson delivered the rehearsal sermons at Paul's cross, and is said to have been appointed to do this on account of his wonderful memory and fine elocution;§ and in her royal visitation in the north, he was the visitor's preacher. In the year 1560, he became dean of Christ-church, Oxford. To procure his settlement in this public situation, the members of the house wrote to Lord Dudley, urging him to prevail upon the queen, in behalf of Sampson. In this letter, subscribed by twenty-two persons of distinguished

* Dr. Sampson having laid a Common Prayer Book, (adorned with fine cuts and pictures, representing the stories of the saints and martyrs,) in the queen's chapel, for her use, it is said, that she severely reprimanded him for so doing, and told him, "That she had an aversion to idolatry, and "to images and pictures of this kind.—That he had forgot her proclama-"tion against images, pictures, and Roman relics in churches.—And she "ordered that no more mistakes of this kind should be committed within "the churches of her realm for the future." It seems difficult to reconcile this, to her majesty's conduct in still retaining idolatrous worship in her own chapel.—*Strype's Annals*, vol. i. p. 239.

† Bishop Parkhurst, who was an exile in the days of Queen Mary, was a person of great learning, a worthy prelate, and always a decided friend to the nonconformists.—*MS. Chronology*, vol. i. p. 273. (2.)

‡ Burnet's Hist. of Refor. vol. iii. p. 291, 292.

§ Strype's Annals, vol. i. p. 238.

learning, they say, "That as for Dr. Sampson, after well considering all the learned men in the land, they found none to be compared to him, for singular learning and great piety, having the praise of all men. And that it was very doubtful, whether there was a better man, a greater linguist, a more complete scholar, or a more profound divine."* Afterwards, Dr. Sampson, Dr. Lawrence Humphrey, and Mr. Andrew Kingsmill, all celebrated puritans, were the only protestant preachers in the university of Oxford.+

Dr. Sampson sat in the convocation of 1562, and subscribed the Articles of Religion. This being finished, many learned members of the lower house, presented to the house a paper of requests, chiefly relating to matters of discipline, in which they desired an allowance in a number of important particulars. His name is among those who subscribed.‡ While the convocation was discussing the subject of discipline, the prolocutor, with Dr. Sampson and Dr. Day, presented to the upper house a book called *Catechismus pucrorum;* to which all the members of the lower house had unanimously given their consent. They left the book with their lordships; but there, unfortunately, it remained without any further notice.§ Afterwards, his scruples and objections against the prescribed habits and ceremonies, being known at court, Secretary Cecil urged him to conform, adding, "That he gave offence by his disobedience, and that obedience was better than sacrifice." To this, Sampson, in a letter to this honourable person, replied, "That in the law, God commanded all idols to be destroyed, with all the ceremonies belonging to them; prohibiting as much the ceremonies, as the idols themselves. That the godly kings of the Jews dealt with idols, idolatry, and the appurtenances accordingly. That the Lord threatened to punish those who should retain such ceremonies and fashions, in time of reformation. That Christ did not communicate in any traditions devised by the pharisees; but reproved them, and warned the apostles to take heed of them. Therefore, all ceremonies devised and used by idolatrous papists, ought to be rejected, destroyed, and forbidden. And though men in authority command otherwise, yet he, who thus followeth the mind of God in his word, doth yield that obedience, which is better

* Strype's Annals, vol. i. p. 432, 433.
+ Wood's Athenæ Oxon. vol. i. p. 193.
‡ Strype's Annals, vol. i. p. 290, 298. ii. Adden. p. 15.
§ Churton's Life of Nowell, p. 96.

than sacrifice." He observed further, "That the conduct of the primitive christians, in refusing such things, was void of blame.—That to prescribe a certain uniform array for ministers, came out of the corrupt state of the church.—That all reformations ought to be framed according to the original and pure state of the church.—That if the reformation would not admit this, but would determine the reverse, he could not see how this should bind him, who knew and desired greater purity.—That these were only some of the reasons which constrained him to do as he did.—And that as he put no restraint upon others, but left them to the Lord, so he desired to be left in like manner."*

In the year 1564, Dr. Sampson and his much esteemed friend, Dr. Humphrey, were cited before the high commission, at Lambeth, an account of which is given in another place.† After being harassed for some time, Humphrey, at length, obtained a toleration; but Sampson suffered deprivation, and was removed from the university. The proceedings of the commissioners were severe enough, even in the opinion of Dr. Heylin; who adds, "that he was worthily deprived, and that, by this *severity*, the puritans found what they might expect."‡ Some of the learned lawyers, however, disputed the legality of his deprivation, and were of opinion, that the commissioners were involved in a premunire. Indeed, Sampson was deprived not only of his deanery, but of his liberty too, and was kept for some time in a state of confinement: nor was he able, without much trouble, to procure his release.§ He was succeeded in the deanery of Christ-church by Dr. Thomas Godwin, afterwards Bishop of Bath and Wells.‖

In the year 1573, our learned divine was struck with the dead palsy on one side; and having enjoyed, for some time, the lecture at Whittington college, London, for which he received ten pounds a year, he resigned it into the hands of his patrons. It was in the gift of the company of cloth-workers, to whom he recommended Mr. Edward Deering, whom they chose for his successor; but this divine being silenced for nonconformity, Archbishop Parker utterly refused his allowance.¶ Mr. Deering was a man of great

* Strype's Annals, vol. i. p. 433, 434. † See Art. Humphrey.
‡ Heylin's Hist. of Presby. p. 250.
§ Strype's Parker, p. 186, 187.
‖ Biog. Britan. vol. iv. p. 2290. Edit. 1747. ¶ Ibid. p. 469, 470.

learning, exemplary piety, and an excellent preacher; and the benefice being very small, it reflects not a little upon the severity of this prelate.

In March this year, Dr. Sampson sent a letter, written by another person, to the Lord Treasurer Burleigh, signifying, that God had been pleased to take from him the use of half his limbs, though not his senses; which was the occasion of his using the hand of another. And though this disease was to him as the messenger of death, he thanked God, that he was ready to depart in peace. He was, indeed, constrained, before his heavenly father called him home, to trouble his lordship once more. He, therefore, earnestly solicited him to use his utmost endeavours to promote the necessary reformation of the church, and herein recommended the directions in Bucer's book on the Kingdom of Christ. "My lord," says he, "though the doctrine of the gospel is preached in the church of England, the *government* of the church, as appointed in the gospel, is still wanting. The doctrine, and the government, as appointed by Christ, are both good; and are to be joined together, and not separated. It is a deformity to see a church, professing the gospel of Christ, governed by those canons and customs, by which antichrist ruleth his synagogue. Martin Bucer wrote a book to King Edward, upon this subject, entitled *De Regno Christi*. There you will see what is wanting of the kingdom of Christ, in the church of England. My lord, I beseech you to read this faithful and brief epitome of the book, which I have sent you; and I beseech you to lay it to heart. It is the cause of Jesus Christ and his church, and very much concerneth the souls of men. Use your utmost endeavours, that, as Christ teacheth us in the church of England, he may also *rule* and *govern* us, even by *the laws of his kingdom*. Help, my lord, in this good work of the Lord your God. By so doing, you will serve him who is King of kings, and he will acknowledge your good service, when all kings and lords shall appear before him. My good lord, use your authority for the glory of Christ, and the peace and welfare of his church. You cannot employ your authority in a better cause."* To this advice, the treasurer returned a christian reply, saying, "that he very much approved of what was urged, but was unable to do all that he recommended." Dr. Sampson, also, returned him a very appro-

* Strype's Annals, vol. ii. p. 365—367.

priate answer, reminding him how much he did at the commencement of the reformation; that his will and his power were not lessened, but increased; and that, seeing others sought a reformation by stopping both preaching and government, the state of the church stood now as much in need of his assistance as ever.*

The following year he wrote to Grindal, formerly his companion in exile, but now advanced to the high dignity of Archbishop of York. Several letters passed betwixt them. Dr. Sampson reminded him of his former low condition, and cautioned him against being too much exalted with his present high title. Grindal, who was certainly different from many of the other dignitaries, told him, he did not value the title of *lord*, but was chiefly concerned to discharge the duties of his function faithfully, until the great day of the Lord Jesus. To this, Sampson replied, "You say, you are not *lordly*, nor value your *lordly estate*, in which, I hope, you say true. Yet I must further observe, that if you whom worldly policy hath made a *lord*, be not *lordly*, but keep an humble and a loving brother, and minister of Christ, shall I say you are a phœnix? I will say that you are by the special grace of God, most happily preserved. Yet your state, your port, your train of waiting-men in the streets, your gentleman-usher going before you with bare head, your family full of idle serving-men, and the rest of your worldly appendages, look very *lordly*. Perhaps the same policy which makes you a *lord*, also charges you with this *lordly state*. But doth the Lord Jesus, whose minister you rejoice to be, charge you with it? Such a number of idle serving-men is unprofitable and unsuitable to the minister of Christ; and, surely, such persons ought not to be maintained by the patrimony of the church. If policy have, therefore, charged you with them, it is very desirable that policy should discharge you; and that the patrimony of Christ may be employed in the support of labourers in the Lord's harvest, and the poor members of his church. But if you take this lordly state upon you, without the charge of policy, your fault is the greater: This is one of the great evils which popery hath left in the church of England."

As the archbishop had pitied his *poverty* and *lameness*, he further adds, "I do not remember that I ever complained of the one or the other. If I did of the first, I was

* Strype's Parker, Appen. p. 177, 178.

to blame; for I must have complained before I suffered want. Touching my *lameness*, I am so far from complaining, that I humbly thank God for it. It is the Lord's hand which hath touched me. He might have smitten or destroyed me: but of his most rich favour and mercy through Jesus Christ, as a loving father, he hath dealt thus tenderly with me. I bless and praise his name for it. If he see that my poor labour will be of any further service in his church, he will heal me: but if he have determined by this lameness, to lead me to my grave, the Lord give me grace to say with Eli, 'It is the Lord, let him do what seemeth him good.' I shall labour, as well as I am able, till I drop into the grave. Though I am in bonds, those bonds are from the Lord; and if it were put to my choice, I would rather carry them to my grave, than be freed from them, and be cumbered with a bishopric."*

Dr. Sampson having been presented to the mastership of the hospital at Leicester, upon his being seized with the palsy, he retired to this situation, where he spent the remainder of his days. Here he was of great service to the hospital, in restoring its privileges and endowments. An account of this is related at some length, to the great honour of his character.† He was intimate with all the leading puritans, with whom he held a friendly correspondence. Among these was the venerable Mr. Gilby of Ashby. His letters to this celebrated divine are now before me, one of which, dated Leicester, March 8, 1584, was as follows:

" My constant salutation in the Lord.

" I do hereby thank you for your loving letter which you " sent me last. I have well advised upon your godly " counsel; but I am not so forward in the matter as you do " think. I do not take upon me to set down a platform of " reformation. I do only desire that meet men may be called " by authority, to consult thereupon. In which assembly " I could find in mine heart to be a door-keeper, though it " were only to keep out dogs. I have a mind to proceed " in that which I proposed. The Lord direct me by his " grace to do that which is good in his sight. Thus " praying you to pray for me, I commit you to God.

" Yours in Christ,

" Tho. Sampson.

" P S. Until ambition and proud Pope xxiii. be pulled " down, there is no hope for any good to be done in con-

* Strype's Parker, Appen. 278—280.
† Strype's Annals, vol. ii. p. 381, 382.

"sultation. Bishops are no meet men. They are too partial; "and the university-men will never yield in disputation. "Pray for reformation by the power of the word preached."*

In the above year, Dr. Sampson was concerned in presenting a supplication to the queen, the council, and the parliament, for a further reformation of the church. It was entitled "A Supplication to be exhibited to our sovereign lady, Queen Elizabeth, to the honourable Lords of her most honourable Privy Council, and to the High Court of Parliament." This supplication, consisting of thirty-four articles at considerable length, enumerates many grievances still retained in the church, and, upon very powerful grounds, humbly solicits a peaceable and speedy redress; but is too long for our insertion.† To this supplication, Dr. Sampson prefixed an address, in which many complaints are enumerated; among which are the following: "We have not vigilant, able, and painful preaching pastors resident among us, to teach us the word of God, by preaching and catechising. We have some kind of pastors, but many of them do not reside on their benefices. Some of them are licensed to two, and some to three benefices. If our bishops provided a remedy for this evil, we would not complain. But they are so far from providing a remedy, that they increase the evil daily. They are constantly making ministers, who will only read out of a printed book, what they are compelled to read; and, with this, the bishops are sufficiently satisfied. Though they want the gift of teaching, they boldly seek to obtain the place of teachers. And, seeing that pastors are commanded to feed the flock of God, over which the Holy Ghost makes them overseers, surely it is very preposterous and presumptuous, to ordain those men to be pastors who cannot feed the flock. The pastors whom the Lord allows and esteems, *are such as feed his people with knowledge and understanding*. Such did our Saviour send forth. Such did his apostles require; that, by sound doctrine, they might convince the gainsayers, apt to teach, rightly dividing the word of truth.

"We might," says he, "greatly increase our complaint. For the good and useful teachers among us, are much discouraged. Some of them are displaced and silenced, not because they do not teach us plainly and faithfully, but because of their nonconformity to the unprofitable ceremonies which men have devised. We most humbly beseech

* Baker's MS. Collec. vol. xxxii. p. 423.
† Strype's Annals, vol. iii. Appen. p. 68—81.

your highness and honours, to call to your remembrance, that they who do well may receive that praise and comfort which they deserve. This hard treatment of our pastors, brings us into great distress. We are sure, that when the bishops deprive our preaching and laborious pastors of their livings, and stop their mouths, so that they cannot teach us the will of our God; they undertake to do that for which they must give an account, in the great day of the Lord. We have great need of such pastors as can and will teach us the way of the Lord. We have no need at all of idle ceremonies, which do not in the least edify in true godliness. Silencing our preaching pastors, who would feed our souls with the provision of God's word; and imposing upon us mere readers, furnished with unprofitable ceremonies, is taking from us the bread of life, which God hath prepared for us, and feeding us with the unprofitable devices of men."* The supplication was sent to the treasurer, followed by two letters from Sampson, entreating his lordship to do every thing in his power to forward the business; but all proved ineffectual.† The ruling prelates, with Archbishop Whitgift at their head, remained inflexible.

Dr. Sampson was a divine highly celebrated for learning, piety, and zeal in the protestant cause, and was greatly esteemed in all parts of the kingdom. Upon his retiring to Leicester, he employed the remainder of his days chiefly in the government of his hospital, and his beloved work of preaching. And having spent his life in much labour, and many troubles, he died in great tranquillity, and comfort in his nonconformity, April 9, 1589, aged seventy-two years.‡ His mortal part was interred in the chapel belonging to his hospital, where was a monumental inscription erected to his memory, of which the following is a translation:§

To the MEMORY
and honour of THOMAS SAMPSON,
a very keen enemy to the Romish hierarchy
and popish superstitions,
but a most constant advocate of gospel truth.
For twenty-one years
he was the faithful Keeper of this Hospital.
Being justly entitled
to the high esteem of the Christian world,

* Strype's Annals, vol. iii. Appen. p. 222—227.
† Strype's Whitgift, p. 184.
‡ Wood's Athenæ, vol. i. p. 193.
§ Wood's Hist. et Antiq. lib. ii. p. 254.

his sons JOHN and NATHANIEL
erected this monument to the memory of their
beloved Father.

HIS WORKS.—1. A Letter to the Professors of Christ's Gospel, in the parish of Alhallows in Bread-street, London, 1564.—2. A Warning to take heed of Fowler's Psalter, 1578.—3. Brief Collection of the Church and the Ceremonies thereof, 1581.—4. Prayers and Meditations Apostolike, gathered and framed out of the Epistles of the Apostles, 1592.—He collected and published several Sermons written by his old friend, Mr. John Bradford.

WILLIAM FULKE, D. D.—This celebrated divine was born in London, and educated in St. John's college, Cambridge, where he was chosen fellow in 1564. He was a youth of great parts, and a very high spirit. When he was a boy at school, having a literary contest with the famous Edmund Campion, and losing the silver pen which was proposed to the victor, he is said to have been angry and mortified to a degree almost beyond conception. Before he became fellow of his college, he spent six years at Clifford's-inn, where, in compliance with the wishes of his father, he was employed in the study of the law. But upon his return to the university, not liking the law, he directed his studies to other objects more congenial to his wishes; with which his father was so exceedingly offended, that though he was a man of considerable property, he refused to afford him support. Young Fulke, not discouraged by the unnatural treatment of his parents, was resolved to persevere in his literary pursuits, and to make his way through the world as well as he could. This he did, by his uncommon endowments, with the greatest ease. He studied with intense application, the mathematics, the languages, and divinity, and became a most celebrated scholar in each of these departments.

This learned divine espoused the principles of the puritans at a very early period; and in the year 1565, he preached openly and boldly against the popish habits and ceremonies incorporated with the ecclesiastical establishment. This presently roused the attention of the ruling ecclesiastics, when he was cited before the chancellor of the university. Though our author does not say what prosecution he underwent, nor what penalty he suffered, the chancellor declared his determination to proceed against him with rigour, and that he should find no comfort while persisting in this wantonness, as he was pleased to call his nonconformity;* and we may suppose he was as good as his word. The deficiency of information is, however, supplied by another author, who observes, that on account of his puritanism, he was expelled from his college; when he took lodgings in the town, and procured a support by the delivery of public lectures.†

Dr. Fulke having gained a most distinguished reputation, so early as the year 1569, he was upon the point of being chosen master of St. John's college, by a very considerable party, who had the highest value for him. This greatly offended Archbishop Parker, who, seasonably interposing, put a stop to his election.‡ The jealous archbishop could not bear that "Fulke's head should be thus stroken," as he expressed it; and he knew it was best to crush puritanism in the bud. About the same time, the Earl of Leicester, a constant friend and patron of such men, received him under his hospitable roof, and made him his domestic chaplain. Also, during the above year, he was charged with being concerned in certain unlawful marriages; but upon his examination by the Bishop of Ely, he was acquitted, and the charge proved to be altogether a calumny. He presently recovered his reputation. Though while he remained under the public odium, he voluntarily resigned his fellowship; yet his innocency was no sooner proved, than he was re-elected by the college.§

In the year 1571, the Earl of Essex presented Dr. Fulke to the rectory of Warley in Essex, and, soon after, to the rectory of Kedington in Suffolk. About this time, he took his doctor's degree at Cambridge, and was incorporated in the same at Oxford. The year following, he accompanied the Earl of Lincoln, then lord high admiral, as ambassador to the court of France.‖ Upon his return, he was chosen master of Pembroke hall, and Margaret professor of divinity, in the university of Cambridge. He was succeeded in his mastership by Dr. Andrews, chaplain to Queen Elizabeth, and afterwards successively Bishop of Chichester and Winchester.¶

Dr. Fulke was particularly intimate with Mr. Thomas

* Strype's Parker, p. 197. Appen. p. 72.
† Middleton's Biographia Evangelica, vol. ii. p. 262. Edit. 1780.
‡ Strype's Parker, p. 280. § Ibid.
‖ Strype's Annals, vol. ii. p. 240.
¶ Baker's MS. Collec. vol. vi. p. 295.

Cartwright; knew well his great worth; and united with other learned divines in warmly soliciting him to answer the Rhemish Testament. But when he found, that by the tyrannical prohibition of Archbishop Whitgift, Mr. Cartwright was forbidden to proceed, he undertook to answer it himself. His work was entitled "A Confutation of the Rhemish Testament," 1589; in which he gave notice, that the reader might some time be favoured with a more complete answer from Mr. Cartwright.* That which occasioned the publication of the Rhemish Testament was as follows:—The English papists in the seminary at Rheims, perceiving, as Fuller observes, that they could no longer "blindfold their laity from the scriptures, resolved to fit them with false spectacles; and set forth the Rhemish translation," in opposition to the protestant versions. Fulke undertook, and successfully accomplished, an entire refutation of the popish version and commentary. The late Mr. Hervey passed a very just encomium on this noble performance: which he styles, "a valuable piece of ancient controversy and criticism, full of sound divinity, weighty arguments, and important observations. Would the young student," he adds, "be taught to discover the very sinews of popery, and be enabled to give an effectual blow to that complication of errors; I scarce know a treatise better calculated for the purpose."†

In the year 1582, Dr. Fulke, with several other learned divines, was engaged in a public disputation with certain papists in the Tower. He was a person in every respect qualified for the undertaking. He had to contend with Campion, his old school-fellow, with whom he had formerly contested for the silver pen. And it is observed, evidently with a view to reproach his principles, and depreciate his memory, that "Dr. Fulke and Dr. Goad, being puritanically inclined, and leaning to Calvin's notions, afforded Campion, on one or two points, an advantage which his cause did not give him over the real principles of the English church."‡ We should have been extremely happy, and it would have been some addition to our stock of knowledge, if our learned author had mentioned those points, and stated the superior advantage they afforded the learned Jesuit, above the real principles of the ecclesiastical establishment. He did not, surely, mean to insinuate, that

* Peirce's Vindication, part i. p. 108.
† Toplady's Historic Proof, vol. ii. p. 196, 197.
‡ Charton's Life of Nowell, p. 278.

puritanism and Calvin's notions approach nearer to popery, than the church of England.

Dr. Fulke was author of a work, entitled "A brief and plain Declaration, containing the desires of all those faithful Ministers who seek Discipline and Reformation of the Church of England, which may serve as a just Apology against the false Accusations and Slanders of their Adversaries," 1584. Here he sufficiently declares his sentiments relative to church discipline and matters of nonconformity. Though Mr. Dudley Finner's name is prefixed to the work, Dr. Fulke was its author.* He was a very holy man, and a divine of uncommon learning and abilities, but ever scrupled some points of conformity. Wood styles him a good philosopher, and a pious and solid divine.† Granger observes, that he gained a great reputation by his writings against Cardinal Allen, and his "Confutation of Heskins, Sanders, and Rastell, three pillars of Popery," 1559. Dr. Fulke was, for a considerable time, says he, a warm advocate for the principles of the nonconformists; but in process of time, got the better of his prejudices, and made a near approach to the doctrine and discipline of the established church.‡ This author, for the satisfaction of his readers, ought to have proved, from good authority, that Dr. Fulke's principles of nonconformity arose from *prejudice*, and to have shewn *how near* he afterwards approached towards the ecclesiastical establishment.

As Dr. Fulke delivered his sentiments openly and freely on this subject, in the works that he published, let him speak in his own language. Giving his opinion of a bishop, according to the use of the church, and of the scripture, he affirms, "That for order and seemly government, there was always one principal, to whom by long use of the church, the name of bishop was applied; yet in the scripture a bishop and an elder is of one order and authority."§ "And," says he, "there ought to be in every church or congregation an eldership, which ought to have the hearing, examination, and determination of all matters pertaining to the discipline and government of that congregation."‖ Giving his sentiments of the cross in baptism, he makes the following observation: "Many, it is

* MS. Chronology, vol. ii. p. 419. (1 | 5.)
† Wood's Athenæ, vol. i. p. 724.
‡ Granger's Biog. Hist. vol. i. p. 215, 216.
§ Petition of Prelates Examined, p. 15. Edit. 1641.
‖ Paget's Church Government, p. 203.

true," says he, "speak of the sign of the cross; but they speak besides the book of God; and therefore their reasons are to be rejected. For men must not compare, or join the cross with the king's stamp; for he appointed no such thing whereby his servants might be known, but only *baptism*."* These sentiments afford sufficient evidence, that he was a puritan in his views of the ceremonies and discipline of the church.

This eminent servant of Christ, after a life of great labour and usefulness in the church of God, was released from all his toils, and received into everlasting joy, in the month of August, 1589; when his remains were interred in the chancel of the church at Kedington already mentioned. Afterwards a monumental inscription was there erected to his memory, of which the following is a translation, with the lines subjoined in English:†

In Memory
of William Fulke, D. D.
Master of Pembroke hall, Cambridge,
and Pastor of this church of Kedington.‡
In testimony of his continued love
hath Robert Wright, Professor of Divinity,
and present pastor of this church,
erected this monument.
His body was committed to the ground
August 28, 1589,
and lies in this chancel in hope of the resurrection
at the coming of Christ.

In deepest learning, with a zealous love,
To Heaven and Truth, could privileges prove
To keep back death, no hand had written here
Lies Reverend Fulke, till Christ in clouds appear.
His Works will shew him more free from all error,
Rome's foe, Truth's champion, and the Rhemist's terror.

Dr. Fulke, the twelfth of the month in which he died, made his last will and testament, which it may not be improper to insert in this place. It was as follows:§

"In the name of God, amen. I William Fulke, clerk, D. D. being of sound mind and memory, God be praised, make here my last will and testament. First, I commend my soul into the hands of Almighty God my Saviour and Redeemer, yielding most humble and hearty thanks unto his majesty for all his mercies bestowed upon me, most vile and

* Sion's Plea, p. 99. † Baker's MS. Collec. vol. ii. p. 292.

‡ Here there appears to have been some mistake in the spelling of the transcriber, which we have taken the liberty to correct.

§ Baker's MS. Collec. vol. iii. p. 327—329.

unworthy wretch, but especially for his mercy shewed unto me in Jesus Christ, in whom I believe to have remission of my sins, and to be justified by his blood. My body I commit to the earth, from whence it was taken, in steadfast hope of a glorious resurrection unto life everlasting, through the mercy and merits of the same Lord Jesus Christ. Concerning my earthly goods, wherewith God hath blessed me, I give all my lands freehold and copy, that are deviseable by law, or the custom of the manor, unto Christopher my eldest son, and to the heirs male of his body lawfully begotten, and for default of such heir, to William Fulke my younger son, and to the heirs male of his body lawfully begotten, and for default of such heirs, unto my heirs female, to be equally divided among them: and this I understand both of such lands as I have in possession, and also of those lands whereof I have the remainder or reversion of the last will of Christopher Fulke my dear father.

"Also I give and bequeath the customary lands that I have in Tanton called the Fullance, to William Leonard my brother-in-law, upon condition that he shall convey them over to my son Christopher, if the custom of the manor will permit it; but if the custom of the manor will not permit such conveyance, then I will that Margaret my wife, within one year after my departure, shall surrender the same to the use of my son Christopher, or else to have no benefit of this my last will and testament.

"I will that my antiquities shall be preserved to the use of Christopher my son, if he shall have delight in them at his full age, or else to the use of my son William at the like age, if he shall have delight in them, or else to be sold to some one that delights in antiquities, and the price to be equally divided among my daughters. Also I will that my books be preserved to the use of Christopher my son, if it shall please God to call him to the study of divinity, or else to the like use of William, if God shall call him to the same study: but if neither of them shall study divinity, I will that they shall be sold to the most advantage, and the price of them to be equally divided among my daughters. Whereas I owe ten pounds and some odd money to Pembroke hall, I will that the same be paid into the hands of him that shall succeed master in my room, in the presence of the treasurer of the college. Also in respect of divers benefits I have received of the said college, for a sign of thankfulness, I give unto the master and fellows of the college of Mary

Valence, one piece of plate made in fashion of an acorn, with a cover, which I will have to be called Dr. Fulke his cup, to be used only at commencements and solemn feasts.

"The rest of all my goods moveable, as money, plate, cattle, household stuff, prized reasonably according to the value, I will to be equally divided between Margaret my wife and my four daughters, Mary, Hester, Elizabeth and Ann, to be delivered unto them at the full age of twenty-four years; or at the day of their marriage, if it shall please God that they shall marry before that age: so that they match in the fear of God, with the consent of their mother, if she be living, or of their uncle Samuel, if he be living. And if any of them depart this life before their marriage, or the year before said, then I will that their portion be equally divided among them that are living. Also where I have a lease for three lives of a farm in Horsheath which is set over to my son Christopher, I will that my three daughters shall enjoy it successively, as they be named in the same, and that my son Christopher shall make conveyance unto them so soon as he shall be of lawful years. I will that the profit of my lands, until my son Christopher come to full age of twenty-one years, my wife's dowry excepted and ten pounds a year abated for the education of my son Christopher, shall be by my executors preserved and equally divided between my wife and my four daughters, in manner and form aforesaid.

"Also, I make Margaret my wife, and Samuel Fulke my brother, executors of this my will, in witness whereof, I have set my hand and seal this twelfth day of August, in the one and thirtieth year of the reign of our sovereign lady Queen Elizabeth.

"William Fulke."

The above will was proved October 9, 1589, before Humphrey Tyndall, deputy to Tho. Nowell, vice-chancellor of Cambridge. Our celebrated divine was author of many other learned works besides those already mentioned, most of which were written against the papists.

His Works.—1. Anti-prognosticon contra Predictiones Nostradami, Lovi, Hilli, &c., 1560.—2. Sermon at Hampton-Court, 1571.—3. Confutation of a Libelle in Forme of an Apology made by Frocknam, 1571.—4. A goodly Gallery, or Treatise on Meteors, 1571.—5. Astrologorum Ludus, 1571.—6. Metpomaxia, sivi, Ludus geometricus, 1578.—7. Responsio ad Tho. Stapletoni Cavillationes, 1579.—8. A Retentive against the Motives of Richard Bristow; also, a

Discovery of the Dangerous Rock of the Popish Church, 1580.—9. A Defence of the Translation of the Holy Scriptures in English, 1583. —10. Confutation of Will. Allen's Treatise in Defence of the Usurped Power of the Popish Priesthood.

JOHN GARBRAND, D. D.—He was born in the city of Oxford, educated in grammar learning at Wickham school, near Winchester, and in 1562, was admitted perpetual fellow of New College, Oxford. Afterwards, he became rector of North-Crowley in Buckinghamshire; and by the favour of Bishop Jewel, obtained some preferment in the church of Sarum. In 1582, he took his degrees in divinity. Upon the death of Jewel, whom he highly admired, he collected and completed several of his learned works: As, 1. A View of a Seditious Bull sent into England from Pius V. Pope of Rome, 1569.—2. A short Treatise of the Holy Scriptures, 1582.—3. An Exposition on the two Epistles to the Thessalonians, 1582.—4. Certain Sermons preached at Paul's Cross, 1583.—5. A Treatise of the Sacraments, gathered out of certain Sermons preached at Salisbury, 1583. Dr. Garbrand died towards the close of the year 1589, and his remains were interred in the church of North-Crowley. Wood says, he was accounted a good poet, an eminent theologian, and a noted preacher, but a severe puritan.* By his last will, he gave a quantity of his books to New College library.

DUDLEY FENNER was a divine of excellent learning and piety, and, for some time a celebrated tutor in the university of Cambridge, where he had Mr. Cartwright, Mr. Travers, and other distinguished persons for his pupils. Upon his removal from the university, he became minister at Cranbrook in Kent; but being dissatisfied with the episcopal ordination of the church of England, he went to Antwerp, and was ordained according to the manner of the reformed churches at that place, renouncing his former ordination.† During his stay at Antwerp, he preached, with Mr. Cartwright, to the English congregation in that city. But upon his return to England, he was brought into many troubles for nonconformity. In the year 1583, universal subscription to Whitgift's three articles being required of the clergy, Mr. Fenner and sixteen of his

* Wood's Athenæ Oxon. vol. i. p. 194, 195.
† Fuller's Church Hist. b. ix. p. 198.—Heylin's Hist of Pres. p. 290.

brethren, all ministers of Kent, waited upon his lordship, and signified that they could not subscribe with a good conscience. Therefore they humbly desired to know the result of his proceedings, and whether they might be favoured with a license to continue in their beloved work of preaching. This they did, in a letter addressed to the archbishop, dated January 30, 1584; in which they express themselves as follows:*—"Our duty in most humble "manner unto your grace presented. Whereas our coming "to your lordship in so great a company, was that every "one might be resolved, being in your lordship's judgment "offensive. Notwithstanding many of our doubts have "been heard, and by your lordship's great pains, favourably "interpreted, we were in the end dismissed without any "certainty of your lordship's pleasure. We have thought "it meet, therefore, to signify these two things to your "grace:—1. That we are not resolved in our consciences, "of the most of our former doubts, and have yet many "others not mentioned, which we judge of equal weight.— "2. That seeing we are not in our consciences, satisfied "to subscribe, we humbly desire to understand your grace's "favourable purpose, in proceeding with us, and whether "we shall receive license to depart or no.

"Your grace's most humble to command in the Lord.

"DUDLEY FENNER, ROBERT GOLLEFORD,
"JOSEPH NICHOLS, JOHN ELVIN,
"JOSEPH MINGE, LEVER WOOD,
"GEORGE CASLOCKE, WILLIAM KNIGHT,
"WILLIAM EVANS, ANTHONY HILTON,
"JAMES GROVE, THEOPHILUS CALVER,
"GEORGE ELY, JOHN MAYO,
"RICHARD HOLDEN, JOHN GRIMESTONE."
"ANTHONY BRIMSTONE,

In the conclusion, the archbishop suspended them all; upon which, Sir Thomas Scot and twenty-six respectable gentlemen in Kent, feeling the great loss of so many excellent ministers being silenced, all waited upon his lordship. From the conversation which they had with the archbishop, now before me, it is manifest how exceedingly solicitous they were to procure their restoration. But his grace being immoveable, their generous endeavours proved ineffectual.† Mr. Fenner continued under suspension many

* MS. Register, p. 326.
† MS. Chronology, vol. i. p. 332. (3 | 1) (3 | 3.)

years, even to the time of his death; and most probably his brethren shared no better fate.*

Upon their suspension, being slanderously aspersed from the press, by one who subscribed himself R. S., they were vindicated against the foul reproaches of this scurrilous writer. This vindication is at considerable length, though probably it was never printed.† Mr. Fenner, that he might silence calumny, gave a written testimony, that he was suspended merely for refusing subscription to Whitgift's articles. This testimony, dated June 12, 1585, was as follows:—"I, Dudley Fenner, was suspended from the "execution of my ministry, for this cause only, that I "refused to subscribe to the two last articles generally pro-"pounded to the ministers at the time of subscription. And "this my suspension was pronounced by the archbishop "himself. Indeed, I appeared before him and the rest "of her majesty's commissioners, to answer unto other "articles, but this was after my suspension; neither did I "receive any censure or other pain in that behalf, after my "answer to the said articles. This, being lawfully called "thereto, I am ready to confirm by oath.

"DUDLEY FENNER."‡

Upon Mr. Fenner's appearance before the archbishop and other commissioners, at the time specified in the above testimony, he received much unkind usage. Though he was a man of distinguished learning and piety, the proud archbishop called him a *boy*, a *knave*, a *slanderer*, a *libeller*, and other foul names, equally contrary to truth, and reproachful to his archiepiscopal character.§ Dr. Grey stigmatizes him "on account of his *vile republican principles*, with holding that it was lawful to take away the life of a king;" for which, if the good man had been punished more severely, than by seven years' suspension, the learned doctor could not but think he would have deserved it.‖ Such were the illiberal notions of these bigotted churchmen!

Some time after Whitgift suspended Mr. Fenner, he was committed to prison for nonconformity. And having suffered twelve months' imprisonment, upon a general subscription to the articles, *as far as the law required*, with a promise to use the Book of Common Prayer, and no other, he is said to have been released. He joined his brethren in

* MS. Register, p. 585. † Ibid. p. 272—290. ‡ Ibid. p. 588.
§ MS. Remarks, p. 403.
‖ Grey's Review of Neal, p. 72.

subscribing the "Book of Discipline."* Afterwards, on account of the severities of the times, there being no prospect of enjoying his liberty in the ministry, or some further troubles awaiting him, he was obliged to flee from the storm, when he went to Middleburgh, where he died towards the close of the year 1589.† His widow became the famous Dr. Whitaker's second wife.

Mr. Fenner, who is styled "an eminent light, yea, a bright-burning candle in his time,"‡ was a man of distinguished learning and abilities, and the author of many excellent works, some of which were upon the controversies of the times. Among these, was "A Defence of the godly Ministers against Dr. Bridges' Slanders, with a true Report of the ill Dealings of the Bishops against them." This work was finished a month only before the author's death.§ Dr. Bridges having asserted, that the puritans were not grievously afflicted, unless it was produced by their own deserts, Mr. Fenner made the following reply:—"Is it no grievous affliction, by suspension to be hung up between hope and despair for a year or two, and in the mean time, to see the wages of our labours eaten up by loiterers? Nay, our righteous souls are vexed with seeing and hearing the ignorance, the profane speeches, and evil examples, of those thrust upon our charges; while we ourselves are defamed, reproached, scoffed at, and called seditious, and rebellious; cited, accused, and indicted, and yet no redress to be found. All this we have patiently borne, though we come daily to the congregations to prayers, to baptisms, and to the sacrament, and by our examples and admonitions have kept many from those excesses whereunto their rashness of zeal would have carried them. And though to such as you, who swarm with *deaneries, double benefices, pensions, advowsons, reversions*, &c. these molestations may seem light; yet, surely, upon every irreligious man's complaint, to be sent for by pursuivants, to pay two-pence for every mile, to find messengers, to defray our own charges, and all this by such as can hardly provide for themselves and their families, it is not only grievous, but heart-burning.

"We will not justify ourselves in all things," says he, "but acknowledge, that when coming by dozens and scores

* Neal's Hist. of Puritans, vol. i. p. 406, 423.
† Wood's Athenæ Oxon. vol. i. p. 172.
‡ Paget's Church Government, p. 86.
§ MS. Register, p. 587.

before the bishop, after half a day's disorderly reasoning, some not being heard to the full, some railed on and miscalled, none with lenity satisfied, but all suspended from our office, because we refused to subscribe to his two last articles, there might afterwards pass from us some unjustifiable expressions. This we are willing to impute to ourselves."* The following is a list of Mr. Fenner's other learned productions.

His Works.—1. An Answer to the Confutation of John Nichols, 1581.—2. A Counter-Poyson, modestlie written for the Time, to make Answere to the Objections and Reproaches, wherewith the Answerer to the Abstract, would disgrace the Holy Discipline of Christ.—3. A Defence of the Reasons of the Counter-Poyson, for maintainance of the Eldershippe, against an Answere made to them by Doctor Copequot, in a publike Sermon at Paules Crosse, upon Psalm lxxxiv., 1584.†—4. A Commentry on Canticles.—5. The Order of Houshold Government.—6. An Interpretation of the Lord's Prayer.—7. An Interpretation of the Epistle to Philemon.—8. A short Table of Religion out of the first Table of the Law.—9. A Treatise of the Sacrament.—10. A profitable Treatise of Lawful and Unlawful Recreations.—11. The Art of Logic and Rhetoric plainly set forth.—12. Sacred Theology, in Ten Books.‡—13. The Consideration of the Admonition of Mr. Vaughan. A MS. copy of this work is now before me, but most probably was never published.

Cuthbert Bainbrigg was fellow of Christ's college, Cambridge, and a popular preacher in the university, but was brought into trouble for nonconformity. Having preached at St. Mary's church, January 5, 1589, he was summoned before the vice-chancellor, Dr. Nevil, and heads of colleges, who, for the dangerous doctrines said to be contained in his sermon, immediately sent him to prison. This affair, with a similar one of Mr. Francis Johnson's,§ excited the attention of the university for a twelvemonth.

Mr. Bainbrigg's text on this occasion was Luke xii. 49., "I am come to send fire upon earth," &c. Certain articles were collected from the sermon, and he was required to declare upon his oath, what he had delivered relative to those articles.‖ Both he and Mr. Johnson appeared before their learned inquisitors, January 23d; and

* Parte of a Register, p. 392, 393.

† The two last articles are published in "A Parte of a Register."—See p. 412—527.

‡ The MS. of this learned work, and apparently in Mr. Fenner's own hand, is still preserved in Dr. Williams's library, Redcross-street, London.

§ See Art. F. Johnson.

‖ Strype's Whitgift, p. 296.

refusing to answer upon their oath, they were committed to prison. The reason of their refusal being demanded, they made this three-fold protestation:—1. "That we do from our hearts, reverence your authority set over us by God.—2. That we refuse not an oath, as if it was unlawful on all occasions.—3. That we are neither afraid, nor unwilling to acknowledge and defend that which we have openly taught, if any person shall impugn it, or charge it to be unlawful."

March 19th, they underwent another examination, when they protested, "That if they had committed any crime, their only objection against taking the oath, was, that by so doing, they might be constrained to bring matter of accusation against themselves, which was contrary both to the word of God, and the laws of the land." And appearing again April 18th, they protested, "That if the oath then offered to them, could be shewn to be warranted by the word of God, and the laws of the land, they were ready to take it."

Their case exciting so much attention, was, at length, sent up to Lord Burleigh, chancellor of the university. Upon this, they further protested, "That if they might be suffered to appear before his lordship, they would clear themselves of the charges brought against them, or willingly suffer any condign punishment.—And that if their accusers would charge them with those things with which his lordship had been made acquainted, they would themselves, or by witness, disprove the charges, or suffer any kind of punishment they deserved: adding, that they were ready to answer, according to their honourable chancellor's letter, which required simply their answer, *without any oath*." They further observe, that they preached their sermons at the usual time and place, as they were required; and in the hearing of many hundreds of persons, both of the town and university, who were sufficiently able to satisfy their judges. But for them, merely by their office, to search what they delivered, by extorting it from them upon their oath; in this case, if they were guilty, they would be obliged to accuse themselves. This they looked upon as contrary to the word of God, and the established laws of the realm.*

The vice-chancellor and heads sent the following information to Burleigh the chancellor, containing, it is

* Strype's Annals, vol. iii. p. 589—591.

said, the chief points relative to the imprisonment of the two divines:—"That the court would have been hard indeed, in these proceedings, if all good means had not been first used.—That their proceeding is according to the canon law and the law of the realm.—That it is according to the former precedents of the university.—That the university, without this course, is hardly to be governed.—That by the relation of the physicians, as well as Mr. Bainbrigg himself, he was not sick.—That they have had liberty to attend their recreations in the fields, and their public exercises in the town."

To each of these points the two prisoners gave the following answers:—The vice-chancellor confesseth the offer of the oath to have been *hard*, but that all gentle means were first used. Let the means, say they, be examined. They were convened upon the delivery of their sermons, when articles were brought against them. They offered to answer these articles, but were refused; and they were required to swear to the truth, the whole truth, and nothing but the truth. They humbly desired that they might not be pressed to swear, because it was impossible for them to deliver every thing uttered in their sermons of an hour and half long. It is very hard to try the conscience of a man, to take the holy name of God in witness of that which he knoweth he cannot perform; and it is contrary to the law of God to offer in his name, to do that which is impossible.

Their reasons not being admitted, the ministers prayed the vice-chancellor, that they might be informed by the law of God and the realm, that they might and ought thus to swear, protesting their willingness to yield thereto; but, if this could not be done, they desired that they might be spared. They were then committed to prison; and, at the time these answers were given, they had been detained upwards of twenty weeks, without being admitted on bail. Hence it may appear, say they, that no very *gentle* means have been used. On the contrary; that all gentle means have been refused, is, indeed, too apparent. For about six weeks after their commitment, Sir Henry Knevett and Sir William Bowes, knights, offered bail to the vice-chancellor and Dr. Perne, which was rejected. Sir William Bowes afterwards renewed his application and his offer, but with no better success. He prayed them to be well informed of the issue, about which, he conceived, they were greatly mistaken. He recommended them to take down the fact concerning the prisoners in writing, then for two lawyers of each party to set down the law; and if the law would justify their proceedings, the prisoners should submit: but if it should appear otherwise, let them be enlarged, and they should complain no further. He also observed, that if the lawyers should not agree in any points of law, the cause, with the reasons of this difference, should be laid before the chancellor, and by him finally determined. These generous proposals the vice-chancellor and his colleagues utterly rejected, and would agree to no determination unless it were by two lawyers whom they should themselves appoint, or by the high commission in the presence of the Archbishop of Canterbury. Certain eminent persons, heads of colleges in the university, became earnest suitors to have them bailed, but all to no purpose.

The two prisoners were informed by their learned counsel, that upon the refusal of the oath, tendered them *ex mero officio*, they ought not to have been detained in prison, without bail, as might be proved by the laws of the land, and by the equity of the statute made 25 Henry VIII. Also, the counsel conceived them greatly mistaken in the whole of their proceedings. For, while they founded these proceedings on the statute of the university, they found therein neither the offer of the oath, which was done *ex mero officio*, being jurisdiction ecclesiastical; nor imprisonment proceeding from civil power; two different authorities compounded in the present action.

Though the above proceedings were said to be according to the precedents of the university, the vice-chancellor refused to shew, or suffer to be shewn, the register of any such precedent. Neither could it be found that any such precedent had ever occurred, excepting one solitary instance when Dr. Bying was vice-chancellor. At the same time, Dr. Goad, provost of King's college; Dr. Whitaker, master of St. John's college; and Mr. Chadderton, master of Emanuel college, all protested that they would have no hand in these proceedings. Also among the *fifteen* heads of colleges, only *five*, and of the *six* other doctors, only *two*, would join in these disgraceful oppressions.

Notwithstanding Mr. Bainbrigg was charged with counterfeiting sickness, the physician whom he employed, declared the contrary under his own hand. And the prisoners, so far from being allowed to go out of their prisons, as was represented to the chancellor, only took the liberty once to go to their college on a special occasion, when their keeper was checked by the vice-chancellor. And having made earnest suit for liberty to attend public service at St. Mary's church, with their keeper, on a Lord's day, their request was rejected by the vice-chancellor, saying, "You must pardon me, I neither can nor will."*

Mr. Bainbrigg and Mr. Johnson having suffered numerous and grievous hardships, laid their distresses before Burleigh the chancellor, in the following letter:†

"Right honourable and very good lord.

"May it please your good lordship once again to "admit the humble suit of us poor prisoners, now having, "as your lordship understandeth, of long time so con-"tinued in the university of Cambridge, without bail "or mainprize. And, first, may it please your honour "to understand, that we are not committed for any thing "uttered by us in our sermons, but only because we "did not yield to take a corporal oath, to deliver the "truth, the whole truth, and nothing but the truth, of "what we spake in our public sermons, and thereby to "accuse ourselves, if in any thing we had offended. "Without oath we have already openly in the consistory "(according to your honour's first letters) answered to "whatsoever we were charged with; notwithstanding "which, we still continue imprisoned, only because we "refuse to take their unlawful oath. We have great cause "to believe, that your honour hath been already a very "good lord unto us, in keeping from us that extremity "which we greatly feared; for which we shall continually "pray the lord to reward sevenfold in your lordship's "bosom. Yet because your lordship's first letters only "(which upon information against us) were imparted to "the rest of the heads of houses, and read also unto us; "but the two late letters sent from your honour, private "only to Mr. Vice-chancellor, were not communicated in "the whole to the heads present in the university. We "see no hope of release, except we yield to that hard "condition, which we have before set down to your "lordship, but are likely to be tired with imprisonment; "although in so good a cause, God witnessing us, we hope "never to give over.

"We are again bold to fly unto your lordship for relief, "desiring your honour to consider of our long impris-

* Baker's MS. Collec. vol. iv. p. 83—85. † Ibid. p. 86, 87.

"ment, only for refusing to take the oath: whereby we "are greatly restrained of that liberty which other scholars "do enjoy; and our bodily health is so endangered as one "of us hath been constrained very inconveniently in the "place to take physic. Our duties, also, to our pupils, "whom their parents have committed unto us, are very "much hindered; besides our common duties as fellows "of our college and scholars of the university, all the "benefits whereof we want, together with the hearing of "the word of God preached, and participation of the "sacrament administered; our private studies in the time "of our preparation for the ministry of the gospel, long "interrupted, and much disappointed; our good name "among our friends abroad and strangers every where, "that hear of our imprisonment, but not of the cause, "greatly impaired; and our exhibition, which should have "been employed to the maintenance of our studies, "exceedingly wasted in the charge of the prison. In all "which considerations we humbly beseech your good lord, "that by your lordship's good favour, we may obtain "at length, some release of that long imprisonment, "which we doubt not your lordship judgeth sufficiently to "have met with our offence.

"We refuse not to answer any matters wherewith we "can be charged, to put in bond or sufficient surety to "appear, either before your lordship, or before our gover-"nors here, when we shall be called. Besides, our fellow-"ships, the only stay of living that we have, will sufficiently "bind us hereunto. This is the whole sum of our suit, "which we refer wholly to your honour's wisdom and "equity. The Lord Almighty bless your honour with "long life, increase of honour in this life, and everlasting "life in the world to come, amen. From our prison in "Camb. May 22, 1589.

Your honour's most humble supplicants,

CUTH. BAINBRIGG, FRAN. JOHNSON."

The vice-chancellor and heads of colleges laid the case before the high commission. This was going the sure way to work. The high commissioners denominated the sermons of the two prisoners, factious, slanderous and offensive, and authorized the vice-chancellor and his colleagues to examine and proceed against the preachers, *according to their discretion*.[a] The dangerous doctrines said to have been

[a] Baker's MS. Collec. vol. vi. p. 185.

contained in Mr. Bainbrigg's sermon, were collected into certain articles; to each of which he delivered his answer in writing, as follows:

Art. 1. That some who seek preferment, pay money for it themselves; and pay their money beforehand.

Ans. I said, that the excellency of a public function in the church or commonwealth, consisted in labour and diligence for the good of the public, rather than in any pomp or outward shew. Jesus Christ came into the world, not to be ministered unto, but to minister unto others. And if the example of Christ were followed, men would, with Moses and Jeremiah, labour for the welfare of their fellow creatures, when they are called so to do, rather than seek preferment with such anxiety, even buying it with money when it cannot be obtained on more easy terms.

2. That there are persons who have a bar standing between them and the fire; that if need be, they may strike the fire out of the hands of those who bring it; and that this bar is your statutes and positive laws.

Ans. That principal word in the article, namely, *your*, I never used at all. I only said, positive laws and statutes had been abused by men in all ages as a bar, either to keep the fire of the word of God from them, or to strike it out of the hands of those who bring it. I observed, that is not a man of wisdom, fearing God, who does not know and acknowledge, that there must be good order, both in church and commonwealth, and will reverence it with all his heart, as one of the excellent appointments of God. He will acknowledge the excellency and necessity of wholesome laws, by which the members of society are united, strengthened, and beautified. Yet I said the wise and learned knew and would acknowledge, that though these laws were useful and necessary, they were imperfect rules of man's obedience, and, therefore, no sufficient bar to keep off the word of God, which requires more obedience than any human laws or statutes whatsoever. The laws of men, being imperfect, should always give place to the perfect laws of God.

I also observed, that when men are reproved for their sins, they should not regard so much how they may acquit themselves before men, and by human laws, though in some cases even this is necessary, as to try all things in the court of conscience, and by the word of God: much less should they strike the fire of the word out of the hands of those who bring it, and require more obedience of man than the laws demand. Offences, indeed, against positive laws must needs be punished, lest others, by too much lenity, be encouraged to do evil; yet with great prudence, especially in the case of a minister, lest the innocent be oppressed and injured. There must be great care, that the church be not deprived of the word, which is so excellent a treasure, and which the Lord hath committed to his ministers.

3. That there is extremity used, especially in the execution of laws.

Ans. I did not say there was extremity in the execution of laws. It seems that they who thus accuse me, wholly misunderstood my meaning when I recommended mutual forbearance; but especially in inferiors towards their superiors.

4. The fire of the word is put out, by stopping the mouths of those who bring it.

Ans. I never used the words, *putting out the fire*, nor *stopping their mouths*.

5. If you mind, indeed, to awake: As if he meant to reflect upon the sleepiness of the doctors' sermons usually delivered there.

Ans. I said thus, directing myself to the doctors, If you desire, indeed, that they (meaning the townsmen) should awake out of sleep; if you would have them forsake the works of darkness, and have Jesus Christ heard among them, provide that Jesus Christ may be more frequently preached among them.

6. That eloquence is base.

Ans. I did not speak against *good* eloquence; because, I said, of all gifts, there were none more excellent in itself, nor more profitable to society. But I spoke against the ridiculous eloquence of some in our days, which consisteth principally in an outward shew, and is disgraceful to the majesty of the word of God.

7. That ceremonies are no sooner spoken of, than they are snatched at.

Ans. I said, I could not help wondering that those men, who, hearing the ceremonies spoken of without distinction, would snatch at the word of God, in order to make a minister a transgressor. Whereas the Lord himself hath spoken against idle and unprofitable ceremonies, both in the Old and the New Testament.*

From the above statement, the reader will be able to

* Strype's Annals, vol. iii. Appen. p. 266, 267.

judge with what degree of justice Mr. Bainbrigg's opinions were denominated factious, slanderous, offensive and dangerous. To put an end to these oppressive measures, the chancellor interposed, and wrote to the vice-chancellor and heads, requiring that the two fellows might not be dealt with so rigorously.* A further account of Mr. Johnson is given under that article, to which the reader is referred. But Mr. Bainbrigg was still in the hands of his enemies; and they were determined to make him feel their smarting rod. The cruel ecclesiastics, contrary to Burleigh's express order, would not release him, till they had thoroughly humbled him. Therefore, they required him to make the following recantation, publicly, before the congregation where he had delivered his sermon:

"Whereas in a sermon made by me in this place, Jan. "5th last past, I was taken to charge the ministry of the "church of England, that they were unlike Moses and "Jeremiah, that refused a charge being called; for that "they do seek for livings, and buy them with their money, "when they do fall. I do acknowledge that howsoever my "words were taken, I think it lawful in a good conscience, "for the good of the church, to desire livings. Neither did "I say, as some did take me, that our statutes of the "university, and positive laws of the realm, are as a bar to "strike the fire of the gospel out of the hands of the "preachers, who be the Lord's messengers; but I think "reverently of good and wholesome laws, such as are "established by the queen's authority, as well in the "university, as in the rest of her dominions.

"And touching preachers, if any of them have by lawful "authority been put to silence, I think as charity requireth, "that the magistrates who have dealt therein, have been "moved thereto by conscience, for the discharge of their "honest duty in that behalf.

"I acknowledge, also, a godly use of eloquence in this "place, and that the ceremonies of our church established "by authority, being in themselves neither impious nor "unprofitable, are not here to be reproved by any private "man's conceit, but redress to be sought where it may be "had, if it be necessary in regard of any ceremony, whereby "offence may be taken."†

The above retraction, it is said, was subscribed by Mr. Bainbrigg's own hand, and he was enjoined to declare the

* Strype's Annals, vol. iii. Appen. p. 592.
† Baker's MS. Collec. vol. vi. p. 185, 186.

same in the pulpit of St. Mary's church; but whether he performed the latter we have not been able to learn. After this, he was most probably released from prison, and was restored to his fellowship in the college, which he appears to have enjoyed in the year 1590.* The year following he was chosen one of the proctors of the university.†

Edmund Littleton was a zealous puritan, who took an active part in promoting the associations. Though it does not appear at what place he exercised his public ministry, he was a man of considerable eminence, and always desirous to obtain a more pure reformation of the church. He united with his brethren in perfecting the "Book of Discipline;" and when it was finished, he joined with them in subscribing it.‡ On account of his zeal and activity to promote the desired ecclesiastical discipline, he was apprehended, with many of his brethren, in the year 1590, and carried before the high commission. He and some others were of opinion, that it was their duty to take an oath in all cases, when required by their superiors. He, therefore, took the oath *ex officio*, and discovered many things relative to the associations; for which he was most probably released.§

When he was apprehended, his papers were seized, and carried away, and produced as evidence against him and his brethren. Among these was the following declaration, subscribed by the persons whose names are subjoined.

"The brethren assembled together in the name of God, having heard and examined by the word of God, and according to their best abilities and judgment, a draught of discipline essential and necessary for all times, have thought good to testify concerning it as follows:—We acknowledge and confess the same to be agreeable to God's most holy word, so far as we are able to judge or discern of it, excepting some few points, which we have sent to our reverend brethren of this assembly, for their further resolution.

"We affirm it to be the same which we desire to be established in this church, by daily prayer to God, which we promise (as God shall offer opportunity, and give us to discern it so expedient) by humble suit unto her majesty, her honourable council and the parliament, and by all

* Strype's Annals, vol. iii. p. 592. † Fuller's Hist. of Cam. p. 149.
‡ Neal's Puritans, vol. i. p. 423. § Strype's Whitgift, p. 331—332.

other lawful and convenient means, to further and advanse, so far as the laws and peace of the present estate of our church will suffer it, and not enforce the contrary. We promise to guide ourselves and to be guided by it, and according to it.

"For a more special declaration of some points more important and necessary, we promise uniformly to follow such order, when we preach the word of God, as in the book is by us set down, in the chapters of the office of ministers of the word, of preaching, of sermons, of sacraments, of baptisms, and of the Lord's supper.

"Further, also, we follow the order set down in the chapters of the meetings, as far as it concerneth the ministers of the word. For which purpose, we promise to meet together every six weeks in classical conferences, with such of the brethren here assembled, as for their neighbourhood may fit us best, and such others as by their advice, we shall desire to be joined with us.

"The like we promise for provincial meetings every half year from our conferences to send unto them, being divided according to the order following. Also, that we will attend the general assembly every year, and at all parliaments, and as often as by order it shall be thought good to be assembled.

"John Oxenbridge,	Thomas Cartwright,
Humphrey Fenn,	Matthew Hulme,
Edward Gellibrand,	Anthony Nutter,
Hercules Cleveley,	Daniel Wight,
Leonard Fetherston,	Edward Lord,
John Ashbye,	Edmund Littleton."*

From the above curious declaration, we have a more clear and correct insight into the proceedings of the puritanical associations, and into the nature and design of their intended ecclesiastical discipline, than from all the raillery and misrepresentation of Dr. Bancroft and other bigotted historians. The private assemblies of the puritans are stigmatized by these writers, as having been dangerous, seditious, and amounting almost to treason; but the above paper will sufficiently refute and expose the shameful slander.

* Baker's MS. Collec. vol. xv. p. 71.

Edward Lord was some years vicar of Woolston in Warwickshire, but greatly persecuted for nonconformity. During Mr. Cartwright's exile at Guernsey and Antwerp, he took care of his hospital at Warwick; for which that reverend divine allowed him part of the profits, and gave the rest to the poor.* He subscribed the "Book of Discipline," and united with his brethren in their private assemblies; for which, in the year 1590, he was apprehended, and convened before the high commission and star-chamber, and cast into prison, where he remained a long time.† He underwent many examinations before his spiritual inquisitors, but refused to take the oath *ex officio*. On one of these occasions, he is said to have inquired "what would become of archbishops, bishops, &c. when the reformation should thrust them from their rich livings, that the country might not be pestered with beggars?" He gave some account of various private meetings and conferences among the brethren; and said, "that the painful preaching ministers now, are worse suppressed, than by the papists in the time of Queen Mary, who professed open enmity against them, and had law against them, which is otherwise now with us."‡ Mr. Lord was an eminently holy man, an able preacher, and an excellent divine. Upon his deprivation at the above period, he was succeeded in the pastoral office at Woolston by Mr. Hugh Clark, another excellent puritan.§

Andrew King was a divine of considerable eminence, but, in 1573, was apprehended and cast into prison for nonconformity. Being brought before the lords of the council and the high commission, and examined concerning some of Mr. Cartwright's opinions, and not answering to the satisfaction of his spiritual inquisitors, he was sent back to prison, and threatened with banishment if he would not conform.‖ What other sufferings he underwent at this time, we have not been able to learn. However, in the year 1590, he was again apprehended, together with Mr. Cartwright and many others, and cast into prison, where he remained a long time. During his imprisonment, he and his brethren were often carried before the high commission and the star-chamber, where they met with

* Clark's Lives annexed to Martyr. p. 20. † See Art. Cartwright.
‡ Baker's MS. Collec. vol. xv. p. 74. § Clark's Lives, p. 20, 129.
‖ Strype's Parker, p. 412, 413.

most tyrannical and cruel usage.* On one of these occasions, the following interrogatories were proposed to him:—"Whether have you refused to use, or have you used in your sermons, the queen's majesty's whole title by law established under her, namely, *defender of the faith*, in all causes, and over all persons, as well ecclesiastical as civil, in these her realms and dominions, and *supreme governor* next and immediately under God? For what cause have you so refused, or not used the said style? and were you admonished to use it?—Whether did you know or had heard before the 19th day of November, 1588, the said day was by and under her majesty's authority appointed to be solemnized and celebrated with thanksgiving unto God, for our happy deliverance from the intended invasion of the Spaniards? And did you that day, nevertheless, absent yourself from the parish church, and neither said divine service, preached, nor procured any other, then and there to do it? What was the cause, and what was your very true and only purpose and intent in so doing?"† Though Mr. King refused the oath *ex officio*, these inquiries were evidently designed to force him to accuse himself, and then to condemn him upon his own confession: but it does not appear what answers he gave, or whether he absolutely refused.

Malancthon Jewel was a zealous minister of Christ, but met with much cruel usage for his nonconformity. He was tried at the public assize at Exeter, and condemned upon the statute for confirming the Book of Common Prayer, to suffer five months' imprisonment. He met with this unjust and inhuman treatment, though he had previously applied to the bishop, for the removal of his doubts and scruples, but could not obtain the favour.‡ In the year 1590, he was again apprehended, and cast into prison; he was frequently taken before the high commission and the star-chamber, and remained under confinement about two years.§

Though he refused the oath *ex officio*, the following inquiries were proposed to him, and he was required to give his answer:—"Whether have you devised, penned, received, or delivered any English books or pamphlets, being contrary to the laws or statutes of this realm, since her majesty's proclamation in that behalf? And have you

* See Art. Cartwright.
† Baker's MS. Collec. vol. xv. p. 73.
‡ MS. Register, p. 585.
§ See Art. Cartwright.

affirmed of them, or some of such books, at Houlsworthy in the county of Devon, or elsewhere, (in commendation of them) that they contained no untruths; nor used words to the like effect? How many of every sort of such books have you had, of whom, and how have you bestowed them? —Whether in your speeches, sermons, or some of them, have you thought or affirmed, that it is of necessity, and in all places, to have churches governed by elderships of pastors, doctors, elders, or such like? Or, that the offices of archbishops and bishops, as they are practised in this realm, are the offices of antichrist; and that the archbishop and lord bishops, as you term them in contempt, were beasts, members of antichrist, and chimney sweepers; and that they persecute godly ministers; and by persecuting them, did purify them, and pollute themselves?—Whether have you taught openly, that no jailer ought to receive any man (though he be committed by any authority) into their prisons, except they first know the cause, that such were certainly offenders? And that her majesty's judges of assize, who affirmed that you have submitted yourself and promised conformity, did belie you, with other terms of reproach? And affirmed in pulpits, that justices were now become tyrants? or have you used any words to the like effect of these, or any of them? when, and where?—Whether did you baptize the child of one Asher, a pretended minister, who then made a public profession of his faith; and amongst other things, said 'he believed Christ had appointed his churches to be governed by pastors, doctors, elders, and deacons,' and in that faith desired baptism for his daughter, whom he named, *The Lord is Near;* and did you thereupon, and in that faith and profession baptize the child?"*—How tyrannical and ridiculous were these proceedings! What answers Mr. Jewel gave, or whether he absolutely refused to answer, we cannot learn.

Edward Snape was educated most probably in the university of Cambridge; afterwards he became minister at St. Peter's church, Northampton. He was a decided nonconformist, a laborious preacher, and a zealous advocate for a more pure reformation of the church. It is observed,

* Baker's MS. Collec. vol. xv. p. 77.

that when the parishioners of St. Peter's in Northampton understood that he did not account himself a full minister, till he should be chosen by some particular congregation, they immediately chose him to be their minister.*

In the year 1576, Mr. Snape and Mr. Thomas Cartwright were invited to the islands of Jersey and Guernsey, to assist the ministers of those places, in framing the necessary discipline for their churches. Dr. Heylin, who could never speak well of such men, charges these two divines with *imposing* their discipline upon the people of those islands; than which he could not have asserted a more palpable falsehood.† They were averse to every species of ecclesiastical imposition, and were called to those places only to give their instructions and advice; and this peevish, calumniating writer, must surely have known this. The two divines were men of distinguished learning and abilities. They laboured to have the discipline of the church wholly regulated by the New Testament; and, therefore, they were admirably qualified for the important undertaking.

After the comfortable settlement of those churches, Mr. Snape returned to England, and preached the gospel for some time in the diocese of Exeter; where, it is said, he sowed the seeds of nonconformity; but it is added, that the vigilant and stout prelate, Dr. Cotton, plucked them up before they came to perfection.‡ This, however, is a very defective account of his labours in those parts. For it is observed, that Mr. Snape, Mr. Eusebius Paget, and Mr. John Holmes, three excellent nonconformists in the diocese of Exeter, were exceedingly zealous and laborious to promote true religion; and, by their frequent and useful preaching, they were made a blessing to very many both of the clergy and common people.§ Mr. Snape having laboured in those parts for some time, returned to his ministerial exercise at Northampton, where he most probably continued several years.‖

About the year 1586, he united with his brethren in subscribing the "Book of Discipline;"¶ and in 1590, he was brought into trouble on account of the associations held in Northamptonshire, Warwickshire, and other counties. He was a zealous and an active member of these assemblies; for

* Bancroft's Dangerous Positions, p. 114.
† Heylin's Hist. of Pres. p. 293. ‡ Fuller's Worthies, part ii. p. 208.
§ MS. Chronology, vol. ii. p. 679. (3.)
‖ Heylin's Hist. of Pres. p. 276, 290. ¶ Neal's Puritans, vol. i. p. 423.

which he was convened before the high commission, when numerous charges were exhibited against him:* as, "That he had certain books in his possession, entitled 'A Defence of the Ecclesiastical Discipline.'—That he refused to baptise a child, unless it was called by some scripture name.†—That in his public ministry, he did not read the confession, absolutions, psalms, lessons, litany, and some other parts of the Book of Common Prayer.—That he renounced his calling to the ministry by the bishop's ordination.—And that he urged others to renounce their calling in like manner."—Such were the crimes with which our divine was charged!

Mr. Snape, and many of his brethren, for crimes like these, were summoned before the high commission at Lambeth, and required to take the oath *ex officio*, to answer all interrogatories which might be proposed to them. This they utterly refused, unless they might first see them. And, says Dr. Heylin, when the interrogatories were even shewed them, Mr. Snape, apprehensive of danger to himself and his brethren, still refused to take the oath. An unpardonable crime was this, in the opinion of this author! It should be recollected, that Mr. Snape and his persecuted brethren did not positively engage to answer, even upon the sight of the interrogatories; they only refused to take the oath, and to give their answer, till they had seen those interrogatories; and, after they had seen them, they should be better able to judge whether it was lawful or unlawful.

Mr. Snape's letters having been intercepted, were produced against him; and when he refused to accuse himself and his brethren, he was immediately sent to prison. Our author adds, "This struck great terror into all the brethren, who now began to apprehend the dangers into which they were fallen by their former insolences."‡ A pitiful triumph, indeed!—Another writer observes, that when Mr. Snape was examined before the high commission at Lambeth, in

* Strype's Whitgift, p. 329—331.

† The following curious tale is told of Mr. Snape:—"There goes a story," says Dr. Heylin, "that one Hodgkingson of Northampton, having a child to be baptized, repaired to Snape, to do it for him; and he consented to the motion, but with promise that he should give it some name allowed in scripture. The holy action being so far forwards, that they were come to the naming of the infant, they named it Richard, being the name of its grandfather. Upon this a stop was made, and he would not be persuaded to baptize the child, unless its name were altered; and the god-father refusing to do this, the child was carried home unchristened."—*Heylin's Hist. of Pres.* p. 293.

‡ Ibid. p. 302, 303.

April, 1590, *thirty-six* articles were delivered to him in writing, which, as an inducement to take the oath, he was allowed to read. These articles related to the persons, places, and times of their associations, and the subjects discussed on those occasions. Upon a second examination, and still refusing the oath, he was committed close prisoner.*

Though we are unable to learn whether he continued to refuse the oath, he certainly gave his answer to at least part of the interrogatories. He underwent many severe examinations before the high commission, and the star-chamber; and on one of these occasions, he gave the following answers, containing, it is said, "a true account of that which Edward Snape confesseth, he wrote and gave forth:"

1. "Touching the substance of my calling to the ministry, I affirm, that I had it of the church of God, being approved by the godly and learned neighbouring ministers, and chosen to the function by the people of my charge. Touching that allowance which I had of the bishop, I take it to be a thing *merely civil*, belonging to a civil magistrate, which authority he hath by act of parliament; and which, therefore, I might lawfully receive at his hands, for the peaceable execution of my ministry.

2. "Touching the use of the Book of Common Prayer, I will use it only in those things which are justifiable by the word of God. And if it can be proved unto me, by sound reasons out of that word, that it is utterly unlawful to use any part of it, I will cease to use it at all.

3. "Touching the calling of elders, I do promise to use all holy and lawful means, for the procuring of it.

4. "Touching the surceasing of my ministry, I do also promise, that though I shall be inhibited by the bishop, yet, if the greater part of the communicants of my charge, shall require the continuance of my ministry; and shall also bind themselves to minister competently to my necessities; and shall have the consent of the godly neighbouring ministers, bonds or liberty, I will not surcease.

5. "Touching obedience to the bishops, I promise not to yield myself subject to them, in any things but such as are *civil;* and otherwise to disclaim any of their authority over me, as they are taken for ministers.

6. "To conclude. Whatever I use in my ministry,

* MS. Chronology, vol. ii. p. 435. (2.)

which shall be proved out of the word of God, to be unlawful, I will leave it: and whatsoever I use not, which may be also proved out of the word of God that I ought to use, I will, God willing, use it."*

Also, on one of these occasions, when Mr. Snape appeared before his ecclesiastical inquisitors, he confessed, and said, "It was agreed upon in the classical and general assemblies, that *dumb* ministers were no ministers of Christ, and that the ministers should preach to promote a pure ecclesiastical government."†

Mr. Snape is said to have confessed in effect the whole of that with which he and his brethren were charged. He acknowledged that he moved the mayor of Northampton to unite with other towns, in presenting a supplication to the queen, humbly beseeching her majesty to hear their cries, and grant them a more pure ecclesiastical discipline. He joined with his brethren in their association at Warwick, in 1588; when they declared against private baptism, reading apocryphal books and homilies in the church, communicating with unlawful ministers and the government of bishops and archbishops, and for the erection of a better discipline.

He is said, also, to have used the following rash expressions, against the persecuting prelates:—"I pray God strengthen our faith, and arm us with patience; and then let the devil and his deputies the bishops, do what they can. In the mean time let us take our pennyworths of them, and not die in their debt. It fareth with us as with the prisoners in popery. God send us their comfort." And he compared the established church, under the oppressions of the bishops, "to Babel and the Red Dragon, dyed red with the blood of the saints."‡ Oppression will make a wise man mad.

At one of Mr. Snape's examinations, the following curious interrogatory was proposed, to which he was required to give his answer:—"Have you said and signified this, viz. 'How say you, if we devise a way to take off all the antichristian yoke and government of bishops, and will jointly erect the discipline and government all in one day, in such sort as they shall never be able to prevail to the contrary? But peradventure, it will not be this year and half?' Or, did you use any words to the like effect, or tending or

* Baker's MS. Collec. vol. xv. p. 72.
† Baxter's Second Plea, p. 32.
‡ Baker's MS. Collec. vol. xv. p. 73, 74.

sounding that way? To whom, when, and where, and what was your meaning, and only meaning thereby?"* Such inquisition was certainly designed to ensnare his conscience, and to compel him to become his own accuser, even in the presence of his judges.

After having suffered eleven months' close imprisonment, Mr. Snape united with many others under similar oppressions, in presenting a supplication to the lord treasurer, humbly desiring to be admitted to give bail. At the same time, Archbishop Whitgift sent them a form of submission, which they unanimously rejected. A particular account of these transactions is given in another place.† But when he was released from prison, we are not able to learn.

The following anecdote is related of this persecuted servant of God. Mr. Snape, it is said, being cast into prison by the bishops for nonconformity; and all his money being expended by his long confinement, he met with much unkind usage from the jailer. The good man being one day on his knees in fervent prayer to God, and the window of his chamber being open, observed something thrown into the room; but he resolved to finish his prayer, before he examined what it was. When he rose from his knees, he found, to his great surprize, a purse full of gold lying on his chamber floor. By this unexpected supply, he was more comfortable in his situation, and enabled to make his keeper *better natured* ever after.‡ *The Lord heareth the young ravens when they cry;* how much more will he hear his afflicted people!

JOHN HOLMES was brought up under Bishop Jewel, and was an excellent preacher, and a man of great piety. Bishop Woolton of Exeter having obtained a good opinion of him, presented him to the benefice of Keane in Devonshire. He no sooner entered upon his public charge, than he began to labour as a faithful steward of the manifold mysteries of God. Being deeply concerned for the welfare of his flock, he manifested a strong affection for their best interests. He embraced every opportunity of affording them the best instruction, particularly by his catechetical exercises, a practice to which they had been very little accustomed. He also faithfully reproved their gross vices and disorders; for which he was complained of to the

* Baker's MS. Collec. vol. xv. p. 76. † See Art. Cartwright.
‡ Mather's Hist. of New Eng. b. iii. p. 10.

bishop; who, though he had been minister of the same place, deprived him of the living. In the year 1590, Humphrey Specot, esq. presented Mr. Holmes to the rectory of Tetcote, in the same county; but the above prelate refused him institution, and put him to numerous troubles, pretending that Mr. Holmes was an inveterate schismatic, merely because he could not with a good conscience observe every punctilio of conformity.

RICHARD GREENHAM, A. M.—This most excellent servant of Christ was born about the year 1531, and educated in Pembroke hall, Cambridge; where he took his degrees in Arts, and was chosen fellow.* Upon his removal from the university, he became pastor to the congregation at Drayton, near Cambridge; where he continued many years, not sparing himself to promote the salvation of souls. He was a hard student, and constantly rose, winter and summer, at four o'clock in the morning. He always preached twice on a Lord's day, and catechised the young people of his parish. He usually preached four times and catechised once, during the week; and for the greater convenience of his people, these week-day services were observed early in the morning. He took such uncommon pains, and was so remarkably ardent, in his preaching, that at the conclusion of the service, his perspiration was so great, that his shirt was usually as wet as if it had been drenched in water. He was more concerned to be useful, than to obtain any worldly emolument whatever; therefore, he refused several lucrative preferments when offered him. He naturally cared for souls, and manifested on all occasions a warm concern for their salvation. At the same time, he was not unmindful of their temporal comfort, but abounded in acts of liberality to the poor and distressed; for which he and his family often suffered want. In addition to his public ministerial labours, he had a remarkable talent for comforting afflicted consciences; and in this department the Lord greatly blessed his endeavours. Having himself waded through the deep waters, and laboured under many painful conflicts, he was eminently qualified for relieving others. The fame of his usefulness in resolving the doubts of inquiring souls, having spread through the country,

* Baker's MS. Collec. vol. ii. p. 378.

multitudes from all quarters, flocked to him as to a wise physician, and by the blessing of God, obtained the desired comfort. Numerous persons who to his own knowledge had laboured under the most racking terrors of conscience, were restored to joy and peace in believing. When any complained of blasphemous thoughts, his advice was "do not *fear* them, but *abhor* them."*

Mr. Greenham was a man remarkable for peace. He was celebrated for promoting peace among those who were at variance, and in labouring incessantly for the peace of the church of God. He was a most exact and conscientious nonconformist, choosing on all occasions to suffer, rather than sacrifice a good conscience. Though he cautiously avoided speaking against conformity, or those things which to him appeared objectionable in the established church; lest he should give the least offence, he was suspended from his ministry, for refusing to subscribe and wear the habits.† He was of opinion that rites and ceremonies introduced into the church of Christ, without the warrant of scripture, were of no real advantage, but productive of much superstition;‡ therefore, he prayed that all such things, as hinderances to the success of the gospel, might be taken away. To subscribe to any thing besides the word of God, or not collected from that sacred volume, he durst not, but peremptorily refused.§

Whoever will read his letter to Dr. Cox, bishop of Ely, will easily perceive what manner of spirit they were of, who could bear hard upon so excellent and peaceable a divine.‖ When he was called before the bishop, upon a complaint of his nonconformity, he discovered at once, his prudence, peaceableness, and good sense. His lordship observing that there was a great *schism* in the church, asked him whether the blame was attached to the conformists, or nonconformists. To which Mr. Greenham immediately replied, "that it might be attached to *either*, or to *neither*. For," said he, "if both parties loved each other as they ought, and did acts of kindness for each other, thereby maintaining love and concord, the blame would be on neither side; but which party soever made the rent, the charge of schism belonged to them." The bishop is said to

* Clark's Lives annexed to his Martyrologie, p. 12—14.
† Parte of a Register, p. 86—93.
‡ Greenham's Works, p. 278. Edit. 1601.
§ Parte of a Register, p. 88, 89.
‖ This letter is preserved, but too long for our insertion.—*Ibid.* p. 86—88.

have been so well satisfied with this answer, that he dismissed him in peace.* Mr. Greenham united with his brethren in subscribing the "Book of Discipline."†

This worthy divine having laboured in the ministry at Drayton about twenty-one years, removed to London, and became minister at Christ-church, where, in about two years, he finished his labours. He died a most comfortable and happy death, in the year 1591, aged sixty years. Fuller, who says he died of the plague, observes, that he was an avowed enemy to nonresidents, and wondered how such men could find any comfort in their wealth. "For," he used to say, "they must see written upon all they have, *this is the price of blood.*" Our author adds, that he was most precise in his conversation, a strict observer of the Lord's day, and that no book made a greater impression upon the minds of the people, than his "Treatise on the Sabbath," which greatly promoted the observance of it through the nation.‡ Mr. Strype denominates him a pious minister, but not well affected to the orders of the established church.§

Mr. Greenham was an excellent writer, for the time in which he lived. His works, including Sermons, Treatises, and a Commentary on Psalm cxix., came forth at different times, but were collected and published in one volume folio, in 1601. The excellent Bishop Wilkins speaks in high commendation of his sermons, classing them with the most valuable in his day.‖ And his commentary, says Dr. Williams, is admirable, for the time in which it was written, both for style and method; and, like all the productions of this author, is full of spiritual unction.¶

The above edition of Mr. Greenham's works was published by Mr. Henry Holland, and dedicated to the Countess of Cumberland and the Countess Dowager of Huntington. In this dedication, it is observed as follows: "I come as in the name of the faithful servant of Christ, Mr. Richard Greenham, a man well known unto your honours, and to those most religious patrons of all piety and good learning, the Right Honourable Earls of Huntington, Warwick, and Bedford, of blessed memory, which now sleep in the Lord. Of them was he much reverenced in his life-time; of your honours much lamented after death; for you know the loss of such to be no small rack unto the church and people of God. Such experience and good liking

* Clark's Lives, p. 13. † Neal's Puritans, vol. i. p. 423.
‡ Fuller's Church Hist. b. ix. p. 219, 220. § Strype's Aylmer, p. 152.
‖ Discourse on Preaching, p. 82, 83. ¶ Christian Preacher, p. 431.

have your honours had of this man of God, of his godliness and gravity, and of the manifold gifts of God in him, that I need say no more, as any way doubting of your honourable acceptation."

In the edition of his works, published in 1612, there is a dedication by Mr. Stephen Egerton, another excellent puritan, to Sir Marmaduke Darrell and Sir Thomas Bloother, knights, part of which is as follows:—"Surely, if one heathen man could gather gold out of the writings of another, how much more may we, being christians, gather not gold only, but pearls and precious stones out of the religious and holy labours of Mr. Richard Greenham, being a most godly brother; yea, more than a brother, even a most painful pastor, zealous preacher, and reverend father in the church of God; of whom I am persuaded that for practical divinity he was inferior to few or none in his time."

This pious divine had a strong and an unceasing attachment to the house of God. He used to say that ministers ought to frequent those places most where God hath made them most useful. Having once found the sweetness of gaining souls, thither should they be most desirous to resort. He had so conscientious a regard for the ordinance of public worship, that, however weak might be the talents of the preacher, he constantly esteemed it his duty, as well as his happiness, to resort to the house of the Lord.

Giles Wigginton, A. M.—This zealous puritan was born at Oundle in Northamptonshire, educated in Trinity college, Cambridge, and, in 1566, made second scholar in the college. He went to the university under the patronage and recommendation of Sir Walter Mildmay,* and was educated under Dr. Beaumont, master of the above college. Afterwards, he was chosen fellow of the house, though much opposed by Dr. Whitgift, then master of the college. He took his degrees in arts in 1571, having made great progress in the knowledge of divinity and the Greek and

* Sir Walter Mildmay was a constant friend to the persecuted nonconformists, and founder of Emanuel college, Cambridge, which afterwards became the very nursery of puritanism. He was surveyor of the court of argumentation in the reign of Henry VIII., and privy counsellor, chancellor, and under-treasurer of the exchequer to Queen Elizabeth. He is celebrated by Camden, and other historians, for his uncommon merit in his private and public character.—*Fuller's Hist. of Cam.* p. 146, 147.—*Granger's Biog. Hist.* vol. i. p. 233.

Hebrew languages. He continued some years longer at Cambridge, and, when he quitted the university, was possessed of great learning and many excellent endowments.

Mr. Wigginton having completed his studies at the university, was presented to the vicarage of Sedburgh, in the North Riding of Yorkshire; but being a zealous nonconformist, he became a great sufferer in the common cause. In the year 1581, Archbishop Sandys, writing to the Bishop of Chester, in whose diocese our divine lived, thus reproaches his nonconformity:—"Your lordship," says he, "shall do well to better Mr. Wigginton, a young man very far out of frame; who, in my opinion, will not accept of you as his ordinary or bishop; neither would I accept of him being in your place, as a preacher of my diocese. He laboureth not to build, but to pull down, and, by what means he can, to overthrow the state ecclesiastical."* He probably thought the ecclesiastical state so far corrupted and decayed, that it was incapable of the amendment that was desired; and, therefore, he might wish and endeavour by all peaceable means, to have it pulled down, and a more pure discipline and government erected.

Being afterwards in London, he was appointed in the year 1584, to preach before the judges, in St. Dunstan's church. Information of this coming to the ears of Whitgift, then Archbishop of Canterbury, he sent a pursuivant to Mr. Wigginton's lodgings in the dead of the night; and, finding him in bed, forbade him preaching, and required him to give bond for his appearance the next day, at Lambeth. All this he did without any written warrant. Upon his appearance at Lambeth, and refusing the oath *ex officio*, to answer certain articles altogether unknown to him, the archbishop, after using much reviling and reproachful language, committed him to the Gatehouse, where he remained nine weeks within one day. At the expiration of this period, the merciful archbishop released him, and gave him canonical admonition, charging him not to preach in his province without further license.†

In the year 1585, upon the information of one Edward Middleton, a man of profane character, and a suspected papist, Whitgift gave orders to his brother Sandys of York, to proceed against Mr. Wigginton, even to deprivation. He was therefore cited before Chadderton, bishop of

* Baker's MS. Collec. vol. xxviii. p. 366. † MS. Register, p. 759.

Chester, when *twelve* charges were exhibited against him; and, in the end, he was deprived of his ministry; and one Colecloth, a minister of immoral character, was sent to take possession of the living. Afterwards, by the favour and influence of several persons of quality, he was again restored.

In the year 1586, our divine, being in London, was again apprehended by one of Whitgift's pursuivants, and carried before his grace at Lambeth; who, for refusing the oath to accuse himself as before, committed him to the White-lion prison, where he was treated with the utmost barbarity. We shall give the account in his own words. "In the month of May," says he, "I was in London; and was sorely vexed by the archbishop's pursuivants, who apprehended me, and took me to Lambeth. At Lambeth, I was shamefully reviled and abused by the archbishop and those about him, as if I had been the vilest rebel against my prince and country. He then committed me to the keeper of the prison in Southwark, who, by the archbishop's strict charge, so loaded me with irons, confined me in close prison, and deprived me of necessary food, that in about five weeks, I was nearly dead." Such were the unfeeling and inhuman proceedings of this persecuting arch-prelate.

While in this deplorable condition, Mr. Wigginton wrote to a certain nobleman, soliciting him to use his utmost endeavours to obtain his deliverance from such cruel usage. In this letter, dated from the White-lion, June 1, 1586, he expressed himself as follows:—"I desire "you to make known my lamentable case to her majesty's "honourable privy council, or to her majesty herself, that "the cause of my imprisonment may be examined, and "that I may be delivered from this hard usage. For I "desire *justice*, and not *mercy*, being conscious of my own "innocency. My old adversary, the archbishop, hath "treated me more like a *Turk*, or a *dog*, than a man, or a "minister of Jesus Christ. I heartily commend you to "God. GILES WIGGINTON."*

He further proceeds in this account of himself, and says, "At length, my life being in so great danger, I was removed to another prison in London. And some time after this, I was brought again to Lambeth; when, for refusing to answer as before, after much slanderous usage, the archbishop suspended me from preaching in his province,

* MS. Register, p. 769.

and, in a certain way, deprived me of my living at Sedburgh: but for my final deprivation, he sent me to Sandys, archbishop of York.

"When by the extremity of my sickness in prison, I was constrained still to abide some time in the city; and when, in the opinion of learned physicians, I was on my death-bed, the archbishop sent two pursuivants, commanding me to appear before him again at Lambeth; which I being unable to do, he pronounced against me the sentence of deprivation and degradation.* After my departure, the Earls of Warwick and Huntington, without my solicitation, did earnestly sue unto him for my restoration; but he absolutely refused, signifying, that he had already written to the patron of the living, for the presentation of another to the place."†

Upon Mr. Wigginton's recovery from sickness, he returned to Sedburgh, and offered himself to preach in the church, but was refused the pulpit. He, therefore, preached in various places, and particularly in his own house, where he had a considerable assembly; and looking upon himself as the pastor set over the people by the Lord, he administered both the ordinances of the gospel. This coming to the knowledge of Whitgift, by his instigation an attachment was sent forth from Archbishop Sandys, "To all justices, mayors, sheriffs, bailiffs, constables, and all other her majesty's officers and subjects, within the province of York, or to any of them, to apprehend him, and commit him to the castle of Lancaster, in the province of York."‡ Accordingly, Mr. Wigginton being soon after on a journey, was apprehended at Boroughbridge, arrested by a pursuivant from the archbishop, and carried to Lancaster castle, being the distance of fifty miles, in a severe, cold winter. There he was shut up in close prison among felons and condemned prisoners, and more basely used than they, or the recusant papists. From hence he sent an account of his case to Sir Walter Mildmay, his worthy patron, and one of the privy council; wherein he expressed himself as follows:§

* Whitgift, says Hume, was a zealous churchman, who had signalized his pen in controversy; and who, having in vain attempted to convince the puritans by argument, was now resolved to open their eyes by power, and by the execution of penal statutes.—*Hist. of Eng.* vol, v. p. 188.

† The person presented to the living, was one Edward Hampton, a man unlearned, and openly profane.—*MS. Register*, p. 760—765.

‡ Ibid. p. 767.

§ Ibid. p. 753, 754.

"Right honourable and beloved in Christ,

"Since my late deprivation at Lambeth, I have both preached and ministered the sacraments, to my flock at Sedburgh; nor could I find any rest in my conscience till I had done this.* And as I have not depended on any man's opinion, in what I have done, so the Lord hath abundantly blessed me with heavenly comforts in my own soul, and under my painful sufferings; and abundantly blessed my labours among those whom he committed to my care.

"I have turned my back upon those antichristian and unlawful proceedings which were used against me, my ministry, and my flock. This was necessary in these days of prelatical and popish superstition. But I must inform you, that as I was lately on my journey as far as Boroughbridge, my wife big with child, and the other branches of my family being with me, I was there arrested by a pursuivant, and brought to this place, a distance of fifty miles, in this cold winter. The chief cause of this usage, is my preaching and administrating the sacraments among my flock, after my deprivation. Dr. Sandys used me hardly, in causing me, and those who were with me, to remain four days at Boroughbridge, and in sending me this distance, to this noisome prison, in cold winter, when there were better prisons near at hand. I am here within the iron gate, in a cold room, among felons and condemned prisoners, and in various ways, worse used than they, or recusant papists. Therefore, my suit to your honour, is, that it would please your honour to use some means, as God shall direct you, whereby I may be delivered out of the hands of my cruel enemies. And that it may please your honour to further the reformation of our English church, especially in this present parliament; that the faithful ministers of Christ may not be silenced by the prelates; that good christians may not be brought into trouble, for refusing those rites and ceremonies which are the inventions of men; and that a learned and godly minister may be appointed to every congregation.

"You are now one of the oldest nobles in our land. Your days are few and wearing out; therefore, let them be spent to the honour of Christ. Thus we shall pray for

* About one hundred and forty of Mr. Wigginton's people, for the sad crime of hearing him preach after his deprivation, were cited to appear at York and other places, at the distance of sixty or eighty miles, most of whom were excommunicated by the ecclesiastical commissioners.—*MS. Register*, p. 770.

you, while you live, and esteem your posterity when you are with Christ in the kingdom of heaven. The Lord both guide and bless your honour, and his whole church. From Lancaster castle, February 28, 1587.

"GILES WIGGINTON, pastor of Sedburgh."

It does not appear what effect was produced by the above letter, nor how long Mr. Wigginton remained a close prisoner; but in about two years, he was brought into other troubles by Whitgift, his old adversary. In the month of December, 1588, being in London, the archbishop's pursuivant apprehended him at his lodgings, while he was in bed, and carried him to Lambeth, upon suspicion of being one of the authors of Martin Mar-Prelate. At Lambeth, he appeared before the Archbishop, the Bishop of Winchester, Dr. Aubery, Dr. Cosin, Dr. Goodman, and other high commissioners; when he underwent the following examination:

Archbishop. There is a book, called Martin Mar-Prelate, a vile, seditious, and intolerable book; and you are suspected to be one of its authors. Therefore, you are to swear what you know concerning it.

Wigginton. You do well to let me know what I have to swear to. But let me know, also, who are my accusers. For I do not mean to accuse myself.

A. We will take your answers upon your word alone. What say you to these articles following? Have you any of those books? or have you read or heard any of them read, or any part of them, at any time?

W. I will not answer to accuse myself. Let my accusers stand forth and proceed against me. You have known my mind upon this point, many years.

A. Have you had any of them, and how many? How came you by them? What did you do with them? In whose hands are they? And by whose means did you obtain them?

W. I had rather accuse myself, than other persons; but I will accuse neither. Let mine accusers, and proper witnesses according to the laws of God and the realm, proceed against me. I expect no comfort in accusing myself, or my neighbour.

A. Have you bought, sold, given, dispersed, handled, or any way dealt in any of them? and in what sort?

W. I account it as unnatural for me to accuse myself, as to thrust a knife into my thigh. The matter, I understand, is doubtful and dangerous; therefore, I will accuse neither myself nor others. "In the mouth of two or three witnesses, let every word be established." The heathen judge said, "I will hear thee when thine *accusers* are come."

A. Do you know the author, writer, or printer of that book? Did you make or help to make, write, or print it, or any part of it, or see any part of it before it was printed?

W. I did neither make, write, nor print it, nor any part of it, nor see any part of it before it was printed.

A. Did you not deliver some copies of it in the country, one to Mr. Moore, and another to Mr. Cartwright?

W. I understand, what you well know, that many lords, and other persons of quality, have obtained and read the book. And supposing I have done the same, it will, in my opinion, be more to your credit, to examine all sorts about it, and not poor persons only, according to your custom.

A. Whom do you believe, think, suspect, or conjecture, to be the author, writer, or printer of it, or any part of it, or any way helper towards it? Did you make any oath, or vow, or promise, to conceal the same?

W. What I believe, think, suspect, or conjecture, or have vowed or promised, I am not bound to make known. I answer as before, I would rather accuse myself, than my neighbour.

A. What printing press, or furniture for printing, have you known, within the two years last past?

W. I know of none, as I told you before.

A. Yes, but you are verily suspected of it. Public fame is against you.

W. I thank God, I am not infamous; nor will I borrow of any man. But, by the grace of God, I will live a true subject, the benefit of whom I claim, and wish to enjoy.

A. But what do you say about the case of Atkinson of Sedburgh, as mentioned in the book? Did not you minister this report of Atkinson, nor any thing else towards the book? Have you the note of Atkinson's hand for it, or who hath it?

W. I did not minister any such thing. For if I had done it, I would have reported the same story in another form. Atkinson told it to many others besides me, whose names I reserve in silence.

A. Did you not say to the pursuivant, as you came in the boat, that you had seen the second Martin, called, "The Epitome?"

W. Let the pursuivant stand forth, and accuse me, if he will.

Bishop. You have preached pernicious doctrine.

W. What do you mean by pernicious doctrine? I preach that doctrine which promotes the glory of God, and the salvation of his people.

B. We have the queen's authority and commission in our hands.

W. I pray for you, that you may do well; but this I tell you, that while I profess to serve God, all that I do is not the service of God: so while you challenge the queen's authority and commission, all that you do is not the queen's authority and commission.

A. The papists answer altogether like you.

W. The papists eat bread, and so do I: and I fear not to do like them in any good thing. Yet I hope you will make a difference betwixt me and papists.

A. Not in that point.

W. It is well known that you mistake my design, and I yours; but I wish you well.

A. I care not for your wishes.

W. My wishes and prayers, though they be sinful, will do you no harm.

A. I desire them not, and would be loath to come under them.

W. Love me not the worse for being plain with you.

Cosin. No, you are not so plain; for you do not directly answer.

W. Martin himself, I understand, will come forth, and defend his matters, if he may have fair trial.

A. Record that, Mr. Hartwell.

W. It is well known that I am as ready to read and lend that book as any person, in a good and lawful manner. Yet I will not accuse myself, and thus do myself hurt, and you no good. And I would rather have to speak well, than ill of you hereafter.

Goodman. If we be ill, whom do you mean?

W. All are ill, and need reformation.

Aubery. Did not you tell Mr. Martin, your keeper at the Compter, that he could not find out the author of the book?

W. Mr. Martin is a simple man, and imagines from the title of the book, that I am the author.

A. Is Mr. Perry then the author of the "Demonstration," or of Martin Mar-Prelate?

W. I think he is not. And I think you are greatly deceived in charging him with it.

A. There are many lies in Martin.

W. You must then confute them.

A. You despise the high commission. Why do you wear a cloak above your gown?

W. As a woman just come out of child-bed, I am just come out of the Compter, and dress thus, fearing the cold.

A. You make a wise comparison of yourself. Such women must be kept warm.

W. Then let them be kept warm.*

The commissioners having finished the examination of Mr. Wigginton, and finding him, after using all the inquisition their wits could devise, unwilling to accuse himself or others, they dismissed him from their presence, while they consulted what they should do. And being again called in, the meek and lowly archbishop thus addressed him:—"Forasmuch as you have refused to swear, and to answer as we have required you, and so, by law, have confessed yourself to be guilty of the accusations charged against you; and as you have at sundry times, and in divers ways, shewed your contempt of our ecclesiastical authority, and of this our high commission, which the queen hath given unto us, and which you shall obey and yield unto, before I have done with you; therefore, your former enlargement shall now be taken away, and you shall be kept close prisoner in the Gatehouse, until you shall yield in these matters; and when you are so disposed, you may send us word. In the mean time go your way. Away with him pursuivant."† He was then carried to the Gatehouse,‡ where he remained a long time; and though repeated intercessions were made to the archbishop for his release, it was all to no purpose. Mr. Wigginton was a pious man, a zealous minister, and a learned divine, and was living in the year 1591; but he most probably continued in the Gatehouse for several years, until the general banishment of the puritans.§

This great sufferer in the cause of nonconformity, during

* MS. Register, p. 843—848. † Ibid.

‡ The warrant sent to the keeper of the Gatehouse, was as follows:—"Herewith we send you one Giles Wigginton, whom we will and require you, and in her majesty's name, do strictly charge and command you to retain in your custody, by virtue of her highness's commission for causes ecclesiastical to us and others directed, and him safely to keep and detain, until you shall have further direction from us. And hereof fail you not, as you will answer to the contrary at your peril. Given at Lambeth, December 6, 1588."—*Ibid.* p. 848, 849.

§ MS. Chronology, vol. ii. p. 441. (8.)

his confinement in prison, had some correspondence with Hacket, the zealous enthusiast, who is said to have devised mad plots against the government; for which he was hanged, drawn and quartered. Whatever acquaintance or correspondence he had with this man, he never approved of his opinions and practice. However, from his slight connection with Hacket, Coppinger, and Arthington, his memory has suffered greatly from the scurrilous pen of Dr. Cosin, one of the high commission in the above examination; and herein he is followed by other historians.* On this account, it will be proper to give a circumstantial statement of the case, even allowing his enemies to be judges.

That Wigginton held correspondence with these men in the matters of their conspiracy, and that there was mutual correspondence betwixt him and them in all their plots for advancing their discipline, is manifest, says our author, by the confession of Arthington, who said, "That he heard Hacket singing certain songs, who wished that Arthington had some of them. For it was a very special thing, and, said he, Mr. Wigginton hath a great many of them." This is one evidence of their mutual and united conspiracy!

Coppinger, it is said, had once a conference with Wigginton, in the presence of Arthington, concerning his extraordinary calling. On this occasion, Mr. Wigginton refused to be made acquainted with Coppinger's secrets, saying, "You are known to be an honest gentleman, and sworn to the queen, and therefore I will not be acquainted with those things which God hath revealed unto you for the good of your sovereign."† Hacket also declared, that he heard Mr. Wigginton say, "That if the magistrates do not govern well, the people might draw themselves together, and see to a reformation." This dangerous opinion, it is said, may be gathered from one of his letters, in which he said, "Mr. Cartwright is in the Fleet, for refusal of the oath, and Mr. K. is sent for, and sundry worthy ministers are disquieted. So that we look for some bickering 'ere long, and then a battle, which cannot long endure." Coppinger and Arthington told Wigginton, "That reformation and the Lord's discipline should now forthwith be established, and therefore charged him in the Lord's name, to put all christians in comfort, that they should see a joyful alteration in the state of church government shortly."‡

* Strype's Whitgift, p. 305.—Collier's Eccl. Hist. vol. ii. p. 327—329.
† Cosin's Conspiracy, p. 57. Edit. 1699. ‡ Ibid. p. 58, 62.

They also told him, "That they were provoked to pronounce him the holiest minister of all others, for dealing so plainly and resolutely in God's cause above all ministers, which God would manifest one day to his comfort." At another time, they came to him and said, "We are come to you now to bring you certain news of great comfort, viz. That we have seen Jesus Christ this day, in lively and extraordinary shape or fashion presented unto us, not in his body; for he sitteth at the right hand of God in heaven, until the last judgment; but in his effectual or principal spirit, whereby he dwelleth in William Hacket, more than in any creature upon the earth."* Such are the grievous crimes with which Mr. Wigginton is charged! These facts, with a few others equally ridiculous, contain all the evidence of his uniting with Hacket and his companions, in their mad plots to overturn the government! As our information is from the pen of one of his bitterest enemies and persecutors, we may presume it is not given at all in his favour, but in some degree to his disadvantage: the impartial reader will, therefore, judge for himself, how far he was guilty.

After the most minute investigation, it appears to me that Mr. Wigginton's character and memory have suffered great injury from the above bigotted historian, and from those who imitated his example. One of them, speaking of Hacket and his companions, observes, "that one of this good brotherhood was Wigginton, as brainsick a teacher as any of the club, and as staunch an enemy to government."† The reader will easily perceive the injustice and falsehood of this representation. For, if this statement be correct, why did not his enemies proceed against him, as well as against the other conspirators? They were in possession of all the evidence that ever appeared against him, and he was now a prisoner in the Gatehouse; why then did they not punish him according to his deserts? This, surely, was not owing to their *too great lenity*, or their want of inclination.

During Mr. Wigginton's imprisonment, he published two pamphlets. One was on "Predestination;" the other was entitled "The Fools Bolt; or, a Fatherly Exhortation to a certain Young Courtier." The latter is said to have been "conceived into an *halting rhyme;*" and written chiefly against the governors of the church.

* Cosin's Conspiracy, p. 87, 88. † Kennet's Hist. of Eng. vol. ii. p. 563.

Thomas Barber was many years the learned and pious minister of Bow-church, London; where he preached four times a week, to a large and affectionate congregation. But his excellent learning, piety, and labours, could not protect him from the persecution of the times. In the month of June, 1584, he was called before Archbishop Whitgift and other high commissioners, and required to take the oath *ex officio*, to answer the interrogatories of the court. Knowing that by taking this oath, he should be liable to accuse himself; therefore, to avoid further trouble, he refused, and was immediately suspended. After receiving the ecclesiastical censure, his parishioners, to the number of one hundred and twenty, whose names are now before me, signed a petition to Sir Edward Osborne, the lord mayor, and the court of aldermen, to procure his release. But that court could do nothing for them.*

Mr. Barber having continued in a state of suspension several years, the archbishop, at length, offered to release him, on condition that he would subscribe with his own hand, the following protestation, dated December, 1587:—"I do faithfully promise, and by these presents subscribed "with mine own hand, do testify, that I will not, by word "or deed, publicly or privately, directly or indirectly, "impugn, deprave, or reprehend, any government, rite, "order, or ceremony, by law established, and retained in this "church of England: But, on the contrary, to my power, "will, by God's grace, observe and seek the peace of the "church of England, and will from time to time, adjoin "myself in public prayer, preaching, and admonitions "thereunto, and will frequent them diligently, and none "other assemblies, meetings, or conventicles."† Mr. Barber was a man of too much learning, piety, and good sense, to bind himself from exercising the right of private judgment, in things sacred. This godly and peaceable divine, therefore, claiming the right of thinking and acting in these things according to the dictates of truth and his own conscience, firmly refused to be tied down with such episcopal cords. But how much longer he continued under suspension, it does not appear.

Mr. Barber was one of the additional members of the presbyterian church erected at Wandsworth in Surrey; and his name is among those learned divines who subscribed the "Book of Discipline."‡ About the year 1591, he was

* MS. Register, p. 458, 459. † Ibid. p. 589, 826.
‡ Neal's Puritans, vol. i. p. 423.

taken into custody, and examined, with several of his brethren, relative to the associations of the puritans; and being required to take the oath *ex officio*, he openly confessed, and discovered their assemblies, with the manner in which they were conducted.*

Robert Cawdrey.—He was a divine of good reputation for learning and piety, but a great sufferer for nonconformity. Having entered into the sacred function about the year 1566, he was presented by Secretary Cecil, to the rectory of South Luffenham in Rutlandshire; but afterwards brought into manifold troubles for refusing to conform. After he had been employed in the ministry about twenty years, he was cited before Bishop Aylmer and other high commissioners; when he was charged with having omitted some parts of the Book of Common Prayer in public worship and the administration of the sacraments, and with having preached against certain things contained in the book. Though he only omitted the cross in baptism, and the ring in marriage, having used the greatest part of the service, he was required to take the oath *ex officio*, to answer all such articles as the tyrannical commissioners should propose; which, says Mr. Strype, he refused; and was, therefore, not only suspended, but utterly deprived of his ministerial exercise.†

He might, indeed, at first refuse the oath; and the statement of our learned historian might so far be correct: yet it is evident from the case at considerable length, now before me, that he afterwards complied, and, accordingly, gave his answers to the various articles. These articles, dated November, 1586, together with his answers, were the following:

1. "That you are a deacon or minister and priest admitted. Declare by whom, and what you were ordered; and likewise that your ordering was according to the book in that behalf by law provided.

Ans. "I am both deacon and priest. I was made deacon by Dr. Bullingham, late bishop of Lincoln, and was made priest by Dr. Scambler, late bishop of Peterborough. I was made deacon about twenty years ago, and minister about sixteen, which, I believe, was done according to the book in that behalf provided.

* Strype's Whitgift, Appen. p. 159—166.
† Strype's Aylmer, p. 129, 130.

2. "That you deem and judge your ordering, admission, and calling into the ministry, to be lawful, and not repugnant to the word of God.

Ans. "If I were now to be made a minister, I would not enter into the ministry according to that order.

3. "That you have sworn as well at your ordering, as at your institution, duty and allegiance to the queen's majesty, and canonical obedience to your ordinary and his successors, and to your metropolitan and his successors, or some of them.

Ans. "When I was instituted, I took an oath, but do not remember the tenour of it; and whether I was sworn at my ordering, or not, I do not remember.

4. "That by a statute made in the first year of the queen's majesty, a virtuous and godly book, entitled 'The Book of Common Prayer and administration of Sacraments, and of other rites and ceremonies in the Church of England,' was authorized and established in full force, and so remaineth.

Ans. "I believe this article to be true in every part.

5. "That by the said statute, all and singular ministers within her majesty's dominions, are bound to say and use a certain form of morning and evening prayer, and administration of each of the sacraments, and all other common and open prayer, in such form and order as is mentioned in the said book, and not otherwise.

Ans. "I believe this article to be true in every part.

6. "That in the said statute, her majesty and parliament assembled, do in God's name, earnestly charge and require all the archbishops, bishops, and other ordinaries, that they shall endeavour, to the utmost of their knowledge, that the due and true execution of the said act may be had throughout their dioceses and charges, as they shall answer before Almighty God.

Ans. "I believe this article to be true.

7. "That within the space of three years, two years, one year, half a year, three months, two months, or one month, last past, you have baptized divers infants, or at least one infant, otherwise and in other manner than the said book prescribeth; and have wittingly added thereunto, diminished therefrom, or altered according to your own fancy, divers or some parts thereof; and especially you have not used the sign of the cross upon the forehead, with the words in the said Book of Common Prayer prescribed to be used. Declare how many you have so baptized; and for what

cause, consideration, and intent, with the circumstance of the words by you used or diminished.

Ans. "I have not used the sign of the cross in the sacrament of baptism. And in reciting the interrogatories to the godfathers, I spoke in the plural number, saying YOU, instead of THOU. I could not have done it according to the order of the said book, or otherwise than as I have done, I think, with a safe conscience. And since I entered upon my benefice, I have baptized divers children, but I cannot remember how many.

8. "That within the time aforesaid, you have divers and sundry times, or at least once, ministered the sacrament of the Lord's supper to the communicants or some of them, standing or walking, and have not used the form of words in that behalf appointed and prescribed in the said Book of Common Prayer. Declare the circumstances thereof, and for what cause or consideration you have done this.

Ans. "I have often ministered the sacrament of the Lord's supper within the time mentioned; and therein I have distributed the bread and wine to the communicants as I found them, some standing, some sitting, and some kneeling; but never to any walking. And as to the prayers appointed in that behalf, and the words at the institution, I have followed the exact order of the book.

9. "Within the time aforesaid, you have used either no form at all, or have used some other than that which the said book prescribeth, in the burial of the dead; and have refused or omitted using or saying divers words appointed and prescribed in that behalf, in the said book. Declare the circumstances thereof, and for what cause or consideration you have done this.

Ans. "Within this year or two, in the burial of the dead, I have not read the whole service; because I am persuaded that some parts of it do nourish superstition. I have omitted this clause, *In sure and certain hope of the resurrection to eternal life*, and some others of the like tendency. And besides reading the chapter appointed, I have expounded some part of the scripture appointed to be read at funerals.

10. "That within the time aforesaid, you have openly in your sermons or sermon, preached or rather inveighed against the Book of Common Prayer, and the authority of archbishops and bishops. You said that the Book of Common Prayer is a wicked thing, fie upon it! fie upon it! that lords spiritual ought not to be lords over their brethren;

and that nonresident ministers are ministers of antichrist. Declare as before, the circumstances thereof, and for what cause or consideration you have done this.

Ans. "About six weeks since, I preached the lecture at Uppingham, being thereto appointed, taking for my text Col. i. 3—7. I then observed, as naturally arising from the words, that there was an equality among the ministers of Christ; and that Epiphras, the faithful minister of Christ, as mentioned in the text, was not a nonresident, and had not one charge in this country and another in another country. I then spoke of the benefits of a faithful ministry, and said that the want of it is the cause of ignorance, superstition, atheism, conspiracy, and rebellion. And in the warmth of my zeal, seeing the book tolerateth an ignorant and unfaithful ministry, I said, 'it is a vile book, fie upon it!'"*

Mr. Cawdrey delivered the above answers upon his oath, in the presence of Bishop Aylmer, Dr. Stanhope, and Dr. Walker. These spiritual rulers thus obliged the good man to take an oath, with a view of making him accuse himself. This was the constant practice of the high commission court. Mr. Cawdrey having given his answers to the charges brought against him, he was ordered to appear again in the month of December, to answer certain articles, mostly the same as those already noticed. Upon his appearance at the time appointed, after a long examination, without coming to any conclusion, he was cited to appear a third time in the month of February following. Upon his third appearance, being required to subscribe, and to enter into an engagement to wear the surplice, he refused, and was kept some time in a state of confinement. During his examination, the Bishop of London, urging him to wear the surplice, thus addressed him:

Bishop. Suppose you were able to keep four or six servants in livery, and one or two of them should refuse to wear your livery, would you take it all in good part? Are not we the queen's servants? And is not the surplice the livery which she hath appointed to be worn? And do you think she will be content if we refuse to wear it? Besides, the long prayer which you use before your sermons, is nothing but *bibble babble, bibble babble*.

Cawdrey. Every kingdom divided against itself must needs come to desolation. So when protestants set themselves

* MS. Register, p. 790—792.

against protestants, and deal more severely with them than with papists, confusion must follow.

B. We do not deal hardly with you, but the laws of the realm. We are only ministers to execute the law.

C. You turn those laws against us, which were made against the papists. We think it is very hard dealing that you and your brethren, the bishops, do punish us for not observing the Book of Common Prayer in every point, especially as neither you, nor most of the bishops in England, have observed it in all points these twenty-eight years.

B. Wherein do we not observe it?

C. Because you do not confirm children, as the book enjoins you to do. By the book we are charged not to receive persons to the communion, until they have been confirmed by the bishop: so we are brought into a painful extremity, and must either offend God, by keeping the people from the communion, or the book, by admitting them without confirmation. If persons can examine themselves, and be able to give a reason of their faith, we may not, we dare not, refuse them the communion, though the book forbids us to admit them till after they have been confirmed by the bishop.

B. Why, what canst thou say against it?

C. More than can be said for it. For, you well know it is a popish ceremony, and not warranted by the word of God; therefore, you justly omit it. And why may not we omit other points, more superstitious and offensive than this, without being brought into trouble?*

B. You shall not depart unless you will subscribe to use the book in every point, and engage to wear the surplice.

C. These are things in which I am not yet resolved. I have not wore the surplice since I entered into the ministry; and if I could be persuaded to wear it, my parishioners would be offended, and all the papists and atheists in the country would triumph. Therefore, I pray you, give me sufficient time to deliberate upon it.

B. I will, if you will give sufficient security for your appearance here next sitting.

C. That I will do.

B. But if thou go home, thou wilt confer with thy fellows, and they will persuade thee not to wear the surplice. Therefore, I will keep thee here, and will not let thee go.†

* Here the bishop was much offended, and immediately suspended Mr. Cawdrey from preaching in any part of the kingdom.

† MS. Register, p. 792—794.

Mr. Cawdrey being kept for some time in a state of confinement, was brought before the high commission, May 5, 1587. Though his case was not then considered; yet seeing a worthy minister out of Essex deprived, for not observing in every point the Book of Common Prayer, and not wearing the surplice; and fearing that he should himself soon share the same fate, he presented a supplication to his worthy friend and patron, the Lord Treasurer Burleigh. This supplication, dated May 10, 1587, was as follows:*

"In most humble and dutiful manner, may it please your honour to be advertised, that as your poor orator, in November last, preaching a sermon at Uppingham, in a lecture regularly holden there, happened to speak against a point of the communion book, and was forthwith accused to the high commissioners; (though by whom he knoweth not) and being sent for by them, was compelled against the law to swear to answer such articles or interrogatories as they ministered unto him. This being done, your humble suppliant did appear again; and after conference with the Bishop of London, he suspended him from his ministry, and so hath been suspended these twelve weeks. And because your said orator hath so answered the said interrogatories, as that by law no advantage can be taken against him, the said bishop doth now urge him to subscribe, and wear the surplice; for refusing to do which, he threateneth to deprive your suppliant, as of late he hath done some others. And seeing that is the only living he hath enjoyed for above sixteen years, and was thereunto presented by your honour, may it please your good lord, even out of a tender regard to the cause of God and his poor suffering church, to extend your lawful favour towards him in this behalf, who hath behaved himself so honestly and uprightly during these sixteen years at Luffenham, every way according to his calling, and as becometh his profession; as, your honour allowing him a convenient time, he doubteth not to procure sufficient testimony from the worshipful and ministers of that county. And so your said orator shall be most dutifully bound to pray unto Almighty God for your good health, with much increase of honour, and your everlasting comfort. Your honour's most obedient servant,

"Robert Cawdrey."

The treasurer, upon the reception of this supplication,

* MS. Register, p. 796, 797.

sent to the bishop, inquiring what were the charges against Mr. Cawdrey, and wishing to know the reasons of his hard dealing with him. He requested, at the same time, that his grace would send him the articles, and Mr. Cawdrey's answers, before any further steps were taken. Notwithstanding this, Mr. Cawdrey appearing before the commission the very same day, and his answers being read, the bishop demanded what he had to say. He then said, "If my answers there set down will not sufficiently acquit me of all accusations, I then crave, as I have a right to do, that I may enjoy the benefit of her majesty's gracious pardon." Dr. Stanhope, the bishop's chancellor, observed, as there was an exception against him in the statute, that would do him no good. But the exception, replied Mr. Cawdrey, related to the papists and recusants only; and the statute being produced and examined, his statement was found correct.

This disappointment being extremely vexatious to his tyrannical persecutors, the angry prelate addressing his brethren upon the commission, said, "It is no matter whether it be so, or not; he shall be sworn to answer new articles." Accordingly, he was constrained to swear, and give direct answers to the two articles following:— "Whether he would hereafter observe the Book of Common Prayer in every point, or not.—And whether he would wear the surplice, or not." To the former of these articles, he said, "I will so far as I may according to the word of God, and with a good conscience." And to the latter, he said, "I am not yet resolved so to do." The bishop then appointed him to appear again on the 30th of the same month. But previous to his next appearance, the lord treasurer, after an impartial hearing of both parties, sent an express order to the bishop, to dismiss him, and trouble him no more. This was extremely galling to Aylmer, who replied, that as he was only one of the commission, he could do nothing without the other commissioners; adding, "he must appear on the day appointed, and we will consider his case according to equity and conscience."* But little equity and conscience was to be expected from Bishop Aylmer and his brethren of the high commission. This will, indeed, appear before the close of the present narrative.

Mr. Cawdrey, in the above painful circumstances, made

* MS. Register, p. 794, 795.

a second application to the treasurer, giving him a correct account of the bishop's proceedings, and further soliciting his favour and assistance. His letter, dated nine days after the former, was as follows:*

"My honourable lord, I am bound most humbly to thank God for your honourable and good favour in this my great vexation, having now for the space of more than nine weeks, been bound over to answer from time to time. It grieveth me to be importunate with you in the midst of so many of your affairs, especially as you are in a poor state of health, from which I beseech God to restore you; but, my good lord, my miserable state even forceth me. Notwithstanding your favourable message and letters to the Bishop of London in my behalf, he still keepeth me from performing those duties which I owe to God, my people, and my wife and children; and he seems as if he meant to wear me out. I having lately claimed before the high commission, the benefit of her majesty's gracious pardon, the bishop then caused me to take a new oath, and to answer new articles; namely, whether I would in every point observe the Book of Common Prayer; and whether I would wear the surplice. These being answered, he appointed me to appear again the 30th of this month, when my case will be further considered. Will it, therefore, please your good lordship, even at this time, to use such means to procure my discharge, as to your godly wisdom shall appear most proper? To you, next under God, I fly for refuge in this case. I protest, I am not obstinate in any one thing, as He knoweth whom I am most loath to displease. I am your honour's, &c.

"Robert Cawdrey."

But the treasurer being sick, Mr. Cawdrey could receive no answer to the above letter; therefore, upon the arrival of the day appointed, he appeared again before the commission. When he was called, and his accusations were read, the bishop asked him what he had to say against their proceeding to pronounce upon him the sentence of deprivation. "To which I answered," says the good man, "that so far as my knowledge and counsel serve, I cannot see how you can deal so hardly with me. For if the rigour of the law should be extended against me for speaking against the book, the penalty, as set down in the statute, is only half a year's imprisonment, and the loss of my living to her

* MS. Register, p. 797.

majesty for one whole year: and the same statute saith it must be wilfully and obstinately persisted in, which is not the case with me. Besides, the said trespass is already remitted by her majesty's gracious pardon; therefore, you have no just cause of deprivation." The bishop, addressing Mr. Cawdrey, said, "If you will abide by such order as I and the other commissioners shall appoint; and will openly recant, in such places as we shall determine, those blasphemous speeches which you have uttered against that holy book, and use it in every point, then we will stay our proceedings." To this tyrannical proposal, Mr. Cawdrey only said, "I would not do that for all the world."

One of the commissioners entreated him not to be obstinate, but to submit to their order; "for," said he, "we hear that you live honestly, are well thought of in your country, are a good housekeeper, and have a wife and many children; therefore, take our good advice." To which he thus replied: "Both my wife and children shall go a begging, rather than I will offend God and my own conscience. And further, if you can justly charge me with any one instance of wickedness in life, or any false doctrine, during the time I have been in the ministry, or at any time before, let the sentence of the law be inflicted with the utmost severity." "False doctrine!" said the angry prelate, "I will stand to it, that whosoever shall say the book is a vile and filthy book, which hath epistles and gospels, psalms and holy prayers in it;* I say flatly he is an *heretic*, take the law upon me who will."

Afterwards, Mr. Cawdrey requested to have some time for further deliberation, but it could not be granted. Then, to give them all the satisfaction in his power, he made the following protestation:—"If you can charge me with holding any point of doctrine, which I cannot prove to be true, both by the word of God, and the judgment of those learned writers, whose works you, the high commissioners, have authorized to be printed and allowed in England; then let me have no favour at all." Notwithstanding all that he could say, the excellence of his character and doctrine was utterly disregarded, so long as he refused to come up to the standard of conformity. The bishop, therefore, pronounced upon him the sentence of deprivation, discharging him from the ministerial exercise in any

* His lordship might, with equal propriety, have observed the same of the popish mass book. For, as our author justly affirms, it contains epistles and gospels, psalms and holy prayers.

part of the kingdom.* Mr. Strype, indeed, observes, that he was not only deprived, but continuing in his disobedience, he was also degraded by the high commission at Lambeth; and that he was charged, not only with nonconformity, but want of learning.†

Mr. Cawdrey, aware of the two-fold charge, presented the following humble vindication of himself to the lord treasurer: "As to my learning," says he, "though I have none to boast of; yet, seeing I have been employed in study, and have exercised myself in expounding the scriptures and preaching the word of God, almost twenty years, I hope God hath blessed me with some small measure of knowledge. I appeal to the people of my charge, and the good success of my ministry among them, which is a great comfort to my soul. I desire your lordship to examine me upon some portion of scripture, and I hope you will not find me so utterly void of learning, as to be wholly unfit to be exercised in the ministry. Indeed, I acknowledge, that, with respect to my important calling, and the ability that is requisite to a proper discharge of it, I am very unfit for the sacred function. Yet it affordeth me some comfort, that God in mercy hath so far blessed my labours, that I hope my people know as well as most, how to "render unto Cæsar the things which are Cæsar's, and unto God the things which are God's."—And as to the charge of not using the Book of Common Prayer, I have always used it, and still purpose to use it. Only I humbly request, that I may not be more narrowly searched into, and more hardly dealt with, than many others ministers in England."‡

Mr. Cawdrey having received the sentence of deprivation, and being dissatisfied with the ecclesiastical censure, was urged to submit his case to the further determination of Archbishop Whitgift and Bishop Aylmer; but he utterly refused, for the following reasons:—"Because he was persuaded in his conscience, and it was manifest from lamentable experience, that the lord bishops countenanced nonresidents, made many ignorant and idle shepherds, and dealt with great severity against many godly ministers for not observing the popish ceremonies:—Because they would allow any papist or atheist, being accused before them, to have a copy of their interrogatories and other proceedings; but the ministers, who could not in conscience observe some

* MS. Register, p. 795.
† Life of Aylmer, p. 130, 131.
‡ Ibid. p. 132, 133.

ceremonies, could neither know their accusers, nor enjoy the benefit of subjects:—Because, though the bishops condemned nonresidence as odious in itself, and injurious to the church of God; yet they tolerated it, and dispensed with it:—And because the said bishops did molest and deprive ministers for preaching the very same doctrines which they had themselves printed and published to the world." On these grounds, he was unwilling to submit his case to the determination of the two ecclesiastical judges, whose tender mercy was cruelty.*

It will be proper also to observe, that he was no sooner brought under the ecclesiastical censure, than he made fresh application to the treasurer. He wrote two letters, the one dated May 31st, being the day following his censure, and the other the 3d of the following month. In these letters he gave an impartial account of the hard usage he had met with, earnestly soliciting his lordship's favourable attention to his unhappy case.† Upon the reception of these letters, the lord treasurer, convinced of the injuries he had received, warmly espoused his cause; and engaged Attorney Morrice,‡ to undertake Mr. Cawdrey's defence, even after his suspension and deprivation. The learned lawyer, therefore, held the bishop's sentence to be null and void in law; because Mr. Cawdrey's benefice was not in Aylmer's diocese, and so not within his jurisdiction; and that the sentence was his lordship's sentence alone, and not the sentence of the commissioners. For by law the sentence should have been given in the name of all the commissioners present, and not in the name of one of them by the consent of the others, as in the present case. In addition to this, the bishop had declared expressly in his decree, that the cause was controverted before him by virtue

* Life of Aylmer, p. 134—138. † MS. Register, p 797, 798.

‡ Attorney James Morrice was a most able and learned barrister, a man of great piety, a zealous opposer of vice, and an avowed friend to the reformation. He was attorney of the court of wards, a member of parliament, and a zealous and courageous defender of the rights and liberties of the people, against all oppression. In the parliament of 1592, he moved the house to inquire into the proceedings of the bishops in spiritual courts, and how far they could justify their inquisition, their subscriptions, and their binding the queen's subjects to their good behaviour, contrary to the laws of God and the realm; their compelling men to take oaths to accuse themselves; and to deprive, degrade, and imprison them, and keep them in prison during their own pleasure. At the same time, he offered two bills to the house; one against the oath *ex officio*, and the other against the illegal proceedings of the bishops, in which he was supported by Sir Francis Knollys and other great statesmen.—*Strype's Whitgift*, p. 387, 388.

of his office, which could not be before the commissioners. And if the cause were depending before his lordship, by virtue of his office, how could the judgment, said Morrice, be any other than his own?

And as to the sentence itself, the attorney held it to be contrary to law. For by law several other censures and punishments, as admonition, excommunication, and sequestration, were to be inflicted previous to deprivation. But in Mr. Cawdrey's case, that sentence which is the most severe, and ought to have been inflicted last, was inflicted first. This, therefore, was contrary to the statute, and not warranted by any of the queen's ecclesiastical laws.* Thus Mr. Attorney Morrice endeavoured to make it appear, that the bishop's proceedings were illegal and oppressive.

But the arguments of the learned barrister proved ineffectual. They were too weak to soften the mind of this relentless prelate. Mr. Cawdrey refusing to submit himself to the illegal and severe proceedings, was brought before Archbishop Whitgift and other high commissioners. He appeared at Lambeth, May 14, 1590; and after being severely threatened, he was degraded and deposed from the ministry, and made a mere layman. On this occasion, Whitgift urging him to conform, Mr. Cawdrey replied, saying, "I never refused to conform, as far as the law requires, and as a minister of Christ is in conscience bound." And one of the commissioners observing, that he was deprived for speaking against the Book of Common Prayer, our divine replied, "that is not true; for it appears from my answers to the articles upon my oath, that it was for speaking against an inconvenience attending the book. If it were taken," says he, "as you have represented, and taken in the worst sense it could be, there was no deprivation by law, for the first offence. And according to law, I should have been indicted at the next assizes following, but was not; therefore, I am clear by the statute."†

Upon these tyrannical proceedings, Mr. Attorney Morrice recommended the lord treasurer to make the Bishop of London feel his lawless severities; and, said he, happily some remorse of conscience may move him to be more favourable. Though it might be offensive, he observed, to find fault with judicial proceedings, there was no evil in seeking to help the injured, to maintain law and justice, and to make ecclesiastical judges more careful of their

* Strype's Aylmer, p. 131, 132. † Ibid. p. 139, 140.

proceedings in future. You need not be afraid of their frowns, especially as you have the law on your side.* But the attorney soon drew down their vengeance upon his own head.† For this bold adventure in defending Mr. Cawdrey against the oppressions of the prelates, and for the motions which he made in parliament, as intimated in the above note, he was seized in the house by a serjeant at arms, discharged from his office in the court of the Duchy of Lancaster, disabled from any practice in his profession as a barrister at law, and kept some years prisoner in Tutbury castle, Staffordshire.‡

Mr. Cawdrey having experienced the above illegal and cruel usage, was advised to appeal to the court of exchequer, and proceed against his diocesan's chaplain, who had taken possession of his living. He made his appeal; and in the year 1591, the jurisdiction of the high commission court, together with its severe proceedings against Mr. Cawdrey, was argued before all the judges. Dr. Aubery, a learned civilian, and one of the high commissioners, confessed that their proceedings were not warrantable by the letter of the statute, and that no statute of the realm would justify the said proceedings; but what they had done was founded upon the *old canon law* still in force. And though their proceeding by way of inquisition, forcing the man to accuse himself, was warranted by no law whatever, the judges being of the same mind as the commissioners, confirmed their tyrannical proceedings, and left Mr. Cawdrey, with his family of eight children, to starve as a mere layman. Besides the good man having *twenty-two* journies to London, the suit cost his friends a round sum of money.§ But, as Mr. Neal justly observes, it was

* Strype's Aylmer, p. 143, 144.

† Heylin's Hist. of Pres. p. 320.

‡ This castle, now in a state of ruin, was formerly a spacious and strong place. Here Mary Queen of Scots, was, for a considerable time, in a state of confinement. This was occasioned by a jealousy and a quarrel arising betwixt her and Queen Elizabeth, when the latter, for her own safety, caused the former to be imprisoned. But what is most curious, during the queen's imprisonment in this castle, her extravagance was so great, that when she bathed, she bathed in wine. And in addition to the immense quantity of wine required for bathing, *two tuns a month* were not sufficient for her ordinary use. The Earl of Shrewsbury, in whose custody the queen was kept, and who appears then to have been governor of the castle, therefore applied to the lord treasurer, stating her extraordinary expenses; at the same time, soliciting some favourable allowance from the public treasure. Also there is preserved a most curious letter, from the Queen of Scots, to Queen Elizabeth, dated from Tutbury castle, March 14, 1569.—*Strype's Annals*, vol. i. p. 538, 539. Appen. p. 61, 62.

§ Heylin's Hist. of Pres. p. 317.—Strype's Aylmer, p. 145, 146.

a brave stand for the rights and liberties of the subject; and it so much staggered the archbishop, that he afterwards declined the business of the commission, and sent most of his prisoners to the star-chamber.

Mr. Cawdrey having endured these troubles for the space of five years, and being almost ruined; the treasurer, his constant friend, compassionately feeling his manifold calamities, still warmly espoused his cause. He not only urged his diocesan, who had sequestered his living, and given it to his chaplain, to allow him some annual pension; but requested that so excellent and useful a preacher might be again restored to his ministry; in each of which, however, he most probably failed.* Mr. Cawdrey united with his brethren in subscribing the "Book of Discipline."†

He was author of "A Treasurie or Store-house of Similies, both Pleasaunt, Delightfull and Profitable for all Estates of Men in generall, newly collected into Heades and Commonplaces," 1609. In the preface to the reader prefixed to this work, the author observes that he had begun another work, which he at first purposed to have united with it. This he calls "A Treatise of Definitions of the principal words, points, and matters that a preacher shall have occasion to speak of;" which he promised, God sparing his life, to publish in a separate work, soon after the former; but whether it ever came forth, or what other things he published, we have not been able to learn.

In the above work, Mr. Cawdrey openly declares his sentiments on the necessity and importance of an exact christian discipline among the churches of Christ, and gives his opinion with great freedom concerning ignorant, idle and insufficient ministers. The minister, says he, who undertakes to feed the flock of Christ, by preaching and catechising, and who has no knowledge to perform this duty, or having sufficient knowledge, yet is nonresident, and absent from them, and thus suffereth the people to perish for want of knowledge, such a one before God, is a *soul-murderer*. Mr. Daniel Cawdrey, ejected in 1662, was his son.‡

* Heylin's Hist. of Pres. p. 140, 147.
† Neal's Puritans, vol. i. p. 423.
‡ Palmer's Noncon. Mem. vol. iii. p. 27.

LEVER WOOD was minister at Brenchley in Kent, but was much persecuted for nonconformity. Upon the publication of Whitgift's three articles, in 1583, he and sixteen of his brethren, all ministers of Kent, waited upon the archbishop at Lambeth. When they appeared before his grace, they declared that they could not, with a good conscience, subscribe to his articles, and desired to know whether they might still proceed in their ministry.* But, instead of obtaining his lordship's approbation, they were all immediately suspended, and Mr. Wood, with some others, if not the whole, was cast into prison, where he continued twelve months. At the expiration of that period, upon his subscription *as far as the law required*, and promising to use the Book of Common Prayer, and no other, he was released from prison.†

His troubles, however, were not over. He still continued under suspension. Therefore, he made interest at court, that he might be restored to his former labours. He applied to Sir Francis Walsingham, secretary of state,‡ who interceded with the archbishop for his restoration to his ministry, but without success. Whitgift would not remove the ecclesiastical censure, and allow Mr. Wood to preach, unless he would subscribe without the least reserve, and practise a perfect conformity.§ And the good man's conscience not allowing him to do this, he remained under suspension at least eight years. He was under his lordship's censure in the year 1591, and whether he was ever restored is extremely doubtful.‖

HUMPHREY FENN.—This most learned and venerable divine was several years minister at Northampton, and above forty years a laborious and faithful preacher in Coventry, and uncommonly successful in his ministry; yet

* See Art. Dudley Fenner. † Neal's Puritans, vol. i. p. 406.

‡ Sir Francis Walsingham was a steady promoter of the reformation; a zealous and constant friend to the puritans; and a most celebrated statesman. His talent for business, his eloquence, insinuating address, universal intelligence, and profound secrecy, are mentioned by all our historians. He was employed by Queen Elizabeth in the most important embassies, and advanced to the post of secretary of state; notwithstanding which, he was so far from accumulating a fortune, that he spent his patrimony in the service of the public, and was buried in the night, at the expense of his friends, through fear of his corpse being arrested for debt: a fault which few statesmen since his time have been guilty of. He died April 6, 1590.—*Welwood's Memoirs*, p. 9—12.—*Granger's Biog. Hist.* vol. i. p. 232.

§ Fuller's Church Hist. b. ix. p. 162, 163.—Strype's Whitgift, p. 226, 227.

‖ MS. Register, p. 585.

he underwent many troubles for nonconformity. While in the former situation, he experienced the cruel oppressions of the times, and was apprehended and committed to close prison, where he remained a long time. During his confinement, the inhabitants at Northampton presented a supplication to Queen Elizabeth, humbly and earnestly beseeching her majesty to grant his release, and his restoration to his beloved ministry. In this supplication they affirmed upon their dutiful allegiance, that during his abode in that place, he had lived an honest and a peaceable life, and gave a high character of his diligence in preaching, his obedience to God, and to those in authority. It does not appear, however, whether this application was at all successful. It is very probable he never returned to his charge at Northampton.

Having at length obtained his release, he most probably entered upon his ministerial charge in the city of Coventry. The oppressed puritans being desirous to be eased of their heavy burdens, Mr. Fenn was unanimously chosen by the London ministers, to accompany the Earl of Leicester, in a presentation of their afflictions and desires to those in authority; but with what success, we have not been able to learn. He consented to this appointment, saying "that he was ready to run, whenever the church commanded him." It is said to have been his opinion, that impropriations, which were attached to her majesty, to colleges, &c. ought to be set to the pastors; and that all tythes, which are appendages by some composition, should be paid to the ministers in specie. It is also observed, that he accounted it unlawful to receive the sacrament at the hands of a dumb minister, or to attend the ordinary service of the church without a sermon.*

Upon the publication of Whitgift's three articles, and the persecutions which followed, he was cited to Lambeth, and, refusing to subscribe, was immediately suspended. When he appeared before the archbishop, he was urged by many arguments, to subscribe; and he, on the contrary, endeavoured to answer those arguments, stating his reasons for refusal. This was as follows:

Archbishop. Your subscription is required by the statute of 13 Eliz.

Fenn. That statute extendeth no further than the confession of christian faith, and the doctrine of the sacraments.

* Baker's MS. Collec. vol. xv. p. 72, 73.

A. There is provision in the statute of 7 Eliz., that the queen, with her high commissioners, or the archbishop, may take further order.

F. The proviso of 7 Eliz. can have no relation to 13 Eliz., which was some years after. And the proviso expresseth how far it is to be extended: not to taking away and establishing ceremonies.

A. But so much of the canon law is still in force, as is not contrary to God's word; and you have promised canonical obedience.

F. But the question is, whether the things required be agreeable to God's word? And not only so, there is no canon which requires us to subscribe to the judgment of our ordinary.

A. That I allow; but the law hath charged the bishop to see that all things for the ministry be duly observed, as by law established; and I take this order for the more effectual execution of things already established.

F. Your care and diligence in the execution of laws must be *according* to law, and not *contrary* to law; that is, by admonition, by suspension, by sequestration, or by deprivation, as the case may require. But these proceedings are not according to law; but an inquisition into our hearts and consciences, for which there is no law.

A. I make this a decree and order for the whole of my province, and, therefore, is to be observed as if it had been made before.

F. No one person, nor any number of persons, hath authority to make decrees or constitutions, except in convocation; which must be called together by the king's writ: As 25 Henry VIII. and 1 Eliz., which is entitled, "The Submission of the Clergy."

A. I have the queen's consent.

F. But that consent was not according to law provided in this behalf. Nor was it done in convocation.

A. I have the consent of my brethren and some others.

F. That was not according to the order of convocation, wherein we are to have our free choice of clerks.*

Mr. Fenn remained under suspension a long time, during the whole of which period his cure was totally neglected.† But by the kind favour of the Earl of Leicester, as appears from his letter to the archbishop, dated July 14, 1585, he was at length restored to his ministry, when he returned to

* MS. Register, p. 592. † Ibid. p. 745.

his charge in Coventry.* The same honourable person also promised, that he would treat with the bishop of Lichfield and Coventry, to obtain his favourable allowance. Though this excellent divine might probably enjoy peace and quietness for a season, his troubles were not ended. In the year 1591, an information was exhibited against him and many of his brethren, for being concerned in the classis, atending their associations, and subscribing the "Book of Discipline;" when they were all apprehended, and committed to prison. A circumstantial account of these proceedings, together with their examinations and endeavours to procure their deliverance, is given in another place.† These worthy sufferers, during their confinement, presented a long letter to the queen, dated April, 1592, in vindication of their own innocency.‡ It does not, indeed, appear how long a time they remained in prison, after that period.

Upon Mr. Fenn's release, he most probably returned to Coventry, where he spent the rest of his days. He died in a firm attachment to those principles for which he suffered. Mr. Clark observes, that he was famous for his ministry and nonconformity in the city of Coventry; and that in his last will and testament, he made so full and open a protestation against the hierarchy and ceremonies, that when his will was tendered to be proved, the prelates, or those of their party, would not allow it to have a place among the records of the court.§

Daniel Wight was a zealous minister of Christ, but greatly harassed for many years, on account of his nonconformity. It is very probable that he preached at some place in London or its vicinity. In the year 1573, when Mr. Johnson and others were sent to the Gatehouse, Mr. Wight and several of his brethren were committed to Newgate. We do not, however, find how long he remained under the bondage of his enemies.‖ As Mr. Johnson afterwards died under the pressure of his rigorous confinement; so Mr. Wight afterwards obtained his liberty, and was restored to his ministry. He subscribed the "Book of Discipline," and took an active part in the associations; for

* Strype's Whitgift, p. 226. † See Art. Thomas Cartwright.
‡ Strype's Annals, vol. iv. p. 85.
§ Clark's Lives annexed to his Martyrologie, p. 160.
‖ Baker's MS. Collec. vol. xxxii. p. 441, 442.

which his study was broken open, and searched, and his private papers were carried away. Those papers contained some of the resolutions agreed upon at their associations; among which were the following:—"That private baptism is unlawful.—That the sign of the cross ought not to be used in baptism.—That the calling of bishops is unlawful.—That the people ought to be taught church discipline.—That ministers ought to be called by their flocks.—And that no minister ought to subscribe to the Book of Common Prayer."* These were the dangerous resolutions and opinions of Mr. Wight and his brethren, for which they were apprehended and cast into prison. They were most shamefully reproached and insulted in the high commission and star-chamber; and were under confinement in the year 1592, having been in prison nearly two years. Whether Mr. Wight continued much longer in bondage, we cannot ascertain.†

WILLIAM PROUDLOVE was a respectable puritan minister, who, about the year 1562, became vicar of Fansley in Northamptonshire; and in 1577, he became rector of Lamport in the same county.‡ He united with his brethren in their private associations, and took an active part in promoting the desired ecclesiastical discipline; for which, in the year 1590, he was apprehended and cast into prison, where he remained a long time.§ He was often carried before the high commission and the star-chamber, when he underwent the severe scrutiny and examination of his ecclesiastical inquisitors; but refused the oath *ex officio*. On one of these occasions, the following interrogatories were proposed to him:

"Whether have not you put in practice that opinion or determination of those that labour for a discipline and government by eldership, whereby they hold, that a godly minister is not to rest in or obey the suspension or deprivation of bishops or their officers, as it is practised in the church of England?—Whether were you suspended or excommunicated by your ordinary, and, nevertheless, did preach and execute your ministry, during such suspension or excommunication; and what moved you so to do?—Whether have you besides the presentation by the patron,

* Strype's Whitgift, p. 291, 292. † See Art. Cartwright.
‡ Bridges's Hist. of Northamptonshire, vol. i. p. 95, 113.
§ See Art. Cartwright.

and institution of the bishop, unto your late benefice, a trial, examination, ordination, calling, and approbation by some of your brethren and neighbouring ministers assembled in classes or conference? In what manner and form was it performed? By whom, when, and where?"* What could his tyrannical judges mean by these iniquitous proceedings, unless it was to force him to become his own accuser, and prove him guilty from his own confession?

John More.—This learned and pious divine was fellow of Christ's college, Cambridge, where he most probably received his education. After his removal from the university, he became a very popular and useful preacher at St. Andrew's church in the city of Norwich; but here he met with persecution on account of his nonconformity. Having refused to wear the surplice, principally on account of the offence which it gave to others, he was convened before the bishop of the diocese, who told him that it was better to offend a few private persons, than to offend God and disobey the prince. His lordship, indeed, gives him this honourable character: "I have not known that he has at any time spoken against her majesty's book of Injunctions, nor can I find any manner of stubbornness in him. And surely," adds the bishop, "he is a godly and learned man, and hath done much good in this city."† He was a zealous champion for the purity of the gospel, and a bold opposer of all false doctrine, as appears from his public contest with the famous Dr. Pern of Cambridge.‡ What a pity then was it, that a divine, endowed with such excellent qualifications, should have been interrupted in his public ministry.

The prelates rigorously imposing the ceremonies upon the clergy, Mr. More, with his brethren in and about Norwich, were among the numerous sufferers. These divines, seeing the approaching storm, prepared for it by presenting their humble supplication to the lords of the council, dated from Norwich, September 25, 1576. In this supplication they declare their great readiness to yield their bodies, their goods, and their lives in the service of

* Baker's MS. Collec. vol. xv. p. 76, 77.
† Strype's Parker, p. 452.
‡ Strype's Annals, vol. ii. p. 282.

their prince; yet they dare not yield to the intended conformity. Having enlarged upon the manifold evils necessarily arising from such rigorous impositions, they conclude in these words: "As to ourselves," say they, "we dare not for all the world yield to those ceremonies. "And if the bishop proceed to urge them upon ministers, "as he hath begun, it will bring the most awful ruin upon "the church. There are already *nineteen* or *twenty* "exercises of preaching and catechizing put down, by "the silencing of ministers in this city. We, therefore, "humbly crave your assistance, both with our prince "and the bishops. The Lord God direct your honours "in this affair, and in all your other concerns, that "they may be for the profit of the church of God and "the advantage of our land. Yours most humbly in the "Lord,

"John More, George Leeds,
"Richard Crick, Richard Dowe,
"Thomas Roberts, William Hart."*

If Mr. More and his brethren were not brought into trouble previous to their application to the council, it is certain they were suspended not long after. This will appear from their own words, in the following submission, dated from Norwich, August 21, 1578, and presented to their diocesan:—"The ministers," say they, "whose names "are underwritten, humbly crave favour to be restored to "their preaching, upon subscription to all those articles "which concern the confession of the true christian faith "and doctrine of the sacraments, according to the words "of the statute. And concerning ceremonies, order, and "government, they acknowledge that they are so far tolerable, that for the same, no man ought to withdraw "himself from hearing the word of God, and receiving the "sacraments; nor, on the same account, ought any minister "to refuse to preach the word of God, and to administer "the sacraments,

"John More, Richard Dowe,
"Richard Crick, George Leeds,
"Thomas Roberts, John Mapes."†
"Vincent Goodwin,

* MS. Register, 256. † Ibid. p. 285.

From the above submission it is obvious that Bishop Maddox had not sufficiently examined the subject, or that his materials of information were defective, when he affirms that Mr. More does not appear to have been suspended.* It is not, indeed, equally clear how long he remained under the episcopal censure, nor whether his submission was at all available. About the year 1584, after the publication of Whitgift's three articles, we find this excellent divine and upwards of sixty others, all ministers of Norfolk, not resolved to subscribe. And about the same time, the ministers of Norwich, being grievously oppressed with the severities laid upon them, presented to the archbishop their reasons for refusing subscription, earnestly soliciting the resolution of their scruples and objections; but I do not find what satisfaction they obtained.† Dr. Ames styles Mr. More a most heavenly man, and the light and glory of the church.‡ Mr. Granger gives the following account of him: "This worthy person," says he, "was about twenty years minister of St. Andrew's in Norwich; where he was held in great veneration for his general knowledge in the sciences, his exact skill in the learned languages, and, above all, for his extensive learning and indefatigable labours as a divine. He constantly preached thrice every Sunday, and was much admired for his excellent talent that way. He refused very considerable preferments, which would have been attended with less labour than his cure at Norwich, only because he thought he could be more useful in that city." This author, giving an account of the different modes of dress at this period, observes, that "Mr. John More of Norwich, one of the worthiest clergymen in the reign of Elizabeth, gave the best reason that could be given for wearing the longest and largest beard of any Englishman of his time; namely, 'That no act of his life might be unworthy of the gravity of his appearance.'"§ He died in the year 1592. Fuller includes him among the learned writers, being fellows of Christ's college, Cambridge; and says, he made the excellent map of the Land of Palestine.‖

In the last will and testament of Mr. Thomas Merburie,

* Vindication of the Church of England, p. 341.
† MS. Register, p. 286, 436.
‡ Ames's Fresh Suit, Appen. p. 18.
§ Granger's Biog. Hist. vol. i. p. 217, 218, 288.
‖ Fuller's Hist. of Camb. p. 92.

of the above college, dated December 1, 1571, and proved the 5th of the same month, honourable mention is made of Mr. More; and Mr. Merburie bequeathed to him all his books in divinity, and made him one of the supervisors of his will.*

* Baker's MS. Collec. vol. iii. p. 314.

END OF VOL. I.

HUGHES, PRINTER, MAIDEN-LANE, COVENT-GARDEN.

CPSIA information can be obtained
at www.ICGtesting.com
Printed in the USA
LVOW13*0047020518
575645LV00016B/350/P